FUNDAMENTALS OF
MARKETING

INTERESTED IN A NEW STUDY AID?

Our Study Guide has been designed to help you understand and apply fundamental marketing concepts. Its features include:

Crossword Puzzles

provide an innovative way to reinforce new terminology.

Real World Readings

from the popular and business press demonstrate how new marketing concepts are applied.

Self-Test Questions

provide an opportunity for you to monitor your own progress.

Notes on the Case Method

summarize the key considerations in solving case-type problems.

The Study Guide to accompany *Fundamentals of Marketing* is available through your bookstore.

ISBN 0-07-549699-2

FUNDAMENTALS OF
MARKETING

Fifth Canadian Edition

Montrose S. Sommers
University of Guelph
James G. Barnes
Memorial University of Newfoundland
William J. Stanton
University of Colorado
Charles Futrell
Texas A & M University

McGraw-Hill Ryerson Limited

Toronto   Montreal   New York   Auckland   Bogotá   Caracas
Hamburg   Lisbon   London   Madrid   Mexico   Milan   New Delhi
Paris   San Juan   São Paulo   Singapore   Sydney   Tokyo

FUNDAMENTALS OF MARKETING
Fifth Canadian Edition

ISBN 0-07-549697-6

 3 4 5 6 7 8 9 0 BP 8 7 6 5 4 3 2 1 0

Book design and illustrations by Daniel Kewley

Printed and bound in Canada

Care has been taken to trace ownership of
copyright material contained in this text. The
publishers will gladly take any information that
will enable them to rectify any reference or credit
in subsequent editions.

Canadian Cataloguing in Publication Data

Main entry under title:

Fundamentals of marketing

5th Canadian ed.
ISBN 0-07-549697-6

1. Marketing.   I. Sommers, Montrose S., date-

HF5415.F86 1989   658.8   C88-094939-2

Dedicated to
Jesse, Annie, and Michael
Jennifer, Stephanie, and Karen

CONTENTS IN BRIEF

CONTENTS

PREFACE

We had two major goals in developing this revision. The first was to ensure that the content reflected what was needed for the future, the 1990s. The second, and equally important, was to ensure that what was needed for the 1990s was presented in a form consistent with what we know will help '90s students learn about the world of marketing.

To achieve our first goal, many changes were made to reflect where we are and where we are going. New concepts have been introduced; established concepts and approaches have been refined; current and emerging developments—be they economic, social, environmental, or strategic—have been emphasized. At the same time that we added material to reflect the future, we revised and reduced other sections to make more effective what we know from the past.

To achieve the goal of presenting Canadian marketing in the right form for the 1990s, we restructured and re-organized sections, chapters, and parts. What will be most obvious are the major changes in presentation style. This edition is designed not only to provide effective topic coverage but also to highlight, to contrast, to illustrate. Above all, it is designed to be a superior learning device, a delight to read and to teach from.

In order to achieve these goals, we went well beyond the "normal" revision. In addition to soliciting comments from a wide range of instructors and students, we conducted a series of focus-group interviews with 24 instructors from a variety of Canadian colleges and universities. Many of the changes in presentation and content are a direct result of this research and we are indeed indebted to our anonymous participants.

THE DESIGN

What is most strikingly new in the fifth edition is the appearance, form, and presentation of the book compared with previous editions as well as competing marketing texts. This "new design for effective learning" features an abundance of colour photographs, which serve to reinforce text material. Graphs and flow-charts strikingly capture and communicate concepts and information traditionally provided in text or tabular form.

These changes in appearance, form, and presentation are not idle atmospherics; they have been carefully developed to increase learning and teaching productivity.

They work to expand the meaning and impact of the written word by creating interest, providing clarity, explaining, illustrating, and reinforcing through the use of colour and design.

REVISED ORGANIZATION

The next most striking feature of the fifth edition is its revised organization and content. We have made significant changes in the content of the book for which we are very much indebted to the instructors who provided comments.

First, there is the matter of organization. Whereas the previous edition contained 25 chapters organized in eight parts, the fifth is made up of 20 chapters organized in seven parts. This re-design allows instructors and students to concentrate more easily on major topics and make use of the whole book in a semester or one-term course.

This trimming and slimming was accomplished in part by integrating service, industrial, not-for-profit, and international marketing concepts and illustrations throughout the text, rather than placing them in separate chapters that can be overlooked due to time constraints; this change allows these critical applications their rightful place. We also eliminated a special treatment of logistics; carefully pruned descriptive materials throughout; and combined two consumer behaviour chapters into one, and three pricing chapters into two.

We expect you will find these organizational changes make a significant overall improvement in the classroom.

NEW AND EXPANDED TOPICS

We added new materials at the same time that we trimmed others. Part 1 contains new information on marketing careers (Chapter 1), and new chapters on the Marketing Environment (2) and on Strategic Marketing Planning (3). The strategic marketing perspective is reinforced throughout the text at a level appropriate for an introductory course. Part 2 now contains redeveloped chapters on marketing research and information systems (6) and market segmentation (7). Part 6 has expanded materials on advertising, sales promotion, and public relations (18). Part 7 now includes coverage of the implementation stage in the management process as well as the previous coverage of the evaluation stage (19).

CANADIAN APPLICATIONS

New to each chapter is an opening vignette and a number of Marketing at Work files. These files provide interesting current detail on recognized Canadian situations, and reinforce basic concepts by demonstrating their wide range of applications. We have included many more illustrations of marketing applied to the non-business and service contexts.

NEW CASES

An exciting feature of the fifth edition is that 21 of the 23 cases are *brand new*. And not only are these new organizations well known, they're real achievers: 15 cases deal with award winners in the 1987 Canada Awards for Business Excellence Program. And since the "case series" treatment has proven to be extremely successful with students, we've presented three of these organizations in the series format.

THE BOOK: ITS BASIC APPROACH Those familiar with the earlier editions will find that, although some major changes have certainly been made, we have retained the essential features that have made this book an outstanding teaching and learning resource. The writing style continues to make the material interesting and easy to read. The basic organization is appropriate in that it reflects new developments as well as the needs of students and instructors. Material flows logically with a section-heading structure that makes for easier reading and outlining.

PEDAGOGICAL FEATURES

We provide many excellent end-of-chapter discussion questions. Most of these are thought-provoking and involve the application of text material rather than simply its recollection. Each of the 23 cases focusses on a topic covered in the text and provides students with an opportunity to apply concepts, practise analysis, and learn decision making.

We have also retained and updated such teaching and learning features as chapter objectives, chapter summaries, marketing arithmetic section, and the glossary. The key terms and concepts are highlighted in bold type throughout the text and are summarized in a list at the end of each chapter.

"A TOTAL SYSTEM"

The central theme and approach has also been retained from previous editions—that marketing is a total system of business action, rather than a fragmented assortment of functions and institutions. To us, this means that the essential marketing ideas are what matters, not lists of terms and functions or specialized formula approaches. While attention is paid to the role of marketing in our system, the book is written largely from the perspective of marketing personnel in an individual organization. This organization may be a manufacturer, a service provider, or an intermediary in a business or non-business field.

The marketing concept is a philosophy that stresses the need for a marketing orientation compatible with society's long-run interests. This philosophy is evident in the framework of the strategic marketing planning process. A company sets its marketing objectives, taking into consideration the environmental forces that influence its marketing effort. Management next selects target markets. The company then has four strategic elements—its product, price structure, distribution systems, and promotional activities—with which to build a marketing program to reach its markets and achieve its objectives. In all stages of the marketing process, management should use marketing research as a tool for problem solving and decision making.

TOPIC SEQUENCE

This framework for the strategic marketing planning process is reflected generally in the organization of the book's content. The text is divided into seven parts. Part

1 serves as an introduction and includes chapters on the marketing environment and strategic marketing planning. Part 2 is devoted to the analysis and selection of target markets—either consumer or industrial markets. It includes marketing information sytems.

Parts 3 through 6 deal with the development of a marketing program, and each of these parts covers one of the above-mentioned components of the strategic marketing mix. In Part 3 various topics related to the product are discussed. The company's price structure is the subject of Part 4, and Part 5 covers the distribution system. Part 6 is devoted to the total promotional program, including advertising, personal selling, and sales promotion. Part 7 deals with the implementation and evaluation of the total marketing effort in an individual firm. It also includes an appraisal of the role of marketing in our society, including the subjects of consumer criticisms and the social responsibility of an organization.

TEACHING AND LEARNING SUPPLEMENTS

The textbook is only the central element in a complete package of teaching and learning resources that has been considerably revised and expanded for this edition. This package includes:

Instructor's Manual

Includes outlines for each chapter, case commentaries, suggested answers to the end-of-chapter questions and the study guide exercises, and a glossary of rental films.

Test Bank

Available in printed and electronic formats. Our test generation software, available for the IBM-PC, Apple, and mainframe, helps make exam creation easier.

Colour Overhead Transparencies

These high-impact visual aids are designed to support your lectures. An extensive collection from our U.S. office.

Newsletter

A semi-annual update on trends, our newsletter is designed with instructors in mind. *Sommers and Barnes On Marketing* is published in early September and early January each year to help fill your need for current examples and applications. Suggestions are welcome!

Annual Case Update

We're committed to providing instructors with additional cases and with updates on cases already in the text. (You'll also find some additional cases from previous editions in the Instructor's Manual.)

McGraw-Hill Ryerson/CBC Venture Videotape

This professionally produced, 90 minute video ties segments from the *Venture* T.V. series to a variety of marketing concepts and applications. Comes with suggestions for classroom use. Fully integrated with the text.

CAD, Inc. Simulation Exercise

Designed for the IBM-PC, this simple, one-product simulation calls for nine decisions.

"Tomorrow's Customer" Booklet and Slides
Through a special agreement with Woods Gordon, we are pleased to make available copies of their glossy annual publication and accompanying high-impact slide show. A superb lecture aid!

Study Guide
Includes outlines for each chapter, sample test questions, crossword puzzles (designed to reinforce terminology), real-world readings for each chapter, and exercises that involve the students in practical marketing experiences.

ACKNOWLEDGEMENTS

Many people—our students, present and past colleagues, business executives, publishers, and other marketing instructors—have contributed greatly to this book over the years.

Specific mention must be made of those who contributed cases: Bill Frisbee, Lanita Carter, Donna Stapleton, and Lynn Morrissey. Tom Clift has once again provided an enormous amount of help with the Instructor's Manual and Study Guide. Michele Shapter was a great help with background research. Ian P. Gadbois, the Business Awards officer for the Canada Awards for Business Excellence Program, was immensely cooperative.

Of course, we are most indebted to the many instructors and students who have provided helpful suggestions for improvement over the years, and specifically to the 24 creative and spirited focus-group participants who helped us develop this new package. Feedback on the current edition and its supplements will be most appreciated. We welcome your letters.

The hundreds of Canadian companies that generously supplied us with photos, promotional materials, and other support are far too many to mention by name, but were clearly instrumental in making this book the effective tool that it is. Also, we want to thank those Canadian companies who allowed us to write such an interesting collection of new cases.

Finally, we would like to recognize, with grateful appreciation, the special efforts and tremendous support provided us by our sponsoring editor, Jackie Kaiser. Special thanks to Norma Christensen for her outstanding management of the photo research. We would also like to acknowledge the creative efforts of the McGraw-Hill Ryerson staff—specifically, Susan Calvert, Clive Powell, and Rachel Mansfield—and Wendy Thomas and Dan Kewley, all of whom did so much to make this book an excellent teaching and learning resource.

Montrose S. Sommers
James G. Barnes

PART 1

MODERN MARKETING AND ITS ENVIRONMENT

An introduction to marketing, the marketing environment, strategic planning, and the role of marketing in business today

The first part of this book is an introduction to the field of marketing. In Chapter 1 we explain what marketing is, how it has developed, and how it is continuing to develop. We look at the role of marketing both in our overall socioeconomic system and in the individual organization. This individual organization may be a business firm or a nonprofit organization; it may be marketing products, services, ideas, people or places; and it may be marketing them locally, provincially, across Canada or internationally.

In Chapter 2 we discuss the environmental forces which shape an organization's marketing program. Then in Chapter 3 we discuss the management process in marketing and introduce the concept of strategic marketing planning.

CHAPTER 1

THE FIELD OF MARKETING

CHAPTER GOALS

This chapter is an answer to the question, "What is marketing?" — and the answer may surprise you. After studying this chapter, you should understand:

- The meaning of marketing — its broad definition and business-system definition.
- The present-day importance of marketing, both in the total economy and in the individual firm.
- The marketing concept.
- The difference between selling and marketing.
- The four-stage evolution of marketing management.
- The broadened view of the marketing concept.

2

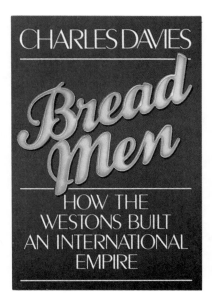

Get a view of the world of jobs today by looking through *The 100 Best Firms to Work for in Canada*; then scan the future by examining *The Next Canadian Economy*; and finally, read *Lessons from Winners in the Canada Awards for Business Excellence*.[1] You'll see that they have something in common — three themes are repeated. The best firms to work for now, the kinds of firms that are expected to succeed in the future, those firms that exhibit excellence, competitive vigour and high productivity all have outstanding leadership; they are populated with "turned-on" people, and they have a strong customer and market orientation.

As we move into the 1990s, into the next era in Canadian business, we can expect it to be more North American and world-based than ever before and more competitive and dynamic than ever before. It's clear that the need for leadership and commitment will continue, as will the need for a strong marketing orientation. The manager in the '90s, whatever else he or she will have to know, will have to understand such concepts as target markets, product life cycles, and market segmentation in order to be part of the pursuit of business excellence.

NATURE AND SCOPE OF MARKETING

One day early last summer two teenagers placed written notices in mailboxes in their neighbourhood announcing a lawn-care service that they had just started. They also went door to door to spread the word in person about their new venture. Whether these young entrepreneurs realized it or not, they were engaging in marketing. At the other end of the size scale, Canadian General Electric also engages in marketing when it realizes that CN and CP need more powerful, yet energy-efficient engines. C.G.E. then develops, sells, and delivers to the railroads a new model of engine to fill that need.

In a business firm, marketing generates the revenues that are managed by the financial people and used by the production people in creating products and services. The challenge of marketing is to generate those revenues by satisfying customers' wants at a profit and in a socially responsible manner.

Broad Dimensions of Marketing

But marketing is not limited to business. Whenever you try to persuade somebody to do something — donate to the Salvation Army, fasten a seat belt, lower a stereo's noise during study hours, vote for your candidate, accept a date with you (or maybe even marry you) — you are engaging in a marketing activity. So-called nonbusiness organizations — they really are in business but don't think of themselves as business people — also engage in marketing. Their ''product'' may be a vacation place they want you to visit, a social cause or an idea they want you to support, a person they are thrusting into the spotlight, or a museum or gallery they want you to attend. Whatever the product is, the organization is engaging in marketing.

As you may gather, marketing is a very broad-based activity, and consequently, it calls for a broad definition. **Now the essence of marketing is a transaction — an exchange — intended to satisfy human needs and wants**. That is, marketing occurs any time one social unit (person or organization) strives to exchange something of value with another social unit. Our broad definition then is as follows:

Marketing consists of all activities designed to generate and facilitate any exchange intended to satisfy human needs or wants.

Marketing at Work

File 1-1

CARE Canada Develops with Marketing

The application of marketing principles to not-for-profit organizations is illustrated through an advertisement recently placed in national newspapers by CARE Canada. This organization, which directs aid and development funding to Third World countries, advertised for a Fund Raising and Marketing Manager. The successful applicant was to be part of the senior management team and his or her duties would include liaison with the media; the acquisition, retention, renewal, and upgrading of donors; the management of fund-raising programs including direct mail, special events, in memoriam and anniversary giving, gift clubs, sponsorships, memberships and telemarketing; and supporting activities including strategic planning, volunteer and paid personnel motivation, and management, research and analysis. Why does CARE Canada need a marketing manager? What ''exchanges'' is CARE Canada interested in stimulating? What is its ''product line''?

In this book the terms *needs* and *wants* are used interchangeably. In a limited physiological sense, we might say that we ''need'' only food, clothing, and shelter. Beyond these requirements we get into the area of ''wants.'' More realistically in our society today, however, many people would say that they ''need'' a telephone or they ''need'' some form of mechanized transportation.

CONCEPT OF EXCHANGE

Now let's examine the concept of **exchange** as this term relates to marketing. Exchange is one of three ways in which a person can satisfy a want. Suppose you want some clothes. You can sew them, knit them, or otherwise produce the clothes yourself. You can borrow them or use some form of coercion to get the clothes. Or you can offer something of value (money, service, other products) to another person who will voluntarily exchange the clothes for what you offer. It is only the third approach that we call an exchange in the sense that marketing is taking place.

Within the context of our definition of marketing, for an exchange to occur the following conditions must exist:

1. Two or more social units (individuals or organizations) must be involved. If you are totally self-sufficient in some area, there is no exchange and hence no marketing.
2. The parties must be involved voluntarily, and each must have wants to be satisfied.
3. Each party must have something of value to contribute in the exchange, and each party must believe it will benefit from the exchange.
4. The parties must be able to communicate with each other. Assume that you want a new sweater and a clothing store has sweaters for sale. But if you and the store are not aware of each other — you are not communicating — then there will be no exchange.

Within this broad definition of marketing, then, (1) the marketers, (2) what they are marketing, and (3) their potential markets all assume broad dimensions. The category of **marketers** might include, in addition to business firms, such diverse social units as (a) a political party trying to market its candidate to the public; (b) the director of an art museum providing new exhibits to generate greater attendance and financial support; (c) a labour union marketing its ideas to members and to the company management; and (d) professors trying to make their courses interesting for students.

In addition to the range of items normally considered as products and services, **what is being marketed** might include (a) *ideas*, such as reducing air pollution or contributing to a charity; (b) *people*, such as a new football coach or a political candidate; and (c) *places*, such as industrial plant sites or a place to go for a vacation.

In a broad sense, **markets** include more than the direct consumers of products, services, and ideas. Thus a college's or university's market includes the legislators who provide funds, the citizens living nearby who may be affected by student activities, and the alumni. A business firm's market may include government regulatory agencies, environmentalists, and local tax assessors.

Our broad (or macro) definition tells us something about the role of marketing in our socioeconomic system. But this is a book about the business of marketing in an individual organization within that system. These organizations may be business firms in the conventional sense of the word *business*. Or they may be what is called a nonbusiness or a nonprofit organization — a hospital, university, Big Brothers, church, police department, or museum, for example. Both groups — business and nonbusiness — face essentially the same basic marketing problems.

CALGARY ZOO

botanical garden & prehistoric park

The category of "what is being marketed" can include some interesting things.

Business Dimensions of Marketing

A nonbusiness "business" also engages in marketing.

Now many executives in those organizations, as well as many household consumers, think they already know a good bit about the business of marketing. After all, churches run newspaper ads and museums sell prints of famous paintings. And people at home watch television commercials that persuade them to buy. These people purchase products on a self-service basis in supermarkets. Some have friends who "can get it for them wholesale." But in each of these examples, we are talking about only one part of the totality of marketing activities. Consequently, we need a micro, business definition of marketing to guide executives in business or nonbusiness organizations in the management of their marketing effort.

BUSINESS DEFINITION OF MARKETING

Our micro definition of marketing — applicable in a business or nonbusiness organization — is as follows:

Marketing is a total system of business activities designed to plan, price, promote, and distribute want-satisfying products, services, and ideas to target markets in order to achieve organizational objectives.[2]

Marketing is:
a system:	for business activities
designed to:	plan, price, promote, and distribute
something of value:	want-satisfying products, services, and ideas
for the benefit of:	the target market — present and potential household consumers or industrial users
to achieve:	the organization's objectives.

This definition has some significant implications:

- It is a managerial, systems definition.
- The entire system of business activities must be customer-oriented. Customers' wants must be recognized and satisfied effectively.
- The marketing program starts with the germ of a product or service idea and does not end until the customer's wants are completely satisfied, which may be some time after the sale is made.
- The definition implies that to be successful, marketing must maximize profitable sales over the *long run*. Thus, customers must be satisfied in order for a company to get the repeat business that ordinarily is so vital to success.

It should be noted that the above definitions, as well as most others commonly used, always include products, services, and ideas in their scope. In discussions, however, products are most frequently referred to and, to a lesser extent, products and services. In fact, the term *product* is now being used in a broader sense than in the past. It stands for various combinations of product, service, and ideas — what could be termed a product/service complex. No longer is it uncommon to hear the term product being used to refer to a "product complex" that consists primarily of services. Recently, when a new member of the board of directors of the Calgary Stampeders was asked how the franchise was going to be saved, his immediate response was, "We're going to put a better product on the field."

PRESENT-DAY IMPORTANCE OF MARKETING

Today most nations — regardless of their degree of economic development or their political philosophy — are recognizing the importance of marketing. Economic growth in developing nations depends greatly upon those nations' ability to develop effective distribution systems to handle their raw materials and their industrial output. Countries with some major state-owned industries are looking to modern marketing practices as a way to improve their economic health. And communist countries are using advertising, pricing, and other marketing activities to improve their domestic distribution systems and to compete more effectively in international trade.

Importance in the Canadian Socioeconomic System

It is in North America and Western Europe that modern marketing has developed to the greatest extent. Aggressive marketing practices have been responsible for a high material standard of living, particularly in Canada and the United States. Today, through mass, low-cost marketing, Canadians enjoy products that once were considered luxuries and that still are so classified in many countries.

In Canada, modern marketing came of age after World War I, when the words *surplus* and *overproduction* became an important part of the economics vocabulary. This is in spite of the fact that the Hudson's Bay Company was incorporated in 1670. Since about 1920, except during World War II and the immediate postwar period, a strong *buyers' market* has existed. That is, the available supply of products and services has far surpassed effective demand. There has been relatively little difficulty in producing most goods. The real problem has been in marketing them. During recession periods, business people soon realize that it is a slowdown in marketing that force cutbacks in production. It becomes evident that ''nothing happens until somebody sells something.''

The importance of marketing in the business world might be more easily understood in quantitative terms. *Between one-fourth and one-third of the civilian labour force is engaged in marketing activities*. Furthermore, over the past century, jobs in marketing have increased at a much more rapid rate than jobs in production. The great increase in the number of marketing workers is a reflection of marketing's expanded role in the economy and the increased demand for marketing services.

Another measure of the importance of marketing is its cost. On the average, about *50 cents of each dollar we spend at the retail level goes to cover marketing costs*. These costs should not be confused with marketing *profits*, however. Nor should it be assumed that products and services would cost less if there were no marketing activities.

AN ECONOMY OF ABUNDANCE

The type of economy we have in Canada and the United States largely explains why marketing is so much a North American phenomenon. Ours is an economy of abundance. This means that as a nation, we produce and consume far beyond our subsistence needs. Although marketing exists in every type of *modern* economy, it is especially important for successful business performance in a highly competitive economy of abundance.

Marketing activity has the task of encouraging the consumption of the vast output of our industry. Although modern marketing has been successful, its success has not been greeted with joy in all quarters. Many social and economic resources are scarce and are becoming more so. A number of respected students of social and economic systems have raised serious questions concerning the influence that marketing has on the allocation of these resources. The question they raise is whether too much marketing is leading to a misallocation of resources. Is marketing accepting its responsibility to guide our use of economic resources toward socially desirable goals? We may be so successful in marketing automobiles and fashionable clothing that we overlook more basic values, such as the provision of education and housing, and the elimination of pollution. In other words, are we marketing the wrong things?

Importance in the Individual Firm

Marketing considerations should be the most critical factor guiding all short-range and long-range planning in any organization, for two reasons. First, the core of marketing is customer want-satisfaction, and that is the basic social and economic

The customer comes first at Mark's Work Wearhouse.

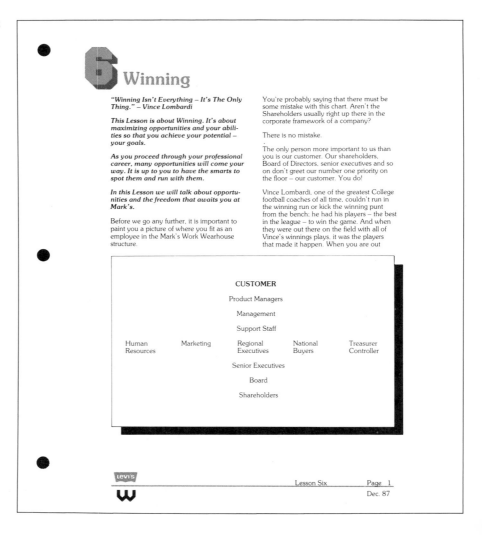

Winning

"Winning Isn't Everything – It's The Only Thing." – Vince Lombardi

This Lesson is about Winning. It's about maximizing opportunities and your abilities so that you achieve your potential – your goals.

As you proceed through your professional career, many opportunities will come your way. It is up to you to have the smarts to spot them and run with them.

In this Lesson we will talk about opportunities and the freedom that awaits you at Mark's.

Before we go any further, it is important to paint you a picture of where you fit as an employee in the Mark's Work Wearhouse structure.

You're probably saying that there must be some mistake with this chart. Aren't the Shareholders usually right up there in the corporate framework of a company?

There is no mistake.

The only person more important to us than you is our customer. Our shareholders, Board of Directors, senior executives and so on don't greet our number one priority on the floor – our customer. You do!

Vince Lombardi, one of the greatest College football coaches of all time, couldn't run in the winning run or kick the winning punt from the bench; he had his players – the best in the league – to win the game. And when they were out there on the field with all of Vince's winnings plays, it was the players that made it happen. When you are out

CUSTOMER

Product Managers

Management

Support Staff

| Human Resources | Marketing | Regional Executives | National Buyers | Treasurer Controller |

Senior Executives

Board

Shareholders

LEVI'S

Lesson Six   Page 1

Dec. 87

justification for the existence of virtually all organizations. Second, marketing is the revenue-generating activity in any organization — nothing happens until somebody sells something.

Too often, unfortunately, business has been oriented toward production. Products are designed by engineers, manufactured by production people, priced by accountants, and then given to sales managers to sell. That procedure generally won't work in today's environment of intense competition and constant change. Just *building* a good product will not result in a company's success, nor will it have much bearing on consumer welfare. The product must be *marketed* to consumers before its full value can be realized.

Today a company must first determine what the customers want and then build a product and marketing program to satisfy those wants, hopefully at a profit. Many organizational departments in a company are essential to its growth, *but marketing is still the sole revenue-producing activity*. This fact sometimes is overlooked by the production managers who use these revenues and by the financial executives who manage them.

File 1-2

Real Products Are for Real Users

A production orientation in business and other organizations is illustrated by a disregard for or lack of attention to the customer or other people upon whom the organization must rely if it is to prosper. For example, when most of Canada's food companies develop new products in their test kitchens, they normally go through a very elaborate series of research projects to determine whether the test products are acceptable to target consumers. Failure to do so amounts to producing whatever the plant is able to turn out, without any regard for whether the consumer finds it attractive or wants to buy it. For several years, a small manufacturer of ice-cream snack items asked family members of employees to try new products that the company was considering adding to its product line. The company also occasionally sent samples to local Cub and Brownie groups. They were confident that their product development process was a sound one, because they rarely received any complaints about the new products. Did this ice-cream manufacturer have a marketing orientation?

Importance to You Okay, so marketing is important in our economy and in an individual organization. But why should you personally study marketing? What's in it for you? Our answer to these questions consists of three points. First, the study of marketing should be fun and exciting to you because you are participating in marketing in so many of your daily activities. You buy various articles in different stores. You watch television with its advertising commercials, and you read magazines and newspaper ads. As a student, you are part of your school's market and you might complain about the price (tuition) of the service (education) that you are receiving. Truly, marketing occupies a large part of your daily life. If you doubt this, just imagine for a moment where you would be if there were no marketing institutions — no retail stores, no advertising to give you information, etc.

A second reason for your studying marketing is to make you a better-informed consumer. When you buy a product, you'll understand something of the company's pricing or branding strategy. You'll understand the role of promotion and the role of middlemen (retailers and wholesalers) in distribution.

The third reason for studying marketing ties in with your career aspirations. If you plan a career in marketing, then of course you are interested in what we have to say — and particularly in the career section at the end of this chapter. Those of you who plan a career in accounting, finance, or some other business field can learn how marketing affects managerial decision making in your field. Finally, some of you may seek a career in a nonbusiness field. You may work in the field of music, psychology, health care, government, education, social work, etc. It is highly likely that organizations in any of those fields will be involved in marketing.

*M*arketing at Work

Marketing Is Route to the Top...

Marketing skill is gaining importance as a prerequisite for appointment to a CEO position in many Canadian industries. Not only in the consumer packaged goods sector, where marketing has traditionally been held in high regard, but in other industries as well, increasing world competition and efforts to improve profitability have increased the allure of a marketing background as the best route to the CEO's office.

A study by Caldwell Partners and the University of Toronto involved interviews with 100 chief executives from the Financial Post 500 corporations. Twenty-two percent of those surveyed cited Marketing as the department most likely to produce their companies' next chief executive, followed by Finance (17%). Marketing and sales are also the recommended launching pads for those just beginning their business careers who already have their long-term sights set on the top job.

Source: Bruce Gates, "Marketing Skills Key in Quest for CEO's," *The Financial Post*, Feb. 22, 1986, p. 24.

THE MARKETING CONCEPT

As business people have come to recognize that marketing is vitally important to the success of a firm, an entirely new way of business thinking — a new philosophy — has evolved. It is called the *marketing concept*, and it is based on three fundamental beliefs (see Fig. 1-1):

- All company planning and operations should be *customer-oriented*.
- The goal of the firm should be *profitable sales volume* and not just volume for the sake of volume alone.
- All marketing activities in a firm should be *organizationally coordinated*.

FIGURE 1-1
The marketing concept is built on three foundation stones.

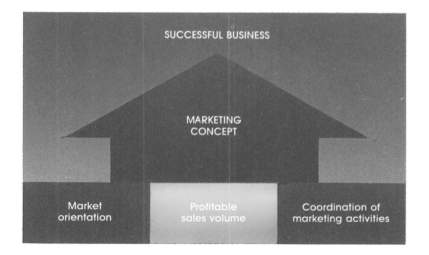

In its fullest sense, the **marketing concept** is a philosophy of business that states that the customers' want-satisfaction is the economic and social justification for a firm's existence. Consequently, all company activities should be devoted to determining customers' wants and then satisfying those wants, while still making a profit over the long run.

Difference between Marketing and Selling

"That's why we switched to Bank of Montreal's New Investment Savings."

Banks also are marketing instead of selling.

Unfortunately, even today many people, including some business executives, still do not understand the difference between selling and marketing. In fact, many people think the terms are synonymous. Instead, these concepts actually have *opposite* meanings.

Under the *selling* concept, a company makes a product and then uses various selling methods to persuade customers to buy the product. In effect, the company is bending consumer demand to fit the company's supply. Just the opposite occurs under the *marketing* concept. The company finds out what the customer wants and then tries to develop a product complex that will satisfy that want and still yield a profit. Now the company is bending its supply to the will of consumer demand.

We can summarize the contrasts between selling and marketing as follows:

Selling	**Marketing**
1. Emphasis is on the product.	**1.** Emphasis is on customers' wants.
2. Company first makes the product and then figures out how to sell it.	**2.** Company first determines customers' wants and then figures out how to make and deliver a product to satisfy those wants.
3. Management is sales-volume-oriented.	**3.** Management is profit-oriented.
4. Planning is short-run-oriented, in terms of today's products and markets.	**4.** Planning is long-run-oriented, in terms of new products, tomorrow's markets, and future growth.
5. Stresses needs of seller.	**5.** Stresses wants and needs of buyers.

MARKETING MANAGEMENT AND ITS EVOLUTION

For a business enterprise to realize the full benefits of the marketing concept, that philosophy must be translated into action. This means that (1) the marketing activities in the firm must be fully coordinated and well managed, and (2) the chief marketing executive must be accorded an important role in company planning. As these two moves occur, marketing management begins to develop. **Marketing management** is the marketing concept in action.

Since the Industrial Revolution, marketing management in North American business has evolved through three stages of development, and a fourth one is emerging. However, many companies are still in the earlier stages. And as yet only a few firms exhibit the managerial philosophies and practices characteristic of the most advanced developmental period.

Production-Orientation Stage

In this first stage, a company typically is production-oriented. Executives in production and engineering shape its planning. The function of the sales department is simply to sell the company's output, at a price set by production and financial executives. This is the ''build a better mousetrap'' stage. The underlying assumption is that marketing effort is not needed to get people to buy a product that is well made and reasonably priced.

During this period, manufacturers have sales departments — marketing is not yet recognized — headed by sales managers whose main job is to operate a sales force. This form of organization predominated in North America until about the start of the Great Depression in the 1930s.

Sales-Orientation Stage

The Depression of the early 1930s made it clear that the main problem in economies no longer was to make or grow enough products, but rather to *sell* the output. Just *producing* a better mousetrap brought no assurance of market success. The product had to be sold, and this called for substantial promotional effort. Thus North American firms entered a period when selling and sales executives were given new respect and responsibilities by company management.

Unfortunately, it was also during this period that selling acquired much of its bad reputation. This was the age of the ''hard sell'' — pictured in terms of the unscrupulous used-car sales person or door-to-door encyclopedia sales people. What is more unfortunate is that even today many organizations still believe that they must operate with a hard-sell philosophy to prosper. And as long as there are companies operating with a hard-sell philosophy, there will be continued (and justified, in the authors' opinion) criticisms of selling and marketing. The sales era generally extended from the 1930s well into the 1950s, although no specific dates sharply define any of the four stages.

Marketing-Orientation Stage

Customers like convenience banking.

Social Responsibility and Human-Orientation Stage

Marketing-Orientation Stage

In the third stage, companies embrace the concept of coordinated marketing management, directed toward the twin goals of customer orientation and *profitable* sales volume. Attention is focussed on marketing, rather than on selling, and the top executive in this area is called a marketing manager or a vice president of marketing. In this stage, several activities that traditionally were the province of other executives become the responsibility of the marketing manager. For instance, inventory control, warehousing, and aspects of product planning are often turned over to the marketing manager. These managers should be brought in at the *beginning*, rather than at the end, of a production cycle. Marketing should influence all short-term and long-range company planning.

The key to implementing the marketing concept successfully is a favourable attitude on the part of top management. The president of Burroughs Corporation caught the spirit of firms that have fully embraced the marketing concept when he said, "Any company is nothing but a marketing organization." The president of Pepsi-Cola said, "Our business is the business of marketing."

We are *not* saying that marketing executives should hold the top positions in a company. The marketing concept *does not* imply that the president of a firm must come up through the marketing department. We say only that the president must be marketing-oriented.

The most progressive Canadian firms are now in this third stage in the evolution of marketing management. The marketing concept continues to be adopted by both large and medium-sized companies. How well many companies have actually implemented the marketing concept, however, is still questionable. Many companies are using the appropriate titles and other external trappings, but they are paying little more than lip service to the concept. In the apparel industry, for example, some observers believe that a combination of foreign competition plus the lack of a marketing orientation will force many manufacturers out of business by 1990.[3] Only the consumer-sensitive firms, such as Sun Ice of Calgary or the Monaco Group of Toronto, have a good chance of escaping the fate of those with obsolete orientations.

Social Responsibility and Human-Orientation Stage

Social and economic conditions in the 1970s and 1980s have led to the fourth stage in the evolution of marketing management — a stage characterized by its societal orientation. It is increasingly obvious that marketing executives must act in a socially responsible manner if they wish to succeed, or even survive. External pressures — consumer discontent, a concern for environmental problems, and political-legal forces — are influencing the marketing problems of countless firms.

Many people are realizing that there are finite limits to our natural resources. We have already experienced shortages of several resources. Consequently, this fourth period might be viewed as a "survival" stage. Marketers must be more broadly environmentally oriented whether we mean the stocks of raw materials, of energy resources, of clean air and water, or of just the "good life" in general.

Perhaps this fourth stage may also be viewed more broadly as a human-orientation period — a time in which there is a concern for the management of human resources. We sense a change in emphasis from materialism to humanism in our society. One mark of an affluent society is a shift from consumption of products to services, and a shift in cultural emphasis from things to people. In this fourth stage, marketing management must be concerned with creating and delivering a better quality of *life*, rather than only a material standard of *living*.[4]

BROADENING THE MARKETING CONCEPT

The wave of consumer protests starting in the late 1960s — the rise of *consumerism* — was an indication to some people that the marketing concept was a failure. Others went so far as to suggest that the marketing concept is an operational philosophy that *conflicts* with a firm's social responsibility.

From one point of view, these charges are true. A firm may totally satisfy its customers (in line with the marketing concept), while at the same time be adversely affecting society. To illustrate, a steel company in Cape Breton might be satisfying its customers in Brazil with the right product, reasonably priced. Yet at the same time this company may be accused of polluting the air and water in Nova Scotia.

The marketing concept and a company's social responsibility can be quite compatible. They need not conflict. The key to compatibility lies in extending the *breadth* and *time* dimensions in the definition of the marketing concept.

Regarding *breadth* — let us assume that a company's market includes not only the buyers of the firm's products, but also other people directly affected by the firm's operations. Then, under this broader definition of customers, the marketing concept and the social responsibility of the firm can indeed be compatible. In our example, the Cape Breton steel mill has several "customer" groups to satisfy. Among these are (1) the Brazilian industrial customers of the steel shipments; (2) the consumers of the air that contains impurities given off by the mill; (3) the recreational users of the local river affected by waste matter from the mill; and (4) the community affected by employee traffic driving to and from work.

This broadening of the marketing concept is consistent with our previously discussed, broad definition of marketing. There we recognized that a given marketer may have several different target markets.

Regarding the extended *time* dimension — we must view consumer satisfaction and profitable business as goals to be achieved *over the long run*. If a company prospers in the long run, it must be doing a reasonably good job of satisfying its customers' current social and economic demands.

*M*arketing at Work

File 1-4

Encouraging Healthy Life-Styles with Marketing

We are all familiar with the application of the marketing concept to retail stores and manufacturers of consumer products such as McCain's French Fries, Nabob Coffee, and Bombardier Ski-Doos. But we are seeing an increasing use of marketing principles in nontraditional organizations. For example, some hospitals in North America have appointed vice presidents of marketing. A major hospital in St. John's appointed a Patient Relations Manager, whose responsibility it is to seek feedback from patients and their families through surveys and interviews. The same hospital has been holding an annual Run for Health since 1978; this is a mass participation event in which several thousand adults and children run, jog, or walk over a five-kilometre course to raise funds for the hospital's health foundation. Why would the hospital need feedback from patients? Other than fund raising, what other objectives might it have in promoting its Run for Health? Is this really marketing?

Thus, the marketing concept and a company's social responsibility are compatible, if management strives *over the long run* to (1) satisfy the wants of product and service buying customers, (2) satisfy the societal wants affected by the firm's activities, and (3) meet the company's profit goals.

CAREERS IN MARKETING

At the beginning of this chapter, we noted that about one-quarter to one-third of all jobs are in the field of marketing. These jobs cover a wide range of activities. Furthermore, this variety of jobs also covers a wide range of qualifications and aptitudes. Jobs in personal selling, for example, call for a set of qualifications that are different from those in marketing research. A person likely to be successful in advertising may not be a good prospect in physical distribution. Consequently, the personal qualifications and aptitudes of different individuals make them candidates for different types of marketing jobs.

In this section we shall briefly describe the major jobs in marketing, grouping them by the title of the job or the activity. As you work through the text, you will see the kinds of activities, characteristics, and responsibilities associated with the major marketing jobs, and the context in which they exist.

Advertising

Advertising jobs are available in three broad types of organizations. First there are jobs with the *advertisers*. Then there are careers with the various *media* (newspapers, TV stations, magazines, etc.) that carry the ads. And, finally, there are the many jobs with *advertising agencies* which specialize in creating and producing individual ads and entire campaigns.

Jobs in advertising encompass a variety of aptitudes and interests — artistic, creative, managerial, research, and sales, for example. There is a real opportunity for the artistic or creative type of person. Agencies and advertising departments need copywriters, artists, photographers, layout designers, printing experts, and others to create and produce the ads.

The account executive occupies a key position in advertising agencies. People in this position are the liaison between the agency and its clients (the advertisers). Account executives coordinate the agency's efforts with the clients' marketing programs.

Another group of advertising jobs involves buying and selling the media time and space. Advertisers and agencies also often need people who can conduct consumer behaviour studies and other types of marketing research.

Brand or Product Management

Brand or product managers are responsible for planning and directing the entire marketing program for a given brand, product, or a group of products.

Early on, product managers are concerned with the packaging, labelling, and other aspects of the product itself. They also are responsible for doing the necessary marketing research to identify the market. They plan the advertising, personal selling, and sales promotional programs and also are concerned with the pricing, physical distribution, and legal aspects of the product. All in all, being a product manager is almost like running your own business.

Typically, the job is a staff position in the organization, rather than a line operating position. Thus, the product manager often has much responsibility for a product's performance but must coordinate with line managers to see that his or her directives and plans are put into effect.

Consumer Affairs and Protection

This broad area encompasses several activities that provide job and career opportunities. Many of these jobs are an outgrowth of the consumer movement discussed in Chapter 2. Many companies, for example, have a consumer affairs department to handle consumer complaints. Various federal and provincial agencies are set up to keep watch on business firms and to provide information and assistance to consumers. Grocery products manufacturers and gas and electric companies regularly hire consumer and marketing specialists to aid consumers in product use. Government and private product-testing agencies hire people to test products for safety, durability, and other features.

Distribution

A large number of jobs exist in this field, and the prospects are even brighter as we look ahead to the 1990s. More and more firms are expected to adopt the systems approach in distribution to control the huge expenses involved in materials movement and warehousing.

Manufacturers, retailers, and all other product-handling firms have jobs that involve two stages of distribution. First, the product must be moved to the firm for processing or resale. Then the finished products must be distributed to the markets. These distribution tasks involve jobs in transportation management, warehousing, and inventory control. In addition, the many transportation carriers and warehousing firms also provide a variety of jobs.

Marketing Research

Marketing research jobs cover a broad range of activities. People are hired for marketing research jobs by manufacturers, retailers, service marketers, government agencies, and other types of organizations. There also are a number of specialized marketing research companies. Generally, however, there are fewer jobs in marketing research than in personal selling or in advertising.

Marketing research people are problem solvers. They collect and analyze masses of information. Consequently, they need an aptitude for methodical, analytical types of work. Typically, some quantitative skills are needed. It helps if you understand statistics and feel comfortable using a computer.

Public Relations

The public or community relations department in an organization is the connecting link between that organization and its various publics. The department especially must deal with, or go through, the news media to reach these publics. Public relations people must be especially good at communications.

In essence, the job of public relations is to project the desired company image to the public. More specifically, public relations people are responsible for telling the public about the company — its products, community activities, social programs, environmental improvement activities, labour policies, views regarding controversial issues, and so on.

Purchasing

The opposite of selling is buying, and here there are a lot of good jobs. Every retail organization needs people to buy the merchandise that is to be sold. Frequently the route to the top in retailing is through the buying (also called merchandising) division of the business. Large retailers have many positions for buyers and assistant buyers. Typically, each merchandise department has a buyer.

The purchasing agent is the industrial market counterpart of the retail-store buyer. Virtually all firms in the industrial market have purchasing departments. People in these departments buy for the production, office, and sales departments in their firms.

Retail buyers and industrial purchasing agents need many of the same skills. They must be able to analyze markets, determine merchandise needs, and negotiate with sellers. It also helps if you have some knowledge of credit, finance, and distribution.

Personal Sales

By far, product and service sales jobs are the most numerous of all the jobs in marketing. These personal selling jobs (1) cover a wide variety of activities, (2) are found in a wide variety of organizations, and (3) carry a wide variety of titles. Consider the following people: a sales clerk in a department store; a sales engineer providing technical assistance in the sales of hydraulic valves; a representative for Canadair selling a fleet of airplanes; a marketing consultant presenting his or her services. All these people are engaged in personal selling, but each sales job is different from the others.

The sales and service representation job is the most common entry-level position in marketing. Furthermore, a sales job is a widely used stepping-stone to a management position. Many companies recruit people for these jobs with the intention of promoting some or all of them into management positions. Personal selling and sales management jobs are also a good route to the top in a firm. This is so because it is relatively easy to measure a person's performance and productivity in selling. Sales results are highly visible.

Sales Promotion   The main function of sales promotion is to tie together the activities in personal selling and advertising. Effective sales promotion requires imagination and creativity, coupled with a sound foundation in marketing fundamentals.

One group of sales promotion activities involves retailer in-store displays and window displays — planning and creating them. Another area of sales promotion jobs involves direct-mail advertising programs. Still another area deals with service demonstrations, trade shows, and other company exhibits. Sales promotion activities also include the development and management of premium giveaways, contests, product sampling, and other types of promotion.

Marketing careers can be pursued in large and small firms, in all parts of Canada as well as abroad in Canadian international marketing activities. Opportunities for marketing careers exist at all levels of the economy, ranging from manufacturing and production organizations through wholesaling, retailing and service provision and marketing. More than ever before, marketing careers exist in nonprofit organizations as well as business.

STRUCTURAL PLAN OF THIS BOOK   The overall plan of this book is to use the managerial-micro approach to study the strategic management of the marketing activities in an individual organization. The book is divided into seven parts consisting of 20 chapters in total.

Part 1 provides us with the background and framework within which we can build our marketing program. The first chapter has covered the nature, importance, and evolution of marketing. In Chapter 2 we see that a company's marketing activity is shaped largely by external, uncontrollable environmental forces, as well as by the environment within the firm. Chapter 3 explains the marketing management process and the fundamentals of strategic planning in a marketing organization.

Part 2 — Chapters 4 through 7 — deals with the identification and analysis of a company's target markets. In Chapters 4 and 5, we examine the demographic, sociological, and psychological influences on buying behaviour in consumer and industrial markets. We discuss the topics of marketing information systems and research and segmentation and target definition in Chapters 6 and 7.

Parts 3 through 6 — Chapters 8 through 18 — are devoted to designing and developing a strategic marketing mix. A marketing mix is a combination of the four elements that constitute the core of a marketing program. The four are an organization's product assortment (Part 3), price structure (Part 4), distribution system (Part 5), and promotional activities (Part 6).

Part 7 deals with the implementation of strategic planning and an evaluation of the performance of the organization's marketing program. In Chapter 19 we use a micro approach to evaluate the performance of the marketing effort in an individual firm. In Chapter 20 we use a macro approach as we evaluate the role of marketing in our socioeconomic system.

For additional help and information we have provided an appendix at the back of the book covering the fundamentals of marketing arithmetic.

SUMMARY   In a broad sense, marketing is any exchange activity intended to satisfy human wants. In this context we need to look broadly at (1) who should be classed as marketers, (2) what is being marketed, and (3) who are the target markets. In a business sense, marketing is a system of business action designed to plan, price, promote, and distribute want-satisfying products, services, and ideas to market in order to achieve organizational objectives.

Marketing is practised today in all modern nations, regardless of their political philosophies. But marketing has developed to the greatest extent in North America. Both Canada and the U.S. have value systems and economies that sustain high-level marketing. One of every three or four people is employed in marketing, and about half of what consumers spend goes to cover the costs of marketing.

The philosophy of the marketing concept holds that a company should (1) be customer-oriented, (2) strive for profitable sales volume, and (3) coordinate all its marketing activities. Marketing management is the vehicle that business uses to activate the marketing concept. Our socioeconomic structure — and marketing management is part of it — has evolved:

- from an agrarian economy in a rural setting,
- through a production-oriented, subsistence-level economy in an urban society,
- and then through a sales-oriented economy,
- into today's customer-oriented economy, featuring a society with a great deal of discretionary purchasing power.

Looking to the future, our attention is shifting to societal relationships:

- to the quality of our life and environment.
- to the conservation and allocation of our scarce resources.
- to a greater concern for people.

These point up the need to broaden the marketing concept to include satisfaction of *all* a company's markets, while generating profits *over the long run*.

NOTES   [1] These three publications, while they approach careers, business excellence, and Canada's future from different perspectives, nevertheless make the same key observations. For the fourth annual look at careers, see Eva Innes, Robert Perry and Jim Lyon, *The 100 Best Firms to Work for in Canada*, Toronto: Collins Publishing Co. Ltd., 1987. For a view of what Canada's economic and business future holds and what is needed to succeed, see Dian Cohen and Kristin Shannon, *The Next Canadian Economy*, Buffalo, N.Y.; Eden Press, 1984. For a close look at excellence in Canadian business and the role of marketing, see Peter Larson, *Improving Competitiveness: Lessons from Winners in the Canada Awards for Business Excellence*, Ottawa, The Conference Board of Canada, July, 1987.

[2] This definition is essentially the same as the one used in all previous editions of this book. We modified our original definition slightly to conform generally with a revised American Marketing Association definition. The AMA definition is as follows: "Marketing is the process of planning and executing the conception, pricing, promotion, and distribution of ideas, goods, and services to create exchanges that satisfy individual and organizational objectives." See "AMA Board Approves New Marketing Definition," *Marketing News*, Mar. 1, 1985, p. 1.

[3] *Marketing News*, Jan. 18, 1985, p. 1. For a report on some other traditionally non-marketing-oriented industries (textiles, transportation, consumer durables, and retailing) and their struggles to become more marketing-oriented, see Edward G. Michaels, ''Marketing Muscle,'' *Business Horizons*, May–June 1982, pp. 63–74.

[4] See Leslie M. Dawson, ''Marketing for Human Needs in a Humane Future,'' *Business Horizons*, June 1980, pp. 72–82.

KEY TERMS AND CONCEPTS

The numbers refer to the pages on which the terms and concepts are defined. In addition, see the glossary at the back of the book.

Marketing (broad definition) 4

Concept of exchange 5

Marketing (micro, business definition) 6

Economy of abundance 7

Marketing concept 10

Marketing management: 12

Production-orientation stage 12

Sales-orientation stage 12

Marketing-orientation stage 13

Social-responsibility stage 13

Broadening the marketing concept 14

QUESTIONS AND PROBLEMS

1. Explain the concept of an exchange, including the conditions that must exist for an exchange to occur.

2. In the following marketing exchanges, what is the ''something of value'' that each party contributes in the exchange?

    a. Your school ⟷ You as a student
    b. Fire department ⟷ People in your hometown.
    c. Flour miller ⟷ Bakery.
    d. CARE Canada ⟷ Contributors.
    e. Delta Hotels ⟷ Publisher's sales meeting.

3. In line with the broader, societal concept of marketing, describe some of the ways in which nonbusiness organizations to which you belong are engaged in marketing activities.

4. For each of the following organizations, describe (1) what is being marketed and (2) who is the target market.

    a. Calgary Stampeders professional football team.
    b. Canadian Auto Workers labour union.
    c. Professor teaching a first-year chemistry course.
    d. Fire department in your city.

5. One writer has stated that any business has only two functions — marketing and innovation. How would you explain this statement to a student majoring in engineering, accounting, finance, or personnel management?

6. One way of explaining the importance of marketing in our economy is to consider how we would live if there were no marketing facilities. Describe some of the ways in which your daily activities would be affected under such circumstances.

7. Explain the three elements that constitute the marketing concept.

8. Explain the difference between marketing and selling.

9. Name some companies that you believe are still in the production or sales stage in the evolution of marketing management. Explain why you chose each of them.

10. The marketing concept does not imply that marketing executives will run the firm. The concept requires only that whoever is in top management be marketing-oriented. Give examples of how a production manager, company treasurer, or personnel manager can be marketing-oriented.

CHAPTER 2

THE MARKETING ENVIRONMENT

CHAPTER GOALS

A variety of environmental forces impinge on an organization's marketing system. Some of these are external to the firm and thus are largely uncontrollable by the organization. Other forces within the firm generally are controllable by management. After studying this chapter, you should understand:

- How the following macroenvironmental factors can influence a company's marketing system:

    a. Demography.
    b. Economic conditions.
    c. Competition.
    d. Social and cultural forces.
    e. Political and legal forces.
    f. Technology.

- How the external microenvironmental factors of the market, suppliers, and marketing intermediaries all can influence an organization's marketing program.
- How the nonmarketing resources within a company can influence that firm's marketing system.
- The need to coordinate the marketing activities within an organization.

Managers and planners of marketing systems must know the past, the present, and the future. They must be aware of the environmental forces that influence the success of the marketing systems they plan for the 1990s.

- What is the impact of the greying of the ''boomers''?
- Where will the microchip cause further changes?
- How will increased global competition affect our markets and industries?
- How will the changing roles of men and women further manifest themselves?
- What will be the impact of continued genetic and biotechnology advances?
- What will be the effect on Canadian companies of less restrictive trade with the United States and other countries?
- Which companies will be most affected by the increasing number of Canadian households containing single adults living alone?
- What will represent the most attractive opportunities in the services sector of the economy, now representing more than 60% of Canadian Gross Domestic Product and accounting for 69% of all jobs in the country?
- How will Canadian companies respond to the growing trend toward deregulation and the privatization of government-owned corporations?

The above questions address part of the external environment of marketing. Determining the answers presents a strong challenge to marketing executives. A company's marketing system operates within the framework of forces that constitute the system's environment. These forces are either external or internal to the firm.

The *internal forces* are inherent in the organization and are controlled by management. The *external forces*, which generally *cannot* be controlled by the firm, may be divided into two groups. The first is a set of broad (*macro*) influences such as culture, laws, and economic conditions. The second group we shall call (for lack of a better term) the firm's *micro*environment. This group includes producer-suppliers, marketing intermediaries, and customers.

EXTERNAL MACROENVIRONMENT

The following six interrelated macroenvironmental forces have considerable effect on any organization's marketing system. Yet they are largely *not* controllable by management. See Fig. 2-1.

- Demography.
- Economic conditions.
- Competition.
- Social and cultural forces.
- Political and legal forces.
- Technology.

Note that we just said that these forces are *largely*, but not *totally*, uncontrollable by management in a firm. That is, a company must be able to manage its external environment to some extent. For example, through company and industry lobbying in Ottawa or provincial capitals, a company may have some influence on the political-legal forces in its environment. Or new-product research and development that is on the technological frontier can influence a firm's competitive position. In fact, it may be *our* company's technology that is the external environmental force of technology that is affecting *other* organizations.[1]

If there is one similarity among the above six environmental factors, it is that

FIGURE 2-1
Major forces in a company's macroenvironment.

they are subject to change — and at different rates. In the remainder of this section, the six major environmental forces will be explored.

We may define **demography** as the statistical study of human population and its distribution. It is especially important to marketing executives, because people constitute markets. Demography will be discussed in greater detail in the section on markets. At this point we shall mention just a couple of examples of how demographic factors influence marketing systems.

In the mid-1980s, for the first time in history, the number of people 65 and older surpassed the number of teenagers — and this gap will widen considerably as we move into the 1990s. The marketing implications of this trend are substantial. Many manufacturers of consumer products added items to their lines aimed at consumers who are in their fifties and sixties. Mature performers are being used to promote various goods and services. Anne Murray has appeared for the Canadian Imperial Bank of Commerce; Gordon Pinsent for Sun Life Insurance; Eddie Shack and Bernie "Boom Boom" Geoffrion for Miller Lite beer. Shoppers Drug Mart advertising features Beatrice Arthur of "Maude" fame. Fast food companies such as Burger King, Harvey's, McDonald's, and A&W often find that they have difficulty hiring teenagers to work in their restaurants. In contrast to the youth-driven promotions of a decade ago, cosmetic firms now feature actresses such as Catherine Deneuve, Sophia Loren, and Joan Collins. Many movies deal with subjects of interest to older people and Famous Players Theatres offer discounts to movie-goers who are over 65.

Another significant demographic development is the growing market segment comprising single people. As recently as 1956, less than 8 percent of adult Canadians lived alone. By 1986, 21.5 percent of Canadian households comprised adults who live alone. A large percentage of these single-person households are made up of older women who have been widowed. Many of these older singles have very active life-styles, enjoying organized activities such as travel tours.

The marketing implications in this demographic force are almost limitless. The frozen-food industry caters to this market with high-quality foods and a great variety of menu offerings. Auto manufacturers are catering to the female singles market. Dealers will even change the angle of the gas pedal to accommodate high heels. Home builders are designing homes, condominium units, and other housing ventures especially for the singles market.

People alone do not make a market. They must have money to spend and be willing to spend it. Consequently, the **economic environment** is a significant force that affects the marketing system of just about any organization. A marketing system is affected especially by such economic considerations as the current stage of the business cycle, inflation, and interest rates.

STAGE OF THE BUSINESS CYCLE

Marketing executives should know what stage of the business cycle the economy currently is in, because this cycle has such an impact on a company's marketing system. The traditional business cycle goes through four stages — prosperity, recession, depression, and recovery. However, various economic strategies have been adopted by the federal government that have averted the depression stage in Canada and other developed countries for over 50 years. Consequently, today we think in terms of a three-stage cycle — prosperity, recession, recovery — then returning full cycle to prosperity.

Essentially, a company usually operates its marketing system quite differently during each stage. Prosperity is characterized typically as a period of economic growth. During this stage, organizations tend to expand their marketing programs as they add new products and enter new markets. A recession, on the other hand, typically is a period of retrenchment for consumers and businesses. People can become discouraged, scared, and angry. Naturally these feelings affect their buying behaviour which, in turn, has major implications for the marketing programs in countless firms.

Recovery finds the economy moving from recession to prosperity: the marketers' challenge is determining how quickly prosperity will return and to what level. As the unemployment rate declines and disposable income increases, companies expand their marketing efforts to improve sales and profits.

INFLATION

Inflation is a rise in price levels. When prices rise at a faster rate than personal income, there is a decline in consumer buying power. During the late 1970s and early 1980s Canada experienced what for us was a high inflation rate of 10 to 15 percent. While inflation has declined in recent years, with economic growth there is a fear that higher rates may return. Consequently, this spectre continues to influence government policies, consumer psychology, and business marketing programs.

Inflation presents some real challenges in the management of a marketing program — especially in the area of pricing and cost control. Consumers are adversely affected as their buying power declines. At the same time, they may overspend today for fear that prices will be higher tomorrow.

INTEREST RATES

Interest rates are another external economic factor influencing marketing programs. When interest rates are high, for example, consumers tend to hold back on long-term purchases such as housing. Consumer purchases also are affected by whether they think interest rates will increase or decline. Marketers sometimes offer below-market interest rates (a form of price cut) as a promotional device to increase business. Auto manufacturers used this tactic extensively in the mid-1980s, for example.

EMPLOYMENT RATES

One of the most important indicators of the strength of an economy is the percentage of people who are employed and the percentage looking for work. During a strong economic period, unemployment rates are generally lower. At other times, or in certain parts of Canada, unemployment is higher. This affects greatly the amount of disposal income which consumers have to spend on products and services, and is of considerable interest to markets.

A marketer must pay considerable attention to the condition of the economy in which his or her company is operating. Purchasers of certain products and services may react quickly to changes or expected changes in economic conditions. The marketer must be ready to respond with changes in the marketing program.[2]

Competition   A company's competitive environment obviously is a major influence shaping its marketing system. Any executives worth their salt should be constantly gathering intelligence and otherwise monitoring all aspects of competitors' marketing activities — that is, their products, pricing, distribution systems, and promotional programs. Under expanded trade with other countries, Canadian firms will have to pay greater attention to *foreign competition*. Two aspects of competition that we shall consider briefly here are the types of competition and the competitive market structure in which companies may be operating.

TYPES OF COMPETITION

A firm generally faces competition from three different sources. The first is the competition from marketers of directly similar products. Thus, in personal computers Tandy competes with Apple, IBM, Compaq, and other brands. Among department stores, The Bay competes with Eaton's and Simpsons in Toronto and with other stores in other markets. The second type of competition is from substitute products. In this situation a manufacturer of vinyl stereo record albums must compete with laser discs, tape cassettes, and even substitute products in the home-entertainment field. In the third type of competition we recognize that every company is competing for the customer's limited buying power. So the competition faced by a producer of tennis rackets might be a new pair of slacks, a garden tool, or a car repair bill.

File 2-1

Competition — Plentiful Where Resources Are Scarce

Competition is not a concept that has application only for businesses. It is clear that Zellers competes with K-Mart, Woolco, Sears, and other stores. While it may not be as obvious, the Canadian Red Cross, the Salvation Army, Big Brothers/Big Sisters, and the Canadian Mental Health Association are all in competition with each other and with other service and charitable organizations. These organizations compete not only for donations, but for the attention of potential contributors, the time of volunteers, and for other resources that they need to carry out their missions.

COMPETITIVE MARKET STRUCTURES

Four basic types of competitive market structures exist in the Canadian economy today. The four are pure competition, monopolistic competition, oligopoly, and monopoly. Figure 2-2 is a summary of the characteristics of each category. A company's marketing program is influenced considerably by the particular type of competitive structure in which the company operates.

Pure competition is a market situation in which there are many small buyers

CHARACTERISTIC	STRUCTURE			
	Pure competition	Monopolistic competition	Oligopoly	Monopoly
Number of competitors	Very many	Many	Few	One
Size of competitors	Small	Varies	Large	There are none
Nature of product	Homogeneous	Differentiated	Homogeneous or differentiated	Unique–no close substitutes
Seller's control over price	None	Some–depends on degree of differentiation	Some–but be careful	Complete (within regulations)
Entry into industry	Very easy	Easy	Difficult	Very difficult

FIGURE 2-2
Characteristics of competitive market structures.

and sellers, each with complete market information. No single buyer or seller controls market demand, market supply, or price. The product or service is homogeneous — i.e., each seller markets the same product or service. It is easy to enter or leave this type of market. Pure competition is rarely, if ever, attained in the real world. Rather, it is a theoretical concept — an ideal. Something close to pure competition often is found in the marketing of farm produce at local markets.

In a market situation of **monopolistic competition** there also are many buyers and sellers, but they lack complete market information. Each seller is attempting to gain a different advantage over its competitors. This advantage may be differences in the product, its brand or packaging, the distribution system, promotional appeals, customer services, personalities, and training of those providing service. The idea is to get the buyer to perceive an attractive difference in what this seller is offering and therefore select this particular seller's offering. Because of these perceived differences, the sellers have more control over their product and price, even though the sellers are marketing essentially similar things. Monopolistic competition is the most prevalent competitive structure in Canada and other western economies. It exists in the marketing of countless products and services.

An **oligopoly** is a market structure in which only a few large sellers, marketing essentially similar products, account for all or almost all of an industry's sales. In Canada and the U.S., we have many common examples of this structure. It exists in cola drinks, autos, breakfast cereals, auto tires, steel, aluminum, cigarettes, beer and other product categories. Usually the strong competition and/or large initial investment will make it very difficult for a new firm to enter an oligopoly.

When planning its marketing strategies, each seller must consider the possible reactions of the few competitors. For example, all sellers tend to charge the same price. If one firm raises its price, its sales drop off considerably. If a firm cuts its price, all competitors will follow and the new market price simply settles at a lower level. Consequently, the last thing an oligopoly wants is a price war.

A **monopoly** is a market structure in which only one firm is marketing or providing a particular product or service, and there are no close substitutes available. This situation is typical, for example, in the telephone, gas and electric utilities market in any given area or province. Because of their unique market positions, public-utility and public service monopolies are regulated by the government. Sometimes patent protections can provide a company with something close to a monopoly position when the product is a significant improvement over existing products. This situation existed for several years in the case of Polaroid cameras and Xerox copiers.

Social and Cultural Forces

The impact of the sociocultural environment on marketing systems is reflected in several sections of this book. Much of two chapters — 2 and 5 — is devoted to the topic. To add to the complexity of the task facing marketing executives, cultural patterns — life-styles, social values, beliefs — are changing much faster than they used to. At this point we shall note just a few that have significant marketing implications.

EMPHASIS ON QUALITY OF LIFE

Our emphasis today is increasingly on the *quality* of life rather than the *quality* of goods. The theme is, ''Not more — but better.'' We seek value, durability, comfort, and safety in the products and services we buy. Looking ahead, we will worry more about inflation, health, and the environment, and less about keeping up with the neighbours in autos, dress, and homes. Our growing concern for the environment and our discontent with pollution and resource waste are leading to significant changes in our life-styles. And when our life-styles change, of course marketing is affected.

ROLE OF WOMEN

One of the most dramatic occurrences in our society in recent years has been the changing role of women. Especially significant is the breaking away from the traditional and sometimes discriminatory patterns that have stereotyped the male-female roles in families, jobs, recreation, product use, and many other areas. Today, women's growing political power, economic power, and new job opportunities have considerably changed their perspectives and those of men as well.

ATTITUDES TOWARD PHYSICAL FITNESS AND EATING

In recent years an increased interest in health and physical fitness seems generally to have cut across most demographic and economic segments of our society. Participation in physical fitness activities from aerobics to yoga (we could not think of any activity beginning with a Z) is on the increase. Stores supplying activity products and service organizations catering to this trend have multiplied. Public facilities (bicycle paths, hiking trails, jogging paths, and playgrounds) have been improved.

Paralleling the physical fitness phenomenon, we are experiencing significant changes in the eating patterns of Canadians. We are becoming more sensitive to the relationship between our diet and major killing diseases such as heart attacks and cancer. Consequently, there is a growing interest in weight-control eating, foods low in salt, additives, and cholesterol, and foods high in vitamins, minerals, and fibre content. Health foods truly have moved into supermarkets.[3]

Oh what a feeling! PARTICIPACTION

Even fitness is marketable.

We Are What We Eat

In recent years, Canadian consumers have changed their eating patterns dramatically. In an effort to overcome the image of an overweight nation that prevailed in the late 1970s, Canadians have joined health clubs, taken up jogging, bought rowing machines, and embarked upon numerous diet plans. But it is in food consumption that we have seen some of the most dramatic changes. Hundreds of new products have been flooding the supermarket shelves, bearing ''light'' and ''lean'' labels. While beef and pork consumption has declined, that of chicken and fish has increased. Nestlé Enterprises has enjoyed great success with its Stouffer's Lean Cuisine line, National Sea Products has its Lite Tonight line of frozen fish products, and McCain Foods even has a Lite Delite frozen pizza. We see ''light'' products in most food and beverage categories, from mayonnaise to beer. Is this a ''fad,'' or do you detect a major change in eating habits?

We want convenient shopping hours.

DESIRE FOR CONVENIENCE

As an outgrowth of the increase in discretionary purchasing power and the importance of time, there has been a continual increase in the consumer's desire for convenience. We want products ready and easy to use, and convenient credit plans to pay for them. We want these products packaged in a variety of sizes, quantities, and forms. We want stores located close by, and open at virtually all hours.

Every major phase of a company's marketing program is affected by this craving for convenience. Product planning is influenced by the need for customer convenience in packaging, quantity, and selection. Pricing policies must be established in conformity with the demand for credit and with the costs of providing the various kinds of convenience. Distribution policies must provide for convenient locations and store hours.[4]

POLITICAL AND LEGAL FORCES

To an increasing extent, every company's conduct is influenced by the political-legal processes in society. Legislation at all levels exercises more influence on the *marketing* activities of an organization than on any other phase of its operations. The political-legal influences on marketing can be grouped into five categories. In each, the influence stems both from legislation and from policies established by the maze of government agencies. The categories are:

1. *General monetary and fiscal policies.* Marketing systems obviously are affected by the level of government spending, the money supply, and tax legislation.

2. *The new constitution, our legislative framework, codes and policies set by government agencies.* Human rights codes and programs to reduce unemployment fall in this category. Also included is legislation controlling the environment.

3. *Social legislation*. Governments often pass legislation that is intended to protect members of society. A ban on smoking in airplanes, mandatory seat belt use, and the prohibition of cigarette advertising are examples of this type of legislation.

4. *Government relationships with individual industries*. Here we find subsidies in agriculture, shipbuilding, passenger rail transportation, culture, and other industries. Tariffs and import quotas also affect specific industries. In the 1980s, government *deregulation* has had a significant effect on financial institutions and on the airline and trucking industries.

5. *Legislation specifically related to marketing*. Marketing executives do not have to be lawyers. But they should know something about these laws, especially the major ones — why they were passed, what are their main provisions, and what are the current ground rules set by the courts and government agencies for administering these laws.

The federal Department of Consumer and Corporate Affairs administers

---

TABLE 2-1   LEGISLATION ADMINISTERED BY CONSUMER AND CORPORATE AFFAIRS CANADA

---

1. Fully Administered by Department of CCA
   - Bankruptcy Act and Bankruptcy Rules
   - Boards of Trade Act
   - Canada Cooperative Associations Act
   - Canada Corporations Act
   - Competition Act
   - Consumer Packaging and Labelling Act
   - Copyright Act
   - Department of Consumer and Corporate Affairs Act
   - Electricity Inspection Act
   - Farmers' Creditors Arrangement Act
   - Gas Inspection Act
   - Hazardous Products Act
   - Industrial Design Act
   - National Trade Mark and True Labelling Act
   - Patent Act
   - Precious Metals Marketing Act
   - Textile Labelling Act
   - Timber Marking Act
   - Trade Marks Act
   - Weights and Measures Act

2. Administered Jointly With Other Departments
   - Canada Agricultural Products Standards Act (with Agriculture)
   - Canada Dairy Products Act (with Agriculture)
   - Fish Inspection Act (with Environment)
   - Food and Drugs Act (with Health and Welfare)
   - Maple Products Industry Act (with Agriculture)
   - Shipping Conferences Exemption Act (with Transport)
   - Winding-up Act (with Finance)

---

much of the legislation which is included in categories 3 and 4 above. Table 2-1 is a summary of the Acts for which the department has responsibility. We shall not continue our discussion of marketing legislation at this point. Instead, we shall cover the relevant legislation in the appropriate places throughout this book.

6. *The provision of information and the purchase of products.* This sixth area of government influence in marketing is quite different from the other five. Instead of telling marketing executives what they must do or cannot do — instead of the legislation and regulations — the government is clearly helping them. The federal government, through Statistics Canada, is the largest source of secondary marketing information in the country. And the government is the largest single buyer of products and services in the country.

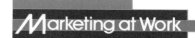

File 2-3

If the Product Is Legal, Can We Prohibit Its Promotion?

One of the most important aspects of the external environment with which the marketer must deal involves the various regulations that are imposed by governments. In Canada, manufacturers of food and beverage products must ensure that their products meet the standards set down by Health and Welfare Canada under the Food and Drugs Act. The wording on and design of the packages in which the products appear are regulated by the Packaging and Labelling Act, and the content of radio and television advertisements must be approved by the Canadian Radio-Television and Telecommunications Commission (CRTC). In some of the most regulated industries such as brewing, a debate continues to rage concerning whether advertising for beer should be permitted and if so, in what form. The critics of such advertising argue that the products are harmful and should not be promoted. Those who defend the right of these companies to advertise maintain that it is legal to sell these products and it should, therefore, be legal to advertise them.

TECHNOLOGY

Technology has a tremendous impact on our lives — our life-styles, our consumption patterns, and our economic well-being. Just think of the effect of major technological developments like the airplane, plastics, television, computers, antibiotics, and birth control pills. Except perhaps for the airplane, all these technologies reached the large-scale marketing stage only in your lifetime or your parents' lifetime. Think how your life in the future might be affected by cures for the common cold, development of energy sources to replace fossil fuels, low-cost methods for making ocean water drinkable, or even commercial travel to the moon.

Major technological breakthroughs carry a threefold market impact. They can:

- Start entirely new industries, as computers, robots, and lasers have done.
- Radically alter, or virtually destroy, existing industries. Television crippled the

radio and movie industries for a long time; wash-and-wear fabrics hurt commercial laundries and dry cleaners; word processors have certainly affected sales of typewriters.

■ Stimulate other markets and industries not related to the new technology. New home appliances and frozen food gave homemakers additional time to engage in other activities.

Technology is a mixed blessing in other ways, also. A new technology may improve our lives in one area, while creating environmental and social problems in other areas. The automobile makes life great in some ways, but it also creates traffic jams and air pollution. Television provides built-in baby-sitters, but it also has an adverse effect on family discussions and on children's reading habits. It is a bit ironic that technology is strongly criticized for creating problems (air pollution, for example), but at the same time we look to technology to solve these problems.

Monitor the Environment

We have finished our discussion of the major external environmental forces that shape an organization's marketing system. When you stop to think about it, you may realize what a monumental task a marketing executive has in adjusting to these external influences. Obviously, the more executives know about their environment and its future development, the better the job they can do in planning and operating their company's marketing systems. One key to learning about the environment is to monitor it in a systematic, ongoing fashion. In each of the six environmental categories, marketing executives should be alert to trends, new developments, and other changes and future scenarios that may present marketing opportunities or problems for their particular firm.

Management should assign this monitoring responsibility specifically to certain people or departments in the organization. Most of the information probably will be derived from a systematic review of existing sources of information such as periodicals, news releases, and government publications. Personal discussions with particular information sources typically are valuable. In some situations, a company may regularly conduct its own marketing field research to determine some aspect of consumer behaviour or competitor activity.

EXTERNAL MICROENVIRONMENT

Three environmental forces are a part of a company's marketing system, but are external to the company. These are the firm's market, producer-suppliers, and marketing intermediaries. While generally classed as noncontrollable forces, these external elements can be influenced to a greater degree than the macro forces. A marketing organization, for example, may be able to exert some pressure on its suppliers or middlemen. And, through its advertising effort, a firm should have some influence on its present and potential market. (See Fig. 2-3.)

The Market

As both an external force and a key part of every marketing system, the market is really what marketing and this book are all about — how to reach the market and serve it profitably and in a socially responsible manner. The market is (or should be) the focal point of all marketing decisions in an organization. This tremendously

FIGURE 2-3
External microenvironment of a company's marketing program.

important factor is the subject of Part 2 (Chapters 4 to 7), and it crops up frequently throughout the text.

WHAT IS A MARKET?

The word *market* is used in a number of ways. There is a stock *market* and an automobile *market*, a retail *market* for furniture, and a wholesale *market* for furniture. One person may be going to the *market*; another may plan to *market* a product. *What, then, is a market?* Clearly, there are many usages of the term in economic theory, in business in general, and in marketing in particular. A *market* may be defined as a place where buyers and sellers meet, products or services are offered for sale, and transfers of ownership occur. A *market* may also be defined as the demand made by a certain group of potential buyers for a product or service. For example, there is a farm *market* for petroleum products. The terms *market* and *demand* are often used interchangeably, and they may also be used jointly as *market demand*.

These definitions of a market may not be sufficiently precise to be useful to us here. Consequently, in this book a **market** is defined as people or organizations with wants (needs) to satisfy, money to spend, and the willingness to spend it. Thus, in the market demand for any given product or service, there are three factors to consider — people or organizations with wants (needs), their purchasing power, and their buying behaviour.

We shall employ the dictionary definition of *needs*: A need is the lack of anything that is required, desired, or useful. As noted in Chapter 1, we do not limit needs to the narrow physiological requirements of food, clothing, and shelter essential for survival. In effect, in our discussion, the words *needs* and *wants* are used synonymously and interchangeably.

A **market** is people or organizations with ⟨ Needs (or wants) to satisfy / Money to spend / Willingness to spend it

Suppliers   You can't sell a product if you can't first make it or buy it. So it is probably rather obvious that **producer-suppliers** of products and services are critical to the success of any marketing organization. In our economy a buyer's market exists for most products. That is, there is no problem in making or buying a product; the problem is usually how to market it.

Marketers often do not concern themselves enough with the supply side. However, the importance of suppliers in a company's marketing system comes into focus sharply when shortages occur. But shortages only highlight the importance of cooperative relationships with suppliers. Suppliers' prices and services are a significant influence on any company's marketing system. At the same time, these prices and services can very often be influenced by careful planning on the part of the buying organization.

Marketing intermediaries are independent business organizations that directly aid in the flow of products and services between a marketing organization and its markets. These intermediaries include two types of institutions: (1) resellers — the wholesalers and retailers — or the people we call ''middlemen'' and (2) various ''facilitating'' organizations that provide transportation, warehousing, financing, and other supportive services sellers needed to complete exchanges between buyers and sellers.

These intermediaries operate between a company and its markets and between a company and its suppliers. Thus they complete what we call ''channels of distribution'' or ''trade channels.''

In some situations it may be more efficient for a company to operate on a ''do-it-yourself'' basis without using marketing intermediaries. That is, a firm can deal *directly* with its suppliers or sell *directly* to its customers and do its own shipping, financing, and so on. But marketing intermediaries do perform a variety of services. They are specialists in their respective fields. Typically, they justify their economic existence by doing a better job at a lower cost than the marketing organization can do by itself.

AN ORGANIZATION'S INTERNAL ENVIRONMENT

The environmental forces that influence a company's marketing program are not limited to external factors. An organization's marketing system is also shaped to some extent by two sets of *internal* forces that are largely controllable by management. One set of these internal factors is the organization's resources in *nonmarketing* areas. The other set of internal influences is the environment and resources *within the marketing department*.

Internal Nonmarketing Resources

A company's marketing system is influenced by the firm's production, financial, and personnel capabilities. If management is considering adding a new product, for example, it must determine whether existing *production facilities* and *expertise* can be used. If the new product requires a new plant or machinery, *financial capability* enters the picture. Other nonmarketing forces are the *company's location*, its *research and development* (R&D) *strength*, and the overall *image* the firm projects to its public. Plant location often determines the geographic limits of a company's market, particularly if high transportation costs or perishable products are involved. The R&D factor may determine whether a company will lead or follow in the industry's technology and marketing. See Fig. 2-4.

Another environmental consideration here is the necessity of coordinating the marketing and nonmarketing activities in a company. Sometimes this can be difficult because of conflicts in activity goals and executive personalities. Production people, for example, like to see long production runs of standardized items. Marketing executives want a variety of models, sizes, and colours to satisfy different market

FIGURE 2-4
A company's internal marketing
environment.

COMPANY'S MARKETING PROGRAM

Production facilities
Financial capability
INTERNAL NONMARKETING RESOURCES
Human resources
Company location
R & D capability
Company image

segments. Financial executives typically want tighter credit and expense limits than the marketing people feel is necessary to be competitive.

Internal Marketing Environment

The notion of encouraging cooperation and minimizing conflicts should not be limited to relationships involving marketing with the other departments in a company. Far from it. The environment *within* the marketing department certainly can have a considerable influence on a company's marketing system. Consequently, we cannot have sales executives fighting with advertising management any more than we can have sales-force executives fighting with production or financial executives.

Nevertheless, occasions may arise when the existing marketing environment will shape or change the marketing planning. To illustrate, management may be considering whether to add a certain new product. The decision is made against it because the firm's distribution system cannot handle the proposed product. A firm may want to enter a new market, but the existing sales force cannot handle this additional assignment, and the company is not prepared to develop a new sales force for the new market.

Environmental Conclusion

To wrap up this chapter, we have designed Fig. 2-5 — a combination of three previous figures — showing the environmental forces as they combine to shape an organization's marketing program. With an understanding of the environment within which they operate, marketing executives now can engage in the strategic planning which hopefully will lead to a successful marketing program. This strategic marketing planning — as part of the total management process in marketing — is the topic of the next chapter.

FIGURE 2-5
A company's marketing environment.

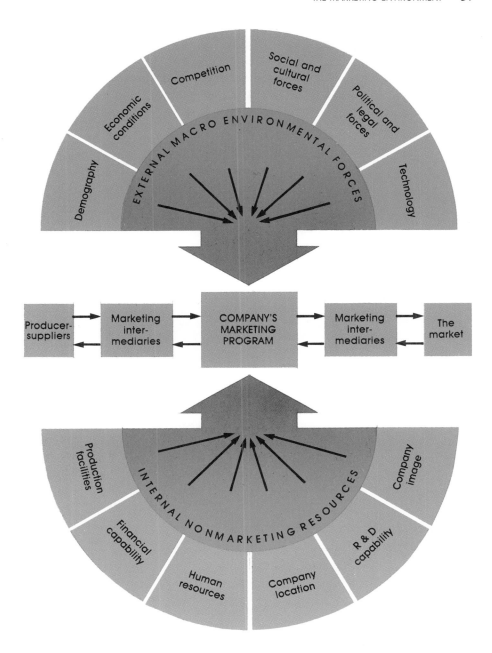

SUMMARY A company operates its marketing system within a framework of ever-changing forces that constitute the system's environment. Some of the forces are broad, external variables that generally cannot be controlled by the executives in a firm. Demographic conditions are one of these macro influences. Another is economic conditions such as the business cycle, inflation, interest rates, and unemployment. Management must be aware of the various types of competitive structure within which a given firm operates. Social and cultural forces, including cultural changes, are other factors to contend with. Political and legal forces, along with technology, round out our group of external macroenvironmental influences. Management should establish a system for monitoring these external forces and assure that the future holds no surprises.

Another set of environmental factors — producer-suppliers, marketing intermediaries, and the market itself — is also external to the firm. But these elements clearly are a part of the firm's marketing system, and they also can be controlled to some extent by the firm. At the same time, a set of nonmarketing resources *within* the firm (production, facilities, personnel, finances, and so on) influences its marketing system. These variables generally are controllable by management, as are the environmental elements within the marketing department.

NOTES [1] For several examples of environmental management strategies that companies can use to influence the uncontrollable environmental forces discussed in this section, see Carl P. Zeithaml and Valarie A. Zeithaml, ''Environmental Management: Revisiting a Marketing Perspective,'' *Journal of Marketing*, Spring 1984, pp. 46–53.

[2] An interesting account of how Canadian consumers responded to the high levels of interest rates and inflation in the early 1980s is presented in James G. Barnes and Lessey Sooklal, ''The Changing Nature of Consumer Behaviour: Monitoring the Impact of Inflation and Recession,'' *The Business Quarterly*, Summer 1983, pp. 58–64.

[3] See Arthur Johnson, ''The Fat of the Land,'' *Report on Business Magazine*, May 1987, pp. 68–74.

[4] ''Presto! The Convenience Industry: Making Life a Little Simpler,'' *Business Week*, April 27, 1987, pp. 86–94.

KEY TERMS AND CONCEPTS

Demography 25
Economic conditions: 25
  Business cycle 25
  Inflation 26
  Interest rates 26
Employment rates 26
Types of competition 27
Competitive market structures: 27
  Pure competition 27
  Monopolistic competition 28
  Oligopoly 28
  Monopoly 28

Social and cultural forces 29
Cultural changes 29
Political and legal forces 30
Technology 32
Environmental monitoring 33
The market 33
Producer-suppliers 34
Marketing intermediaries 35
Nonmarketing resources in a firm 35

1. It is predicted that college enrolments will decline during the next several years. What marketing measures should your school take to adjust to this forecast?

2. For each of the following companies, give some examples of how its marketing program is likely to differ during periods of prosperity as contrasted with periods of recession.

   a. McCain's orange juice.
   b. CCM skates.
   c. Adidas athletic shoes.
   d. Sony television.

3. If interest rates are high, how is the situation likely to affect the market for the following products?

   a. Roots sweatshirts.
   b. Building materials.
   c. Videocassette recorders.

4. Compare the economic characteristics of the competitive market structures of oligopoly and monopolistic competition.

5. Give some examples of how the changing role of women has been reflected in marketing.

6. What are some of the marketing implications of the increasing public interest in health and physical fitness?

7. What should be the role of marketing in treating the following major social problems?

   a. Air pollution.
   b. The depletion of irreplaceable resources.
   c. Seasonal unemployment.

8. Give some examples of the effects of marketing legislation in your own buying, recreation, and other everyday activities. Do you believe these laws are effective? If not, what changes would you recommend?

9. Using examples other than those in this chapter, explain how a firm's marketing system can be influenced by the environmental factor of technology.

10. Explain how each of the following resources within a company might influence that company's marketing program.

    a. Plant location.
    b. Company image.
    c. Financial resources.
    d. Personnel capability.

11. Specify some internal environmental forces affecting the marketing program of:

    a. Shoppers Drug Mart.
    b. Your school.
    c. A local disco.
    d. Air Canada.

CHAPTER 3

STRATEGIC MARKETING PLANNING

The marketing system must be managed — and its activities must be planned — for effective operation within its environment. After studying this chapter, you should understand:

- The management process as it applies to marketing.
- The meanings of some basic management terms.
- The nature, scope, and importance of planning in marketing.
- Some fundamentals of strategic company planning and strategic marketing planning.
- The concept of the marketing mix.

In April 1987, A&W Food Services of Canada tore down its 25-year-old drive-in restaurant on North Vancouver's Marine Drive. To mark the occasion, the company decided to hold a wake. It invited local high school students and car-club members to a feast of Teenburgers and root beer. It was the end of an era in Canadian fast-food retailing.

From the mid-1950s to the mid-1970s, A&W was the dominant fast-food chain in Canada. In 1975, McDonald's Restaurants of Canada finally moved ahead of A&W as the market leader, after a five-year assault on the market based on low prices and an appeal to family values — ''You deserve a break today.'' In comparison, A&W evoked memories of car hops and teenagers who met in the back seat of a Chevy. By 1975, these same '50s and '60s teens were bringing their own children to McDonald's for Big Macs. In 1975 alone, A&W profits fell by 40 percent.

While A&W was never in danger of going into the red, McDonald's quickly became the market leader, leaving A&W, Harvey's, and Burger King far behind. Seeing that their restaurants were not competing effectively with the family and children orientation of McDonald's, the management team at A&W began a major evaluation of corporate strategy. It soon became obvious that the company had to change its whole approach to doing business; it had to be repositioned.

In looking for an appropriate market niche, the management group at A&W identified a gap that looked promising. While other burger chains were building free-standing restaurants that were still dependent on cars to get customers to them, A&W management decided to take its burgers to the customers by locating in the high-traffic markets of regional shopping malls. In order to raise the capital necessary to expand into such high-cost locations, the company made the difficult decision to sell off several of its company-owned restaurants in eastern Canada.

In 1983, A&W entered into an agreement with Coca-Cola Canada Limited to bottle and distribute A&W Root Beer to retail outlets across Canada. By 1986,

A&W Root Beer had become the leading brand in Canada and accounted for sales of more than $15 million.

By late 1987, A&W had 125 of its 315 outlets in major shopping malls across the country. Sales had reached more than $160 million, up from $82 million in 1977, and profits had increased six-fold over that period. Basing its strategy on the fact that the A&W name stood for quality food and beverages, the company took deliberate steps to appeal to an adult market, with a different appeal to that of McDonald's. With plans to revamp or rebuild its remaining 190 free-standing restaurants, complete with telephone extensions and video monitors at the booths, the company is turning the local A&W into an adult hang-out with a definite difference from McDonald's.

Source: Adapted from ''A Toast to a Comeback'' by Anne Collins, *Canadian Business*, November 1987, pp. 48–50, 137–140.

Whatever the future outcome may be for A&W Canada, that company provided us with a classic example of how environmental and competitive forces can shape a company's strategic marketing program. In the preceding chapter we saw that a company's marketing system is strongly influenced by external environmental forces and also by the firm's internal environment. Now in this chapter we shall consider how a company manages its marketing activities within its environment. Specifically, we shall discuss the management process as it applies to a marketing program, and one major part of this management process — namely, strategic planning. Our coverage will be brief and at a level that seems reasonable for your first course in marketing.

MANAGING A MARKETING SYSTEM

Within its environment, a company must plan, implement, and evaluate its marketing system. That is, the organization must *manage* its marketing effort — and must do this effectively.

The ''marketing'' part of the term *marketing management* was defined in Chapter 1, but what about the ''management'' part? The terms *management* and *administration* are used synonymously here. They may be defined as the process of planning, implementing, and evaluating the efforts of a group of people toward a common goal. Through management, the combined group output surpasses the sum of the individual outputs.

The Management Process

The management process, as applied to marketing, consists basically of (1) planning a marketing program, (2) implementing it, and (3) evaluating its performance. The **planning** stage includes setting the goals and selecting the strategies and tactics to reach these goals. The **implementing** stage includes forming and staffing the marketing organization and directing the actual operation of the organization according to the plan. The **performance-evaluation** stage is a good example of the interrelated, continuing nature of the management process. That is, evaluation is both a look back and a look ahead — a link between past performance and future planning and operations. Management looks back to analyze performance in light of organi-

FIGURE 3-1

The management process in marketing systems.

Plans are implemented, and performance results are evaluated to provide information used to plan for the future. The process is continuous and allows for adapting to changes in the environment.

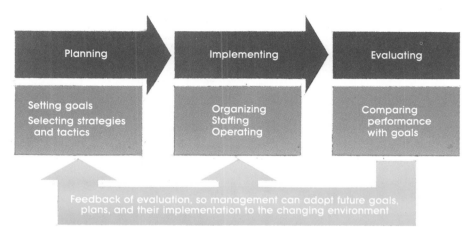

zational goals. The findings from this evaluation of past performance then are used to look ahead in setting the goals and plans for future periods. (See Fig. 3-1.)[1]

Throughout the past 20 years a tremendous amount of attention in business has been devoted to the planning phase of the management process. Several planning models were developed and most of the large companies used one or more of these models. The popular term for this activity — virtually a buzzword in business — is strategic planning. In the next major section of this chapter, we shall briefly discuss strategic planning — especially strategic marketing planning. Business also typically devotes much time and effort to the performance-evaluation activities in the management process.

In Parts 2 through 5 of this book we shall be discussing the planning and development of a marketing program in an organization. Periodically throughout those chapters we shall be dealing with the implementation of marketing plans. Then, near the end of the book, we devote an entire chapter (Chapter 19) to the implementation and evaluation stages of the marketing management process.

Some Basic Management Terminology

Several basic terms continually appear in discussions of the management of a marketing system. These terms sometimes are used carelessly, and they may mean different things to different people. Consequently, at this point let's look at the way these terms will be used in this book.

OBJECTIVES AND GOALS

We shall treat these two terms — objectives and goals — as synonymous and to be used interchangeably in all our discussions. An **objective** (or **goal**) is something that is to be attained. Effective planning must begin with a series of objectives that are to be reached by carrying out the plans. The objectives are, in essence, the reasons for the plans. Furthermore, the objectives should be stated in writing, to minimize (1) the possibility of misunderstanding and (2) the risk that managerial decisions and activities will not be in accord with these goals.

To be effective, the goals also should be stated as specifically as possible:

Too vague, too general	More specific
1. Increase our market share.	1. Next year, increase our market share to 25 percent from its present 20 percent level.
2. Improve our profit position.	2. Generate a return on investment of 15 percent next year.

STRATEGIES

A **strategy** is a broad, basic plan of action by which an organization intends to reach its goal. The word *strategy* (from the Greek word *strategia*) originally was related to the science or art of military generalship. A strategy is a grand plan for winning a battle as a step toward achieving the objective of winning the war.

In marketing, the relationship between goals and strategies may be illustrated as follows:

Goals	Possible strategies
1. Reduce marketing costs next year by 15 percent below this year's level.	1a. Reduce warehouse inventories and eliminate slow-moving products.
	1b. Reduce number of sales calls on small accounts.
2. Increase sales next year by 10 percent over this year's figure.	2a. Intensify marketing efforts in domestic markets.
	2b. Expand into foreign markets.

Two companies might have the same goal, but use different strategies to reach that goal. For example, two firms might each aim to increase their market share by 20 percent over the next three years. To reach this goal, one firm's strategy might be to intensify its efforts in the domestic markets. The other company might select the strategy of expanding into foreign markets.

Conversely, two companies might have different goals but select the same strategy to reach them. As an illustration, suppose one company's goal is to increase its sales volume next year by 20 percent over this year's sales. The other company wants to earn a 20 percent return on investment next year. Both companies might decide that their best strategy is to introduce a major new product next year.

TACTICS

A **tactic** is an operational means by which a strategy is to be implemented or activated. A tactic typically is a more specific, detailed course of action than is a strategy. Also, tactics generally cover shorter time periods — are more closely oriented to short-term goals than are strategies.

Let's look at some examples:

Strategies	Tactics
1. Direct our promotion to males, age 25-40.	1a. Advertise in magazines read by this market segment.
	1b. Advertise on television programs watched by these people.

2. Increase sales-force motivation.

2a. Conduct more sales contests.

2b. Increase incentive features in pay plans.

2c. Use more personal supervision of sales people.

To be effective, the tactics selected must parallel or support the strategy. It would be a mistake, for example, to adopt a strategy of increasing our sales to the women's market — and then advertise in men's magazines or use advertising messages that appeal to men.

POLICY

A **policy** is a course of action adopted by management to routinely guide future decision making in a given situation. Policies typically are used on all levels in an organization — from the presidential suite down to new employees. It may be company *policy*, for example, to have a union leader on the board of directors. Sales managers may follow the *policy* of hiring only college graduates for sales jobs. In the office, our *policy* may be that the last person leaving must turn off the lights and lock the door.

A policy typically is an "automatic decision-making mechanism" for some situation. That is, once a course of action is decided upon in a given situation, then that decision becomes the *policy* that we follow every time the same situation arises. For example, to reach the goal of a certain sales volume in our company, suppose we decided on a strategy of offering quantity discounts in pricing. The relevant tactic we selected was a certain detailed discount schedule. Now, once those decisions have been made, we can follow the pricing *policy* of routinely granting a quantity discount according to our predetermined schedule.

File 3-1

Marketing at Work

Sun Ice Promotions Shine

Sun Ice is a Calgary company that designs, manufactures, and markets ski wear, casual outerwear, active sportswear, and leisure wear. It distributes its products throughout all ten provinces and 31 states of the United States. A recent marketing goal of the company has been to expand its markets in Ontario and Quebec and throughout the United States. The marketing strategies used by Sun Ice include offering no discounted or "off-price" goods, assisting retailers in the merchandising of Sun Ice products, and investing heavily in marketing "Canadian manufactured products." Sun Ice also promotes its products through sponsorship of athletic events such as the Calgary Winter Olympics and through projects such as "Adult Lift Ticket Hang Tags" and the "Junior Learn-to-Ski Program." These promotions give purchasers the right to ski free for a day when they buy a Sun Ice product. Can you contrast these strategies with those used by competing manufacturers of similar clothing products?

CONTROL

Many writers and business executives refer to the management process as consisting of planning, implementation, and *control*. In this book we use the term *performance evaluation* to represent the third activity in the management process. To speak of *control* as only one part of the management process seems to be a misleading and unduly restricted use of the term.

Control is not an isolated managerial function — it permeates virtually all other managerial activities. For example, management *controls* its company operations by virtue of the goals and strategies it selects. The type of organizational structure used in the marketing department determines the degree of *control* over marketing operations. Management *controls* its sales force by means of the compensation plan, the territorial structure, and so on.

Levels of Goals and Strategies

When discussing objectives, strategies, and tactics, it is important to identify the organizational level that we are talking about. Otherwise, we run the risk of creating confusion and misunderstanding, for a very simple reason: What is an *objective* for an executive on one organizational level may be a *strategy* for management on a higher level.

As an illustration, suppose one executive says, "Our goal is to enter the four-province Western market next year and generate a sales volume of at least $1 million." A second executive says, "No — entering that new market is only a strategy. Our goal is to increase our market share to 15 percent next year." A third executive says that the second is wrong. "Increasing our market share is our

Life's an adventure. Live it!

L'HOMME Roger & Gallet®
PARIS

Tactic: Run this ad in a men's magazine unless you want her to buy it for him.

strategy,'' is this person's argument. ''Our goal is to earn a 20 percent return on investment.''

Actually, all three executives are correct. They simply are speaking from the perspectives of different organizational levels in their firm. These relationships may be summarized as follows:

- *Company goal:* To earn a 20 percent return on investment next year.
- *Company strategy (and marketing goal):* To increase our share of the market to 15 percent next year.
- *Marketing strategy (and sales-force goal):* To enter the four-province Western market next year and generate a minimum sales volume of $1 million.

And so on down to an individual sales representative. This person's goal may be to exceed quota by 15 percent, and the proposed strategy may be to average three more sales calls per day.

In any case, for a particular *level of objective*, a *strategy* is a plan of action designed to reach that objective. *Tactics* then are the operational details that implement this plan.

NATURE AND SCOPE OF PLANNING

We now are ready to talk about developing a marketing program in an organization. To do an effective job in developing such a program, however, management first should prepare a strategic plan for the total organizational effort. Then this total-company planning should be followed by strategic planning in the organization's various functional divisions, including marketing. The success of a company's marketing effort depends largely upon management's ability to strategically plan a marketing program within the environmental framework discussed earlier in this chapter and then to carry out that plan.

But before we discuss strategic company planning, let's first understand the concept of planning in general.

What Is Planning?

There's an old saying to the effect that if you don't know where you're going, then any road will take you there. That is, you need a plan. If you don't have a plan, you cannot get anything done — because you don't know what needs to be done or how to do it. In simple English, **planning** is studying the past to decide in the present what to do in the future. Or deciding what we are going to do later, when and how we are going to do it, and who will do it.

In business management, one type of planning that we find very useful is the more formal concept called strategic planning. **Strategic planning** may be defined as the managerial process of matching an organization's resources with its marketing opportunities over the long run. Note (1) that strategic planning is a total-company concept and (2) that it involves a long-run orientation.

The concept of planning is not new. However, market and economic conditions in recent years have led to a better understanding of the need for formal planning. Truly, any success that management has in increasing the profitability of marketing operations depends in large part upon the nature of its marketing planning. Formal planning is one of the most effective management tools available for reducing risks.

Planning may cover long or short periods of time. **Long-range planning** (for 3, 5, 10, or even 25 years) usually involves top management and special planning staffs. It deals with broad, company-wide issues such as plant, market, or product expansion. **Short-term planning** typically covers a period of one year or less and is the responsibility of lower- and middle-echelon executives. It involves such issues as planning next year's advertising campaign, making merchandise-buying plans in a store, or setting sales quotas for a sales force.

The planning activities in an organization may be conducted on three or four different levels, depending upon the size of the organization and the diversity of its products or services. These planning levels are as follows:

1. **Strategic company planning.** At this level, management defines the organization's mission, sets the organization's long-range goals, and decides on broad strategies formulated to achieve the goals. These long-range, company-wide goals and strategies then become the framework within which departmental planning is done. This total-company planning takes into consideration an organization's financial requirements, production capabilities, labour needs, research and development effort, and marketing capabilities.

2. **Strategic business unit planning.** In large, diversified organizations, a modification of strategic company-wide planning has emerged in recent years. For more effective planning and operation, the total organization is divided into separate divisions called *strategic business units* (SBUs). Each SBU is, in effect, a separate ''business,'' and each SBU conducts its own strategic ''business-wide'' planning.

3. **Strategic marketing planning.** At this level, management is engaged in setting goals and strategies for the marketing effort in the organization. In smaller or nondiversified organizations, the SBU planning and marketing planning may be combined into one strategic planning activity. Or, in small, single-business organizations, the top three levels of planning (company, SBU, marketing) may be combined into one planning activity.

    Strategic marketing planning includes (1) the selection of target markets and (2) the development of the four major ingredients in a company's marketing program — the product, the distribution system, the pricing structure, and the promotional activities. In Parts 3 to 6 of this book, these four ingredients will be considered individually.

4. **Annual marketing planning.** The annual marketing plan is one part, covering one time segment, of the ongoing strategic marketing planning process. It is a master plan covering a year's marketing operations for a given product line, major product, brand, or market. Thus, this plan serves as a tactical operational guide to the executives in each phase of the marketing effort for the given product or market.

Strategic company planning is the managerial process of matching an organization's resources with its marketing opportunities over the long run. This process consists of (1) defining the organization's mission, (2) setting organizational objectives, (3)

FIGURE 3-2
The strategic planning process for the total organization.

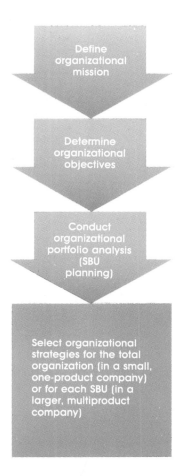

evaluating the strategic business units (this is called *business portfolio analysis*), and (4) selecting appropriate strategies so as to achieve the organizational objectives. (See Fig. 3-2.) The strategic planning process will be influenced considerably by the external macroenvironmental forces that we discussed earlier in Chapter 2. It probably is obvious that management's planning also will be influenced by the organization's internal resources such as its financial condition, production facilities, research and development capabilities, etc.

Define Organizational Mission

The first step in the strategic planning process, as applied to the organization as a whole, is to clearly define the company's mission. For some firms, this step requires only the review and approval of a previously published mission statement. But, for most firms, this step in formal planning really has never been clearly articulated.

Defining an organization's mission means answering the question, ''What business are we in?'' And further, management may also ask, ''What business *should* we be in?'' Unless the organization's basic purpose is clear to all executives, any efforts at strategic planning are likely to be ineffective.

Kodak's mission is to market memories.

An organization's purpose, or mission, should be stated in writing and well publicized. A properly prepared statement of company mission can be an effective public relations tool. The statement should not be too broad or vague — nor should it be too narrow or specific. To say that our mission is "to benefit consumers" is too broad and vague. To say that our business is "to make tennis balls" is too narrow. Neither statement provides sufficient guidance to management.

Traditionally, companies have stated their mission in production-oriented terms: "We make telephones (or furnaces, or skis)." Management might say, "We are in the railroad business (or in furniture manufacturing, or in the mutual funds business)."

Marketing with a Mission

Compare and discuss the following mission statements, and explore the implications of each for the marketing programs of the respective companies:

Sun Ice: to market fashion outerwear and leisure wear that performs.

Jungle Interiors: to market "silk" plants and trees to take the place of "live" plants in homes, offices or any other indoor space and in some outdoor situations.

A&W: to be an energetic, consumer-driven growth company, which builds on earning the trust of all its business partners.

Today, in line with the marketing concept, organizations are urged to be marketing-oriented in their mission statements. Executives should be thinking of the benefits they are marketing and the wants they are satisfying. (See Table 3-1.) Thus, instead of saying, "We make telephones," a phone company should define its mission as the marketing of communication services. Instead of "making furnaces," the Lennox Company's mission should be stated as the marketing of home climate control. Not only are these marketing-oriented mission statements more attractive to the public, but also they serve to broaden a company's market and extend the company's life. If your mission is to make furnaces, you will be out of business when furnaces are replaced by heat pumps or solar heating units. But if your mission is to market climate control, then you can discontinue furnace production, switch to alternative energy sources, and continue competing with the new generation of heating and air-conditioning companies.

TABLE 3-1   **WHAT BUSINESS ARE YOU IN?**

	Production-oriented answer	**Marketing-oriented answer**
Bell Canada	We operate a phone company.	We market a communications system.
Esso	We produce oil and gasoline products.	We market energy.
Via Rail	We run a railroad.	We provide a transportation system.
Roots Canada	We make sweatshirts.	In wearing apparel we offer comfort, fashion, and durability.
Xerox Canada	We make copy machines.	We market automated office systems.
Kodak Canada	We make cameras and film.	We market beautiful memories.
Revlon Cosmetics — the president said:	"In the factory we make cosmetics."	"In the drugstore, we sell hope."

Determine Organizational Objectives

The next step in the strategic planning process is for management to decide upon a set of objectives that will guide the organization in accomplishing its mission. These objectives can also serve as guides for managerial planning at lower levels in an organization. And they provide standards for evaluating an organization's performance.

In effect, the definition of what business we are in and a statement of our goals are critically important to the marketing effort in our organization. The mission statement tells us something about the markets to be served, and the objectives give us some direction in determining how we will implement the marketing concept. Together, the statements of mission and objectives should help us to be marketing-oriented rather than production- or sales-oriented.

At any level of strategic planning, the objectives should be clearly stated *in writing*. Such statements should avoid meaningless platitudes. Objectives should be action-stimulators, because objectives are achieved by actions that carry out plans.

The organization's objectives should be realistic and mutually consistent. To be effective, each objective should be stated in *specific* terms, and wherever possible, the objectives should be *quantitatively measurable*. Some examples of objectives that illustrate these criteria are as follows:

Too general: To increase the company's profitability.

More specific: To increase the company's return on investment to 18 percent within two years.

Not measurable: To improve the company's public image.

Measurable: To receive favourable recognition awards next year from at least three consumer or environmental groups.

Conduct Organizational Portfolio Analysis: Strategic Business Unit (SBU) Planning

Many organizations are so diversified that total-company planning cannot serve as an effective guide for the executives who manage the component divisions of the organizations. Certainly at Imasco, for example, the mission, objectives, and strategies of the tobacco division are quite different from those of the Shoppers Drug Mart division. Most large and medium-sized companies — and even many small firms — are multiproduct, and even multibusiness, organizations.

Consequently, for more effective planning and operation, the total organization should be divided into major product or market divisions. These divisions are called *strategic business units* (SBUs) — a term coined some years ago by a major consulting firm in its work with General Electric. Each SBU may be a major division in an organization, a group of related products, or even a single major product, or brand.

To be identified as an SBU, a unit should possess these characteristics:

- It is a separately identifiable business.
- It has its own distinct mission.
- It has its own competitors.
- It has its own executives and profit responsibility.
- It may have its own strategic plan.

To illustrate, some possible SBU divisions are as follows:

General Electric: Electrical motors, major appliances, jet engines, medical equipment, lighting equipment, electronic supplies, etc.

A university: Different schools (engineering, business, education, law, etc.) *or* different teaching methods (on-campus courses, television courses, correspondence courses).

Dylex: Retail stores throughout Canada, operated under a variety of different names, including Tip Top Tailors, Harry Rosen, Braemar, Big Steel, Fairweather, L A Express, Suzy Shier, Thrifty's, Diva, Fantasia, Feathers, Ruby's, and Town and Country.

Sears' retail stores: Auto supplies, furniture, large appliances, plumbing and heating equipment, home furnishings, women's apparel, men's apparel, sporting goods, hardware, etc.

The trick here is to set up the proper number of SBUs in an organization. If there are too many, then the management can get bogged down in the planning, operating, and reporting details. If there are too few SBUs, each unit covers too broad an area to be useful for managerial planning and control.

The total organization may then be viewed as a "portfolio" of these businesses. And a *key step in strategic planning* is an evaluation of the individual businesses in the organization's portfolio. This evaluation is called a **business** (or **product**) **portfolio analysis**. Or we can use the broader term **organizational portfolio** analysis, to imply the use of this planning concept in nonbusiness, nonprofit organizations.

A portfolio analysis is made to identify the present status of each SBU and to determine its future role in the company. This evaluation also provides guidance to management in designing the strategies and tactics for an SBU. Management typically has limited resources to use in supporting its SBUs. Consequently, management needs to know how to allocate these limited resources. Which SBUs should be stimulated to grow, which ones maintained in their present market position, and which ones eliminated? A business portfolio analysis is designed to aid management in this decision making.

Selected Organizational Strategies

By this point in its strategic planning, presumably the organization has determined where it wants to go. The next step in strategic planning is to design the ways to get there. These are the organizational strategies — the broad, basic plans of action by which an organization intends to achieve its goals and fulfil its mission. We are speaking about selecting strategies (1) for the total organization in a small, one-product company or (2) for each SBU in a larger, multiproduct or multibusiness organization.

Several models have been developed that management can use as a guide in its selection of appropriate organizational strategies. To illustrate the possible strategic use of these models, at this point we shall describe very briefly three of them. Any further discussion of these and other planning models really is outside the scope of this book.

PORTER'S GENERIC-STRATEGIES MODEL

Professor Michael Porter of the Harvard Business School has developed a model in which he identifies the following three generic strategies to achieve success in a competitive market.[1]

- *Overall cost leadership:* Produce a standardized product at a low price and then underprice everybody else.
- *Differentiation:* Market at a higher-than-average price something that customers will perceive as being unique in quality, design, brand, or some other feature.
- *Focus:* Concentrate on a small specialty market (particular consumer group, geographic market) or a segment of the product line.

Porter's model is shown in Fig. 3-3. Companies in the upper left-hand end of the curve are profitable even with a small market share, because their products and/or markets are specialized and command above-average prices. Firms at the upper right-hand end of the curve also are successful. This is because they differentiate their products or they have a large market share because of low prices and low costs. It is the firms in the middle (low) part of the curve that are in trouble. They have low profits and a modest share because they have nothing going for them.

FIGURE 3-3
Porter's generic-strategies model.

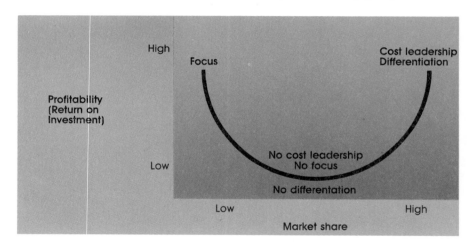

BOSTON CONSULTING GROUP MATRIX

The Boston Consulting Group (BCG), a well-known management consulting firm, has developed a new strategic planning matrix.[2] This new matrix replaces an earlier, widely used one that had been shown to have some shortcomings in the competitive environment of the late 1970s. See Fig. 3-4.

On the vertical axis is plotted the number of ways the company can obtain a marketing advantage, from few to many. On the horizontal axis we plot the size of the advantage, ranging from small to large. The resulting model may be divided into four cells, each identifying a different strategic industrial situation, as follows:

- *Stalemate (stagnant) industries:* Very few advantages, and they are small — steel or uncoated paper, for example.

FIGURE 3-4
Boston consulting group's
strategic planning matrix.

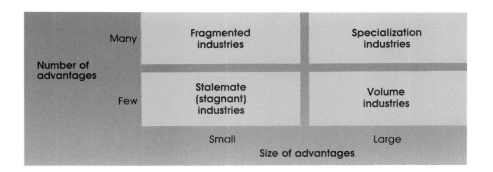

- *Volume industries:* Very few advantages, but they are big — such as the cost advantage in a large aluminum plant.
- *Fragmented industries:* Many competitive advantages, but each one is limited in size — as in the restaurant industry.
- *Specialization industries:* Many competitive advantages, and they are large — Japanese automobile manufacturers or television manufacturers, for example.

PRODUCT/MARKET EXPANSION STRATEGIES

Most statements of mission and objectives reflect an organization's intention to grow — to increase its revenues and profit. In such cases, an organization may take either of two routes in its strategy design. It can continue to do what it is now doing with its products and markets — only do it better. Or the organization can venture into new products and/or new markets. These two routes, when applied to markets and products, result in the following four strategic alternatives.[3] See Fig. 3-5.

- *Market penetration:* A company tries to sell more of its present products to its present markets. Supporting tactics might include an increase in expenditure for advertising or personal selling.
- *Market development:* A company continues to sell its present products, but to a new market. Thus, a manufacturer of power tools now selling to industrial users might decide to sell its small portable tools to household consumers.

FIGURE 3-5
Organizational strategies for
product/market expansion.

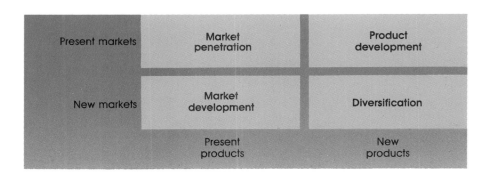

■ *Product development:* This strategy calls for a company to develop new products to sell to its existing markets. A stereo records company recently introduced laser discs to its present customers.

■ *Diversification:* A company develops new products to sell to new markets. Sears, for example, diversified into insurance, financial services, and a credit-card program.

STRATEGIC MARKETING PLANNING

After completing the strategic planning for the total organization and for each SBU, then management can do the planning for each major functional division, such as marketing or production. The planning for marketing (or for any functional division, for that matter) should be guided by the total organizational or the SBU mission and objectives.

The Planning Process

The **strategic marketing planning process** consists of these steps: (1) conduct a situation analysis; (2) determine marketing objectives; (3) select target markets and measure the market demand; (4) design a strategic marketing mix; (5) prepare an annual marketing plan. See Fig. 3-6.

A *situation analysis* is a review of the company's existing marketing program. By analyzing where the program has been and where it is now, management can

FIGURE 3-6
The strategic marketing planning process.

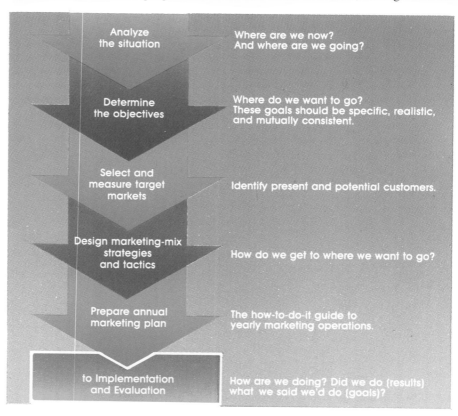

Analyze the situation	Where are we now? And where are we going?
Determine the objectives	Where do we want to go? These goals should be specific, realistic, and mutually consistent.
Select and measure target markets	Identify present and potential customers.
Design marketing-mix strategies and tactics	How do we get to where we want to go?
Prepare annual marketing plan	The how-to-do-it guide to yearly marketing operations.
to Implementation and Evaluation	How are we doing? Did we do (results) what we said we'd do (goals)?

determine where the program should go in the future. A situation analysis normally includes an analysis of the external environmental forces and the nonmarketing resources that surround the organization's marketing program. A situation analysis also includes a detailed review of the company's present marketing mix — its product and pricing situation, its distribution system (including suppliers and middlemen), and its promotional program.

The next step in the marketing planning process is to *determine the marketing objectives*. As with organizational objectives, the marketing goals should be realistic, specific, measurable, and mutually consistent. And they should be clearly stated in writing.

The goals at the marketing level are closely related to the company-wide goals and strategies. In fact, a company strategy often translates into a marketing goal. For example, to reach an organizational objective of a 20 percent return on investment next year, one organizational strategy might be to reduce marketing costs by 15 percent. This organizational strategy would then become a marketing goal.

The *selection of target markets* is obviously a key step in marketing planning. Management should analyze existing markets in detail and identify potential markets. At this point, management also should decide to what extent, and in what manner, it wants to segment its market. As part of this step in the planning process, management also should forecast its sales in its various markets.

The Marketing Mix

Management next must *design a strategic marketing mix* that enables the company to satisfy the wants of its target markets and to achieve its marketing goals. The design, and later the operation, of the marketing mix constitutes the bulk of the company's marketing effort.

Marketing mix is the term that is used to describe the combination of the four inputs that constitute the core of an organization's marketing system. These four elements are the product offerings, the price structure, the promotional activities, and the distribution system. While the marketing mix is largely controllable by company management, this mix still is constrained by external environmental forces. The mix also is both influenced and supported by a company's internal nonmarketing resources. Figure 3-7 reflects a company's total marketing system as being a combination of these environmental and internal forces.

The four "ingredients" in the marketing mix are interrelated. Again we see the *systems* concept; decisions in one area usually affect actions in the others. Also, each of the four contains countless variables. A company may market one item or several — related or unrelated. They may be distributed through wholesalers or directly to retailers, and so on. Ultimately, from the multitude of variables, management must select the combination that will (1) best adapt to the environment, (2) satisfy the target markets, and (3) still meet the organizational and marketing goals.

Product   Managing the product ingredient includes planning and developing the right products and/or services to be marketed by the company. Strategies are needed for changing existing products, adding new ones, and taking other actions that affect the assortment of products carried. Strategic decisions are also needed regarding branding, packaging, and various other product features.

FIGURE 3-7
A company's complete marketing system: a framework of internal resources operating within a set of external forces.

Price In pricing, management must determine the right base price for its products. It must then decide on strategies concerning discounts, freight payments, and many other price-related variables.

Promotion Promotion is the ingredient used to inform and persuade the market regarding a company's products. Advertising, personal selling, and sales promotion are the major promotional activities.

Distribution Even though marketing intermediaries are primarily a noncontrollable environmental factor, a marketing executive has considerable latitude when working with them. Management's responsibility is (1) to select and manage the trade channels through which the products will reach the right market at the right time and (2) to develop a distribution system for physically handling and transporting the products through these channels.[4]

Marketing at Work

File 3-3

Back to Our Marketing Roots

Roots retail stores are operated by Natural Footwear Limited. This company, established in 1973, began by marketing a line of "natural" shoes. Over the years, the company has expanded its product line so that shoes represent a very small portion of total sales. The **product** component of the company's marketing mix now includes a complete line of leisure clothing and accessories, from the well-known Roots sweatshirts, to sweaters, leather goods, and outer clothing. The company's products would be in the medium to upper **price** range; **promotion** is done primarily through advertising in newspapers and through point-of-sale materials (although the company's own sweatshirts, bearing the Roots brand, might themselves be considered a form of advertising); and **distribution** is accomplished through more than 20 company-owned and franchised stores in Canada and 10 in the United States. Compare this marketing mix with the approach taken by other manufacturers of similar product lines.

NONBUSINESS MARKETING MIX

The concept of a marketing mix is also applicable to nonbusiness and/or nonprofit organizations. To illustrate, the marketing mix for the Winnipeg Symphony might include:

- *"Product":* Concerts of classical, semiclassical, and even "pop" music that provide product benefits of social uplifting, music appreciation, enjoyment, relaxation, and use of leisure time.
- *Price:* Public donations and admission charges.
- *Distribution:* Direct from the orchestra to its market; no intermediaries (middlemen) are used.
- *Promotion:* Advertisements in the media telling about the forthcoming season,

Nonbusiness firms also need a marketing mix.

or ads for individual concerts; signs outside the concert hall; an advertising campaign to sell season tickets.

Annual Marketing Plans Periodically, the ongoing strategic marketing planning process in an organization culminates in the preparation of a series of short-term marketing plans. These plans usually cover the period of a year — hence the name ''annual marketing plan.'' However, in some industries it is necessary to prepare these plans for even shorter time periods because of the nature of the product or market. A separate or annual plan should be prepared for each product line, major product, brand, or market.

An **annual marketing plan** is the master guide covering a year's marketing activity for the given business unit or product. The plan then becomes the how-to-do-it document that guides executives in each phase of their marketing operations. The plan includes (1) a statement of objectives, (2) the identification of the target markets, (3) the strategies and tactics pertaining to the marketing mix, and (4) information regarding the budgetary support for the marketing activity.

In an annual marketing plan, more attention can be devoted to tactical details than is feasible in longer-range planning. As an example, long-range marketing planning may emphasize the role of personal selling in the promotional mix. The annual plan then might be concerned, for example, with increased college recruiting as a source of sales people.

In conclusion, let's sum up the role of marketing in an individual organization. To fulfil its mission and achieve its goals, a company should start and end its marketing effort with a consideration of its customers and their wants (see Fig. 3-8). Thus, management first should select and analyze its markets. Then, within a framework of the environmental constraints that face the organization, management should develop a marketing program to provide want-satisfaction to those markets. Permeating the planning and operation of this model is the company's marketing

FIGURE 3-8
Marketing in the firm begins and ends with the customers.

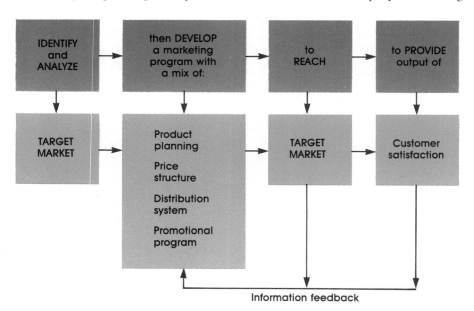

information system — a key marketing subsystem intended to aid management in its decision making. The next section deals with customers — their characteristics and behaviour; gathering customer and market information; and the structure of the marketing information system which supports marketing planning, implementation, and evaluation.

SUMMARY

Within its external and internal environment, a company must develop and operate its marketing system. That is, the organization must *manage* its marketing effort. The management process, as applied to marketing, involves (1) *planning* the company's goals and strategies, (2) *implementing* these plans, and (3) *evaluating* the marketing performance. Executives need to understand the management concepts of objectives, strategies, tactics, and policies.

Strategic planning is a major key to a company's success. With regard to the organizational level on which it is conducted, we find company-wide planning, strategic business unit planning, and strategic marketing planning. Strategic *company* planning is the process of matching an organization's resources with its marketing opportunities over the long run. The organization-wide strategic planning process consists of (1) defining the organization's mission, (2) setting organizational objectives, (3) conducting an organizational portfolio analysis, and (4) designing organizational strategies to achieve the objectives.

Strategic *marketing* planning should be done within the context of the organization's overall strategic planning. The strategic marketing planning process consists of (1) conducting a situation analysis, (2) setting marketing goals, (3) selecting target markets, (4) designing a strategic marketing mix to satisfy those markets and achieve those goals, and (5) preparing an annual marketing plan to guide the tactical operations.

A company's marketing mix is the core of its marketing system. The mix is a combination of the firm's product offerings, price structure, distribution system, and promotional activities.

NOTES

[1] This discussion is adapted from Walter Kiechel, III, ''Three (Or Four, or More) Ways to Win,'' *Fortune*, Oct. 19, 1981, p. 181; and by same author, ''The Decline of the Experience Curve,'' *Fortune*, Oct. 5, 1981, p. 146. See also Michael E. Porter, *Competitive Strategy: Techniques for Analyzing Industries and Competitors*, The Free Press, New York, 1980.

[2] This discussion is based on Kiechel, ''Three . . . Ways to Win,'' pp. 184, 188.

[3] H. Igor Ansoff, ''Strategies for Diversification,'' *Harvard Business Review*, September–October 1957, pp. 113-124.

[4] For a historical perspective on the marketing mix, see G. Ray Funkhouser, ''Technological Antecedents of the Modern Marketing Mix,'' *Journal of Macromarketing*, Spring 1984, pp. 17–28.

QUESTIONS AND PROBLEMS

1. Which, if any, of the main topics discussed in this chapter are useful to a small manufacturer or retailer?

2. Explain the relationship among the three main stages of the management process.

3. a. Explain the terms *strategy* and *tactic*, using examples.
   b. What is the difference between a strategy and a policy in marketing management?

4. Explain the difference between organizational objectives and marketing objectives in strategic planning. Give some examples of each.

5. Using a marketing approach (benefits provided or wants satisfied), answer the question, "What business are you in?" for each of the following companies:

   a. Holiday Inn.
   b. Adidas sports shoes.
   c. Apple computers.
   d. National Sea Products.
   e. Goodyear Tire.
   f. Roots clothing.

6. Using examples, explain the concept of a strategic business unit (SBU).

7. What criteria should an organizational division meet in order to be classified as a strategic business unit?

8. For each of the following Porter generic strategies, give some examples of organizations that might employ the particular strategy.

   a. Cost leadership.
   b. Differentiation.
   c. Focus.

9. For each of the following product/market growth strategies, give some examples (other than those in this chapter) of how a company might employ the particular strategy.

a. Market penetration.
b. Market development.
c. Product development.
d. Diversification.

10. In the situation-analysis stage of the marketing planning process, what are some points that should be analyzed by a manufacturer of backpack equipment for wilderness camping?

11. Explain how the concept of the marketing mix might be applied to:

a. The Salvation Army.
b. An art museum.
c. Your school.
d. Your local police force.

CASE 1.1

UPPER CANADA BREWING
COMPANY (A)

Evaluating the Market
Opportunity

Of all possible entrepreneurial endeavours, few can be as daunting as brewing beer. The heavy capital outlay for plant and equipment in a sector dominated by established giants could deter even the most determined of adventurers. But not Frank Heaps! In October 1983, Frank invested in the Granville Island Brewing Company, and now, only two months later, he was evaluating the market opportunity of starting a similar cottage brewery in his hometown, Toronto, Ontario. To enable him to make a good decision, he knew he needed reliable information; market research was undertaken for this purpose. He carefully analyzed the information before him to make this important decision — should he put this deal together and start the Upper Canada Brewing Company?

THE MARKET

In Canada, the brewing industry is dominated by three large brewers that supply 98 percent of the domestic Canadian market. The big three national brewers — Molson Breweries of Canada Ltd., John Labatt Ltd., and Carling O'Keefe Breweries of Canada Ltd. — all engage in a fierce struggle for a greater share of a large but essentially stable market. To compete, the brewing industry in Canada paid six-figure sums for market research and boosted their combined advertising expenditures from $52.4 million in 1982. Despite these efforts, 1983 sales were still dropping, accompanied by serious declines in profit. (See Figure A-1.)

The greatest threats to the big brewers are demographic and life-style changes. Many male ''baby boomers'' drank less as they got older, and there were fewer young men to take their place. As well, some customers were bypassing beer for other types of beverages. The result was a market that was flat, with no anticipated significant rise in consumption in the near future.

Nevertheless, beer is still big business. According to Statistics Canada, in 1983 Canadians spent nearly $7 billion on beer, with 99 percent of that amount going to domestic brewers; sales of imported beer accounted for only $14 million. However, sales of the higher-priced imported beers had been growing in Ontario over the past few years and represented the only segment of the beer market that showed an increase (See Table A-1.) This increased demand for premium-priced imports was taken to indicate that tastes were changing in some market segments toward specialty alternatives rather than mass-produced products.

MARKET RESEARCH

THE GRANVILLE ISLAND BREWING VENTURE

Market research was an important element in the decision to establish Granville Island Brewing, a cottage brewery in downtown Vancouver, British Columbia. This

This case was prepared by Donna M. Stapleton and is intended to stimulate discussion of an actual management problem and not to illustrate either effective or ineffective handling of that problem. The author wishes to acknowledge the support provided by The Upper Canada Brewing Company, and particularly by Frank Heaps, President.

FIGURE A-1

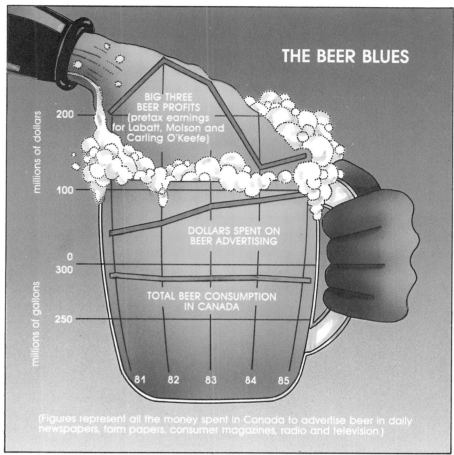

Source: Media Measurement Services Inc.

TABLE A-1   **ONTARIO BEER CONSUMPTION (MILLIONS OF GALLONS)**

Distributors	1981	1982	1983
Brewers' Warehousing	168.3	168.4	164.5
Liquor Control Board of Ontario— Domestic	8.0	7.8	7.8
— Imported*	1.1	1.3	1.4
TOTAL	177.4	177.5	173.7

*Heineken, Lowenbrau, Tuborg, Kronenburg and other European lagers comprising about 65%.

Source: Liquor Control Board of Ontario (L.C.B.O.)

micro brewery, scheduled to open during the spring of 1984, was expected to be the first retail cottage brewery in Canada. The owners' concept was to make beer that would be noticeably different from the mass-produced products dominating the market. The products would be different in taste, like the products of small traditional breweries in Europe; different in quality, being carefully crafted in small

Frank Heaps

quantities with special all-natural ingredients; different in price, where high price would support the perception (and fact) of superior quality; and different in organization, where the new small and independent brewery would be closer to the customer and thus have the advantage of appealing to consumers' desires. Market research supported the perceived need for something different and identified the market opportunity as a relatively small, upscale niche.

Frank Heaps, a management consultant working in Vancouver at the time, liked the concept, decided to invest in the Granville Island Brewing venture, and immediately began thinking of the feasibility of introducing the concept into his hometown market, Toronto. If the concept could work in Vancouver, why not Toronto? He did not believe there was a significant difference in beer drinkers in the two markets. As an investor in Granville Island, he knew that the principals had conducted extensive market research before reaching their decision to enter the Vancouver market. He felt that the data collected on the attitudes of the general public for the Vancouver market were also relevant to his decision. A copy of the research report showed that the public were:

—increasingly interested in returning to more traditional elements of life-styles, particularly with regards to food and beverage products;

—increasingly supportive of products perceived to be more wholesome;

—part of the "small is beautiful" trend, resulting in significant commercial support for goods which were more handcrafted and of a higher quality than those which were mass produced;

—prepared to give trial support for the products of small local entrepreneurs as an alternative to those of diversified national corporations.

UPPER CANADA BREWING VENTURE

Granville Island as the "pioneering venture" served as the precedent for Frank Heaps to evaluate the potential viability of the Upper Canada Brewing proposal. His premise was that "if the Toronto market showed as good a potential as the Vancouver market then the decision would be to go ahead." Research was designed to compare the Toronto and Vancouver markets. The analysis consisted of a comparison of published statistical data on the two markets and the results of 100 group and one-on-one interviews. The interviews were conducted by frequenting taverns and other licensed establishments in the Toronto area and talking with individuals and groups as they enjoyed their beer or ale.

A comparison of published statistical reports showed similarities and differences in the two markets (see Table A-2). There were obvious population differences of persons 20 years of age and older between the Vancouver Census Metropolitan Area (CMA) and the Toronto CMA. As well, a comparison of the population by sex and age revealed that the Toronto marketplace showed significantly greater potential than the Vancouver marketplace, especially with the heavy beer drinkers (males 20-34 years). The large ethnic population in Toronto, especially those of European origin, also indicated greater market potential for the European-style products of the proposed new brewery. Income levels and current growth rate were comparable for the two markets.

A comparison of the number and concentration of taverns and other licensed establishments in the two markets revealed that there was a significantly larger

TABLE A-2   **MARKET RELATED DATA (1981 CENSUS)**

	The Toronto Marketplace		The Vancouver Marketplace	
Population				
Sex and age group	City	CMA	City	CMA
Male				
20-24	29,180	140,255	20,435	58,780
25-34	62,225	262,590	41,245	115,180
35-44	38,610	198,115	24,370	83,650
45-54	33,280	174,985	23,215	69,885
55-64	27,040	130,865	20,850	57,525
65-69	10,375	43,190	9,110	22,870
70 years & older	18,335	65,100	16,800	37,955
Female				
20-24	31,645	146,545	22,440	61,005
25-34	63,820	279,690	40,020	117,330
35-44	36,990	200,085	23,385	81,460
45-54	31,690	171,680	22,070	66,665
55-64	30,220	141,595	24,455	65,650
65-69	13,160	52,965	11,640	28,135
70 years & older	32,955	112,180	25,680	56,985
Total Population	599,217	2,998,947	414,281	1,268,183
Current Growth Rate	−0.054	6.5%	1.1%	8.3%
Income				
Average Family Income	$29,794	$31,238	$30,252	$31,634
Median Family Income	23,608	27,775	25,525	28,292
Mother Tongue				
English		2,136,975		982,465
French		45,455		20,470
Italian		219,925		66,555
Portuguese		78,785		41,315
Chinese		67,910		19,385
German		58,390		18,265
Other		391,505		119,730
Retail Sales (1983 as a percentage above national average)		11%		7%

Source: Statistics Canada

number in Toronto (concentrated in a typical retail three-mile radius). In addition, many more licensees were open on Sunday, allowing another day of sale.

The interviews indicated that similar attitudes existed with regard to natural, wholesome, "small batch," and more traditional products. While this attitude appeared more prevalent in Vancouver, other research with retail food outlets suggested that the larger market of Toronto provided more potential. Torontonians also appeared to be willing to try new beer products at least as readily as Vancouverites. This seemed to be as true with tavern and restaurant owners as with the general public. Furthermore, tavern owners, because of the very competitive environment in the Toronto market, were prepared to provide "whatever the customer wanted."

In addition, there existed in Toronto a very large network of Brewers' Retail Stores, which were conveniently located with ample parking. These stores, equipped with refrigerated storage and selling capacity, would be very important in the distribution of the product because its "all natural," "non-pasteurized" nature required refrigeration during storage and display. In Vancouver, such cold beer stores were not available and this restricted distribution to the brewery site alone.

From the data, Mr. Heaps concluded that the Toronto market potential was as great as, and probably greater than, that of Vancouver. However, he was also aware of the "brewery wars" so evident in the Toronto market. With the strength and financial resources of the large brewers, Mr. Heaps wondered whether he would be able to compete. With a total Ontario beer market of about 175 million gallons a year, a market share of 0.1 percent in the first year, growing to less than 0.3 percent in five years, was a conservative estimate of the volume of business needed to be viable. Did the Ontario market have the potential for the Upper Canada Brewing venture to achieve this volume? Given the hostile nature of this market, what should he do?

QUESTIONS

1. Do you think the Toronto market represented a "good opportunity" for Mr. Heaps? Why or why not?
2. What additional information do you think would be required in assessing this market opportunity? How and where would you obtain it?
3. Which market segment(s) would you say have the greatest potential for the Upper Canada Brewing Company? Why?
4. What types of retaliation by competitors should Mr. Heaps expect?

CASE 1.2

VANCOUVER SYMPHONY
ORCHESTRA (A)

Applying the Marketing
Concept

On Tuesday evening, January 27, 1988 — after 59 years of operation — the Vancouver Symphony Orchestra suspended its season. Symphony officials, facing a debt of $1.7 million and finding no way out of their dilemma, made their announcement as 84 musicians tuned up in the rehearsal hall prior to a concert. The audience was dumbfounded. Michael Adam, sitting in a choice seat, had known that the VSO was in trouble but the announcement shocked him as well. He also knew that as Vice President of Marketing for Pan Pacific Forest Products, he would have to deal with some of the fallout of the suspension of operations within the next few

This case was prepared by Montrose S. Sommers. The material that deals with the Vancouver Symphony Orchestra, the city task force, and comments concerning VSO problems was drawn from: *Globe and Mail*, "Troubled VSO to Be Studied by City Task Force" March 5, 1988, p. C10; Stephen Godfrey, "Audience Tells Task Force to Move Quickly on VSO," March 25, 1988, p. C11; and *Maclean's*, "The Day the Music Died," Feb. 8, 1988, p. 50.

weeks. Specifically, he would have to deal with Jesse Saunders, Pan Pacific's legal counsel and member of both the Pan Pacific and the VSO boards of directors.

Jesse Saunders had met with Michael a number of times in the last year. At each meeting it was clear to Michael that not only was Jesse interested in learning more about the kind of marketing ideas Michael was bringing to Pan Pacific but also what it could mean for the Vancouver Symphony. In the three years since Michael had been with Pan Pacific, he had never really thought too much about marketing beyond consumer and industrial products. He knew that he would shortly be stretching his mind in a new direction as Jesse Saunders looked for advice.

By the next morning, the Vancouver media were full of the news of the suspension of the orchestra's season and by Saturday, there were news reports and commentaries across the country. On the following Monday morning, Michael began tracking what was being said so that he would be prepared for his next meeting with Jesse.

There was a lot of comment and activity during the next few days. Vancouver's mayor gave a ringing endorsement for the future of the VSO and called it the cornerstone of the city's future. The mayor also reported that he had received many messages and phone calls essentially telling him that the public believed in music. He said that many people approached him with the comment that while they hadn't been to the symphony in years, it was important to have it.

From reviewing reports in local and eastern newspapers, a number of things became obvious. First, orchestras across the country had had their problems over the last few years; the Atlantic Symphony, the Windsor Symphony, and others had faced financial difficulties. Secondly, it frequently appeared as if the difficulties were the result of increasing costs and salaries for performers and musicians. Thirdly, a popular approach to resolving the financial problems seemed to be to work harder to get increased donations from public and private sources; strong local action seemed to save the troubled orchestras — at least in the short run.

Within a few days of the beginning of Michael's tracking efforts, Vancouver's mayor had appointed a task force to report to city council on the VSO's future and hearings began almost immediately. Everyone seemed to feel a sense of urgency, for if immediate action was not forthcoming, members of the orchestra would have to leave Vancouver in search of other jobs, and first-class musicians would be hard to recruit. In spite of the fact that a great deal of media attention was focussed on the suspension and the beginning of hearings, and that public petitions of support for the orchestra had quickly been circulated and signed by at least 10,000 people, the task force's first public forum attracted a rather small audience of about 125. It was reported that of those attending, 32 spoke about the symphony.

Michael found the reports on the meeting and comments made to him by a few people who attended to be intriguing in general and very certainly in professional marketing terms. It seemed that the case of the VSO ran true to form. It was thought by some that the problems started in 1985 when federal, provincial, and corporate grants reduced the orchestra's deficit from $2.5 million to $1.5 and gave the organization some breathing space to recover from its financial problems and try and get back to the good old days of the previous decade. At that time, the VSO performed in front of near-capacity audiences. But by the fall of 1987, attendance had fallen to 51 percent of capacity and a campaign to sell 50,000 season tickets for the 1987-88 season had resulted in only 16,000 being sold before the suspension was announced. While there were as many reasons advanced to explain the VSO's difficulties as there were members of the orchestra and people who attended the task force's public forum, to Michael they seemed to boil down to a small number.

One attributed the problems to the 1985 appointment of Rudolph Barshai as musical director and conductor. He arrived in Vancouver in the middle of a wage dispute between symphony management and orchestra members, and some believed he never recovered from this introduction. Mr. Barshai's problems as musical director and conductor were such that by 1987, many musicians were demanding he be ousted, and the VSO Board decided not to renew his contract for the 1988–89 season. Some said Barshai was too autocratic with orchestra members. Others felt that he was not in Vancouver often enough to impress either the "cultural" community or the media — that he either didn't bother with or didn't have star quality or charisma and thus did not sell the orchestra.

A second explanation offered was that the musical fare being presented was just not as appealing as in the past — too much classical and not enough "pops." Some commentators had noted that not only was Vancouver a richer leisure and entertainment market then ever before but also it offered more choice to residents. Some symphony supporters had difficulty believing that the VSO had to compete with the Vancouver Canucks, the B.C. Lions, events at Vancouver's covered stadium, B.C. Place, not to mention the attractions of beaches, parks, ski hills, theatres, clubs and, of course, Stanley Park.

The consensus explanation given the task force was that the problem lay in the changing nature of Vancouver's population. It was noted that 41 percent of the city's population and 53 percent of its school population listed English as a second language; these were high percentages compared with the past. One alleged result was that not only did teachers have difficulty in being understood but also they were unable to instil an appreciation of music in their students. It was also pointed out that it had been a long time since the orchestra had played at either Simon Fraser University or the University of British Columbia or given concerts in schools, parks, and other public locations.

In pondering the VSO problems, Michael was struck by how similar they seemed to the problems at Pan Pacific when he first arrived as marketing manager. At that time, the company was still being buffeted by recessionary economic conditions. The demand for traditional forest products had dropped out of sight because of the fall in new construction. The company saw itself as a producer of lumber and plywood and knew that there were good times and bad. Its response to hard times was to tighten its belt, cut costs, and sell harder. Since it had a good and secure supply of logs, senior executives felt it was only a matter of time before conditions would change and sales would improve. Michael had worked hard in the last few years to get across to his department and senior management the difference it made if you were production, sales or marketing oriented. It had not been easy since many in the firm believed that lumber was lumber and that builders and people involved in do-it-yourself work bought raw lumber or plywood by grade and price and delivery and that was that.

Michael was not sure about Jesse Saunders. Jesse was a very astute lawyer, but he had never worked in line management. Among the things that he did as a board member was to be responsible for Pan Pacific's donations program. Michael wanted very much to provide Jesse with some sound professional advice. He needed to develop an approach to get his ideas across to Jesse as well as to organize a presentation to convince him of what modern marketing thinking could contribute to Pan Pacific and the Vancouver Symphony Orchestra.

As he began putting his reference materials into a pile, his eye caught the tail-end of a magazine piece on the VSO; it concluded with the announcement that the artistic director of the Vancouver Opera Company was resigning at the end of the 1988-89 season because of low attendance.

QUESTIONS

1. What kind of marketing orientation existed at Pan Pacific and in what manner can it evolve?
2. Does it make sense for Michael to compare Pan Pacific with the VSO in order to convince Jesse Saunders of what could be done?
3. What kind of marketing orientation, if any, has existed at the VSO? If the task force meeting consensus view is pursued, what kind of marketing orientation would this represent?
4. What should be the outline of Michael's presentation?

CASE 1.3

NABOB FOODS

Marketing Goals, Objectives and Strategies

By 1980, things at Nabob Foods had got to the point where the question had become: "Can this company survive? And if so, how?" This was the issue that faced the management with stark clarity.

Nabob Foods had evolved over 90 years as a wholly owned manufacturing arm of Kelly Douglas, which in turn was owned by Weston Foods. In 1976, Nabob was acquired by Jacobs Suchard of Zurich, Switzerland, known in Europe as a dynamic food company. At the time of the acquisition, the Nabob multi-product line of coffee, peanut butter, jam, tea, crystals, spices, and desserts had been distributed through Super Valu, the company-owned supermarket chain, as well as other Weston companies. Ninety-five percent of Nabob sales were made in Western Canada.

Because the Nabob brands had always been guaranteed distribution in Super Valu and other outlets belonging to the Weston group, none of the numerous products had been developed with unique selling features other than the fact that they were above average in quality. In addition, very little in the way of advertising and promotional dollars had been invested in them. But after the acquisition in 1976, all of this changed. No longer did Nabob have the captive retail trade of Weston companies to provide it with a guaranteed retail base. Nabob now had to market

This case was prepared by Montrose S. Sommers and is intended to stimulate discussion of an actual management problem and not to illustrate either effective or ineffective handling of that problem. The author wishes to acknowledge the support provided by Nabob Foods, Inc., and particularly by John R. Bell, President.

to the retailer rather than be just a supplier. In the face of strong competition from well known and heavily supported national brands and other retail outlets — principally Canada Safeway and their store brands — the Nabob line became increasingly weaker. The products continued to be vulnerable since they were sold at relatively low prices and thus produced low returns. The low returns made it difficult to respond to the continued heavy competitive pressures with the result that Nabob volume, market share, and profits continued to deteriorate. Between 1977 and 1980, losses were $13 million. Nabob Coffee, the flagship brand, dropped from a 53 percent share of the Western Canada market in 1968 to 27 percent in 1978. Coffee sales accounted for 55 percent of Nabob's $79 million in total sales in 1978.

Management, acting under instructions from the board of directors, set about developing a series of objectives, issues, and options. Each one required some hard data on which to base judgements and, regardless of the data, there was much room for disagreement. It was crucial that there be a clear view of the future ten years from the present. Questions about objectives, options, and issues were:

1. Should Nabob be a conglomerate company similar to General Foods or Nabisco or should it be cut down to a focussed coffee company? Nabob Coffee products represented 55 percent of all sales; non-coffee products represented 45 percent of sales and 60 percent of profits; non-coffee products had market share dominance where distributed in the West but 50-70 percent of sales were in Weston controlled outlets; 95 percent of Nabob's coffee volume was in the West and 5 percent in the East.

2. Should Nabob deal only in high value-added, higher priced and high quality products or maintain its low value-added better-than-average lower price position? High value-added products require heavy advertising and promotion support; high value-added brands require more innovation and creativeness; low value-added products do not require heavy investments and long pay-back periods.

3. Should there be expansion to the eastern Canadian food market or should Nabob consolidate its position in the West? The eastern Canadian food market represented 65 percent of the Canadian total; it was heavily dominated by large conglomerate food companies and was the home of some of the country's most powerful retail chains; selling prices of coffee were lower; advertising and promotion costs were higher and margins lower.

4. With respect to coffee, should Nabob consolidate its existing roast coffee business or switch to the highly profitable instant coffee market? Instant coffee represented 60 percent of coffee consumption and 90 percent of coffee profits; instant received 90 percent of coffee advertising dollar support.

5. In consideration of the ground coffee business, should Nabob convert to the high quality vacuum can or remain with the existing lower cost bag? Consumers perceived the vacuum can to be the gold standard for coffee; the can added $.25/lb. to costs, bags added $.05/lb.; both Nabob and Maxwell House had failed to successfully introduce a vacuum pack in 1977-78; vacuum pack cost was $.10/lb; vacuum bags were perceived by consumers to be of somewhat better quality. Half the ground coffee in Canada used the standard bag format, and 90% of Nabob sales were in this format.

In order for these objectives, issues, options, and supporting key facts to be considered, and in order to determine what else should be included in a useful strategic plan, the material had to be converted into another form and organized into a logical sequence.

1. What is the proposed company mission? In what sense is it different from the previous mission?
2. What goals have been set out for consideration? How do they differ from what was in place?
3. What strategies are associated with the goals?
4. What tactical options are available for the strategies?
5. What steps remain to be taken in order to have the main ingredients for a strategic plan?

PART 2

TARGET MARKETS

An analysis of the people and
organizations who buy, why they buy,
and how they buy

In Part 1 we stressed the importance of customer orientation in an organization's marketing efforts. We also defined strategic planning as the process of matching an organization's resources with its marketing opportunities. These notions suggest that early in the strategic marketing process, an organization should determine who its potential customers are. Only then can management develop a marketing mix intended to satisfy the wants of these customers. Therefore, in Part 2 we discuss the selection of an organization's intended customers — that is, its target market.

In Chapter 4 we review the concept of a target market, and we discuss the demographic and buying-power dimensions of consumer markets. Chapter 5 is devoted to the buying behaviour and the buying process in consumer and industrial markets. Chapter 6 covers the processes by which consumer and market information is collected and organized. In Chapter 7 we discuss the concepts of market segmentation and market demand forecasting.

CHAPTER 4

MARKET DEMOGRAPHICS AND BUYING POWER

This is the first of four chapters on target markets — ultimate consumers and industrial users. After studying this chapter, you should understand:

- Some fundamentals regarding the selection of target markets.
- The difference between ultimate-consumer markets and industrial-user markets.
- The marketing implications of the distribution and composition of populations and industrial users.
- The influences of consumer-income distribution and sales volumes on marketing.
- Consumer spending patterns and the way they affect marketing.

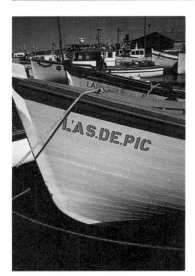

People *are* different in different parts of the country, and regional differences *do* exist in product preferences, purchase patterns, product ownership, and brand preferences. In the home baking product category, for example, flour and other baking ingredients sell in much greater volumes and in larger package sizes in rural areas of the country, such as rural Quebec and the Atlantic provinces, where there is still a great deal of home baking done, as compared with large cities, where flour may be used primarily for making gravies and sauces. Coca-Cola is the leading cola drink in most provinces, except in Quebec and Newfoundland, where Pepsi outsells Coke by a wide margin. Down-filled clothing sells better in ski regions than it does on the Pacific coast.

On the next page is a list of product ownership, household characteristics, and other indicators that illustrate differences that exist across provincial markets. These are all 1986 per-capita expenditure data, collected by Statistics Canada.[1] Each of these indicators represents important information for marketers in particular businesses.

Why do you suppose people in British Columbia spend so much money in restaurants, and why do so many of the households in Newfoundland have home freezers? In addition to obvious regional differences that result from climate and geography, many marketers find that purchase patterns and consumer preferences are influenced by age, ethnic background, cultural influences and other demographic factors. Food consumption patterns of people who live in Quebec, downtown Toronto, or the Prairie provinces, for example, are greatly influenced by their ethnic backgrounds. (Remember, in Chapter 2, we defined *demography* as the statistical study of human population and its distribution.)

PRODUCT/ INDICATOR	NUMBER ONE MARKET	LEAST DEVELOPED MARKET	TOTAL CANADIAN MARKET
Per capita expenditures in restaurants annually	British Columbia $602	Newfoundland $233	$506
Percentage of single detached homes	Newfoundland 78.8%	Quebec 41.5%	56.1%
Percentage of homes without mortgages	Newfoundland 59.4%	Quebec 24.4%	31.5%
Percentage with dishwashers	Alberta 52.6%	Newfoundland 16.4%	37.9%
Percentage with cable television	British Columbia 81.4%	Prince Edward Island 44.2%	64.9%
Percentage with videocassette recorders	Alberta 39.5%	Prince Edward Island 27.9%	35.1%
Percentage with microwave ovens	Alberta 48.6%	Newfoundland 18.2%	33.6%
Percentage with home freezers	Newfoundland 75.8%	Quebec 46.1%	57.7%

In short, any marketer who hopes to be successful in the changing markets of the 1990s must be fully aware of the changing demographic situation that Canadian companies and other organizations will be facing. It is impossible for a marketer to be on top of the market without an appreciation for demographic trends. It is the demographic characteristics of a market that help shape preferences, determine attitudes, mould values, and ultimately influence purchase decisions. Unless marketers monitor the shifting market and interpret the implications of the changes for their companies, they face a very real danger of being left behind.

The demographic basis for characterizing markets at the consumer and industrial levels is a large part of what we shall be talking about in this chapter. Before an organization develops a marketing program to achieve its marketing goals, management first must select its target market(s). In Chapter 2 we defined a **market** as people or organizations with (1) wants (needs) to satisfy, (2) money to spend, and (3) the willingness to spend it. A **target market** is a group of customers (people or organizations) at whom the seller specifically intends to aim its marketing efforts.

Theoretically, a market opportunity exists any time and any place there is a person or an organization with an unfilled need or want. Realistically, of course, a company's market opportunity is much more restricted. Consequently, selecting a target market requires an appraisal of the market opportunities available to the organization. A market opportunity analysis involves, first, a study of the various environmental forces (as discussed in Chapter 2) that affect a firm's market program. Then the organization must analyze the three components of a market — people (or organizations), their buying power, and their willingness to spend. Analysis of the ''people'' component involves a study of the geographic distribution and demographic composition of the population. The second component is analyzed through the distribution of consumer income and consumer expenditure patterns. These first two components are discussed more fully later in this chapter. Finally, to determine consumers' ''willingness to spend,'' management must study their buying behaviour. This involves the sociological and psychological factors that influence buyer behaviour — the topics covered in Chapter 5.

In defining the market or markets it will sell to, an organization has its choice of two general approaches. In one, the total market is viewed as a single unit — as one mass, aggregate market. This approach leads to the strategy of *market aggregation*. In the other approach, the total market is seen as being composed of many smaller, homogeneous segments. This approach leads to the strategy of *market segmentation*, in which one or more of these segments are selected as target markets.

Deciding which of these two strategies to adopt is a key step in selecting target markets. We shall discuss market aggregation and segmentation in more detail in Chapter 7, after we have a better understanding of the three components of a market. That is, segmentation decisions are based on the demographic characteristics of the marketplace, plus some understanding of customer buying behaviour, and the buying process. However, for our discussion of the three market components, it will be helpful at this point to divide the total potential market into two broad categories — ultimate consumers and industrial users.

The sole criterion for placement in one or other of these categories is the customer's *reason for buying*. **Ultimate consumers** buy and/or use products or services for their own personal or household use. They are satisfying strictly nonbusiness wants, and they constitute what is called the ''consumer market'' — the first part of this chapter.

Industrial users are business, industrial, or institutional organizations that buy products or services to use in their own businesses or to make other products. A manufacturer that buys chemicals with which to make fertilizer is an industrial user of these chemicals. Farmers who buy the fertilizer to use in commercial farming are industrial users of the fertilizer. (If homeowners buy fertilizer to use on their yards, they are ultimate consumers because they buy it for personal, nonbusiness use.) Supermarkets, hospitals, or paper manufacturers that buy floor wax are industrial users of this product because they use it in a business or institution. Industrial users in total constitute the ''industrial market'' — the topic of the last part of this chapter.

The segmentation of all markets into two groups — consumer and industrial — is significant from a marketing point of view because the two markets buy differently in certain important respects. Consequently, the composition of a seller's marketing mix — the products, distribution, pricing, and promotion — will depend upon whether it is directed toward the consumer market or the industrial market. However, in terms of the basic principles of marketing, industrial and consumer markets can be approached with the same ideas.[2]

POPULATION: ITS DISTRIBUTION AND COMPOSITION

According to our definition, people are the main component of a consumer market. Therefore, marketers should analyze the geographic distribution and demographic composition of the population as a first step toward understanding it.

Total Population

A logical place to start is with an analysis of total population, and here the existence of a ''population explosion'' that has fizzled becomes evident. The population of Canada did not reach 10 million until about 1930. However, it took only another 35 years to double, and by 1966 the total population of the country stood at just over 20 million. But then the rapid growth in population that had been experienced during the baby boom years from 1945 to the early 1960s began to slow down and by 1986 the Canadian population had reached only 25.3 million. With the current low birth rate expected to continue, projections are that the total population will not go beyond 29 million by 2006. Unless the federal government relaxes restrictions on immigration, Canada could face a situation of *declining* population early in the twenty-first century. The result of a decline in the birth rate from almost four children per family to 1.7 and reduced immigration levels is a static, aging population.

The total market is so large and so diverse that it must be analyzed in segments. Significant shifts are occurring in regional and urban-rural population distribution patterns. Market differences traceable to differences in age, gender, household arrangements, life-styles, and ethnic backgrounds pose real challenges for marketing executives.

Regional Distribution

Figure 4-1 shows the distribution of Canadian population in 1986 and its projected growth to 2006 by province. The biggest markets and the largest urban areas are located in central Canada, where the provinces of Ontario and Quebec together account for almost 62 percent of Canadian population. However, the greatest rate of population growth since 1976 has occurred in Western Canada, in particular in the provinces of Alberta and British Columbia.

The regional distribution of population is important to marketers, because people within a particular geographic region broadly tend to share the same values, attitudes, and style preferences. However, significant differences do exist among the various regions, because of differences in climate, social customs, and other factors.

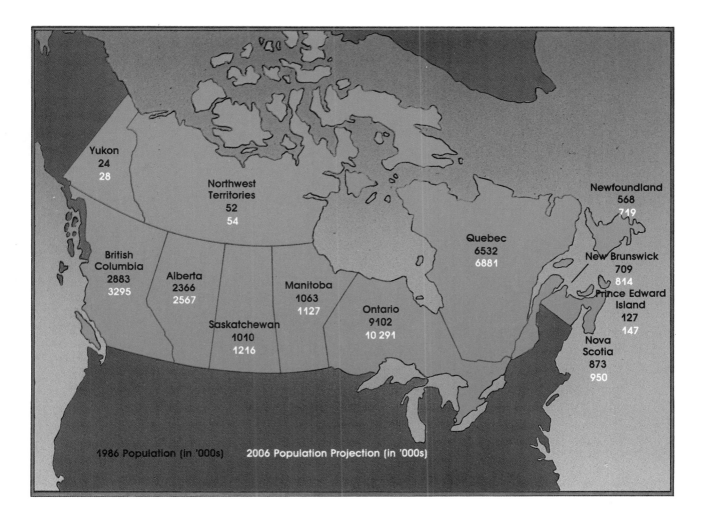

Yukon
24
28

Northwest
Territories
52
54

Newfoundland
568
719

British
Columbia
2883
3295

Alberta
2366
2567

Manitoba
1063
1127

Quebec
6532
6881

New Brunswick
709
814

Prince Edward
Island
127
147

Saskatchewan
1010
1216

Ontario
9102
10 291

Nova
Scotia
873
950

1986 Population (in '000s)   2006 Population Projection (in '000s)

FIGURE 4-1

Provincial distribution of Canadian population, 1986, and projected growth to 2006.

Ontario is a more urbanized province and represents the greatest concentration of people in Canada, especially in the corridor between Oshawa and Niagara Falls. This market is attractive to many marketers because of its sheer size and the diversity of consumers living there. On the other hand, the Atlantic region and the Prairie provinces are characterized by a much more relaxed and rural life-style, which suggests demand for different types of products and services. People in the West tend to be more relaxed and less formal than Eastern Canadians, and they spend more time outdoors. As this Western Canadian market grows, there will be a growth in demand for products associated with an outdoors life-style.

Urban, Rural, and Suburban Distribution

For many years in Canada there has been both a relative and an absolute decline in the farm population, and this decline in the rural market is expected to continue. The declining farm population has led some people to underestimate the importance of rural markets. However, both as an industrial market for farm machinery and other resource industry equipment and supplies, and as a consumer market with increased buying power and more urban sophistication, the rural market is still a major one. Sociological patterns (such as average family size and local customs) among rural people differ significantly from those of city dwellers. These patterns have considerable influence on buying behaviour. Per capita consumption of cosmetics and other beauty aids, for example, is much lower in farm and rural markets than in city markets.

Census Metropolitan Areas

As the farm population has shrunk, the urban and suburban population has expanded. In recognition of the growing urbanization of the Canadian market, some years ago the federal government established the concept of a Census Metropolitan Area (CMA) as a geographic market-data-measurement unit. A CMA is defined by Statistics Canada as the main labour market of a continuous built-up area having a population of 100,000 or more. Table 4-1 indicates the growth in the population of the 25 CMAs in Canada from 1979 to 1986. By 1986, these 25 city areas accounted for 60 percent of the total population of Canada, and this percentage is

Table 4-1   CENSUS METROPOLITAN AREAS
POPULATION, 1979 AND 1986 (in thousands)

	1979	1986
Calgary, Alberta	530.9	671.3
Chicoutimi-Jonquiere, Quebec	132.3	158.5
Edmonton, Alberta	608.2	785.5
Halifax, Nova Scotia	274.1	296.0
Hamilton, Ontario	537.5	557.0
Kitchener, Ontario	281.8	311.2
London, Ontario	279.4	342.3
Montreal, Quebec	2,799.8	2,921.4
Oshawa, Ontario	149.4	203.5
Ottawa-Hull, Ontario-Quebec	712.6	819.3
Québec, Québec	562.4	603.3
Regina, Saskatchewan	159.6	186.5
St. Catharines-Niagara Falls, Ontario	305.5	343.3
St. John's, Newfoundland	148.8	161.9
Saint John, New Brunswick	114.0	121.3
Saskatoon, Saskatchewan	143.7	200.7
Sherbrooke, Québec	—	130.0
Sudbury, Ontario	151.5	148.9
Thunder Bay, Ontario	121.8	122.2
Toronto, Ontario	2,910.0	3,427.2
Trois-Rivières, Quebec	—	128.9
Vancouver, British Columbia	1,207.6	1,380.7
Victoria, British Columbia	223.5	255.5
Windsor, Ontario	250.4	254.0
Winnipeg, Manitoba	583.0	625.3

Source: *Market Research Handbook*, Revised Edition, 1987–88, Statistics Canada, Ottawa, December 1987, p. 398. Reproduced with permission of Supply and Services Canada.

expected to continue to increase. Obviously, these Census Metropolitan Areas represent attractive, geographically concentrated market targets with considerable sales potential.

In several places in Canada the metropolitan areas have expanded to the point where there is no rural space between them. This joining of metropolitan areas has been called ''interurbia.'' Where two or more city markets once existed, today there is a single market. For example, there is virtually no space between Quebec City and Niagara Falls that is not part of a major urban area.

Suburban Growth As the metropolitan areas have been growing, something else has been going on *within* them. The central cities are growing very slowly, and in some cases the older established parts of the cities are actually losing population. The real growth is occurring in the fringe areas of the central cities or in the suburbs outside these cities. For the past 40 years, one of the most significant social and economic trends in Canada has been the shift of population to the suburbs. As middle-income families have moved to the suburbs, the economic, racial, and ethnic composition of many central cities (especially core areas) has changed considerably, thus changing the nature of the markets in these areas.

The growth of the suburban population has some striking marketing implications. Since a great percentage of suburban people live in single-family residences, there is a vastly expanded market for lawn mowers, lawn furniture, home furnishings, and home repair supplies and equipment. Suburbanites are more likely to want two cars than are city dwellers. They are inclined to spend more leisure time at home, so there is a bigger market for home entertainment and recreation items.

As we enter the 1990s, marketing people are watching two possible counter-trends. One is the movement from the suburbs back to the central cities by older people whose children are grown. Rather than contend with commuting, home maintenance, and other surburban challenges, older people are moving to new apartments located nearer to downtown facilities. And it is not just older people who are returning to the downtown areas. In many Canadian cities, young professional families are locating close to their downtown places of work, preferring to renovate an older home, rather than contend with commuting and other perceived shortcomings of suburban living.

The other reversal is that there has been an increase in the rural population near larger cities. Although the rural population of Canada increased by less than 1 percent from 1981 to 1986, much of that growth occurred in close proximity to the large Census Metropolitan Areas. This growth has been brought about, not only because some people wish to live in a more rural setting, but also because of rising real estate prices in and near many Canadian cities.

Age Groups Analyzing the consumer market by age groups is a useful exercise in the marketing of many products. But marketing executives must be aware of the changing nature of the age mix. Looking ahead again to the year 2006, we can see an aging population and one which will grow very slowly, if at all. In 1986, for example, there were 3.71 million people in Canada aged between 10 and 19. By 1996, this age group will have become slightly smaller at 3.68 million. But by 2006, there will be only 3.31 million Canadians in this age bracket. On the other hand, in 1986 there were only 2.7 million Canadians aged 65 and older. By 1996, this group will have increased to 3.58 million, and by 2006 to 4.14 million.

The *youth* market (roughly aged 5 to 13) carries a three-way market impact. First, these children can influence parental purchases. Second, millions of dollars are spent on this group by their parents. Third, these children themselves make purchases of goods and services for their own personal use and satisfaction, and the volume of these purchases increases as the children get older. Promotional programs are often geared to this market segment. Manufacturers of breakfast cereals, snack foods, and toys often advertise on television programs that are directed at children — except on the CBC television network, which prohibits advertising on children's programs.

The *teenage* market is also recognized as an important one, and yet many companies find it difficult to reach. The mistake might be in attempting to lump all teenagers together. Certainly, the 13 to 16 age group is very different from the 17 to 20 age bracket. Yet marketers must understand the teenage market because of the size of the segment and because its members have a great deal of money to spend. This group has considerable discretionary buying power, because of their part-time jobs and allowances which often come from two income-earning parents. Although the total number of teens has decreased since the 1970s, this group still represents a major market segment for marketers of clothing, cosmetics, fast food, stereo records and tapes, driving lessons, and other products.

In the 1990s, the early *middle-age* population segment (35 to 50) will be an especially large and lucrative market. These people are the products of the post-World War II baby boom and were the rebels of the 1960s and 1970s. They also were a very big and profitable teenage and young adult market for many companies during those years. Now, as they move toward middle age in the 1990s, they are reaching their high earning years. Typically, their values and life-styles are far

---

Marketing at Work   File 4-1

The Boom Still Echoes

North American marketers have had a love affair with the baby boom ever since they noticed that birth rates had begun to increase rapidly soon after the end of World War II. Birth rates remained high until the early 1960s, producing a generation of baby boomers, many of whom are now in their thirties or early forties. This group will continue to have a considerable impact on the economy as they get older. Through the 1980s and 1990s, the children of the baby boomers themselves will create a ''mini baby boom,'' which will lead to an increased demand for many products directed at a decidedly upscale children's and teens' markets. The more affluent among the baby-boom families purchase designer baby clothing and high-tech toys. While their own teenage years were characterized by Levi's jeans and the Pepsi Generation, the baby boomers' teenage children have already adopted as their uniform such brands as Ralph Lauren, Roots, and Esprit.

different from those found among the people of the same age category in previous generations. Already, companies are adjusting to these changing demographics. While toothpaste manufacturers like Procter & Gamble and Colgate-Palmolive capitalized on concern about cavity prevention in children's teeth in the 1950s and 1960s, twenty years later they are producing toothpaste to fight tartar — an adult dental problem. This generation, with more dual-income families and fewer children, have more money to spend on themselves. As a result, they are a prime market for products that promise convenience and for home and garden services.

At the older end of the age spectrum are two market segments that should not be overlooked. One is the group of people in their fifties and early sixties. This *mature* market is large and financially well off. Its members are at the peak of their earning power and typically no longer have financial responsibility for their children. Thus, this segment is a good target for marketers of high-priced, high-quality products and services.[3]

The other older age group comprises people over 65 — a segment that is growing both absolutely and as a percentage of the total population. Manufacturers and middlemen alike are beginning to recognize that people in this age group are logical prospects for small, low-cost housing units, cruises and foreign tours, health prod-

Responding to an aging market.

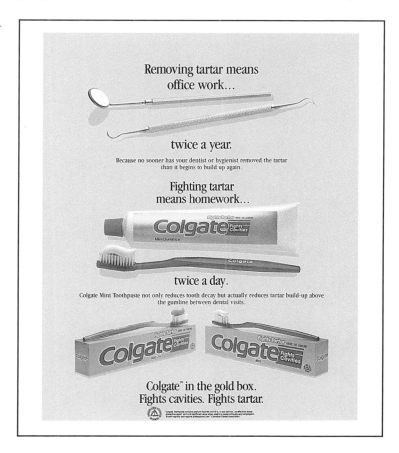

Marketing at Work

As We All Age Gracefully

The average age of the Canadian population is increasing, so —

- Crest and Colgate toothpastes are now available in a plaque-fighter formulation;
- Shoppers Drug Mart run a national ''Salute to Seniors Day'' promotion twice a year, with special seniors' discounts and information brochures, and have featured Bea Arthur as their advertising spokesperson.
- most large travel agencies offer special travel and tour packages for seniors.
- the Royal Bank of Canada offers ''60 Plus'' savings accounts for older customers, giving them a higher rate of interest, no-charge service for the payment of bills, the purchase of money orders, or the writing of cheques, and sit-down service.
- fast-food restaurants are finding it increasingly difficult to hire teenagers as part-time employees. As a result, many are employing senior citizens to serve Big Macs and Papaburgers.

ucts, and cosmetics developed especially for older people. Many firms are also developing promotional programs to appeal to this group because their purchasing power is surprisingly high. Also, the shopping behaviour of the over-65 market typically is different from that found in other age segments. On a per capita basis, seniors are increasing their spending faster than average in areas such as health care, entertainment, recreation, gifts, and contributions. In this latter category, seniors give more dollars than the average Canadian, making them an attractive market segment for charities and religious groups.[4]

Gender   Gender is an obvious basis for consumer market analysis. Many products are made for use by members of one gender, not both. In many product categories — autos, for example — women and men typically look for different product benefits. Market analysis by gender is also useful because many products have traditionally been purchased by either men only or women only.

However, some of these traditional buying patterns are breaking down, and marketers certainly should be alert to changes involving their products. Not too many years ago, for example, the wife did practically all the grocery shopping for her family, and the husband bought the products and services needed for the automobile. Today, men are frequent food shoppers, and women buy the gas and arrange for repair and maintenance. Many products and activities once considered limited to the male market are now readily accepted by women.

The number of working women, both married and single, is increasing dramatically. By 1986, more than 55 percent of women in Canada were employed outside the home. Almost three-quarters of women in the age group from 25 to 44 were in the labour force. By 1996, it is expected that more than 87 percent of women in this age bracket will be employed outside the home. These facts are significant

The main market is men, but women may buy it as a gift.

for marketers. Not only are the life-style and buying behaviour of women in the labour force quite different from those of women who do not work outside their homes, but many of those women are members of households where their spouses also are employed, thereby producing Canadian households with considerable buying power.

Family Life Cycle Frequently, the factor accounting for differences in consumption patterns between two people of the same age and gender is that they are in different life-cycle situations. The concept of the **family life cycle** implies that there are several distinct stages in the life of an ordinary family. A six-stage family cycle, with two alternative stages, is shown in Fig. 4-2. Life-cycle position is also a major determinant of

FIGURE 4-2
The family life cycle.

1. Bachelor stage: young, single people

2. Young married couples with no children

3. Full nest I: young married couples with children

ALTERNATIVE STAGES

A. Divorced person without dependent children

B. Young or middle-aged person with dependent children – the single parent.

4. Full nest II: older married couples still with dependent children

5. Empty nest: older married couples with no children living with them

6. Older single people, still working or retired

buying behaviour. A young couple with two children (the full-nest stage) has quite different needs from those of a couple in their mid-fifties with children no longer living at home (the empty-nest stage). A single-parent family (divorced or widowed) with dependent children faces social and economic problems quite different from those of a two-parent family. The financial position and buying behaviour of these two families usually are quite different. Typical buying patterns in the various stages are discussed later in this chapter in connection with consumer buying patterns.

One of the most rapidly growing segments among the Canadian population is the *singles*. In 1961, only 9.3 percent of Canadian households consisted of just one person — a **single**. By 1986, just 25 years later, more than 21 percent of Canadian homes had only a single occupant. The total number of one-person households is increasing at a much faster rate than that of family units. Among the reasons for this increase in one-person households are:

- The growing number of working women.
- People marrying at a later age.
- The reduced tendency for single people to live with their parents.
- A rising divorce rate.

The impact that single people of both sexes have on the market is demonstrated by such things as apartments for singles, social clubs for singles, and special tours, cruises, and eating places seeking the patronage of singles. Even in the mundane field of grocery products the growing singles market (including the divorced and widowed) is causing changes by retailers and food processors.[5]

The singles in the 25 to 39 age bracket are especially attractive to marketers

Singles constitute an attractive market.

Marketing at Work

File 4-3

Counting on Singles Adds Up Faster

Inter-Continental Gourmet Adventures Inc. is an Ottawa-based company that exists to cater to single adults. The principal element of the company's operations is the Single Gourmet, a dues-paying club where singles meet over good food and fine wines. The club provides approximately 12 events each month for its members, ranging from elegant dinners to barbecues to white-water rafting expeditions. To quote co-owner David Muller, "We're targeting a certain type of people. The price dictates who belongs and we attract sophisticated professionals, not just anyone off the streets. Hard-working single people get bored sometimes, and turned off by the bar scene. We fill the void by providing social events without pressure."

The formula seems to have worked. In the first three years of operation, membership reached 1,500 in Ottawa alone. David and Ruthy Muller are planning expansion of the concept to other Canadian cities and in late 1987 held their first Gourmet Couple event, identical to the singles club, but aimed at pairs.[6]

because they are such a large group. Also, compared with the population as a whole, this singles group is:

- More affluent.
- More mobile.
- More experimental and less conventional.
- More fashion- and appearance-conscious.
- More active in leisure pursuits.
- More sensitive to social status.

Other Demographic Bases for Segmentation

The market for some consumer products is influenced by such factors as education, occupation, religion, or ethnic origin. With an increasing number of people attaining higher levels of **education**, for example, we can expect to see (1) changes in product preferences and (2) buyers with more discriminating taste and higher incomes. **Occupation** may be a more meaningful criterion than income in segmenting some markets. Truck drivers or auto mechanics may earn as much as young retailing executives or college professors. But the buying patterns of the first two are different from those of the second two because of attitudes, interests, and other life-style factors.

For some products, it is useful to analyze the population on the basis of *religion* or *ethnic origin*. The most important distinction in Canada is between the two founding races. French-English differences are fundamental to doing business in Canada and will be dealt with in much greater detail in Chapter 5. Marketers have known for some time that certain products such as instant coffee and tomato juice sell much better in Quebec.

In larger Canadian cities, the cultural diversity of the population creates an

File 4-4

The Mosaic at Work

The ethnic market in certain areas of Canada is becoming increasingly important. Here are some examples of the attention being paid to this segment of the population.

- The Government of Ontario has chosen a Toronto advertising agency, Ethnic/Ad, which specializes in ethnic advertising, to coordinate and place all government advertising in ethnic publications in 36 languages and on ethnic radio and television stations.
- The T. Eaton Company now ensures that 15 to 20 percent of its print advertising in newspapers, catalogues, and direct mail features non-white models.
- Ford of Canada directs a television advertising campaign to the large Toronto ethnic community by featuring on-camera endorsements from satisfied Ford owners who represent the Chinese, Caribbean, and other ethnic communities.

increasing marketing opportunity for companies that specialize in products and services that are directed toward a particular ethnic community. In Toronto, for example, more than half of the population have non-British roots. Persons of Italian heritage represent more than six percent of the population of Ontario and more than 10 percent in Toronto. More than 10 percent of the population of Alberta have German roots, as do more than 17 percent of people in Saskatchewan. Almost 10 percent of the population of Manitoba are Ukrainian.

In certain areas of some provinces, such as the large German population around Kitchener, Ontario, and in some areas of the larger cities, ethnic groups represent a viable target market for certain specialty products and services. In Toronto, Chinese immigrants have established their own neighbourhoods as did immigrants from Portugal, Italy, and the Caribbean before them. They, and other new Canadians from Asian countries, including India and Pakistan, represent a growing ethnic market. With a declining rate of population growth in Canada, the federal government can be expected to relax its restrictions on immigration into the country in coming years. This will contribute to a rapidly growing and diversified ethnic community in Canada. Developing marketing programs to meet the needs of ethnic market segments can be a very successful initiative for some marketers.

CONSUMER INCOME AND ITS DISTRIBUTION

People alone do not make a market; they must have money to spend. Consequently, income, its distribution, and how it is spent are essential factors in any quantitative market analysis.

Nature and Scope of Income

What is income? There are so many different concepts of income that it is good to review some definitions. The following outline is actually a "word equation" that shows how the several concepts are related.

National income: Total income from all sources, including employee compensation, corporate profits, and other income
> *Less*: Corporate profits and pension and social program contributions
> *Plus*: Dividends, government transfer payments to persons, and net interest paid by government
> *Equals*:

Personal income: All forms of income received by persons and unincorporated businesses; including wages, salaries, and supplementary labour income; military pay and allowances; net income of nonfarm business including rent; net income of farm operators from farm production; interest, dividends, and miscellaneous investment income; and transfer payment income from government, corporations, and non-residents
> *Less*: All personal federal, provincial, and municipal taxes
> *Equals*:

Personal disposable income: Personal income less personal direct taxes and other current transfers to government from persons; represents the amount available for personal consumption expenditures and savings
> *Less*: (1) Essential expenditures for food, clothing, household utilities, and

local transportation and (2) fixed expenditures for rent, house mortgage payments, insurance, and instalment debt payments

Equals:

One way to use your discretionary income.

Discretionary purchasing power: The amount of disposable personal income that is available after fixed commitments (debt repayments, rent) and essential household needs are taken care of. As compared with disposable personal income, discretionary purchasing power is a better (more sensitive) indicator of consumers' ability to spend for *nonessentials*.

In addition, we hear the terms "money income," "real income," and "psychic income." **Money income** is the amount a person receives in actual cash or cheques for wages, salaries, rent, interest, and dividends. **Real income** is what the money income will buy in goods and services; it is purchasing power. If a person's money income rises 5 percent in one year but the cost of purchases increases 8 percent on the average, then real income decreases about 3 percent. **Psychic income** is an intangible, but highly important, income factor related to comfortable climate, a satisfying neighbourhood, enjoyment of one's job, and so on. Some people prefer to take less real income so they can live in a part of the country that features a fine climate — greater psychic income.

As measured by income, the Canadian market has grown dramatically in recent years. Until the economic downturn of the early 1980s, the economy had enjoyed almost uninterrupted growth since the end of the Second World War. Personal disposable income had grown to more than $323 *billion* by 1985. This represents an increase of almost 300% in just ten years. Discretionary purchasing power increased at approximately the same rate between 1975 and 1985. Even after allowing for the increases in prices which occurred over that period, the increase in consumer buying power is impressive indeed.

Income Distribution

To get full value from an analysis of income, we should study the variations and trends in the distribution of income among regions and among population groups. Regional income data are especially helpful in pinpointing the particular market to which a firm wishes to appeal. Income data on cities and even on sections within cities may indicate the best locations for shopping centres and suburban branches of downtown stores.

There has been a genuine income revolution going on in Canada over the past thirty years or so. During the second half of the twentieth century, the pattern of income distribution has been dramatically altered. (See Table 4-2.) There has been a tremendous growth in the middle-income and upper-income markets and a corresponding decrease in the percentage of low-income groups.

The purchasing power of the average Canadian family is expected to continue to increase over the next ten years. We will see the effects of higher personal incomes and higher participation rates in the labour force. It is entirely possible that half of all Canadian families will have a total annual income in excess of $50,000 by the year 2000. This anticipated increase in the number of affluent households is the result of several factors. These include (1) the large growth in the number of people in the prime earning years 25 to 45, (2) the increase in dual-income families, and (3) the wider distribution of inherited wealth. We will still have low-income families. However, there will be fewer below the poverty line, even though that level (by government definition) is moving up, in recognition of both inflation and a society that is generally better able to provide its members with a reasonable income.

Marketing Significance of Income Data

The declining percentage of families in the poverty bracket, coupled with the sharp increases in the upper-income groups, presages an explosive growth in discretionary purchasing power. And, as discretionary income increases, so too does the demand for items that once were considered luxuries.

The middle-income market is a big market and a growing market, and it has forced many changes in marketing strategy. Many stores that once appealed to low-income groups have traded up to the huge middle-income market. These stores are upgrading the quality of the products they carry and are offering additional services.

In spite of the considerable increase in disposable income in the past 30 years, many households are still in the low-income bracket or find their higher incomes inadequate to fulfil all their wants. Furthermore, many customers are willing to forgo services in order to get lower prices. One consequence of this market feature has been the development of self-service retail outlets, discount houses, and the more recent superstores such as those operated by furniture and appliance retailers like the Brick Warehouse in Ontario and Western Canada and by specialists in electronic sound equipment such as Majestic Electronic Stores, which operate almost 40 stores in Ontario.

Earlier in this chapter we noted the dramatic increase in the number of working women. This demographic factor also has had a tremendous impact on family income levels. The increase in two-income families has significant marketing and sociological implications. Dual incomes generally enable a family to offset the ravages of inflation. But more than that, two incomes often enable a family to buy within a short time the things that their parents worked years to acquire.

Table 4-2   **PERCENTAGE DISTRIBUTION OF FAMILIES BY INCOME GROUPS IN CANADA Annual income 1982 and 1985**

Income Group	1982	1985
less than $10,000	7.5	5.8
$10,000 to $14,999	10.8	8.7
$15,000 to $19,999	9.9	9.5
$20,000 to $24,999	10.9	8.9
$25,000 to $34,999	22.0	18.9
$35,000 to $44,999	17.1	17.0
$45,000 and over	21.6	31.1

Source: Statistics Canada. Reproduced with permission of Supply and Services Canada.

CONSUMER EXPENDITURE PATTERNS

How consumers' income is spent is a major market determinant for most products and services. Consequently, marketers need to study consumer *spending patterns*, as well as the *distribution* of consumer income. Marketers also should be aware of the significant *shifts* in family spending patterns that have occurred over the past two or three decades. Energy costs, inflation, and heavy consumer debt loads have had a major impact on our spending patterns. As examples, let's consider just a few of the changes in spending patterns that have occurred between the 1960s and the late 1980s. Over that time span, families have *increased* the percentage of their total expenditures going for housing, health, and utilities. Spending (as a percentage of total) has *decreased* for food, beverage, clothing, and home expenses (except utilities).

But expenditure patterns are not the same for all families. These patterns vary considerably, depending upon family income, life-cycle stage, and other factors.

Relation to Stage of Family Life Cycle

Consumer expenditure patterns are influenced by the consumer's stage in the life cycle. There are striking contrasts in spending patterns between, say, people in the full-nest stage with very young children and people in the empty-nest stage. Table 4-3 summarizes the behavioural influences and the spending patterns for families in each stage of the cycle. (This table expands the number of stages shown earlier in Fig. 4-2.) Young married couples with no children typically devote large shares of their income to clothing, autos, and recreation. When children start arriving, expenditure patterns shift as many young families buy and furnish a home. Families with teenagers find larger portions of the budget going for food, clothing, and educational needs. Families in the empty-nest stage, especially when the head is still in the labour force, are attractive to marketers. Typically, these families have more discretionary buying power.[7]

Relation to Income Distribution

The size of a family's income is an obvious determinant of how that family spends its income. Consequently, marketers should analyze the expenditure patterns of the various income classes (under $10,000, $10,000 to $15,000, and so on). Some of the findings from Statistics Canada's studies of consumer expenditures are summarized below. These findings suggest the type of information that marketers might get from analyses of spending patterns by income groups.

■ There is a high degree of uniformity in the expenditure patterns of *middle-income* spending units. As we shall note in Chapter 5, however, social-class structure is often a more meaningful criterion for determining expenditure patterns.

■ For each product category, there is a considerable *absolute increase* in dollars spent as income rises (or, more correctly, as we compare one income group with a higher income group). In other words, people in a given income bracket spend significantly more *dollars* in each product category than those in lower brackets. However, the lower-income households devote a larger *percentage* of their total expenditures to some product categories, such as food. Marketers are probably more concerned with the total *dollars* available from each income group than with the *percentage* share of total expenditures.

■ In each successively higher income group, the amount spent for food declines as a *percentage* of total expenditures.

■ The percentage of expenditures devoted to housing, household operation, and utilities totals approximately 21 percent. This varies from more than 33 percent for the lowest income consumers to 17 percent for those whose family incomes are among the top 20 percent in the country.

■ Dramatic differences are observed across income groups in their actual dollar

TABLE 4-3   BEHAVIOURAL INFLUENCES AND BUYING PATTERNS, BY FAMILY LIFE-CYCLE STAGE

Bachelor stage; young single people not living at home	Newly married couples; young, no children	Full nest I; youngest child under 6	Full nest II; youngest child 6 or over	Full nest III; older married couples with dependent children
Few financial burdens. Fashion opinion leaders. Recreation-oriented. Buy: Basic kitchen equipment, basic furniture, cars, equipment for the mating game, vacations.	Better off financially than they will be in near future. Highest purchase rate and highest average purchase of durables. Buy: Cars, refrigerators, stoves, sensible and durable furniture, vacations.	Home purchasing at peak. Liquid assets low. Some wives work. Dissatisfied with financial position and amount of money saved. Interested in new products. Like advertised products. Buy: Washers, dryers, TV sets, baby food, chest rubs and cough medicine, vitamins, dolls, wagons, sleds, skates.	Financial position better. Many wives work. Less influenced by advertising. Buy larger-sized packages, multiple-unit deals. Buy: Many foods, cleaning materials, bicycles, music lessons, pianos.	Financial position still better. Many wives work. Some children get jobs. Hard to influence with advertising. High average purchase of durables. Buy: New, more tasteful furniture, auto travel, nonnecessary appliances, boats, dental services, magazines.

Empty nest I; older married couples, no children living with them, head in labour force	Empty nest II; older married couples, no children living at home, head retired	Solitary survivor, in labour force	Solitary survivor, retired
Home ownership at peak. Most satisfied with financial position and money saved. Interested in travel, recreation, self-education. Make gifts and contributions. Not interested in new products. Buy: Vacations, luxuries, home improvements.	Drastic cut in income. Keep home. Buy: Medical appliances, medical care, products which aid health, sleep, and digestion.	Income still good but likely to sell home.	Same medical and product needs as other retired group; drastic cut in income. Special need for attention, affection, and security.

Source: William D. Wells and George Gubar, "Life Cycle Concept in Marketing Research," *Journal of Marketing Research*, November 1966, p. 362.

expenditures on recreation. Whereas a family in the lower income bracket may spend as little as $400 annually, the higher income family will spend $3,000 or more.

■ The percentage spent on clothing remains fairly constant across income groups, ranging from 5.8 percent to 6.3 percent. Dollar expenditures, however, range from $500 to well over $3,000 annually.

■ A major difference between low-income and higher-income Canadian families lies in the percentage of their total income which goes to government in the form of taxes. Whereas a family whose total income is in the top 20 percent in Canada will pay 25 percent or more of total personal income in taxes, lower-income families may pay no tax at all.

■ Major differences in expenditure patterns are also found when the Canadian population is examined across geographic regions. This is related in part to income differences, but also is caused to a degree by the differences in the cost of certain items in different areas of the country. For example, the average family in Montreal spends 15.8 percent of total expenditures on food, while a family in Calgary spends only 12.6 percent. On the other hand, the Calgary family will spend more than 20 percent of its total expenditures on housing, as compared with only 15.5 percent for a family in St. John's.

Generalizations such as these provide a broad background against which marketing executives can analyze the market for their particular product or service. People with needs to satisfy and money to spend, however, must be *willing* to spend before we can say a market exists. Consequently, in the next chapter we shall look into consumer motivation and buying behaviour — the "willingness-to-buy" factor in our definition of a market.

THE DEMOGRAPHICS OF INDUSTRIAL MARKET DEMAND

The factors affecting the market for industrial products are the number of potential industrial users and their purchasing power, buying motives, and buying habits. In the following discussion we identify several basic *differences* between consumer markets and industrial markets.

Number and Types of Industrial Users

TOTAL MARKET

The industrial market contains relatively few buying units when compared with the consumer market. There are approximately a half million industrial users, in contrast to about 25 million consumers divided among more than 6 million households. The industrial market will seem even more limited to most companies, because they sell to only a segment of the total market. A firm selling to meat processing plants, for example, would have about 45 potential customer plants. If you were interested in providing services to battery manufacturers, you would find about 25 companies as basic prospects. Consequently, marketing executives must try to pinpoint their market carefully by type of industry and geographic location. A firm marketing hard-rock mining equipment is not interested in the total industrial market, or even in all firms engaged in mining and quarrying.

One very useful source of information is the Standard Industrial Classification system (SIC), which enables a company to identify relatively small segments of its industrial market.[8] All types of businesses in Canada are divided into 12 groups, as follows:

1. Agriculture.
2. Forestry.
3. Fishing and trapping.
4. Mines, quarries, and oil wells.

5. Manufacturing industries (20 major groups).
6. Construction industry.
7. Transportation, communication, and other utilities.
8. Trade.
9. Finance, insurance, and real estate.
10. Community, business, and personal service industries (8 major groups).
11. Public administration and defence.
12. Industry unspecified or undefined.

A separate number is assigned to each major industry within each of the above groups; then, three- and four-digit classification numbers are used to subdivide each major category into finer segments. To illustrate, in division 5 (manufacturing), major group 4 (leather) contains:

SIC code	Industrial group
172	Leather tanneries
174	Shoe factories
175	Leather-glove factories
179	Luggage, handbag, and small-leather goods manufacturers

SIZE OF INDUSTRIAL USERS

While the market may be limited in the total number of buyers, it is large in purchasing power. As one might expect, industrial users range in size from very small companies with fewer than five employees to firms with over 1,000 workers. A relatively small percentage of firms account for the greatest share of the value added by a given industry. For example, Statistics Canada data on the manufacturing sector in Canada indicate that slightly more than 1 percent of manufacturing firms — those with 500 or more employees — account for approximately 40 percent of the total value added by manufacturing and for more than 30 percent of the total employment in manufacturing. The firms with fewer than 50 employees, while accounting for more than 80 percent of all manufacturing establishments, produce less than 15 percent of the value added by manufacturing.

The marketing significance in these facts is that the buying power in the industrial market is highly concentrated in relatively few firms. This market concentration has considerable influence on a seller's policies regarding its channels of distribution. Middlemen are not as essential as in the consumer market.

REGIONAL CONCENTRATION OF INDUSTRIAL USERS

There is a substantial regional concentration in many of the major industries and among industrial users as a whole. A firm selling products usable in oil fields will find the bulk of its market in Alberta, the Northwest Territories, offshore Newfoundland, and the U.S. and abroad. Rubber products manufacturers are located mostly in Ontario, shoes are produced chiefly in Quebec, and most of the nation's garment manufacturers are located in southern Ontario and Quebec. There is a similar regional concentration in the farm market.

While a large part of a firm's market may be concentrated in limited geographic areas, a good portion may lie outside these areas. Consequently, a distribution policy must be developed that will enable a firm to deal directly with the concentrated market and also to employ middlemen (or a company sales force at great expense) to reach the outlying markets.

IMPORTANCE OF THE SERVICE SECTOR

There is a very real danger, when we refer to the industrial sector, to assume that we are discussing only manufacturing companies. In fact, we probably should look for new terminology, or at least refer to this important market as *industrial and commercial*. Over time, less and less of the output of Canadian business is being accounted for by manufacturing. In fact, the *service* sector in this country has grown to the point where it now accounts for more than 60 percent of the Gross Domestic Product and almost 70 percent of all jobs.

When we consider all those Canadians who are working for various government departments and agencies, for the banks and other financial institutions, for retail stores, hotels and restaurants, for universities, colleges and other not-for-profit organizations, it is not difficult to understand how almost nine million Canadians are now working in service sector jobs.

Many service companies are quite small, partly because of the low cost of going into business. There is considerable *ease of entry* for many service firms, especially in the provision of personal services such as child care and home cleaning and in certain professional services such as management consulting. While these service firms do not purchase raw materials for further manufacture, they nevertheless represent a major market for office supplies and furnishings, computer software, and communications equipment. In fact, the dramatic advances which have been made in technology and communications have enabled service companies to locate in fairly remote areas of the country. Toll-free telephone lines, facsimile machines, and computer networks mean that there is no need for airline reservations offices and similar services to be located in major cities.

Buying Power of Industrial Users

The volume of concrete sold is an indicator of construction activity and industrial demand.

Another determinant of industrial market demand is the purchasing power of industrial users. This can be measured, either by the expenditures of industrial users or by their sales volume. Many times, however, such information is not available or is very difficult to estimate. In such cases it is more feasible to use an **activity indicator** — that is, some market factor that is related to income generation and expenditures. Sometimes an activity indicator is a combined indicator of purchasing power and the number of industrial users. Following are examples of activity indicators that might be used to estimate the purchasing power of industrial users.

MEASURES OF MANUFACTURING ACTIVITY

Firms selling to manufacturers might use as market indicators such factors as the number of employees, the number of plants, or the dollar value added by manufacturing. One firm selling work gloves used the number of employees in manufacturing establishments to determine the relative values of various geographic markets. Another company that sold a product that controls stream pollution used two indicators — (1) the number of firms processing wood products (paper mills, plywood mills, and so forth) and (2) the manufacturing value added by these firms.

MEASURES OF MINING ACTIVITY

The number of mines operating, the volume of their output, and the dollar value of the product as it leaves the mine all may indicate the purchasing power of mines. This information can be used by any firm marketing industrial products to mine operators.

MEASURES OF AGRICULTURAL ACTIVITY

A company marketing fertilizer or agricultural equipment can estimate the buying power of its farm market by studying such indicators as cash farm income, acreage planted, or crop yields. The chemical producer that sells to a fertilizer manufacturer might study the same indices, because the demand for chemicals in this case is derived from the demand for fertilizer.

MEASURES OF CONSTRUCTION ACTIVITY

If an enterprise is marketing building materials, such as lumber, brick, gypsum products, or builders' hardware, its market is dependent upon construction activity. This may be indicated by the number and value of building permits issued or by the number of construction starts by type of housing (single-family residence, apartment, or commercial).

File 4-5

*M*arketing at Work

Demanding More Services Than Ever Before

The service sector is expected to continue to expand within the Canadian economy. Woods, Gordon, a national management consulting firm, has predicted that the following services will grow in the next four years:

- *Electronic database services*: This industry will provide an expanded array of financial, credit, corporate, and marketing information.
- *Temporary employment agencies*: This service allows companies to be flexible in their employment patterns in that they no longer need to make long-term commitments to some employees. The employees themselves can obtain variety and gain control over working hours, an advantage not possible in routine jobs.
- *Home shopping*: As time becomes an increasingly scare commodity for many Canadians, shopping can be as close as the living-room television set, especially for products that are low-risk and that require minimal pre-purchase inspection.
- *Mega stores*: It is expected that stores larger than 100,000 square feet will be built in many cities, as Canadians continue to appreciate the wide selection of foods, drugs, furniture, and other products that they offer.
- *Financial supermarkets*: The deregulation of the financial services industry in this country will lead to a blurring of the distinction between banks, trust companies, insurance companies, and investment dealers. We will see more

"cross selling" of services as many of the companies in these industries will now offer services that they were unable to offer in the past.

Source: Adapted from Woods, Gordon, *Competing for Tomorrow's Customers*, 1987, p. 19.

Buying Patterns of Industrial Users

Overt buying behaviour in the *industrial and commercial* market differs significantly from *consumer* behaviour in several ways. These differences obviously stem from the differences in the products, markets, and buyer-seller relationships.

DIRECT PURCHASE

Direct sale from the producer to the ultimate consumer is rare. In the industrial market, however, direct marketing from the producer to the industrial user is quite common. This is true especially when the order is large and the buyer needs much technical assistance. From a seller's point of view, direct marketing is reasonable, especially when there are relatively few potential buyers, they are big, and they are geographically concentrated.

FREQUENCY OF PURCHASE

In the industrial market, firms buy certain products very infrequently. Large installations are purchased only once in many years. Smaller parts and materials to be used in the manufacture of a product may be ordered on long-term contracts, so that an actual selling opportunity exists only once every year. Even standardized operating supplies, such as office supplies or cleaning products, may be bought only once a month.

Because of this buying pattern, a great burden is placed on the advertising and personal selling programs of industrial sellers. Their advertising must keep the company's name constantly before the market. The sales force must call on potential customers often enough to know when a customer is considering a purchase.

SIZE OF ORDER

The average industrial order is considerably larger than its counterpart in the consumer market. This fact, coupled with the infrequency of purchase, spotlights the importance of each sale in the industrial market. Losing the sale of a pair of shoes to a consumer is not nearly as devastating as losing the sale of 10 airplanes.

LENGTH OF NEGOTIATION PERIOD

The period of negotiation in an industrial sale is usually much longer than in a consumer market sale. Some of the reasons for the extended negotiations are (1) several executives are involved in the buying decision; (2) the sale often involves a large amount of money; (3) the industrial product is often made to order, and considerable discussion is involved in establishing the specifications.

DEMAND FOR PRODUCT SERVICING

The user's desire for excellent service is a strong industrial buying motive that may determine buying patterns. Consequently, many sellers emphasize their service as much as their products. Frequently a firm's only attraction is its service, because the product itself is so standardized that it can be purchased from any number of companies.

Sellers must stand ready to furnish services both before and after the sale. A manufacturer of computers may study a customer firm's accounting operations and suggest more effective systems that involve using the seller's products. The manufacturer will also arrange to retrain the present office staff. After the machines have been installed, other services, such as repairs, may be furnished.

QUALITY AND SUPPLY REQUIREMENTS

Another industrial buying pattern is the user's insistence upon an adequate quantity of uniform-quality products. Variations in the quality of materials going into finished products can cause considerable trouble for manufacturers. They may be faced with costly disruptions in their production process if the imperfections exceed quality-control limits. Adequate *quantities* are as important as good quality. A work stoppage that is caused by an insufficient supply of material is just as costly as one that is caused by inferior quality of material. In one study of problems faced by purchasing agents for smaller manufacturers, the problem most often reported was sellers failing to deliver on schedule.[9]

Adequacy of supply is a problem especially for sellers and users of raw materials such as agricultural products, metal ores, or forest products. Climatic conditions may disrupt the normal flow of goods — logging camps or mining operations may become snowbound. Agricultural products fluctuate in quality and quantity from one growing season to another. These "acts of God" create managerial problems for both buyers and sellers with respect to warehousing, standardizations, and grading.

LEASING INSTEAD OF BUYING

A growing behavioural pattern among firms in the industrial and service sector is that of **leasing** products instead of buying them outright. In the past, this practice was limited to large equipment, such as computers and heavy construction equipment. Today, industrial firms are expanding leasing arrangements to include delivery trucks, sales-force automobiles, machine tools, and other items generally less expensive than major installations.

Leasing has several merits for the firm leasing out its equipment. Total net income — after charging off pertinent repair and maintenance expenses — is often higher than it would be if the unit were sold outright. Also, the market may be expanded to include users who could not afford to buy the product, especially large equipment. Leasing offers an effective method of getting distribution for a new product. Potential users may be more willing to rent a product than to buy it. If they are not satisfied, their expenditure is limited to a few monthly payments.

Sometimes it's better to rent than to buy.

SUMMARY   A sound marketing program starts with the identification and analysis of the target market for a product or service. A market is people or organizations with needs or wants, money to spend, and the willingness to spend it. In preparation for target-market selection, it is helpful first to divide the total market into ultimate-consumer and industrial-user submarkets.

In the consumer market, the makeup of the population — its distribution and composition — has a major effect on target-market selection. For some products it is useful to analyze population on a regional basis. Another useful division is by urban, suburban, and rural segments. In this context, the bulk of the population is concentrated in metropolitan areas. Moreover, these areas are expanding and joining together in several parts of the country.

The major age groups of the population make up another significant basis for market analysis — young adults, teenagers, the over-65 group, and so on. The stage of the family life cycle influences the market for many products. Other demographic bases for market analysis include education, occupation, religion, and ethnic origin.

Consumer income — especially disposable income and discretionary income — is a meaningful measure of buying power and market potential. The distribution of income affects the market for many products. Income distribution has shifted considerably during the past 25 years. Today, a much greater percentage of families are in the over-$35,000 bracket and a much smaller percentage earn under $10,000. A family's income level and life cycle are, in part, determinants of its spending patterns.

Industrial market demand is analyzed by evaluating the same three basic factors as those in the consumer market: (1) the number and kinds of industrial users, (2) their buying power, and (3) their motivation and buying behaviour. Buying patterns (habits) of industrial users often are quite different from patterns in the consumer market. In the industrial market, the negotiation period usually is longer, and purchases are made less frequently. Orders are larger, and direct purchases (no middlemen) are more common. Leasing (rather than product ownership) are quite common in industrial marketing.

NOTES

[1] *Market Research Handbook*, Revised Edition, 1987–88, Statistics Canada, Ottawa, December 1987. Reproduced with permission of Supply and Services Canada.

[2] For a thoughtful analysis which proposes that the traditional distinction between consumer marketing and industrial marketing is not justified, see Edward F. Fern and James R. Brown, "The Industrial/Consumer Marketing Dichotomy: A Case of Insufficient Justification," *Journal of Marketing*, Spring 1984, pp. 68–77.

[3] Fabian Linden, "New Money and the Old," *Across the Board*, July–August, 1985, pp. 43–49.

[4] *Competing for Tomorrow's Customers*, 21st edition, Toronto: Clarkson Gordon/Woods Gordon, 1987, p. 8.

[5] See Valarie A. Zeithaml, "The New Demographics and Market Fragmentation," *Journal of Marketing*, Summer 1985, pp. 64–75.

[6] Adapted from André Picard, "Couple Has Hit Recipe for the Appetites of Upscale Singles," *Globe and Mail Report on Business*, August 10, 1987, p. B7.

[7] For a view of the family life cycle that reflects the growing numbers of single adults, with or without dependent children, see Patrick E. Murphy and William A. Staples, "A Modernized Family Life Cycle," *Journal of Consumer Research*, June 1979, pp. 12–22.

[8] Statistics Canada, *Standard Industrial Classification Manual*, cat. no. 12–501. Information Canada, Ottawa, 1980. Both Statistics Canada and the Treasury Board publish a large number of sector and industry reports that provide basic industrial demographics.

[9] Monroe M. Bird, ''Small Industrial Buyers Call Late Delivery Worst Problem,'' *Marketing News*, Apr. 4, 1980, p. 24.

KEY TERMS AND CONCEPTS

Market 79	Discretionary purchasing power 91
Target market 79	Types of income: money, real, psychic 91
Market aggregation 79	
Market segmentation 79	Expenditure patterns 92
Industrial market 79	Income distribution 93
Ultimate consumers 79	Industrial users 95
Population distribution by regions 80	Demography 95
Urban-suburban-rural distribution 81	Standard industrial classification (SIC) 95
Census Metropolitan Area 82	
Population distribution by age group 83	Activity indicators of buying power 97
Market segmentation by *gender* 86	Service sector 97
Stages in the family life cycle 87	Direct purchase 99
Disposable personal income 90	Leasing 100

QUESTIONS AND PROBLEMS

1. Give several examples of products whose market demand would be particularly affected by each of the following population factors:

   a. Regional distribution.
   b. Marital status.
   c. Gender.
   d. Age.
   e. Urban-rural-suburban distribution.

2. Cite some regional differences in product preferences caused by factors other than climate.

3. Suppose you are marketing automobiles. How is your marketing mix likely to differ when marketing to each of the following market segments?

   a. High school students.
   b. Husbands.
   c. Blue-collar workers.
   d. Homemakers.
   e. Young single adults.

4. Using the demographic and income segmentation bases discussed in this chapter, describe the segment likely to be the best market for:

   a. Snow skis.
   b. Good French wines.
   c. Power hand tools.
   d. Birthday cards.
   e. Outdoor barbecue grills.

5. List three of the major population trends noted in this chapter (for instance, a growing segment of the population is over 65 years of age). Then carefully explain how *each* of the following types of retail stores might be affected by *each* of the trends.

   a. Supermarket.
   b. Sporting goods store.
   c. Drugstore.
   d. Restaurant.

6. In which stage of the life cycle are families likely to be the best prospects for each of the following products or services?

   a. Braces on teeth.
   b. Suntan lotion.
   c. Second car in the family.
   d. Vitamin pills.
   e. Refrigerators.
   f. Life insurance.
   g. Jogging suits.
   h. 14-day Caribbean cruise.

7. In what ways has the rise in disposable personal income since 1960 influenced the marketing programs of a typical department store? A supermarket?

8. Give examples of products whose demand is substantially influenced by changes in discretionary purchasing power.

9. What are the marketing implications for a seller in the fact that customers are geographically concentrated and limited in number?

10. Select three advertisements for industrial products and identify the buying motives stressed in the ads.

CHAPTER 5

SOCIAL-GROUP AND PSYCHOLOGICAL INFLUENCES ON BUYER BEHAVIOUR

CHAPTER GOALS

In Chapter 4 we discussed the population and buying-power (income) components of the consumer market and similar characteristics of industrial markets. In this chapter we consider consumers' *willingness to buy*, as influenced by their motivation, perception, social environment, and psychological forces. We then consider industrial buyers and their approaches to purchasing. After studying this chapter, you should understand:

- The roles of motivation and perception in consumer behaviour.
- Culture as an influence on perceptions.
- The influence of social classes on buyer behaviour.
- The effects of small reference groups on buyer behaviour.
- Family and organization buying behaviour.
- The psychological forces that influence buyer behaviour, especially the consumer's learning experiences, personality, attitudes and beliefs, and self-concept.
- The decision-making process in consumer buying, especially patronage buying motives and postpurchase behaviour (cognitive dissonance).
- The buying motives and buying processes of industrial users.

Allan and Karen Ritchie are a young married couple living in Halifax. Both hold responsible positions with local companies, Allan as a junior marketing manager for a local fish processing company, and Karen as a foreign exchange trader with the regional office of a major bank. Late on a Monday afternoon, having collected their five-year-old son, Jason, from day care, Allan stopped at a nearby Sobey's supermarket to pick up a few groceries. He specifically knew the family needed coffee and cereal for tomorrow's breakfast. As he wheeled Jason through the aisles of the store, Allan selected a box of Kellogg's Rice Krispies, a package of Nabob ground coffee, a can of Clover Leaf tuna, a loaf of bread, some fresh strawberries, and (at Jason's suggestion) a package of Oreo cookies. To the casual observer — and possibly even to Allan himself — this may appear to have been a simple, routine shopping experience. Yet, each apparently simple purchase decision was, in fact, a product of a much more complex process. Why did Allan buy Rice Krispies rather than some other brand of cereal? Why Nabob coffee instead of the Maxwell House the family had been buying for the past year or more? Why did he buy the canned tuna, the bread and the strawberries, when he apparently had not intended to when he entered the store? Why Oreo cookies? Why did he shop at this particular Sobey's supermarket and why did he and Karen not buy these items when they had done the weekly grocery shopping on Saturday?

In this chapter we try to shed some light on consumer and industrial buying behaviour to help explain buying decisions. First, we consider how buying behaviour is influenced by motivations and perceptions. Next we discuss how perceptions are determined to a great extent by culture and by the various groups of people with whom we associate. Then our focus shifts to the psychological forces that influence our perceptions. In the final section on consumer buying behaviour, we tie together these discussions as we examine the decision-making process that we go through when making a purchase. We conclude the chapter with a discussion of the buying motives and buying processes of industrial users.

IMPORTANCE AND DIFFICULTY OF UNDERSTANDING CONSUMER BEHAVIOUR

We have reasonably good quantitative data on the number of people living in each geographic region, what their incomes are, and so on. For some products (snow shovels, oil filters), demographic and economic factors alone may explain why a consumer bought the product. Most consumer purchases, however, are also likely to be influenced by psychological or sociological factors.

We know very little about what goes on in a buyer's mind before, during, and after a purchase. Sometimes the explanation for buyers' behaviour is not even discernible to the buyers themselves. To illustrate, buying motives may be grouped on three different levels depending upon the consumers' awareness of them and their willingness to divulge them. At one level, buyers recognize, and are quite willing to talk about, their motives for buying certain products. At a second level, they are aware of their reasons for buying but will not admit them to others. (A family may buy a backyard swimming pool because they feel it adds to their social position in the neighbourhood. Or a businessperson may buy a new coat to keep up with his or her peer group. But when questioned about their motives, they offer other reasons that they think will be more socially acceptable.) The most difficult motives to uncover are those at the *third* level, where even the buyers themselves do not know the real factors motivating their buying actions.

A purchase is rarely the result of a single motive. Furthermore, various motives may conflict with one another. In buying a new dress, a woman may want to (1) please herself, (2) please her boyfriend, (3) be considered a fashion leader by other women in her social circle, and (4) strive for economy. To do all these things in one purchase is truly a difficult assignment. Also, a person's buying behaviour changes over a period of time because of changes in income, changes in life-cycle stage, and other factors.

If we add to this complexity the countless variations occurring because each consumer has a unique personality, our task of understanding consumer behaviour may seem an impossible dream. Yet try we must, because an understanding of buyer behaviour is critical to the success of a marketing program. Fortunately, marketing people, working with behavioural scientists, have been able to develop some generalizations about what influences consumer buying behaviour.

Motivation

To understand why consumers behave as they do, we first must ask why a person acts at all. The answer is, "Because he or she is motivated." That is, all behaviour starts with motivation. A **motive** (or drive) is a stimulated need that an individual seeks to satisfy. Thus hunger, a need for security, and a desire for prestige are examples of motives.

In discussing the behavioural forces that influence consumer buying activity, our model will be as follows: One or more motives within a person trigger behaviour toward a goal that is expected to bring satisfaction.

Which of Maslow's levels of needs does this ad appeal to?

It is important to note that need must be *aroused or stimulated* before it becomes a motive. People sometimes have needs that are dormant and therefore do not activate behaviour because these needs are not sufficiently intense. That is, they have not been aroused. The source of this arousal may be internal (we get hungry) or enivronmental (we see an ad for food). Or just thinking about a need (food) may cause arousal of that need (hunger).

CLASSIFICATION OF MOTIVES

No single classification of motives is generally accepted by psychologists, simply because we do not know enough about human motivation. However, psychologists generally do agree that motives can be grouped into two broad categories. They are (1) aroused **biogenic needs** (such as the needs for food and bodily comfort), which arise from *physiological* states of tension, and (2) aroused **psychogenic needs** (such as the needs for affection and self-respect), which arise from *psychological* states of tension.

A.H. Maslow has formulated a useful theory of motivation. He calls it a "holistic-dynamic" theory because it fuses the points of view of different schools of psychological thought. It also conforms to known clinical, observational, and experimental facts.[1] Maslow identified a hierarchy of five levels of needs, arrayed in the order in which a person seeks to gratify them. This hierarchy is shown in Fig. 5-1.

Maslow contended that people remain at one level until all their needs at that level are satisfied. Then new needs emerge on the next higher level. To illustrate, as long as a person is hungry or thirsty, the physiological (biogenic) needs dominate. Once they have been satisfied, the needs in the safety category become important. When safety needs have been largely gratified, new (and higher-level) needs arise, and so on.

For the relatively few people who move through all five levels, even to fulfilling

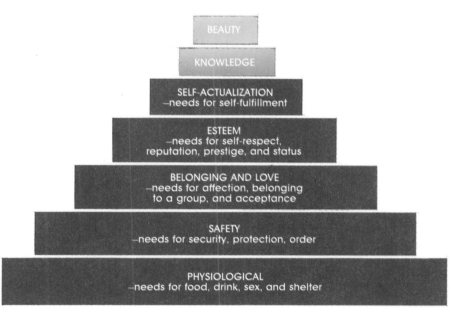

FIGURE 5-1
Maslow's hierarchy of needs.

a need for self-actualization, Maslow identified two additional classes of cognitive needs:

- The need to know and understand.
- The need for aesthetic satisfaction (beauty).

Maslow recognized that in real life there is more flexibility than his model seems to imply at first glance. Actually, a normal person is most likely to be working toward need satisfaction on several levels at the same time. And rarely are all needs on a given level ever fully satisfied. Thus it becomes a question of how much effort is expended for each needs level.

While the Maslow construct has much to offer us, it still leaves some unanswered questions and disagreements. For one thing, there is no direct consideration of multiple motives or needs for the same behaviour. Thus, a teacher may go on a ship's cruise to acquire a better knowledge of foreign countries, to meet new people, and to rest frazzled nerves. Other possibilities not included in the model are (1) identical behaviour by several people resulting from quite different motives and (2) quite different behaviour resulting from identical motives.

Perception   A motive is an aroused need. It, in turn, acts as a force that *activates* behaviour intended to satisfy that aroused need. But what *influences* or *shapes* this behaviour? What determines the direction or path this behaviour takes? The answer is our perceptions. We define **perception** as the process whereby we receive stimuli (information) through our five senses, we recognize this information, and then we assign a meaning to it. In other words, perception is the meaning we give to stimuli, or the way we interpret stimuli.

This interpretation, or meaning, that we attribute to stimuli — that is, our perceptions — is shaped by our sociocultural environment and by psychological conditions within us. Our behaviour, in turn, is determined by what stimuli we respond to and how we interpret those stimuli. That is, our behaviour is determined by our perceptions.

Every day an almost infinite number of marketing stimuli exist that conceivably we could be exposed to. These include brand names, signs, retail stores, advertisements, packages, and direct experiences with products. In reality, however, a process of **selectivity** that limits our perceptions is occurring continuously. As an illustration, consider that:

- We are exposed to only a portion of all marketing stimuli (products, ads, stores). We cannot read every magazine or visit every store. Or we perceive only part of what we are exposed to. We can read a newspaper and not notice an ad. (This is selective exposure.)
- We may alter information when it is inconsistent with our beliefs or attitudes. Thus, someone may say, "I don't believe smoking is hazardous to my health." (This is selective distortion.)
- We retain only part of what we selectively perceive. We may read an ad but later forget it. (This is selective retention.)

There are many marketing implications in this selectivity process. To illustrate, if a marketing stimulus — a product or a store — falls outside your range of perception, then for you that product or store does not exist. In another situation, a perceived product stimulus such as a videocassette recorder (VCR) may be understood (have meaning) quite differently by various consumers. A child perceives a VCR as a source of entertainment. Mother may view it as a baby-sitter, a source of information and entertainment, and a teacher for her child. Father may view it as an overpriced luxury that prevents him from buying a new outboard motor. (The colour TV set was perfectly okay for entertainment.)

Marketers cannot afford the expense of unlimited exposure of their marketing stimuli — products, ads, stores, etc. Consequently, they strive for the exposure that will fall within the perception range of the target market. This means, for example, carefully selecting the right stores to carry the product or the right magazines to carry the ads. In the case of advertising stimuli, the message must be sufficiently meaningful and strong to survive the customers' selective retention processes. Thus, the seller may run an extra large ad or a colour ad placed in a sea of black-and-white ads.

File 5-1

Marketing at Work

Beauty Is Still in the Eye of the Beholder

A major retailer operated quality department stores under the Glover's name in a number of Canadian cities. In order to compete with the expanding discount chains, it had opened several Big Buy discount stores. After several years of relatively unsuccessful operation, the decision was made to close most of the discount operations. However, one store was kept open and responsibility for its operation was transferred to the management team that managed one of the company's nearby Glover's department stores.

Over time, the Glover's management team converted the Big Buy store, which was in an excellent location, to a Glover's operation in all but name. The two stores carried essentially the same merchandise, followed the same pricing policies, and even used a similar advertising style. Management could not understand why the Big Buy store was unable to generate the level of sales produced at the Glover's store. As the company president, Jack Glover, put it, ''Can't customers understand they are the same store?''

A marketing research study commissioned by Mr. Glover revealed that customers clearly did not perceive the Big Buy store to be similar to Glover's. It was considered to be a discount store that carried lower quality merchandise. Potential customers were driving past the Big Buy location to shop at Glover's. The consultant who conducted the research recommended that the Big Buy name be dropped and that the company announce the opening of a ''new'' Glover's location. Even though literally nothing was changed but the name on the front of the store, within six months sales per square foot at the renamed Big Buy store had increased by 30 percent.

Although the merchandise, prices, and other elements of the store were identical in the two locations before the name change, customers perceived them to be different. To them, Big Buy was still a discount store. Perception really is as important as reality.

CULTURAL INFLUENCES   The structure for the remainder of our dicussion of consumer buying behaviour in this chapter is illustrated in Fig. 5-2. How we perceive things — and how we think, believe, and act — are determined to a great extent by our experiences. And this means by the various groups of people with whom we interrelate. All the social-group influences on consumer buying behaviour start with the *culture* in which the consumer lives.

FIGURE 5-2
Sociocultural and psychological forces that influence consumers' buying behaviour.

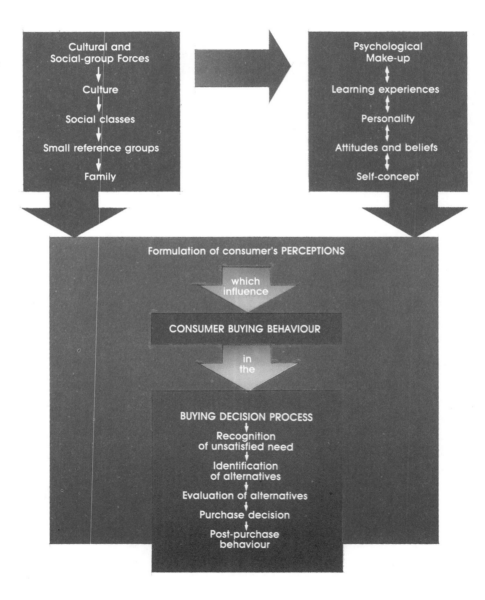

Definition of Culture and
Cultural Influence

A **culture** is the complex of symbols and artifacts created by a given society and handed down from generation to generation as determinants and regulators of human behaviour. The symbols may be intangible (attitudes, beliefs, values, languages, religions) or tangible (tools, housing, products, works of art). A culture implies a totally learned and "handed-down" way of life. It does *not* include instinctive acts. However, standards for performing instinctive biological acts (eating, eliminating body wastes, and sexual relationships) can be culturally established. Thus everybody gets hungry, but what people eat and how they act to satisfy the hunger drive will vary among cultures.

Actually, much of our behaviour is culturally determined. Our sociocultural institutions (family, schools, churches, and languages) provide behavioural guidelines. Years ago, Kluckhohn observed: "Culture . . . regulates our lives at every turn. From the moment we are born until we die there is constant conscious and unconscious pressure upon us to follow certain types of behaviour that other men have created for us."[2] People living in a culture share a whole set of similarities — and these can be different from those in or from another culture.

Cultural Change

Cultural influences do change over time, as old patterns gradually give way to the new. During the past 10 to 25 years, cultural changes — that is, life-style changes — of far-reaching magnitude have been occurring. Marketing executives must be alert to these changing life-styles so that they can adjust their planning to be in step with, or even a little ahead of, the times. In Chapter 2 we mentioned some of these cultural changes when we discussed social and cultural forces as an environmental factor influencing a company's marketing system. Now at this point we shall simply summarize a few of the sociocultural changes that significantly affect consumer buying behaviour.[3]

- From a thrift and savings ethic to spending more freely and buying on credit.
- From a work ethic to more self-indulgence and having fun.
- From a husband-dominated family towards equality in husband-wife roles; or, in a broader context, the changing role of women.

- From emphasis on *quantity* of goods to emphasis on *quality* of life.
- From self-reliance to more reliance on government and other institutions.
- From postponed gratification to immediate gratification.
- More concern about the pollution of our natural environment.
- A concern for more safety in our products and in our occupations.
- A concern for the conservation of irreplaceable resources.

Subcultures

Reaching Canada's Greek community.

Given the multicultural nature of Canadian society, marketers should understand the concept of subcultures and analyze them as potentially profitable market segments. Any time there is a culture as heterogeneous as ours, there are bound to be significant subcultures based upon factors such as race, nationality, religion, geographic location, age, and urban-rural distribution. Some of these were recognized in Chapter 4, when we analyzed the demographic market factors. Ethnicity, for example, is a cultural factor that has significant marketing implications. Concentrations of Middle or Eastern Europeans in the Prairies provide a market for some products that would go unnoticed in Italian or Chinese sections of Toronto.

The cultural diversity of the Canadian market has taken on increased importance for some companies in recent years. Twenty years ago, most companies ignored the ethnic market, but the 1986 Census showed that almost 40 percent of Canada's population had origins other than British, French, or native. Almost four million Canadians claimed a mother tongue other than English or French.

The most obvious efforts to reach ethnic market segments are, of course, found in major urban markets such as Toronto and Vancouver. In Toronto, for example, a multicultural television channel, MTV, carries European soccer and other programming directed to ethnic markets. These and similar media represent attractive advertising outlets for companies who wish to reach this growing market segment.

The sharpest subcultural differences are portrayed in behavioural differences between English- and French-Canadian communities on a country-wide basis, although to the urban dweller in Toronto or Montreal the acceptance (or ritual avoidance) of the obvious differences between a diversity of ethnic minorities is now a matter of course. As indicated in Chapter 4, marketing to French Canada involves considerably more than cursory acknowledgement of ethnic differences.

The Changing Nature of the French-Canadian Market

French Canada, as a subculture, has undergone a revolution during the past 25 years. This cultural revolution — sometimes termed the Quiet Revolution — has had a profound effect on the nature of the French-Canadian market.

With the beginning of the Quiet Revolution, French Canadians took major steps to preserve their cultural identity in the English-dominated North American society and to prevent the assimilation of French Canada into this society. It has been a modern, progressive movement that has been manifest in programs to preserve the French language, improved health and education programs, renewed interest in French-Canadian crafts and culture, and the confidence shown in Quebec's hosting of Expo '67 and the 1976 Summer Olympics. As a movement, it has been exemplified in the slogan *Maîtres Chez Nous* — masters in our own house. The roles of religion, the family, and women have changed dramatically. No longer do the traditional professions of the priesthood, law, and medicine dominate the cultural hierarchy. A new middle class has developed in French Canada that is less traditional in its outlook and is more attuned to youth and business. The Quebec business scene is vibrant and entrepreneurial. New, exciting opportunities are developing for Quebec-owned businesses and hundreds of new businesses have been established in the province in recent years. Quebec now accounts for more than one-third of all business graduates from Canadian universities.

Differences in Consumption Behaviour

Cultural differences lead to differences in consumption behaviour between English- and French-Canadians. Certain products sell in much larger quantities in Quebec than in other provinces, while other products that sell well in English Canada are rarely purchased by French-Canadians. Some examples of differences in product preferences and buying behaviour follow:[4]

- There is a better acceptance in Quebec of premium-priced products such as premium-grade gasoline and expensive liquors.
- French Canadians spend more per capita on clothing, personal care items, tobacco, and alcoholic beverages.
- The French Canadian consumes more soft drinks, maple sugar, molasses, and candy per capita than does the English Canadian.
- French Canadians have much higher consumption rates for instant and decaffeinated coffee.
- French Canadians watch more television and listen to radio more than do English Canadians.
- Premiums and coupons are more popular in Quebec.
- French Canadians buy more headache and cold remedies than do English Canadians.
- In many Quebec homes a full meal is served both at noon and in the evening.
- French-Canadian consumers may experience higher levels of dissatisfaction with repairs and general consumer services and with professional and personal services than is the case for English-speaking Canadians.[5]

Factors Influencing French-English Consumption Differences

While it is relatively easy to determine where actual differences in consumption behaviour exist between French and English Canadians, it is somewhat more difficult to identify reasons for the existence of such differences. And yet, it is important for marketers to have some understanding of the factors that contribute to these differences if they are to market effectively to both market segments.

In the past, authors have pointed out that French Canadians have a lower per capita income than do English Canadians, that they have lower average education levels, and that they are a much more rural population. These differences along income and other demographic lines might suggest that the differences in product purchase rates and shopping behaviour between French Canadians and English Canadians may be attributable simply to demographic differences and that the consumption behaviour of French Canadians is really no different from that of

Special media for special markets.

English Canadians of similar demographic characteristics. At least two studies have refuted this argument.

An early one indicated that consumption behaviour was significantly different between Quebec and Ontario households when households of *similar size and income levels were compared.*[6] A second study found significant differences in household expenditure levels between English-Canadian and French-Canadian households for eight consumption expenditure categories after certain noncultural differences (such as the rural-urban breakdown of the groups and stage of the family life cycle) between the two groups were controlled.[7] Such findings suggest that the consumption behaviour differences between French and English Canadians are not attributable solely to demographic differences but, rather, are more likely explained by cultural differences.

Certain characteristics of the French-Canadian culture and directions in which that culture appears to have changed were discussed earlier. The important message for the marketer is that French Canada is culturally distinctive from English Canada and that certain products and other elements of the marketing mix are perceived quite differently by the French Canadian than they are by the English Canadian. As has been suggested, the *function* and *meaning* of products sold to French Canada must be perceived by the French-Canadian culture as consistent with that culture.

The Impact of Cultural Differences on Marketing

The fact that French Canada represents a distinctively different culture from that found in English Canada requires that marketers who wish to be successful in the French-Canadian market develop unique marketing programs for this segment. There must be an appreciation of the fact that certain products will not be successful in French Canada simply because they are not appropriate to the French-Canadian culture and life-style. In other cases, products that are successful in English Canada must be marketed differently in French Canada because the French Canadian has a different perception of these products and the way in which they are used. It may be necessary for companies to develop new products or appropriate variations of existing products specifically for the French-Canadian market. Similarly, the retail buying behaviour of French Canadians may necessitate the use of different channels of distribution in Quebec.

In the area of advertising, many national companies have encountered problems in reaching the French-Canadian market. Much of the national advertising in Canada was prepared by English-Canadian advertising agencies (usually based in Toronto) that developed advertisements for use in both English and French Canada. These agencies generally employed translators whose responsibility it was to translate the advertisements, which had been developed by English Canadians for the English culture, so that they might be used in the Quebec market. In many cases, literal translations were demanded and the end results were inappropriate for the French market.

The challenges of advertising in French Canada go far beyond those of translating English to French. Even where the translation is a good one and English expressions and slang are converted into expressions that are meaningful to French Canadians, the problem still remains that the basic approach to the advertisement is based in English-Canadian or even American culture. Many advertisements contain illustrations, themes, and representations of life-styles that are quite appropriate in English

Canada but quite inappropriate in Quebec. What is needed is that advertising which is to be directed to the French-Canadian market be planned from "scratch" with that market in mind. The advertising content must be consistent with the culture of the market, and this requires that it be developed and written by French Canadians. Many national advertisers now place their English-language advertising with an English-Canadian agency, but use a Montreal-based French-language agency to develop advertising for the Quebec market.[8]

In the packaging and labelling of consumer products there have also been recent developments that are important for marketing in French Canada. For many years, Canadian companies made no special effort to prepare product labels for use in French Canada, with the result that most of the products on the shelves of Quebec retail stores bore English labels. Since 1967, however, it has been a requirement of the Quebec government that all labels on food products sold in that province give at least equal prominence to the French language. Similarly, the federal government's Consumer Packaging and Labelling Act and its regulations require that all label information on consumer products produced in Canada or imported into this country be conveyed in both English and French.

SOCIAL-GROUP INFLUENCES

Consumers' perceptions and buying behaviour are also influenced by the social groups to which they belong. These groups include the large social classes and smaller reference groups. The smallest, yet usually the strongest, social-group influence is a person's family.

Influence of Social Class

People's buying behaviour is often influenced by the class to which they belong, or to which they aspire, simply because they have values, beliefs and life-styles that are characteristic of a social class. This occurs whether they are conscious of class notions or not. The idea of a social-class structure and the terms *upper*, *middle*, and *lower* class may be repugnant to many Canadians. However, it does represent a useful way to look at a market. We can consider social class as another useful basis for segmenting consumer markets.[9]

More than 40 years ago, Warner and Lunt conducted a study that identified a six-class system within the social structure of a small American town.[10] The placement of people in the structure was based on their *type*, not amount, of income, and on their occupation, type of house, and area of residence within the community. Through the years, other researchers have made similar social-class studies in other locations, sometimes using different bases of measurement.

A social-class structure currently useful to marketing managers is one developed by Richard Coleman and Lee Rainwater, two respected researchers in social-class theory. The placement of people in this structure is determined primarily by such variables as *education, occupation, and type of neighbourhood of residence.*[11]

Note that "amount of income" is *not* one of the placement criteria. There may be a general relationship between amount of income and social class — people in the upper classes usually have higher incomes than people in the lower classes. But *within* each social class there typically is a wide range of incomes. Also, the same amount of income may be earned by families in different social classes.

For purposes of marketing planning and analysis, marketing executives and researchers often divide the total consumer market into five social classes. These classes and their characteristics, as adapted from the Warner and Coleman structures previously noted, are summarized below. The percentages are only approximations and may vary from one city or region to another.

SOCIAL CLASSES AND THEIR CHARACTERISTICS

The **upper class**, about 2 percent of the population, includes two groups: (1) the socially prominent "old families" of inherited wealth and (2) the "new rich" of the corporate executives, owners of large businesses, and wealthy professionals. They live in large homes in the best neighbourhoods and display a sense of social responsibility. They buy expensive products and services, but they do not conspicuously display their purchases. They patronize exclusive shops.

The **upper-middle class**, about 12 percent of the population, is composed of moderately successful business and professional people, and owners of medium-sized companies. They are well educated, have a strong drive for success, and want their children to do well. Their purchases are more conspicuous than those in the upper class. This class buys status symbols that show their success, yet are socially acceptable. They live well, belong to private clubs, and support the arts and various social causes.

The **lower-middle class**, about 32 percent of the population, consists of the white-collar workers — office workers, most sales people, teachers, technicians, and small-business owners. The **upper-lower class**, about 38 percent of the population, is the blue-collar "working class" of factory workers, semiskilled workers, and service people. Because these two groups together represent the mass market and thus are so important to most marketers, the attitudes, beliefs, and life-styles they exhibit are the focus for much marketing research.

File 5-2

Marketing at Work

Education and Occupation Tell Us Who We Are

Education and occupation provide a more accurate explanation of consumer purchase behaviour than does income, a study conducted in Ottawa in the early 1980s confirmed.

This study found that families with lower education and job status owned larger cars, had more and larger television sets, watched TV more frequently, ate more convenience foods, drank more whisky and beer, were more likely to own electric frying pans, and bought better-known national brands.

On the other hand, upper-middle class families spent less time watching TV, placed greater emphasis on meal preparation and nutrition, more often bought economy-sized packages, drank more Scotch and imported wine, and owned more blenders and drip coffee makers.

Source: Jo Marney, "Status: The Subtle Force That Still Sells," *Marketing*, January 16, 1984, pp. 13, 15.

YUPPIES: A CLASS UNTO THEMSELVES?

Are "yuppies" a separate social class or part of the upper-middle class? There is no doubt that the concept of a "yuppie" segment is well known to marketers, primarily because of the considerable buying power represented by the group. Yuppies (young urban professionals) are the most visible members of the baby-boom generation. They are the consumers who are in their thirties, are university educated, hold down professional or managerial jobs, are from dual-income households, and have a total family income of $50,000 or more. They may or may not have children. But, if they do, they also have lots of money to spend on them.

While there are more than seven million Canadians in the baby-boom generation (those born between 1946 and the late 1960s), the yuppies are the leading edge of that group, although they represent only about 4 percent of the total adult population. Their influence is, however, much greater than their numbers would imply.

These young consumers have the buying power to forge new market trends. They are the opinion leaders, the ones who can make or break new products and brands. Their life-style has been responsible for the success of certain products and even for the establishment of certain sectors of markets for import cars, light foods and beverages, exercise equipment and clothing, and consumer electronics. If it were not for the influence of the yuppies, what would be the current success of Perrier, BMW, white wine spritzers, fitness classes, cappuccino, the Sony Walkman, and the compact disc?

Catering to the needs of this segment of the market has meant success for many Canadian companies. More important is the influence which these style-setters have had on the preferences and purchase behaviour of less wealthy consumers. They are probably best defined as a segment within the upper-middle class group — for many companies, a very attractive segment.

The **lower-lower class**, about 16 percent of the population, is composed of unskilled workers, the chronically unemployed, unassimilated immigrants, and people frequently on welfare. They typically are poorly educated, with low incomes, and live in substandard houses and neighbourhoods. They tend to live for the present and often do not purchase wisely. The public tends to differentiate (within this class) between the ''working poor'' and the ''welfare poor.''

MARKETING SIGNIFICANCE OF SOCIAL CLASSES

Now let's summarize the basic conclusions from social-class research that are highly significant for marketing:

- A social-class system can be observed whether people are aware of it or not. There are substantial differences between classes regarding their buying behaviour.
- Differences in beliefs, attitudes, and orientations exist among the classes. Thus the classes respond differently to a seller's marketing program.
- For many products, class membership is a better predictor of buyer behaviour than is income.

This last point — the relative importance of income versus social class — has generated considerable controversy. There is an old saying that ''a rich man is just a poor man with money — and that, given the same amount of money, a poor man would behave exactly like a rich man.'' Studies of social-class structure have proved that this statement simply is not true. Two people, each earning the same income but belonging to different social classes, will have quite different buying patterns. They will shop at different stores, expect different treatment from sales people, and buy different products and even different brands. Also, when a family's income increases because more family members get a job, this increase almost never results in a change in the family's social class.

Influence of Small Reference Groups

Small reference groups influence our buying behaviour.

Small-group influence on buyer behaviour introduces to marketing the concept of reference-group theory, which we borrow from sociology. A **reference group** may be defined as a group of people who influence a person's attitudes, values, and behaviour. Each group develops its own standards of behaviour that then serve as guides, or ''frames of reference,'' for the individual members. The members share these values and are expected to conform to the group's normative behavioural patterns. It is likely that a person's reference groups are to be found in their own social class category.

Consumer behaviour is influenced by the small groups to which consumers belong or aspire to belong. These groups may include family, fraternal organizations, labour unions, church groups, athletic teams, or a circle of close friends or neighbours. Studies have shown that personal advice in face-to-face groups is much more effective as a behavioural determinant than advertising in newspapers, television, or other mass media. That is, in selecting products or changing brands, we are more likely to be influenced by word-of-mouth advertising from satisfied customers in our reference group. This is true especially when the speaker is considered to be knowledgeable regarding the particular product.

A person may agree with all the ideas of the group or only some of them. Also, a person does not have to belong to a group to be influenced by it. Young people frequently pattern their dress and other behaviour after that of an older group which the younger ones aspire to join.

Another useful finding pertains to the flow of information between and within groups. For years marketers operated in conformity with the ''snob appeal'' theory. This is the idea that if you can get social leaders and high-income groups to use your products, the mass market will also buy them. The assumption has been that influence follows a *vertical* path, starting at levels of high status and moving downward through successive levels of groups. Contrary to this popular assumption, studies by Katz and Lazarsfeld and by others have emphasized the *horizontal* nature of opinion leadership. Influence emerges on each *level* of the socioeconomic scale, moving from the opinion leaders to their peers.[12]

The proven role of small groups as behaviour determinants, plus the concept of horizontal information flow, suggests that a marketer is faced with two key problems. The first is to identify the relevant reference group likely to be used by consumers in a given buying situation. The second is to identify and communicate with two key people in the group — the innovator (early buyer) and the influential person (opinion leader). Every group has a leader — a tastemaker, or **opinion leader** — who influences the decision making of others in the group. The key is for marketers to convince that person of the value of their products or services. The opinion *leader* in one group may be an opinion *follower* in another. Married women with children may be influential in matters concerning food, whereas unmarried women are more likely to influence fashions in clothing and makeup.

Family Buying Behaviour (Buying Habits)

Christmas packaging reflects when people buy some products.

Of all the small groups that we belong to through the years, one group normally exerts the strongest and most enduring influence on our perceptions and behaviour. That group is our family.

In addition to understanding *why* people buy, marketers also need to know *when*, *where*, and *how* they buy. We are talking now about consumers' buying *habits*, or overt buying *patterns*, in contrast to their buying *motives* (why they buy). This section on buying habits applies to consumers living alone as well as to families. For families we need to answer an additional question — who does the family buying?

WHEN CONSUMERS BUY

Marketing executives should be able to answer at least three questions about *when* people buy their products or services: During what season do they buy? On what day of the week do they buy? At what time of the day do they buy? If seasonal buying patterns exist, marketing executives should try to extend the buying season. There is obviously little opportunity for extending the buying season for Easter bunnies or Christmas-tree ornaments. But the season for vacations has been shifted to such an extent that winter and other ''off-season'' vacations are now quite popular.

When people buy may influence the product-planning, pricing, or promotional phases of a firm's marketing program. After-shave lotion and alcoholic beverages often are distinctly packaged at Christmastime because they are purchased for gifts. To smooth the seasonal peaks and valleys in production, a fishing tackle manufacturer may want retailers to buy well in advance of the summer season. To get retailers to do this, the manufacturer may offer them ''seasonal datings.'' This is a pricing strategy whereby retailers take delivery in April but do not have to pay for the merchandise until July.

WHERE CONSUMERS BUY

A firm should consider two factors with respect to *where* people buy — where the buying decision is made and where the actual purchase occurs. For many products and services the decision to buy is made at home. For others, the decision is often made in whole or in part at the point of purchase. A man shopping in a sporting goods store for golf clubs may see some tennis balls on sale. Knowing he needs some, he decides on the spot to buy them. A woman may decide at home to buy a birthday gift for her husband. But she will wait until she gets to the store before deciding whether it will be a shirt or a book.

A company's promotional program, and its product planning, must be geared to carry the greatest impact at the place where the buying decision is made. If this decision is made in the store, then attention must be devoted to packaging and point-of-purchase display materials, particularly in self-service stores. A shopper may decide at home to buy some cold cereal, but the key decisions regarding which type and which brand may be made at the store.

HOW CONSUMERS BUY

The *how* part of consumers' buying habits encompasses several areas of behaviour and, consequently, many marketing decisions. Long ago, for example, many firms found that consumers prefer to buy such products as pickles, cookies, and butter already packaged. The advantage of cleanliness and ease of handling offset the higher unit price.

The trend toward one-step shopping has encouraged retailers to add related and even unrelated lines of merchandise to their basic groups of products. The increase of credit-card buying has led many stores to accept Visa or MasterCard credit cards. In the past, these retailers would accept only their own charge-account cards.

WHO DOES THE FAMILY OR HOUSEHOLD BUYING?

Marketers should treat this question as four separate ones, because each may call for different marketing strategies and tactics. The four questions are:

1. Who influences the buying decision? (This may be a member of the family, or the influence may come from an outside reference group.)
2. Who makes the buying decision?
3. Who makes the actual purchase?
4. Who uses the product?

Four different people may be involved, or only one member may do all four, or there may be some other combination of influences.

For many years, women have done most of the family buying. They still exert substantial influence in buying decisions and do a considerable amount of the actual purchasing. However, men have increasingly entered the family buying picture. Self-service stores are especially appealing to men. Night and Sunday openings in various parts of the country also encourage men to play a bigger role in the family purchasing.

In recent years, teenagers and young children have become decision makers in family buying, as well as actual purchasers. The amount of money teenagers spend now is substantial enough to be considered in the marketing plans of many manufacturers and middlemen. Even very young children are an influence in buying decisions today because they watch television programs or shop with their parents.

Purchasing decisions are often made jointly by husband and wife (sometimes even the children are included). Young married people are much more likely to make buying decisions on a joint basis than are older couples. Apparently the longer a husband and wife live together, the more they feel they can trust each other to act unilaterally.

Who buys a product will influence a firm's marketing policies regarding its product, channels of distribution, and promotion. If children are the key decision makers, as is often the case in purchasing breakfast cereals, then a manufacturer may include some type of premium with the product. In a department store, the men's department is often located on the street floor near a door. This permits men

One-stop shopping can lead to some interesting product assortments.

Sometimes a little guy can influence a buying decision — especially when there is a premium in the box.

to enter, shop, and leave the store without having to wade through crowds of shoppers. The entire advertising campaign — media, appeals, copy, radio and television programming, and so forth — is affected by whether the target consists of men, women, or children.

PSYCHOLOGICAL DETERMINANTS OF BUYER BEHAVIOUR

In discussing the psychological forces in consumer behaviour, we shall continue to use the model we set up near the beginning of this chapter. That is, one or more motives within a person trigger behaviour toward a goal that is expected to bring satisfaction. This goal-oriented behaviour is influenced by the person's perceptions. In this section, we discuss the effects that learning experiences, personality, attitudes and beliefs, and self-concept have on perceptions. (Recall Fig. 5-2.) These psychological variables help to shape a person's life-style and values. The term **psychographics** is being used by many researchers as a collective synonym for these psychological variables and life-style values.[13]

Learning Experiences

As a factor influencing a person's perceptions, **learning** may be defined as changes in behaviour resulting from previous experiences. However, also by definition, learning does *not* include behaviour changes attributable to instinctive responses, or temporary states of the organism such as hunger or fatigue.[14]

The ability to interpret and predict the consumer's learning process is a real key to understanding buying behaviour. Therefore, it is unfortunate that no simple learning theory has emerged as universally workable and acceptable. The principal learning theories described here are (1) stimulus-response (S-R) theories, (2) cognitive theories, and (3) gestalt and field theories.

STIMULUS-RESPONSE THEORIES

These theories were first formulated by psychologists such as Pavlov, Skinner, and Hull on the basis of their laboratory experiments with animals. This school of theorists holds that learning occurs as a person (or animal) (1) responds to some stimulus and (2) is reinforced with need satisfaction for a correct response or penalized for an incorrect one. When the same correct response is repeated in reaction to a given stimulus, behavioural patterns are established.

Today we realize that attitudes and other factors (not just the mechanical stimulus-response) also influence a consumer's response to a given stimulus. Nevertheless, the stimulus-response model, with reinforcement as an essential element, is a useful explanation of the learning process. Four factors — drive, cue, response, and reinforcement — are fundamental to the process. A **drive** (or motive) is a strong stimulus that requires satisfaction — a response of some sort. The **cues** are weaker stimuli that determine the pattern of this response — the "when," "where," and "how" of the response behaviour. For instance, a TV commercial or a change in price is a cue that might shape a consumer's behaviour in seeking to satisfy an aroused hunger drive. The **response** is simply the behavioural reaction to the cues and drive. **Reinforcement** results when the response is rewarding (satisfying).

If the response is gratifying, a connection between cue and response will be established; that is, a behavioural pattern will be learned. Learning, then, emerges from reinforcement. Continual reinforcement leads to habit or brand loyalty. Once a habitual pattern of behaviour is established, it replaces conscious, willful behaviour. The stronger the habit, the more difficult it is for a competitive product to break the habit and enter a consumer's learning field. On the other hand, if the original response action is not rewarding, the consumer's mind is open to another set of cues leading to another response. For example, the consumer will buy a substitute product or switch to another brand.

COGNITIVE THEORIES

Cognitive learning theories reject the S-R model as being too mechanistic. In S-R theory, behaviour is the result of *only* the degree of reinforcement stemming from a response to some stimulus. No other influences are recognized as intervening in the S-R channel. Proponents of cognitive theory insist that learning is influenced by factors such as attitudes, beliefs, and an insightful understanding of how to achieve a goal. Cognitive theorists believe that a person can use thinking ability to solve a current problem, even if there are no historical precedents in the person's experience. Habitual behavioural patterns, then, are the result of perceptive thinking and goal orientation.

GESTALT AND FIELD THEORIES

Gestalt is a German word which roughly means "configuration," "pattern," or "form." Gestalt psychologists are concerned with the "whole" of a thing — the total scene — rather than its component parts. They maintain that learning and behaviour should be viewed as a total process, in contrast to the individual-element approach in the S-R model.[15]

Field theory, as formulated by Kurt Lewin, is a useful refinement of gestalt psychology.[16] This theory holds that the only determining force accounting for a person's behaviour at any given time is that person's psychological "field" at that time. A person's *field* or *life space* may be defined as the totality of facts pertaining to the individual and his or her environment at the time of the behaviour. Gestalt psychologists believed that people perceive the whole — their total environment — rather than its parts. Thus, the properties of the *total field* influence people's perceptions of the stimuli in that field. To illustrate, a distinguished-looking man in a white coat can speak in a serious tone in a TV commercial advertising a pain reliever. Many viewers will perceive him as a doctor or a pharmacist, because that is how they interpret the total scene in light of their past experience.

Several field principles, which have applications in marketing, deal with the ways in which properties of stimuli affect our perception of them. The principle of **closure** postulates that we tend to complete (close) figures to make them meaningful. Thus, "13 0" will be "closed" by the viewer to get "B O." A change in spacing (illustrating the principle of **proximity**) can give different results — "13 0" will be viewed as the number "130" rather than as two letters.

According to another field principle, marketing messages must be placed in a reasonable **context** — a smartly dressed woman should not be shown painting her house. Ads should also be **simple** in both structure and content. Because of **locational properties**, some items will stand out in a sea of similar-looking products.

This principle places a premium on eye-level shelf position in a supermarket, for example. And all parts of a marketing program — price, type of ads, product quality, and the like — must be in **harmony**, that is, consistent with consumers' expectations.

Personality

The study of human personality has given rise to many, sometimes widely divergent schools of psychological thought. Yet, perhaps because of this multifaceted attention, we still lack even a consensus definition of the term. Attempts to inventory and classify personality traits have understandably produced many different structures. In this discussion, **personality** is defined as an individual's pattern of traits that are a determinant of behavioural responses. Thus we speak of people having personality traits such as being self-confident, aggressive, shy, domineering, dynamic, secure or insecure, extroverted or introverted, easygoing, friendly, flexible or stubborn, etc.

It is generally agreed that consumers' personality traits do influence their perceptions and so are related to their buying behaviour. Unfortunately, however, the nature of this relationship — that is, *how* personality influences behaviour — is frequently situation- or issue-specific. We know that people's personalities often are reflected in the clothes they wear, the brand and type of car they drive (or whether they use a bike or motorcycle instead of a car), the restaurants they eat in, etc. What is clear is that, from time to time, a personality trait pattern or a trait can prove to be a useful segmentation variable.

Attitudes and Beliefs

An **attitude** may be defined as a person's enduring cognitive evaluation, emotional feeling, or action tendency toward some object or idea. Attitudes involve thought processes as well as emotional feelings, and they vary in intensity. Attitudes influence beliefs, and beliefs influence attitudes. In fact, for the purpose of our generalized, introductory-level discussion of buying behaviour, we shall use the two concepts interchangeably. They both reflect value judgements and positive or negative feelings toward a product, service, or brand.

Attitudes and beliefs are strong and direct forces affecting consumers' perceptions and buying behaviour. Attitudes significantly influence people's perceptions by selectively screening out any stimuli that conflict with those attitudes. They also can distort the perception of messages and affect the degree of their retention.

Various studies uniformly report a very close relationship between consumers' attitudes and their buying decisions in regard to both the type of product and the brand selection. Surely, then, it is in a marketer's best interests to understand how attitudes are formed, measured, and changed. Attitudes are **formed**, generally speaking, by the information individuals acquire (1) through their past learning experiences with the product or idea or (2) through their relations with their reference groups (family, social and work groups, etc.). The perception of this information is influenced by personality traits.

Attitude **measurement** is far from easy. In limited instances a researcher may simply employ the direct-question, survey technique. The most widely used techniques, however, have been some form of attitude scaling. Respondents may be asked, for instance, to rank several models or products by order of preference. Or they may be asked to rate some item according to a verbal scale ranging from one extreme to another (from ultramodern to very old-fashioned, for example). Many features in a company's marketing program lend themselves to attitude measurement. A seller may measure, for example, what people think about various product features (brand, package, colour), middlemen's activities (store hours or location, helpfulness of sales clerks), or promotional activities (advertisements, TV programs).

We need to note that measuring attitudes is *not* the same as measuring buying intentions or forecasting sales. You can have a very favourable attitude toward a product, but never buy it. Maybe the item is too expensive, or some other reason may block your purchase, regardless of your highly favourable attitude.

It is *extremely* difficult to **change** consumers' attitudes, regardless of marketing critics' opinions to the contrary. As far as attitudes are concerned, to get consumers to buy his product a seller has two choices. The first is to change consumers' attitudes to be favourable towards the service or product. The second is to determine what consumers' attitudes are and make the product or service consistent with those attitudes. Ordinarily it is much easier to change the product than it is to change the consumers' attitudes.

Nevertheless, in some situations attitudes have been changed in recent years. Consider, for instance, the cultural changes discussed earlier in this chapter. Every one of those situations involved a change in people's attitudes. Consider further how formerly negative attitudes have changed in favour of small cars, yellow tennis balls and oversized racquets, off-season vacations, adults getting their teeth straightened, and women wearing glasses.

Closely related to the concept of attitude is **image**. Retailers and brand managers should be very interested in the image of their brands or stores. Marketers regularly measure brand, store, and corporate image through various research techniques. Essentially, they are examining what consumers think of their products and their companies, acting on the premise that attitude guides behaviour. People are not likely to buy a brand which they consider to be inferior or shop at a store which they believe treats their customers poorly. The attitude toward or image of a brand or store is very much influenced by the consumer's perception. Once a marketing manager realizes that his or her brand has a negative image, then steps can be taken to change the marketing program so as to alter the brand's personality or image — the way it is perceived by consumers.

The Self-Concept Another personality based notion is the self-concept, or self-image. Your **self-image** is the way you see yourself. At the same time, it is the picture you think others have of you. Some psychologists distinguish between (1) the *actual* self-concept (the way you really see yourself) and (2) the *ideal* self-concept (the way you want to be seen or would like to see yourself). A person's self-image is influenced, for instance, by innate and learned physiological and psychological needs. It is conditioned also by economic factors, demographic factors, and social-group influences.

Studies of actual purchases show that people generally prefer brands and products that are compatible with their own self-concept. There are mixed reports concerning the degree of influence of the actual and ideal self-concepts on brand and product preferences. Some psychologists contend that consumption preferences correspond to a person's *actual* self-image. Others hold that the *ideal* self-image is dominant in consumers' choices.

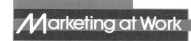

Attitudes Make a Point

Canadian marketers, whether they are major retailers, producers of food products, government departments, or manufacturers of hospital equipment, are interested in the attitudes of their "customers." This is consistent with the view that the better you know your customers, the better you can tailor your marketing program to meet their needs. Also, attitudes represent a major determinant of the purchase decision. Marketers generally use some form of marketing research to measure attitudes.

The Potato Marketing Board of Prince Edward Island is interested in the attitudes of residents of southern Ontario toward P.E.I. potatoes. A government department that is planning new labour legislation may be interested in finding out current attitudes toward labour unions. The B.C. Tourism department would want to know the attitudes of residents of the northwest United States concerning British Columbia vacations.

In all of these cases, the "marketer" wishes to introduce a new product or service, or is considering a change in the present marketing program. Information concerning attitudes is valuable in guiding the development of marketing plans.

Describe her self-image.

Perhaps there is no consensus here because in real life we often switch back and forth between our actual and our ideal self-concepts. A middle-aged man may buy some comfortable, but not fashionable, clothing to wear at home on a weekend where he is reflecting his actual self-image. Then later he buys some expensive, high-fashion exercise clothing as he envisions himself (ideal self-image) as a young, active, upwardly mobile guy. Or this same fellow may drive a beat-up pickup truck for his weekend errands (actual self-concept). But he'll drive his new foreign sports car to work where he wants to project a different (ideal) self-image.[17]

One of the most important developments for marketers with respect to self-concept relates to how women feel about themselves. This has involved a major change over the past 20 years or so and it has influenced the attitudes and behaviour of women of all ages and from all walks of life. The fundamental change is that women have an identity of their own. They no longer represent a ''segment'' of the market who can be identified only through their roles as wife or mother. The changing role of women and its implications for family composition, decision making, and purchase behaviour are considerable.

Values and Life-styles

One of the most valuable ways of looking at a market and its potential involves consideration of consumer life-styles and values. Marketers now develop marketing programs based not only on how old their customers are or where they live, but also on how they spend their leisure time, what type of movies they like to watch,

Convenience for breakfast.

and what things they consider important in their lives. This is an integral part of the concept of market segmentation, which we will discuss in Chapter 7. Essentially, the Canadian market is made up of many different types of people. Once we can identify how these various groups think and live, we can do a better job of developing products, services, advertising, and other marketing techniques to appeal to them.

The field of psychographic research was developed in the 1960s and initially examined consumer activities, interests, and opinions. A more recent development has been the use of a program known as VALS (Values, Attitudes, and Life-style), which was developed in the United States at the Stanford Research Institute. VALS research involves the study of thousands of consumers and measures their opinions, interests, attitudes, values, beliefs, and activities in a variety of different areas. Using sophisticated computer-based data analysis techniques, the developers of VALS have identified nine different segments or clusters of consumers in the U.S. population. In Canada, a similar study has revealed 14 different "life-style segments," eight female and six male (see box). The company that developed this way of looking at the market, Canada Lifestyle, has given each segment a name and can describe personal attributes of its members.

These life-style or psychographic definitions of market segments are much more interesting and useful to the marketer than are segments based only on demographic characteristics such as age, income levels, and marital status. For example, groups for which convenience is of considerable importance represent target segments for home cleaning services and automatic teller machines.

File 5-4

Marketing at Work

Life-styles: Everything You Ever Wanted to Know

In the late 1970s, Canada Lifestyle did a study of Sara Lee frozen desserts. The advertising agency that was handling the Sara Lee account knew that the main consumers of Sara Lee products were mothers with children and thought of them as traditional housewives, represented in the Canada Lifestyle typology by Fran (estimated to be 9% of the female population). "We found that Fran won't buy a frozen dessert because she thinks it's a real sin to buy what she can make better herself," said Canada Lifestyle president Barry Thornton. "If Fran bought a chocolate cake, she'd smuggle it home, so the neighbours wouldn't see, whereas Diana and Sue don't have time for domestic chores. Diana would say, 'The last time I was in the kitchen was to get a beer.' " The Canada Lifestyle survey found that more than half of the frozen dessert users were Dianas, the working moms, and Sues, their unmarried counterparts. As a result, Sara Lee launched a major transportation advertising campaign to reach all the Dianas and Sues on their way to and from work.

Source: Ian Pearson, "Social Studies," *Canadian Business*, December 1985, p. 69.

CANADIANS AS LIFE-STYLE SEGMENTS

Trying to get a fix on the real you? Canada Lifestyle can help. According to the company, English Canadians over the age of 18 can be neatly divided into the following 14 "lifestyle segments":

Diana, "The Working Mother" (20%): Not a "mother who works" but a "worker with kids." Aggressively social, active, mobile and practical.

Sue, "The Social Single" (17%): A remnant of the "Me Generation." Well educated and a voracious cultural consumer but incapable of making commitments and fearful of marriage, family and romance.

Liz, "The Upscale Pacesetter" (15%): An affluent, sophisticated homemaker who runs her home as if it were a business. Cultured, well educated, well informed and confident.

Sara, "The Traditionalist" (12%): A middle-aged, middle-class housewife who lives according to the values she was brought up on. Thoughtful and articulate, she is constantly looking for ways to improve herself.

Brenda, "Blue Jeans Mother" (10%): A young, lower-income homemaker trying to cope with the transition from being a carefree single to the responsibilities of family life. Depends on a "strong leader" — either husband or father — and exercises thrift in her spending.

Fran, "The Happy Homemaker" (9%): Her interests are the family, home and church, and she pours most of her energy into the home. Traditional, security conscious and sceptical of women's lib.

Gran, (9%): Old-fashioned and traditional, she lives morally in the nineteenth century. More family oriented than any other segment.

Edna, "The Malcontent" (8%): Emotionally and intellectually negative, she is a homebody who hides within the fortress of her family. She sees only deterioration in the world around her.

Steve, "The Hardhat" (21%): Usually employed in a skilled trade, he is well paid but depressed by the routine of the working day. Conservative and materialistic, he admires strong leaders and can be prone to violence.

Ross, "The Urban Businessman" (20%): Well educated and status conscious, he is probably in a professional or executive position. Although he observes some traditions, he is progressive and modern in his thinking. He enjoys competition but lives in constant fear of failure.

Dave, "The Playboy" (17%): Extremely social, a swinger and a sportsman. Sensitive about his self-image, he avoids personal commitment but is determined to succeed professionally.

Henry, "The Old Guard" (16%): A gentleman, a churchman and a traditionalist. Ultraconservative, he is disillusioned by the decline of morals in the contemporary world but is content with his own achievements.

Bert, "The Egotist" (13%): Chauvinistic and macho, he is obsessed with his masculinity. Most likely to work at a job that requires more strength than skill, he harbours fantasies about becoming a person of great strength who defies danger and wins the day.

Roy, "The Homespun Handyman" (13%): Canada's cowboy, fisherman, farmer or artisan. Dedicated to his trade and his family, he has no illusions about social status and is happy with the old-fashioned way he has chosen to live.

Reprinted with permission from Ian Pearson, "Social Studies," *Canadian Business*, December 1985, p. 73.

**DECISION-MAKING
PROCESS IN BUYING**

It is time now to tie together some of our points regarding consumer behaviour and to describe the process consumers go through when making purchasing decisions. The process is a problem-solving approach consisting of the following five stages, also shown in the lower half of Fig. 5-2:

1. *Recognition of an unsatisfied need:* A family needs a new auto.
2. *Identification of alternative ways of achieving satisfaction:* They can buy a sports car or a station wagon.
3. *Evaluation of alternatives:* They consider pros and cons of the two types of autos.
4. *Purchase decision:* They buy a sports car.
5. *Postpurchase behaviour:* They wonder if they made the right decision.

Once the process has been started, potential buyers can withdraw at any stage prior to the actual purchase, and some stages can be skipped. A total-stage approach is likely to be used only in certain buying situations — a first-time purchase of a product, for instance, or in buying high-priced, infrequently purchased articles. For many products the purchasing behaviour is a routine affair in which the aroused need is satisfied in the usual manner by purchasing the same brand. That is, past reinforcement in learning experiences leads directly to the buying response-act, and thus the second and third stages are bypassed. However, if something changes appreciably (price, product, services), buyers may reopen the full decision process and consider alternative brands or products.

**Recognition of
Unsatisfied Need**

The process starts when an unsatisfied need (motive) creates inner tension. This may be a biogenic need, aroused internally (the person feels hungry). Or the need may have been dormant until it was aroused by an external stimulus, such as an ad or the sight of the product. Or perhaps dissatisfaction with the present product created the tension.

Once the need has been recognized, often consumers become aware of conflicting or competing uses for their scarce resources of time or money. Let us say that a consumer has a desire to install a hot tub in the backyard at a cost of $5,000. Family members may point out that they need new furniture for the living room. Or they may think that their neighbours (a key reference group) would not approve. A person must resolve these conflicts before proceeding. Otherwise, the buying process stops at this point.

**Identification of
Alternatives**

Once a need has been recognized, both product and brand alternatives must be identified. Suppose a woman wants to make her hands feel softer. Some alternative solutions include buying a dishwasher, using rubber gloves, or trying a different detergent or a new hand cream. Or she can get family members to wash the dishes and scrub the floors. If one of the product alternatives is selected, then there still are several brand alternatives to choose from.

The search for alternatives is influenced by such factors as (1) what the time and money costs are (not much time is spent buying a hamburger, in comparison with the time spent buying a new winter coat); (2) how much information the consumer already has from past experience and other sources; and (3) the amount of the perceived risk if a wrong selection is made.

Evaluation of Alternatives

Once all the reasonable alternatives have been identified, the consumer must evaluate each one preparatory to making a purchase decision. The factors that consumers use in their evaluations should be familiar by now. They include past experiences with and attitudes toward various brands. Consumers also use the opinion of members of their families and other reference groups as guidelines in these evaluations.

Purchase Decisions

After searching and evaluating, the consumer at some point must decide whether or not to buy. If the decision is to buy, the buyer must make a series of decisions regarding brand, price, store, colour, and so on.

Anything marketers can do to simplify decision making will be attractive to buyers, because most people find it very hard to make a decision. Sometimes several decision situations can be combined and marketed as one package. A travel agency simplifies travellers' decisions concerning transportation, hotels, and which tours to take by selling a packaged tour.

At this point in the buying process, marketers are trying to determine the consumers' **patronage buying motives**. These are the reasons that a consumer shops at (patronizes) a certain store. These are different from *product buying motives*, which are reasons for buying a certain product. Some of the more important patronage buying motives are:

- Convenience of location.
- Rapidity of service.
- Ease of locating merchandise.
- Uncrowded conditions.
- Price.
- Assortment of merchandise.
- Services offered.
- Attractive store appearance.
- Calibre of sales personnel.

Patronage motives and choice of stores are related to the concept of social-class structure. Studies of social classes show definitely that people match their own values and expectations with the perceived status of the store. Not all people want to shop at glamorous, high-status stores. People know that they will be punished in subtle ways by the clerks and other customers if they go into certain exclusive shops. ''The clerk treats you like a crumb,'' was one response.

Postpurchase Behaviour

All the steps in the buying process up to this point occur *before* or *during* the time a purchase is made. However, a buyer's feelings *after* the sale are also significant for the marketer. They can influence repeat sales and what the buyer tells others about the product.

Typically, buyers experience some postpurchase anxieties in all but routine purchases. We refer to this state of anxiety as **cognitive dissonance**. The theory is that people strive for internal harmony and consistency among their *cognitions* (knowledge, attitudes, beliefs, values). Any inconsistency in these cognitions is called *dissonance*.

Postpurchase cognitive dissonance occurs because each of the alternatives con-

An ad like this can reduce cognitive dissonance.

GO AHEAD.
MAKE MY DAY.

It's quiet in the Maytag repair shop. Too quiet. Because Maytag washers are on the job, and they're known to last longer and need fewer repairs.

In fact, every appliance that wears the Maytag name is built to incredibly exacting standards. We make many of our own parts, to be sure you get Maytag quality, inside and out. And every single Maytag appliance is tested to prove it can meet our high standards—before it leaves our door. So whether you need a quality washer, dryer, microwave, range, dishwasher, or disposer, treat yourself to the highest standard: the one that's built like a Maytag.

Not all Maytag repairmen are this lonely, but it takes a special kind of individual to handle a job like this. Waiting for that first break in the case, staked out by the phone, where it's quiet. Too quiet.

MAYTAG
THE DEPENDABILITY PEOPLE

sidered by the consumer usually has both advantages and limitations. Thus, when the purchase decision is finally made, the selected alternative has some drawbacks, while the rejected alternatives each possess some attractive features. That is, *negative* aspects of the item *selected*, and the *positive* qualities of the *rejected* products, create cognitive dissonance in the consumer.

Dissonance typically increases as (1) the dollar value of the purchase increases; (2) the relative attractiveness of the unselected alternatives increases; and (3) the relative importance of the decision increases (buying a house or car creates more dissonance than buying a candy bar).

To restore internal harmony and minimize discomfort, people will try to reduce their postpurchase anxieties. Thus they are likely to avoid information (such as ads for the rejected products) that is likely to increase dissonance. Prior to making the purchase, they may shop around quite a bit, especially for high-priced, infrequently purchased articles. In this way they seek to minimize postdecision dissonance by spending more time in predecision evaluations.

Some useful generalizations can be developed from the theory. For example, anything sellers can do in their advertising or personal selling to reassure buyers — say, by stressing desirable features of a product — will reduce dissonance. This reduction will reinforce consumers and increase the likelihood of repeat purchases. When the product in question is expensive and infrequently purchased, the sellers' postsale service program can be a significant factor in reducing dissonance.

In general, we might consider the consumer moving through the various stages from being unaware of the need for a certain product or service to being loyal to a particular brand or store. The marketing program should be designed to move consumers along this process from the stage where they do not even know the company's brand or store exists, to the point where they have tried the brand or visited the store several times and have been satisfied to the point where **loyalty** develops. It is the stage of brand or store loyalty that marketers would like to achieve.

Many marketing programs that have been introduced in recent years are intended to establish consumer loyalty. Air Canada and Canadian Airlines International have introduced frequent flyer programs and give passengers points every time they fly with these airlines. These points may be accumulated and are redeemable for free flights at a later date. Zeller's Department Store has borrowed the concept and has introduced a frequent shopper program, "Club Z," which provides points for each dollar spent at Zeller's. The points are redeemable for merchandise. These programs are designed to encourage customers to keep coming back again and again — to establish loyalty.

Buying Motives of Industrial Users

In general terms, everything we have said about the factors that influence the buying behaviour of consumers applies to industrial users. The difference is the importance of some factors in the buying process. These differences make industrial buying like a very organized form of family influenced buying. The person responsible for buying equipment, materials, supplies, and services for others to use in service agencies, manufacturing or retailing organizations is truly a family purchasing agent.

Industrial buying behaviour, like consumer buying behaviour, is initiated when an aroused need (a motive) is recognized. This leads to goal-oriented activity designed to satisfy the need. Once again, marketing practitioners must try to determine what motivates the buyer.

Industrial buying motives, for the most part, are presumed to be rational, and an industrial purchase normally is a methodical, objective undertaking. Industrial buyers are motivated primarily by a desire to satisfy the various users or "specifiers" within the organization (family) and, at the same time, to maximize their firms' profits. More specifically, their buying goal is to achieve the optimal combination of price, quality, and service in the products they buy for others. On the other hand, sales people would maintain that some industrial buyers seem to be motivated more toward personal goals that are in conflict with their employers' goals.

Actually, industrial buyers do have two goals — to improve or secure their positions in their firms (self-interest) and to further their company's position (in profits, in acceptance by society). Sometimes these goals are mutually consistent, and sometimes they are in conflict. Obviously, the greater the degree of consistency, the better for both the organization and the individual. When very little mutuality of goals exists, the situation is poor. Probably the more usual situation is to find some overlap of interests, but also a significant area where the buyer's goals do not coincide with those of the firm. In these cases, a seller might appeal to the buyer both on a rational, "what's-good-for-the-firm" basis and on an ego-building basis. Promotional efforts attuned to the buyer's self-concept are particularly useful when two or more competing sellers are offering essentially the same products, prices, and services.

The Industrial
Buying Process

Competition and the compexity of industrial marketing have encouraged companies to focus attention on the *total* buying process. Buying is treated as on ongoing relationship of mutual interest to both buyer and seller. As one example of this approach, researchers in a Marketing Science Institute study developed a framework to explain different types of industrial buying situations.[18] The model for this framework — called a **buy-grid** — is illustrated in Table 5-1. The model reflects two major aspects of the industrial buying process: (1) the classes of typical buying situations and (2) the sequential steps in the buying process.

TABLE 5-1   **THE BUY-GRID FRAMEWORK**

Stages in the industrial buying process (buy phases) in relation to buying situations (buy classes)

Buy phases (stages in buying-decision process)	Buy classes		
	New class	Modified rebuy	Straight rebuy
1. Recognize the problem.	Yes	Maybe	No
2. Determine product needs.	Yes	Maybe	No
3. Describe product specifications.	Yes	Yes	Yes
4. Search for suppliers.	Yes	Maybe	No
5. Acquire supplier proposals.	Yes	Maybe	No
6. Select suppliers.	Yes	Maybe	No
7. Select an order routine.	Yes	Maybe	No
8. Evaluate product performance.	Yes	Yes	Yes

Source: Adapted from Patrick J. Robinson, Charles W. Faris, and Yoram Wind, *Industrial Buying and Creative Marketing*, Allyn and Bacon, Inc., Boston, 1967, p. 14.

Buying a corporate aircraft is usually a new-task buying situation.

Three typical buying situations (called **buy classes**) were identified as follows: new tasks, modified rebuys, and straight rebuys. The **new task** is the most difficult and complex of the three. More people influence the new-task buying-decision process than influence the other two types. The problem is that new-information needs are high, and the evaluation of alternatives is critical. Sellers are given their best opportunity to be heard and to display their creative ability in satisfying the buyer's needs.

Straight rebuys — routine purchases with minimal information needs and no real consideration of alternatives — are at the other extreme. Buying decisions are made in the purchasing department, usually from a list of acceptable suppliers. Suppliers, especially those from new firms not on the list, have difficulty getting an audience with the buyer. **Modified rebuys** are somewhere between the other two in time required, information needed, alternatives considered, and other characteristics. It is not too hard to see these three buy classes in the context of family-influenced buying behaviour.

The other major element in the buy-grid reflects the idea that the industrial buying process is a sequence of eight stages, called **buy phases**. The process starts with the recognition of a problem. It ranges through the determination and description of product specifications, the search for an evaluation of alternatives, and the buying act. It ends with postpurchase feedback and evaluation. This surely is reminiscent of the consumer's buying-decision process previously outlined in this chapter.

Multiple Buying Influences — The Buying Centre

One of the biggest problems in marketing to an industrial user is determining who in the organization buys the product. That is, who influences the buying decision, who determines the product specifications, who makes the buying decision, and who does the actual buying (places the order). In the industrial market, these activities typically involve several people — there is a **multiple or family type buying influence** — particularly in medium-sized and large firms. Even in small companies where the owner-managers make all major decisions, they usually consult with knowledgeable employees before making some purchases.

Understanding the concept of a buying centre is helpful in identifying the multiple buying influences and understanding the buying process in industrial organizations. A **buying centre** may be defined as all the individuals or groups who are involved in the purchasing decision-making process. Thus a buying centre includes the people who play any of the following roles.[19]

- **Users:** The people who actually use the product — perhaps a secretary, a production-line worker, or a truck driver.
- **Influencers:** The people who set the specifications and aspects of buying decisions because of their technical expertise, their financial position, or maybe even their political power in the organization.
- **Deciders:** The people who make the actual buying decision regarding the product and the supplier. A purchasing agent may be the decider in a straight rebuy situation. But someone in top management may make the decision regarding whether to buy an expensive computer.
- **Gatekeepers:** The people who control the flow of purchasing information within the organization and between the buying firm and potential vendors. These people may be purchasing agents, secretaries, receptionists, or technical personnel.
- **Buyers:** The people who select the suppliers, arrange the terms of sale, and process the actual purchase orders. Typically, this is the purchasing department's role. But again, if the purchase is an expensive, complex new buy, the buyer's role may be filled by someone in top management.

This secretary may be a user, influencer, gatekeeper, or all the above.

Several people in an organization may play the same role — for example, there may be several users of the product. Or the same person may occupy more than one role. A secretary may be a user, an influencer, and a gatekeeper in the purchase of an office machine.

The size and composition of a buying centre will vary among business organizations. Also, within a given organization, the size and makeup of the buying centre will vary depending on the product's expense, complexity, and length of life. The buying centre for a straight rebuy of office supplies will be quite different from the centre handling the purchase of a building or a fleet of trucks.

It is probably obvious that the variety of people involved in any industrial buying situation, plus the differences among companies, present some real challenges to sales people. As they try to determine ''who's on first'' — that is, determine who does what in a buying situation — the sales reps often will call on the wrong executives. Even knowing who the decision makers are is not enough — these people may be very difficult to reach.

SUMMARY

In our early chapters, we defined consumer markets as people with money to spend and the willingness to spend it. It is important that marketers understand the ''willingness-to-buy'' factor — that is, consumer buying behaviour. It is also very difficult to interpret consumer behaviour, because we do not know what goes on in a person's mind.

The simplified consumer behaviour model we followed is this one: Buying behaviour is initiated when aroused needs (motives) create inner tensions that lead to behaviour designed to satisfy the needs and thus reduce the tensions. This goal-oriented behaviour is shaped by our perceptions. Our perceptions, in turn, are shaped by the cultural, social-group, and psychological forces that constitute a person's frame of reference.

Marketers must be aware of cultural change and of the importance of segmenting the market into subcultures. Large and small reference groups to which we belong, or aspire to belong, also influence our perceptions. Reference groups stress conformity to the behavioural standards set for the groups' members and often enforce these standards. Most groups have opinion leaders. A company's marketing effort should be directed toward identifying and communicating with these leaders. The family is the smallest social group to influence our perceptions, and often it is the most powerful social force affecting buyer behaviour. Marketers need to know *who* does the family buying and *when*, *where*, and *how* people buy — that is, the buying habits of consumers.

One of the psychological forces affecting perceptions and buying behaviour is a person's learning experience. Three sets of learning theories — the stimulus-response model, cognitive theory, the gestalt and field theory — describe learning and its effect on behaviour. Another psychological influence on perceptions is personality, although there is no agreement as to how personality influences behaviour. Finally, perceptions are also influenced by attitudes and beliefs and by self-image.

Consumers often go through a logical, five-stage process in the course of making a buying decision. First, the unsatisfied need is recognized. Next, the reasonable alternatives are first identified and then evaluated. The actual decision to purchase is then made. (This stage involves patronage buying motives and retail-store image.) In the final stage, postpurchase behaviour may involve some cognitive dissonance on the part of the buyer.

The industrial market differs from the consumer market in a number of important ways. Industrial buying is more like family decision making in the consumer market. The buy-grid framework indicates the industrial buying-decision process for each of the buy classes: new, modified rebuy, straight rebuy. The buying centre concept helps in identifying the influences commonly brought to bear on the industrial-buying decision. The logical five-stage process the consumer goes through in making a buying decision is very similar to the eight stages in the industrial buying process.

Marketers must be aware that while industrial users are more deliberate in their buying than are many consumers, they are also human and influenced by their work, family, recreational, and other large and small reference groups. Thus, in general terms, the factors that influence consumer perceptions also influence those of industrial buyers. While there are important differences in detail, the same general principles of buyer behaviour apply to both consumer and industrial markets.

NOTES

[1] A.H. Maslow, *Motivation and Personality*, Harper & Row, Publishers, Inc., New York, 1954, pp. 80-106.

[2] Clyde Kluckhohn, "The Concept of Culture," in Richard Kluckhohn (ed.), *Culture and Behaviour*, The Free Press, New York, 1962, p. 26.

[3] For some major life-style trends and how marketers can react to them, see Ronald D. Michman, "New Directions for Lifestyle Behavior Patterns," *Business Horizons*, July-August 1984, pp. 59-64; and William Lazer, "Turning Changing Consumers into Profitable Market Opportunities," *Sales & Marketing Management*, July 25, 1983, pp. A-30ff.

[4] See Nariman K. Dhalla, *These Canadians: A Sourcebook of Marketing and Socioeconomic Facts*, McGraw-Hill, Toronto, 1966, pp. 287-300; Frederick Elkin and Mary B. Hill, "Bicultural and Bilingual Adaptations in French Canada: The Example of Retail Advertising," *Canadian Review of Sociology and Anthropology*, August 1965, pp. 132-148; M. Brisebois, "Marketing in Quebec," in W.H. Mahatoo (ed.), *Marketing Research in Canada*, Thomas Nelson and Sons, Toronto, 1968, pp. 88-90; Bruce Mallen, "The Present State of Knowledge and Research in Marketing to the French-Canadian Marketing," in Donald N. Thompson and David S.R. Leighton (eds.), *Canadian Marketing: Problems and Prospects*, Wiley Publishers of Canada Limited, Toronto, 1973, pp. 100-101; and Jean-Charles Chebat and Georges Hénault, "The Cultural Behavior of Canadian Consumers," in Vishnu H. Kirpalani and Ronald H. Rotenberg (eds.), *Cases and Readings in Marketing*, Holt, Rinehart and Winston of Canada Limited, Toronto, 1974, pp. 178-180.

[5] S.B. Ash, Carole P. Duhaime, and John A. Quelch, "Consumer Satisfaction: A Comparison of English- and French-Speaking Canadians," in Vernon J. Jones (ed.), *Marketing*, vol. 1, part 3, *Proceedings* of the Administrative Sciences Association of Canada, Marketing Division, Montreal, 1980, pp. 11-20.

[6] Kristian S. Palda, "A Comparison of Consumer Expenditures in Quebec and Ontario," *Canadian Journal of Economics and Political Science*, February 1967, p. 26.

[7] Dwight R. Thomas, "Culture and Consumption Behavior in English and French Canada," in Bent Stidsen (ed.), *Marketing in the 1970s and Beyond*, Canadian Association of Administrative Sciences, Marketing Division, Edmonton, 1975, pp. 255-261.

[8] For a discussion of the evolution of advertising agencies in Quebec, see Madeleine Saint-Jacques and Bruce Mallen, "The French-Canadian Market," in Peter T. Zarry and Robert D. Wilson (eds.), *Advertising in Canada: Its Theory and Practice*, McGraw-Hill Ryerson Limited, Toronto, 1981, pp. 349-368; and Robert MacGregor, "The Impact of the Neo-Nationalist Movement on the Changing Structure and Composition of the Quebec Advertising Industry," in the *Proceedings* of the Marketing Division, Administrative Sciences Association of Canada, 1980, p. 237.

[9] D.W. Greeno and W.F. Bennett, "Social Class and Income as Complementary Segmentation

Bases: A Canadian Perspective," in *Proceedings* of the Marketing Division, Administrative Sciences Association of Canada, 1983, p. 113-122.

[10] W. Lloyd Warner and Paul Lunt, *The Social Life of a Modern Community*, Yale University Press, New Haven, Conn., 1941; and W. Lloyd Warner, Marchia Meeker, and Kenneth Eells, *Social Class in America*, Science Research Associates, Inc., Chicago, 1949.

[11] See Richard P. Coleman, "The Continuing Significance of Social Class to Marketing," *Journal of Consumer Research*, December 1983, pp. 265-280.

[12] See Elihu Katz and Paul Lazarsfeld, *Personal Influence*, Free Press, New York, 1955, especially p. 325.

[13] No universally accepted definition of the term *psychographics* has as yet been developed. See William D. Wells, "Psychographics: A Critical Review," *Journal of Marketing Research*, May 1975, pp. 196-213.

[14] For a discussion of other definitions of learning, see John F. Hall, *Psychology of Learning*, J.B. Lippincott Company, Philadelphia, 1966, pp. 3-6.

[15] See K. Koffka, *Principles of Gestalt Psychology*, Harcourt, Brace, & World, Inc., New York. 1935; Wolfgang Kohler, *Gestalt Psychology*, Liveright Publishing Corporation, New York, 1947.

[16] See Kurt Lewin, *A Dynamic Theory of Personality* (1935) and *Principles of Topological Psychology* (1936), McGraw-Hill Book Company, New York.

[17] For an analytical review of self-concept studies, the research problems connected with these studies and a comprehensive bibliography, see M. Joseph Sirgy, "Self-Concept in Consumer Behavior: A Critical Review," *Journal of Consumer Research*, December 1982, pp. 287-300.

[18] Patrick J. Robinson, Charles W. Faris, and Yoram Wind, *Industrial Buying and Creative Marketing*, Allyn and Bacon, Boston, 1967. For a different perspective on the buy-grid concept, see Joseph A. Belizzi and Phillip McVey, "How Valid Is the Buy-Grid Model?" *Industrial Marketing Management*, February 1983, pp. 57-62.

[19] Frederick E. Webster, Jr., and Yoram Wind, "A General Model for Understanding Organizational Buying Behavior," *Journal of Marketing*, April 1972, pp. 12-19. Also see Webster and Wind, *Organizational Buying Behavior*, Prentice-Hall, Englewood Cliffs, N.J., 1972, especially pp. 75-87; and Thomas V. Bonoma, "Major Sales: Who *Really* Does the Buying," *Harvard Business Review*, May-June 1982, pp. 111-119.

KEY TERMS AND CONCEPTS

Buyer behaviour 106
Motivation 106
Hierarchy of needs 107
Perception 108
Selectivity in perceptions 108
Culture 111
Cultural changes 111
Subcultures 112
Social-class structure 115
Small reference group 118
Consumer buying habits 119
Psychographics 121
Learning 121

Attitudes and beliefs 123
Image 124
Self-concept (self-image) 124
Values and life-styles 126
Buying-decision process 127
Patronage buying motives 130
Cognitive dissonance 130
Buy-grid 133
Buy classes 133
Buy phases 133
Multiple buying influences (buying centre) 134
Users 134

1. Which needs in Maslow's hierarchy might be satisfied by each of the following products or services?

   a. Home burglary alarm system.
   b. Pepsi-Cola.
   c. *World Book Encyclopedia*.
   d. Body lotion.
   e. Chartered accountant.
   f. Starting your own business.

2. Explain what is meant by the selectivity process in perception.

3. Discuss the concept of a small reference group, explaining the meaning of the concept and its use in marketing.

4. Explain how factors of *when* and *where* people buy might affect the marketing program for each of the following products:

   a. House paint.
   b. High-quality sunglasses.
   c. Outboard motors.
   d. Room air conditioners.

5. Distinguish between *drives* and *cues* in the learning process.

6. Describe the differences you would expect to find in the self-concepts of an insurance sales person and an assembly-line worker in an automobile plant. Give some examples of resultant buying behaviour. (Assume that both have the same income.)

7. Following is a series of headliners or slogans taken from advertisements of various retailers. To what patronage motive does each appeal?

   a. "Factory-trained mechanics at your service."
   b. "We never close."
   c. "One dollar down, no payments until the strike is over."
   d. "We treat you like a somebody."
   e. "We won't be undersold."

8. What causes cognitive dissonance to increase in a buying situation? What can a seller do to decrease the level of dissonance in a given purchase of the seller's product?

9. Select four of the buy phases in the industrial buying process and explain how the relative importance of each one changes, depending upon whether the buying situation is a new task or a straight rebuy.

10. What suggestions do you have for industrial sellers to help them determine who influences the buying decision among industrial users?

11. In the buying centre in an industrial organization, discuss briefly the role of each of the following:

    a. Influencers.
    b. Buyers
    c. Gatekeepers.

12. Explain how industrial buying is like family-influenced buying of consumer goods.

CHAPTER 6

MARKETING INFORMATION SYSTEMS AND MARKETING RESEARCH

A marketing system runs on current, accurate information — about the market, the macroenvironment, and internal and external operations. This chapter is concerned with the sources and uses of such information. After studying this chapter, you should understand:

- Marketing information systems — what they are, why they are needed, and how they are used.
- The difference between a marketing information system and marketing research.
- The procedure in marketing research investigations.
- The current status of marketing research.

Moosehead Breweries is trying to decide how to increase sales of its Moosehead Special brand by changing its image. A ski resort in Collingwood, Ontario, wants to find out how it can attract more university and college students. On a flight between Vancouver and Ottawa, an Air Canada flight attendant distributes questionnaires to a number of passengers and asks that they complete them before landing in Ottawa. A manufacturer of chocolate bars interviews 300 children at a shopping centre in Winnipeg, asking them a series of questions about their preference for chocolate bars and having them taste four different versions of the company's leading brand. Students from Ryerson Polytechnical Institute and the University of Toronto are invited to attend a series of group interviews at a research company in downtown Toronto. They spend 90 minutes discussing their preferences and purchase patterns for soft drinks, and they are paid $20 for attending. A publisher of marketing textbooks conducts a series of hour-long interviews with faculty members at selected universities and colleges to better understand the process that is followed in the selection of a textbook for use in a marketing course.

The above companies all had one thing in common. They needed information to aid them in decision making regarding their stated problems. Some years ago, Marion Harper, Jr., then president of a large advertising agency, said, "To manage a business well is to manage its future; and to manage the future is to manage information." That statement applies today in any organization — business or nonbusiness, profit or nonprofit, domestic or international.

Management in any organization needs information — and lots of it — about potential markets and environmental forces. In fact, *one essential requirement for success in strategic marketing planning is information — effectively managed.* Today a mass of information is available both from external sources and from within a firm. The problem, however, is to sort it out and use it effectively — to manage it. This is the role of a marketing information system. The use of this tool should permeate every phase of a company's marketing program. For this reason, we discuss information management after we have introduced the marketing environment, market demographics and buying power, and consumer and industrial buying behaviour. It is the effective use of marketing information that makes possible market segmentation strategy — Chapter 7 — and programming the marketing mix elements — Parts 3, 4, 5 and 6 which follow.

WHAT IS A MARKETING INFORMATION SYSTEM?

A **marketing information system (MkIS)** is an ongoing, future-oriented structure designed to generate, process, store, and later retrieve information to aid decision making in an organization's marketing program.

A marketing information system to some extent resembles a military or diplomatic intelligence operation. It gathers, processes, and stores potentially useful information that exists in open and available form in several locations inside and outside the company. In an MkIS, however, we are *not* suggesting the use of undercover intelligence methods such as industrial espionage or hiring competitors' personnel to learn their secrets. In most cases a company does not need to rely on such clandestine methods. The information a company needs is usually available by socially acceptable means, if the firm will just establish a marketing information system.

A MARKETING INFORMATION SYSTEM IS:

1. The systems concept applied to information handling, to:
   a. determine what data you need for decision making.
   b. generate (gather) this information.
   c. process the data (with the aid of quantitative analytical techniques).
   d. provide for the storage and future retrieval of the data.
2. Future-oriented. It anticipates and prevents problems as well as solving them. It is preventive as well as curative medicine for marketing.
3. Operated on a continuing basis, not a sporadic, intermittent one.
4. Wasted if the information is not used.

A marketing information system is especially characterized by its use of a computer and personnel possessing quantitative analytical capabilities. A modern MkIS is not possible without a computer because of the masses of data to be handled. Fortunately, the wide variety in types and prices of computer hardware and software available today brings an MkIS capability to almost any organization.

NEED FOR A MARKETING INFORMATION SYSTEM

Today, many environmental forces make it imperative that every firm manage its marketing information as effectively as possible. Let's consider a few of these forces and their relationship to information management.

- *There is a shortening of the time span allotted to an executive for decision making.* Product life cycles frequently are shorter than they used to be. Also, companies are being forced to develop and market new products more quickly than ever before.
- *Marketing activity is becoming more complex and broader in its scope.* Com-

panies are expanding their markets, even to the point of engaging in multinational marketing. Our insights into buyer behaviour, while limited, are still sufficient to tell us there is a world of behavioural data we need to acquire and understand.

■ *Shortages of raw materials* mean that we must make more efficient use of our resources and labour power. A company needs to know which of its products are profitable and which ones should be eliminated.

■ *Growing consumer discontent* is often intensified because management lacks adequate information about some aspect of its marketing program. Maybe the firm does not realize that its product is not up to consumer expectations or that its middlemen are not performing adequately.

■ *The knowledge explosion (the information explosion)* is fantastic. We have more than an adequate supply of information. We simply need to figure out what to do with it — how to manage it. Fortunately, with the continued improvement of computers and other data processing equipment, management has a fast, inexpensive means of processing masses of marketing information.

A marketing information system can help marketers to cope with each of these dynamic forces. Yet many firms seem to be doing little or nothing toward managing information in a sophisticated manner. Even today, most companies do not have a formal marketing research department.

BENEFITS AND USES OF AN MkIS

An organization generates and gathers much information in its day-to-day operations, and much more information is available to it. But unless the company has some system to retrieve and process this information, it is unlikely that it is using its marketing information effectively. Without such a system, information flowing from these sources is frequently lost, distorted, or delayed.

In contrast, a well-designed MkIS can provide a fast, less expensive, and more complete information flow for management decision making. The storage and retrieval capability of an MkIS allows a wider variety of data to be collected and used. Management can continually monitor the performance of products, markets, sales people, and other marketing units in greater detail.

A marketing information system is of obvious value in a large company where information is likely to get lost or distorted as it becomes widely dispersed. However, experience also tells us that integrated information systems can also have beneficial effects on management's performance in small and medium-sized firms. Figure 6-1 illustrates the use of an MkIS in connection with two marketing activities — sales forecasting and the evaluation of territorial sales performance.

RELATIONSHIP BETWEEN MARKETING INFORMATION SYSTEMS AND MARKETING RESEARCH

The relationship between marketing information systems and marketing research is perceived quite differently by various people. Some see an MkIS as simply a logical, computer-based extension of marketing research. (The first marketing information systems were developed in the 1960s, while marketing research as a separate activity predates this by some 40 years.) Others see the two as distinctly different activities,

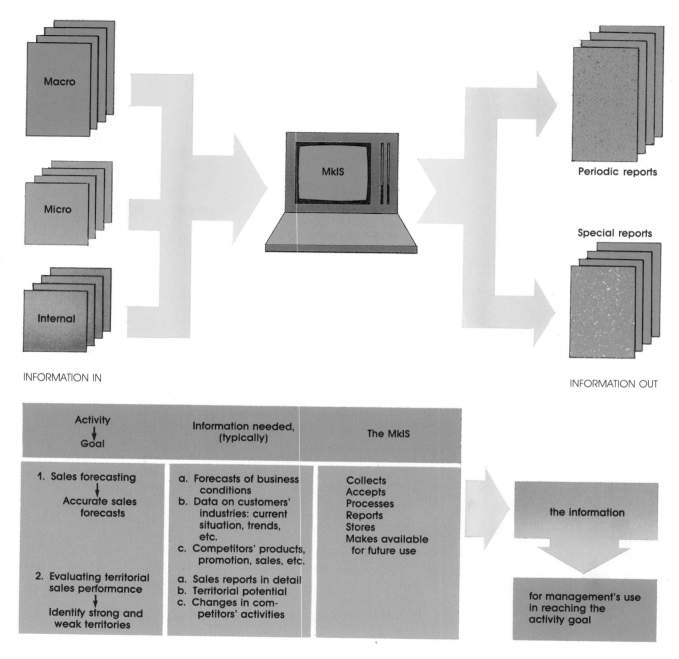

INFORMATION IN

INFORMATION OUT

Activity ↓ Goal	Information needed, (typically)	The MkIS		
1. Sales forecasting ↓ Accurate sales forecasts	a. Forecasts of business conditions b. Data on customers' industries: current situation, trends, etc. c. Competitors' products, promotion, sales, etc.	Collects Accepts Processes Reports Stores Makes available for future use	the information	
2. Evaluating territorial sales performance ↓ Identify strong and weak territories	a. Sales reports in detail b. Territorial potential c. Changes in competitors' activities			for management's use in reaching the activity goal

FIGURE 6-1
A marketing information system, with two examples of its use.

related only to the extent that they both deal with the management of information. Firms without an MkIS will perceive a broader role for their marketing research group. If a company has a formal MkIS, then the marketing research activity is probably treated as just one part of this information system.

Marketing research may be defined as the function which links the consumer and the customer to the organization through information — information used to identify and define marketing problems; generate, refine, and evaluate marketing actions; monitor marketing performance; and improve our understanding of marketing as a process.[1] This definition suggests a *systematic* activity, thus sounding like the essence of an MkIS. Yet, as traditionally practised, marketing research has tended to be *unsystematic*. (See Table 6-1 for a comparison of the two activities as they are usually practised.)

TABLE 6-1   **CONTRASTING CHARACTERISTICS OF MARKETING RESEARCH AND A MARKETING INFORMATION SYSTEM**

Marketing research	Marketing information system
1. Emphasizes the handling of external information.	1. Handles both internal and external data.
2. Is concerned with solving problems.	2. Is concerned with preventing as well as solving problems.
3. Operates in a fragmented, intermittent fashion — on a project-to-project basis.	3. Operates continuously — is a system.
4. Tends to focus on past information.	4. Tends to be future-oriented.
5. Need not be computer-based.	5. Is a computer-based process.
6. Is one source of information input for a marketing information system.	6. Includes other subsystems besides marketing research.

Marketing research tends to be conducted on a project-to-project basis, with each project having a starting point and an end. Projects often seem to deal with unrelated problems on an intermittent, almost "brush-fire" basis. This is in contrast to the continuous information flow in a marketing information system. Marketing research tends to stress the collection of past data to solve problems. Information systems perform future-oriented activities designed to prevent problems from arising.

Parenthetically, we should recognize that many marketing research practitioners would not agree with these distinctions. They would contend that they already are doing much of what we have attributed to MkIS. And they may be correct *if* the firm has no formal MkIS. Then the scope of the marketing research activity is likely to be much broader. It may well include some sales-volume analysis, demand forecasting, and so on.

In firms that have an MkIS, a separate marketing research activity can be extremely valuable. Marketing research projects are a significant source of data for an MkIS. Consequently, at this point we turn to the subject of marketing research. We shall discuss (1) its scope, (2) the typical procedure in a marketing research investigation, (3) the organizational structures typically used for marketing research, and (4) the current status of the field.

SCOPE OF MARKETING RESEARCH ACTIVITIES

For the past 50 years, there has been steady growth in marketing research activity in Canada, reflecting management's recognition of the importance of research information. A study of more than 200 larger Canadian companies has shown that slightly more than 20 percent of them have a formalized marketing research function. This usually means a small department with responsibility for research. Much of the

TABLE 6-2   MARKETING RESEARCH ACTIVITIES OF CANADIAN COMPANIES

	Percentage which undertake each activity
SALES AND MARKET RESEARCH	
Measurement of market potential	59
Market share analysis	61
Determination of market character	60
Sales analysis	58
Establishment of sales quotas, etc.	54
Distribution channels and costs	49
Test markets, store audits	35
Consumer panel studies	33
Sales compensation studies	37
Studies of premiums, coupons, etc.	28
ADVERTISING RESEARCH	
Motivation research	25
Copy research	33
Studies of effectiveness	42
Studies of competitive advertising	39
Media research	36
BUSINESS ECONOMICS AND CORPORATE RESEARCH	
Short-range forecasting	51
Long-range forecasting	50
Studies of business trends	49
Pricing, profit and/or value analysis	50
Location studies	35
Acquisition/diversification studies	41
Export and international studies	33
MIS	41
Operations research	34
Internal employee studies	39
CORPORATE RESPONSIBILITY RESEARCH	
Consumers' "right to know" studies	16
Ecological impact studies	16
Studies of legal constraints	29
Social values and policies studies	18
PRODUCT RESEARCH	
New product modelling/optimization	48
Competitive product studies	54
Product testing (existing products)	52
Packaging research design characteristics	41

Source: Joyce Cheng, David Conway, and George H. Haines, Jr., "A Comparison of Business Use of Marketing Research in Canada and the United States," in Thomas E. Muller (ed.), *Marketing*, Volume 7, Part 3, Proceedings of the Annual Conference of the Administrative Sciences Association of Canada — Marketing Division, 1986, p. 284.

research that they carry out would, in fact, be supplied by professional marketing research companies. The scope of marketing research activities in which these Canadian companies would be engaged and the percentage of firms engaged in each is summarized in Table 6-2. The most common activities are determination of market characteristics, measurement of market potential, market-share analysis, and sales analysis.

PROCEDURE IN MARKETING RESEARCH

The general procedure illustrated in Fig. 6-2 is applicable to most marketing research projects. However, some of the steps listed there are not needed in every project. (The numbers in the following section headings correspond to the steps in the research procedure in Fig. 6-2.)

FIGURE 6-2
Procedure in a marketing research investigation.

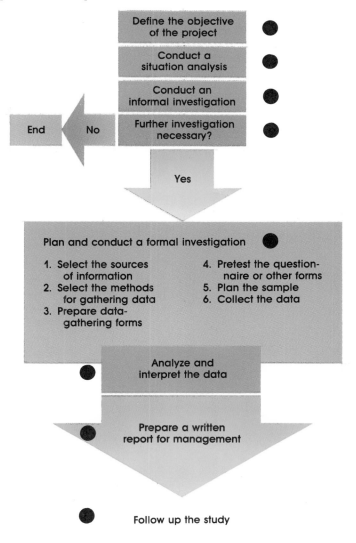

When You Can't Afford to Be Wrong

Bootlegger, a Vancouver-based clothing chain, was considering undertaking a marketing research project. The marketing manager explained, ''We have a good idea of who our clientele is, but we want to know for sure. The biggest mistake in the retail business is to make an assumption about who your customer is and then sell to that assumption. And mistakes are extremely expensive in this game. What with the cost of buying media and opening stores, we can't afford to be wrong.''*

Source: Barbara Aarsteinsen, ''Growth Rate in Research Is Soaring,'' *The Globe and Mail Report on Business*, June 9, 1986, pp. B1, B9.

1: Define the Objective

Researchers should have a clear idea of what they are trying to accomplish in a research project — that is, what is the goal of the project. Usually the objective is to solve a problem, but this is not always so. Often the purpose is to *define* the problem, or to determine whether the firm even *has* a problem. To illustrate, a manufacturer of commercial air-conditioning equipment had been enjoying a steady increase in sales volume over a period of years. Management decided to do a sales analysis. This research project uncovered the fact that, although the company's volume had been increasing, its share of the market had declined. In this instance, marketing research uncovered a problem that management did not know existed.

The case history of Photo Accessory (an actual company but a fictitious name) can be used to illustrate the first three steps in a marketing research project — namely, problem definition, situation analysis, and informal investigation. Photo Accessory was a small manufacturer of camera accessory equipment. Its engineering department developed a rechargeable power cell for use by professional photographers. The prototype was 18 centimetres thick, 16 wide and 24 centimetres long. It weighed 1.8 kg. A photographer would hang it from a belt and have a 1 metre wire connecting it to the camera. Approximately 300 flashes were possible before recharging it by plugging it into an electrical wall outlet.

The general problem, as presented to an outside marketing research firm, was to determine whether the company should add this product to its line. A breakdown of the problem into parts that could be handled by research resulted in the following specific questions:

- What is the market demand for such a product?
- What additional features are desired, if any?
- What channels of distribution should be used for such a product?
- What will technology be like in the next five years?
- What will the competition be like in the next five years?

With this tentative restatement of the problem, the researchers were ready for the next procedural step, the situation analysis.

2: Conduct Situation Analysis

The **situation analysis** involves obtaining information about the company and its business environment by means of library research and extensive interviewing of company officials. The researchers try to get a "feel" for the situation surrounding the problem. They analyze the company, its market, its competition, and the industry in general. In the Photo Accessory case, the researchers studied several trade magazine articles in the library and held extensive discussions with company executives and workers.

In the situation analysis, the researchers also try to define the problem more clearly and to develop hypotheses for further testing. In a research project, a **hypothesis** is a tentative supposition or a possible solution to a problem. It is something that is assumed or conceded merely for purposes of argument or action. In a well-run project, each hypothesis should be proved or disproved on the way to fulfilling the project's objectives.

In the Photo Accessory case, the situation analysis suggested the following hypotheses:

- There is an adequate market demand for the product.
- Marketing channels should concentrate on selling through traditional retail stores in order to reach the mass market.
- Advancing technology will not quickly make the project obsolete.
- Competition is not a threat to the success of the product.

<table>
<tr><td>

3 and 4: Conduct
Informal Investigation

</td><td>

Having gotten a feel for the problem, the researchers are now ready to conduct an informal investigation. To some extent this step overlaps the preceding one, which involves getting background information from *within* the company or from a library. The **informal investigation** consists of talking to people *outside* the company — middlemen, competitors, advertising agencies, and customers.

</td></tr>
</table>

The researchers in the Photo Accessory case talked with many people. From their situation analysis plus telephone conversations with officials of a number of trade associations representing photographers and photo equipment manufacturers, the researchers developed an estimate of the potential market for the product. This estimate suggested that the market was large enough to warrant a further investigation. Next, 15 photographers in three cities were interviewed to get their evaluation of the product itself, plus photographic practices in general. All liked the product, but they did suggest some product modifications.

To investigate channels of distribution, the researchers talked on the telephone with several photo retailers across the country. The consensus was that the retailers would not stock this new product for various reasons. The researchers then visited the annual Photo Marketing trade show to talk with more retailers and to get a line on the competition. Again, the retailers' reaction was negative. Also, the researchers learned that three major competitors — Vivitar, Quantum, and Bogen – soon would introduce rechargeable batteries that would compete directly with Photo Accessory's new product. Furthermore, there was a rumour that the Japanese soon would be entering the market.

The informal investigation is an important step in a research project because it often will determine whether further study is necessary. Decisions on the main problem in a research project frequently are made after the informal investigation is completed. As a matter of fact, at this point Photo Accessory decided not to market its portable power cell.

Marketing at Work

Research Supports the Attaché Case

Competition in the less-regulated Canadian airline industry has become increasingly keen in recent years. Surveys conducted by Canadian Airlines International (formerly CPAir) revealed that business travellers were not bothered as much by the fact that they usually paid full fare as they were by the fact that they were often seated next to other travellers who paid less but received the same service. The surveys found that business travellers wanted instant baggage pickup, more seat space, palatable food, and the company of other business travellers. On the basis of this research, the airline introduced its Attaché service in late 1984, offering business passengers on non-stop business flights fewer and wider seats, free newspapers and drinks, multicourse meals, and more flight attendants, all for a surcharge of five percent above regular economy airfare.*

Source: Ian Allaby, "Dogfight: The Domestic Airlines Are in a Battle Royal, and Business Travellers Are the Spoils of the War," *Canadian Business*, Vol. 59, No. 8, August 1986, pp. 65-72.

5: Plan and Conduct Formal Investigation

If the informal investigation has shown that the project is economically feasible, management then determines what additional information is needed. The next step for the researchers is to plan where and how to get the desired data.

SELECT THE SOURCES OF INFORMATION

Primary data, secondary data, or both can be used in an investigation. **Primary data** are original data gathered specifically for the project at hand. **Secondary data** have already been gathered for some other purpose. For example, when researchers stand in a supermarket and observe whether people use shopping lists, they are collecting primary data. When they get information from Statistics Canada, they are using a secondary source.

One of the biggest mistakes made in marketing research is to collect primary data before exhausting the information available in secondary sources. Ordinarily, secondary information can be gathered much faster and at far less expense than primary data.

Sources of Secondary Data   Several readily available, excellent sources of secondary information are at the disposal of a marketing researcher.

1. *Internal company records.* Companies regularly maintain orderly records of sales people's daily reports, call reports, sales orders, and customers' complaints. Companies also usually keep sales records for each territory, product, and class of customer. When a problem must be solved, the first place a company should go for information is to its own files. In many cases, this source may well be the only place where the needed information can be found.

2. *Parent company records.* Foreign parents of Canadian subsidiaries (mainly U.S. parents) are able to provide useful data on activities in the American market. If the parent is involved in multinational operations, experiences and data on worldwide market conditions and consumer reactions to marketing programs can be available. In those cases where the Canadian company has a market posture that is similar to that of the parent and where Canadian strategy and market conditions are viewed as lagging the parent's by a number of years, then access to such data is an invaluable asset. The problem of comparability of data and situations is, however, a constant one.

3. *Government.* The Canadian government regularly furnishes more marketing data than any other single source. These data are available at very low prices, even though there is a tremendous cost involved in collecting them. Also, the government has access under the law to types of information (company sales and profits, personal income, etc.) that it is impossible for a private company to obtain.

   Statistics Canada is the statistical arm of the Government of Canada. Statistics Canada was established in 1918 and regularly collects and publishes information on agriculture, construction and housing, education, fisheries, forestry, health and welfare, international commodity trade, employment, labour income, tourist travel, manufacturing, retail and wholesale trade, service trades, mining, national income and expenditure, prices and public finance, public utilities, and transportation, as well as the Census of Canada. Most government departments also publish both regular and incidental papers independently. The data published are both historical and on a forecast basis. The annual *Canadian Government Publications* lists all federal government publications according to the agency or department that prepared them. In addition, Statistics Canada publishes an annual catalogue.

   Of the numerous reports published by Statistics Canada, one of the most useful to marketers is the *Market Research Handbook*. It is published regularly and contains a considerable amount of data under the following headings: selected economic indicators; merchandising and services; population characteristics; personal income and expenditure; housing, motor vehicles, and household facilities and equipment; Metropolitan Area data; and Census Agglomeration data.

   The *Canada Year Book* is an annual publication that contains somewhat less detailed historical data on many aspects of Canada's economy and population. In addition, much information of interest to marketers is contained in the decennial census. Many volumes of data are published following each census, and Statistics Canada publishes a separate catalogue of census publications. The marketer should be aware, however, that despite the availability and detail of census data, these data should be used with caution since they are often not published until one or two years after the census is taken. For example, most of the reports from the 1986 Census were not published until 1987 or 1988. Consequently, appropriate adjustments must be made in census data before they can be used for marketing purposes.

   Statistics Canada also provides CANSIM, its computerized data bank and information retrieval service, and Telichart, an information service that links the CANSIM database with colour graphics. Using Telichart, the marketer can obtain data on more than 5,000 continually updated economic and social indicators.

One department of the Government of Canada that produces reports and studies of particular interest to marketing managers is the Department of Consumer and Corporate Affairs. This department regularly conducts studies on such topics as consumer problems, energy usage, and regulation. The department also publishes a quarterly *Misleading Advertising Bulletin* that contains valuable information to guide advertising decisions, particularly those of small businesses.

A number of provinces also publish many reports and statistical summaries that are of interest. These provincial data are often not as well catalogued or easily located as are Government of Canada and Statistics Canada publications. However, many provinces do publish annual catalogues of their reports and publications, and these are available from provincial government offices.

4. *Trade, professional, and business associations.* Associations are excellent sources of information for their members. They also supply data for outside groups. Through trade journals and periodic reports, members of associations can also keep up to date on activities in their given trades.

5. *Private business firms.* Private marketing research firms, advertising agencies, and individual manufacturers and middlemen may be able to provide information needed by a researcher. Companies such as the A.C. Nielsen Company, Canadian Facts, and Market Facts of Canada conduct various kinds of marketing research. In addition, the various management consulting firms such as Woods, Gordon; Stevenson, Kellogg; and Peat, Marwick regularly conduct marketing research projects on behalf of their clients. The types of reports prepared by these research companies are many and diverse. The Nielsen Company, for example, prepares a food-drug index giving information on a client's sales and on its competitors' sales for particular products. Data regarding inventories, retail prices, and promotional activity at the retail level are also published. Daniel Starch (Canada) regularly measures readership of advertisements in various magazines and newspapers. Elliott Research Corporation, through its subsidiary, Media Measurement Limited, collects and supplies national advertising data by media for a large variety of major industries.

Marketing research companies such as Market Facts of Canada, International Surveys Limited (ISL), and Omnifacts Research Limited operate consumer mail panels from which data are collected on a regular basis, dealing with media patterns, purchase, usage, and attitudes toward various products.

6. *Advertising media.* Many magazines, newspapers, radio and television networks and stations, and outdoor advertising companies publish information that marketing researchers may not find available elsewhere. *The Financial Post* publishes its *Canadian Markets* annually. It is a handbook of marketing data and facts gleaned mainly from Statistics Canada sources.

Many media publish circulation data, station reach and coverage maps, and statistics on their trading areas. Researchers should be aware that much of the data published by the media are produced for the purpose of attracting advertising revenue. For this reason, these data may not be appropriate in certain marketing research situations. Accurate data on circulation, reach, and rates for all advertising media in Canada are published monthly in Maclean-Hunter's *Canadian Advertising Rates and Data*.

7. *University research organizations.* Some of our universities operate research units and publish findings that are of value to the business community. Business research units play a leading role in this activity, although marketers may also obtain useful reports from a bureau of agricultural research or social research.

8. *Foundations.* Nonprofit research foundations and related groups carry out many kinds of research projects. Statistical analyses and reports on special topics of interest to Canadian business, or specifically Canadian in content, are published by such groups as the Conference Board of Canada (which produces an excellent overview of the Canadian market entitled *Handbook of Canadian Consumer Markets*), the Institute for Research in Public Policy, the Fraser Institute, the Hudson Institute, and the C.D. Howe Institute. While national and international foundations, such as Ford, Carnegie, and Killam, are not limited to business research, many of their reports are of interest to marketers.

9. *Royal Commissions and the Economic Council of Canada.* Many federal and provincial royal commissions conduct studies that are of direct interest to business, and often to marketers in particular. Royal Commission reports on Corporate Concentration, Banking and Finance, and Canada's Economic Prospects are examples of such studies. The Economic Council of Canada issues an annual report as well as occasional studies on general economic conditions and on specific topics such as population and labour-force projections, wage trends, and international trade. Such reports are usually available in the Government Documents section of most municipal and university libraries.

10. *Libraries.* For the marketing researcher and the student of marketing, a good library is probably the best, single, all-around source of secondary information. It will contain publications from practically all of the sources mentioned here. All researchers and students should be familiar with such resources as the *Business Periodicals Index*, the *Canadian Periodicals Index*, and the *Canadian Business Index*. These indices contain references to articles that have appeared in various business publications. The *ProFile Index* contains references to provincial government publications and reports that are available on microfiche in many libraries. The ability to use bibliographies, card indices, and periodical indices is virtually a prerequisite for anyone hoping to do any kind of research.

There are literally hundreds of databases in existence. Most of them can be searched by computer, which can save hours of torturous labour in the library. For example, the Canadian Online Enquiry (CAN/OLE) system offers the Canadian Business and Current Affairs (CBCA) and Materials Business File (MBF) databases. In general, electronic databases contain information on market research reports which are available for purchase; describe markets in terms of companies, products, sales, prices, and advertising expenditures; identify companies that might be prospective customers or competitors; and provide technical information about industries, markets, products, and companies. Most of these databases are available to Canadian users over the telephone lines, using appropriate microcomputers or terminals and software. They represent a valuable source of secondary information.[2]

Sources of primary data   After exhausting all reasonable secondary sources of information, researchers may still lack sufficient data. Then they will turn to primary sources and gather the information themselves. In a company research project, for instance, a researcher may interview that firm's sales people, middlemen, or customers to obtain the pertinent market information.

DETERMINE METHODS FOR GATHERING PRIMARY DATA

There are three widely used methods of gathering primary data: survey, observation, and experimentation. Normally, all three are not used on one project. The choice of method will be influenced by the availability of time, money, personnel, and facilities.

Survey method   A **survey** consists of gathering data by interviewing a limited number of people (a sample) selected from a larger group. A survey has the advantage of getting to the original source of information. In fact, this may be the *only* way to find out the opinions or buying intentions of a group.

While interviewing is still the most widely used method of collecting primary data, there may be a trend away from it. Other methods have been improved and their value has been more fully realized. The survey method contains certain inherent limitations. There are opportunities for error in the construction of the survey questionnaire and in the interviewing process. Surveys may be very expensive, and they are time-consuming. Another key weakness is that respondents often cannot or will not give true answers.

The interviewing in a survey may be done by the researcher in person, by telephone, or by mail.

Personal interviews are more flexible than the other two types because interviewers can alter the questions to fit the situation as they see it. They are able to probe more deeply if an answer is not satisfactory. Ordinarily, it is possible to obtain more information by personal interview than by telephone or mail. Also, the interviewer can, by observation, obtain data regarding the respondents' socio-economic status — their home, neighbourhood, and apparent standard of living.

The rising costs and other problems associated with door-to-door interviewing have prompted many market researchers to interview in central locations, typically regional shopping centres. This new technique is called the **shopping mall intercept** method of interviewing.[3] Another currently popular tool for face-to-face interviewing is the **focus group**. In a focus-group interview usually six to ten people meet

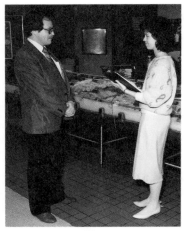

In a survey you can collect primary data by personal interviews.

with the researcher. Open-ended questions are often used to prompt participants into freely discussing the topic. The researcher can ask follow-up questions of the people in order to probe deeper into their attitudes and opinions.[4]

In addition to their high cost and time-consuming nature, personal interviews also face the possible limitation that the researcher may introduce personal bias into an interview. Sometimes, for example, respondents will answer a question in a way that they perceive the interviewer wants that question answered.

Marketing at Work

File 6-3

Focus Groups: Research in the Depths

The Tourism Branch of the Government of Newfoundland had been conducting consumer research with target segments of the vacation market for many years in the Maritime provinces, Ontario, and the Northeast United States. A great deal was known about the image of the province as a vacation destination, but no in-depth information was available about why tourists *really* decided to vacation in Newfoundland. In collaboration with Marine Atlantic, the operators of the ferry service between Nova Scotia and Newfoundland, the Tourism Branch conducted a series of focus group interviews with vacationers on board the new Marine Atlantic ferry, the *Caribou*. These depth interviews provided considerable insight into why vacationers from other provinces and the United States had decided to vacation in Newfoundland, what factors had been most important to them in making their decision, and what they expected to see and do while in the province.

— or by telephone interviews.

In a **telephone survey**, the respondent is approached by telephone, and the interview is completed at that time. Telephone surveys can usually be conducted more rapidly and at less cost than either personal or mail surveys. Since a few interviewers can make any number of calls from a few central points, this method is quite easy to administer. The use of computer-assisted techniques has broadened the scope of telephone interviewing. These techniques involve automatic random-number dialing, a recorded voice asking the questions, and a machine to record the respondents' answers.

A telephone survey can be timely. For instance, people may be asked whether they are watching television at the moment and, if so, the name of the program and the sponsor. One limitation of the telephone survey is that interviews must be short. Lengthy interviews cannot be conducted satisfactorily over the phone. Also, as many as 20 percent of the households in some cities either have unlisted numbers, have moved since the last directory was printed, or have no telephone at all.

Interviewing by mail involves mailing a questionnaire to potential respondents and having them return the completed form by mail. Since no interviewers are involved, this type of survey is not hampered by interviewer bias or problems connected with the management of interviewers. Mailed questionnaires are more economical than personal interviews and are particularly useful in national surveys.

— or by a mail questionnaire.

Also, if the respondents remain anonymous, they are more likely to give true answers because they do not feel the need to impress the interviewer.

A major problem with mail questionnaires is the compilation of a good mailing list, especially for a *broad-scale* survey. If the sample can be drawn from a *limited* list, such as property taxpayers in certain cities or subscribers to a certain magazine, the list presents no problem. Another significant limitation concerns the reliability of the questionnaire returns, particularly when the returns are anonymous. If the respondents have characteristics that differentiate them from nonrespondents, the survey results will be invalid.

Still another limitation is that typically there is a very low response rate in a mail survey. Some of the more successful inducements to improve the response rate include sending questionnaires by first-class mail, sending follow-up questionnaires, and enclosing incentives — monetary or nonmonetary — with the questionnaires. Using incentives is particularly effective in improving response rates, apparently since people receiving them feel obligated to cooperate.[5]

Observational method   In the **observational method**, the data are collected by observing some action of the respondent. No interviews are involved, although an interview may be used as a follow-up to get additional information. For example, if customers are observed buying beer in cans instead of bottles, they may be asked why they prefer that one form of packaging to the other.

Information may be gathered by personal or mechanical observation. In one form of personal observation, the researcher poses as a customer in a store. This technique is useful in getting information about the calibre of the sales people or in determining what brands they promote. Mechanical observation is illustrated by an electric cord stretched across a highway to count the number of cars that pass during a certain time period.

The observation method has several merits. It can be highly accurate. Often it removes all doubt about what the consumer does in a given situation. The consumers are unaware that they are being observed, so presumably they act in their usual fashion.

The observation technique reduces interview bias. However, the technique is limited in its application. Observation tells *what* happened, but it cannot tell *why*. It cannot delve into motives, attitudes, or opinions.

To overcome the biases inherent in the survey method, some firms are using sophisticated observational techniques that involve a combination of cable TV, electronic scanners in supermarkets, and computers. For example, some marketing research companies in Canada and the United States have established "scanner panels." Selected households are invited to participate in a program that involves recording electronically every TV commercial watched in participants' homes; every purchase the participants make in supermarkets which are equipped with checkout scanners is electronically recorded. With this observational method, researchers can measure which product members of the households are buying and determine which TV commercials they have seen. It provides an improved link between advertising and purchase that allows for more accurate measurement of which advertising works and which does not.

In 1988, the A.C. Nielsen Company and the BBM Bureau of Measurement installed "people meters" in more than 2000 Canadian homes. These devices record

Let a scanner be your observer.

electronically the channels to which TV sets are tuned and who is watching the programs. Computers are already programmed with data on each member of the households that participate in the panel. Data are recorded continuously and fed to a central computer each night, providing the TV networks and advertisers with detailed, timely, and accurate information concerning program ratings and the exposure of TV commercials. The CBC and Radio-Canada were the first networks to sign up for the new service.[6]

Test your market with a taste test.

Experimental method   The **experimental method** of gathering primary data involves the establishment of a controlled experiment that simulates the real market situation as much as possible. The theory is that the small-scale experiment will furnish valuable information for designing a large-scale marketing program.

The experimental method may be used in several different ways. In one instance, a firm may manufacture a few units of a product and give them to employees or consumers to try out. Probably the major application of the experimental method has been in market testing. This technique consists of establishing (1) a control market, in which all factors remain constant, and (2) one or more test markets, in which one factor is varied. A firm may be considering a change in the colour of its package. In city A, the product is marketed in its existing colour. In each of cities B, C, and D, a different colour is used. All other factors are kept constant. By measuring sales in the four markets over a period of time, the manufacturer hopes to determine which colour is most effective.

The outstanding merit of the experimental method is its realism. It is the only one of the three methods of gathering primary data that simulates an actual market situation.

Two big problems are encountered in market testing: selecting the control and test markets and controlling the variables. It is difficult — though necessary — to select markets that are identical in all significant socioeconomic factors. Some variables are really uncontrollable, and these may upset the comparability of results. Competitors may get word of the test and try to confuse the picture by suddenly increasing their advertising, for example. Furthermore, the experimental method is expensive; it requires long periods of careful planning and administration.

Because of its inherent limitations, the use of traditional test marketing is declining as faster, less expensive alternatives are being developed. One such method, for example, is to simulate test marketing by using fewer people in a more controlled environment. Another alternative is the computer-based analysis of market information provided by electronic scanners in supermarkets.[7]

PREPARE DATA-GATHERING FORMS

When the interviewing or observation method is used, the researcher must prepare standard forms to record the information. However, the importance of the questionnaire in the survey method and the difficulty of designing it cannot be overemphasized. In fact, most of the problems in data collection, whether it is done by personal interview, mail, or telephone survey, centre on the preparation of the questionnaire. Extreme care and skill are needed in designing questionnaires to minimize bias, misunderstanding, and respondent anger.

SOME TYPICAL ERRORS IN QUESTIONNAIRE DESIGN

- The respondent feels the information requested is none of your business: What is your family's income? How old are you? What percentage of your home mortgage remains to be paid?
- Questions lack a standard of reference: Do you like a large kitchen? (What is meant by "large"?) Do you attend church regularly?
- The respondent does not know the answer: What is your spouse's favourite brand of ice cream?
- The respondent cannot remember and, therefore, guesses: How many calls did you (as a sales rep) make on office supply houses during the past year?
- Questions are asked in improper sequence. Save the tough, embarrassing ones for late in the interview. By then, some rapport ordinarily has been established with the respondent. A "none-of-your-business" question asked too early may destroy the entire interview.

PRETEST THE QUESTIONNAIRE OR OTHER FORMS

No matter how good a researcher thinks the questionnaire is, it still should be pretested. This process is similar to field-testing a product. In pretesting, a questionnaire is simply tried out on a small number of people similar to those who will be interviewed. Their responses should tell the researcher whether there are any problems with the questionnaire.

PLAN THE SAMPLE

Normally, it is unnecessary to survey every person who could shed light on a given research problem. It is sufficient to survey only some of these people, if their reactions are representative of the entire group. However, before the data can be gathered, the researchers must determine whom they are going to survey. That is, they must plan or establish a sample. Sampling is no stranger to us because we employ it frequently in our everyday activities. We often base our opinion of a person on only one or two conversations with that person. We often take a bite of food before ordering a larger quantity.

The fundamental idea underlying the concept of **sampling** is as follows: If a small number of items (the sample) is selected at random from a larger number of items (called a "universe"), then the sample will have the same characteristics, and in about the same proportion, as the universe. In marketing research, sampling is another procedural step whose importance is difficult to overestimate. Improper sampling is a source of errors in many survey results. A survey of New Brunswick residents that was conducted only in English created a very biased picture of public opinion. By not surveying the French-speaking population of the province, the researchers had tapped a biased (unrepresentative) sample.

One of the first questions asked regarding sampling is: How large should the sample be? To be statistically reliable, a sample must be large enough to be truly representative of the universe or population.

To be statistically reliable, a sample must also be proportionate. That is, all types of units found in the universe must be represented in the sample. Also, these units must appear in the sample in approximately the same proportion as they are found in the universe. Assume that a manufacturer of power lawn mowers wants to know what percentage of families in a certain metropolitan area own this product. Further, assume that one-half the families in the market live in the central city, and the other half in the suburbs. Relatively more families in the suburbs have power mowers than do families in the city. If 80 percent of the sample is made up of suburban dwellers, the percentage of families owning power mowers will be overstated because the sample lacks proportionality.

Several sampling techniques can be used in marketing research. Some of these are quite similar, and some are hardly ever used. For a basic understanding of sampling, we shall consider three types: (1) simple random samples, (2) area samples, and (3) quota samples. The first two are probability (random) samples, and the third is a nonrandom sample. A random sample is one that is selected in such a way that every unit in the predetermined universe has a known and equal chance of being selected.

In a **simple random sample**, each unit in the sample is chosen directly from the universe. Suppose we wished to use a simple random sample to determine department store preferences among people in Ottawa, Ontario. We would need an accurate and complete listing of all people within the city limits. This would be our universe. Then in some random fashion we would select our sample from this universe.

A widely used variation of the simple random sample is the **area sample**. An area sample may be used where it is not economically feasible to obtain a full list of the universe. In the Ottawa department store study, for example, one way to conduct an area sample would be first to list all the blocks in the city. Then select a random sample of the blocks. Then every household or every other household in the sample blocks could be interviewed.

A **quota sample** is both nonrandom and stratified (or layered). Randomness is lost because the sample is "forced" to be proportional in some characteristic. Every element in the universe does *not* have an equal chance of being selected. To select a quota sample, the researchers first must decide which characteristic will serve as the basis of the quota. Then they determine in what proportion this characteristic occurs in the universe. The researchers then choose a sample with the same characteristic in the same proportion.

As an example, let us consider a research study of tourists who visit Nova Scotia during the summer of 1990. Interviewers might be stationed at airports, ferry terminals, and tourist information centres. The research company conducting the survey could decide to use a quota sample based on the tourists' place of residence. If we assume that the Nova Scotia Department of Tourism has secondary information — probably from earlier studies — that approximately 25 percent of the tourists who visit Nova Scotia are from Ontario, 15 percent from Quebec, 20 percent from other Atlantic provinces, 10 percent from Western provinces, and 30 percent from the United States, the researcher might then select a sample of vacationers in which 25 percent of the sample is from Ontario, 15 percent from Quebec, and so on. The sample is constructed on a nonrandom basis according to the place of residence of the tourist. That is, every tourist to Nova Scotia during the summer of 1990 does not have an equal chance of being included in the survey.

Random sampling has one big advantage. Its accuracy can be measured with mathematical exactness. In quota sampling, much reliance is placed on the judgement of those designing and selecting the samples. There is no mathematical way of measuring the accuracy of the results.

COLLECT THE DATA

The actual collection of primary data in the field — by interviewing, observation, or both — normally is the weakest link in the entire research process. Ordinarily, in all other steps, reasonably well-qualified people are working carefully to ensure the accuracy of the results. The fruits of these labours may be lost if the fieldworkers (data gatherers) are inadequately trained and supervised. The management of fieldworkers is a difficult task because they usually are part-time workers with little job motivation. Also, their work is done where it cannot be observed, often at many widely separated locations.

A myriad of errors may creep into a research project at this point, and poor interviewers only increase this possibility. Bias may be introduced because people in the sample are not at home or refuse to answer. In some instances, fieldworkers are unable to establish rapport with respondents. Or the interviewers revise the wording of a question and thus obtain untrue responses. Finally, some interviewers just plain cheat in one way or another.

File 6-4

Marketing at Work

The Favourite Among Nonusers

A manufacturer of home baking products had been regularly conducting a series of "usage and attitude" surveys. Information was collected concerning purchase and usage patterns for its products and consumer attitudes toward the various brands of flour and related products available in the Canadian market. In one of its recent surveys, the company found that its brand's share of market was continuing to slip in the rural areas of a particular province. While the company's product was still quite strong in urban markets, where consumers are less likely to do much home baking, it had lost share among more traditional rural consumers. In essence, the brand had become the market leader among those consumers who use very little flour, but had lost many of the rural heavy users to the competition.

6 and 7: Analyze the Data and Prepare a Written Report

The final steps in a marketing research project are to analyze the data, interpret the findings, and submit a written report. Today sophisticated computers and software enable a researcher to tabulate and analyze masses of data quickly and inexpensively. The end product of the investigation is the researcher's conclusions and recommendations, submitted in written form.

8: Follow Up the Study

For their own best interests, researchers should follow up each study to determine whether their recommendations are being followed. Too often, the follow-up is omitted. Actually, an analyst's future relations with an organization can depend on this follow-up, whether the analyst works in the organization or for an outside agency. Unless there is a follow-up, the company may not pay much attention to the report. It may be filed and forgotten.

WHO DOES MARKETING RESEARCH?

When a firm wishes to carry out a research project, the job can be done by the company's own personnel or by an outside organization.

Within the Company

Separate marketing research departments exist primarily in larger companies and are usually quite small. The marketing research department may consist of only a single manager or may be as large as four or five professionals in large consumer products companies. In most such situations, the marketing research department rarely conducts research utilizing its own staff, but rather contracts the work out to suppliers outside the company. The primary role of the marketing research department, therefore, is to organize, monitor, and coordinate marketing research, which may be done by a number of different suppliers throughout the country. The manager of the marketing research department reports either to the chief marketing executive or directly to top management. The researchers who staff this department must be well versed in company procedures and know what information is already available within the company. They must also be familiar with the relative strengths and weaknesses of potential marketing research suppliers.

Outside the Company

A sign of maturity in marketing research is the fact that it has already developed many institutions from which a company may seek help in marketing research problems. There exist in Canada today more than 100 companies that operate in the field of marketing research. When a marketing manager requires information on Canadian marketing research suppliers, a number of sources exist that may be consulted in order to obtain a list of potential suppliers. One listing of such suppliers is the *Directory of Canadian Marketing Research Organizations*, produced by the Professional Marketing Research Society. This directory provides detailed information on well over 100 companies that operate in Canada in marketing research and related fields.

There are approximately 30 full-service marketing research companies in Canada. These companies include such firms as the Creative Research Group, Canadian Facts, Market Facts of Canada, and Daniel Starch (Canada) Limited. These companies provide a full range of marketing research services, from the design of a research study to the submission of a final report. In addition to the full-service marketing research companies, there are in Canada dozens of smaller firms that operate in various specialized areas of marketing research. These companies are usually small and may specialize by geographic region, by industry, or by service performed. Some concentrate in either consumer or industrial research or carry out studies that involve the application of specialized techniques. Other companies provide specialized marketing research services, such as the analysis of survey data. Some marketing research is also conducted in Canada by advertising agencies and by management consulting firms such as Woods, Gordon and Stevenson, Kellogg.

Canadian business is just beginning to realize the potential of marketing research. Significant advances have been made in both quantitative and qualitative research methodology, to the point where researchers are making effective use of the behavioural sciences and mathematics. Still, however, far too many companies are spending dollars on manufacturing research, but only pennies to determine the market opportunities for their products.

Several factors account for this less-than-universal acceptance of marketing research. Unlike the results of a chemical experiment, the results of marketing research cannot always be measured quantitatively. The research director or brand manager cannot conduct a research project and then point to x percent increase in sales as a result of that project. Also, if management is not convinced of the value of marketing research, it will not spend the amount of money necessary to do a good job. Good research costs money. Executives may not realize that they cannot always get half as good a job for half the amount of money.

Marketing research cannot predict future market behaviour accurately in many cases, yet often that is what is expected of it. In fact, when dealing with consumer behaviour, the researcher is hard-pressed to get the truth regarding *present* attitudes or motives, much less those of next year.

Possibly a more fundamental reason for the modest status of marketing research has been the failure of researchers to communicate adequately with management. Admittedly, there are poor researchers and poor research. Moreover, sometimes the mentality of the quick-acting, pragmatic executive may be at odds with the cautious, complex, hedging-all-bets mentality of a marketing researcher. However, researchers, like many manufacturers, are often product-oriented when they should be market-oriented. They concentrate on research methods and techniques, rather than on showing management how these methods can aid in making better marketing decisions. Executives are willing to invest heavily in technical research because they are convinced there is a payoff in this activity. Management is not similarly convinced of a return on investment in marketing research.

Another basic problem is the apparent reluctance of management (1) to treat marketing research as a continuing process and (2) to relate marketing research and decision making in a more systematic fashion. Too often, marketing research is viewed in a fragmented, one-project-at-a-time manner. It is used only when management realizes it has a marketing problem. One way to avoid such a view is to incorporate marketing research as one part of a marketing information system — a system that provides a continuous flow of data concerning the changing marketing environment.[8]

Looking to the future, however, we think the prospects for marketing research are encouraging. As more top marketing executives embrace the concept of strategic marketing planning, we should see a growing respect for marketing research and marketing information systems. The strategic planning process requires the generation and careful analysis of information. Marketing researchers have the particular training, capabilities, and systems techniques that are needed for effective information management.[9]

SUMMARY   For a company to operate successfully today, management must develop an orderly method for gathering and analyzing the mass of information that is relevant to the organization. A marketing information system is such a method. It is a structure designed to generate and process an information flow to aid managerial planning and decision making in a company's marketing program. A marketing information system is a future-oriented, continuously operating, computer-based process. It is designed to handle internal and external data and to prevent problems as well as to solve them.

Marketing research is a major component or subsystem within a marketing information system. It is used in a very wide variety of marketing situations. Typically, in a marketing research study, the problem to be solved is first identified. Then a researcher normally conducts a situation analysis and an informal investigation. If a formal investigation is needed, the researcher decides whether to use secondary or primary sources of information. To gather primary data, the researcher may use the survey, observation, or experimental method. Normally, primary data are gathered by sampling. Then the data are analyzed, and a written report is prepared.

NOTES   [1] Peter Bennett, ed., *Glossary of Marketing Terms*, American Marketing Association, Chicago, forthcoming.

[2] Stephen Arnold, "Electronic Databases and Market Research," *Imprints: PMRS Newsletter*, Toronto: Professional Marketing Research Society, November 1987.

[3] Alan J. Bush and Joseph F. Hair, Jr., "An Assessment of the Mall Intercept as a Data Collection Method," *Journal of Marketing Research*, May 1985, pp. 158–167.

[4] Jared Mitchell, "The Truth Is Not for the Squeamish," *Report on Business Magazine*, March 1987, pp. 75–76.

[5] For suggestions on increasing the response rate, see Milton M. Pressley, "Try These Tips to Get 50% to 70% Response Rate from Mail Surveys of Commercial Populations," *Marketing News*, Jan. 21, 1983, p. 16.

[6] John Haslett Cuff, " 'People Meters' Measure Up at CBC," *The Globe and Mail*, January 22, 1988, p. A18.

[7] Eleanor J. Tracy, "Testing Time for Test Markets," *Fortune*, Oct. 29, 1984, pp. 75–76. See also "Test Marketing," a Special Section in *Sales & Marketing Management*, Mar. 10, 1986, pp. 87ff.

[8] For some suggestions on how to improve the effectiveness of marketing research departments, see David J. Luck and James R. Krum, *Conditions Conducive to the Effective Use of Marketing Research in the Corporation*, Marketing Science Institute, Cambridge, Mass., 1981. Also see David A. Aaker and George S. Day, "Increasing the Effectiveness of Marketing Research," *California Management Review*, Winter 1980, pp. 59–65.

[9] See Linden A. Davis, Jr., "What's Ahead in Marketing Research?" *Journal of Advertising Research*, June 1981, pp. 49–51.

KEY TERMS AND CONCEPTS

Marketing information system 142	Shopping mall intercept 154
Marketing research 143	Focus group 154
Situation analysis 148	Telephone survey 155
Hypothesis 149	Mail questionnaire 155

QUESTIONS AND
PROBLEMS

1. Why does a company need a marketing information system?

2. How does a marketing information system differ from marketing research?

3. "The marketing information executive — rather than an operating, decision-making executive — should be the one to identify marketing problems, delineate the area to be studied, and design the research projects." Do you agree? Explain.

4. A group of wealthy business executives regularly spends some time each winter at a popular ski resort — Whistler, British Columbia; Banff, Alberta; or Grey Rocks, Quebec. They were intrigued with the possibility of forming a corporation to develop and operate a large ski resort in the B.C. Rockies near the Alberta border. This would be a totally new venture and would be on federal park land. It would be a complete resort with facilities appealing to middle- and upper-income markets. What types of information might they want to have before deciding whether to go ahead with the venture? What sources of information would be used?

5. A manufacturer of a liquid glass cleaner competitive with Windex and Glass Wax wants to determine the amount of the product that he can expect to sell throughout the country. To help him in this project, prepare a report that shows the following information for your province and, if possible, your home city or municipality. Carefully identify the source you use for this information, and state other sources that provide this information.
   a. Number of households or families.
   b. Income or buying power per family or per household.
   c. Total retail sales in the most recent year for which you can find reliable data.
   d. Total annual sales of food stores, hardware stores, and drugstores.
   e. Total number of food stores.

6. Explain, with examples, the concepts of a situation analysis and an informal investigation in a marketing research project.

7. Evaluate surveys, observation, and experimentation as methods of gathering primary data in the following projects:
   a. A sporting goods retailer wants to determine college students' brand preferences for skis and tennis rackets.
   b. A supermarket chain wants to determine shoppers' preferences for the physical layout of fixtures and traffic patterns, particularly around checkout stands.
   c. A manufacturer of conveyor belts wants to know who makes buying decisions for his product among present and prospective users.

8. Carefully evaluate the relative merits of personal, telephone, and mail surveys on the bases of flexibility, amount of information obtained, accuracy, speed, cost, and ease of administration.

9. Explain and differentiate among a random sample, an area sample, and a quota sample.

10. What kind of sample would you use in each of the research projects designed to answer the following questions?

   a. What brand of shoes is most popular among the female students on your campus?

   b. Should the department stores in or near your hometown be open all day on Sundays?

   c. What percentage of the business firms in the large city nearest your campus have automatic sprinkler systems?

CHAPTER *7*

MARKET SEGMENTATION AND FORECASTING MARKET DEMAND

CHAPTER GOALS

This is the last of four chapters dealing with target markets. We have analyzed the components of consumer and industrial markets. We have indicated the nature of marketing information systems and the process of marketing research. To conclude our discussion of target-market selection, we consider the concepts of market segmentation and demand forecasting. After studying this chapter, you should understand:

- The concept of market segmentation — its meaning, benefits, limitations, and conditions for use.
- The bases for segmenting consumer markets.
- The bases for segmenting industrial markets.
- Target-market strategies — aggregation, concentration, and multiple segmentation.
- The nature and importance of demand forecasting in marketing.
- The major methods used in forecasting market demand.

Traditionally, women's fashion clothing has been designed for women of medium height and weight — generally in a size range of 8 to 14. Very small women shopped in the junior or girls' department for dresses and often in the boys' department for jeans, parkas, and other sportswear. Large women similarly were ignored by the fashion designers, manufacturers, and retailers. *Very* few retail clothing stores catered to large-sized women.

But times are changing. Today, clothing designers, manufacturers, and retailers are finally realizing that there is great profit potential in the market segments comprising very small or very large women. Town and Country, a large ladies' clothing chain and part of the Dylex group of companies, now has a "petite" division. The Town and Country Petite stores feature clothing designed by well-known fashion designers, as well as the company's own brands. These stores carry clothing in sizes 3 to 12 and serve customers who are 5 feet 4 inches and under. Another ladies' clothing chain that has a "petites" division in all of its stores is Irene Hill, carrying many designer labels in sizes 2 to 14.

At the other end of the size spectrum, there are probably three million Canadian women who wear clothing in size 16 or larger. This segment represents a very large annual market which many companies in the clothing industry are now beginning to address. In so doing, these companies realize that they simply cannot take a size 8 dress design and manufacture it as a size 26. Totally new designs are being developed. In retailing, Pennington's has been specializing for many years in ladies' clothing in sizes 14 to 52. Addition-Elle carries items in the 14 to 26 size range.

By catering separately to small and large women, the apparel industry in effect is engaging in market segmentation. Not all consumers want to wear the same type of clothing, use the same hair shampoo, or participate in the same recreational activities. Nor do all business firms want to buy the same type of word processors or delivery trucks. At the same time, a marketer usually cannot afford to tailor-make a different product for every single customer. Consequently, some form of market segmentation is the strategy that most marketers adopt as a compromise between the extremes of one product for all and a different product for each customer. A major key to a company's success is its ability to select the most effective location on this segmentation spectrum between the two extremes.

In our discussion of selecting target markets, we have completed the phase of market opportunity analysis in which we analyzed the three components of a market — people or organizations with wants to satisfy, the money to spend, and the willingness to spend it. With this analysis plus our understanding of how to collect and organize market and consumer information as well as our earlier environmental analysis as a guide, a company can start to zero in on its selection of target markets. Two main tasks that remain are to decide on a market segmentation strategy and to estimate the demand in the selected segments. These tasks are discussed in this chapter.[1]

GUIDELINES IN MARKET SELECTION

There are some general guidelines to follow when selecting target markets. The first one is that the target markets should be compatible with the organization's goals and image. A firm that is marketing high-priced personal computers should not sell through discount chain stores in an effort to reach a mass market.

A second guideline — consistent with our definition of strategic planning — is to match the marketing opportunity with the company's resources. The Kellogg Salada company has done this by staying close to the technology of flaked cereals. Kellogg has developed many new products by using different grains, by spraying honey, nuts, and sugar onto these grains, and by adding raisins, nuts, and apples in the box. The incremental cost of producing these new products and of addressing different market segments has been minimal. Kellogg has optimized the consumer perception of difference while minimizing the real cost.[2]

Over the long run, a business must generate a profit if it is to continue in existence. This rather obvious, third guideline translates into what is perhaps an obvious market-selection guideline. That is, an organization should consciously seek markets that will generate a sufficient sales volume at a low enough cost to result in a profit. Unfortunately, through the years, companies often overlooked the profit factor in their quest for high-volume markets. The goal often was sales volume alone, not *profitable* sales volume.

Finally, a company ordinarily should seek a market wherein the number of competitors and their size are minimal. An organization should not enter a market that is already saturated with competition unless it has some overriding competitive advantage that will enable it to take customers away from existing firms.

NATURE OF MARKET SEGMENTATION

The total market for most types of products is too varied — too heterogeneous — for management to consider it as a single, uniform entity. To speak of the market for vitamin pills, or electric razors, or tractors is to ignore the fact that the total market for each product consists of submarkets that differ significantly from one another. This lack of uniformity may be traced to differences in buying habits, in ways in which the product is used, in motives for buying, or in other factors. Market segmentation takes these differences into account.

What Is Market Segmentation?

Market segmentation is the process of dividing the total heterogeneous market for a product into several segments, each of which tends to be homogeneous in all significant aspects. Management then selects one or more of these market segments

FIGURE 7-1

Demand curves representing market aggregation and market segmentation.

The object of aggregation is to fit the market to the product. Segmentation is an attempt to fit the product to the market.

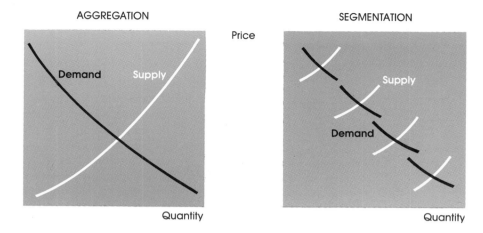

as the organization's target market. Finally, a separate marketing mix is developed for each segment or group of segments in this target market.

Market segmentation is the opposite of market aggregation. **Market aggregation** is the strategy whereby an organization treats its total market as a unit — that is, as one mass, aggregate market whose parts are considered to be alike in all major respects. This organization then develops a single marketing mix to reach as many customers as possible in this aggregate market.

In the language of economic theory, in market aggregation the seller assumes there is a single demand curve for its product. In effect, the product is assumed to have a broad market appeal. In contrast, in market segmentation the total market is viewed as a series of demand curves. Each one represents a separate market segment calling for a different product, promotional appeal, or other element in the marketing mix. See Fig. 7-1. Thus, instead of speaking of one aggregate market for personal computers, we can segment this total market into several submarkets. We then will have, for example, a college-student market segment for personal computers. Other submarkets might consist of segments representing homemakers, professors, travelling executives, travelling sales people, small businesses, etc.

Benefits of Market Segmentation

Market segmentation is a customer-oriented philosophy and thus is consistent with the marketing concept. We first identify the needs of the customers within a sub-market (segment) and then satisfy those needs. Stated another way, in market segmentation we employ a "rifle" approach (separate programs, pinpointed targets) in our marketing activities. In contrast, market aggregation is a "shotgun" approach (one program, broad target).

By tailoring marketing programs to individual market segments, management can do a better marketing job and make more efficient use of marketing resources. A small firm with limited resources might compete very effectively in one or two market segments, whereas the same firm would be buried if it aimed for the total market. By employing the strategy of market segmentation, a company can design products that really match the market demands. Advertising media can be used more effectively because promotional messages — and the media chosen to present them — can be more specifically aimed toward each segment of the market.

Marketing at Work

Segmentation for Profit, Not Volume

Explore one of the last unexplored frontiers on earth. Join one of our all day jeep tours into the jungles and mountains and discover miles of remote beaches along the coast of South America. Or be among the very few to set eyes on the world's highest waterfall "Angel Falls" (19 times higher than Niagara Falls). Sunquest offers 1 and 2 week charter package holidays every week. Imagine an adventure to another world.

*Price shown is per person based on double occupancy and will vary depending on departure and choice of accommodation. Taxes and service charges are not included. Refer to the Sunquest Spring/Summer 1988 brochure for full selection of rates and accommodation

Sunquest Vacations Limited, one of Canada's largest vacation tour wholesalers, doesn't offer trips to Florida. Pat Brigham's company packages hotel rooms and airline seats into vacation holidays and markets them through travel agents throughout Canada, but he got out of Florida more than ten years ago. Sunquest caters to a growing pool of sophisticated travellers who aren't thinking only about how much they will have to pay. Brigham explains that, even though 1.5 million Canadians go to Florida every year, the destination tends to attract vacationers who are extremely cost conscious. In his words, "It didn't make any sense. We were moving a lot of passengers, but by the time we had taken in $199, we earned $19 on the transaction." Now Sunquest flies only to 11 tried and true vacation spots in the Caribbean, California, and Latin America. Sunquest ads feature upscale young couples, never a photograph of anyone with grey hair. Good-looking singles of the baby-boomer generation are pictured lounging in beach chairs or leaping over tennis nets. To cater to the clientele he wants — the great Canadian middle and upper-middle class — Brigham has developed new and interesting destinations, including Venezuela and the Dominican Republic.

Source: Ross Fisher, "Sell Those Seats, Fill That Plane," *Report on Business Magazine*, February 1988, pp. 77–83.

Limitations of Market Segmentation

While market segmentation can provide a lot of marketing benefits to an organization, this strategy also has some drawbacks with respect to costs and market coverage. In the first place, market segmentation can be an expensive proposition in both the production and marketing of products. In production, it obviously is less expensive to produce mass quantities of one model and one colour than it is to produce a variety of models, colours, and sizes.

Segmentation increases marketing expenses in several ways. Total inventory costs go up because adequate inventories of each style, colour, etc., must be maintained. Advertising costs go up because different ads may be required for each market segment. Or some segments may be too small for the seller to make effective use of television or some other advertising medium. Administrative expenses go up when management must plan and implement several different marketing programs.

Conditions for Effective Segmentation

Ideally, management's goal should be to segment its markets in such a way that each segment responds in a homogeneous fashion to a given marketing program. Three conditions will help management move toward this goal.

- The basis for segmenting — that is, the characteristics used to categorize customers — must be *measurable*, and the data must be *accessible*. The "desire for ecologically compatible products" may be a characteristic that is useful in segmenting the market for a given product. But data on this characteristic are neither readily accessible nor easily quantified.

- The market segment itself should be *accessible* through existing marketing institutions — middlemen, advertising media, company sales force, and so on — with a minimum of cost and waste. To aid marketers in this regard, some national magazines, such as *Maclean's* and *Chatelaine*, publish separate regional editions. This allows an advertiser to run an ad aimed at, say a Western segment of the market, without having to pay for exposure in other, non-market areas.

■ Each segment should be *large enough* to be profitable. In concept, management could treat each single customer as a separate segment. (Actually, this situation may be normal in industrial markets, as when Canadair markets passenger airplanes to corporations and commercial airlines.) But in segmenting a consumer market, a firm must not develop too wide a variety of styles, colours, sizes, and prices. Usually, the diseconomies of scale in production and inventory will put reasonable limits on this type of oversegmentation.

BASES FOR MARKET SEGMENTATION

In Chapter 4 we discussed the segmentation of the entire Canadian market into two broad categories — ultimate consumers and industrial users. That was a worthwhile start toward useful segmentation, but it still leaves too broad and heterogeneous a grouping for most products, either consumer or industrial. Consequently, we need to identify some of the widely used bases for further segmenting these two broad markets. We shall start with the consumer market.

Bases for Segmenting Consumer Market

The commonly used bases for segmenting the consumer market may be grouped into the following four broad categories:

■ Geographic.
■ Demographic.
■ Psychographic.
■ Behaviour toward product (product-related bases).

Table 7-1 summarizes the segmentation bases for the consumer market. Four main categories are shown along with typical subcategories under each of the four. Then for each subcategory there are some examples of typical market segments.

In using these bases to segment markets, we should note two points. First, buying behaviour is rarely traceable to only one segmentation factor. Useful segmentation typically is developed by including variables from several bases. To illustrate, the market for a product rarely consists of all the people living in British Columbia or all people over 65. Instead, the segment is more likely to be described with several of these variables. Thus a market segment might be British Columbia families with young children, and earning above a certain income. As another example, one clothing manufacturer's target market was affluent young women (income, age, gender).

The other point to observe is the interrelationships among these factors, especially among the demographic factors. For instance, age and life-cycle stage typically are related. Income depends to some degree on age, life-cycle stage, education, and occupation.

GEOGRAPHIC SEGMENTATION

Many organizations segment their market on some geographic basis such as census region, city size, urban-suburban-rural, or climate. Many companies market only

TABLE 7-1   SEGMENTATION BASES FOR CONSUMER MARKETS

Segmentation basis	Examples of typical market segments
Geographic:	
Region	Atlantic provinces; Quebec; Ontario; Prairie provinces; B.C. census regions.
City or CMA size	Under 25,000; 25,000 to 100,000; 100,000 to 250,000; 250,000 to 500,000; 500,000 to 1,000,000; over 1,000,000.
Urban-rural	Urban; rural; suburban; farm.
Climate and topography	Mountainous; seacoast; rainy; cold and snowy; etc.
Demographic:	
Age	Under 6, 6–12, 13–19, 20–34, 35–49, 50–64, 65 and over.
Gender	Male, female.
Family life cycle	Young single, young married no children, etc.
Education	Grade school only, high school graduate, college graduate.
Occupation	Professional, manager, clerical, craftsman, sales, student, housewife, unemployed.
Religion	Protestant, Catholic, Jewish, other.
Ethnic background	White; black; oriental. British; French; Chinese; German; Ukrainian; Italian; Indian; etc.
Income	Under $10,000, $10,000–$25,000, $25,000–$35,000, $35,000–$50,000, over $50,000.
Psychographic:	
Social class	Upper class, upper middle, lower middle, upper lower, etc.
Personality	Ambitious, self-confident, aggressive, introverted, extroverted, sociable, etc.
Life-style	Conservative, liberal, health and fitness oriented, "straight," "swinger," adventuresome.
Behaviour toward product (or product-related bases):	
Benefits desired	Examples vary widely depending upon product: appliance: cost, quality, life, repairs, toothpaste: no cavities, plaque control, bright teeth, good taste, low price.
Usage rate	Nonuser, light user, heavy user.

Many companies select the largest cities as their market segment.

in a limited geographic area. Mary Brown's Fried Chicken, for example, operates stores only in Ontario and Atlantic Canada. The chain has to be confident that a store can draw on a population base of 7,500 or more before a store will be opened. Tabi International, a ladies' clothing chain, prefers to locate in shopping centres where the Tabi stores can benefit from upmarket anchor stores that draw the type of clientele Tabi seeks. The Body Shop, a chain specializing in fragrances and soaps, also will open stores primarily in malls and other busy locations which will provide a certain level of passing traffic.

DEMOGRAPHIC SEGMENTATION

Probably the most widely used basis for segmenting consumer markets is some demographic factor such as age, gender, income, stage in family life cycle, ethnic background, etc. Again, see Table 7-1. The reason for this is simply that so often consumers' wants or product use are related to one or more of these factors. Also most demographic factors can serve as the bases for *operational* market segments, because they meet the conditions for effective segmentation — measurable, accessible, and large enough.

Let's look briefly at a few demographic factors to illustrate how they can serve as segmentation bases.

Age   We all are well aware that our needs and wants change as we go through life. In recognition of this fact, countless firms use age categories as a basis for segmenting the markets for their products. Procter & Gamble now market several varieties of Crest toothpaste, each aimed at a distinct market segment. To the existing flavours of Crest, P&G recently added Crest for Kids and Tartar Control Crest. The children's version of the leading toothpaste brand competes head on with Aqua Fresh for Kids, Muppets and Sesame Street toothpastes. Other manufacturers also have tartar-control versions that are directed to a distinctly adult market for which tartar buildup is more likely to be a problem.[3] Cosmetic manufacturers market acne creams for teenagers and hair shampoo for people over 40. Attractive women over 40 are featured in cosmetic ads aimed at this age market.

Gender   For many years gender has been a commonly used segmentation basis for many products such as clothing, shoes, autos, personal care products, and magazines. In recent years, however, there have been some interesting variations on traditional sex-based segmentation. In clothing, for example, several traditionally male products have been redesigned and repositioned for the female segment of the market.[4] Jockey markets a line of Jockey Underwear for Her. Calvin Klein designs a line of men's-style underwear for women. Blue jeans and T-shirts, once for men

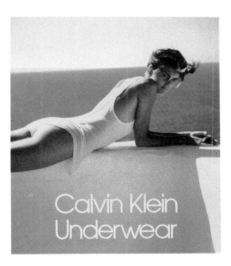

Some traditionally single-gender products now are targeted at both men and women.

only, today are unisex items. Some cosmetics and personal care products originally targeted only at the women's market are today also marketed to men. Clairol, a leading supplier of women's hair care products, has launched a new line of hair products for men called New Vitalis.

Income   Segmenting markets on the basis of income is commonly done by firms selling such products and services as autos, housing, travel, jewellery, and furs. A Rolls-Royce or a yacht obviously is intended for a different income market than is a Lada or a rowboat. Income also typically is combined with some other base in market segmentation. In Chapter 5 we pointed out, for example, that social class may be a better predictor of consumer buying behaviour than income alone.

PSYCHOGRAPHIC SEGMENTATION

Three common bases for the psychographic segmentation of consumer markets are social-class structure, personality characteristics, and life-styles.

Social class   As we observed in Chapter 5, a person's social class has a considerable influence on that person's choice in many product categories. Consequently, many companies will select one or two social classes as target markets and then develop a product and marketing mix to reach those segments.

Personality characteristics   *Theoretically*, personality characteristics should form a good basis for segmenting markets. Compulsive people buy differently from cautious consumers. Quiet introverts presumably make product choices different from those made by gregarious, outgoing people. *Realistically*, however, personality characteristics pose some problems that limit their usefulness in practical market segmentation. These characteristics typically are difficult to measure accurately in a quantitative sense. Many studies have been made of consumer attitudes and personality traits in relation to product and brand preferences in a wide variety of product categories. But the results generally have been too limited to be of value when companies want to implement their market segmentation strategies.

Nevertheless, it is interesting that many firms in their advertising do appeal to consumers who have certain personality traits. Thus we see a brand advertised to consumers who "are on the way up," or who are "people of distinction," or who "don't want their family left helpless."

Life-styles   The term *life-style* is a very broad concept and sometimes overlaps personality characteristics. Being cautious, sceptical, ambitious, a workaholic, a copy-cat — are these personality or life-style traits? Life-styles relate to your activities, interests, and opinions. They reflect how you spend your time and what your beliefs are on various social, economic, and political issues.[5]

There is no commonly accepted terminology of life-style categories for segmenting markets. Researchers often develop a different category terminology to fit the market or product being studied. As we discussed in Chapter 5, one widely respected study of values and life-styles (VALS) segmented consumers into the following nine life-style categories:[6]

- Survivors.
- Sustainers.

Segmenting by life-style.

- Belongers.
- Emulators.
- Achievers.
- I-Am-Me.
- Experiential.
- Socially conscious.
- Integrated.

Regardless of the imprecision in terminology, people's life-styles undoubtedly do affect their choice of product types and their brand preferences within these product categories. Marketers are well aware of this and often attempt to segment their markets on a life-style basis. Similar to the VALS approach, several Canadian research companies regularly conduct life-style segmentation studies on behalf of clients. Goldfarb Consultants produced six "attitude segments" from its surveys of 1,400 Canadians. This study described the largest segment (25 percent of the sample) as the Day-to-Day Watchers — "They watch the world around them, and they tend to be bandwagoners as opposed to leaders." The next largest group (18 percent) were conservative, traditional, and somewhat inflexible, and were labelled "Old-fashioned Puritans." Psychographic research was used to create the concept behind the famous "Fred and the boys" television commercials for Molson Export, as well as campaigns for luxury hotels.[7] Many retailers are successful, in part, because they regularly determine the latest consumer life-style trends and then design strategies to reach specific market segments.[8]

PRODUCT-RELATED BASES

Some marketers regularly attempt to segment their markets on the basis of a consumer behavioural characteristic related to the product. In this section we shall briefly consider two of these product-related segmentation bases — benefits desired and product usage rate.

Benefits desired   Conceptually it is very logical to segment a market on the basis of the different benefits that customers want from the product. Certainly benefit segmentation is consistent with the idea that a company should be marketing product *benefits* and not simply the physical or chemical characteristics of a product. From the consumers' point of view, they really are buying product *benefits* and not the product itself. That is, a customer wants a smooth surface (the benefit) and not sandpaper (the product).

For benefit segmentation to be effective, two tasks must be accomplished. First, a company must be able to identify the various benefits that people seek in the product or service. To illustrate, in segmenting the market for its ocean cruises, the Viking Steamship Line might identify such benefit segments as (1) the opportunity to meet people, (2) recreation, (3) education, (4) rest and relaxation. In his classic study which originated the concept of benefit segmentation, Russell Haley identified the following benefit segments for toothpaste and the benefits sought by these segments: (1) sensories — flavour and appearance; (2) sociables — brightness of teeth; (3) worriers — decay prevention; (4) independents — low price. Today Haley might add "tartar control" as a fifth benefit segment.[9]

Once these separate benefits are identified, the second task is to describe the demographic and psychographic characteristics of the people in each segment. Then the seller is in a position to launch a product and marketing program to reach a selected target segment.

Usage rate   Another product-related basis for market segmentation is the rate at which people use or consume a product. Thus we can have categories for nonusers, light users, medium users, and heavy users. Normally a company is most interested in the heavy users of its product. The 50 percent of the people who are the ''heavy half'' of the users of a product typically account for 80 to 90 percent of the total purchases of a given product. The remarkable feature of these usage patterns is that they seem to remain reasonably constant over time. Thus this segmentation base becomes an effective predictor of future buying behaviour. Comparable studies in the 1960s and 1980s showed similar patterns in the percentage of total purchases accounted for by the heavy-user half of the market in each product category. Some sample products and percentages of the total market accounted for by the heavy half in 1962 and 1982 were as follows: shampoo, 81 and 79 percent; cake mixes, 85 and 83 percent; beer, 88 and 87 percent; soaps and detergents, 80 and 75 percent.[10]

Sometimes the target market is the nonuser or light user, where the objective is to woo these customers into a higher use category. Once the characteristics of these light users are identified, management can go to them directly with an introductory low-price offer. Or a seller might increase usage rates by promoting (1) new uses for a product (baking soda as a deodorant); (2) new times for uses (off-season vacations); or (3) multiple packaging (a six-pack of soft drinks).

Bases for Segmenting Industrial Market

Several of the bases that were used to segment the consumer market could also be used to segment the broad industrial market. For example, we can segment industrial markets on a geographical basis. Several industries are geographically concentrated, so any firm selling to these industries could nicely use this segmentation basis. Sellers also can segment on product-related bases such as usage rate or benefits desired.

At this point, let's look at some of the bases that are used solely when segmenting industrial markets. Three in particular that deserve our attention are type of customer, size of customer, and type of buying situation.[11]

TYPE OF CUSTOMER

Any firm that sells to customers in a variety of industries may want to segment this market on the basis of customer types. In Chapter 4 we discussed the Standard Industrial Classification (S.I.C.) code as a very useful tool for identifying industrial and commercial target markets. A firm selling display cases or store fixtures to the retail market, for example, might start out with potential customers included in the two-digit code number 61 for shoe, apparel, fabric and yarn industries — retail. Then the three-digit code 612 identifies potential customers in the retail clothing business. Finally, the four-digit code number 6121 pinpoints men's clothing specialty stores.

A firm selling janitorial supplies or small electric motors would have a broad potential market among many different industries. Management in this firm could

Industrial markets can be segmented by type of customer.

segment its market by type of customer and then perhaps decide to sell to firms in only a limited number of these segments.

File 7-2

Segmenting Business Markets: A Suite Deal

In an attempt to cater to the growing market segment of business travellers, a number of companies have established hotels which offer only suites, rather than conventional hotel rooms. In Halifax, the Cambridge Suites, an all-suite hotel, offers the business traveller separate working and sleeping rooms and a small kitchen. The business person has room to hold a business meeting or to write a sales report, without spreading papers over the bed. Breakfast is complimentary, a convenience store is nearby, and the kitchen is equipped with dishes, cutlery, toasters, spices, and other items. More all-suite hotels, offering rooms at reasonable prices, are being established in other major Canadian cities.

SIZE OF CUSTOMER

In this situation size can be measured by such factors as sales volume, number of production facilities, or number of sales offices. Many industrial sellers divide their potential market into large and small accounts, using separate distribution channels to reach each segment. The large-volume accounts, for example, may be sold to directly by the company's sales force. But to reach the smaller accounts, the seller will use a manufacturers' agent or some other form of middleman.

TYPE OF BUYING SITUATION

Referring back to Chapter 5, we discussed three types of buying classes — new buy, modified rebuy, and straight rebuy. We also recognized in that discussion that a new buy was significantly different from a straight rebuy in several important respects. Consequently, an industrial seller might well segment its market into these three buy-class categories. Or the seller could at least set up two segments by combining new buy and modified rebuy into one segment. Then different marketing programs would be developed to reach each of these two or three segments.[12]

TARGET-MARKET STRATEGIES

Let's assume that a company is aware of the opportunities for segmenting its market, having analyzed the various segmentation bases in relation to the company's product. Now management is in a position to select one or more segments as its target markets. The company can follow one of three broad strategies in this selection process. The three alternatives are market aggregation, single-segment concentration, and multiple-segment segmentation. See Fig. 7-2.

Market Aggregation

By adopting a strategy of **market aggregation** — also known as a *mass-market* or an *undifferentiated-market* strategy — an organization treats its total market as a single given. This unit is one mass, aggregate market whose parts are considered to be alike in all major respects. Management then develops a single marketing

FIGURE 7-2
Alternative target-market strategies.

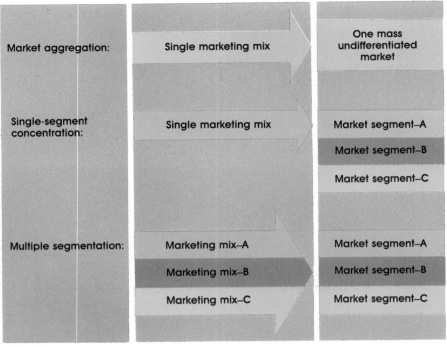

mix to reach as many customers as possible in this aggregate market. That is, the company develops a single product or service for this mass audience; it develops one pricing structure and one distribution system for its product; and it uses a single promotional program that is aimed at the entire market.

When is an organization likely to adopt the strategy of market aggregation? Generally, when a large group of customers in the total market tends to have the same perception of the product or service's want-satisfying benefits. Therefore, this strategy often is adopted by firms that are marketing a nondifferentiated, staple product such as gasoline, salt, or sugar. In the eyes of many people, cane sugar is cane sugar, regardless of the brand. All brands of table salt are pretty much alike, and one unleaded gasoline is about the same as another. Firms that provide laundry and dry cleaning services on a chain basis also adopt this strategy.

Basically, market aggregation is a production-oriented strategy. It enables a company to maximize its economies of scale in production, physical distribution, and promotion. Producing and marketing one product for one market means longer production runs at lower unit costs. Inventory costs are minimized when there is no (or a very limited) variety of colours and sizes of products. Warehousing and transportation efforts are most efficient when one product is going to one market.

Market aggregation will work only as long as the seller's single marketing mix continues to satisfy enough customers to meet the company's sales and profit expectations. The strategy of marketing aggregation typically is accompanied by the strategy of product differentiation in a company's marketing program. **Product differentiation** is the strategy by which one firm attempts to distinguish its product from competitive brands offered to the same aggregate market. By differentiating

Some products are suited for a market-aggregation strategy.

its product, an organization hopes to convince potential customers that its product is better than the competitors' brands. The seller also hopes to engage in nonprice competition and thus avoid or minimize the threat of price competition.

A seller implements this strategy either (1) by changing some feature of the product — the package or colour, for example — or (2) by using a promotional appeal that features a differentiating benefit. Crest says that its toothpaste now fights tartar formation on teeth. Scotian Gold puts its apple juice in aseptic packages which keep fresh without refrigeration. Lever Brothers uses a cuddly bear named Snuggle to promote its fabric softener of the same name, while Downy stresses its "April fresh smell." Dry Idea is differentiated from other roll-on deodorants by the fact that it has "almost no water."

Marketing at Work

File 7-3

Differentiation: Not Just Another Mall

Promenade Shopping Centre.

Differentiation is just as important for a shopping centre developer as it is for the manufacturer of detergent or toothpaste. The objective is to give the customer a reason to buy our brand or shop at our mall.

The shopping centre was introduced into Canadian retailing with the opening of Toronto's Yorkdale Shopping Centre in 1954. The first-generation of shopping centres looked like large boxes — they were rows of stores with a roof over them.

The second generation of centres were larger and contained more variety to attract customers — open spaces, theatres, and creative floor plans. But the second generation came to be criticized for their "sameness." Most attracted the same mix of tenants, so that most centres across the country offered customers approximately the same choice of shopping at the same chain outlets.

We are now seeing the opening of the third generation of Canadian shopping centres, the forerunner of which is the West Edmonton Mall, the equivalent of 24 city blocks, with its indoor beach, ice rink, and amusement park. Other smaller malls have been developed with the objective of creating an impression that these centres are not like all the others, that they offer a special shopping experience.

One of Canada's largest shopping centre developers, Cadillac Fairview, in its Promenade shopping centre in Vaughan, Ontario, has reproduced as natural a setting as possible, with arched skylights, an interior street with trees and plants, water running through man-made streams, and floors of gleaming marble. The Food Hall is intended to recreate the atmosphere of Harrod's in London or a European shopping arcade.

Source: Karen Howlett, "Mall Looks Change but Stay the Same," *The Globe and Mail Report on Business,* October 9, 1987, pp. B1, B2.

Single-Segment Concentration Strategy

A strategy of **single-segment concentration** involves selecting as the target market one homogeneous segment from within the total market. One marketing mix is then developed to reach this single segment. A small company may want to concentrate on a single market segment, rather than to take on many competitors in a broad market. Many service organizations use the single segment approach because of the flexibility of personnel compared with physical product. For example, an Alberta guest ranch got started by appealing only to horseback riders who also enjoyed square dancing. A large cruise-ship company, offering a round-the-world luxury cruise, targets its marketing effort at one market segment — the older, financially well-off people who also have time to travel.

When the manufacturers of foreign automobiles first entered the North American market, they typically targeted a single market segment. The Volkswagen *Beetle* was intended for the low-priced, small-car market, and as we enter the 1990s Yugo and Lada continue that tradition. Honda originally sold only lower-powered motorcycles, and Mercedes-Benz targeted the high-income market. Today, of course, most of the original foreign car marketers have moved into a multisegment strategy. Only a few, such as Rolls Royce and Ferrari, continue with a concentration strategy.

This strategy enables a company to penetrate one small market in depth and to acquire a reputation as a specialist or an expert in this limited market. A company can enter such a market with limited resources. And as long as the single segment remains a small market, large competitors are likely to leave the single-segment specialist alone. However, if the small market should show signs of becoming a large market, then the big boys may well jump in. This is exactly what happened in the market for herbal and specialty teas. Prior to the early 1980s, rose-hip, camomile, Earl Grey, and similar specialty teas were sold primarily in health food stores and specialty shops and were available from only a small number of manufacturers and importers. With changing consumer tastes and preferences through the 1980s, specialty teas became more popular. The growth of the herbal and specialty segment was such that new tea companies entered this expanding corner of the market, including some major competitors such as Tetley and Lipton.

The big risk and limitation to a single-segment strategy is that the seller has all its eggs in one basket. If that single segment declines in market potential, the seller can suffer considerably. Also, a seller with a strong name and reputation in one segment may find it difficult to expand into another segment. Eaton's encountered problems in the 1970s when it opened its Horizon discount stores to compete with Woolco and K-Mart. IBM experienced consumer resistence to its PCjr. microcomputer which was directed to the family market. Both Volkswagen and Honda have traded their lines up to compete with the higher-priced models of BMW and Mercedes: VW with its Audi line, and Honda with its Acura. Nestlé has successfully marketed its instant coffees Nescafé and Taster's Choice for many years and is now challenging the ground coffee segment with its Taster's Choice ground.

Special tea markets.

Multiple-Segment Strategy

In the strategy of **multiple segmentation**, two or more different groups of potential customers are identified as target-market segments. Then a separate marketing mix is developed to reach each segment. A marketer of personal computers, for example, might identify three separate market segments — college students, small businesses, and homemakers — and then design a different marketing mix to reach each segment. In segmenting the passenger automobile market, General Motors of Canada develops separate marketing programs built around its five brands — Chevrolet, Pontiac, Buick, Oldsmobile, and Cadillac. General Motors, in effect, tries to reach the total market for autos, but does so on a segmented basis.

As part of the strategy of multiple segmentation, a company frequently will develop a different variety of the basic product for each segment. However, market segmentation can also be accomplished with no change in the product, but rather with separate marketing programs, each tailored to a given market segment. A producer of cosmetics, for instance, can market the identical product to the teenage market and to the 25 to 30 age segment. But the promotional programs for the two markets will be different.

A multiple-segment strategy normally results in a greater sales volume than a single-segment approach. Multiple segmentation also is useful for a company facing a seasonal demand for its product. In England during the summer, several universities market their empty dormitory space to the tourists — another market segment. A firm with excess production capacity may well seek additional market segments to absorb this capacity. Probably the biggest drawback to the multiple-segment strategy is that the unit costs of production and marketing typically increase when multiple segments are targeted.

FORECASTING MARKET DEMAND

As the final step in selecting its target markets, a company should forecast the market demand for its product or service. Forecasting market demands means to estimate the sales-volume size of a company's total market and the sales volume expected in each market segment. This step involves estimating the total industry potential for the company's product in the target market. (This industry figure is called the *market potential* for the product.) Then the seller should estimate its share of this total market. (This company figure is called the *sales potential*.)

The key requirement in demand forecasting is the preparation of a sales forecast, usually for a one-year period. A sales forecast is the foundation of all budgeting and operational planning in all departments of a company — marketing, production, and finance.

Definition of Some Basic Terms

Before we discuss forecasting methods, we need to define several terms, because they often are used loosely in business.

MARKET FACTOR AND MARKET INDEX

A **market factor** is an item or element that (1) exists in a market, (2) may be measured quantitatively, and (3) is related to the demand for a product or service. To illustrate, the "number of cars three years old and older" is a market factor underlying the demand for replacement tires. That is, this element affects the number of replacement tires that can be sold. A **market index** is simply a market factor expressed as a percentage, or in some other quantitative form, relative to some base figure. To illustrate, one market factor is "households owning appliance X"; in 1990, the market index for this factor was 132 (relative to 1975 equals 100). An index may also be composed of multiple market factors, such as the number of cars three years old and older, population, and disposable personal income.

MARKET POTENTIAL AND SALES POTENTIAL

The **market potential** for a product is the total expected sales of that product by all sellers during a stated period of time in a stated market. **Sales potential** (synonymous with **market share**) is the share of a market potential that an individual company expects to achieve.

Thus we may speak of the "market potential" for automatic washing machines, but the "sales potential" (or market share) for one company's brand of machine. In the case of either market potential or sales potential, the market may encompass the entire country, or even the world. Or it may be a smaller market segmented by income, by geographic area, or on some other basis. For example, we may speak of the *market potential* for washing machines in the Atlantic provinces, or the *sales potential* for Whirlpool washers in homes with incomes of $25,000 to $35,000. The market potential and sales potential are the same when a firm has a monopoly in its market, as in the case of some public utilities.

SALES FORECAST

A **sales forecast** may be defined as an estimate of sales (in dollars or product units) during some specific future period of time and under a predetermined marketing plan in the firm. A sales forecast can ordinarily be made more intelligently if the company first determines its market and/or sales potential. However, many firms start their forecasting directly with the sales forecast. See Fig. 7-3.

The sales forecast and the marketing plan   The marketing goals and broad strategies — the core of a marketing plan — must be established before a sales forecast is made. That is, the sales forecast depends upon these predetermined goals and strategies. Certainly, different sales forecasts will result, depending upon whether the marketing goal is (1) to liquidate an excess inventory of product A or (2) to expand the firm's market share by aggressive advertising.

FIGURE 7-3
Business application of some of our definitions.

```
              MARKET SHARE WORKSHEET FOR 1990

Dan's Diaper Deliveries
Regina, Saskatchewan

Market factor: _____        Number: _____

Base period: _____          Number: _____


Market index: _____ + _____  _____


Market potential @ 6 dozen per child per month:

    6X _____ = _____ dz/mo


Sales projection: _____ dz/mo


Market share: _____ + _____ = _____
```

However, once the sales forecast is prepared, it does become the key controlling factor in all *operational* planning throughout the company. The forecast is the basis of sound budgeting. Financial planning for working-capital requirements, plant utilization, and other needs is based on anticipated sales. The scheduling of all production resources and facilities, such as setting labour needs and purchasing supplies and materials, depends upon the sales forecast.

Sales-forecasting periods   The most widely used period for sales forecasting is one year, although many firms will review annual forecasts on a monthly or quarterly basis. Annual sales forecasts tie in with annual financial planning and reporting, and are often based on estimates of the coming years' general economic conditions.

Forecasts for less than a year may be desirable when activity in the firm's industry is so volatile that it is not feasible to look ahead for a full year. As a case in point, many firms engaged in fashion merchandising — producers and retailers alike — prepare a forecast that covers only one fashion season.

Methods of Forecasting Demand   A company can forecast its sales by using either of two basic procedures — the ''top-down'' or the ''buildup'' approach.

Using the **top-down** (or **breakdown**) approach, management generally would:

1. *start with a forecast of general economic conditions*, as the basis to
2. *determine the industry's total market potential for a product or service*; then
3. *measure the share of this market the firm is getting*; the measurements in items 2 and 3 form the basis to
4. *forecast the sale of the product or service*.

In the **buildup** technique, management would generate estimates of future demand in segments of the market or from organizational units (sales people or branches) in the company. Then management would simply add the individual estimates to get one total forecast.

Predictions of future market demand — whether they are sales forecasts or estimates of market potential — may be based on techniques ranging from uninformed guesses to sophisticated statistical methods. Marketing executives do not need to know how to do the statistical computations. However, they should understand enough about a given technique to appreciate its merits and limitations. They should also know when each method is best used, and they should be able to ask intelligent questions regarding the assumptions underlying the method.

Here are some of the commonly used methods of predicting demand.

MARKET-FACTOR ANALYSIS

This method is based on the assumption that the future demand for a product is related to the behaviour of certain market factors. If we can determine what these factors are and can measure their relationship to sales activity, we can forecast future sales simply by studying the behaviour of the factors.

The key to the successful use of this method lies in the selection of the appropriate market factors. It is also important to minimize the number of market factors used. The greater the number of factors, the greater the chance for erroneous estimates and the more difficult it is to tell how much each factor influences the demand. The two procedures used to translate market-factor behaviour into an estimate of future sales are the direct-derivation method and the correlation-analysis technique.

Direct derivation   Let's illustrate the use of this method to estimate *market potential*. Suppose that a manufacturer of automobile tires wants to know the market potential for replacement tires in Canada in 1991. The primary market factor is the number of automobiles on the road. The first step is to estimate how many cars are likely prospects for new tires. Assume (1) that the seller's studies show that the average car is driven about 16,000 km a year and (2) that the average driver gets about 45,000 km from a set of four tires. This means that all cars that become three years old during 1991 can be considered a part of the potential market for replacement tires during that year. The seller can obtain a reasonably accurate count of the number of cars sold in 1988. (These are the cars that will become three years old in 1991.) The information sources are provincial vehicle licensing offices or private organizations. In addition, the seller can determine how many cars will become 6, 9, or 12 years old in 1991. (These ages are multiples of three. That is, in 1991, a six-year-old car presumably would be ready for its second set of replacement tires.) The number of cars in these age brackets times four (tires per car) should give a fair approximation of the market potential for replacement tires in 1991. We are, of course, dealing in averages. Not all drivers will get 45,000 km from a set of tires, and not all cars will be driven exactly 16,000 km per year.

The direct-derivation method has much to recommend it. It is relatively simple and inexpensive to use, and it requires little statistical analysis. It is reasonably easy to understand, so that executives who are not statistics-oriented can follow the method and interpret the results.

Correlation analysis   This technique is a mathematical refinement of the direct-derivation method. When correlation analysis is used, the degree of association between potential sales of the product and the market factor is taken into account. In effect, a correlation analysis measures, on a scale of 0 to 1, the variations between two series of data. Consequently, this method can be used only when a lengthy sales history of the industry or firm is available, as well as a history of the market factor.

Correlation analysis gives a more exact estimate of market demand, provided that the method is applied correctly. In direct derivation, the correlation measure is implicitly assumed to be 1.00. But rarely does this perfect association exist between a market factor and the sales of a product. Correlation analysis therefore takes the past history into account in predicting the future. It also allows a researcher to incorporate more than one factor into the formula.

There are at least two major limitations to this method. First, as suggested above, a lengthy sales history must be available. To do a really good job, researchers need about 20 periods of sales records. Also, they must assume that approximately the same relationship has existed between the sales and the market factors during this entire period. And, furthermore, they must assume that this relationship will continue in the next sales period. These can be highly unrealistic assumptions. The other major drawback is that not all marketing people understand correlation analysis

Computers enable you to employ more complex forecasting methods.

and can actually do the necessary computations. Thus a statistical staff may be necessary.

SURVEY OF BUYER INTENTIONS

Another commonly used method of forecasting is to survey a sample of potential customers. These people are asked how much of the stated product or service they would buy or use at a given price during a specified future time period. Some firms maintain consumer panels on a continuing basis to act as a sounding board for new-product ideas, prices, and other features.

A major problem is that of selecting the sample of potential buyers. For many consumer products, a very large, and thus very costly, sample would be needed. Aside from the extremely high cost and large amount of time that this method often entails, there is another very serious limitation. It is one thing for consumers to *intend to buy* a product, but quite another for them to *actually buy* it. Surveys of buying intentions inevitably show an inflated measure of market potential.

Surveys of buying intentions are probably most effective when (1) there are relatively few buyers; (2) these buyers are willing to express their buying intentions; and (3) their past record shows that their follow-up actions are consistent with their stated intentions.

Some forecasting starts with talking to prospective customers.

TEST MARKETING

In using this technique, a firm markets its product in a limited geographic area. Then, from this sample, management projects the company's sales potential (market share) over a larger area. Test marketing is frequently used in deciding whether sufficient sales potential exists for a new product. The technique also serves as a basis for evaluating various product features and alternative marketing strategies. The outstanding benefit of test marketing is that it can tell management how many people *actually buy* the product, instead of only how many *say they intend* to buy. If a company can afford the time and money for this method, and can run a valid test, this is the best way of measuring the potential for its product.

These are big "ifs," however. Test marketing is expensive in time and money. Great care is needed to control the test-marketing experiment. A competitor, learning you are test marketing, is usually adept at "jamming" your experiment. That is, by unusual promotional or other marketing effort, a competitor can create an artificial situation that distorts your test results. To avoid such test-market "wars," some companies are using simulations of test markets. In effect, these marketers are conducting a test market in a laboratory, rather than in the field.[13]

PAST SALES AND TREND ANALYSIS

A favourite method of forecasting is to base the estimate *entirely* on past sales. This technique is used frequently by retailers whose main goal is to "beat last year's figures." The method consists simply in applying a flat percentage increase to the volume achieved last year or to the average volume of the past few years.

This technique is simple, inexpensive, and easy to apply. For a firm operating in a stable market, where its market share has remained constant for a period of years, past sales alone might be used to predict future volume. On balance, however, the method is highly unreliable.

Trend analysis is a variation of forecasting based on past sales, but it is a bit more complicated. It involves either (1) a long-run projection of the sales trend, usually computed by statistical techniques, or (2) a short-run projection (forecasting for only a few months ahead) based upon a seasonal index of sales. The statistical sophistication of long-run trend analysis does not really remove the inherent weakness of basing future estimates only on past sales activity. Short-run trend analysis may be acceptable if the firm's sales follow a reliable seasonal pattern. For example, assume that sales reach 10,000 units in the first quarter (January–March) and, historically, the second quarter is always about 50 percent better. Then we can reasonably forecast sales of 15,000 units in the April–June period.

SALES-FORCE COMPOSITE

This is a buildup method that may be used to forecast sales or to estimate market potential. As used in sales forecasting, it consists of collecting from all sales people and middlemen an estimate of sales in their territories during the forecasting period. The total (the composite) of these separate estimates is the company's sales forecast. This method can be used advantageously if the firm has competent, high-calibre sales people. The method is also useful for firms selling to a market composed of relatively few, but large, customers. Thus, this method would be more applicable to sales of large electrical generators than small general-use motors.

The sales-force composite method takes advantage of the sales people's specialized knowledge of their own market. Also, it should make them more willing to accept their assigned sales quotas. On the other hand, the sales force usually does not have the time or the experience to do the research needed in forecasting future sales.

EXECUTIVE JUDGEMENT

This method covers a wide range of possibilities. Basically, it consists of obtaining opinions regarding future sales volume from one or more executives. If these are really informed opinions, based on valid measures such as market-factor analysis, then the executive judgement is useful and desirable. Certainly all the previously discussed forecasting methods should be tempered with sound executive judgement. On the other hand, forecasting by executive opinion alone is risky. In some instances, such opinions are simply intuition or guesswork.

This ends our discussion of the consumer and industrial markets. Once a company's executives know their market or markets, they are in a position to capture their desired share of those markets. They have the four components of the marketing mix — product, price, distribution system, and promotion — with which to attain that goal. Each of Parts 3 to 6 is devoted to one of these components.

SUMMARY Some form of market segmentation is the strategy that most marketers adopt as a compromise between the extremes of an aggregate, undifferentiated market and a different product tailor-made for each customer. Market segmentation is the process of dividing the total heterogeneous market into several homogeneous segments. Then a separate marketing mix is developed for each segment that the seller selects as a target market. Market segmentation is a customer-oriented philosophy that is consistent with the marketing concept.

Market segmentation enables a company to make more efficient use of its marketing resources. Also, this strategy allows a small company to compete effectively in one or two segments. The main drawback to market segmentation is that it requires higher production and marketing costs than if a one-product, mass-market strategy were used. The requirements for effective segmentation are that (1) the bases for segmentation be measurable with accessible data; (2) the segments themselves be accessible to existing marketing institutions; and (3) the segments be large enough to be potentially profitable.

The total Canadian market may be divided into two broad segments — ultimate consumers and industrial and commercial users. The four broad categories for further segmenting the consumer market are geographic bases, demographic bases, psychographic bases, and product-related bases. Each of these four typically is further divided into several segments. Firms selling to the industrial market may use several of these same bases for segmentation. In addition, the industrial market may be segmented on the bases of type of customer, size of customer, and type of buying situation. Normally, in either the consumer or industrial market, a seller will use a combination of two or more segmentation bases.

There are three alternative segmentation strategies that a marketer can choose from when selecting a target market. The three are market aggregation, single-segment concentration, or multiple segmentation. Market aggregation involves using one marketing mix to reach a mass, undifferentiated market. In single-segment concentration, a company still uses only one marketing mix, but it is directed at only one segment of the total market. The third alternative involves selecting two or more segments and then developing a separate marketing mix to reach each one.

Before deciding on a target market, the company should forecast the demand in the total market and in each segment under consideration. Demand forecasting involves measuring the industry's market potential, then determining the company's sales potential (market share), and finally preparing a sales forecast. The sales forecast is the foundation of all budgeting and operational planning in all major departments of a company. There are several major methods available for forecasting market demand.

NOTES

[1] For the classic article on market segmentation, and one foundation for much of today's research on the subject, see Wendell R. Smith, "Product Differentiation and Market Segmentation as Alternative Marketing Strategies," *Journal of Marketing*, July 1956, pp. 3–8.

[2] John Oldland, "Segmentation: Where Does the Future Lie?" *Marketing*, Vol. 91, No. 20, May 19, 1986, p. 32.

[3] Skip Wollenberg, "Toothpaste Makers Catering to Kids' Market," *The Globe and Mail Report on Business*, January 5, 1988, p. B10.

[4] To help us understand the new segmentation of the women's market, Judith Langer traces the development of the women's movement through five phases, starting with the traditional

premovement phase. See "At Last, Marketers Acknowledge Women's New Role," *Marketing News*, Nov. 8, 1985, p. 45.

[5] See Joseph T. Plummer, "The Concept and Application of Life Style Segmentation," *Journal of Marketing*, January 1974, pp. 33–37.

[6] See Arnold Mitchell, *The Nine American Lifestyles*, Macmillan, New York, 1983. Mitchell was the founding director of the VALS study, an ongoing project sponsored by SRI International, a research firm formerly associated with Stanford University.

[7] Ian Pearson, "Social Studies," *Canadian Business*, December 1985, pp. 67–72.

[8] See Max L. Densmore and Sylvia Kaufman, "How Leading Retailers Stay on Top," *Business*, April–June 1985, pp. 28–35; and Roger D. Blackwell and W. Wayne Talarzyk, "Life-Style Retailing: Competitive Strategies for the 1980s," *Journal of Retailing*, Winter 1983, pp. 7–27.

[9] See Russell J. Haley, "Benefit Segmentation: A Decision Oriented Research Tool," *Journal of Marketing*, July 1963, pp. 30–35. For an update on this classic article and the concept of benefit segmentation, see Haley, "Benefit Segmentation — 20 Years Later," *The Journal of Consumer Marketing*, vol. 1, no. 2, 1983, pp. 5–13.

[10] Victor J. Cook, Jr., and William A. Mindak, "A Search for Constants: The 'Heavy User' Revisited," *The Journal of Consumer Marketing*, vol. 1, no. 4, 1984, pp. 79–81.

[11] For some additional approaches to industrial marketing segmentation, see Benson P. Shapiro and Thomas V. Bonoma, "How to Segment Industrial Markets," *Harvard Business Review*, May–June 1984, pp. 104–110. See also James G. Barnes and Ronald McTavish, "Segmenting Industrial Markets by Buyer Sophistication," *European Journal of Marketing*, vol. 17, no. 6, 1983, pp. 16–33.

[12] For an excellent review of the literature on industrial market segmentation — some 30 articles spanning 20 years — see Richard E. Plank, "A Critical Review of Industrial Market Segmentation," *Industrial Marketing Management*, May 1985, pp. 79–91.

[13] For a series of articles on the practical aspects of test marketing, see Aimée L. Stern, "Test Marketing Enters a New Era," *Dun's Business Month*, October 1985, p. 86; and "Special Report on Test Marketing," *Advertising Age*, Feb. 28, 1985, pp. 15–16ff, and Feb. 13, 1986, pp. 11–12ff.

KEY TERMS AND CONCEPTS

Market segmentation   168
Market aggregation   169
Conditions for effective
  segmentation   170
Bases for consumer market
  segmentation: 171
  Geographic   171
  Demographic   173
  Psychographic   174
  Product-related   175
Bases for segmenting industrial
  markets   176

Market aggregation strategy   177
Product differentiation   178
Single-segment concentration
  strategy   179
Multiple-segment strategy   180
Market factor and market index   181
Market potential   181–182
Sales potential (market
  share)   181–182
Sales forecast   182
Methods of demand
  forecasting   183–186

QUESTIONS AND PROBLEMS

1. Distinguish between market aggregation and market segmentation.

2. What benefits can a company expect to gain from segmenting its market?

3. Explain, with examples, the conditions required for effective market segmentation.

4. a. Select three demographic segmentation bases and then describe your marketing class in terms of these demographic characteristics.

   b. List six products or services for which your marketing class would be a good market segment. Explain your reasoning in each case.

5. Describe what you believe to be the demographic characteristics of heavy users of:
   a. Dog food.
   b. Ready-to-eat cereal.
   c. Videocassette recorders.
   d. Pocket calculators.

6. Explain how the concept of benefit segmentation might be applied by the marketing executives for a symphony orchestra or an art museum.

7. How would you segment the market for copying machines such as Xerox or Canon copiers?

8. Explain the similarities and differences between a single-segment and a multiple-segment target-market strategy.

9. How might the following organizations implement the strategy of market segmentation?
   a. Manufacturer of personal computers.
   b. Canadian Red Cross.
   c. CBC.
   d. Producer of laser-disc style of stereo records.

10. Assume that a company has developed a new type of portable headphone-type cassette player in the general product category of a Sony Walkman. Which of the three target-market strategies should this company adopt?

11. Carefully distinguish between market potential and a sales forecast, using examples of consumer or industrial products.

12. What are some logical market factors that you might use in estimating the market potential for each of the following products?
    a. Central home air conditioners.
    b. Electric milking machines.
    c. Golf clubs.
    d. Sterling flatware.
    e. Safety goggles.

13. How would you determine the market potential for a textbook written for the introductory course in marketing?

14. Explain the direct-derivation method of sales forecasting, using a product example other than automobile tires. How does this forecasting method differ from the correlation-analysis method?

15. What are some of the problems a researcher faces when using the test-market method for determining market potential or sales potential?

CASE 2.1

CN HOTELS INC. (A)
Identifying the Best
Market Opportunity

February 1984 would be a date to remember at CN Hotels. To combat increasing competitive pressure, Brian Richardson, vice president of marketing, decided to embark on a strategy of market segmentation. Realizing that the end consumers who purchased hotel rooms were a very heterogeneous group, this decision to segment the market was an easy one. The more difficult question facing the company, and indeed the real challenge, was to identify and characterize the market segments which represented the best opportunities for CN Hotels.

THE HOTEL INDUSTRY

The hotel industry was dominated by approximately ten companies all with worldwide operations. Because the barriers to entry in the hotel industry were quite high, very few new companies entered this market. However, expansion by existing companies occurred at a relatively fast pace, even though demand for hotel accommodations over the past two or three years was relatively stagnant. This resulted in an increasingly competitive environment in which, because of declining profit margins, hotel companies were forced to undertake strategies which created more economic efficiencies and synergy. As a result, the smaller independent companies were slowly being squeezed out of the marketplace.

Within Canada, a large portion of the market was held by non-Canadian chains, although several Canadian chains, such as Delta Hotels, Four Seasons Hotels, Canadian Pacific Hotels, and Venture Inns, in addition to CN Hotels, did exist. The highly competitive nature of the hotel industry in Canada resulted in a greater amount of retail-type promotions and programs, greatly affecting the industry's profit margins.

CN Hotels Inc. owned and managed a chain of ten hotels and resorts across Canada (see Table 1). The company provided primarily hotel accommodation to the travelling public as well as food service outlets to travellers and local communities.

CN Hotels recognized that in order to remain competitive in this highly competitive industry it was necessary to develop a unique marketing approach. Observation of other industries (such as airlines and consumer product and service companies) revealed that they were pursuing a strategy of increased market segmentation. To adopt such a strategy at CN Hotels, Mr. Richardson knew it would first be necessary to understand the "reasons and methods" the end consumer had for using a hotel room. To obtain this information, CN Hotels undertook a major marketing research study of the travelling public.

This case was prepared by Donna M. Stapleton and is intended to stimulate discussion of an actual management problem and not to illustrate either effective or ineffective handling of that problem. The author wishes to acknowledge the support provided by CN Hotels, and particularly by Brian Richardson, Vice President, and Sandra Diem, Director, System Marketing.

TABLE 1   **CN HOTELS PROPERTIES**

Hotel Name	Location	No. of Rooms	Maximum Capacity for Banquets/ Meetings
Hotel Vancouver	Vancouver	506	1400
Jasper Park Lodge	Jasper	400	1000
The Guild Inn	Toronto	96	150
L'Hotel	Toronto	600	750
Chateau Laurier	Ottawa	448	700
Mont Ste. Marie	Lac Ste. Marie	138	200
The Queen Elizabeth	Montreal	1045	3000
Hotel Beausejour	Moncton	314	1000
Citadel Halifax	Halifax	270	200
Hotel Newfoundland	St. John's	306	1100

THE MARKET RESEARCH STUDY

The market research project began in early 1984, immediately following the decision to segment the market. Information was gathered to identify who the customers were, why they bought and how they bought. To collect this information, consumers were asked to identify the reason for their purchase, as well as the factors influencing the purchase and the method of purchase.

Based on the traveller's reason for purchase, it was found that the total consumer market for hotels could be divided into two segments — the business group and the leisure group. Not surprisingly, data indicated that in Canada 73 percent of hotel stays resulted from business travel and 27 percent from leisure travel.

The data collected further indicated that both the business and leisure markets were heterogeneous. Each was composed of smaller market segments which were similar in the factors influencing the purchase and the method of purchase. The business travel market was found to be composed of three major market segments: the individual business traveller, the largest segment, comprised 55 percent of the total business market; contract business (airline and government staff) comprised 20 percent; and the meetings market accounted for 25 percent (see Table 2). The leisure market was also found to be composed of three major market segments: transient travellers accounted for 42 percent; weekend package vacationers accounted for 28 percent; and tour participants accounted for 12.5 percent. The remaining 17.5 percent were a group of miscellaneous travellers (see Table 3).

After careful study of these research findings, Mr. Richardson determined that the best market opportunity for CN Hotels was the individual business traveller. This market segment was by far the largest, comprising 40 percent of the total market and was also the least price sensitive. Mr. Richardson realized, however, that this segment was in itself quite diverse; the business traveller displayed a number of similarities and differences with respect to needs, value, life-styles, likes/ dislikes, and buying patterns. Further information on these travellers was required to allow CN to specifically tailor its products to reach and satisfy this market.

TABLE 2   BUSINESS MARKET 73%

	Individual 55%	Contract 20%	Meetings Market	
			Small Meeting 5%	Convention 20%
Who decides on purchase	Individual 58% Company 30% Travel agent 4%	Government airline 100%	Meeting Planners 100%	Meeting Planners 100%
Factors influencing purchase	Location Image Quality service	Price Location	Price Quality service Environment hassle-free	Destination Quality service Space Price
Purchase made through	Central reservation 40% Hotel reservation 60%	Sales department	Sales & catering department	Sales department

TABLE 3   LEISURE MARKET 27%

	Weekend Package 28%	Transient 42%	Tour 12.5%
Who decides on purchase	Individual 85% Travel agent 15%	Individual 85% Travel agent 15%	Tour operator 100%
Factors influencing purchase	Product Price	Location Value	Destination Price
Purchase made through	Central reservation 10% Hotel reservation 90%	Central reservation 20% Hotel reservation 80%	Sales department

THE FREQUENT BUSINESS TRAVEL MARKET

To develop an understanding of frequent business travellers, CN Hotels undertook, during the summer of 1984, an in-depth survey of 451 Canadian frequent travellers (those taking at least six business trips per year). The objectives of this study were to determine the demographic and psychographic profiles of frequent business travellers and to establish their preferences, needs, attitudes, and behaviours.

The data showed very clearly who the frequent travellers were. Their demographic profile is given in Table 4. Their attitudes toward staying in a hotel are presented in Table 5. Data also showed that there were some significant differences between the very frequent travellers, those taking at least 30 business trips per year, and the frequent business travellers, those taking at least six trips per year. In general it was found that the very frequent travellers placed less value than frequent travellers on (i) touches such as fruit basket in the room and breakfast included in the price; (ii) elegant dining facilities and 24-hour coffee shop; (iii) indoor swimming pool, sauna, and health club; (iv) availability of photocopier and secretarial services; and

TABLE 4   **WHO ARE THE FREQUENT TRAVELLERS?**

Age:	39% between 35 and 44 70% between 45 and 54 Average: 44 years
Status:	90% married 92% male; 8% female
Family Size:	4.37
Smoking:	72% non-smoking
Occupation:	54% senior management 20% middle management 21% professionals
Personal Income:	28% made $70M+ in 1983 46% made between $35M and $70M
Room Rate Paid:	11% paid $45 or less 25% paid $46 – $55 28% paid $56 – $75 15% paid $76 – $85 9% paid $86 – $99 8% paid $100 +

(v) airport shuttle. On the other hand, these very frequent travellers placed more value on (i) comfort: queen- or king-sized bed; (ii) convenience services: valet parking and newspaper delivery by 7 a.m.; and (iii) frequent guest recognition. A presentation of additional differences is given in Table 6.

The research findings also revealed that there were some behavioural and attitudinal differences among the hotel users based on the price paid for the hotel room. The travellers' preferences toward hotels based on the price paid are given in Table 7 and the psychographic and demographic characteristics are given in Table 8.

RESEARCH CONCLUSIONS

Mr. Richardson carefully studied the research findings; it was clear that there were some similarities and differences among the frequent business travellers. After careful analysis and much thought, he concluded that the business market should be further divided into three sub-segments. The three relatively homogeneous groups he identified were (1) the "Affluent" group, the 5 percent of the market who demanded only the most luxurious accommodations; (2) the "Cost Plus" group, that 10 percent of the market who were willing to pay extra for business class accommodation; and (3) the "No Frills" group, the 85 percent of the market who wanted deluxe accommodation and good service at the corporate rate.

TABLE 5   **FREQUENT TRAVELLERS' ATTITUDES TOWARD STAYING IN A HOTEL (numbers indicate percentage agreeing)**

I like to feel pampered at a hotel	33%
I like to be left alone	61%
I prefer to eat breakfast in my room	21%
I prefer eating breakfast in the coffee shop	76%
I like to eat good plain food in a hotel	70%
I like to eat exotic food	23%
I want a hotel that's ''plain and simple''	28%
I want one with some frills	71%
A hotel should be a home away from home	59%
It should be ritzier	36%
I prefer to be left alone in a hotel	64%
I sometimes like to mingle	33%
I prefer to stay in a bustling hotel	18%
I prefer a calm atmosphere	78%
I like my room set up like an office	18%
I just want a room to relax in	79%
I need my room to be large	39%
I'm content with an average size room	59%
I really use a hotel for work, meeting . . .	27%
A hotel is just somewhere to rest	64%
I enjoy trying different hotels in a city	27%
I find a favourite and stick to it	73%
I prefer to stay at a hotel which is part of a chain	24%
It makes no difference	76%

TABLE 6   **A PROFILE OF THE VERY FREQUENT HOTEL USER COMPARED TO THE FREQUENT HOTEL USER**

	Very frequent traveller (> 30 trips)	Frequent traveller (> 6 trips)
No company policy dictates where you can stay	83%	73%
Company gets a corporate rate	86%	78%
Use room service	35%	29%
Use swimming pool	10%	14%
Use sauna	6%	8%
Use exercise equipment	3%	6%
Price insensitive	38%	26%
Frequent guest recognition	85%	81%

TABLE 7   HOTEL PREFERENCES BY PRICE PAID

	$56–75	$76–85	$86 +
Prefer a chain	25%	28%	24%
Try a different hotel	30%	28%	23%
Find a favourite	70%	71%	76%
Use hotel for meetings	32%	25%	27%
Just place to rest	59%	68%	67%
Need a large room	37%	30%	51%
Prefer room like office	15%	19%	25%
Prefer a calm atmosphere	77%	84%	72%
Prefer a bustling hotel	19%	12%	24%
Prefer to be left alone	65%	65%	70%
Like to mingle	31%	33%	27%
Prefer a hotel that is ritzier than home	33%	43%	42%
Prefer exotic food	23%	16%	34%
Want to be pampered	30%	39%	38%
Prefer a hotel with some frills	65%	72%	89%

TABLE 8   PSYCHOGRAPHIC AND DEMOGRAPHIC CHARACTERISTICS BY PRICE PAID

	$56–75	$76–85	$86 +
Enjoy dynamic environment	69%	80%	89%
Enjoy business travel	45%	54%	48%
Care about fitness	71%	70%	82%
Fascinated with politics	48%	57%	56%
Want to achieve more	51%	52%	63%
Dress fashionably	33%	38%	35%
Enjoy quiet evening home	74%	77%	68%
Price no object when travelling	27%	22%	42%
First to try new product	70%	70%	72%
Mean income	$57,000	$68,000	$69,000
Mean age	45.3	46.0	42.6

QUESTIONS

1. Given the market research data available, did CN Hotels segment the consumer hotel market appropriately? Why or why not?
2. What additional information, if any, do you feel would help to segment this market?
3. From the marketing research information given, identify the criteria and factors important to CN Hotels' target market when choosing the hotel product.

CASE 2.2

The information was in! Jerry White, president of Mother's Restaurants Limited, was looking forward to this morning's management meeting. He was confident that the results of the consumer research gave valuable insight into their consumers' needs. After a year of research and approximately $100,000 spent, Mother's had the information it needed to gain the competitive edge. Mr. White was certain that today, August 5, 1986, would be a day to remember. He looked at his watch — one hour to go — just time enough to review the results once more.

While reviewing the files, Mr. White's mind wandered back to when it all began. Who would have thought that Mother's would become Canada's largest pizza and pasta chain serving 18 million Canadians every year?

Mother's offered a complete line of products including pizza, soups, lasagna, salads, and soups, free of any chemicals, additives, or preservatives. All dough and toppings were produced fresh daily. Nothing was frozen or mass produced. As well, all products were available for home delivery. Mother's had an innovative line of packaging that allowed the entire menu to be "sent out." Mother's was acutely aware of the problems that could occur with staffing and attempted to develop a stable and competent team of employees.

The restaurants were fully serviced, fully licensed units with upwards of 200 seats and 6000 square feet. Management in each unit could decide to have a smoke-free area. Most units were located in urban areas. With 120 units (including two in the United States) and sales in excess of $100 million, constituting 10 percent of the entire industry, the company had an admirable record. Unfortunately, past accomplishment was no guarantee of future success.

It was well known that although the food service and hospitality sector was one of the fastest growing business sectors, it was also one of the most volatile and competitive. In fact, it appeared that the competition was increasing. In Canada, other pizza chains including Pizza Pizza and Pizza Delight were competing with Mother's for the same market. As well, Mother's was competing with chains positioned against them such as Swiss Chalet and Ponderosa. Compounding this problem was the fact that the United States' chains were making major inroads into Canada — Pizza Hut, Domino's, Little Caesar's, and Red Lobster. Identifying a market niche through proper positioning would allow Mother's to keep in tune with changing consumer needs.

Mr. White smiled. With the consumer research, Mother's could select its positioning strategy. Looking at the final report, he was impressed with the results. He admitted that he had shown scepticism about the preliminary findings. The sheer volume of information had been intimidating.

Information had been collected by independent consultants through in-depth consumer research studies, focus groups, telephone interviews, and in-home interviews. Mr. White remembered how some of the management had questioned the need for such extensive means of data collection. He was confident that the findings would erase any doubts.

This case was prepared by Lynn Morrissey and is intended to stimulate discussion of an actual management problem, and not to illustrate either effective or ineffective handling of that problem. The author wishes to acknowledge the support provided by Mother's Restaurants, and particularly by Jerry White, President.

A major component of the research involved determining usage and attitudes towards the restaurant sector in general (mainly with respect to family-style restaurants) and Mother's in particular. For this component, 400 telephone interviews were conducted in the Toronto metropolitan area.

The research determined that in the past six months, almost 40 percent of the respondents had eaten at a restaurant for either lunch or dinner more than once a week. The percentage of usage by age is given in Table 1. Mr. White remembered the fact that no significant differences in usage were shown between male and female.

TABLE 1   % WHO ATE IN ANY RESTAURANT IN THE LAST THREE MONTHS BY AGE (n = 301)

	18–24	25–34	35–44	45–59	60+
Daily	4.6	9.2	25.1	5.1	0.0
Several times a week	22.2	38.7	31.0	21.5	32.3
Once a week	30.6	25.6	18.9	24.7	42.2
A few times a month	16.7	13.1	5.9	18.6	0.0
About once a month	26.0	13.5	19.2	30.1	25.5

Source: Ronald Rotenberg and Associates Canada Ltd. 1986. "Image Study of Mother's Restaurants," p. 15.

Anyone not eating in a restaurant at least once a month was eliminated from the study. Sixty-eight percent of those in the study were found to be heavy users (more than once a month) of family-style restaurants (restaurants that have an average menu price between $5 and $7 and that welcome and cater to children). This fact pleased Mr. White as Mother's was considered to be in this category. By age, the percentage of heavy users is shown in Table 2.

TABLE 2   % OF HEAVY USERS OF FAMILY-STYLE RESTAURANTS BY AGE (n = 206)

	18–24	25–34	35–44	45–59	60+
Percentage heavy users	51.2%	77.8%	78.4%	62.2%	74.5%

Source: Ronald Rotenberg and Associates Canada Ltd. 1986. "Image Study of Mother's Restaurants," p. 21.

Knowing that customers frequented family-style restaurants, Mr. White had asked the consultants to determine the respondent's unaided top-of-mind awareness of restaurants in this category. Responses showed that Swiss Chalet had the most first mentions (25.6 percent) followed by Ponderosa (11.6 percent). Mother's was rated first by 4.4 percent. This low top-of-mind awareness had bothered Mr. White. His anxiety was reduced somewhat by the fact that 97.9 percent had heard of Mother's. As well, Pizza Hut had received only a 0.7 percent unaided top-of-mind awareness rating.

Responses on actual patronage of family-style restaurants indicated that 3.7 percent went to Mother's most often as compared to 24.4 percent for Swiss Chalet, 4.6 percent for Ponderosa, and 1.6 percent for Pizza Hut.

Mr. White was particularly interested in the factors identified as important ones when choosing a family-style restaurant. Table 3 ranks these factors according to respondents' age. Mr. White noted that across all ages the desire for "high quality food" had been rated as the most important; however, the percentage weighting within each age bracket differed. As well, additional information gleaned from personal interviews showed that the majority of those interviewed perferred to eat in the no-smoking section and also liked home delivery.

TABLE 3   MOST IMPORTANT FACTOR WHEN CHOOSING A FAMILY-STYLE RESTAURANT BY AGE (n = 300)

	18–24	25–34	35–44	45–59	60+
Serves high quality food	27.1	37.6	41.3	53.1	24.5
Has good tasting food	13.7	22.3	12.5	18.8	24.3
Is a clean restaurant	25.1	14.2	20.9	25.4	8.8
Provides good value for money	10.6	15.9	12.8	2.6	7.8
Has a wide variety of foods	10.4	2.4	6.1	0.0	16.7
Staff gives good service	8.3	7.6	6.4	0.0	7.8
Is licensed to serve liquor	4.7	0.0	0.0	0.0	7.8

Source: Ronald Rotenberg and Associates Canada Ltd. 1986. "Image Study of Mother's Restaurants," p. 103.

Respondents had also been asked to rate Mother's, Pizza Hut, and Swiss Chalet according to their strengths on these important factors. Table 4 highlights the responses. Mr. White was bothered that Mother's had low ratings in the "strongly agree" categories. He would have liked these ratings to be higher.

TABLE 4   RATING OF MOTHER'S, PIZZA HUT, AND SWISS CHALET ON VARIOUS FACTORS

	Mother's		Pizza Hut		Swiss Chalet	
	Strongly Agree	Agree	Strongly Agree	Agree	Strongly Agree	Agree
Serves high quality food	2.9	59.9	6.3	49.3	15.9	62.6
Has good tasting food	5.8	66.0	5.7	55.1	15.8	70.8
Is a clean restaurant	6.5	75.4	10.2	60.9	21.3	73.3
Provides good value for money	5.9	68.5	6.5	62.4	20.2	74.5
Has a wide variety of foods	3.2	51.9	1.3	30.3	0.0	18.2
Staff gives good service	7.4	67.4	6.0	54.2	7.5	79.0

Source: Ronald Rotenberg and Associates Canada Ltd. 1986. "Image Study of Mother's Restaurants," pp. 104, 108, 112.

Through the research, the distinct characteristics of Mother's users were identified. Generally, it was found that a large number of Mother's users were out of the house a lot, liked simple, relaxed social occasions, liked to try new things, were not really careful with their money, and were personally involved in active sports. Interestingly, when these user characteristics were compared with those of non-users, very few differences between the two groups were shown. For Mr. White, this fact was quite encouraging.

Mr. White looked at his watch — time to go! He rose slowly from his chair, his mind still on the research findings. With this information, target markets could be identified and marketing strategies could be designed properly. With confidence, Mr. White entered the board room.

QUESTIONS

1. Which segmentation variables are of most importance to Mother's? Based on these variables, what market segment(s) would you identify as the target(s) for Mother's?
2. Given the market research data, what positioning strategy is most appropriate? Why?
3. How should Mother's implement its repositioning strategy?
4. What is the marketing problem which the marketing research was designed to resolve? What additional information is needed, if any, to resolve Mother's marketing problem?

CASE 2.3

BOOKENDS, LIMITED*

PLANNING A MARKETING
RESEARCH PROJECT

Late one August morning, Katie Martin, co-owner of Bookends, Limited, sat at her desk near the back wall of her cluttered office. With some irritation, she had just concluded that the calculator on her desk could help no more. "What we still need," she thought, "are estimates of demand and market share . . . but at least we have two weeks to get them."

Martin's office was located at the rear of Bookends, a 200-square-metre bookstore specializing in quality paperbacks. The store carried over 10,000 titles and had sold more than $600,000 worth of books in 1988. Titles were stocked in 18 categories ranging from art, biography, and cooking to religion, sports, and travel.

Bookends was located in a small strip shopping centre, across the street from the main entrance of Prairie University (PU). The university had a student population of approximately 10,000 students, enrolled in arts and science programs and in a number of professional schools (including Business, Engineering, Social Work, and Education). Despite downward trends in enrolment in many Canadian universities, the PU admissions office had predicted that the number of students entering first year would grow at about 1 percent a year until the mid 1990s. The city in which PU was located, with a population of approximately 150,000, was expected to grow at about twice that rate.

*This case was adapted by James G. Barnes from a case originally developed by James E. Nelson. Used with permission.

Bookends carried no textbooks, even though many of its customers were PU students. Both Martin and her partner, Susan Campbell, felt that the PU campus bookstore had too firm a grip on the textbook market in terms of price, location, and reputation to allow Bookends to make any inroads into that market. Bookends also carried no classical records. They had been part of the regular stock of the store until two months earlier, when that area of the store was converted to an expanded fitness and nutrition section. Martin recalled with some discomfort the $15,000 or so they had lost on classical records. "Another mistake like that and the bank will end up running Bookends," she thought. "And, despite what Susan thinks, the photocopy service could just be that final mistake."

The idea for a photocopy service had come from Susan Campbell. She had seen the candy store next door to Bookends go out of business in July. She had immediately asked the owner of the shopping centre, Angus Anderson, about the future of the 80-square-metre space. Upon learning it was available, she had met with Martin to discuss her idea for the photocopy service. She had spoken excitedly about the opportunity: "It can't help but make money. I could work there part-time and the rest of the time we could hire students. We could call it 'Copycats' and even use a sign with the same type of letters as we do in 'Bookends.' I'm sure we could get Angus to knock out the wall between the two stores, if you think it would be a good idea. Probably we could rent most of the copying equipment, so there's not much risk."

Martin was not so sure. A conversation yesterday with Anderson had disclosed his preference for a five-year lease (with an option to renew) at $1,000 per month. He had promised to hold the offer open for two weeks before attempting to lease the space to anyone else. Representatives from copying equipment suppliers had estimated that charges would run between $200 and $2,000 per month, depending on equipment, service, and whether the equipment was bought or leased. The photocopy service would also incur other fixed costs — utility expenses, interest, and insurance. Further, Bookends would have to invest a sizeable sum in fixtures and inventory (and possibly equipment). Martin concluded that the service would begin to make a profit at about 20,000 copies per month under best-case assumptions, and at about 60,000 copies per month under the worst-case scenario.

Further formal investigation had identified two major competitors. One was the copy centre located in the university library on the west side of the campus, about a kilometre away. The other was a private firm, Goodland's Stationery, located on the northern boundary of the campus, also about a kilometre from Bookends. Both offered service "while you wait," on several copying machines. The library's price was about $1/2$ cent per copy higher than Goodland's. Both offered collating, binding, colour copying, and other services. The library copying centre was open seven days a week; Goodland's was closed on Sundays.

Actually, Martin had discovered in talking with a number of students and faculty members that a third major "competitor" consisted of the photocopying machines scattered throughout the university's various departments and faculties. Most faculty and administrative copying was done on these machines, but students were also allowed the use of some, at cost. In addition, at least 20 self-service coin-operated copying machines were located on campus in the library, the student centre, and several other buildings.

Moving aside a stack of books on her desk, Katie Martin picked up the telephone and dialled her partner. When Campbell answered, Martin asked, ''Susan, do you know how many copies a student might make in a semester? I mean, according to my figures, we would break even somewhere between 20,000 and 60,000 copies per month. I don't know if this is half the market or what.''

''You know, I have no idea,'' Campbell answered. ''I suppose when I was going to university I probably made 10 copies a month — for articles, class notes, old exams, and so on.''

''Same here,'' Martin said. ''But some of the graduate students I knew made at least that many copies each week. I think we ought to do some marketing research before we go much farther with this. What do you think?''

''Sure. But we can't afford to spend much time or money on it. What do you have in mind, Katie?''

''Well, we could easily interview our customers as they leave the store and ask them how many copies they have made in the past week or so. Of course, we would have to make sure they were students.''

''What about a telephone survey?'' Campbell asked. ''That way we can have a random sample. We would still ask about the number of copies, but now we would know for sure that they were students.''

''Or, what about interviewing students in the cafeteria in the student centre? There's always a large crowd there at lunchtime, and that would be even quicker.''

''I just don't know,'' Campbell replied. ''Why don't I come in this afternoon? We can talk about it some more.''

''Good idea,'' Martin responded. ''Between the two of us, we should be able to come up with something.''

QUESTIONS

1. What sources of information should Martin and Campbell use?
2. How should Martin and Campbell collect the information they need?
3. What questions should they ask?
4. How should they select a sample of people to interview?

CASE 2.4

THE IMPERIAL PROVINCIAL BANK OF CANADA
Targeting a New Service to the Rural Consumer

Frank Smith, assistant vice president of marketing for the Imperial Provincial Bank of Canada (IPBC), was wondering whether his bank should offer a new service to customers living in more rural areas. Two months ago, a proposal concerning the new service had been made to the bank's new product committee, of which Mr. Smith is chairman. Since then, there has been much discussion and many differing opinions expressed on whether or not the service should be offered by the IPBC.

The Imperial Provincial Bank of Canada is one of Canada's smaller domestic

---

This case was prepared by James G. Barnes and is intended to stimulate discussion of an actual management problem, and not to illustrate either effective or ineffective handling of that problem.

(Schedule A) banks. It has been a regional bank, with its base in Western Canada, but recently opened a number of branches in Ontario. The senior management of the IPBC intended that the bank would eventually be national in scope, with branches in Quebec and the Atlantic region as well. Since its establishment in the 1950s, the IPBC has served primarily the farming communities of the three Prairie provinces, although it opened branches in Vancouver and Victoria in the late 1960s. It currently has 43 branches in Western Canada and three in Ontario.

The proposed new service would involve the IPBC entering into agency contracts with retail convenience stores throughout its territory, with a view to having the stores offer certain services to IPBC customers. Mr. Smith thought of the idea as being something like franchising, whereby the bank would contract with the small retailers to deliver services in areas where the bank did not have a branch and at times when IPBC's branches were not open. He also thought of this as a way to get some of the advantages of automated teller machines to people who did not have access to these machines.

The bank's customers who wished to use the new service would be issued a card that looked like a credit card, but had the photograph of the account holder printed right on the card. It could be used as identification for cheque cashing at branches of the bank and at retail stores. More importantly, the card could be used at any of the bank's convenience store "agency" branches throughout the three Prairie provinces. In time, Frank thought that the IPBC could license as many as 200 retail stores as agencies. At these convenience stores, many of which would be open 24 hours a day, customers could withdraw cash up to a certain pre-determined limit and could pay their utility bills. To be eligible for this identification card, a customer of the bank would have to maintain both a chequing and a savings account with the bank. There would be a charge added to the customer's monthly statement for each transaction involving use of the "agency" card.

The manufacture of the card required a Polaroid photograph of the account holder which was then transferred to the surface of the card by a patented process. The card also had a magnetic strip on the back, similar to many credit cards. The operations department of the bank had completed a cost study that indicated that the cost of producing the card was approximately $8. This cost did not include floor space requirements in the bank's branches for the photograph to be taken or the time of IPBC staff to collect customer information on an application form and to take the photograph.

Fred Blake, vice president of the bank's mortgage division, liked the idea of the new service, but suggested that customers be charged $5 or $10 for the card. Emily Gorman, the bank's director of customer service, raised some questions about the market for the new service. She asked whether the primary target market was present customers, or whether the bank intended to use the "agency" service as a promotional device to attract new customers. She also did not like the idea of requiring the holder of an "agency" card to have both a chequing and a savings account at the IPBC. "And one more thing," said Ms. Gorman, "if we are going to offer this new service, then let's do it right. That means we first have to come up with a catchy name for it."

Frank Smith realized that the Imperial Provincial Bank of Canada was a relatively small player in the extremely competitive Canadian banking industry. He also knew that other financial institutions were quite capable of matching any new competitive device that IPBC might introduce. He wondered whether the bank's customers even needed a service such as this, considering the many innovations that have been made in retail banking in recent years. He also wondered whether his bank was in a position to take a lead in new product introductions in its market.

Finally, he realized that the bank's operations people would still have to undertake a cost-benefit study to determine the economic feasibility of contracting with convenience stores to deliver the new service. In the meantime, the new product committee had been asked to consider the concept and to get back to the vice president of marketing with a recommendation on whether the bank should proceed to the next stage of having the feasibility study done. The vice president had asked Mr. Smith to let him have the committee's recommendations today so that he might consider them before the next meeting of the senior management group at the end of next week.

QUESTIONS

1. Should the new product development committee of the Imperial Provincial Bank of Canada recommend that the bank proceed with further study into the introduction of the proposed "agency" store service? Why?
2. Assuming your decision is "yes," then:
   a. what information should be collected in order to allow a final decision to be made concerning the launch of the new service?
   b. what, in your opinion, are the major factors that the senior management group of the bank should consider in deciding whether or not to establish the new service?
3. If a decision is made to proceed with the introduction of the new "agency" service through convenience stores:
   a. what should the bank call its new service?
   b. should there be a charge for the card and, if so, how much?
   c. to whom should the service be promoted?
   d. should the "agency" card holder be required to maintain both a chequing and a savings account at the bank? Should there be other criteria?

PART 3

THE PRODUCT

The planning, development, and management of the want-satisfying goods and services that are a company's products

Part 2 was concerned with using information for the selection and identification of target markets in accordance with the firm's marketing goals. The next step in the strategic marketing planning process is to develop a marketing mix that will achieve these goals in the selected target markets. The marketing mix is a strategic combination of four variables — the organization's product, pricing structure, distribution system, and promotional program. Each of these is closely interrelated with the other three variables in the mix.

Part 3, consisting of three chapters, is devoted to the product phase of the marketing mix. In Chapter 8 we define the term *product*, consider the importance of product planning and innovation, and discuss the new-product development process. Chapter 9 deals mainly with product-mix strategies, the management of the product life cycle, and a consideration of style and fashion. Chapter 10 is concerned with branding, packaging, labelling, and other product features.

CHAPTER 8

PRODUCT PLANNING AND DEVELOPMENT

This chapter will show you why "building a better mousetrap" is *not* enough to ensure success. After studying this chapter, you should understand:

- The meaning of the word *product* in its fullest sense.
- What a "new" product is.
- The classification of consumer and industrial products.
- The relevance of these product classifications to marketing strategy.
- The nature and characteristics of services.
- The importance of product innovation.
- The steps in the product-development process.
- The criteria for adding a product to a company's line.
- The new-product adoption and diffusion processes.
- Organizational structures for new-product planning and development.

206

For years, Fishery Products International (FPI) and many other companies in Canada's east coast fishing industry were considered to be marginally successful, production oriented, and focussed primarily on exporting raw fish to the large United States market. All that has changed in recent years, as FPI has emerged as an innovative, consumer-driven marketer of seafood to Canadian and export markets.

The success of Fishery Products International in the last half of the 1980s results in part from environmental factors and from certain strategic decisions made by senior management. The United States market for seafood became increasingly attractive in recent years as growing consumer awareness of the nutritional value of fish products created strong demand and higher prices for the products which FPI and other Canadian seafood exporters could supply to the U.S. market. Per capita consumption of seafood in the U.S. increased by 24 percent from 1982 to 1988, to 15.3 pounds annually.

In addition, the management group at FPI, under chairman Vic Young, took steps to increase the volume of the company's products exported in finished-product, ready-to-serve form. As a result, considerable emphasis was placed on new product development, resulting in FPI becoming the largest foreign supplier of seafood to the U.S. market in 1987 and the selection of its "Cajun Style Scrod" as new product of the year. It was the third time in four years that FPI products had earned that award.

Fishery Products International continues to develop and introduce new seafood products for export to the growing U.S. market. At the same time, the company has expanded its line of products sold to Canadian retail and food-service companies and its private-label products, which are produced for such quality-conscious retailers as Loblaws and Marks and Spencer. The company's most exciting marketing opportunity for the future lies in Japan, where per capita consumption of seafood is the highest in the world, five times the U.S. level. Eleven new frozen fish products were developed to meet Japanese tastes and were launched in 1988 through a marketing arrangement with Nichiro Gyogyo Kaisha, a leading Japanese seafood company.

As Fishery Products International shifts its new product strategy, two points stand out. First, the most senior levels of management within the company are committed to and involved in product innovation. This is an absolutely essential ingredient for success with new products. Second, the product planning component of the marketing mix is a difficult, complex task, requiring intimate knowledge of markets, both domestic and export.

THE MEANING OF PRODUCT

In a very *narrow* sense, a product is a set of tangible physical attributes assembled in an identifiable form. Each product carries a commonly understood descriptive (or generic) name, such as apples, steel, or baseball bats. Product attributes appealing to consumer motivation or buying patterns play no part in this narrow definition. A Cuisinart and a La Machine are one and the same product — a food processor.

A *broader* interpretation recognizes each *brand* as a separate product. In this sense an Eaton's man's suit and a Tip Top man's suit are two different products. Lantic sugar and St. Lawrence sugar are also separate products, even though their only tangible difference may be the brand name on the package. But the brand name suggests a product difference to the consumer, and this brings the concept of consumer want-satisfaction into the definition.

Any change in a physical feature (design, colour, size, packaging), however minor it may be, creates another product. Each such change provides the seller with an opportunity to use a new set of appeals to reach what essentially may be a new market. Pain relievers (Tylenol, Anacin) in capsule form are a different product from the same brand in tablet form, even though the chemical contents of the tablet and the capsule are identical.

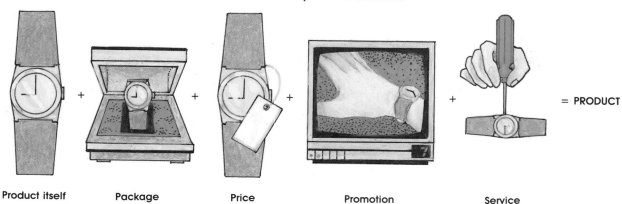

Product itself   +   Package   +   Price   +   Promotion   +   Service   = PRODUCT

We can broaden this interpretation still further. A Panasonic television set bought in a discount store on a cash-and-carry basis is a different product from the identical model purchased in a department store. In the department store, the customer pays a higher price for the TV set. But he buys it on credit, has it delivered free of extra charge, and receives other store services. Our concept of a product now includes services accompanying the sale, and we are close to a definition that is valuable to marketing people.

Our traditional definition is as follows: A **product** is a set of tangible and intangible attributes, including packaging, colour, price, manufacturer's prestige, retailer's prestige, and manufacturer's and retailer's services.

But the key idea in this definition is that the consumers are buying more than a set of physical attributes. Fundamentally, they are buying want-satisfaction. Thus, a wise firm sells **benefits** rather than just products. As Elmer Wheeler, an author and sales training consultant, said, "Don't sell the steak, sell the sizzle."

Our "Product" May Not Be a Product

Actually the "product" being sold by a company to provide benefits and customer want-satisfaction may not be a physical, tangible article at all. Within our brand definition, a product may be a service, a place, a person, or an idea.

As we indicated in earlier chapters of this book, the entertainment provided by a sports team such as the Calgary Flames is a product. The Delta Hotels' product is a service that provides the benefit of a comfortable night's rest in a pleasant room, with good service, at a reasonable price. The product of the Prince Edward Island Tourism Department is an attractive tourist destination that provides relaxation, sun and sand, attractions for children, theatre and other entertainment, and lobster suppers in church halls. In a political campaign, the products of the Progressive Conservative, Liberal, and New Democratic parties are their candidates and the platforms that they put forth. The Canadian Cancer Society is selling the idea and benefits of not smoking. Throughout this entire book, when we speak of *products*, we intend that the term be used broadly.

What Is a "New" Product?

Just what is a "new" product? Are the new models that auto manufacturers introduce each autumn new products? If a firm adds a wrinkle-remover cream to its assortment of women's cosmetics, is this a new product? Or must an item be totally new in concept before we can class it as a *new* product?

File 8-1

Users Think Benefits, Producers Think Features, Marketers Think Both

A product is more than its tangible, obvious features. It is, in fact, a means to an end. When we buy sandpaper, we don't want sandpaper; we want a smooth surface. We don't want a 1/4-inch drill; we want a 1/4-inch hole. We don't buy a car, we buy a means of transportation, which also offers many other benefits.

So the challenge to the marketer is to tell us what the product can do for us — what the end benefits are.

- Calvin Klein, Lee, and GWG jeans are not items of clothing. They are a sex symbol and a fashion status symbol.
- Labatt's Blue beer isn't a beer. It's a blue-collar macho symbol.
- Visa and American Express cards are not credit cards that let you charge what you buy. They are a security blanket.
- Canada's Wonderland is not simply an amusement park with rides and shows. It is an escape from reality.
- West Edmonton Mall is not a shopping centre. It is a multi-faceted experience.
- Birks is not a chain of jewellery stores. It is a place that takes the risk out of buying diamonds and lets you buy with confidence.
- Dinner at a fine restaurant isn't just a meal. It's . . .

A "product" may be an idea or a social cause.

Here, we need not seek a very limited definition. Instead, we can recognize several possible categories of new products. What is important, however, is that each separate category may require a quite different marketing program to ensure a reasonable probability of success.

Three recognizable categories of *new products* are as follows:

- Products that are *really* innovative — truly unique. Examples would be a hair restorer or a cancer cure — products for which there is a real need but for which no existing substitutes are considered satisfactory. In this category we can also include products that are quite different from existing products but satisfy the same needs. Thus, microwave ovens compete with conventional ovens and solar power competes with other energy sources.
- Replacements for existing products that are *significantly* different from the existing goods. For many people instant coffee replaced ground coffee and coffee beans; then freeze-dried instant replaced instant coffee. Compact-disc players are replacing conventional stereo records and players. Automatic 35 mm cameras and cordless telephones are replacing some traditional models. In some years annual model changes in autos and new fashions in clothing are different enough to fit into this category.
- Imitative products that are new to a particular company but not new to the market. The company simply wants to capture part of an existing market with a "me-too" product.

Perhaps the key criterion as to whether a given product or service is new is how the intended market perceives it. If buyers perceive that a given item or service is significantly different (from what is being replaced) in some characteristic or benefit (appearance, performance), then it is a new product or service.

CLASSIFICATION OF PRODUCTS

Just as it is necessary to segment markets to improve the marketing programs in many firms, so also it is helpful to separate *products* into homogeneous classification. First we shall divide all products into two groups — consumer goods and industrial goods — in a classification that parallels our segmentation of the market.

STILL TO COME

Woods, Gordon, a leading Canadian firm of management consultants, predict that these products and services will represent growth areas over the next ten years or so.

■ *Upscale baby products*: "posture perfect" baby strollers, designer baby clothes, sophisticated toys.

■ *"Make it snappy" products*: designed to reduce the time it takes to do household chores; built-in vacuum systems, cleaning and gardening services.

■ *Quality above all*: move toward higher-priced quality merchandise; upscale kitchen and laundry appliances, extended warranties, luxury and exotic foods.

■ *More "fad" and "technology as toy" products*: demand for novelty will result in products with short life cycles, more home entertainment centres.

■ *Customized products*: increasing fragmentation of the market will lead to the ultimate segmentation, custom clothing, shoes, programmable electronics.

■ *Re-emergence of style*: a return to products with flair, convertible cars, clothing, hairstyles, designer appliances.

Source: Woods Gordon, *Tomorrow's Customers*, 21st edition, 1987, p. 10.

Then we shall divide each of these two product categories still further. In the section that follows, we will highlight the unique characteristics of services.

Consumer Goods and Industrial Goods

Consumer goods are products intended for use by ultimate household consumers for nonbusiness purposes. **Industrial goods** are products intended to be sold primarily for use in producing other goods or for rendering services in a business. The fundamental basis for distinguishing between the two groups is the *ultimate use* for which the product is intended in its present form.

Particular stages in a product's distribution have no effect upon its classification. Cornflakes and children's shoes are classed as consumer products, even if they are in the manufacturer's warehouse or on retailer's shelves, *if ultimately they will be used in their present form by household consumers*. Cornflakes sold to restaurants and other institutions, however, are classed as industrial goods.

Often it is not possible to place a product only in one class or the other. A personal computer may be considered a consumer good if it is purchased by a student or a homemaker for nonbusiness use. But if the computer is bought by a travelling sales representative for business use, it is classed with industrial goods. The manufacturer of such a product recognizes that the product falls into both categories and therefore develops separate marketing programs for the two markets.

The two-way product classification is a useful framework for the strategic planning of marketing operations. Each major class of products ultimately goes to a different type of market and thus requires different marketing methods.

Classification of Consumer Products

The marketing differences between consumer and industrial goods make this two-part classification of products valuable. Yet, the range of consumer goods is still too broad for a single class. Consequently, consumer products are further classified as convenience goods, shopping goods, specialty goods, and unsought goods. (See Table 8-1.) This subdivision is based on consumer *buying habits* rather than on *types of products*.

TABLE 8-1   CHARACTERISTICS OF CLASSES OF CONSUMER PRODUCTS AND SOME MARKETING CONSIDERATIONS

Characteristics and marketing considerations	Type of product*		
	Convenience	Shopping	Specialty
Characteristics:			
1. Time and effort devoted by consumer to shopping	Very little	Considerable	Cannot generalize; consumer may go to nearby store and buy with minimum effort or may have to go to distant store and spend much time and effort
2. Time spent planning and purchase	Very little	Considerable	Considerable
3. How soon want is satisfied after it arises	Immediately	Relatively long time	Relatively long time
4. Are price and quality compared?	No	Yes	No
5. Price	Low	High	High
6. Frequency of purchase	Usually frequent	Infrequent	Infrequent
7. Importance	Unimportant	Often very important	Cannot generalize
Marketing considerations:			
1. Length of channel	Long	Short	Short to very short
2. Importance of retailer	Any single store is relatively unimportant	Important	Very important
3. Number of outlets	As many as possible	Few	Few; often only one in a market
4. Stock turnover	High	Lower	Lower
5. Gross margin	Low	High	High
6. Responsibility for advertising	Manufacturer's	Retailer's	Joint responsibility
7. Importance of point-of-purchase display	Very important	Less important	Less important
8. Advertising used	Manufacturer's	Retailer's	Both
9. Brand or store name important	Brand name	Store name	Both
10. Importance of packaging	Very important	Less important	Less important

*Unsought products are not included. See text explanation.

CONVENIENCE GOODS

The significant characteristics of convenience goods are (1) that the consumer has complete knowledge of the particular product wanted *before* going out to buy it and (2) that the product is purchased with a minimum of effort. Normally, the gain resulting from shopping around to compare price and quality is not considered worth the extra time and effort required. A consumer is willing to accept any of several brands and thus will buy the one that is most accessible. For most buyers, this subclass of goods includes groceries, tobacco products, inexpensive candy, drug sundries, such as toothpaste, and staple hardware items such as light bulbs and batteries.

Convenience goods typically have a low unit price, are not bulky, and are not greatly affected by fad and fashion. Convenience goods usually are purchased

Many people like to shop around for shoes.

frequently, although this is not a necessary characteristic. Items such as Christmas-tree lights or Mother's Day cards are convenience goods for most people, even though they may be bought only once a year.

Marketing considerations   A convenience good must be readily accessible when the consumer demand arises so the manufacturer must secure wide distribution. But, since most retail stores sell only a small volume of the manufacturer's output, it is not economical to sell directly to all retail outlets. Instead, the producer relies on wholesalers to reach part of the retail market.

The promotional strategies of both the manufacturer and the retailer are involved here. Retailers typically carry several brands of a convenience item, so they are not able to promote any single brand. They are not interested in doing much advertising of these articles because many other stores carry them. Thus, any advertising by one retailer may help its competitors. As a result, virtually the entire advertising burden is shifted to the manufacturer.

SHOPPING GOODS

Shopping goods are products for which customers usually wish to compare quality, price, and style in several stores before purchasing. This search continues only as long as the customer believes that the gain from comparing products offsets the additional time and effort required. Examples of shopping goods include women's apparel, furniture, major appliances, and used cars.

Marketing considerations   The buying habits that consumers demonstrate in the purchase of shopping goods affect the distribution and promotional strategy of both manufacturers and middlemen. Manufacturers of shopping goods require fewer retail outlets because consumers are willing to look around a bit for what they want. To increase the convenience of comparison shopping, manufacturers try to place their products in stores located near other stores carrying competing items. Similarly, department stores and other retailers who carry primarily shopping goods like to be bunched together.

Manufacturers usually work closely with retailers in the marketing of shopping goods. Since manufacturers use fewer retail outlets, they are more dependent upon those they do select. Retail stores typically buy shopping goods in large quantities. Thus, distribution direct from manufacturer to retailer is common. Finally, store names often are more important to buyers of shopping goods than are manufacturers' names. This is true particularly for items such as some wearing apparel, where the average customer often does not know or care who made the product.

SPECIALTY GOODS

Specialty goods are those products for which consumers have a *strong* brand preference and are willing to expend special time and effort in purchasing them. The consumer is willing to forgo more accessible substitutes in order to obtain the wanted brand, even though this may require a significant expenditure of time and effort. Examples of products usually classified as specialty goods include expensive men's suits, stereo sound equipment, health foods, photographic equipment, and, for many people, new automobiles and certain home appliances.

For some people an auto is a specialty product.

Marketing considerations   Since consumers *insist* on a particular brand and are willing to expend considerable effort to find it, manufacturers can afford to use fewer outlets. Ordinarily, the manufacturer deals directly with these retailers. The retailers are extremely important, particularly if the manufacturer uses only one in each area. And, where the franchise to handle the product is a valuable one, the retailer may become quite dependent upon the producer. Thus, they are interdependent; the success of one is closely tied to the success of the other.

Because brand is important and because only a few outlets are used, both the manufacturer and the retailer advertise the product extensively. Often the manufacturer pays some portion of the retailer's advertising costs, and the retailer's name frequently appears in the manufacturer's advertisements.

UNSOUGHT GOODS

The very title of this category suggests a somewhat unusual type of product that does not parallel the three categories already discussed. For this reason we did not try to include unsought goods in Table 8-1.

There are two types of unsought products: (1) new products that the consumer is not yet aware of and (2) products that right now the consumer does not want. For some people, products in the first group might include disposable cameras, computers that speak, cellular telephones, or methanol as a fuel for autos. Examples of the second type of product might include prepaid burial insurance, gravestones, and foreign vacations.

The title of this product category also suggests that a seller faces a monumental advertising and personal selling job when trying to market these products.

Classification of
Industrial Products

As was the case with consumer products, the general category "industrial products" is too broad to use in developing a marketing program. The practices used in marketing the various industrial goods are just too different. Consequently, we separate industrial goods into five categories: raw materials, fabricating materials and parts, installations, accessory equipment, and operating supplies. (See Table 8-2.) This classification is based on the broad *uses* of the product.

RAW MATERIALS

Raw materials are industrial goods that will become part of another physical product. They have not been processed in any way, except as necessary for economy or protection during physical handling. Raw materials include (1) goods found in their natural state, such as minerals, land, and products of the forests and the seas; and (2) agricultural products, such as wheat, potatoes, fruits, vegetables, livestock, and animal products — eggs and raw milk. These two groups of raw materials are marketed quite differently.

Clay is an industrial raw material.

Marketing considerations   The marketing of raw materials in their natural state is influenced by several factors. The supply of these products is limited and cannot be substantially increased. Usually only a few large producers are involved. The products must be carefully graded and, consequently, are highly standardized. Because of their great bulk, their low unit value, and the long distance between producer and industrial user, transportation is an important consideration.

These factors necessitate short channels of distribution and a minimum of physical

TABLE 8-2   CLASSES OF INDUSTRIAL PRODUCTS: SOME CHARACTERISTICS AND MARKETING CONSIDERATIONS

Characteristics and marketing considerations	Type of product				
	Raw materials	Fabricating parts and materials	Installations	Accessory equipment	Operating supplies
Example:	Iron ore	Engine blocks	Blast furnaces	Storage racks	Paper clips
Characteristics:					
1. Unit price	Very low	Low	Very high	Medium	Low
2. Length of life	Very short	Depends on final product	Very long	Long	Short
3. Quantities purchased	Large	Large	Very small	Small	Small
4. Frequency of purchase	Frequent delivery; long-term purchase contract	Infrequent purchase, but frequent delivery	Very infrequent	Medium frequency	Frequent
5. Standardization of competitive products	Very much; grading is important	Very much	Very little; custom-made	Little	Much
6. Limits on supply	Limited; supply can be increased slowly or not at all	Usually no problem	No problem	Usually no problem	Usually no problem
Marketing considerations:					
1. Nature of channel	Short; no middlemen	Short; middlemen only for small buyers	Short; no middlemen	Middlemen used	Middlemen used
2. Negotiation period	Hard to generalize	Medium	Long	Medium	Short
3. Price competition	Important	Important	Not important	Not main factor	Important
4. Presale/postsale service	Not important	Important	Very important	Important	Very little
5. Demand stimulation	Very little	Moderate	Sales people very important	Important	Not too important
6. Brand preference	None	Generally low	High	High	Low
7. Advance buying contract	Important; long-term contracts used	Important; long-term contracts used	Not usually used	Not usually used	Not usually used

handling. Frequently, raw materials are marketed directly from producer to industrial user. At most, one intermediary may be used. The limited supply forces users to assure themselves of adequate quantities. Often this is done either (1) by contracting in advance to buy a season's supply of the product or (2) by owning the source of supply. Advertising and other forms of demand stimulation are rarely used. There is very little branding or other product differentiation. Competition is built around price and the assurance that a producer can deliver the product as specified.

Agricultural products used as industrial raw materials are supplied by many small producers located some distance from the markets. The supply is largely controllable by producers, but it cannot be increased or decreased rapidly. The product is perishable and is not produced at a uniform rate throughout the year.

Close attention must be given to transportation and warehousing. Transportation costs are high relative to unit value, and standardization and grading are very important. Because producers are small and numerous, many middlemen and long channels of distribution are needed. Very little promotional activity is involved.

FABRICATING MATERIALS AND PARTS

Fabricating materials and parts are industrial goods that become an actual part of the finished product. They have already been processed to some extent (in contrast to raw materials). Fabricating **materials** will undergo further processing. Examples include pig iron going to steel, yarn being woven into cloth, and flour becoming part of bread. Fabricating **parts** will be assembled with no further change in form. They include such products as windows in houses and semiconductor chips in computers.

Marketing considerations Fabricating materials and parts are usually purchased in large quantities. To ensure an adequate, timely supply, a buyer may place an order a year or more in advance. Because of such buying habits, most fabricating products are marketed on a direct-sale basis from producer to user.

Middlemen are used most often where the buyers are small or where they place small fill-in orders for a rapid delivery. Normally, buying decisions are based on the price and the service provided by the seller. Branding is generally unimportant. However, some firms have made successful attempts to pull their products out of obscurity by identifying them with a brand. Pella windows and the NutraSweet brand of sweetener are notable examples.

INSTALLATIONS

Installations are manufactured industrial products — the long-lived, expensive, major equipment of an industrial user. Examples include large generators in a dam, a factory building, diesel engines for a railroad, blast furnaces for a steel mill, and jet airplanes for an airline. The *differentiating characteristic of installations is that they directly affect the scale of operations in a firm*. Adding 12 new microcomputers will not affect the scale of operations of Canadian Airlines International, but adding 12 new jet airplanes certainly will. Therefore, the airplanes are classed as installations, but the microcomputers are not.

These steel reinforcing bars are classed as fabricating parts.

This B.C. pulp and paper mill is an installation.

Marketing considerations   The marketing of installations presents a real challenge to management because every single sale is important. Usually no middlemen are involved; sales are made directly from producer to industrial user. Typically, the unit sale is large, and often the product is made to the buyer's detailed specifications. Much presale and postsale servicing is required. A high-calibre sales force is needed to market installations, and often sales engineers are used. Promotional emphasis is on personal selling rather than advertising, although some advertising is used.

ACCESSORY EQUIPMENT

Accessory equipment is used in the production operations of an industrial firm, but it does not have a significant influence on the scale of operations in the firm. Accessory equipment does not become an actual part of the finished product. The life of accessory equipment is shorter than that of installations and longer than that of operating supplies. Examples include cash registers in a retail store, small power tools, forklift trucks, and the microcomputers mentioned above.

Forklifts are accessory equipment in a lot of firms.

Marketing considerations   It is difficult to generalize about the distribution policies of firms that market equipment. In some cases, direct sale is used. This is true particularly where the order is for several units of the product or where the product is of relatively high unit value. A firm which manufactures forklift trucks may sell directly because the price of a single unit is large enough to make this distribution policy profitable. In the main, however, manufacturers of accessory equipment use middlemen. They do so because (1) the market is geographically dispersed, (2) there are many different types of potential users, and (3) individual orders may be relatively small.

OPERATING SUPPLIES

Operating supplies are the "convenience goods" of the industrial field. They are short-lived, low-priced items usually purchased with a minimum of effort. They aid in a firm's operations but do not become a part of the finished product. Examples are lubricating oils, pencils and stationery, registration supplies in a university, heating fuel, and washroom supplies.

Marketing considerations   Like consumer convenience products, industrial operating supplies must be distributed widely. The producing firm makes extensive use of wholesale middlemen. This is done because the product is low in unit value, is bought in small quantities, and goes to many users. Price competition is heavy because competitive products are quite standardized and there is little brand insistence.

NATURE AND CHARACTERISTICS OF SERVICES

In concept, product marketing and service marketing are essentially the same. In each case, the marketer must select and analyze its target markets. Then a marketing program must be built around the parts of the marketing mix — the product (or service), the price structure, the distribution system, and the promotional program. Moreover, there often are substantial similarities in practice. At the same time, however, the basic characteristics that differentiate services from products must be appreciated in order to develop marketing programs in service organizations.

Here is an expanded definition of services that we shall use in this section in order to focus on some of the unique characteristics of services.

Services are those separately identifiable, essentially intangible activities that provide want-satisfaction, and that are not necessarily tied to the sale of a product or another service. To produce a service may or may not require the use of tangible goods. However, when such use is required, there is no transfer of the title (permanent ownership) to these tangible goods.

Now let's elaborate a bit on that definition, to reduce any possibility of confusion:

- We include such activities as medical care, entertainment, and repair services (but not the medicines or repair parts purchased).
- We *exclude* credit, delivery, and other services that exist only when there is the sale of a product or another service.
- The consumer of a service can take only *temporary* possession or make only *temporary* use of any goods required in the production of the service — a hotel room or a rented car, for example. (An exception here would include such tangible goods as insurance policies, legal papers, or a consultant's reports that supplement but do not comprise the service.) Service organizations are those that do not have as their *principal* aim the production of tangible products that buyers will possess permanently.

The definitional problem will continue. Some statistics on services may be misleading because it is becoming more difficult to separate products and services in our economy. We rarely find situations in which services are marketed without any product involvement whatsoever. Most products are accompanied by services, and most services require supporting products. It is this product-service mix that really is growing in importance in our economy.

We are concerned here primarily with the services marketed by business or professional firms with profit-making motives — commercial services. This is in contrast to services of nonbusiness organizations, such as churches, public schools, and the government. One useful classification of commercial services by industry is given below. No attempt is made to separate these into consumer and industrial services, as we did with products in the first part of this chapter. In fact, most services are purchased by both market groups.[1]

- Housing (includes rentals of hotels, motels, apartments, houses, and farms).
- Household operations (includes utilities, house repairs, repairs of equipment in the house, landscaping, and household cleaning).
- Recreation and entertainment (includes rental and repair of equipment used to participate in recreation and entertainment activities; also admission to all entertainment, recreation, and amusement events).
- Personal care (includes laundry, dry cleaning, beauty care).
- Commercial medical and other health care (excludes all medical service, dental, nursing, hospitalization, optometry, and other health care which a consumer does not directly pay for).

- Private education.
- Business and other professional services (includes legal, accounting, management consulting, and computer services).
- Insurance, banking, and other financial services (includes personal and business insurance, credit and local service, investment counselling, and tax service).
- Transportation (includes freight and passenger service on common carriers, automobile repairs and rentals).
- Communications (includes telephone, telegraph, computer, and specialized business communication services).

Importance of Services

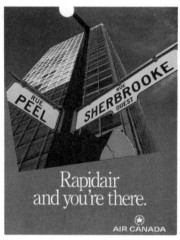

When you can't touch it, you have to sell the benefits of it.

North America has genuinely become a service economy. Almost 70 percent of all jobs in Canada are now accounted for by the service sector, and over 60 percent of the country's gross domestic product is accounted for by services. Also, service jobs typically hold up better during a recession than do jobs in industries that produce tangible products. Canadians have become more dependent on the service sector for their jobs. Much of that employment, particularly in retail organizations, is now on a part-time basis.

Close to one-half of all consumer expenditures are for the purchase of services. During the 1950s and 1960s, much of the employment growth in services involved jobs in government and other public sector organizations, such as education and health. Since the early 1970s, most of the growth has been in business and personal services. We have seen dramatic growth, for example, in the financial services industry and in the provision of household and personal services. The growth in the market for *personal services* is at least partially explained by the relative prosperity that Canadians have enjoyed during the past 40 years. As consumers became better able to satisfy their demand for tangible items, they turned to services either to provide things that they could not afford before or to do things for them that they no longer wished to do for themselves.

The growth of *business services* may be attributed to the fact that business has become increasingly complex, specialized, and competitive. As a consequence, management has been forced to call in experts to provide services in research, taxation, advertising, labour relations, and a host of other areas.

The rate of growth has not been uniform for all categories of consumer services. As disposable personal incomes have increased and life-styles have changed, the demand for some services has grown relatively faster than for others. Projections into the 1990s suggest that high growth rates in jobs and spending will occur especially in temporary employment, auto repairs, banking and finance fields, leisure-time industries, and home shopping.

Characteristics of Services

The special nature of services stems from several distinctive characteristics. These characteristics create special marketing challenges and opportunities. They also often result in strategic marketing programs that are substantially different from those found in product marketing.

INTANGIBILITY

Since services are essentially intangible, it is impossible for customers to sample

— to taste, feel, see, hear, or smell — services *before* they buy them. This feature of services places some strain on a marketing organization. The burden falls mainly on a company's promotional program. The sales force and the advertising department must concentrate on the *benefits* to be derived from the service, rather than emphasizing the service itself. An insurance company thus may promote service benefits such as guaranteed payment of a child's college expenses, or a retirement income of so many dollars per month. The telephone companies tell us how business users can cut selling costs by using long-distance calling.[2]

INSEPARABILITY

Services often cannot be separated from the person of the seller. Moreover, some services must be created and dispensed simultaneously. For example, dentists create and dispense almost all their services at the same time.

From a marketing standpoint, inseparability frequently means that direct sale is the only possible channel of distribution, and a seller's services cannot be sold in very many markets. This characteristic also limits the scale of operation in a firm. One person can repair only so many autos in a day or treat only so many eye-care patients.

As an exception to the inseparability feature, the service may be sold by a person who is representing the creator-seller. A travel agent, insurance broker, or rental agent, for instance, may represent and help promote the service that will be sold by the institution producing it.

HETEROGENEITY

It is impossible for a service industry, or even an individual seller of services, to standardize output. Each "unit" of the service is somewhat different from other "units" of the same service. For example, an airline does not give the same quality of service on each trip. All repair jobs a mechanic does on automobiles are not of equal quality. An added complication is the fact that it is often difficult to judge the quality of a service. (Of course, we can say the same for some products.) It is particularly difficult to forecast the quality in advance of buying a service. A person pays to see a Montreal Expos baseball game without knowing whether it will be an exciting one, well worth the price of admission, or a dull performance.

Service companies should therefore pay particular attention to the "product-planning" stage of their marketing programs. From the beginning, management must do all it can to ensure consistency of quality and to maintain high levels of quality control. Turning the provision of services over to machines helps to achieve consistency. For the most part, the automatic teller machines now used by all major banks and trust companies provide the same level of service to each customer, every time.

PERISHABILITY AND FLUCTUATING DEMAND

Services are highly perishable, and they cannot be stored. Unused electric power, empty seats in a stadium, and idle mechanics in a garage all represent business that is lost forever. Furthermore, the market of services fluctuates considerably by season, by day of the week, and by hour of the day. Many ski lifts lie idle all

If he isn't pitching tomorrow, it's a different ball game.

There is no tomorrow for selling seats to this game.

summer, and golf courses go unused in the winter. The use of city buses fluctuates greatly during the day.

There are some notable exceptions to this generalization regarding the perishability and storage of services. In health and life insurance, for example, the service is purchased. Then it is held by the insurance company (the seller) until needed by the buyer or the beneficiary. This holding constitutes a type of storage.

The combination of perishability and fluctuating demand offers product-planning, pricing, and promotion challenges to service company executives. Some organizations have developed new uses for idle plant capacity during off-seasons. Thus, during the summer, several ski resorts operate their ski lifts for hikers and sightseers who want access to higher elevations. Advertising and creative pricing are also used to stimulate demand during slack periods. Hotels offer lower prices and family packages for weekends. Telephone companies offer lower rates during nights and weekends. In some university and college towns, apartment rates are lowered in the summer.

File 8-2

Marketing at Work

Services Can't Be Returned

If Sunquest Vacations has chartered 50 seats on a flight to Puerta Vallarta, they must be sold! Unlike a tangible product, if the charter seats aren't sold, they do not go back into inventory, they disappear. Pat Brigham, chairman of Sunquest, describes the dilemma. "It drives me absolutely crazy when we have unsold seats. If on Monday I still have 50 seats to Venezuela, I can't sell them. The tour left on Saturday. I have to throw them in the garbage, but I still have to pay the airline and the hotel for the guests who never arrived."

Source: Ross Fisher, "Sell Those Seats, Fill That Plane," *Report on Business Magazine*, February 1988, pp. 77-83.

IMPORTANCE OF
PRODUCT INNOVATION

The social and economic justification for the existence of a business is its ability to satisfy its customers. A company meets this basic responsibility to society through its products. In this section we point out some of the reasons why effective new product planning and development are so important to a company today. Good executive judgement elsewhere cannot offset weaknesses in product planning. A company cannot successfully sell a poor product over the long run.

Products Have Life
Cycles

Like people, products go through a life cycle. They grow (in sales), then decline, and eventually are replaced. From birth to death, a product's life cycle can generally be divided into four stages — introduction, growth, maturity, and decline. The sales-volume curve in Fig. 8-1 illustrates the typical pattern of sales growth and decline for products as they go through their life cycle. The concept of the product life cycle is discussed in more detail in the next chapter.

Two points related to the life-cycle concept help to explain why product innovation is so important. First, every company's present products will eventually become obsolete as their sales volume and market share are reduced by competitive products. Second, as a product ages, its profit generally declines (as shown in Fig. 8-1). If those products are not changed or replaced, the company's sales volume and profit will be reduced.

Product Is a Basic Profit
Determinant

New products are essential for sustaining a company's expected rate of profit. Figure 8-1 illustrates a typical relationship between the sales-volume curve and the profit curve through the life cycle of a product. Note that the profit curve for most new products is negative through most of the introductory stage. Also, the profit curve

FIGURE 8-1
Typical life cycle of a product — sales and profit curves.

Profit usually starts to decline while a product's sales volume is still increasing. How does the relationship between these curves influence the time at which additional new products should be introduced?

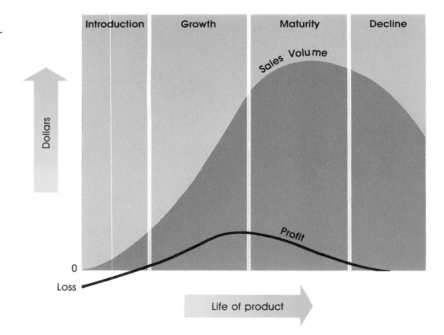

starts to decline while the sales volume is still ascending. This occurs because a company usually must increase its advertising and selling effort or cut its prices (or do both) to continue its sales growth during the maturity stage in the face of intensifying competition. The introduction of a new product at the proper time will help to maintain the company's desired level of profits.

New Products Are Essential to Growth

A useful watchword for management is to "innovate or die." Truly, an innovating attitude is a philosophy almost paralleling that of the marketing concept. Many companies will get a substantial portion of their sales volume and net profit this year from products that did not exist 5 to 10 years ago. Moreover, various studies have shown that growth industries are those that are oriented to new products.

Increased Consumer Selectivity

In recent years consumers have become more selective in their choice of products. As consumers' disposable income has increased, and as an abundance of products has become available, consumers have fulfilled many of their wants. The big middle-income group is reasonably well fed, clothed, housed, transported, and equipped. If market satiation — in terms of quantity — does exist to some extent, it follows that consumers may be more critical in their appraisal of new products. While the consumer is being increasingly selective, the market is being deluged with products that are imitations or that offer only marginal competitive advantages. This situation may be leading to "product indigestion." The cure is to develop *really* new products — to *innovate*, and not just *imitate*.

Resources and Environmental Considerations

We are finally realizing that the supply of many of our natural resources is limited and irreplaceable. These two conditions clearly point up the importance of careful new-product planning. Environmental factors will increasingly influence product decisions because we simply cannot afford to waste our natural resources or pollute our environment. As a corollary, business must make effective use of its human resources — particularly its scarce scientific and technical talent.

File 8-3

Marketing at Work

Sometimes Benefits Just Aren't

Marketers are sometimes faced with ethical considerations about certain products in their product lines. Fast-food restaurants have become concerned about the environmental impact of the disposable food trays that they use. These moulded polyurethane trays have been linked to a deterioration of the ozone layer around the earth. Should these restaurants switch to biodegradable trays?

A major Canadian brewer was testing consumer reaction to several packaging innovations, one of which was a new "rip cap" that allowed the consumer to open a bottle of beer with a pull on a ring tab, similar to those used to open cans of soft drinks. The company discontinued testing of the cap when a number of people interviewed expressed concerns about safety implications of walking on discarded rip caps on beaches and in other public places.

Possibly the most controversial of all consumer products at the present time is cigarettes. Although it is perfectly legal to sell these products, public concern about the health hazards of cigarette use has led to bans on smoking in public places and in airplanes and to legislation to restrict advertising and promotion of the products. A small number of retailers now refuse to sell cigarettes in their stores. This is a particularly contentious point for drugstores, whose product lines generally are associated with health. Should drugstores sell cigarettes?

DEVELOPMENT OF NEW PRODUCTS

It has been said that nothing happens until somebody sells something. This is not entirely true. First, there must be something to sell — a product, a service, or an idea — and that "something" must be developed.

The development process for new products should begin with the selection of an explicit new-product strategy. This strategy then can serve as a meaningful guideline throughout the step-by-step development process used for each individual new product.

Selection of New-Product Strategy[4]

The purpose of an effective overall new-product strategy is to identify the strategic role that new products are to play in helping the company achieve its corporate and marketing goals. For example, a new product might be designed to defend a market-share position or to maintain the company's position as a product innovator. In other situations, the product's role might be to meet a specific return-on-investment goal or to establish a position in a new market.

A new product's intended role also will influence the *type* of product to be developed. To illustrate:

Company goal	**Product strategy**
1. To defend a market-share position.	**1.** Introduce an addition to an existing product line, or revise an existing product.
2. To further the company's position as an innovator.	**2.** Introduce a *really* new product — not just an extension of an existing one.

Only in recent years have many companies consciously identified new-product strategies as a separate and explicit activity in the development process. Since then, however, there has been a dramatic increase in the efficiency of the development process. To illustrate, a survey by the Booz, Allen & Hamilton management consulting firm reported that in 1968 there were 58 new-product ideas considered for every successful new product introduced. In 1981, only seven new-product ideas were required to generate one successful new product — truly a dramatic improvement in the mortality rate for new-product ideas.[5]

Steps in the Development Process

With the company's new-product strategy as a guide, the development of a new product can proceed through a series of six steps (or stages). (See Fig. 8-2.) During each stage, management must decide whether to move on to the next stage, abandon the product, or seek additional information.

The first two steps — generating new-product ideas and evaluating them — are tied especially to the overall new-product strategy. This strategy can provide (1) a focus for generating new-product ideas and (2) a criterion for screening and evaluating these ideas.

FIGURE 8-2
Major stages in new-product development process.

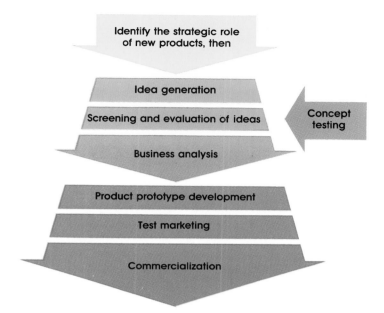

1. *Generation of new-product ideas*. New-product development starts with an idea. The particular source of ideas is not nearly so important as the company's system for stimulating new ideas and then acknowledging and reviewing them promptly.
2. *Screening and evaluation of ideas*. In this stage new-product ideas are evaluated to determine which ones warrant further study.
3. *Business analysis*. A new-product idea that survives to this stage is expanded into a concrete business proposal. Management (*a*) identifies product features, (*b*) estimates market demand and the product's profitability, (*c*) establishes a program to develop the product, and (*d*) assigns responsibility for further study of the product's feasibility.

   These first three steps are together referred to as *concept testing*. This is pretesting the product *idea*, as contrasted to later pretesting of the product itself and its market.[6]
4. *Product development*. The idea-on-paper is converted into a physical product. Pilot models or small quantities are manufactured to designated specifications. Laboratory tests and other necessary technical evaluations are made to determine the product feasibility of the article.
5. *Test marketing*. Market tests, in-use tests, and other commercial experiments in limited geographic areas are conducted to ascertain the feasibility of a full-scale marketing program. In this stage, design and production variables may have to be adjusted as a result of test findings. At this point, management must make a final decision regarding whether or not to market the product commercially.
6. *Commercialization*. Full-scale production and marketing programs are planned, and then the product is launched. Up to this point in the development process, management has virtually complete control over the product.

Once the product is "born" and enters its life cycle, however, the external competitive environment becomes a major determinant of its destiny.

In this six-step evolution, the first three — the idea, or concept, stages — are the critical ones. Not only are they least expensive — each stage becomes progressively more costly in dollars and scarce human resources. But more important, many products fail because either the idea or the timing is wrong — and those three stages are designed to identify such situations.[7]

File 8-4

Test, Test, Test!

In Canada, more than 500 new consumer products are introduced each year, and most of these are tested and retested with consumers at several stages before they actually reach the shelves of the supermarket. It's easy to see how a new food product might be tested, but how does a retailer test a new retailing concept?

A major furniture retailer in an eastern Canadian city had a large warehouse building quite close to a regional shopping centre. The company planned to move its warehouse operation to a new facility several miles away and planned to expand its present retail furniture operation. Several members of the management team developed a concept that would make use of the large warehouse building and take advantage of the high traffic location adjacent to the regional shopping centre, with its 200 stores. The concept involved converting the building into a "home centre" to house a number of small specialty stores around a central core, with the company's large furniture store as an "anchor."

With the assistance of a marketing research company, a series of focus group interviews were held with homeowners who were asked to discuss their shopping patterns for furniture and home furnishings. The 90-minute group interviews confirmed the acceptability and attractiveness of the retail "home centre" concept and provided the management group with many ideas on the mix of stores that would be most acceptable and how the plan should be implemented.

Manufacturer's Criteria for New Products

When should a proposed new product be added to a company's existing product assortment? Here are some guidelines that some manufacturers use in answering that question:

■ There should be an *adequate market demand*. This is by far the most important criterion to apply to a proposed product. Too often, management begins with a question such as, "Can we use our present sale force?" or "Will the new item fit into our production system?" The basic question is, "Do enough people really want our product?"

■ The product must be compatible with current *environmental and social standards*. Do the manufacturing processes heavily pollute air or water (as steel or paper mills do)? Will the use of the finished product be harmful to the environment (as automobiles are)? After being used, is the product harmful to the environment (as some detergents are)? Does the product have recycling potential?

What products can Harvey's add to their menu and still be Harvey's?

- The product should fit into the company's present *marketing* structure. The general marketing experience of the company is important here. Alfred Sung probably would find it easy to add designer sheets and towels to his clothing line, whereas paint manufacturers would find it quite difficult to add margarine to theirs. More specific questions may also be asked regarding the marketing fit of new products: Can the existing sales force be used? Can the present channels of distribution be used?

- A new-product idea will be more favourably received by management if the item fits in with existing *production* facilities, labour power, and management capabilities.

- The product should fit from a *financial* standpoint. At least three questions should be asked: Is adequate financing available? Will the new item increase seasonal and cyclical stability in the firm? Are the profit possibilities worthwhile?

- There must be no *legal* objections. Patents must be applied for, labelling and packaging must meet existing regulations, and so on.

- *Management* in the company must have the time and the ability to deal with the new product.

- The product should be in keeping with the *company's image* and objectives. A firm stressing low-priced, high-turnover products normally should not add an item that suggests prestige or status.

Middleman's Criteria for New Products

When retailers or wholesalers are considering whether to take on a new product, they should use all the above criteria except those related to production. In addition, a middleman should consider:

- *The relationship with the manufacturer*: The manufacturer's reputation, the

It helps when the new product fits in with existing marketing and production facilities.

possibility of getting exclusive sales rights in a given geographic territory, and the type of promotional and financial help given by the manufacturer.

- *In-store policies and practice*: What type of selling effort is required for the new product? How does the proposed product fit with store policies regarding repair service, alterations (for clothing), credit, and delivery?

NEW-PRODUCT ADOPTION AND DIFFUSION PROCESSES

The opportunity to market a new product successfully is increased if management understands the adoption and the diffusion processes for that product. The **adoption process** is the decision-making activity of *an individual* through which the new product — the innovation — is accepted. The **diffusion** of the new product is the process by which the innovation is spread through a *social system* over time.[8]

Stages in Adoption Process

A prospective user goes through the following six stages during the process of deciding whether to adopt something new:

Stage	Activity in That Stage
Awareness	Individual is exposed to the innovation; becomes a prospect.
Interest	Prospect is interested enough to seek information.
Evaluation	Prospect mentally measures relative merits.
Trial	Prospect adopts the innovation on a limited basis. A consumer buys a small sample; for example, if for some reason (cost or size) an innovation cannot be sampled, the chances of its being adopted will decrease.
Adoption	Prospect decides whether to use the innovation on a full-scale basis.
Postadoption confirmation	The innovation is adopted; then the user continues to seek assurance that the right decision was made.

Adopter Categories

Researchers have identified five categories of individuals, based on the relative time when they adopted a given innovation. Figure 8-3 illustrates the proportion of adopters in each category. The categories are rather arbitrarily partitioned on a time scale to represent unit standard deviations from the average time of adoption. Also, *nonadopters are excluded*.

INNOVATORS

Innovators, a *venturesome* group, constitute about 2.5 percent of the market and are the first to adopt an innovation. In relation to later adopters, the innovators are likely to be younger, have a higher social status, and be in a better financial position. Innovators also tend to have broader, more cosmopolitan social relationships. They

FIGURE 8-3
Distribution of innovation adopters.

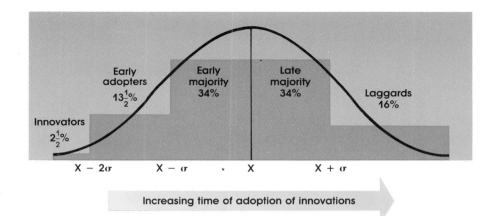

Innovators $2\frac{1}{2}$%
Early adopters $13\frac{1}{2}$%
Early majority 34%
Late majority 34%
Laggards 16%

$X - 2\sigma$ $X - \sigma$ X $X + \sigma$

Increasing time of adoption of innovations

are likely to rely more on impersonal sources of information, rather than on sales people or other word-of-mouth sources.

EARLY ADOPTERS

Early adopters — about 12.5 percent of the market — tend to be a more integrated part of a local social system. That is, whereas innovators are cosmopolites, early adopters are localites. Thus the early-adopter category includes more opinion leaders than any other adopter group. Early adopters are greatly *respected* in their social system. An ''agent of change'' is a person who is seeking to speed up the diffusion of a given innovation. This change agent will often try to work through the early adopters because they are not too far ahead of others in their peer group. As information sources, sales people are probably used more by the early adopters than by any other category.

EARLY MAJORITY

The more *deliberate* group, the early majority, represents about 34 percent of the market. This group tends to accept an innovation just before the ''average'' adopter in a social system. This group is a bit above average in social and economic measures. Its members rely quite a bit on advertisements, sales people, and contact with early adopters.

LATE MAJORITY

Representing about another 34 percent of the market, the late majority is a *sceptical* group. Usually its members adopt an innovation in response to an economic necessity or to social pressure from their peers. They rely on their peers — late or early majority — as sources of information. Advertising and personal selling are less effective with this group than is word-of-mouth.

LAGGARDS

This *tradition-bound* group — 16 percent of the market — includes those who are the last to adopt an innovation. Laggards are suspicious of innovations and innovators. By the time laggards adopt something new, it may already have been discarded by the innovator group in favour of a newer idea. Laggards are older and are at the low end of the social and economic scales.

At this point we might recall that we are discussing only *adopters* (early or late) of an innovation. For most innovations, there are still many people who are *not* included in our percentages. These are the people who *never do* adopt the innovation — the nonadopters.

Characteristics of Innovations Affecting Adoption Rate

Five characteristics of an innovation, as perceived by individuals, seem to influence the adoption rate.[9] One is **relative advantage** — the degree to which an innovation is superior to preceding ideas. Relative advantage may be reflected in lower cost, higher profitability, or some other measure. Another characteristic is **compatibility** — the degree to which an innovation is consistent with the cultural values and experiences of the adopters.

The degree of **complexity** of an innovation will affect its adoption rate. The more complex an innovation is, the less quickly it will be adopted. The fourth characteristic — **trialability** — is the degree to which the new idea may be sampled on some limited basis. On this point, a central home air-conditioning system is likely to have a slower adoption rate than some new seed or fertilizer, which may be tried on a small plot of ground. Finally, the **observability** of the innovation affects its adoption rate. A weed killer that works on existing weeds will be accepted sooner than a preemergent weed killer. The reason is that the latter — even though it may be a superior product — produces no dead weeds to show to prospective adopters.

ORGANIZING FOR PRODUCT INNOVATION

For new-product programs to be successful, they *must* be supported by a strong and continuing commitment from top management over the long term. Furthermore, this commitment must be maintained even in the face of the failures that are sure to occur in some individual new-product efforts. To effectively implement this commitment to innovation, the new-product programs must be effectively organized.

There is no "one best" organizational structure for new-product planning and development. In fact, many companies use more than one type of such structures to manage these activities. Four of the most widely used organizational structures for planning and developing new products are:

- *Product-planning committee*: The members usually include the company president and executives from major departments — marketing, production, finance, engineering, and research.
- *New-product department*: Generally these units are small, consisting of four or five or even fewer people, and usually the department head reports to the president.
- *Venture team*: A venture team is a small, multidisciplinary group, organizationally segregated from the rest of the firm. It is composed of representatives of engineering, production, finance, and marketing research. The team oper-

ates in an entrepreneurial environment, in effect being a separate small business. Typically the group reports directly to top management.

■ *Product manager*: We discuss this concept later in this section.

Upon the completion of the development process, responsibility for marketing a new product usually is shifted to another organizational unit. This unit may be an existing department, or a new department established just for this new product. In some cases, the team that developed the product may continue as the management nucleus of a newly established division in the company.

Which of these particular organizational structures is chosen is not the critical point here — each has its strengths and weaknesses. The key point is to make sure that some person or group has the specific organizational responsibilities for new-product development — and is backed by top management. Product innovation is too important an activity to let it be handled in an unorganized, nonchalant fashion, figuring that somehow the job will get done.

At least two risks are involved in the course of organizationally integrating new products into departments now marketing established, mature products. First, the executives involved with ongoing products may have a short-term outlook as they deal with day-to-day problems of existing products. Consequently, they tend to put the new products on the back burner, so to speak. Second, managers of successful existing products often are reluctant to assume the risks involved in marketing new products.[10]

PRODUCT MANAGER

In many companies a product manager — sometimes called a brand manager or a merchandise manager — is the executive responsible for planning related to *new* products as well as to *established* ones. A large company may have several product managers, who report to a top marketing executive. The wealth of discussion in business regarding the product manager's function is some indication of management's interest in this organizational structure.

In many large firms — Procter & Gamble, Canada Packers and General Foods, for example — the product manager's job is quite broad. This executive is responsible for *planning the complete marketing program* for a brand or group of products. Thus, he or she may be concerned with new-product development as well as the improvement of established products. Responsibilities include setting marketing goals, preparing budgets, and developing plans for advertising and field selling activities. At the other extreme, some companies limit product managers' activities essentially to the areas of selling and sales promotion.

Probably the biggest problem in the product-manager system is that a company will saddle these executives with great responsibility, yet it will *not* give them the corresponding authority. They must develop the field selling plan, but they have no line authority over the sales force. Product managers do not select advertising agencies, yet they are responsible for developing advertising plans. They have a profit responsibility for their brands, yet they are often denied any control over product costs, prices, or advertising budgets. Their effectiveness depends largely on their ability to influence other executives to cooperate with their plans.

Interestingly enough, there are some indications that the product-manager system may change considerably as we head into the 1990s. The product-manager system was widely adopted and thrived particularly during the period of economic growth and market expansion in the 1950s to 1970s. In the 1980s, however, many industries experienced slow economic growth in maturing markets, coupled with a trend toward strategic planning that stresses centralized managerial control. Because of these environmental forces, one careful study concluded that the product-manager system will be greatly modified in many companies and eventually abolished in some firms.[11]

WHY NEW PRODUCTS FAIL OR SUCCEED

Why do some products fail while others succeed? In the various research studies regarding this question, we find some consistently recurring themes. The key reasons typically cited for the failure of new products are as follows.[12]

File 8-5

Marketing Research: You Can Get What You Pay For

The importance of good marketing research was not lost on Jerry White, former president of Mother's Restaurants. Mr. White has compiled his ten rules of effective marketing. For him, Rule No. 1 is: "You cannot market effectively without market research and this is a field in which you always get what you pay for. Using secondary data and other people's work generally will produce second-rate results. Because the world is dynamic, your research must be as current and comprehensive as possible and of the best quality you can afford. This research is the foundation for the entire marketing plan. A poor foundation inevitably leads to collapse."

Source: Jerry White, "Marketing," *En Route*, November 1985, p. 46.

- *Poor marketing research*: Misjudging what products the market wanted; over-estimating potential sales of the new product; and lack of knowledge of buying motives and habits.
- *Technical problems in the new product's design or in its production*: Poor product quality and performance; products that were too complicated; and especially products that did not offer any significant advantage over competing items already on the market.
- *Poor timing in product introduction*: Delays in bringing the product to the market; or, conversely, rushing the product too quickly to the market.
- *Other poor management practices*: Lack of a well-defined new-product strategy; lack of a strong, long-term commitment by top management to new-product development; ineffective organization for new-product development.

Now let's look at the good news. Corrective actions to remedy these deficiencies have increased the systemization and effectiveness of the new-product development process. Specifically, we can attribute new-product success to these product factors and management characteristics.[13]

- The product satisfies one or more market needs.
- The product is technologically superior, and it enjoys a competitive cost advantage.
- The product is compatible with the company's internal strengths in key functional areas such as selling, distribution, and production.
- Top management makes a long-term commitment to new-product development. The experience thus gained enables management to improve its performance in introducing new products over a period of years.
- Strategies for new products are clearly defined. They enable a company to generate and select new products that specifically meet internal strategic needs and external market needs.
- There are an effective organization and a good management style. The organization structure is consciously established to promote new-product development. The management style encourages new-product development and can adjust to changing new-product opportunities.

One authority on new products observed that in the history of every successful product he studied, he always found at least one of three advantages — a product advantage, a marketing advantage, or a creative advertising advantage.[14] Without at least one of these three, it appeared there simply was no chance for success. Here are some examples of these features as developed by companies you'll probably recognize.

Product advantage. NutraSweet artificial sweetener (tastes more like sugar without the fattening and cavity-causing effects); facsimile machine (sends printed messages instantaneously over the telephone lines); *Financial Post Daily* (a proven business newspaper, now delivered daily); Pizza Experts restaurant (pizza cooked to your order and delivered to your home in 35 minutes or you get it free).

Marketing advantage: Tupperware and Regal Stationery (products are distributed to customers in their own homes); Sears Canada (offers the convenience of catalogue shopping as well as large department stores); Royal LePage Real Estate (nationwide computer listings of homes for sale).

Creative advertising advantage. Harvey's Restaurants ("makes a hamburger a beautiful thing"); Panasonic ("just slightly ahead of our time"); Ford of Canada ("At Ford, Quality Is Job 1"). These companies developed attention-getting advertising that assisted in differentiating them from the competition and in repositioning them in their respective markets.

SUMMARY

If the first commandment in marketing is "Know thy customer," then the second is "Know thy product." A firm can fulfil its socioeconomic responsibility to satisfy its customers by producing and marketing truly want-satisfying products or services. In light of a scarcity of resources and a growing concern for our environment, socially responsible product innovation becomes even more important. The new products or services marketed by a firm are a prime determinant of that company's growth rate, profits, and total marketing program.

To manage their product assortments and services effectively, marketers should understand the full meaning of the term *product* and the different concepts of what a *new product* is. Products can be classified into two broad categories — consumer products and industrial products. Then each of these two major groups should be further subdivided, because a different marketing program is required for each subgroup.

Services are those separately identifiable, essentially intangible activities that provide want-satisfaction, and that are not necessarily tied to the sale of a product or another service. In the broadest sense, product marketing and service marketing are the same.

There are seven steps in the development process for new products, starting with a clear statement of the intended new-product strategy. The early stages in this process are important. If a firm can make an early (and proper) decision to drop a product, a lot of money and labour can be saved. In its decision regarding whether to accept or reject a new product, there are several criteria for a manufacturer or a middleman to consider. The product should fit in with marketing, production, and financial resources. But the key point is that there *must* be an adequate market demand for the product. Management should understand the adoption and diffusion processes for a new product. Adopters of a new product can be divided into five categories, depending upon how quickly they adopt a given innovation. In addition, there usually is a group of nonadopters.

Organizational relationships are typically reported as a major problem in new-product planning and development. Top management must be deeply committed to product innovation and must support this activity in a creative fashion. Most firms that report reasonable success in product innovation seem to use one of these four organizational structures for new-product development: product-planning committee, new-product department, venture team, or product-manager system. Successful products typically have an advantage in at least one of three areas — as a want-satisfying product, in their marketing program, or their advertising.

NOTES

[1] For a series of five classification schemes, each of which separates services into clusters that share certain marketing characteristics, see Christopher H. Lovelock, "Classifying Services to Gain Strategic Marketing Insights," *Journal of Marketing*, Summer 1983, pp. 9–20. This article also includes a summary of several service-classification schemes proposed by other authors.

[2] For suggestions on how to offset the marketing problems created by intangibility in services (and also in products), see Theodore Levitt, "Marketing Intangible Products and Product Intangibles," *Harvard Business Review*, May–June 1981, pp. 94–102. See also Betsy D. Gelb, "How Marketers of Intangibles Can Raise the Odds for Consumer Satisfaction," *The Journal of Consumer Marketing*, Spring 1985, pp. 55–61.

[3] See Leonard L. Berry, Valarie A. Zeithaml, and A. Parasuraman, "Quality Counts in Services, Too," *Business Horizons*, May–June 1985, pp. 44–52.

[4] See *New Products Management for the 1980s*, Booz, Allen & Hamilton, New York, 1982, pp. 10–11. Also see Earl L. Bailey (ed.), *Product-Line Strategies*. The Conference Board, New York, report no. 816, 1982, pp. 6–23.

[5] *New Products Management for the 1980s*, p. 14. For a report on several new-product strategies and their impact on performance results, see Robert G. Cooper, "Industrial Firms'

New Product Strategies,'' *Journal of Business Research*, April 1985, pp. 107–121; and Robert G. Cooper, ''Overall Corporate Strategies for New Product Programs,'' *Industrial Marketing Management*, August 1985, pp. 175–193.

⁶ For a further discussion of concept testing, with an excellent bibliography, see William L. Moore, ''Concept Testing,'' *Journal of Business Research*, September 1982, pp. 279–294; and David A. Schwartz, ''Concept Testing *Can* Be Improved — and Here's How to Do It,'' *Marketing News*, Jan. 6, 1984, p. 22.

⁷ For a report on the criteria used in marketing go/no-go decisions at major stages in the product-development process, see Ilkka A. Ronkainen, ''Criteria Changes across Product Development Stages,'' *Industrial Marketing Management*, August 1985, pp. 171–178.

⁸ For some foundations of diffusion theory, a review of landmark studies on diffusion of innovation, and extensive bibliographical references, see Everett M. Rogers, *Diffusion of Innovations*, 3d ed. The Free Press, New York, 1983.

⁹ Rogers op. cit., chap. 6.

¹⁰ For more of this problem, see Roger C. Bennett and Robert G. Cooper, ''The Product Life Cycle Trap,'' *Business Horizons*, September–October 1984, pp. 7–16.

¹¹ See Victor P. Buell, ''Firms to Modify, Abolish Product Manager Jobs Due to Sluggish Economy, Centralized Planning,'' *Marketing News*, Mar. 18, 1983, p. 8. For a report on the role of product managers in the strategic planning process, see Thomas J. Cossé and John E. Swan, ''Strategic Marketing Planning by Product Managers — Room for Improvement?'' *Journal of Marketing*, Summer 1983, pp. 92–102.

¹² See David S. Hopkins, *New-Product Winners and Losers*, The Conference Board, New York, report no. 773, 1980, pp. 12–20. Also see Valerie S. Folkes and Barbara Kotsos, ''Buyers' and Sellers' Explanations for Product Failure: Who Done It?'' *Journal of Marketing*, April 1986, pp. 74–80.

¹³ *New Products Management for the 1980s*, pp. 17–23.

¹⁴ Harry W. McMahan, ''Alltime Ad Triumphs Reveal Key Success Factors behind Choice of '100 Best,' '' *Advertising Age*, Apr. 12, 1976, p. 72.

KEY TERMS AND CONCEPTS

1. In what respects are the products different in each of the following cases?
   a. An Inglis dishwasher sold at an appliance store and a similar dishwasher sold by Sears under its Kenmore brand name. Assume Inglis makes both dishwashers.
   b. A Sunbeam Mixmaster sold by a leading department store and the same model sold by a discount house.

2. a. Explain the various interpretations of the term *new product*.
   b. Give some examples, other than those stated in this chapter, of products in each of the three new-product categories.

3. ''As brand preferences are established with regard to women's ready-to-wear, these items, which traditionally have been considered shopping goods, will move into the specialty-goods category. At the same time, women's clothing is moving into supermarkets and variety stores, thus indicating that some articles are convenience goods.'' Explain the reasons involved in these statements. Do you agree that women's clothing is shifting away from the shopping-goods classification? Explain.

4. In what way is the responsibility for advertising a convenience good distributed between the manufacturer and the retailers? A shopping good? A specialty good?

5. Compare the elements of a manufacturer's marketing mix for a convenience good with those of the mix for a specialty good.

6. In which of the five subclassifications of industrial products should each of the following be included? Which products may belong in more than one category?
   a. Trucks.
   b. Medical X-ray equipment.
   c. Typing paper.
   d. Copper wires.
   e. Printing presses.
   f. Nuts and bolts.
   g. Paper clips.
   h. Land.

7. What are some of the marketing implications in the fact that services possess the characteristic of intangibility?

8. Services are highly perishable and are often subject to fluctuations in demand. In marketing its services, how can a company offset these factors?

9. Cite some examples of service marketers that seem to be customer-oriented, and describe what these firms have done in this vein.

10. Present a brief analysis of the market for each of the following service firms. Make use of the components of a market as discussed in Chapters 4 to 6.
    a. Laundry and dry-cleaning firm located in a shopping centre close to your campus.

  b. Four-bedroom house for rent at a major seashore resort.
  c. Bowling alley.
  d. Nursing home.

11. What are some of the ways in which each of the following service firms might expand its line?
  a. Advertising agency.
  b. Telephone company.
  c. Automobile repair garage.

12. What factors account for the growing importance of product planning?

13. In planning and developing new products, how can a firm make sure that it is being socially responsible in regard to scarce resources and our environment?

14. What are some of the questions that management is likely to want answered during the business-analysis stage of new-product development?

15. Assume that the following organizations are considering the following additions to their product lines. In each case, should the proposed product be added?
  a. McDonald's — pizza.
  b. Safeway supermarkets — automobile tires.
  c. Petro-Canada — personal computers.
  d. Bank of Montreal — life insurance.
  e. General Motors — outboard boat motors.

16. In the "trial" stage of deciding whether to adopt an innovation, the likelihood of adoption is reduced if the product cannot be sampled because of its cost or size. What are some products that might have these drawbacks? How might these drawbacks be overcome?

17. What are some of the problems typically connected with the product-manager organizational structure?

18. Why do so many new products turn out to be failures in the market?

CHAPTER 9

PRODUCT-MIX STRATEGIES

At any given time, a firm may be marketing some new products and some older products, while others are being planned and developed. This chapter is concerned with the managing of the entire range of products. After studying this chapter, you should understand:

- The difference between product mix and product line.
- The major product-mix strategies, such as:
  a. Expansion.
  b. Contraction.
  c. Alterations.
  d. Positioning.
  e. Trading up and trading down.
- A product's life cycle and its management.
- Planning obsolescence, including:
  a. Style and fashion.
  b. The fashion-adoption process.

The Campbell Soup Company introduced a new Rich and Creamy line of soups. The same company combined the convenience of canned soup with the nutrition of stew to come up with its Chunky line. Bata Limited, the world's largest shoe company, plans to open new retail stores to sell children's clothing. Alfred Sung, the fashion designer, launches a new line of fragrances. Carling O'Keefe introduces a new import beer, Stella Artois from Belgium, now brewed in Canada. Coca-Cola made the first change in its product in 99 years when it introduced New Coke. Diet Pepsi, Diet Coke and Diet 7-Up substituted NutraSweet for saccharin. Levi's introduced a new line of maternity clothing.

Canadian General Electric rejuvenated a very mature product by introducing new refrigerator models with features such as ice-water dispensers. General Foods combined the fun of the Popsicle with the nutrition of pudding when they created Jell-O Pops. Procter & Gamble extended its detergent line with the introduction of Tide Liquid. Makers of video games suffered when that market declined in popularity, while other firms took advantage of the popularity of videocassette recorders and the revitalization of skateboards.

One common thread permeates this wide variety of product situations. All of these cases involve strategies related to the company's assortment of products and services. The management of that assortment is the topic of this chapter.

PRODUCT MIX AND PRODUCT LINE

A broad group of products, intended for essentially similar uses and possessing reasonably similar physical characteristics, constitutes a **product line**. Wearing apparel is one example of a product line. But in a different context, say, in a small specialty shop, men's furnishings (shirts, ties, and underwear) and men's ready-

FIGURE 9-1

Product mix — breadth and depth.

Part of the product mix in a lawn and garden store.

	Breadth (different lines)		
	Lawnmowers	Gardening tools	Lawn furniture
Depth (assortment within a line)	Power rotary	Rakes	Chairs
	Power reel-type	Hoes	Chaise longues
	Hand-powered	Pruning shears	Benches
	_____	Shovels	
	each in 40 cm		_____
	50 cm	each in various sizes	Various sizes in redwood or aluminum with plastic webbing

to-wear (suits, sport jackets, topcoats, and slacks) would each constitute a line. In another context, men's apparel is one line, as contrasted with women's apparel, furniture, or sporting goods. (See. Fig. 9-1.)

The **product mix** is the full list of all products offered for sale by a company. The structure of the product mix has dimensions of both breadth and depth. Its *breadth* is measured by the *number* of product lines carried; its *depth*, by the assortment of sizes, colours, and models offered *within* each product line.

MAJOR PRODUCT-MIX STRATEGIES

Several major strategies used by manufacturers and middlemen in managing their product mix are discussed below. A discussion of planned obsolescence as a product strategy, and of fashion as an influence on the product mix, is deferred until later in the chapter.

Expansion of Product Mix

A firm may elect to expand its present product mix by increasing the number of

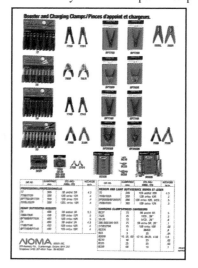

NOMA, long-time manufacturers of Christmas tree lights, has expanded into many electrical products.

lines and/or the depth within a line. New lines may be related or unrelated to the present products.

The *Globe and Mail*, remaining within the publishing business, began to publish a series of magazines, including *Report on Business Magazine, Destinations*, a travel magazine, and *Domino*, a high-fashion publication. Labatt's launched Blue Light as an extension to its popular Labatt's Blue brand. Campbell's moved a little away from soup with its Belgian-made Godiva chocolates. Pillsbury launched a number of premium frozen vegetable mixes under its Green Giant label.

Expanding into somewhat unrelated lines, Bata moved into kids' clothing, Coca-Cola bought Columbia Pictures, and General Mills owns Eddie Bauer, the retailer of outdoor gear. McCain's, a major food manufacturer, branched into transportation and courier services.

Contraction of Product Mix

Another product strategy is to thin out the product mix, either by eliminating an entire line or by simplifying the assortment within a line. The shift from fat and long lines to thin and short lines is designed to eliminate low-profit products and to get more profit from fewer products. IBM discontinued the PC*jr* when it did not meet volume expectations in the personal computer market. After a six-year stint in the wine business, Coca-Cola sold its wine brands when the products did not meet profit expectation. RJR Nabisco decided to get out of the ocean-shipping and energy-generating businesses and concentrate on cigarettes, food products (Del Monte, Oreo, Ritz, Kentucky Fried Chicken), and drinks (Canada Dry, liqueurs and wines).

The practice of slimming the product mix has long been recognized as an important product strategy. However, during the past decade it has been used extensively to cope with economic and competitive conditions as well as to retrench from the highly expansionary strategies of earlier years.

Here we see both breadth and depth in the product mix.

Alteration of Existing Products

As an alternative to developing a completely new product, management should take a fresh look at the company's existing products. Often, improving an established product can be more profitable and less risky than developing a completely new one. Most of you are probably familiar with the story of how Coca-Cola altered its existing product when the company came out with New Coke. Whether this move will prove to be a profitable strategy in the long run remains to be seen.

A common strategy is resizing an existing product.

However, we know already that the substitution of NutraSweet for saccharin in diet soft drinks (Coke, Pepsi, 7-Up, and others) clearly was a successful alteration.

For some products, *redesigning* is the key to their renaissance. Gillette reformulated and relaunched Silkience Shampoo and Conditioner. *Packaging* has been a popular area for product alteration, especially for consumer products. Colgate increased its sales of toothpaste considerably when this product was repackaged in a pump dispenser. Even something as mundane as bread, glue, or cheesecloth can be made more attractive by means of creative packaging and display.

Positioning the Product

Management's ability to position a product appropriately in the market is a major determinant of company profit. A product's **position** is the image that the product projects in relation to competitive products and to other products marketed by the same company. Unfortunately, the term *product positioning* has no generally accepted definition, so this important concept in product management is loosely applied and difficult to measure.

Marketing executives can choose from a variety of positioning strategies, some of which are as follows:[1]

- *Positioning in relation to a competitor.* For some products (Coca-Cola and Pepsi-Cola, for example), the best position is directly against the competition. For other products, head-to-head positioning is exactly what *not* to do, especially when a competitor has a strong market position. Avis became successful only after it stopped positioning itself directly against Hertz, readily admitted that it was Number 2, and advertised that it was trying harder. Midas Muffler, went head-to-head with Speedy Muffler King, terming its mechanics the "top guns."

- *Positioning in relation to a target market.* In the face of a declining birth rate, Johnson & Johnson repositioned its mild baby shampoo for use by mothers, fathers, and people who must wash their hair frequently. Air Canada and Canadian Airlines International aim their frequent flyer programs at regular business travellers in an attempt to build "brand" loyalty. When Labatt Breweries introduced the first light beer in the Canadian market, its Labatt's Lite appealed primarily to diet-conscious consumers who drank relatively little beer. Molson Light was introduced as light beer with the taste of a regular beer — a beer with ''heart.'' Miller Lite was positioned as a beer with a great taste, but less filling.

■ *Positioning in relation to a product class.* Sometimes a company's positioning strategy involves associating its product with (or disassociating it from) a common class of product. The soft drink 7-Up was positioned as an un-cola with no caffeine, to set it apart from Coca-Cola and the other cola drinks. Libby's, Del Monte, Campbell Soups, Kellogg's cereals, and other food processors introduced product lines with one common denominator — no salt (or very little) was added. Thus these items were positioned against the food products that are packed with the conventional (larger) amounts of salt.

■ *Positioning by price and quality.* Some retail stores are known for their high-quality merchandise and high prices (Harry Rosen, Birks). Positioned at the other end of the price and quality scale are discount stores such as K-Mart and Zellers.

Positioning by quality.

Trying to reposition a company on the price and quality spectrum can be a tricky proposition. In the 1970s, Woolco and other discount department stores tried to upgrade their fashion and quality image by adding lines of brand-name fashion clothing, while at the same time trying to retain their image for low price and ''good value for the money.'' The move met with varying degrees of success, serving in some cases to blur the corporate image and to confuse some customers. Zellers, similarly, has been working on trading up its image toward becoming a family department store, rather than a discount store. Zellers has added designer-label clothing lines to the store's own labels and has introduced well-known brand names in a new cosmetics section.[2]

Marketing at Work

Clear Positioning: Better Than Gold

The launch of the American Express Platinum Card in Canada is an example of a successful positioning strategy. The development of this new product by American Express Canada was predicated on identifying a need in a well understood target market. American Express targeted their existing customer base, recognizing that "loyal customers are much more profitable because acquiring a new prospect costs about five times more than keeping one." Marketing research in the form of focus groups and surveys played an important role in assisting American Express to target their product at a specific group of customers who have displayed purchasing behaviour that warranted a more specialized product.

Source: Carolyn R. Farquhar, "Taking Aim at Target Markets," *Canadian Business Review*, Summer 1986, p. 36.

Trading Up and Trading Down

As product strategies, trading up and trading down involve, essentially, an expansion of the product line and a change in product positioning. **Trading up** means adding a higher-priced, prestige product to a line in the hope of increasing the sales of existing lower-priced products. In the automobile industry some years ago, Ford introduced the Thunderbird, and Chevrolet the Corvette. More recently, we have seen the Toyota Cressida and the Honda Prelude, all positioned in such a way that the lower-priced cars produced by these companies will benefit from the reflected image of the higher-priced models.

When a company embarks upon a policy of trading up, at least two avenues are open with respect to promotional emphasis: (1) The seller may continue to depend upon the older, lower-priced product for the bulk of the sales volume and promote it heavily, or (2) the seller may gradually shift promotional emphasis to the new product and expect it to produce the major share of sales volume. In fact, the lower-priced line may be dropped altogether after a transition period.

A company is said to be **trading down** when it adds a lower-priced item to its line of prestige products. The company expects that people who cannot afford the original product will want to buy the new one because it carries some of the status of the higher-priced good. In line with this strategy, major manufacturers of 35 mm single lens reflex (SLR) cameras, such as Pentax, Canon, and Minolta, have in recent years introduced smaller, simplified cameras for photography buffs who want to be seen to be using the major brands but who do not want to be bothered with the intricacies of 35 mm photography. Mont Blanc, the West German manufacturer of the "world's most famous fountain pen," introduced a lower-priced ballpoint pen, thereby allowing its purchasers to own a Mont Blanc without having to pay more than $300 for the top-of-the-line fountain pen.

Trading up and trading down are perilous strategies because the new product may simply confuse buyers, so that the net gain is negligible. Nor is any useful purpose served if sales of the new item are generated at the expense of the older products. When *trading down* is used, the new article may permanently hurt the firm's reputation and that of its established high-quality product.

In *trading up*, on the other hand, the seller's major problem is to change the firm's image enough so that new customers will accept the higher-priced product. At the same time, the seller does not want to lose its present customers. The real risk is that the company will lose *both* customer groups through this change in its product positioning: The former customers may become confused because the company has clouded its image; and the new target market may not believe that the company is marketing high-quality merchandise.

CONCEPT OF THE PRODUCT LIFE CYCLE

This concept was introduced briefly in Chapter 8. There we noted that products have life cycles that can be divided into four stages: introduction, growth, maturity, and decline. A company's marketing success can be affected considerably by its ability to understand and manage the life cycle of its products. The product life cycle can be illustrated with the sales-volume and profit curves, as in Fig. 9-2. The *shapes* of these curves will vary from product to product. However, the basic shapes and the relationship between the two curves are usually as illustrated. (The relationship between these two curves was explained in Chapter 8 in connection with Fig. 8-1.)

FIGURE 9-2
Sales-volume curve and profit-margin curve in relationship to a product's life.
Profit margin usually starts to decline while a product's sales volume is still increasing.

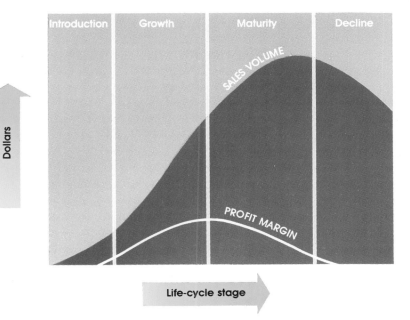

Characteristics of Each Stage

It is quite important that management recognize what part of the life cycle its product is in at any given time. The competitive environment and the resultant marketing strategies ordinarily will differ depending upon the stage.

For some markets this product is already in the growth stage; for others it is in the introductory stage.

INTRODUCTION

During the first stage of a product's life cycle, it is launched into the market in a full-scale production and marketing program. It has gone through the embryonic stages of idea evaluation, pilot models, and test marketing. The entire product may be new, like a machine that cleans clothes electronically without using any water. Or the basic product may be well known but have a new feature or accessory that is in the introductory stage — a gas turbine engine in an automobile, for example.

There is a high percentage of product failures in this period. Operations in the introductory period are characterized by high costs, low sales volume, net losses, and limited distribution. In many respects, the pioneering stage is the most risky and expensive one. However, for really new products, there is very little direct competition. The promotional program is designed to stimulate *primary*, rather than *secondary*, demand. That is, the *type of product*, rather than the *seller's brand*, is emphasized.

GROWTH

In the growth, or market-acceptance, stage, both sales and profits rise, often at a rapid rate. Competitors enter the market — in large numbers if the profit outlook is particularly attractive. Sellers shift to a "buy-my-brand" rather than a "try-this-product" promotional strategy. The number of distribution outlets increases, economies of scale are introduced, and prices may come down a bit. Typically profits start to decline near the end of the growth stage.

MATURITY

During the first part of this period, sales continue to increase, but at a decreasing rate. While sales are levelling off, the profits of both the manufacturer and the retailers are declining. Marginal producers are forced to drop out of the market. Price competition becomes increasingly severe. The producer assumes a greater share of the total promotional effort in the fight to retain dealers and the shelf space in their stores. New models are introduced as manufacturers broaden their lines, and trade-in sales become significant.

DECLINE AND POSSIBLE ABANDONMENT

For virtually all products, obsolescence sets in inevitably as new products start their own life cycles and replace the old ones. Cost control becomes increasingly important as demand drops. Advertising declines, and a number of competitors withdraw from the market. Whether the product has to be abandoned, or whether the surviving sellers can continue on a profitable basis, often depends upon management's abilities.

Length of Product Life Cycle

The length of the life cycle varies among products. It will range from a few weeks or a short season (for a fad or a clothing fashion) to several decades (for, say, autos or telephones). In general, however, product life cycles are getting shorter as the years go by. Rapid changes in technology can make a product obsolete. Or, if competitors can quickly introduce a "me-too" version of a popular product, this product may move quickly into the maturity stage.

Figure 9-2 suggests that the life-cycle stages cover nearly equal periods of time. That is *not* the case, however. The stages in any given product's life cycle usually last for *different* periods of time. Also, the duration of each stage will vary among products. Some products take years to pass through the introductory stage, while others are accepted in a few weeks. Moreover, not all products go through all the stages. Some may fail in the introductory stage, and others may not be introduced until the market is in the growth or maturity stage. In virtually all cases, however, decline and possible abandonment are inevitable. This is because (1) the need for the product disappears (as when frozen orange juice generally eliminated the market for juice squeezers); (2) a better or less expensive product is developed to fill the same need (electronic microchips made possible many replacement products); or (3) the people simply grow tired of a product (a clothing style, for example), so it disappears from the market.

Life Cycle Is Related to a Market

When we say a product is in its growth stage, or some other stage, implicitly we are referring to that product's relation to a specific market. That is, a product may be well accepted (growth or maturity stage) in some markets but be in the introductory stage in other markets. Microwave ovens, for example, were in the maturity stage in the airline and industrial in-plant feeding markets while they were still in the introductory stage in most consumer markets.

The definition, or identity, of the product also is involved in this life–cycle market relationship. To illustrate, computers, broadly defined, are in the growth stage of their life cycle. But personal computers are still in the introductory stage in most consumer markets.

Management of the Product Life Cycle

The shape of a product's sales and profit curves is not predetermined. To a surprising extent, the shape can be controlled by effective managerial action. One key to successful life-cycle management is (1) to predict the shape of the proposed product's cycle even before it is introduced and then, at each stage, (2) to anticipate the marketing requirements of the following stage. The introductory period, for instance, may be shortened by broadening the distribution or by increasing the promotional effort.

File 9-2

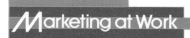

Staying Alive with Repositioning

Faced with a decline in its share of market, Gillette decided to relaunch its Silkience Shampoo and Conditioner in a reformulated version. The brand had occupied a leadership position in the very competitive Canadian shampoo industry. Charles Daigle, senior product manager at Gillette, explained that a relaunch of the brand was less expensive than dropping the brand and replacing it with a new one. ''The life cycle of a shampoo is roughly three years,'' he explained. ''It takes about two or three years to peak, then it starts to decline. Some shampoos decline at a faster rate than others. We are in a situation where, rather than see the brand starting to decline, we decided to revitalize and relaunch it.''

Gillette's repositioning strategy for Silkience involved the addition of ''silk protein essentials'' to strengthen hair and help prevent breakage. The package was redesigned, with a new bottle and graphics — and a new ''flanker'' brand was added, ''Silkience for Frequent Use.'' Gillette spent more than $500,000 in television and print advertising and distributed more than 500,000 trial-size samples to support the relaunch.

Source: Randy Scotland, ''Gillette Reformulates Silkience in Hope of Regaining Lost Share,'' *Marketing,* June 3, 1987.

MANAGING DURING MATURITY STAGE

A product's life may be extended during the maturity stage of its life cycle if the product is rejuvenated through product modifications, new promotion, or repricing. We find one example of this in the appliance industry — an industry considered dull and mature, even by some people in it. Proctor-Silex, a company that manufactures small electrical appliances, rejuvenated the basic toaster by adding features such as electronic browning controls and slots that accept wide slices of bread. Colgate and other toothpaste manufacturers added a tartar-fighter ingredient and a toothpaste for children, both packaged in pump dispensers. Campbell's have low-sodium and calorie-reduced soups. The introduction of Ultra Pampers helped the manufacturer, Procter & Gamble, slow declining sales and market share in the maturity stage of the disposable diaper market. To boost the image of a tired brand, GWG brought out a line of 1911's jeans, which were made of heavier denim and bore a distinctive leather patch with the GWG logo.[3]

Design is one way of rejuvenating a product at maturity stage.

MANAGING DURING SALES-DECLINE STAGE

Perhaps it is in the sales-decline stage that a company finds its greatest challenges in life-cycle management. At some point in the product's life, management may have to consider whether to abandon the product. The costs of carrying profitless products go beyond the expenses that show up on financial statements. The real burdens are the insidious costs accruing from managerial time and effort that are diverted to sick products. Unfortunately, management often seems reluctant to discard a product. Sometimes, the reasons are emotional and sentimental.

When sales are declining, management has the following alternatives, some of which are reflected in ''A 10-Point Vitality Test . . .'' in the nearby box:

- Improve the product in a functional sense, or revitalize it in some manner.

A 10-POINT VITALITY TEST FOR OLDER PRODUCTS, OR HOW TO GET THAT SALES CURVE TO SLOPE UPWARD AGAIN

1. Does the product have new or extended uses? Sales of Cow Brand baking soda increased considerably after the product was promoted as a refrigerator deodorant.
2. Is the product a generic item that can be branded? Sunkist put its name on oranges and lemons, thus giving a brand identity to a formerly generic item.
3. Is the product category "underadvertised?" Condoms were in this category until Julius Schmid of Canada and other manufacturers started spending large advertising appropriations and the product was displayed more openly.
4. Is there a broader target market? Procter & Gamble increased the sales of Ivory soap by promoting it for adults, instead of just for babies.
5. Can you turn disadvantages into advantages? Several small regional Canadian companies have been able to prove to customers that, while they may not have the extensive product line of a national company, they almost certainly know the needs of their region better.
6. Can you build volume and profit by cutting the price? This is what has happened with many of the new technologies of recent years. Sales of digital watches and home computers increased dramatically as prices fell.
7. Can you market unused by-products? Lumber companies market sawdust as a form of kitty litter.
8. Can you sell the product in a more compelling way? Procter & Gamble's Pampers disposable diapers were only a moderate success in the market when they were sold as a convenience item for mothers. Sales increased, however, after the advertising theme was changed to say that Pampers kept babies dry and happy.
9. Is there a social trend to exploit? Many companies have been successful in taking advantage of the national interest in fitness and nutrition. Yoplait yoghurt and Fleischmann's corn-oil margarine are merely two examples of products that have been successful as a result of an increased diet-consciousness among Canadians.
10. Can you expand distribution channels? Hanes Hosiery Company increased its sales of L'eggs panty hose by distributing this product through supermarkets.

Source: Adapted from *The Wall Street Journal*, February 18, 1982, p. 25.

- Make sure that the marketing and production programs are as efficient as possible.
- Streamline the product assortment by pruning out unprofitable sizes and models. Frequently, this tactic will *decrease* sales and *increase* profits.
- "Run out" the product; that is, cut all costs to the bare-minimum level that will optimize profitability over the limited remaining life of the product.

In the final analysis the only reasonable alternative may be simply to abandon the product. Knowing when and how to abandon products successfully may be as important as knowing when and how to introduce new ones. Certainly management should develop a systematic procedure for phasing out its weak products.[4]

<table>
<tr><td>

PLANNED OBSOLESCENCE AND FASHION

</td><td>

The North American consumer seems to be on a constant quest for the "new" but not "*too* new." The market wants newness — new products, new styles, new colours. However, people want to be moved gently out of their habitual patterns, not shocked out of them. This has led many manufacturers to develop the product strategy of planned obsolescence. Its objective is to make an existing product out of date and thus to increase the market for replacement products.

</td></tr>
</table>

Nature of Planned Obsolescence

The term **planned obsolescence** may be used in two ways:

- *Technological or functional obsolescence*. Significant technical improvements result in a more effective product. For instance, pocket calculators made slide rules technologically obsolete. This type of obsolescence is generally considered to be socially and economically desirable.
- *Style obsolescence*. This is sometimes called "psychological" or "fashion" obsolescence. Superficial characteristics of the product are altered so that the new model is easily differentiated from the previous model. The intent is to make people feel out of date if they continue to use old models.

When people criticize planned obsolescence, they are usually referring to the second interpretation — style obsolescence. In our discussion, planned obsolescence will mean only style obsolescence, unless otherwise stated.

Nature of Style and Fashion

Although the word *style* and *fashion* are often used interchangeably, there is a clear distinction between the two. A **style** is defined as a distinctive manner of construction or presentation in any art, product, or endeavour (singing, playing, behaving). Thus we have styles in automobiles (sedans, station wagons), in bathing suits (one-piece, bikinis), in furniture (Early American, French Provincial), and in dancing (waltz, rumba).

A **fashion** is any style that is popularly accepted and purchased by several successive groups of people over a reasonably long period of time. Not every style becomes a fashion. To be rated as a fashion, or to be called "fashionable," a style must become popularly accepted.

A **fad** normally does not remain popular as long as a fashion, and it is based on some novelty feature.

Basic styles never change, but fashion is always changing. Fashions are found in all societies, including primitive groups, the great Oriental cultures, and the societies of ancient and medieval Europe.

Origin of Fashion

Fashion is rooted in sociological and psychological factors. Basically, people are conformists. At the same time, they yearn to look, act, and be a *little* different from others. They are not in revolt against custom; they simply wish to be a bit different and still not be accused of bad taste or insensitivity to the code. Fashion discreetly furnishes them the opportunity for self-expression.

Stanley Marcus, the president of Nieman-Marcus, the high-fashion women's store in Dallas, Texas, once observed:[5]

If, for example, a dictator decreed feminine clothes to be illegal and that all women should wear barrels, it would not result in an era of uniformity, in my opinion. Very shortly, I think you'd find that one ingenious woman would color her barrel with a lipstick, another would pin paper lace doilies on the front of hers, and still another would decorate hers with thumbtacks. *This is a strange human urge toward conformity, but a dislike for complete uniformity.*

Fashion-Adoption Process   The fashion-adoption process reflects the concepts of (1) large-group and small-group influences on consumer buying behaviour and (2) the diffusion of innovation, as discussed in Chapters 5 and 8. People usually try to imitate others in the same social stratum or those on the next higher level. They do so by purchasing the fashionable product. This shows up as a wave of buying in that particular social stratum. The **fashion-adoption process** then, is a series of buying waves that arise as the given style is popularly accepted in one group, then another and another, until it finally falls out of fashion. This wavelike movement, representing the introduction, rise, popular culmination, and decline of the market's acceptance of a style, is referred to as the **fashion cycle**.

Three theories of fashion adoption are recognized (see Fig. 9-3):

- **Trickle-down**, where a given fashion cycle flows *downward* through several socioeconomic classes.
- **Trickle-across**, where the cycle moves *horizontally* and *simultaneously within* several social classes.
- **Trickle-up**, where the cycle is initiated in lower socioeconomic classes, then later the style becomes popular among higher-income and social groups.

Traditionally, the trickle-down theory has been used as the basic model to explain the fashion-adoption process. As an example, designers of women's apparel first introduce a style to the leaders — the tastemakers who usually are the social leaders in the upper-income brackets. If they accept the style, it quickly appears in leading fashion stores. Soon the middle-income and then the lower-income markets want to emulate the leaders, and the style is mass-marketed. As its popularity wanes, the style appears in bargain-price stores and finally is no longer considered fashionable.

To illustrate the trickle-across process, let us again use the example of women's apparel. Within a few weeks at the most, at the beginning of the fall season, the same style of dresses appears (1) in small, exclusive dress shops appealing to the upper social class, (2) in large department stores appealing to the middle social

FIGURE 9-3
Fashion-adoption processes.

Exclusive Stores

Department Stores

Discount Stores

Product introduced at same time in all three types of stores

TRICKLE DOWN

TRICKLE ACROSS

TRICKLE ACROSS

TRICKLE ACROSS

TRICKLE UP

THE "TRICKLE-UP" PROCESS

Blue jeans, denim jackets, T-shirts, and "soul" food in the 1980s. Years earlier there were popular styles of music we call jazz and the blues. These all have one thing in common. They are styles that *trickled up* in popularity; that is, they were popular first with lower socioeconomic groups. Later, their popularity trickled up as these styles gained wide acceptance among higher-income markets. T-shirts — once the domain of beer-drinking blue-collar workers and radicals — have moved up considerably in social respectability and price. Now they are designed by Yves Saint Laurent, Calvin Klein, Ralph Lauren, and others.

Some styles remain in fashion for a long time.

class, and (3) in discount houses and low-priced women's ready-to-wear chain stores, where the appeal is to the upper-lower social class. Price and quality mark the differences in the dresses sold on the three levels — *but the style is basically the same. Within each class* the dresses are purchased early in the season by the opinion leaders — the innovators. If the style is accepted, its sales curve rises as it becomes popular with the early adopters, and then with the late adopters. Eventually, sales decline as the style ceases to be popular. This cycle, or flow, is a horizontal movement occurring virtually simultaneously within each of several social strata.

Today the trickle-across concept best reflects the adoption process for most fashions. Granted, there is some flow downward, and obviously there is an upward influence. But market conditions today seem to foster a horizontal flow. By means of modern production, communication, and transportation methods, we can disseminate style information and products so rapidly that all social strata can be reached at about the same time. In the apparel field particularly, manufacturing and marketing programs tend to foster the horizontal movement of fashions. Manufacturers produce a wide *variety* of essentially one style. They also produce various *qualities* of the same basic style so as to appeal to different income groups simultaneously. When an entire cycle may last only one season, sellers cannot afford to wait for style acceptance to trickle down. They must introduce it into many social levels as soon as possible.

File 9-3

Marketing at Work

Retail Control Can Mean Fashion Success

Some of Canada's most successful fashion designers are also successful retailers. When Robin Kay and David Rothberg opened a small fashion boutique in Toronto's trendy Yorkville district in 1981, they had no intention of becoming clothing manufacturers. But, becoming increasingly frustrated by dealing with suppliers, they soon began to design and manufacture their own garments. They now own a seven-store chain under the name of Robin Kay Clothing, stocked exclusively with their own label, produced in their own Toronto factory.

The ability to control their own costs, quality, design, and delivery is leading other retailers to establish their own production facilities. As many discount stores now carry the same labels as are available at the major department stores, some of the larger retailers now offer private label lines that are exclusive to them. Eaton's offers its own labels in men's and ladies' clothing, and Harry Rosen has dramatically increased the percentage of its merchandise that bears the Harry Rosen label. The Toronto-based Monaco Group manufacturers and retails its Alfred Sung, Sung Sport, and Club Monaco labels through its own stores. In some cities, designers such as Ralph Lauren have opened their own specialty stores.

Marketing Considerations in Fashion

When a firm's products are subject to the fashion cycle, management must know what style the cycle is in at all times. Managers must decide at what point to get into the cycle, and when they should get out.

Accurate forecasting is of inestimable value in achieving success in fashion merchandising. This is an extremely difficult task, however, because the forecaster is often dealing with complex sociological and psychological factors. Frequently a retailer or a manufacturer operates largely on intuition and inspiration, tempered by considerable experience.

ANOTHER "LAW OF FASHION"

The same dress is indecent 10 years before its time, daring 1 year before its time, chic in its time, dowdy 3 years after its time, hideous 20 years after its time, amusing 30 years after its time, romantic 100 years after its time, and beautiful 150 years after its time.

Source: James Laver, British costume historian, in *Today's Health*, October 1973, p. 69.

The executives also must know what market they are aiming for. Ordinarily, a retailer cannot successfully participate in all stages of the fashion cycle at the same time. A high-grade specialty store selling apparel — whose stocks are displayed in limited numbers without price tags — should get in at the start of a fashion trend. A department store appealing to the middle-income market should plan to enter the cycle in time to mass-market the style as it is climbing to its peak of popularity.

SUMMARY

To make the product-planning phase of a company's marketing program most effective, it is imperative that management select appropriate strategies for the company's product mix. One strategy is simply to expand the product mix by increasing the number of lines and/or the depth within a line. An alternative is to prune out the product mix by eliminating an entire line or by simplifying the assortment within a line. Another strategy is to alter the design, packaging, or other features of existing products. Still another is appropriate ''positioning'' of the product, relative to competing products or to other products sold by the firm. In other strategies, management may elect to trade up or trade down, relative to its existing products.

Executives need to understand the concept of a product's life cycle and the characteristics of each stage in the cycle. The task of managing a product as it moves through its life cycle presents both challenges and opportunities — perhaps most frequently in the sales-decline stage.

An especially controversial product strategy is that of planned obsolescence, built around the concepts of style, fashion, and the fashion cycle. Fashion — essentially a sociological and psychological phenomenon — follows a reasonably predictable pattern. With advances in communications and production, the fashion-adoption process has moved away from the traditional trickle-down pattern. Today the process is better described as trickle-across. There also are some noteworthy examples of fashions trickling up. Style obsolescence, in spite of its critics, is based on consumer psychology.

NOTES

[1] Adapted from David A. Aaker and J. Gary Shansby, ''Positioning Your Product,'' *Business Horizons*, May-June 1982, pp. 56-58.

[2] For a step-by-step procedure to follow in selecting a positioning strategy, see Aaker and Shansby, op. cit., pp. 58-62; and William D. Neal, ''Strategic Product Positioning: A Step-by-Step Guide,'' *Business*, May-June 1980, pp. 34-42. See also Kenneth G. Hardy, ''The Power of Positioning Your Product Lines,'' *Business Quarterly*, vol. 51, no. 3, November 1986, pp. 90-92.

[3] Wayne Mouland, ''How to Promote Sales of Mature Brands,'' *Marketing*, November 17, 1986, p. CP and 14.

[4] For a discussion of strategies for reviving declining products and also some ideas for reintroducing abandoned products, see William Lazer, Mushtaq Liqmani, and Zahir Quraeshi, ''Product Rejuvenation Strategies,'' *Business Horizons*, November-December 1984, pp. 21-28; and Mark N. Vamos, ''New Life for Madison Avenue's Old-Time Stars,'' *Business Week*, Apr. 1, 1985, p. 94.

[5] Stanley Marcus, ''Fashion Merchandising,'' a Tobé lecture on retail distribution, Harvard Business School, Mar. 10, 1959, pp. 4-5.

KEY TERMS AND CONCEPTS

Product line 239
Product mix 239
Product-mix breadth and depth 240
Expansion of product mix 240
Contraction of product mix 241
Product alteration 241
Product positioning 242
Trading up/trading down 244
Product life cycle 245
Planned obsolescence 249

Fashion (style) obsolescence 250
Style 250
Fashion 250
Fad 250
Fashion-adoption process 251
Fashion cycle 251
Trickle-down 251
Trickle-across 251
Trickle-up 251

1. "It is inconsistent for management to follow concurrently the product-line strategies of *expanding* its product mix and *contracting* its product mix." Discuss.

2. "Trading up and trading down are product strategies closely related to the business cycle. Firms trade up during periods of prosperity and trade down during depressions or recessions." Do you agree? Why?

3. Name some products that you believe are in the introductory stage of their life cycles. Identify the market that considers your examples to be new products.

4. Give examples of products that are in the stage of market decline. In each case, point out whether you think the decline is permanent. What recommendations do you have for rejuvenating the demand for the product?

5. How might a company's pricing strategies differ, depending upon whether its product is in the introductory stage or maturity stage of its life cycle?

6. What advertising strategies are likely to be used when a product is in the growth stage?

7. What products, other than wearing apparel and automobiles, stress fashion and style in marketing? Do styles exist among industrial products?

8. Select a product and trace its marketing as it moves through a complete fashion cycle. Particularly note and explain the changes in the distribution, pricing, and promotion of the product in the various stages of the cycle.

9. Is the trickle-down theory applicable in describing the fashion-adoption process in product lines other than women's apparel? Explain, using examples.

10. Planned obsolescence is criticized as a social and economic waste because we are urged to buy things we do not like and do not need. What is your opinion in this matter? If you object to planned obsolescence, what are your recommendations for correcting the situation?

11. What effects might a recession have on:
   a. Product life cycles?
   b. Planned obsolescence?
   What marketing strategies might a firm employ to counter (or take advantage of) these effects?

CHAPTER **10**

BRANDS, PACKAGING, AND OTHER PRODUCT FEATURES

CHAPTER GOALS

The title of this chapter could be ''Product Presentation'' — because the way in which a physical product is presented to potential customers is very much a part of the product itself. After studying this chapter, you should understand:

- The nature and importance of brands, including the characteristics of a good brand and the problem of generic brand names.
- Brand strategies of manufacturers and middlemen.
- The ''battle of the brands.''
- The nature and importance of packaging.
- Major packaging strategies.
- Types of labelling.
- The marketing implications in some other product features — design, colour, quality, warranty, and servicing.

256

When you hear the term "beer market," do you think immediately of the well-known products of Canada's national brewers? Do you put on your investor hat and anticipate a downturn in stock prices ("bear market")? Or do you wonder why so many companies seem to be using friendly teddy bears to promote their products? In all cases, the marketing implications are important.

The Canadian beer industry is characterized by a high level of segmentation. There is literally a brand for every taste, although most beer drinkers can't tell their own regular brand from a competing brand in a blind taste test. There are domestic national brands such as Labatt's Blue, Molson Golden, and OV. There are the light brands that now account for more than 20 percent of the market — Blue Light, Miller Lite, Molson Light, and several others. There are regional brands, available only in certain provinces — Kokanee on the west coast, O'Keefe's Extra Old Stock in several provinces, Brador in Quebec, Moosehead and Black Horse in the east. Then there are the brands whose origins are in other countries, but which are brewed in Canada under licence from the original brewer — Coors, Miller, Lowenbrau, Budweiser, Carlsberg, and Foster's Lager. With such variety, how do consumers decide which brand is "theirs"?

And what of the phenomenon of the "bear market"? More and more companies are using stuffed bears as a means of brand and corporate identification. Lever Brothers uses "Snuggle" to promote its fabric softener of the same name. Shoppers Drug Mart has a Life bear; McGuinness Distillers has a Polar Ice bear; and Dare Foods employs Professor Bear. Zellers has its "Zeddy" bear, and we all remember the A&W Root Bear. Ultramar uses a whole family of bears to advertise its home heat services. Why bears?

For many products the brand image is all-important. Otherwise, how do you account for some people wanting Bayer Aspirin and others preferring a private label ASA brand, when both are physically and chemically the identical product? Some people buy Esso motor oil, while others choose the Petro-Canada brand. Yet many people contend that there are no significant differences among the well-known brands of motor oils.

Why do some people use certain brands and not others? The buyer's choice may be affected by the package, warranty, colour, design, or some other feature of the product. In packaging, for example, Rothmans, Players, and other brands try to increase sales by putting 25 cigarettes into a package, instead of the traditional 20. Colgate, Maclean's, and Crest toothpaste increased sales when they marketed this product in a pump-dispenser package. Holiday Inn found that by offering a money-back guarantee, the company gained a second chance with unhappy customers and also improved its own service. The effective use of product quality as a marketing tool by Panasonic, Sony, and other Japanese manufacturers is known worldwide. All these product characteristics combined project an image to prospective customers. Consequently, because these product features are such important elements in a company's marketing program, we devote this chapter to them.

INFLUENCES OF PRODUCT FEATURES ON BUSINESS FUNCTIONS

Branding, packaging, and the other product features are interrelated with, and affect, the production and financial functions of a firm as well as other marketing activities. If a product is manufactured in six colours instead of one, the *production* runs are shorter, there are more of them, and therefore they are more costly. A product made in small units and packaged in an attractive wrapper is ordinarily more costly than one put up in large, bulk-packaged units.

Financial risks increase as the variety of sizes and colours is increased. Packaging products in special Christmas containers exposes a company to a financial loss on merchandise that is unsold after December 26. A business that offers a generous warranty — ''Double your money back if not entirely satisfied'' — has greater financial risks than a firm whose policy is ''All sales are final.''

Product features are also interrelated with other marketing elements. Products to be sold on a self-service basis must be carefully packaged and labelled to attract the customer at the point of purchase. And, normally, branding increases price rigidity. At the same time, however, well-known brands are most likely to have their prices cut to attract customers to the seller's establishment.

BRANDS

The word *brand* is a comprehensive term, and it includes other, narrower terms. A **brand** is a name, term, symbol, or special design, or some combination of these elements, that is intended to identify the goods or services of one seller or a group of sellers. A brand differentiates one seller's products or services from those of competitors.[1] A brand **name** consists of words, letters, and/or numbers that can be *vocalized*. A brand **mark** is the part of the brand that appears in the form of a symbol, design, or distinctive colouring or lettering. It is recognized by sight but may not be expressed when a person pronounces the brand name. Ski-Doo, du Maurier, Gillette, and Robin Hood are brand names. Brand marks are illustrated by the picture of Robin Hood on the flour package, the distinctive CN logo of

Robin Hood is a brand *name*. The illustration of the Robin Hood character is a brand mark. Together they are a brand that is protected as a trademark.

Canadian National, and the Root Bear character who promotes A&W. These marks, logos, or designs are usually registered and may be used only by the company that owns the mark.

A **trademark** is defined as a brand that is given legal protection because, under the law, it has been appropriated by one seller. Thus *trademark* is essentially a legal term. All trademarks are brands and thus include the words, letters, or numbers that can be pronounced. They may also include a pictorial design (brand mark). Some people erroneously believe that the trademark is only the pictorial part of the brand.

One major method of classifying brands is on the basis of who owns them — producers or middlemen. IBM, Arrow, Bick's, York, and GWG are producers' brands, while Pride of Arabia, Viking, Motomaster, Birkdale, and Ann Page are middlemen's brands.

The terms *national* and *private* have been used to describe producer and middleman brand ownership, respectively. However, marketing people prefer the producer-middleman terminology. To say that the brand of a small manufacturer of poultry feed in British Columbia, who markets only in two or three western provinces, is a *national* brand, while the brands of Sears, Eaton's, Loblaws, Woodwards, and Steinberg are *private* brands, seems to be stretching the meaning of the terms *national* and *private*.

Importance of Branding

Brands make it easy for consumers to identify products or services. Brands also assure purchasers that they are getting comparable quality when they reorder.

For sellers, brands are something that can be advertised and that will be recognized when displayed on shelves in a store. Branding also helps sellers to control their market because buyers will not confuse one branded product with another. Branding reduces price comparisons because it is hard to compare prices on two items with different brands. Finally, for sellers, branding can add a measure of prestige to otherwise ordinary commodities (Sunkist oranges, Sifto salt, Lantic sugar, Highliner fish, Chiquita bananas).

Reasons for Not Branding

The two major responsibilities inherent in brand ownership are (1) to promote the brand and (2) to maintain a consistent quality of output. Many firms do not brand their products because they are unable or unwilling to assume those responsibilities.

Some items are not branded because of the difficulty of differentiating the products of one firm from those of another. Clothespins, nails, and industrial raw materials (coal, cotton, wheat) are examples of goods for which product differentiation (including branding) is generally unknown. The physical nature of some items, such as fresh fruits and vegetables, may discourage branding. However, now that these products are often packaged in typically purchased quantities, brands are being applied to the packages.

Producers frequently do not brand that part of their output that is below their usual quality. Products graded as seconds or imperfects are sold at a cut price and are often distributed through channels different from those used for usual-quality goods.

Selecting a good brand name is not an easy task. In spite of the acknowledged importance of a brand, it is surprising how few really good brand names there are. In a study made many years ago, it was found that only 12 percent of the names helped sell the product; 36 percent actually hurt sales. The other 52 percent were "nonentities — contributing nothing to the sales appeal of the product." There is no reason to believe that the situation has improved materially since that study was made.

Is this a good brand name?

CHARACTERISTICS OF A GOOD BRAND

A good brand should possess as many of the following characteristics as possible. It is extremely difficult, however, to find a brand that has all of them. A brand should:

- Suggest something about the product's characteristics — its benefits, use, or action. Some names that suggest desirable benefits include Beautyrest, Coldspot, Motomaster, and La-Z-Boy. Product use and action are suggested by Minute Rice, Dustbuster, Spic and Span, Gleem, and Reddi-Whip.
- Be easy to pronounce, spell, and remember. Simple, short, one-syllable names such as Tide, Ban, Aim, and Raid are helpful.
- Be distinctive. Brands with names like National, Star, Ideal, or Standard fail on this point.
- Be adaptable to new products that may be added to the product line. An innocuous name such as Kellogg, Lipton, or Jelinek may serve the purpose better than a highly distinctive name suggestive of product benefits. Frigidaire is an excellent name for a refrigerator and other cold-image products. But when the producer expanded its line of home appliances and added Frigidaire kitchen ranges, the name lost some of its sales appeal.
- Be capable of being registered and legally protected under the Trade Marks Act and other statutory or common laws.

GENERIC USAGE OF BRAND NAMES

Over a period of years, some brands become so well accepted that the brand name is substituted for the **generic** name of the particular product. Examples of brand names that legally have become generic are linoleum, celluloid, cellophane, kerosene, shredded wheat, and nylon. Originally, these were trademarks limited to use by the owner.

A brand name can become generic in several ways. Sometimes the patent on a product expires. There is no simple generic name available, and so the public continues to use the brand name as a generic name. This happened with shredded wheat, nylon, and cellophane. Sometimes a firm just does too good an advertising and selling job with an outstanding brand name. While not yet legally generic, names such as Xerox, Band-Aid, Scotch Tape, Ski-Doo and Kleenex are on the

Marketing at Work

Brand Care Equals Strong Share

These brands have been market leaders for a long time.

A study by the A.C. Nielsen Company showed that 24 of the top 25 grocery product brands in Ontario had been established in the market for more than ten years. These are brands with which we are all familiar — Kellogg's Corn Flakes, Carnation evaporated milk, Campbell's Soup. What distinguishes such well-known, established brands from others with a short life cycle? Nielsen concluded that the marketers of these successful brands have built an element of trust among the users of their brands. This trust has been carefully nurtured, in part through heavy advertising support. Also, each of these leading brands tends to undergo periodic renewal, through packaging changes, line extensions, product improvements, or image enhancement. When brands have established such a strong consumer franchise, their manufacturers use a wide variety of marketing tools in order to encourage consumer loyalty, thereby maintaining market position.

Source: Adapted from Wayne Mouland, "How to Promote Sales of Mature Brands," *Marketing*, November 17, 1986, p. CP & I 4.

Well-known company logos.

borderline. They are outstanding brand names for the original product and have been promoted so well that many people use them generically.

It is the responsibility of the trademark owner to assert the company's rights in order to prevent the loss of the distinctive character of the trademark. A number of strategies are employed to prevent the brand name from falling into generic usage. The most common strategy is to ensure that the words "trade mark" or the letters "TM"® appear adjacent to the brand name wherever it appears.

A second strategy is to use two names — the brand name together with either the company's name or the generic name of the product. An example of this is the name "Thermos Vacuum Bottle," which is designed to suggest to the public that "Thermos" is but one brand of vacuum bottle and that the name "Thermos" should not be applied to all products in that product category.

A third strategy for protecting a trademark involves the incorporation into the trademark of a distinctive signature or logo. Many companies have adopted dis-

XEROX

Six things you shouldn't hear at the office:

1. "Deal me in."

2. "We'll just add it to the expense account."

3. "Let's end this coffee break, it's time for lunch."

4. "Alright, who phoned Mozambique 7 times?"

5. "It's o.k., the boss is on jury duty."

6. "Will you Xerox these memos, please?"

Actually, it's the last statement of the list we're most interested in. You see, whoever used that phrase used our name incorrectly. The Xerox trademark is not a verb. So you can't "Xerox a memo." But you certainly can copy a memo on your Xerox copier.

In fact, we wish you would make a copy of *this* message and use it to remind your office friends not to say things they shouldn't....At least as far as Xerox is concerned.

TeamXerox

XEROX® is a trademark of XEROX CORPORATION.

tinctive ways of presenting the brand name of their products so that the consumer is able to identify their products whenever they encounter the particular brand written in a certain script or type face.

Finally, the owner of a registered trademark must be willing to prosecute any other companies attempting to market products under a brand name that is identical to or similar to the registered brand name. By prosecuting such infringements of the trademark protection, the company is demonstrating to the courts that it is actively protecting its right to use of the brand and is guarding against the brand falling into generic usage. If the owner company fails to prosecute infringements, even if it decides to prosecute at a later date after other companies have adopted the brand, the distinctive character of the trademark will be lost and the courts are likely to rule that the original owner no longer has exclusive right to use of the brand name, as it is in the public domain. Some companies seek to show competitors or others who wish to make use of registered trademarks that they are willing to take legal action to protect their trademarks. An example of advertising that is designed to achieve this purpose is presented above.

Brand Strategies

MANUFACTURERS' STRATEGIES

Manufacturers must decide whether to brand their products and whether to sell any or all of their output under middlemen's brands.

Marketing entire output under manufacturer's own brands   Companies that market their entire output under their own brands typically are very large, well financed, and well managed. Polaroid, Maytag, and IBM are examples. They typically have broad product lines, well-established distribution systems, and large shares of the market. Probably only a small percentage of manufacturers follow this policy, and their number seems to be decreasing.

Many of the reasons for adopting this policy have already been covered in the section on the importance of branding to the seller. In addition, middlemen often prefer to handle manufacturers' brands, especially when the brands have high consumer acceptance.

Branding of fabricating parts and materials   Some producers of industrial fabricating materials and parts (products used in the further manufacturing of other goods) will brand their products. This strategy is used in the marketing of Fiberglas insulation, Pella windows, Acrilan fabrics, and many automotive parts — spark plugs, batteries, oil filters, and so on.

Underlying this strategy is the seller's desire to develop a market preference for its branded part or material. For instance, G.D. Searle wants to build a market situation in which customers will insist on food products sweetened with Nutra-Sweet. In addition, the parts manufacturer wants to persuade the producer of the finished item that using the branded materials will help sell the end product. In our example, the Searle Company hopes to convince food manufacturers that their sales will increase if their products contain NutraSweet.

Certain product characteristics lend themselves to the effective use of this strategy. First, it helps if the product is also a consumer good that is bought for replacement purposes. This factor encourages the branding of Champion spark plugs, Atlas batteries, and Fram oil filters, for example. Second, the seller's situation is improved if the item is a major part of the finished product — a television picture tube, for example.

The qualities of DuPont-produced Antron Nylon Fibres are emphasized in the carpets produced by other firms.

Marketing under middlemen's brands   A widespread strategy is for manufacturers to brand part or all of their output with the brands of their middlemen customers. For the manufacturer, this middlemen's-brand business generates additional sales volume and profit dollars. Orders typically are large, payment is prompt, and a manufacturer's working-capital position is improved. Also, manufacturers may utilize their production resources more effectively, including their plant capacities. Furthermore, refusing to sell under a retailer's or wholesaler's brand will not eliminate competition from this source. Many middlemen want to market under their own brands, so if one manufacturer refuses their business, they will simply go to another.

Probably the most serious limitation to marketing under middlemen's brands is that a manufacturer may be at the mercy of the middlemen. This problem grows as the proportion of that producer's output going to middlemen's brands increases.

MIDDLEMEN'S STRATEGIES

The question of whether or not to brand must also be answered by middlemen. There are two usual strategies, as follows:

Carry only manufacturer's brands   Most retailers and wholesalers follow this policy because they are not able to take on the dual burdens of promoting a brand and maintaining its quality. Even though manufacturers' brands usually carry lower gross margins, they often have a higher rate of turnover and a better profit possibility.

Carry middlemen's brands along with manufacturer's brands   Many large retailers and some large wholesalers have their own brands. Middlemen may find it advantageous to market their own brands for several reasons. First, this strategy increases their control over their market. If customers prefer a given middleman's brand, they can get it only from that middleman's store. Furthermore, middlemen can usually sell their brands at prices below those of manufacturers' brands and still earn higher gross margins. This is possible because middlemen can buy at lower costs. The costs may be lower because (1) manufacturers' advertising and selling costs are not included in their prices, or (2) producers are anxious to get the extra business to keep their plants running in slack seasons.

Middlemen have more freedom in pricing products sold under their own labels. Products carrying a retailer's brand become differentiated products, and this hinders price comparisons that might be unfavourable to that retailer. Also, prices on manufacturer's brands can be cut drastically by competing retail stores. This last point is what has been happening in recent years in the marketing of clothing with designer labels such as Calvin Klein, Simon Chang, Ralph Lauren, and Alfred Sung. Some of the large retailers in their upper-priced clothing departments have increased their stocks of apparel carrying the store's own brand. These stores (Eaton's, Simpsons, The Bay, Harry Rosen, for example), have cut back on products with designer brands such as Calvin Klein, Pierre Cardin, and others. The reason for this brand-switching is that some designer-labelled products are now available at much lower prices in stores such as K-Mart, Zellers, and other "off-price retailers."[2]

STRATEGIES COMMON TO MANUFACTURERS AND MIDDLEMEN

Manufacturers and middlemen alike must adopt some strategy with respect to branding their product mix and branding for market saturation.

Branding a line of products   At least four different strategies are widely used by firms that sell more than one product.

- The same "family" or "blanket" brand may be placed on all products. This policy is followed by Heinz, Catelli, Campbell, McCain's and others in the food field, as well as by Proctor-Silex and Black & Decker.
- A separate name may be used for each product. This strategy is employed by Procter & Gamble and Carling O'Keefe.
- A separate family brand may be applied to each grade of product or to each group of similar products. Sears groups its major home appliances under the Kenmore name, its paints and home furnishings under Harmony House, and its insurance under Allstate.

Catelli gives the "family" brand name to a variety of products.

- The company trade name may be combined with an individual name for the product. Thus there is Johnson's Pledge, Kellogg's Rice Krispies, Molson Golden, and Ford Mustang.

When used wisely, a family-brand strategy has considerable merit. This strategy makes it much simpler and less expensive to introduce new related products to a line. Also, the general prestige of a brand can be spread more easily if it appears on several products rather than on only one. A family brand is best suited for a marketing situation where the products are related in quality, in use, or in some other manner. When Black & Decker, a manufacturer of power tools, purchased General Electric's line of small appliances, the Black & Decker brand was put on those appliances, *but* not immediately. Because of the perceived differences between kitchen products and workroom products, Black & Decker realized it was a risky proposition to switch brands. Consequently, the company mounted a year-long brand-transition campaign before making the change. Also, during those years, Black & Decker introduced several other houseware products, and this helped in the General Electric-Black & Decker brand transition.[3]

On the other hand, the use of family brands places a greater burden on the brand owner to maintain consistent quality among all products. One bad item can reflect unfavourably, and even disastrously, on all other products carrying the same brand.

Branding for market saturation Frequently, to increase its degree of market saturation, a firm will employ a multiple-brand strategy. Suppose, for example, that a company has built one type of sales appeal around a given brand. To reach other segments of the market, the company can use other appeals with other brands. Procter & Gamble's two detergents, Tide and Dreft, illustrate this point. Some people feel that if Tide is strong enough to clean soiled work clothes, it cannot be used on lingerie and other fine clothing. For these people, Procter & Gamble has marketed Dreft, a detergent whose image is more gentle than that of Tide. To penetrate the middle-income market or a different segment altogether, several designers of higher-priced women's apparel have introduced a lower-priced line, usually under a different brand name. Some examples of the original designer label with their "second" brand are Alfred Sung (Monaco), Yves Saint Laurent (Variation), and Ralph Lauren (Chaps).[4]

Marketing at Work

File 10-2

Despite the Clutter, Strong Brands Keep Marching On

With the proliferation of brands in the marketplace, there has been much comment about a decline in brand loyalty. Some writers have observed that the fragmentation of the consumer market has resulted in much greater variety. Consumers now have more choice — from the long-established major brands to newer "niche" brands, introduced to appeal to a particular segment of the market. Despite the arguments about whether brand loyalty is or is not dying, many of the most successful brands remain strong and continue to be the first or second choice of the majority of consumers. Many product categories are still dominated by one or two leading brands, which together may account for 60 to 70 percent of total sales.

In the service sector, promotions run by airlines, hotels, and retailers are intended to build loyalty. Air Canada's Aeroplan frequent-flyer program and Zellers' "Club Z" both give customers points based on the volume of their purchases. These points can be redeemed for free flights or merchandise.

The Battle of the Brands

Now *this* is a battle of the brands.

Middlemen's brands have proved to be eminently successful in competing with manufacturers' brands. However, neither group has demonstrated a convincing competitive superiority over the other in the marketplace. Consequently, the "battle of the brands" shows every indication of continuing and becoming more intense.

About 15 years ago several supermarket chains introduced products sold under their generic names. That is, the products were simply labelled as pork and beans, peanut butter, cottage cheese, paper towels, and so on. These unbranded products generally sell for 30 to 40 percent less than manufacturers' brands and 20 percent less than retailers' brands. While they are the nutritional equivalent of branded products, the generics (graded "standard" in industry terms) may not have the colour, size, and appearance of the branded items (graded "fancy"). Most of the chains sell these products completely unbranded — referring to them as "generic" or "generic products" in the store's advertising. In effect, "generic" becomes an unofficial brand name in that it is the identifying name used by the stores and consumers. Generic products now account for a large enough share of total sales in their respective product lines to be a major factor in the battle of the brands.

Several factors account for the success of middlemen's brands and generic-labelled products. The thin profit margins on manufacturers' brands have encouraged retailers to establish their own labels. The improved quality of retailers' brands has boosted their sales. Consumers have become more sophisticated in their buying and their brand loyalty has declined, so they do consider alternative brands. It is quite generally known that retailers' brands usually are produced by large, well-known manufacturers. Generic labels, with their low-price, no-frills approach, appeal to price-conscious consumers.

Manufacturers do have some effective responses to combat generic labels and retailers' brands. Producers can, for example, devote top priority to product innovation and packaging, an area in which retailers are not as strong. Manufacturers' research and development capacity also enables them to enter the market in the early stages of a product's life cycle, whereas retailer brands typically enter after a product is well established.

Trademark Licensing

An effective branding strategy that has grown by leaps and bounds in recent years is brand (or trademark) licensing. Under this strategy, the owner of a trademark grants permission (a licence) to other firms to use the owner's brand name, logotype (distinctive lettering and colouring), and/or character on the licensee's products. To illustrate, Coca-Cola has allowed (licensed) Murjani International to use the Coca-Cola name and distinctive lettering on a line of clothing(blue jeans, sweaters, shirts, jackets). The owner of the trademark characters in the ''Peanuts'' cartoon strip (Snoopy, Charlie Brown, Lucy, etc.) has licensed the use of these characters on many different products and services. Sears has introduced McKids, a line of children's clothing featuring McDonald's characters. The licensee typically pays a royalty of about five percent on the wholesale price of the product that carries the licensed trademark. However, this figure can vary depending upon the perceived strength of the licensor's brand.

Strategy decisions must be made by both parties — the licensor and the licensee. Pierre Cardin (a licensor) must ask, ''Should we allow other firms to use our designer label?'' A manufacturer of eyeglasses (a licensee) must ask, ''Do we want to put out a line of high-fashion eyeglasses under the Pierre Cardin name?''

Owners of well-known brands are interested in licensing their trademarks for various reasons. First, it can be very profitable since there is no expense involved on the part of the licensor. Second, there is a promotional benefit, because the licensor's name gets wider circulation far beyond the original trademarked article. Third, licensing can help protect the trademark. If Coca-Cola licenses its brand for use in a variety of product categories, it can block any other company from using that brand legally in those product categories.

For the company receiving the licence — the licensee — the strategy is a quick way to gain market recognition and to penetrate a new market. Today there is a high financial cost involved in establishing a new brand name. Even then there is no guarantee of success. It is a lot easier for an unknown firm to gain consumer acceptance of its product if that item carries a well-known brand.

PACKAGING

Packaging may be defined as all the activities involved in designing and producing the container or wrapper for a product. There are three reasons for packaging:

■ Packaging serves several *safety* and *utilitarian purposes*. It protects a product on its route from the producer to the final customer, and in some cases even while it is being used by the customer. For example, effective packaging can help to prevent ill-intentioned persons from tampering with products. Some protection is provided by "child-proof" closures on containers of medicines and other products that are potentially harmful for children. Also, compared with bulk items, packaged goods generally are more convenient, cleaner, and less susceptible to losses from evaporation, spilling, and spoilage.

■ Packaging may *implement a company's marketing program*. Packaging helps to identify a product and thus may prevent substitution of competitive products. At the point of purchase, the package can serve as a silent sales person. Furthermore, the advertising copy on the package will last as long as the product is used in its packaged form. Also, a package may be the only significant way in which a firm can differentiate its product. In the case of convenience goods or industrial operating supplies, for example, most buyers feel that one well-known brand is about as good as another.

Some feature of the package may serve as a sales appeal — a no-drip spout, a reusable jar, or a self-applicator (Gillette's shaving brush with built-in lather, for example). When Campbell's Soup introduced its Swanson Gourmet line of premium quality frozen dinners, the price of the product was kept low by an inexpensive packaging innovation. The meals are cooked in and can be eaten from the paper carton they come in, reducing packaging costs by 30 percent.

■ Management may package its product in such a way as to *increase profit possibilities*. A package may be so attractive that customers will pay more just to get the special package — even though the increase in price exceeds the additional cost of the package. Also, an increase of handling or a reduction in damage losses, due to packaging, will cut marketing costs, again increasing profit.

Importance of Packaging in Marketing

Historically, packaging was a production-oriented activity in most companies, performed mainly to obtain the benefits of protection and convenience. Today, however, the marketing significance of packaging is fully recognized, and packaging is truly a major competitive force in the struggle for markets. The widespread use of self-service selling and automatic vending means that the package must do the selling job at the point of purchase. Shelf space is often at a premium, and it is no simple task for manufacturers even to get their products displayed in a retail outlet. Most retailers are inclined to cater to producers that have used effective packaging.

In addition, the increased use of branding and the public's rising standards in health and sanitation have contributed to the importance of packaging. Safety in packaging has become an especially important marketing and social issue in recent years.

New developments in packaging, occurring rapidly and in a seemingly endless flow, require management's constant attention to packaging design. We see new packaging materials replacing the traditional ones, new shapes, new closures, and other new features (measured portions, metered flow). These all make for increased convenience for consumers and additional selling points for marketers. One new development in packaging is the aseptic container — a "paper bottle" made of laminations of paper, aluminum foil, and plastic. Its airtight feature keeps perishables fresh for five months without refrigeration, and it costs about one-half as

Packaging innovation expands markets.

much as cans and 30 percent as much as bottles. Already it is being used to package many different drink products, and its future prospects are exceptionally bright.

CHANGING THE PACKAGE

In general, management has two reasons for considering a package change — to combat a decrease in sales and to expand a market by attracting new groups of customers. More specifically, a firm may want to correct a poor feature in the existing container, or a company may want to take advantage of new materials. Some companies change their containers to aid in promotional programs. A new package may be used as a major appeal in advertising copy, or because the old container may not show up well in advertisements.

PACKAGING THE PRODUCT LINE

A company must decide whether to develop a family resemblance in the packaging of its several products. **Family packaging** involves the use of identical packages for all products or the use of packaging with some common feature. Campbell's Soup, for example, uses virtually identical packaging on its condensed soup products. Management's philosophy concerning family packaging generally parallels its feelings about family branding. When new products are added to a line, promotional values associated with old products extend to the new ones. On the other hand, family packaging should be used only when the products are related in use and are of similar quality.

File 10-3

Marketing at Work

Standing Out in a Flat Market

The Canadian beer industry in recent years has been (excuse the expression!) flat. There has been little or no growth in per capita beer consumption since the early 1980s. As a result, the major brewers have been competing fiercely to increase their respective shares of a stable market. Since beer is a relatively undifferentiated product, the industry has turned to packaging to set one brand apart from the others. One of the first moves to differentiate brands on the basis of packaging was the abandonment of the ''stubby'' brown bottle in favour of what is known in the industry as ''private mould glass'' — in other words, each brand is packaged in its own distinctive bottle. Soon to follow were packaging innovations such as twist caps and the bottom bottle opener, all designed to give beer drinkers a reason to switch brands.

REUSE PACKAGING

Another strategy to be considered is reuse packaging. Should the company design and promote a package that can serve other purposes after the original contents have been consumed? Glasses containing cheese can later be used to serve fruit juice. Baby-food jars make great containers for small parts like nuts, bolts, and screws. Reuse packaging also should stimulate repeat purchases as the consumer attempts to acquire a matching set of containers.

MULTIPLE PACKAGING

For many years there has been a trend toward multiple packaging, or the practice of placing several units in one container. Dehydrated soups, motor oil, beer, golf balls, building hardware, candy bars, towels, and countless other products are packaged in multiple units. Test after test has proved that multiple packaging increases total sales of a product.

A variety of packages increases sales.

Criticisms of Packaging

Packaging is in the forefront today because of its relationship to environmental pollution issues. Perhaps the biggest challenges facing packagers is how to dispose of used containers, which are a major contributor to the solid-waste disposal problem. Consumers' desire for convenience (in the form of throw-away containers) conflicts with their desire for a clean environment.

Other criticisms of packaging are:

- Packaging depletes our natural resources. This criticism is offset to some extent as packagers increasingly make use of recycled materials. Another offsetting point is that effective packaging reduces spoilage (another form of resource waste).
- Packaging is excessively expensive. Cosmetic packaging is often cited as an example here. But even in seemingly simple packaging — beer, for example — as much as half the production cost goes for the container. On the other hand, effective packaging reduces transportation costs and losses from product spoilage.
- Health hazards occur from some forms of plastic packaging and some aerosol cans. Government regulations have banned the use of several of these suspect packaging materials.
- Packaging is deceptive. Government regulation plus improvements in business

practices regarding packaging have reduced the intensity of this criticism, although it is heard on occasion.

Truly, marketing executives face some real challenges in satisfying these complaints while at the same time retaining the marketing-effectiveness, consumer-convenience, and product-protection features of packaging.

LABELLING

Labelling is another product feature that requires managerial attention. The **label** is the part of a product that carries verbal information about the product or the seller. A label may be part of a package, or it may be a tag attached directly to the product. Obviously there is a close relationship among labelling, packaging, and branding.

Types of Labels

Typically, labels are classified as brand, grade, or descriptive. A **brand label** is simply the brand alone applied to the product or to the package. Thus, some oranges are brand-labelled (stamped) Sunkist or Jaffa, and some clothes carry the brand label Sanforized. A **grade label** identifies the quality with a letter, number, or word. Canadian beef is grade-labelled A, B, or C and each grade is subdivided by number from 1 to 4 indicating an increasing fat content. **Descriptive labels** give objective information about the use, construction, care, performance, or other features of the product. On a descriptive label for a can of corn, there will be statements concerning the type of corn (golden sweet), the style (creamed or in niblet kernels), and the can size, number of servings, other ingredients, and nutritional contents.

RELATIVE MERITS

Brand labelling creates very little stir among critics. While it is an acceptable form of labelling, its severe limitation is that it does not supply sufficient information to a buyer. The real fight centres on grade versus descriptive labelling and on whether grade labelling should be made mandatory.

The proponents of grade labelling argue that it is simple, definite, and easy to use. They also point out that if grade labels were used, prices would be more closely related to quality, although grade labelling would not stifle competition. In fact, they believe that grade labelling might increase competition, because consumers would be able to judge products on the basis of both price and known quality.

Those who object to grade labelling point out that a very low score on one grading characteristic can be offset by very high scores on other factors. Companies selling products that score high *within* a given grade would be hurt by grade labelling. These companies could not justify a higher price than that charged for a product that scored very low in the same grade. And some people feel that grades are an inaccurate guide for consumer buying. It is not possible to grade the differences in flavour and taste, or in style and fashion, yet these are the factors that often influence consumer purchases.

Statutory Labelling Requirements

The importance of packaging and labelling in terms of its potential for influencing the consumer's purchasing decision is reflected in the large number of federal and provincial laws that exist to regulate this marketing activity. At the federal level, the Competition Act regulates the area of misleading advertising and a number of companies have been convicted of misleading advertising for the false or deceptive statements that have appeared on their packages. In this case, the information that appears on a package or label has been considered to constitute an advertisement.

The Hazardous Products Act gives the federal government the power to regulate the sale, distribution, advertising, and labelling of certain consumer products that are considered dangerous. A number of products have been banned from sale under this Act and all hazardous products, such as cleaning substances, chemicals, and aerosol products, must carry on their labels a series of symbols that indicate the danger associated with the product and the precautions that should be taken with its use. The symbols illustrate that the product is poisonous, inflammable, explosive, or corrosive in nature.

Similarly the federal Food and Drugs Act regulates the sale of food, drugs, cosmetics, and medical devices. Under this Act, regulations deal with the manufacture, sale, advertising, packaging, and labelling of such products. Certain misleading and deceptive packaging and labelling practices are specifically prohibited.

The Textile Labelling Act requires that manufacturers label their products, including wearing apparel, yard goods, and household textiles, according to the fibre content of the product. In the past, more than 700 fabric names have appeared on products, but most of these were brand names of individual companies. For example,

The labels on these products must be printed in both French and English and quantity must be expressed in metric units.

the fibre known generically as polyester has been labelled as Terylene, Trevira, Dacron, Kodel, Fortrel, Tergal, Tetoron, and Crimplene, all of which are manufacturers' brand names for polyester. In order to reduce confusion among the buying public, products now have to be labelled according to the generic fibre content, with the percentage of each fibre in excess of five percent listed.

There also exist in Canada two government-sponsored consumer product labelling schemes that are informative in nature. These programs are the Canada Standard Size program and the Textile Care Labelling program. The Textile Care Labelling program involves the labelling of all textile products with symbols that indicate instructions for washing and dry cleaning the product.

The Consumer Packaging and Labelling Act regulates all aspects of the packaging and labelling of consumer products in this country. The regulations that have been passed under this Act require that most products sold in Canada must bear bilingual labels. The net quantity of the product must appear on the label in both metric and imperial units. If the quantity of a food product is expressed in terms of a certain number of servings, the size of the servings must also be stated. Where artificial flavourings are used in the manufacture of a food product, the label must contain the information that the flavour is imitation or simulated. The Act also makes provision for the standardization of container sizes. The first set of regulations to be passed under the Act set down the standard package sizes for toothpaste, shampoo, and skin cream products and it is in contravention of the regulations to manufacture these products in other than the package sizes approved.

The Consumer Packaging and Labelling Act requires that manufacturers of consumer products, especially in the food industry, incorporate the bilingual and metric requirements into the design of their labels.

The provinces have also moved into the field of regulating packaging and labelling. A number of provinces have passed legislation regarding misleading advertising and any information that appears on a package or label is considered an advertisement. In Quebec, that province's Official Language Act requires that all labels be written in French or in French and another language. If both English and French appear on the label, at least equal prominence must be given to the French.

File 10-4

Franchising Means Branding Service

When we think of packaging and brands, we normally think of tangible products. But services can be packaged and branded as well. In fact, there has been a recent trend, through the establishment of franchise operations, to market a consistent, branded service across the country.

One of the best examples is found in the home service industry, which has been growing rapidly through the 1980s. When Adrienne Stringer founded Molly Maid Home Care Services in Toronto in 1978, she paid particular attention to packaging (each of her employees wears a uniform) and to consistent, professional service. Now, with almost 300 franchises throughout Canada, the United States, and Great

Britain, the company name is as synonomous with home cleaning as McDonald's is with hamburgers.

Source: Adapted from Rona Maynard, ''Mop Your Way to Millions,'' *Report on Business Magazine*, September 1987, pp. 38-44.

OTHER IMAGE-BUILDING FEATURES

A well-rounded program for product planning and development will include a company policy on several additional product attributes: product design, colour, quality, guarantee, and servicing.

Product Design

Some companies use a computer to aid in designing a product.

One way to build an image of a product is through its design. In fact, a distinctive design may be the only feature that significantly differentiates a product. Many firms feel that there is considerable glamour and general promotional appeal in product design and the designer's name. In the field of industrial products, *engineering* design has long been recognized as extremely important. Today there is a realization of the marketing value of *appearance* design as well. Office machines and office furniture are examples of industrial products that reflect recent conscious attention to product design, often with good sales results. The marketing significance of design has been recognized for years in the field of consumer products, from big items like automobiles and refrigerators to small products like fountain pens and apparel.

Good design can improve the marketability of a product in many ways. It can make the product easier to operate. It can upgrade the product's quality or durability. It can improve product appearance and reduce manufacturing costs.

Colour

Colour often is the determining factor in a customer's acceptance or rejection of a product, whether that product is a dress, a table, or an automobile. Colour by itself, however, is no selling advantage because many competing firms offer colour. The marketing advantage comes in knowing the right colour and in knowing when to change colours. If a garment manufacturer or a retail store's fashion coordinator guesses wrong on what will be the fashionable colour in women's clothing, this error can be disastrous.[5]

Product Quality

In recent years, manufacturers have been increasingly concerned about the quality of their products. And well they should be! For many years, a major consumer complaint has concerned the poor quality of some products — both materials and workmanship. Some foreign products — Japanese cars, for example — have made serious inroads into the North American market because these products are perceived as being of better quality than their North American counterparts.

The quality of a product is extremely important, but it is probably the most difficult of all the image-building features to define. Users frequently disagree on what constitutes quality in a product, from a cut of meat to a piece of music. Personal tastes are deeply involved. Nevertheless, a marketing executive must make several decisions about product quality. First, the product should reach only that level of quality compatible with the intended use of the item; it need not be any better. In fact, *good* and *poor* are misleading terms. *Correct* and *incorrect* or *right* and *wrong* would be much more appropriate. If a person is making a peach cobbler, grade B or C peaches are the correct quality. They are not necessarily the *best* quality, but they are *right* for the intended use. It is not necessary to pay grade A prices for large, well-formed peaches when these features are destroyed in making the cobbler.[6]

Product Warranty and Product Liability

The general purpose of a warranty is to give buyers some assurance that they will be compensated in case the product does not perform up to reasonable expectations. In years past, courts seemed generally to recognize only **express warranties** — those stated in written or spoken words. Usually these were quite limited in what they covered and seemed mainly to protect the seller from buyers' claims.

But times have changed! Consumer complaints have led to a governmental campaign to protect the consumer in many areas, one of which is product liability. Today, courts and government agencies are broadening the scope of warranty coverage by recognizing the concept of **implied warranty**. This is the idea that a warranty was *intended* by the seller, although not actually stated. Manufacturers are being held responsible, even when the sales contract is between the retailer and the consumer. Warranties are considered to "run with the product." Manufacturers are held liable for product-caused injury, whether or not they are to blame for negligence in manufacturing. It all adds up to "Let the seller beware."

In recent years manufacturers have responded to legislation and consumer complaints by broadening and simplifying their warranties. Many sellers are using their warranties as promotional devices to stimulate purchase by reducing consumers' risks. The effective handling of consumers' complaints related to warranties can be a significant factor in strengthening a company's marketing program.[7]

The Hazardous Products Act indicates how the law has changed regarding product liability and injurious products. This law prohibits the sale of certain dangerous products and requires that other products which may be potentially dangerous carry an indication on their labels of the dangers inherent in their use. As further indication of the growing interest on the part of consumer groups and governments in the protection that existing forms of warranties offer the consumer, the Ontario Law Reform Commission in 1972 issued its Report on Consumer Warranties and Guarantees in the Sale of Goods. This report recommended broad and sweeping changes in the law respecting warranties and guarantees, which would provide the consumer with greater protection. Since the mid-1970s, two provinces, Saskatchewan and New Brunswick, have passed Consumer Products Warranty Acts. The Saskatchewan Act provides for statutory warranties that are deemed to be given by the retailer to the original purchaser and to subsequent owners. It also prescribes the form that written warranties must take.[8]

Product Servicing

A related problem is that of adequately providing the services guaranteed by the warranty. Product servicing requires management's attention as products become more complex and consumers grow increasingly dissatisfied and vocal. To cope with these problems, management can consider several courses of action. For instance, a producer can establish several geographically dispersed factory service centres, staff them with well-trained company employees, and strive to make servicing a separate profit-generating activity. Or the producer can shift the main burden to middlemen, compensate them for their efforts, and possibly even train their service people.

Today the provision of adequate product servicing should be high on the list of topics calling for managerial action. A perennial major consumer complaint is that manufacturers and retailers do *not* provide adequate repair service for the products they sell. Oftentimes, the situation is simply that the consumers wish to be *heard*. That is, they simply want someone to listen to them regarding their complaints. In response to this situation, a number of manufacturers have established toll-free (800-number) telephone lines to their customer service departments.

SUMMARY

The management of the various features of a product — its brand, package, labelling, design, colour, quality, warranty, and servicing — is an integral part of effective product planning. A *brand* is a means of identifying and differentiating the products or services of an organization. Branding aids sellers in managing their promotional and pricing activities. Brand ownership carries the dual responsibilities of promoting the brand and maintaining a consistent level of quality. Selecting a good brand name — and there are relatively few really good ones — is a difficult task. A good name should suggest a product's benefits, be easy to pronounce and remember, lend itself to product-line additions, and be eligible for legal registration and protection.

Manufacturers must decide whether to brand their products and whether to sell under a middleman's brand. Middlemen must decide whether to carry manufacturers' brands alone or whether to establish their own brands as well. Both groups of sellers must set policies regarding branding of groups of products and branding for market saturation. Customer acceptance of generic-labelled products has heated up the "battle of the brands." Another branding strategy is trademark licensing, which is being employed to an increasing extent by owners of well-known brands. The owner allows the use of (licenses) its name or trademarked character to another firm that is looking for a quick, relatively low-cost way of penetrating a market.

Packaging is becoming increasingly important as sellers recognize the problems, as well as the marketing opportunities, involved in packaging. *Labelling* is a related activity. Marketers should understand the merits and problems of grade labelling and of descriptive labelling. Many consumer criticisms of marketing have involved packaging and labelling, and there are federal laws regulating these marketing activities.

Companies are now recognizing the marketing value of product *design* — especially appearance design. Two related factors are product *colour* and product *quality*. Selecting the right colour is a marketing advantage. Projecting the appropriate quality image is essential. In addition, *warranties* and *servicing* require considerable management attention these days because of consumer complaints and governmental regulations in these areas.

NOTES

[1] Adapted from *Marketing Definitions: A Glossary of Marketing Terms*, American Marketing Association, Chicago, 1960, p. 8.

[2] See Hank Gilman, ''Retailers Bet Their Designer Wear Can Lure You Past Calvin Klein,'' *The Wall Street Journal*, Feb. 1, 1985, p. 17; and ''Why Designer Labels Are Fading,'' *Business Week*, Feb. 21, 1983, p. 70. See also Barbara Aarsteinsen, ''Clothing Makers, Retailers Venturing into Each Other's Turf,'' *The Globe and Mail Report on Business*, November 9, 1987, p. B3.

[3] For a discussion of the strategy of using a familiar, established brand on products that are in a product category that is new to a company, see Edward M. Tauber, ''Brand Franchise Extension: New Product Benefits from Existing Brand Names,'' *Business Horizons*, March-April 1981, pp. 36-41. See also Aimée Stern, ''New Payoff from Old Brand Names,'' *Dun's Business Month*, April 1985, p. 42.

[4] See Pamela G. Hollie, ''Cheaper Lines by Designers: Offshoots Spur Sales,'' *New York Times*, July 27, 1985, p. 19-Y.

[5] See Ronald Alsop, ''Color Grows More Important in Catching Consumers' Eyes,'' *The Wall Street Journal*, Nov. 29, 1984, p. 33.

[6] For some suggestions on how quality can be used strategically to position and sell products, see David A. Garvin, ''Product Quality: An Important Strategic Weapon,'' *Business Horizons*, March–April 1984, pp. 40–43.

[7] See John Koten, ''Aggressive Use of Warranties Is Benefiting Many Concerns,'' *The Wall Street Journal*, Apr. 5, 1984, p. 33.

[8] For a good review of the product-liability problem, see Fred W. Morgan, ''Marketing and Product Liability: A Review and Update,'' *Journal of Marketing*, Summer 1982, pp. 69–78.

KEY TERMS AND CONCEPTS

Brand 258	Trademark licensing 267
Brand mark 258	Packaging 267
Brand name 259	Grade label 271
Trademark 259	Descriptive label 271
Producer's brand (national brand) 259	Statutory labelling requirements 271
Middleman's brand (private brand) 259	Consumer Packaging and
Brand names becoming	Labelling Act 273
generic names 260	Product design 274
Branding of parts and materials 263	Product colour 274
Family (blanket) brands 264	Product quality 274
Branding for market saturation 265	Product warranty 275
Battle of the brands 266	Product liability 275
No-name (generic) brands 266	Hazardous Products Act 275

QUESTIONS AND PROBLEMS

1. List five brand names that you think are good ones and five that you consider poor. Explain the reasoning behind your choices.

2. Evaluate each of the following brand names in light of the characteristics of a good brand, indicating the strong and weak points of each name.
   a. Xerox (office copiers).
   b. Kodak (cameras).
   c. Bauer (skates).

    d. Hartt (shoes).

    e. A-1 (steak sauce).

    f. Far West (clothing).

3. Suggest some brands that are on the verge of becoming generic. What course of action should a company take to protect the separate identity of its brand?

4. Under what conditions would you recommend that a manufacturer brand a product that will be used as a part or material in the production of another product?

5. In which of the following cases should the company adopt the strategy of family branding?

    a. A manufacturer of men's underwear introduces essentially the same products for women.

    b. A manufacturer of women's cosmetics adds a line of men's cosmetics to its product assortment.

    c. A manufacturer of hair-care products introduces a line of portable electric hair dryers.

6. Suppose you are employed by the manufacturer of a well-known brand of skis. Your company is planning to add skates and water skis to its product line. It has no previous experience with either of these two new products. You are given the assignment of selecting a brand name for the skates and water skis. Your main problem is in deciding whether to adopt a family-brand policy. That is, should you use the snow-ski brand for either or both of the new products? Or should you develop separate names for each of the new items? You note that Campbell's (soups) and McCain (french fries) use family brands. You also note that Sears and Procter & Gamble generally do the opposite. They use different names for each *group of products* (Sears) or each *separate product* (P&G). What course of action would you recommend? Why?

7. A manufacturer of a well-known brand of ski boots acquired a division of a company that marketed a well-known brand of skis. What brand strategy should the new organization adopt? Should all products (skis and boots) now carry the boot brand? Should they carry the ski brand? Is there still some other alternative that you feel would be better?

8. Why do some firms sell an identical product under more than one of their own brands?

9. Assume that a large department-store chain proposed to the manufacturers of Maytag washing machines that Maytag supply the department store with machines carrying the store's brand. What factors should Maytag's management consider in making a decision? If the product were General Foods' Jell-O, to what extent would the situation be different?

10. Give examples of products that are excellently packaged. Mention some that are very poorly packaged.

11. What changes would you recommend in the typical packaging of these products?
    a. Soft drinks.
    b. Hairspray.
    c. Potato chips.
    d. Toothpaste.

12. If grade labelling is adopted, what factors should be used as bases for grading the following products?
    a. Lipstick.
    b. Woollen sweaters.
    c. Diet-food products.

13. Give examples of products for which the careful use of the colour of the product has increased sales. Can you cite examples to show that poor use of colour may hurt a company's marketing program?

14. Explain the relationship between a product warranty on small electric appliances and the manufacturer's distribution system for these products.

15. How would the warranty policies set by a manufacturer of skis differ from those adopted by an automobile manufacturer?

Cases for Part 3

CASE 3.1

UPPER CANADA BREWING COMPANY (B) Developing a Product Strategy

The deal was finally together! Frank Heaps, founder and president of the Upper Canada Brewing Company, Toronto, had by June 1984 put the management team in place and by December 1984 completed the major task of raising the $3.5 million in start-up capital. He was now ready to begin the challenge of putting together his marketing plan. The major task facing him at present was to plan and develop the actual product itself and to finalize the various product strategies. These decisions had to be made immediately if he was to have the products on the market by the targeted date, June 1985. Given the cyclical nature of this industry, where summer peak sales must compensate for winter lows, this target date was critical to ensuring financial viability.

BACKGROUND

The marketing strategy of the Upper Canada Brewing Company was to make beer pure and simple. Mr. Heaps wanted to carve a market niche for his firm based on the product itself, not advertising and marketing gimmickry. It was his perception that most Canadian beers were made the "same." In fact, he believed, as did others, that most beer drinkers often could not identify their favourite brands in blind taste tests. As well, he felt that a segment of the beer market wanted more than these bland alternatives — they wanted beer that was truly different. He proposed developing a product that would cater to this changing market demand.

The Upper Canada Brewing Company did not endeavour to compete with the major producers for the mass market. Instead it was intended to build market appeal and support within a specialized segment. The target market for the Upper Canada Brewing Company was viewed as a combination of the import and domestic beer markets. The market segment included knowledgeable beer drinkers, yuppies, ethnic groups, natural food enthusiasts, and college/university groups. Mr. Heaps also had an objective to expand the market abroad by exporting the product to countries like the United States, Germany, and maybe even Japan.

The competitive strength of the new company lay in its form — being a small cottage brewery. Its commitment was to a more traditional and natural brewing method that produced a superior quality product, different from the "hi-tech" brews of the major breweries. Cottage breweries also strived to portray a "feeling" for the brewery craft that the major breweries could not impart. The Upper Canada Brewing Company was the first cottage brewery to open in Toronto but was one of several which had re-appeared in Canada after being absent for some 20 years.

THE PRODUCT DECISIONS

THE PRODUCT MIX

The first major product strategy decision facing Mr. Heaps was to determine what type of beer product(s) to produce. He knew that the beer had to be different, but

This case was prepared by Donna M. Stapleton and is intended to stimulate discussion of an actual management problem and not to illustrate either effective or ineffective handling of that problem. The author wishes to acknowledge the support provided by the Upper Canada Brewing Company, and particularly by Frank Heaps, President.

not too different. He also knew that the product(s) had to be of consistently high quality to be accepted by the consumer. Beer, being a very perishable food product, had to be brewed under strict guidelines to achieve these results.

The strictest of all brewing legislation — the Bavarian Purity Act of 1516 — was adopted to ensure product excellence. Under this code, only the finest barley malt, hops, yeast, and water can be used in beer production. No "adjuncts" (corn, rice, or other grains) or chemical additives can be used to assist fermentation. The Act also forbids the common practice of adding sugar or corn syrup to artificially speed up the brewing process; all products must be naturally aged to enhance the beer flavour. The products are also unpasteurized since this process adversely affects the taste of beer and may interfere with the natural carbonation process. The result is that beer brewed under these guidelines produces dual benefits for the consumer — true beer taste and no headaches or hangovers.

To determine what product lines of beer to produce, Mr. Heaps did his homework to find out the facts about beer. Research showed that two brewing styles dominated the world production of beer. Almost all beer made was either an ale product or a lager beer product. Indeed, all North American "light" beer products were lager beers. Ale was a generic term for English-style top-fermented beers, while lager was a generic term for all bottom-fermented beers. One advantage of brewing ale products as opposed to lager products was that an ale took only half the time to mature — three weeks as opposed to five. Mr. Heaps wondered what product lines he should brew — an ale, or a lager, or both? In addition, he had to decide whether to include a line of light beer. The company was new and therefore had limited resources. But, he also wanted to offer a variety of products which would meet the needs of his target market.

An equally important decision concerned the depth of the product lines. Most beer products were available in kegs for the licensee trade and 6-, 12-, and 24-packs for the ultimate consumer. One higher-priced domestic premium beer was also available in a 20-pack to compensate for the higher price. He wondered which of these alternatives would be most advantageous for his company.

PACKAGING

There were a number of packaging decisions facing Mr. Heaps. First he had to decide what bottle size would be most appropriate for his new brew. The traditional bottle size used by the major breweries was 341 mL. The Granville Island Brewery also used this bottle size and the mould was available to Mr. Heaps for use at Upper Canada; one advantage of this alternative was that it avoided the up-front $16,000 expense of a custom-made mould. The other common bottle sizes included the litre-sized bottles used for a number of European beers that were sold in Ontario and the half-litre size (500 mL) used in Germany. The advantage of these other sizes was the import image that they projected. Other bottle decisions facing Mr. Heaps concerned the shape and colour. Granville Island Brewery used a tall, traditional bottle, a replica of a 30-year-old British Columbia beer bottle design, in amber glass. The bottles of the other breweries were undergoing change, with many of the mass breweries moving to the non-stubby bottles desired by the consumer. The colour of most North American beer bottles was amber. Import bottles varied in shape and colour; most were tall, traditional-styled in either amber or green. The amber glass was preferred by many brewers because it was the best for screening natural or artificial light and thus offered the beer the best protection when it was out of its case.

Mr. Heaps also had to decide on the type of cap to be used on the bottle. There were basically three alternatives: (i) the new twist-off caps being adopted by the mass brewers; (ii) the standard compression caps; and (iii) the corks with wire holders, available on some European beers. The major advantage of the twist-off cap was customer convenience. The problem, however, was that to be tamper-evident a twist-off cap should have a protective foil or paper label around it. This would mean that the company would need a new labeller or foiler — an additional expense. The compression style cap did not have this disadvantage but was considered old-fashioned and inconvenient by some consumers. The cork with the wire holder had the advantage of a European image and convenience but was more expensive.

The final packaging decision concerned the cartons in which the beer would be packed. Mr. Heaps had two objectives which he felt the package must achieve: it had to "say something," and be bright and interesting to attract attention. He proposed including a brief description about the specifications of the product, including a mention of the Bavarian Purity Act of 1516, as well as the company logo — a beaver building a dam with pine forests in the background (see Exhibit 1). The major breweries followed a completely different strategy — their cases featured a brand name and little else.

Exhibit 1

POSITIONING

Positioning the product(s) correctly in the marketplace was of critical importance if the Upper Canada Brewing Company was to achieve a competitive advantage. Mr. Heaps felt that the target market wanted a high quality product with taste. This market segment was not being satisfied by existing mass-produced alternatives, thus the products of the Upper Canada Brewing Company would be positioned to reach and satisfy this market niche. The positioning would be done by product attribute, emphasizing the all-natural, high quality, traditional "beer" taste and price/quality — value for money.

The target date to get the products on the market was only six months away. The product mix decisions, the related packaging decisions, and positioning strategy needed to be finalized soon if Mr. Heaps was to meet this deadline.

1. Does the target market identified by Mr. Heaps represent the best market opportunity for this new venture? Why or why not?
2. What would you recommend to Mr. Heaps in each of the following product strategy areas? Substantiate your recommendations.
   a. Breadth of the product mix (number of lines to brew).
   b. Number of package sizes (depth).
   c. Bottle size, shape, and colour.
   d. Type of cap.
   e. Product positioning.
3. Are there any other decisions that Mr. Heaps should make in the product strategy area? What are they?
4. Evaluate the packaging approach Mr. Heaps has proposed for the Upper Canada Brewery. Will the "informative" approach and proposed logo design appeal to the target market?
5. How important is the Bavarian Purity Act of 1516 to the competitive position of the Upper Canada Brewery's product(s)? What advantage will this offer the company in the short and long term?

CASE 3.2

CN HOTELS INC. (B) Tailoring the Hotel Product

Brian Richardson, vice president of marketing at CN Hotels, concentrated as he reviewed the final specifications for the Entrée line of products. The Entrée product concept resulted from a year of extensive marketing research and innovative market segmentation. The changes proposed with the Entrée line were designed to give CN Hotels a competitive advantage in a highly competitive industry. He wondered if CN Hotels was finally ready to implement the proposed changes. February 1985 was the targeted date for the launching of the Entrée line; a decision was needed in the next week if this deadline was to be met. Mr. Richardson reviewed the research data and the unique features of each Entrée product to determine if they were sufficiently tailored to meet the needs of the target markets before he made his final decision on the launch of the new concept.

THE ENTRÉE LINE

ENTRÉE GOLD

Entrée Gold was designed for the traveller who wanted the satisfaction of choosing only the best and was willing to pay more to stay in highly personalized surroundings. This unique product was developed to meet the needs of affluent Canadian business travellers including corporate presidents, vice presidents, and senior executives.

Entrée Gold guests would experience a warm, personal, but elegant atmosphere on a private floor. They would be treated with individual attention by the Entrée Gold Concièrge and have the privacy of direct check-in on the Entrée Gold floor;

This case was prepared by Donna M. Stapleton and is intended to stimulate discussion of an actual management problem and not to illustrate either effective or ineffective handling of that problem. The author wishes to acknowledge the support provided by CN Hotels, and particularly by Brian Richardson, Vice President, and Sandra Diem, Director, System Marketing.

a private lounge would be open all day and serve complimentary breakfast and canapés at the cocktail hour. The product image and quality was depicted in the tasteful advertisement developed to reach the target market and promote this product concept (see Exhibit 1).

EXHIBIT 1

ENTRÉE SILVER

Entrée Silver was designed to satisfy the needs of frequent travellers who felt they wanted to reward themselves with a little extra. Frequent travellers in this category would include executives, senior managers, professionals, or entrepreneurs who have the flexibility, because of their position, to pay a little more for a hotel room.

Entrée Silver offered comfortable, more informal surroundings with special features to meet the needs of business travellers. It also offered a special speedier check-in desk in the main lobby, plus a lounge on the Silver floor, open for breakfast and serving canapés at the cocktail hour. The rooms were tastefully decorated with more amenities and features than Entrée Première. Again the product image and quality were presented in the advertisement developed to promote this product and reach the target market (see Exhibit 2).

ENTRÉE PREMIÈRE

Entrée Première was designed to give a touch above the usual, while offering value to the customer. Its potential market included corporate rate business travellers,

EXHIBIT 2

EXHIBIT 3

and couples and families travelling for pleasure during holidays or weekends. These accommodations provided premium comfort, convenience, quality, and accommodation for the price. Entrée Première also included public spaces and facilities where guests could eat, drink, and relax. An advertisement was developed to promote this product image of quality and style to the market (see Exhibit 3).

Many other hotels offered different types of accommodations and upgraded rooms, but with the Entrée line, CN Hotels would be the first company to have branded the different room types, thereby allowing the customer to identify and purchase a specific level of accommodation for his or her particular needs. In addition, CN Hotels developed a fourth product, Entrée Plus, which would satisfy the needs of all three target groups by allowing them to accumulate points that could be redeemed for valuable merchandise or complimentary room nights.

THE DECISION

Mr. Richardson understood the importance of his decision; if the Entrée line did not give CN Hotels a competitive advantage, CN could lose to the competition. He must decide if the time was right for CN Hotels to launch the Entrée line. The question he faced was: given the marketing research data on the target groups (see CN Hotels Inc. [A]), was the Entrée line of products sufficiently different in features, quality, style, image, packaging, and price to reach and satisfy these markets?

QUESTIONS

1. Given the target markets that CN Hotels have identified as their best market opportunity, does the Entrée line of products satisfy the need of these markets? Why?
2. Is CN Hotels ready to launch the Entrée line? What changes if any would you make to the Entrée products before putting them on the market?
3. Do the advertisements communicate the distinctive features of each product in the Entrée line?

CASE 3.3

NATIONAL SEA PRODUCTS

National Sea Products is a very successful seafood processing company with headquarters in Halifax, Nova Scotia. The company owns and operates the world's largest fish-processing operation in Lunenberg, Nova Scotia. National Sea owns 18 plants that operate year round and process groundfish such as cod, haddock, sole, halibut, Boston blue fish, and ocean perch, as well as lobster, scallops, shrimp, crab, squid, herring, mackerel, and fish meal. These plants package and ship fresh fish, as well as filleting and preparing fish for marketing in frozen, smoked, precooked, canned, and other value-added forms, including the frozen entrées packaged under the Highliner label.

National Sea is a strong competitor in the growing seafood market. The company's

This case was prepared by Lanita Carter and is intended to stimulate discussion of an actual management problem, and not to illustrate either effective or ineffective handling of that problem. The author wishes to acknowledge the support provided by National Sea Products, and particularly by Ronald G. Whynacht, Vice President of Product Development.

sales increased from $268.1 million in 1979 to $452.2 million in 1983. National Sea has moved aggressively from a fish-based enterprise to an international food processing company. The mission statement, shown in Exhibit 1, reflects the company's commitment to a market-driven approach.

EXHIBIT 1:   **Mission Statement**

''The objective of National Sea Products Limited is to increase shareholders' value through planned growth, profit performance and dominance in the marketing of food, particularly seafood.

''The Company will be recognized as the best in the industry by offering its customers the highest quality for value sought and by being a good employer and a good corporate citizen.''

In 1979, National Sea Products launched a new frozen entrée product, Fillets in Sauce, under the Highliner label. This product weighed 14 oz. and was packed in a foil pan inside a box with a picture of the product on the front. Fillets in Sauce were available in five flavours: mushroom sauce, cheese sauce, lemon butter, parsley sauce, and white sauce. Though many new competitive items were introduced following the launch of this product, these five Highliner flavours managed to capture 65 percent of the frozen entrée market.

The seafood market had begun to grow at a rapid rate in the late 1970s. As more people became health conscious, they turned to seafood as a low-fat, low-calorie alternative to beef. United States' per capita consumption increased from 12.2

pounds in 1975 to 13.8 pounds in 1983. These trends created an excellent opportunity for National Sea to enter the frozen entrée market in 1979, especially since 65 percent of their products were sold to the U.S.

After the success of their new product, National Sea decided to introduce Fillets in Sauce in a new 250 g single-serving size. The 450 g package design had proven to be more than enough for one and could often be used as an entrée along with a salad for two people. However, the market was changing and the number of single-person households was increasing. Two new target groups emerged based on these trends: the young singles and the over-54 population. Based on National Sea's research, this product appealed to the young singles because of the taste and ease of preparation, and to the 55 and over population because of smaller portion sizes which meant no leftovers. These two groups also gave favourable responses to a retail price of about $2. This new 250 g format was offered in three of the most popular flavours: fillets in mushroom sauce, fillets in cheese sauce, and fillets in lemon butter with rice. This product, like the 14 oz. package, was also very successful.

However, by 1983 many new competitors had entered the frozen entrée market. Ron Whynacht, the vice president for product development, had been trying to figure out how the company could meet this new competition in the market. Stouffer's had just launched their Lean Cuisine line including several new fish entrées. Campbell's had also announced plans to market a frozen, microwaveable entrée-meal called Le Menu under their Swanson brand.

Mr. Whynacht has to decide how National Sea will compete with these new products. He has been reading the results of the tracking study conducted by the company. The results of this study indicate that consumers liked the new single serving size, though they preferred a slightly larger serving, such as the new Lean Cuisine packages with a net weight of 270 g.

The results of the study also indicated that there were four market segments in this growing seafood market. The first group liked the fillets in sauce that were on the market. They liked the quality of the product and the value for their money. The second segment preferred a low-calorie entrée like the one introduced under the Lean Cuisine label. The third segment had more upscale tastes and preferred a gourmet entrée, such as the Le Menu entrée-meal. The fourth segment identified in the study were more adventuresome in their preferences and wanted new varieties of entrées. The conclusions of this study suggested that consumers wanted new convenient seafood products that were not breaded or battered.

Based on the findings of this study, Mr. Whynacht has to develop a marketing plan for the Highliner frozen entrée line for the coming year. He feels that the seafood market may be ready for several new products, but he's not sure which market segment will be the best choice for new product development.

QUESTIONS

1. What new products might Mr. Whynacht develop to meet the emerging market segments in the seafood market?
2. Should these new products be branded under the Highliner label (brand extension) or introduced under another label (new product)?

CASE 3.4

DEPENDABLE DRUGS*
Brand Strategy

Two brothers, Ed and Jim Henderson, owned and operated a chain of five retail drugstores, doing business under the name of Dependable Drugs. From the time they started in business, Ed and Jim had consistently followed the policy of carrying only nationally branded merchandise — that is, well-known manufacturers' brands. During the past few years, however, they had noticed a change in the way many of their customers shopped at the stores. They felt that these customers had become much more price-conscious than they had been several years ago, partly because of the inflation that had been experienced during the 1980s, and partly because of the increased availability of discount prices at competing stores. More and more, customers were comparing the prices at Dependable Drugs with those charged by competing chain drugstores and by the pharmacy departments of chain stores such as Zellers and Woolco.

The brothers also had observed that some supermarket chains had introduced, with apparent success, a line of products being sold without any brand name. These products were simply labelled with the generic name of the article — beans, peanut butter, or paper towels, for example. As a result of these various developments, the Henderson brothers were wondering whether they should add a line of products under their own store name — in effect, their own "private brand."

The Dependable Drugs stores were located in small shopping centres and residential areas in the Halifax-Dartmouth metropolitan area of Nova Scotia. Ed Henderson was a registered pharmacist, and his brother, Jim, had a degree in Business Administration from a local university.

The brothers started in business about 20 years ago when they purchased their father's drugstore, which was located in an old, established residential neighbourhood. Several years later, an uncle, who also owned a retail drug business, died very suddenly. His widow offered his store to Ed and Jim at a relatively low price. The remaining three units in the Dependable Drugs chain were started as new stores in nearby suburban shopping centres.

The first two stores in the Dependable Drugs chain were being successfully operated as full-service businesses when the Henderson brothers acquired them. The other three stores, however, had presented quite a different business situation. These stores were started from scratch as far as location, customers, fixtures, reputation, and managerial policies were concerned. Consequently, they had presented a series of challenging elements of entrepreneurship not experienced in the first two stores.

Business in the new stores initially was slow, despite elaborate "grand opening" promotional efforts. During succeeding months, the sales volume increased moderately. However, neither the sales volume nor the profit had yet come up to the owners' expectations.

The original store had a large cellar, which the company still used as its main storage area. For two reasons, however, this storage area was rapidly becoming overcrowded. First, Dependable Drugs had to buy some products in large amounts in order to obtain the quantity discounts that helped meet the keen price competition.

*This case was adapted by James G. Barnes from a case originally developed by Walter F. Rohrs. Used with permission.

Second, there was a stream of new sizes, colours, and varieties of existing products, plus a flow of new products, which the Hendersons felt they had to carry.

The Hendersons believed that their policy of stocking only national (manufacturers') branded merchandise was a good one. With such a policy, they could trade on the general consumer acceptance of national brands as well as the fine reputation of large, well-known organizations. Furthermore, these products typically were heavily advertised and otherwise promoted by the manufacturers.

Within the past year or so, clerks in all of the Dependable Drugs stores had observed that customers were becoming more aware of the prices being charged by the stores and by the competition. In some instances, they even brought in flyers and newspaper ads from drug chains such as Shoppers Drug Mart and Lawton's Drugs, showing nationally branded products at prices considerably lower than those charged by Dependable Drugs. The prices that seemed to cause the greatest concern among customers were those charged for frequently purchased items such as shampoo, toothpaste, tissues, and other paper products. Some customers said they did not mind paying a few cents more at Dependable Drugs, but 15 to 20 percent on an item was just too much. Consequently, the sales of some proprietary (nonprescription) medicines had been declining.

During their recent regular Friday afternoon business meetings, Ed and Jim had been discussing this problem of lost sales caused by intense price competition. They had explored several options, one of which was to market a line of products under their own private brand — the Dependable Drugs brand. At the same time, however, they were uncertain regarding whether or not they should go the private-brand route.

Jim had gathered detailed information and samples from a number of sources that could provide top-grade products under the Dependable Drugs brand. The prices of these products were generally much lower than the prices of similar products carrying the manufacturers' brands. This was the case even though the product-quality specifications on the private-branded merchandise were as good as, or better than, the specifications for the national brands.

Jim and Ed recognized there were advantages to their marketing a group of products under the Dependable Drugs brand. These products could be sold at lower prices than the nationally branded items. Also, by using a private brand, Dependable Drugs largely eliminated price comparisons with competitive products. The Hendersons were impressed by the fact that the large national drug chains, such as Shoppers Drug Mart, had been marketing under a private brand for years. In fact, the brothers were enthusiastic enough to have selected a brand name — "Double D" — in the event they decided to go the private-brand route.

At the same time, Ed and Jim recognized they were likely to encounter problems with a private brand. Ed pointed out that consumer resistance was likely to be strong, at least in the beginning. He said that strong emotional considerations were involved in the purchase of many drugstore products. Dependable Drugs would have to educate its customers and build consumer confidence in the Double D brand. Store personnel would have to explain to customers that Dependable Drugs' products were, by law, at least the equivalent of the better-known national brands. Ed also stressed that Dependable Drugs would need a carefully planned promotional effort and a strong money-back guarantee of quality.

Both brothers were concerned with the potential warehousing, inventory control, and financing problems that they might face. Already their cellar warehouse often was close to being full. Financing pressures might increase because private-brand suppliers often required large minimum orders.

Jim then raised another question. ''Supposing we decide to go the private-brand route,'' he said. ''Then we have to consider how extensively we should apply the Double D brand. Do we put it on just a few products where we face the greatest price competition? Or, do we use our brand over a wider range of products and product lines?''

Ed suggested they might start by using the Double D brand on about 20 fast-moving items such as vitamins, rubbing alcohol, and talcum powder.

Jim recalled the experiences of a drug retailer in another city who had plunged in with a private brand on a broad assortment of products. And, he pointed out, the guy had been pretty successful at it.

Ed was wondering if Dependable Drugs could draw on the recent experiences that supermarket chains were having with generic brands. ''They started out with only a few items,'' he observed, ''and now they have generic toothpaste, suntan lotion, paper products, and lots of other non-food items. Should we follow their policy?''

QUESTIONS

1. Should Dependable Drugs adopt a private-brand policy?
2. If your decision is yes, what products should carry the Double D brand?
3. Should Dependable Drugs add a line of generic ''branded'' products?

PART 4

THE PRICE

The development and use of a pricing structure as part of the firm's marketing mix

We are in the process of developing a strategic marketing mix to reach our target markets and achieve our marketing goals. With our product planning completed, we now turn our attention to the pricing ingredient in the marketing mix. In the strategic planning for — and development of — the pricing structure, we face two broad tasks. First, we must determine the base price for a product, including a decision on our pricing objectives. These topics are covered in Chapter 11. Second, we must decide on the strategies (such as discounts) to employ in modifying and applying the base price. These strategies are discussed in Chapter 12.

CHAPTER 11

PRICE DETERMINATION

CHAPTER GOALS

In this chapter we discuss the role of price in the marketing mix — what price is, how it can be used, and how it is set relative to product costs, market demand, and competitive prices. This chapter is somewhat more difficult and quantitative than previous ones. After studying this chapter, you should understand:

- The meaning of price.
- The importance of price in our economy and in an individual firm.
- The major pricing goals.
- The idea of an ''expected'' price.
- The several types of costs that are incurred in producing and marketing a product.
- The cost-plus method of setting a base price.
- The use of break-even analysis in setting a price.
- Prices established by considering both supply and demand (costs and anticipated revenues).
- Prices established in relation only to the competitive market price.

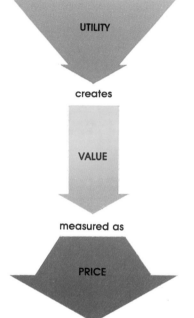

UTILITY

creates

VALUE

measured as

PRICE

''How much do you think we ought to sell it for?'' Marketing executives with Procter & Gamble had to ask this question when they were planning the introduction of Liquid Tide. So did the marketing people at Colgate-Palmolive when they introduced Colgate toothpaste in a pump dispenser. The same question is asked by the board of the Newfoundland Symphony Orchestra and the business manager of the Royal Winnipeg Ballet when pricing season tickets. The management of Maple Leaf Gardens has to decide each season whether to raise the prices of tickets to Leafs games. Accountants, musicians, and hair-stylists have to decide what to charge for their services. In effect, the question is asked any time an organization introduces a new product or service. This question of how much to charge comes up because so often we do not have any easy formula or model to follow in setting a price. Pricing still remains an art, not a science, and much intuition is sometimes involved. How else do you account for the fact that some companies are able to *increase* sales by *raising* prices? For some fashion products, perfumes, and luxury cars, it often seems that the higher their price, the more desirable these products become.

Perhaps our opening question would be more accurately worded if we asked, ''How much do you think people will pay for this item?'' The question then would be in accord with the generalization that *prices are always on trial.* A price is simply an offer or an experiment to test the pulse of the market. If customers accept the offer, then the price is fine. If they reject it, the price usually will be changed quickly, or the product may even be withdrawn from the market. In this chapter we shall discuss some of the major methods used to determine a price — that is, to answer our opening question. Before being concerned with actual price determination, however, executives should understand the meaning and importance of price, and they should decide on their pricing objectives.

MEANING OF PRICE

Undoubtedly, many of the difficulties associated with pricing start with the rather simple fact that often we really do not know what we are talking about. That is, we do not know the meaning of the word *price*, even though it is true that the concept is quite easy to define in familiar terms.

In economic theory, we learn that price, value, and utility are related concepts.

Wonder what the price would be at the orchard if you picked them yourself.

Utility is the attribute of an item that makes it capable of satisfying human wants. **Value** is the quantitative measure of the worth of a product to attract other products in exchange. We may say the value of a certain hat is three baseball bats or 25 litres of gasoline. Because our economy is not geared to a slow, ponderous barter system, we use money as a common denominator of value. And we use the term *price* to describe the money value of an item. **Price** is value expressed in terms of dollars and cents, or any other monetary medium of exchange.

Practical problems arise in connection with a definition of price, however, when we try to state simply the price of a product — say, an office desk. Suppose the price quoted to Helen for an office desk was $525, while Bill paid only $275. At first glance it looks as if Bill got a better deal. Yet, when we get all the facts, we may change our opinion. Helen's desk was delivered to her office, she had a year to pay for it, and it was beautifully finished. Bill bought a partially assembled desk with no finish on it. (He was a do-it-yourself fan.) He had to assemble the drawers and legs and then painstakingly stain, varnish, and hand-rub the entire desk. He arranged for the delivery himself, and he paid cash in full at the time of purchase. Now let us ask who paid the higher price in each case. The answer is not as easy as it seemed at first glance.

This example illustrates how difficult it is to define price in an everyday business situation. Many variables are involved. The definition hinges on the problem of

THE PRICE IS WHAT YOU PAY FOR WHAT YOU GET

"That which we call a rose by any other name would smell as sweet."
— *Romeo and Juliet*, Act II, Scene 2

Tuition ....Education	Contribution ...Appreciation from your alumni fund
Interest ....Use of money	
Rent ....Use of living quarters or a piece of equipment for a period of time	Toll ....Long-distance phone call or travel on some highways or bridges
Fare ....Taxi or bus ride	Salary ....Services of an executive or other white-collar worker
Fee ....Services of a lawyer	
Retainer ....Accountant's services over a period of time	Wage ....Services of a blue-collar worker
Donation ......Thanks from a charity	Commission ...Sales person's services
Subscription ...Magazines or a concert series	Honorarium ....Guest speaker
Fine ....Parking on an expired parking meter	Dues ....Membership in a union or a club

— then in socially undesirable situations, some people pay a price called blackmail, ransom, or bribery.

Source: Suggested, in part, by John T. Mentzer and David J. Schwartz, *Marketing Today*, 4th ed., Harcourt Brace Jovanovich, San Diego, 1985, p. 599.

determining exactly what is being sold. This relates to a problem posed in Chapter 8, that of trying to define a product. In pricing, we must consider more than the physical product alone. A seller usually is pricing a combination of the physical product and several services and want-satisfying benefits. Sometimes it is difficult even to define the price of the physical product or service alone. On one model of automobile, a stated price may include radio, power steering, and power brakes. For another model of the same make of car, these three items may be priced separately.

In summary, price is the value placed on goods and services. **Price** is the amount of money and/or products that are needed to acquire some combination of another product and its accompanying services.

Marketing at Work

File 11-1

Price Means Cost and Value

There is no question that the pricing decision is a very important one for the company trying to decide what to charge for its product or service. But how important is it to the consumer who is expected to buy that product or service? Marketers occasionally fall into the trap of believing that price is all-important in influencing the consumer's decision of whether or not to buy. Such is not always the case. Just a few years ago, a study was conducted of the retail price of food products in 50 cities and towns in Newfoundland to determine what factors contributed to differences in the prices paid by consumers in different towns. The main conclusion of the study was that the level of food prices is attributable mainly to factors such as the presence of large chain stores, the amount of competition, and the distance from main wholesale distribution centres. What was more surprising was that consumers in small, more isolated towns did not express as much concern about the level of food prices as had been expected. Consumers were more concerned about the variety of food products available and the quality of fresh fruit and vegetables. Many said that they would be prepared to pay even more for better quality and greater variety. Although consumers may complain about *price*, what they really want is better *value*.

IMPORTANCE OF PRICE

In the Economy

Pricing is considered by many to be the key activity within the capitalistic system of free enterprise. The market price of a product influences wages, rent, interest, and profits. That is, the price of a product influences the price paid for the factors of production — labour, land, capital, and entrepreneurship. Price thus is a basic regulator of the economic system because it influences the allocation of these factors of production. High wages attract labour, high interest rates attract capital, and so on. As an allocator of scarce resources, price determines what will be produced (supply) and who will get the goods and services that are produced (demand).

Criticism of the free enterprise system, and the public's demand for further restraints on the system, are often triggered by a reaction to price or to pricing policies.

Price — doctors call it a fee and universities and colleges call it tuition.

In the Individual Firm

The price of a product or service is a major determinant of the market demand for the item. Price affects the firm's competitive position and its share of the market. As a result, price has a considerable bearing on the company's revenue and net profit.

At the same time, there usually are forces that limit the importance of pricing in a company's marketing program. Differentiated product features or a favourite brand may be more important to consumers than price. In fact, as noted in Chapter 10, one object of branding is to decrease the effect of price on the demand for a product. To put the role of pricing in a company's marketing program in its proper perspective, then, let us say that price is important, but not all-important, in explaining marketing success.

PRICING OBJECTIVES

Every marketing task — including (and perhaps, especially) pricing — should be directed toward the achievement of a goal. In other words, management should decide on its pricing *objective* before determining the price itself. Yet, as logical as this may be, very few firms consciously establish, or explicitly state, their pricing objective.

THE MAIN GOALS IN PRICING ARE:

Profit-oriented — to:	*Sales-oriented — to:*	*Status quo-oriented — to:*
Achieve target return on investment or net sales. Maximize profit.	Increase sales. Maintain or increase market share.	Stabilize prices. Meet competition.

The pricing goal that management selects should be entirely compatible with the goals set for the company and its marketing program. To illustrate, let's assume that the company's goal is to increase its return on investment from the present level of 15 percent to a level of 20 percent at the end of a three-year period. Then it follows that the pricing goal during this period must be to achieve some stated percentage return on investment. It would not be logical, in this case, to adopt the pricing goal of maintaining the company's market share or of stabilizing prices.

Profit-Oriented Goals   By selecting profit maximization or a target return, management focusses its attention on profit generation. Profit goals may be set either for the short run or for longer periods of time.

ACHIEVE TARGET RETURN

A firm may price its products or services to achieve a certain percentage return on its *investment* or on its *sales*. Such goals are used by both middlemen and manufacturers.

Many retailers and wholesalers use target return on *net sales* as a pricing objective for short-run periods. They set a percentage markup on sales that is large enough to cover anticipated operating costs plus a desired profit for the year. In such cases, the *percentage* of profit may remain constant, but the *dollar* profit will vary according to the number of units sold.

Achieving a target return on *investment* is typically selected as a goal by manufacturers that are leaders in their industry — companies such as General Motors and Union Carbide (Prestone antifreeze, Eveready batteries). Target-return pricing is used frequently by industry leaders because they can set their pricing goals more independently of competition than can the smaller firms in the industry.

MAXIMIZE PROFITS

The pricing objective of making as much money as possible is probably followed by a larger number of companies than any other goal. The trouble with this goal is that the term *profit maximization* may have an ugly connotation. It is sometimes connected in the public mind with profiteering, high prices, and monopoly. Extra billing doctors as well as auto insurers in some provinces are accused of greedy maximizing. In economic theory or business practice, however, there is nothing wrong with profit maximization. Theoretically, if profits become unduly high because supply is short in relation to demand, new capital will be attracted into the field. This will increase supply and eventually reduce profits to normal levels. Or it can lead to provincial government fee and rate setting. In the marketplace, it is difficult to find many situations where profiteering has existed over an extended period of time. Substitute products are available, purchases are postponable, and competition can increase to keep prices at a reasonable level. Where prices may be unduly high and entry into the field is severely limited, public outrage soon balances the scales. If market conditions and public opinion do not do the job directly, government restraints will soon bring about moderation.

A profit maximization goal is likely to be far more beneficial to a company and to the public if practised over the *long run*. To do this, however, firms sometimes have to accept short-run losses. A company entering a new geographic market or introducing a new product frequently does best by initially setting low prices to build a large clientele.

The goal should be to maximize profits on *total output* rather than on each single item marketed. A manufacturer may maximize total profits by practically giving away some articles in order to stimulate sales of other goods. Through its sponsored broadcasts and telecasts of athletic events, the Gillette Company frequently promotes razors at very low, profitless prices. Management hopes that once customers acquire Gillette razors, they will become long-term profitable customers for Gillette blades.

File 11-2

Price by Any Other Name Is Still Price

In many organizations, particularly in the not-for-profit sector, the objective of pricing decisions may not be the maximization of profits. A public art gallery sets a token admission charge to help it defray some of its expenses, relying on grants from government and public donations for the bulk of its revenues. A public library certainly does not consider the maximization of revenues when it decides what fines to levy on patrons who return books late. The fine is a deterrent to encourage the tardy borrower to return books on time. The local amateur theatre group sets its ticket prices so as to generate revenues, while at the same time trying not to discourage any interested member of the public from attending its performances. Universities and colleges set their tuition fees in much the same way — setting them high enough to recoup a reasonable portion of the operating costs, while at the same time wishing to ensure that no student finds it impossible to attend because of the cost. Pricing really is an art, and often not at all scientific.

Sales-Oriented Goals

In some companies, management's pricing attention is focussed on sales volume. In these situations, the pricing goal may be to increase sales volume or to maintain or increase the firm's market share.

INCREASE SALES VOLUME

This pricing goal is usually stated as a percentage increase in sales volume over some period of time, say, one year or three years. However, to increase sales volume may or may not be consistent with the marketing concept that advocates *profitable* sales volume. Management may decide to increase its volume by discounting or some other aggressive pricing strategy, perhaps incurring a loss. Thus, management is willing to take a short-run loss if the increased sales enable the company to get a foothold in its market.

MAINTAIN OR INCREASE MARKET SHARE

In some companies, both large and small, the major pricing objective is to maintain or increase the share of the market held by the firm. Market share may be a better indicator of corporate health than target return on investment, especially when the total market is growing. Then a firm might be earning a reasonable return. But if management is not aware that the market is expanding, the company may be getting a decreasing share of that market.

Status Quo Goals

These two closely related goals — to stabilize prices and to meet competition — are the least aggressive of any of the pricing goals.

STABILIZE PRICES

Price stabilization often is the goal in industries where a large firm is the price leader and the product is highly standardized — for example, steel, gasoline, copper, or bulk chemicals. A major reason for seeking price stability is to avert price wars. However, adherence to the industry leader's price is not as rigid today as it used to be, especially during periods of sluggish demand. Smaller firms sometimes are cutting below the industry price and are not suffering reprisals from the large firms in the industry.

MEET COMPETITION

Countless firms, regardless of size, consciously price their products simply to meet the competition. In concentrated industries where there is a price leader and where the product is highly standardized, most firms have a follow-the-leader policy.

Gas stations' pricing goal usually is to meet competition.

FACTORS INFLUENCING PRICE DETERMINATION

Knowing their objective, executives then can move to the heart of price management — the actual determination of the base price of a product or service. By **base price** (or list price) we mean the price of one unit of the product at its point of production or resale. This is the price before allowance is made for discounts, freight charges, or any other modification such as those discussed in the next chapter.

The same general procedure is followed in pricing both new and established products. However, the pricing of an established product usually involves little difficulty, because the exact price or a narrow range of prices may be dictated by the market. In the pricing of new products, though, the decision called for in the pricing process typically are important and difficult.

In the price-determination process, several factors usually influence the final decision. The key factors, however, are as follows:

- Demand for the product.
- Target share of the market.
- Competitive reactions.
- Other parts of the marketing mix — the product, distribution channels, and promotion.

Estimated Demand for the Product

An important step in pricing a product is to estimate the total demand for it. This is easier to do for an established product than for a new one. Two steps in demand estimation are, first, to determine whether there is a price that the market expects and, second, to estimate the sales volume at different prices.

ELASTICITY OF DEMAND
A Review of a Basic Economic Concept

Elasticity of demand refers to the effect that unit-price changes have on the number of units sold and the total revenue. (The total revenue — that is, the total dollar sales volume — equals the unit price times the number of units sold.) We say that the demand is **elastic** when (1) reducing the unit price causes an increase in total revenue or (2) raising the unit price causes a decrease in total revenue. In the first case, the cut in unit price results in a boost in quantity sold and more than offsets the price cut — hence the increase in total revenue.

These situations are illustrated in Fig. 11-A. We start with a situation wherein, at $5 a unit, we sell 100 units and the total revenue equals $500. When we lower the price to $4 a unit, the quantity sold increases to 150 and the resultant total revenue also goes up — to $600. When the unit price is boosted to $6, however, the quantity sold drops off so much (to 70 units) that the total revenue also declines (to $420).

Demand is **inelastic** when (1) a price cut causes total dollar sales volume to decline or (2) a price raise results in an increase in total revenue. In each of these two situations the changes in unit price more than offset the relatively small changes in quantities sold. That is, when the price is cut, the increase in quantity sold is not enough

When the unit price is raised, it more than offsets the decline in quantity sold, so total revenue goes up.

In Fig. 11-B, again we start with a unit price of $5, we sell 100 units, and our total revenue is $500. When we lower the unit price to $4, our quantity sold increases to 115. But this is not enough to offset the price cut, so our total revenue declines to $460. When we raise our unit price to $6, our quantity sold falls off to 90. But the price increase more than offsets the drop in quantity sold, so our total revenue goes up to $540.

As a generalization, the industry demand for necessities (salt, sugar, gasoline, telephone service, gas and electric service) tends to be inelastic. If the price of gasoline, for example, goes up or down say, 4 or 8 cents a litre, the total number of litres sold does not change very much. On the other hand, the demand for products purchased with our discretionary income (luxury items, large appliances, furniture, autos) typically is much more elastic. Moreover, the demand for individual *brands* is much more elastic than is the demand for the broader *product* category. Thus, the demand for Air Canada seats or Hertz rental cars is far more elastic (price-sensitive) than is the demand for air travel or rented cars in general.

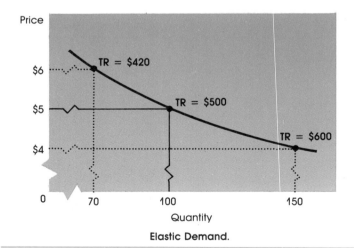

Elastic Demand.

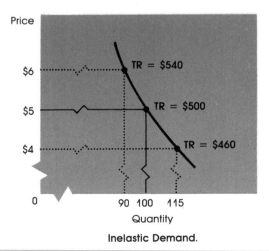

Inelastic Demand.

THE "EXPECTED" PRICE

The "expected" price for a product is the price at which customers consciously or unconsciously value it — what they think the product is worth. The expected price usually is expressed as a *range* of prices, rather than as a specific amount. Thus,

What is the expected price?

Computers can help a company to estimate the demand for its products.

the expected price might be "between $250 and $300" or "not over $20." Consumers sometimes can be surprisingly shrewd in evaluating a product and its expected price.

A producer must also consider the middlemen's reaction to the price. Middlemen are more likely to give an article favourable treatment in their stores if they approve of its price. Retail or wholesale buyers can frequently examine an item and make an accurate estimate of the selling price that the market will accept.

It is possible to set a price too low. If the price is much lower than that which the market expects, sales may be lost. For example, it would probably be a mistake for a well-known cosmetics manufacturer to put a 49-cent price tag on its lipstick or to price its imported perfume at $2.29 a millilitre. Either customers will be suspicious of the quality of the product or their self-concepts will not let them buy such low-priced merchandise. More than one seller has raised the price of a product and experienced a considerable increase in sales. This situation is called **inverse demand** — the higher the price, the greater the unit sales. This inverse demand situation usually exists only within a given price range and only at the lower price levels. Once a price rises to some particular point, inverse demand ends and the usual-shaped demand curve takes over. That is, demand then declines as prices rise.

How do sellers determine expected prices? They may submit articles to experienced retailers or wholesalers for appraisal. A manufacturer of industrial products might get price estimates by showing product models or blueprints to engineers working for prospective customers. A third alternative is to survey potential consumers. They may be shown an article and asked what they would pay for it. Often, however, there is a considerable difference between what people say a product is worth and what they will actually pay for it. A more effective approach is to market the product in a few limited test areas. By trying different prices under controlled test-market conditions, the seller can determine at least a reasonable range of prices.

ESTIMATES OF SALES AT VARIOUS PRICES

It is extremely helpful to estimate what the sales volume will be at several different prices. By doing this, the seller is, in effect, determining the demand curve for the product and thus determining its demand elasticity. These estimates of sales at different prices also are useful in determining break-even points — a topic that we discuss later in this chapter.

There are several methods that sellers can use to estimate potential sales at various prices. Some of these methods were suggested in the preceding section on expected prices. Other methods were discussed in the sales forecasting section of Chapter 7. To illustrate, a company can conduct a survey of buyer intentions to determine consumer buying interest at different prices. Or management can conduct test-market experiments, offering the product at a different price in each market and measuring consumer purchases at these different prices. For an established product, management can measure sales of competitors' products, especially when reasonably similar models are offered at different prices.

A seller may be able to design a computerized model that would simulate field selling conditions and sales responses at various prices. Some firms can get these estimates by surveying their wholesalers and retailers. For some industrial products,

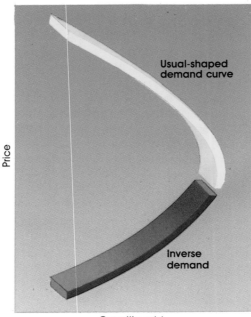

Price

Usual-shaped
demand curve

Inverse
demand

Quantity sold

the sales estimates can be generated by using the sales-force composite method of
forecasting.

Target Share of Market   The market share targeted by a company is a major factor to consider in determining
the price of a product or service. A company striving to increase its market share
may price more aggressively (lower base price, larger discounts) than a firm that
wants to maintain its present market share.

The expected share of the market is influenced by present production capacity
and ease of competitive entry. It would be a mistake for a firm to aim for a larger
share of the market than its plant capacity can sustain. So, if management will not
expand its plan (because ease of competitive entry will drive down future profits),
then the initial price should be set relatively high.

Competitive Reactions   Present and potential competition is an important influence in determining a base
price. Even a new product is distinctive for only a limited time, until the inevitable
competition arrives. The threat of *potential* competition is greatest when the field
is easy to enter and the profit prospects are encouraging. Competition can also come
from three other sources:

- *Directly similar products:* Nike running shoes versus Adidas or Reebok shoes.
- *Available substitutes:* Air freight versus truck or rail freight.
- *Unrelated products seeking the same consumer dollar:* Videocassette recorder
  (VCR) versus a bicycle or a weekend excursion.

Other Parts of the   The base price of a product normally is influenced considerably by the other major
Marketing Mix   ingredients in the marketing mix.

THE PRODUCT

We have already observed that the price of a product is influenced substantially by whether it is a new item or an older, established one. The importance of the product in its end use must also be considered. To illustrate, there is little price competition among manufacturers of packaging materials or producers of industrial gases, and a stable price structure exists. These industrial products are only an incidental part of the final article, so customers will buy the least expensive product consistent with the required quality. The price of a product is influenced also (1) by whether the product may be leased as well as purchased outright, (2) by whether or not the product may be returned to the seller, and (3) by whether a trade-in is involved.

CHANNELS OF DISTRIBUTION

The channels selected and the types of middlemen used will influence a manufacturer's pricing. A firm selling both through wholesalers and directly to retailers often sets a different factory price for each of these two classes of customers. The price to wholesalers is lower because they perform activities (services) that the manufacturer otherwise would have to perform itself — activities such as providing storage, granting credit to retailers, and selling to small retailers.

PROMOTIONAL METHODS

The promotional methods used, and the extent to which the product is promoted by the manufacturer or middlemen, are still other factors to consider in pricing. If major promotional responsibility is placed upon retailers, they ordinarily will be charged a lower price for a product than if the manufacturer advertises it heavily. Even when a manufacturer promotes heavily, it may want its retailers to use local advertising to tie in with national advertising. Such a decision must be reflected in the manufacturer's price to these retailers.

BASIC METHODS OF SETTING PRICES

In our price-determination discussion we now are at the point where we can talk about setting a *specific* selling price. Most of the approaches used by companies to establish base prices for their products are variations of one of the following methods:

- Prices are based on total cost plus a desired profit. (Break-even analysis is a variation of this method.)
- Prices are based on a balance between estimates of market demand and supply (the costs of production and marketing).
- Prices are based only on competitive market conditions.

COST-PLUS PRICING

Cost-plus pricing means setting the price of one unit of a product equal to the unit's total cost plus the desired profit on the unit. As an example, suppose a contractor figures that the labour and materials required to build and sell 10 houses will cost $750,000, and that the other expenses (office rent, depreciation on equip-

House builders often start with cost-plus pricing.

ment, wages of management, and so on) will equal $150,000. On this total cost of $900,000, the contractor desires a profit of 10 percent of cost. The cost plus the profit amount to $990,000, so each of the 10 houses is priced at $99,000.

While this is a very simple and easily applied pricing method, it has one serious limitation. It does not account for the fact that there are different types of costs, and that these costs are affected differently by increases or decreases in output. In our housing example, suppose the contractor built and sold only eight houses at the cost-plus price of $99,000 each. Total sales would be $792,000. Labour and material chargeable to the eight houses would total $600,000 ($75,000 per house). Since the contractor would still incur the full $150,000 in overhead expenses, however, the total cost would be $750,000. This would leave a profit of only $42,000, or $5,250 per house instead of the anticipated $9,000. On a percentage basis, the profit would be only 5.6 percent of total cost rather than the desired 10 percent. This example of the cost-plus pricing of the houses is summarized in Table 11-1.

TABLE 11-1   EXAMPLE OF COST-PLUS PRICING

Actual results often differ from the original plans because the various types of costs react differently to changes in output.

Costs, selling prices, profit	Number of houses built and sold	
	Planned = 10	Actual = 8
Labour and material costs ($75,000 per house)	$750,000	$600,000
Overhead (fixed) costs	150,000	150,000
Total costs	$900,000	$750,000
Total sales at $99,000 per house	990,000	792,000
Profit: Total	$90,000	$42,000
Per house	$9,000	$5,250
As % of cost	10%	5.6%

The Cost Concepts

The total unit cost of a product is made up of several types of costs. These costs react differently to changes in the quantity produced. Thus, the total unit cost of the product changes as output expands or contracts. A more sophisticated approach to cost-plus pricing takes such changes into consideration.

The cost concepts in the nearby box are important to our discussion. These nine cost concepts and their interrelationships may be studied in Table 11-2 and in Fig. 11-1, which is based on the table.

The interrelationships among the various *average unit* costs is displayed graphically in Fig. 11-1 and explained briefly as follows (again the data come from Table 11-2):

1. The **average fixed cost curve** declines as output increases because the total of the fixed costs is spread over an increasing number of units.
2. The **average variable cost curve** usually is U-shaped. It starts high because average variable costs for the first few units of output usually are high. The variable costs per unit then decline as the company realizes efficiencies in

TABLE 11-2   COSTS FOR INDIVIDUAL FIRM

Total fixed costs never change, despite increases in quantity. Variable costs are the costs of inputs — materials, labour, power. Their total increases as production quantity rises. Total cost is the sum of all fixed and variable costs. The other measures in the table are simply methods of looking at costs per unit; they always involve dividing a cost by the number of units produced.

(1)	(2)	(3)	(4)	(5)	(6)	(7)	(8)
Quantity output	Total fixed costs	Total variable costs	Total costs (2) + (3)	Marginal cost per unit	Average fixed cost (2) ÷ (1)	Average variable cost (3) ÷ (1)	Average cost per unit (4) ÷ (1)
0	$256	$ 0	$256	$ 0	**Infinity**	$ 0	**Infinity**
1	256	64	320	⊢→ 64	$256.00	64	$320.00
2	256	84	340	⊢→ 20	128.00	42	170.00
3	256	99	355	⊢→ 15	85.33	33	118.33
4	256	112	368	⊢→ 13	64.00	28	92.00
5	256	125	381	⊢→ 13	51.20	25	76.20
6	256	144	400	⊢→ 19	42.67	24	66.67
7	256	175	431	⊢→ 31	36.57	25	61.57
8	256	224	480	⊢→ 49	32.00	28	60.00
9	256	297	553	⊢→ 73	28.44	33	61.44
10		400	656	⊢→ 103	25.60	40	65.60

FIGURE 11-1

Unit cost curves for an individual firm.

This figure is based on data in Table 11-2. Here we see how unit costs change as quantity increases. Using cost-plus pricing, four units of output would be priced at $92 each, while eight units would sell for $60 each.

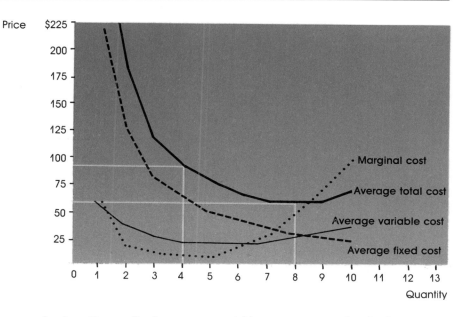

production. Eventually the average variable cost curve reaches its lowest point, reflecting the optimum output as far as variable costs (not total costs) are concerned. In Fig. 11-1, this point is at six units of output. Beyond that point, the average variable cost rises, reflecting the increase in unit variable costs caused by overcrowded facilities and other inefficiencies. If the variable

THE DIFFERENT KINDS OF COSTS

A **fixed cost** is an element, such as rent, executive salaries, or property tax, that remains constant regardless of how many items are produced. Such a cost continues even if production stops completely. It is called a fixed cost because it is difficult to change in the short run (but not in the long run, over several years).

Total fixed cost is the sum of all fixed costs.

Average fixed cost is the total fixed cost divided by the number of units produced. It is the amount of the total fixed cost that is allocated to each unit.

A **variable cost** is an element, such as labour or material cost, that is directly related to production. Variable costs can be controlled in the short run simply by changing the level of production. When production stops, for example, all variable production costs become zero.

Total variable cost is the sum of all variable costs. The more units produced, the higher this cost is.

Average variable cost is the total variable cost divided by the number of units produced. Average variable cost is usually high for the first few units produced. It decreases as production increases, owing to such things as quantity discounts on materials and more efficient use of labour. Beyond some optimum output it increases, owing to crowding of production facilities, overtime pay, etc.

Total cost is the sum of total fixed cost and total variable cost (for a specific quantity produced).

Average total cost is the total cost divided by the number of units produced.

Marginal cost is the cost of producing and selling one more unit; it is the cost of the last unit produced. Usually the marginal cost of the last unit is the same as the variable cost of that unit.

---

costs per unit were constant, then the average variable cost curve would be a horizontal line at the level of the constant unit variable cost.

3. The **average total cost curve** is the sum of the first two curves — average fixed cost and average variable cost. It starts high, reflecting the fact that total *fixed* costs are spread over so few units of output. As output increases, the average total cost curve declines, because the unit fixed cost and unit variable cost are decreasing. Eventually, the point of lowest total cost per unit is reached (eight units of output in Fig. 11-1). Beyond that optimum point, diminishing returns set in and the average total cost curve rises.

4. The **marginal cost curve** has a more pronounced U-shape than the other curves in Fig. 11-1. The marginal cost curve slopes downward until the fifth unit of output, at which point the marginal costs start to increase.

Now note the relationship between the marginal cost curve and the average total cost curve. The average total cost curve slopes downward *as long as the marginal cost is less than the average total cost*. Even though the marginal cost increases after the fifth unit, the average total cost curve continues to slope downward until after the eighth unit. This is so because marginal cost — even when it is going up — is still less than average total cost.

The marginal cost curve and the average total cost curve intersect at the lowest point of the average total cost curve. Beyond that point (the eighth unit in the example), the cost of producing and selling the next unit is higher than the average cost of all units. Therefore, from then on the average total cost rises. The reason for this is that the average variable cost is increasing faster than the average fixed cost is decreasing. Table 11-2 shows that producing the ninth unit reduces average fixed cost by $3.56 (from $32 to $28.44), but causes average variable cost to rise by $5.

Refinements in Cost-Plus Pricing

Once management understands that not all costs react in the same way to output increases or decreases, refinements in cost-plus pricing are possible. Let's assume that the desired profit is included either in the fixed cost or in the variable cost schedule. That is, profit is included as a cost in Table 11-2 and Fig. 11-1. Then management can refer to the table or graph to find the appropriate price, once a decision has been made regarding output quantity. If the executives decide to produce six units in our example, the selling price will be $66.67 per unit. A production run of eight units would be priced at $60 per unit. (Refer to Table 11-2 or Fig. 11-1.)

The user of this pricing method assumes that all the intended output will be produced and sold. If fewer units are produced, each would have to sell for a higher price in order to cover all costs and show a profit. But, obviously, if business is slack and output must be cut, it is not wise to raise the unit price. Thus the difficulty in this pricing approach is that no attention is paid to market demand.

Prices Based on Marginal Costs Only

Another approach to cost-plus pricing is to set a price that will cover only the marginal costs, not the total costs. Refer again to the cost schedules shown in Table 11-2 and Fig. 11-1, and assume that a firm is operating at an output level of six units. Under marginal cost pricing, this firm can accept an order for one unit at $31, instead of the total unit cost of $66.67. The firm is then trying to cover only its variable costs. If the firm can sell for any price over $31 — say, $33 or $35 — the excess contributes to the payment of fixed costs.

Obviously, not all orders can be priced to cover only variable costs. Marginal cost pricing may be feasible, however, if management wants to keep its labour force employed during a slack season. Marginal cost pricing may also be used when one product is expected to attract business for another. A department store, for example, may price meals in its tearoom at a level that covers only the marginal costs. The reasoning is that this tearoom will bring shoppers to the store, where they will buy other merchandise.

Cost-Plus Pricing by Middlemen

Cost-plus pricing is widely used by retailing and wholesaling middlemen. At least it seems this way at first glance. A retailer, for example, pays a given amount to buy products and have them delivered to the store. Then the retailer adds an amount (a markup) to the acquisition cost. This markup is estimated to be sufficient to cover the store's expenses and still leave a reasonable profit. To simplify pricing

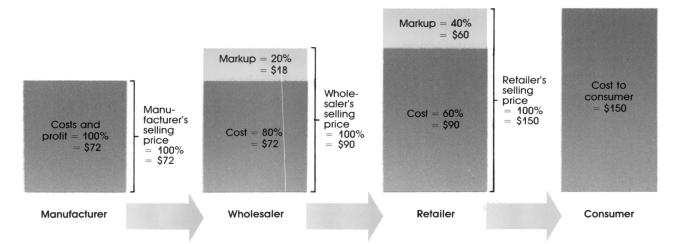

Manufacturer

Costs and
profit = 100%
= $72

Manu-
facturer's
selling
price
= 100%
= $72

Wholesaler

Markup = 20%
= $18

Cost = 80%
= $72

Whole-
saler's
selling
price
= 100%
= $90

Retailer

Markup = 40%
= $60

Cost = 60%
= $90

Retailer's
selling
price
= 100%
= $150

Consumer

Cost to
consumer
= $150

FIGURE 11-2
Examples of markup pricing by retailers and wholesalers.

and accounting, the retailer may add the same *percentage* markup to every product. This is an average markup that the retailer's experience has shown is large enough to cover the costs and profit for the store. Thus, a clothing store may buy a garment for $30 including freight, and then price the item at $50. The price of $50 reflects a retailer markup of 40 percent based on the selling price, or $66\frac{2}{3}$ percent based on the merchandise cost.

Different types of retailers will require different percentage markups because of the nature of the products handled and the services offered. A self-service supermarket has lower costs and thus a lower average markup than a full-service delicatessen. Figure 11-2 shows an example of markup pricing by middlemen. The topic of markups is discussed in more detail in Appendix A.

To what extent is cost-plus pricing truly used by middlemen? At least three significant indications suggest that what seems to be cost-plus pricing is really market-inspired pricing:

1. Most retail prices set by applying average percentage markups are really only price offers. If the merchandise does not sell at the original price, that price will be lowered until it reaches a level at which the merchandise will sell.

2. Many retailers do not use the same markup on all the products they carry. A supermarket will have a markup of 6 to 8 percent on sugar and soap products, 15 to 18 percent on canned fruit and vegetables, and 25 to 30 percent on fresh meats and produce. These different markups for different products definitely reflect competitive considerations and other aspects of the market demand.

3. The middleman usually does not actually set a base price but only adds a percentage to the price that has already been set by the manufacturer. The manufacturer's price is set to allow each middleman to add the customary markup and still sell at a retail price that is competitive. That is, the key price is set by the manufacturer, with an eye on the market.

**Evaluation of
Cost-Plus Pricing**

We have emphasized that a firm must be market-oriented and must cater to consumers' wants. Why, then, are we now considering cost-plus pricing? Actually, it provides a good point of departure for our discussion of price determination. Also, cost-plus pricing is mentioned so widely in business that it must be understood. Adherents of cost-plus pricing point to its simplicity and its ease of determination. They say that costs are a known quantity, whereas attempts to estimate demand for pricing purposes are mainly guesswork.

This opinion is questionable on two counts. First, it is doubtful whether adequate, accurate cost data are available. We know a fair amount about cost-volume relationships in production costs, but what we know is still insufficient. Furthermore, our information regarding marketing costs is woefully inadequate. Second, it is indeed difficult to estimate demand — that is, to construct a demand schedule that shows sales volume at various prices. Nevertheless, sales forecasting and other research tools can do a surprisingly good job in this area.

Critics of cost-plus pricing do not say that costs should be disregarded in pricing. Costs should be a determining influence, they maintain, but not the only one. Costs are a floor under a firm's prices. If goods are priced under this floor for a long time, the firm will be forced out of business. But when used by itself, cost-plus pricing is a weak and unrealistic method, because it ignores the influences of competition and market demand.

BREAK-EVEN ANALYSIS

One way to use market demand in price determination, and still consider costs, is to conduct a break-even analysis and determine break-even points. A **break-even point** is that quantity of output at which the sales revenue equals the total costs, *assuming a certain selling price*. Thus, there is a different break-even point for each different selling price. Sales of quantities above the break-even output result in a profit on each additional unit. The further the sales are above the break-even point, the higher the total and unit profits. Sales below the break-even point result in a loss to the seller.

**Determining the
Break-Even Point**

The method of determining the break-even point is illustrated in Table 11-3 and Figs. 11-3 and 11-4. In our hypothetical situation, the company's fixed costs are $250, and its variable costs are constant at $30 a unit. Recall that in our earlier example (Table 11-2 and Fig. 11-1), we assumed that the unit variable costs were *not* constant; they fluctuated. Now, to simplify our break-even analysis, we are assuming that the unit variable costs *are* constant.

Thus the total cost of producing one unit is $280. For five units the total cost is $400 ($30 multiplied by 5, plus $250). In Fig. 11-3 the selling price is $80 a unit. Consequently, every time a unit is sold, $50 is contributed to overhead (fixed costs). That is, the variable costs are $30 per unit, and these costs are incurred in producing each unit. But any revenue over $30 can be used to help cover the fixed costs. At a selling price of $80, the company will break even if five units are sold. This is so because a $50 contribution from each of five units will just cover the total fixed costs of $250.

Stated another way, the variable costs for five units are $150 and the fixed costs

TABLE 11-3 COMPUTATION OF BREAK-EVEN POINT

At each of several prices, we wish to find out how many units must be sold to cover all costs. At a unit price of $100, the sale of each unit contributes $70 to cover the overhead expenses. We must sell about 3.6 units to cover the $250 fixed cost. See Figs. 11-3 and 11-4 for a visual portrayal of the data in this table.

(1) Unit price	(2) Unit variable costs, AVC	(3) Contribution to overhead (1) − (2)	(4) Overhead (total fixed costs)	(5) Break-even point (4) ÷ (3)
$ 60	$ 30	$ 30	$250	8.3 units
80	30	50	250	5.0 units
100	30	70	250	3.6 units
150	30	120	250	2.1 units

FIGURE 11-3
Break-even chart with selling price of $80 per unit.

Here the break-even point is reached when the company sells five units. Fixed costs, regardless of quantity produced and sold, are $250. The variable cost per unit is $30. If this company sells five units, total cost is $400 (variable cost of 5 × $30, or $150, plus fixed cost of $250). At a selling price of $80, the sale of five units will yield $400 revenue, and costs and revenue will equal each other. At the same price, the sale of each unit above five yields a profit.

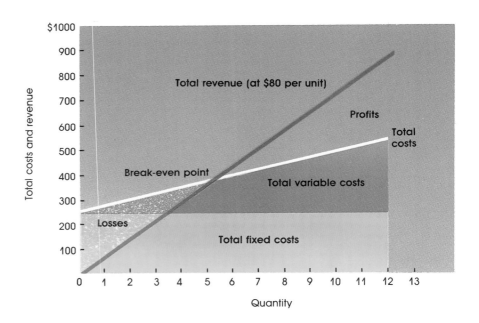

are $250, for a total cost of $400. This is equal to the revenue from five units sold at $80 each. So, for an $80 selling price, the break-even volume is five units.

The break-even point may be found with this formula:

$$\text{Break-even point in units} = \frac{\text{total fixed costs}}{\text{unit contribution to overhead}}$$
$$= \frac{\text{total fixed costs}}{\text{selling price} - \text{average variable cost}}$$

FIGURE 11-4
Break-even chart showing four different selling prices.

Here the company is experimenting with several different prices in order to determine which is the most appropriate. There are four different prices and four break-even points. At a price of $60, the company will start making a profit after it has sold 8.3 units. At the opposite extreme, the break-even point for a price of $150 is about 2.1 units.

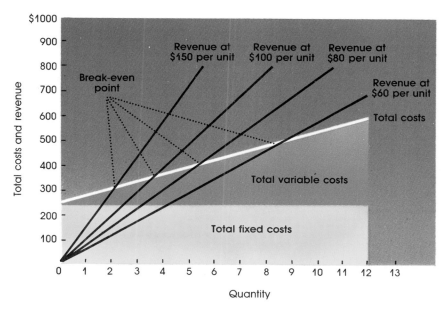

It is important to note the assumptions underlying the computations in the preceding paragraph and in Fig. 11-3. First, we assume that total fixed costs are constant. This is true only over a short period of time and within a limited range of output. It is reasonably easy, however, to develop a break-even chart wherein the fixed costs, and consequently the total costs, are stepped up at several intervals. A second assumption in our example is that the variable costs remain constant per unit of output. In the earlier discussion of the cost structure of the firm, we noted that the average variable costs in a firm usually fluctuate.

Another limitation of Fig. 11-3 is that it shows a break-even point only if the unit price is $80. It is highly desirable to compute the break-even points for several different selling prices. Therefore, in Fig. 11-4 the break-even point is determined for four prices — $60, $80, $100, and $150. Figure 11-4 is also based on Table 11-3. If the price is $60, it will take sales of approximately 8.3 units to break even; at $150, only about 2.1 units. Every different selling price will result in a different break-even point. A company could use these break-even points as the basis for setting the selling price — say, by choosing the price that results in the most reasonable break-even point.

Evaluation of
Break-Even Analysis

Certainly no one should claim that break-even analysis is the perfect pricing tool. Many of its underlying assumptions are unrealistic in a practical business operation. It assumes that costs are stable (that is, nonfluctuating). Thus, break-even analysis has limited value in companies where the average (unit) cost fluctuates frequently.

The major limitation of break-even analysis as a realistic pricing tool is that it ignores the market demand at the various prices. It is still essentially a tool for cost-plus pricing. The revenue curves in Figs. 11-3 and 11-4 show only what the revenue will be at the different prices *if* (and it is a big if) the given number of units can be sold at these prices. The completed break-even charts show only the amount that must be sold at the stated price to break even. The charts do not tell us whether we *can* actually sell this amount. The amount the market will buy at a given price could well be below the break-even point. For instance, at a selling price of $80 per unit, the break-even point is five units. But competition and/or a volatile market may prevent the company from actually selling those five units. If the company can sell only three or four units, the firm will not break even. It will show a loss.

These limitations, however, should not lead management to dismiss break-even analysis as a pricing tool. Even in its simplest form, break-even analysis is very helpful because, in the short run, many firms are faced with reasonably stable cost and demand structures.

PRICES BASED ON A BALANCE BETWEEN SUPPLY AND DEMAND

Another method of price setting involves balancing demand with costs to determine the best price for profit maximization. This method of price determination is thus best suited for companies whose pricing goal is to maximize profit. However, companies with other pricing goals might use this method in special situations or perhaps to compare prices determined by different methods.

In discussing demand, we should distinguish between the demand curve or schedule facing an individual seller and the one facing the entire industry. Theoretically, when a firm operates in a market of perfect competition, its demand curve is horizontal at the market price. That is, the single seller has no control over the price. And the seller's entire output can be sold at the market price. However, the industry as a whole has a downward-sloping curve. That is, the industry can sell more units at lower prices than at higher prices.

The market situation facing most firms today is one of monopolistic, or imperfect, competition. This is characterized by product differentiation and nonprice competition. By differentiating its products, an individual firm gains some control over its prices. In effect, each firm becomes a separate "industry"; its product is to some extent unlike any other. Thus an individual firm in monopolistic competition has a downward-sloping demand curve. That is, it will attract some buyers at a high price, but to broaden its market and to sell to more people, it must lower the price.

Determining the Price

To use this pricing method, the price setter must understand the concepts of average and marginal revenue, in addition to average and marginal cost. **Marginal revenue** is the income derived from the sale of the last unit — the marginal unit. **Average revenue** is the unit price at a given level of unit sales. It is calculated by dividing total revenue by the number of units sold. Referring to the hypothetical demand schedule in Table 11-4 we see that the company can sell one unit at $80. To sell two units, it must reduce its price to $75 for each unit. Thus, the company receives an additional $70 (marginal revenue) by selling two units instead of one. The fifth unit brings a marginal revenue of $53. After the sixth unit, however, total revenue declines each time the unit price is lowered to sell an additional unit. Hence, there is a negative marginal revenue.

The price-setting process that involves the balancing of supply and demand is

TABLE 11-4   DEMAND SCHEDULE FOR INDIVIDUAL FIRM

At each market price, a certain quantity of the product will be demanded. Marginal revenue is simply the amount of additional money gained by selling one more unit. In this example, the company no longer gains marginal revenue after it has sold the sixth unit at a price of $60.

Units sold	Unit price (average revenue)	Total revenue	Marginal revenue
1	$80	$ 80	
2	75	150	$ 70
3	72	216	66
4	68	272	56
5	65	325	53
6	60	360	35
7	50	350	− 10
8	40	320	− 30

FIGURE 11-5
Price setting and profit maximization through marginal analysis.

illustrated in the three-part Fig. 11-5. We assume that a firm will continue to produce units as long as the revenue from the last unit sold exceeds the cost of producing this last unit. That is, output continues to increase as long as marginal revenue exceeds marginal cost. At the point where they meet (quantity Q in Fig. 11-5a), output theoretically should cease. Certainly management will not want to sell a unit at a price less than the out-of-pocket (variable) costs of production. Thus the *volume of output* is the quantity level at which **marginal costs equal marginal revenue**, or quantity Q.

The unit price is determined by locating the point on the average revenue curve that represents an output of Q units. Remember that average revenue represents the unit price. The average revenue curve has been added in Fig. 11-5b. The unit price at which to sell quantity Q is represented by point C. It is the price B in Fig. 11-5b.

The average total (unit) cost curve has been added in Fig. 11-5c. It shows that,

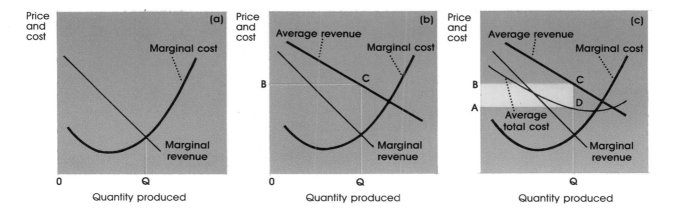

for output quantity Q, the average unit cost is represented by point D. This average unit cost is A. Thus, with a price of B and an average unit cost of A, the company enjoys a unit profit given by AB in the future. The total profit is represented by area ABCD (quantity Q times unit profit AB).

Evaluation of Supply-Demand Pricing

Supply and demand analysis as a basis for price setting has enjoyed only limited use. Business people usually claim that better data are needed for plotting the curves exactly. Supply and demand analysis can be used, they feel, to study past price movements, but it cannot serve as a practical basis for setting prices.

On the brighter side, management's knowledge of costs and demand is improving. Data processing equipment is bringing more complete and detailed information to management's attention all the time. Earlier we pointed out that management usually can estimate demand within broad limits, and this is helpful. Also, experienced management in many firms can do a surprisingly accurate job of estimating marginal and average costs and revenues.

Marginal analysis can also have practical value if management will adjust the price in light of some conditions discussed earlier in this chapter. In Fig. 11-5, the price was set at point B. But, in the short run, management may price below B, or even below A, adopting an aggressive pricing strategy to increase its market share, or to discourage competition.

PRICES SET IN RELATION TO MARKET ALONE

Cost-plus pricing is one extreme among pricing methods. At the other end of the scale is a method whereby a firm's prices are set in relation *only* to the market price. The seller's price may be set right at the market price to meet the competition, or it may be set either above or below the market price.

Pricing to Meet Competition

Management may decide to price a product right at the competitive level in several situations. One such situation occurs when the market is highly competitive and the firm's product is not differentiated significantly from competing products. To some extent, this method of pricing reflects market conditions that parallel those found under perfect competition. That is, product differentiation is absent, buyers and sellers are well informed, and the seller has no discernible control over the selling price. Most producers of agricultural products and small firms producing well-known, standardized products ordinarily use this pricing method.

The sharp drop in revenue that occurs when the price is raised above the prevailing level indicates that the individual seller faces a *kinked demand* (see Fig. 11-6). The prevailing price is at A. If the seller tries to go above that price, the demand for the product drops sharply, as indicated by the flat average revenue curve above point P. At any price above A, then, the demand is highly elastic — that is, total revenue declines. Below price A, the demand is highly inelastic, as represented by the steeply sloping average revenue curve and the negative marginal revenue curve. That is, the total revenue decreases each time the price is reduced to a level below A. The prevailing price is strong. Consequently, a reduction in price by one firm will not increase the firm's unit sales very much — certainly not enough to offset the loss in average revenue.

FIGURE 11-6

Kinked demand curve facing manufacturer of products sold at prevailing price (the same type of curve faces individual oligopolist).

The kink occurs at the point representing the prevailing price A. Above A, demand declines rapidly as the price is increased. A price set below A results in very little increase in volume, so revenue is lost. That is, the marginal revenue is negative.

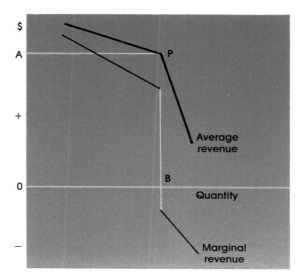

Up to this point in our discussion of pricing to meet competition, we have observed market situations that involve many sellers. Oddly enough, the same pricing method is often used when the market is dominated by only a few sellers. This type of market is called an **oligopoly**. The demand curve facing an individual seller in an oligopoly is a kinked one, as in Fig. 11-6.

An oligopolist must price at market level to maximize profits. Selling *above* market price will result in a drastic reduction in total revenue because the average revenue curve is so elastic above point P. If an oligopolist cuts its price *below* the market price, all other members of the oligopoly must respond immediately. Otherwise the price cutter will enjoy a substantial increase in business. Therefore, the competitors do retaliate with comparable price cuts, and the net result is that a new market price is established at a lower level. All members of the oligopoly end up with about the same share of the market that they had before. However, unit revenue is reduced by the amount of the price cut.

File 11-3

arketing at Work

Running Down the Price to Stay in the Same Place

The type of pricing situation discussed in this section is precisely what happens whenever businesses engage in a price war. This will occur most often in a highly competitive market environment where the competitors are dealing in a product or service that is not easily differentiated. We are all familiar with gasoline price wars. The same thing is common among manufacturers of non-differentiated products such as flour and even among airlines. If a gasoline retailer on a busy intersection were to drop prices by five cents a litre in an attempt to gain market share from its competitors, the service stations on the other three corners would probably immediately match the lower price. The result is usually that no one gains market share, and all lose money because they all must charge the lower price in order to retain customers. Deregulation of the airline business in the United States has brought about similar developments. On heavily travelled routes, some airlines dropped return fares to as low as $99. These no-frills flights were money-losers, but competitors had to match them or lose business. We see much the same process at work in Canada, where airlines compete with seat sales and frequent flyer programs, a form of price promotion.

Theoretically, oligopolists gain no advantage by cutting their prices. For their own good, they should simply set their prices at a competitive level and leave them there. In reality, price wars often are touched off in an oligopoly because it is not possible to fully control all sellers of the product. In the absence of collusion, every so often some firm will cut its price. Then all others usually will follow to maintain their respective market shares.

Pricing to meet competition is rather simple to do. A firm ascertains what the going price is, and after allowing for customary markups for middlemen, it arrives at its own selling price. To illustrate, a manufacturer of men's quality dress shoes is aware that retailers want to sell the shoes for $150 a pair. The firm sells directly to retailers, who want an average markup of 40 percent of their selling price. Consequently, after allowing $60 for the retailer's markup, the producer's top price is about $90. This manufacturer then decides whether $90 is enough to cover its costs and still leave it a reasonable profit. Sometimes a manufacturer faces a real squeeze in this regard, particularly when its costs are rising but the market price is holding firm.

Pricing below Competitive Level

A variation of market-based pricing is to set a price at some point *below* the competitive level. This method of pricing is typically used by discount retailers. These stores offer fewer services, and they operate on the principle of low markup and high volume. They typically price nationally advertised brands 10 to 20 percent below the suggested retail list price, or the price actually being charged by full-service retailers. Even full-service retailers may price below the competitive level by eliminating specific services. For example, some gas stations offer a discount to customers who use the self-service pumps or who pay cash instead of using a credit card.

Pricing above Competitive Level

Manufacturers or retailers sometimes set their prices *above* the market level. Usually, above-market pricing works only when the product is distinctive or when the

Some firms price above the competition.

seller has acquired prestige in its field. Most cities have a prestige clothing or jewellery store where price tags are noticeably above the competitive level set by other stores that handle similar products.

SUMMARY

In our economy, price is a major regulator because it influences the allocation of scarce resources. In individual companies, price is one important factor in determining marketing success. The problem is that it is difficult to define price. A rather general definition is this: Price is the amount of money (plus possibly some goods or services) needed to acquire, in exchange, some assortment of a product and its accompanying services.

Before setting the base price on a product, management should identify its pricing goal. Major pricing objectives are (1) to earn a target return on investment or on net sales, (2) to maximize profits, (3) to increase sales, (4) to gain or hold a target share of the market, (5) to stabilize prices, and (6) to meet competition's prices.

The key factors that should influence management's decision when setting the base price for a product or service are (1) demand for the product or service, (2) desired market share, (3) competitive reactions, (4) other major elements in the marketing mix, and (5) the costs of producing the product or of delivering the service.

The major methods used to determine the base price are (1) cost-plus pricing, (2) balancing market demand with costs (supply), and (3) setting the price in relation only to the market.

For cost-plus pricing to be at all effective, a seller must consider the several types of costs and their different reactions to changes in the quantity produced. A producer usually sets a price to cover total cost. In some cases, however, the best policy may be to set a price that covers marginal cost only. The major weakness in cost-plus pricing is that it completely ignores the market demand. To partially offset this weakness, a company may use break-even analysis as a tool in price setting.

In real-life situations, virtually all price setting is market-inspired to some extent. Consequently, marginal analysis is a useful method for setting a price. Prices are set and output level is determined at the point where marginal cost equals marginal revenue.

For many products, price setting is a relatively easy job because management simply sets the price at the market level established by the competition. Two variations of market-level pricing are to price below or above the competitive level.

KEY TERMS AND CONCEPTS

Price 296
Pricing objectives: 298
   Target return 299
   Maximize profit 299
   Increase sales 300
   Market share 300

Cost-plus pricing 305
Fixed cost 306
Variable cost 306
Marginal cost 308
Average cost 308
Total cost 308

QUESTIONS AND
PROBLEMS

1. Two students paid $2.49 for identical tubes of toothpaste at a leading store. Yet one student complained about paying a much higher price than the other. What might be the basis for this complaint?

2. Explain how a firm's pricing objective may influence the promotional program for a product. Which of the six pricing goals involves the largest, most aggressive promotional campaign?

3. What marketing conditions might logically lead a company to set "meeting competition" as a pricing objective?

4. What is the expected price for each of the following articles? How did you arrive at your estimate in each instance?
   a. A new type of carbonated cola beverage that holds its carbonation long after it has been opened; packaged in 355-mL and 2-litre bottles.
   b. A nuclear-powered 55 cm table-model television set, guaranteed to run for years without replacement of the original power-generating component; requires no battery or electric wires.
   c. An automatic garage-door opener for residential housing.

5. Name at least five products for which you think an inverse demand exists. For each product, within which price range does this inverse demand exist?

6. In Fig. 11-1, what is the significance of the point where the marginal cost curve intersects the average total cost curve? Explain why the average total cost curve is declining to the left of the intersection point and rising beyond it. Explain how the marginal cost curve can be rising, while the average total cost curve is still declining.

7. In Table 11-2, what is the marginal cost of the seventh unit produced?

8. What are the merits and limitations of the cost-plus method of setting a base price?

9. In a break-even chart, is the total *fixed* cost line always horizontal? Is the total *variable* cost line always straight? Explain.

10. In Table 11-3 and Fig. 11-3, what would be the break-even points at prices of $50 and $90, if the variable costs are $40 per unit and the fixed costs remain at $250?

11. A small manufacturer sold ball-point pens to retailers at $8.40 per dozen. The manufacturing cost was 50 cents for each pen. The expenses, including all selling and administrative costs except advertising, were $19,200. How many dozen must the manufacturer sell to cover these expenses and pay for an advertising campaign costing $6,000?

12. In Fig. 11-5, why would the firm normally stop producing at quantity Q? Why is the price set at B and not at D or A?

13. Are there any stores in your community that generally price above the competitive level? How are they able to do this?

CHAPTER 12

PRICING STRATEGIES AND POLICIES

CHAPTER GOALS

This chapter is concerned with the ways in which a base price can (and sometimes must) be modified. After studying this chapter, you should understand:

- Price discounts and allowances.
- Geographic pricing strategies.
- Skimming and penetration pricing strategies.
- One-price and flexible-price strategies.
- Unit pricing.
- Price lining.
- Resale price maintenance.
- ''Leader'' pricing.
- Psychological pricing.
- Price competition versus nonprice competition.

As the Canadian airline business has moved toward greater deregulation during the 1980s, we have seen greater price competition. But Canadian airlines have generally avoided the wholesale price wars that marked the early years of the deregulated industry in the United States. In Canada, the two major national airlines, Air Canada and Canadian Airlines International, tended to engage in price competition on a selective basis, using the device of the ''seat sale.'' Rather than reduce all prices, the airlines would offer low prices for a limited time period and on certain routes only and would limit the number of seats available at sale prices on each flight.

When Air Canada returned from a labour dispute which shut down operations in late 1987, the airline immediately announced a sale for a two-month period on most of its North American and European routes. In an attempt to win back customers who had switched to other airlines while Air Canada was shut down, prices were cut dramatically. But there were restrictions. For example, travel would have to take place on Tuesdays, Wednesdays, or Thursdays and reservations would have to be made at least seven days prior to departure, 21 days for flights to Europe. No changes or refunds were permitted. Canadian Airlines International and Wardair immediately responded with their own seat sales.

In order to capture a share of the growing business travel market during the mid-1980s, all major airlines introduced *frequent flyer programs*. Air Canada's *Aeroplan* and Canadian Airlines International's *Canadian Plus* programs are designed to establish a loyalty to a particular airline. Each offers frequent travellers a certain number of points each time they fly with that airline, or with one of its affiliated regional commuter airlines. The number of points obtained is linked to the length of the trip and the class of service taken. Points can also be obtained by renting cars from certain rental car companies and staying at certain hotels with which the airlines have reciprocal agreements. Accumulated points may be redeemed for free flights and other gifts. Such programs are really a form of price promotion in much the same way as a manufacturer of shampoos will give a retailer a volume discount or deal — buy 10, get one free.

The strategy of engaging in price competition — as the airlines have been doing — is just one of the pricing strategies that we shall discuss in this chapter. In managing the price portion of a company's marketing mix, management first decides on its pricing goal and then sets the base price for a product or service. The next task is to design the appropriate strategies and policies concerning several aspects of the price structure. What kind of discount schedule should be adopted? Will the company occasionally absorb freight costs? In this chapter we shall discuss several pricing topics that require strategy decisions and policy making. We also shall consider some legal aspects of these activities. A company's success in pricing may depend upon management's ability to design creative pricing strategies that reflect a customer orientation, rather than the traditional cost-oriented pricing methodology.

We shall be using the terms *policy* and *strategy* frequently in this chapter. So let's review the meaning of these terms as they were defined in Chapter 3. A **strategy** is a broad plan of action by which an organization intends to reach its goal. A **policy** is a managerial guide to future decision making when a given situation arises. Thus a policy becomes the course of action followed routinely any time a given strategic or tactical situation arises. To illustrate, suppose management adopts the *strategy* of offering certain quantity discounts in order to achieve the goal of a 10 percent increase in sales next year. Then, routinely, every time the company receives an order of a given size, it is company *policy* to grant the customer the prescribed quantity discount.

DISCOUNTS AND ALLOWANCES

Discounts and allowances result in a deduction from the base (or list) price. The deduction may be in the form of a reduced price or some other concession, such as free merchandise or advertising allowances.

Quantity Discounts

Quantity discounts are deductions from the list price offered by a seller to encourage customers to buy in larger amounts or to make most of their purchases from that seller. The discounts are based on the size of the purchase, either in dollars or in units.

A **noncumulative** discount is based upon the size of an *individual order* of one or more products. Thus a retailer may sell golf balls at $1 each or at three for $2.50. A manufacturer or wholesaler may set up a quantity discount schedule such as the following, which was used by a manufacturer of industrial adhesives.

Boxes purchased on single order	% discount from list price
1–5	0.0
6–12	2.0
13–25	3.5
Over 25	5.0

Noncumulative quantity discounts are expected to encourage large orders. Many expenses, such as billing, order filling, and the salaries of sales people, are about the same whether the seller receives an order totalling $10 or $500. Consequently, selling expense as a percentage of sales decreases as orders become larger. The seller shares such savings with the purchaser of large quantities.

Cumulative discounts are based on the total volume purchased *over a period of time*. These discounts are advantageous to a seller because they tie customers more closely to that seller. They really are patronage discounts, because the more total business a buyer gives a seller, the greater is the discount. Cumulative discounts are especially useful in the sale of perishable products. These discounts encourage customers to buy fresh supplies frequently so that the merchandise will not grow stale.

Retailers, too, offer quantity discounts.

Quantity discounts can help a manufacturer effect real economies in production as well as in selling. Large orders can result in lower-cost production runs and lower transportation costs. A producer's cumulative discount based on total orders from all the stores in a retail chain may increase orders from that chain substantially. This enables the producer to make much more effective use of production capacity, even though the individual orders are small and do not generate savings in marketing costs.

Trade Discounts **Trade** discounts, sometimes called **functional** discounts, are reductions from the list price offered to buyers in payment for marketing functions that they will perform. A manufacturer may quote a retail list price of $400 with trade discounts of 40 percent and 10 percent. This means that the retailer pays the wholesaler $240 ($400 less 40 percent), and the wholesaler pays the manufacturer $216 ($240 less 10 percent). The wholesaler is given the 40 and 10 percent discounts. The wholesaler keeps the 10 percent to cover the costs of the wholesaling functions and passes on the 40 percent discount to the retailers. Note that the 40 and 10 percent discounts do not constitute a total discount of 50 percent off the list price. Each discount percentage in the ''chain'' is computed on the amount remaining after the preceding percentage has been deducted.

Cash Discounts A **cash** discount is a deduction granted to buyers for paying their bills within a specified period of time. The discount is computed on the net amount due after first deducting trade and quantity discounts from the base price. Let's say a buyer owes $360 after the other discounts have been granted and is offered terms of 2/10, n/30 on an invoice dated November 8. This buyer may deduct a discount of 2 percent ($7.20) if the bill is paid within 10 days after the date of the invoice (by November 18). Otherwise the entire bill of $360 must be paid in 30 days (by December 8).

Every cash discount includes three elements: (1) the percentage discount itself, (2) the time period during which the discount may be taken, and (3) the time when the bill becomes overdue. (See Fig. 12-1 below.) There are many different terms

FIGURE 12-1

The parts of a cash discount.

(Source: Don L. James, Bruce J. Walker, and Michael J. Etzel, *Retailing Today*, 2d ed., Harcourt Brace Jovanovich, Inc., New York, 1981, p. 199)

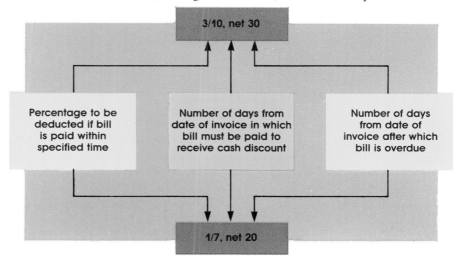

of sale because practically every industry has its own traditional combination of elements.

Normally, most buyers are extremely eager to pay bills in time to earn cash discounts. The discount in a 2/10, n/30 situation may not seem like very much. But management must realize that this 2 percent is earned just for paying 20 days in advance of the date the entire bill is due. If buyers fail to take the cash discount in a 2/10, n/30 situation, they are, in effect, borrowing money at a 36 percent annual rate of interest. (In a 360-day year, there are 18 periods of 20 days. Paying 2 percent for one of these 20-day periods is equivalent to paying 36 percent for an entire year.)

Other Discounts and Allowances

A firm that produces articles, such as air conditioners, that are purchased on a seasonal basis may consider the policy of granting a **seasonal** discount. This is a discount of, say, 5, 10, or 20 percent given to a customer who places an order during the slack season. Off-season orders enable manufacturers to make better use of their production facilities and/or avoid inventory carrying costs.

Forward dating is a variation of both seasonal and cash discounts. A manufacturer of fishing tackle, for example, might seek and fill orders from wholesalers and retailers during the winter months. But the bill would be dated, say, April 1, with terms of 2/10, n/30 offered as of that date. Orders that the seller fills in December and January help to maintain production during the slack season for more efficient operation. The forward-dated bills allow the wholesale or retail buyers to pay their bills after the season has started and some sales revenue has been generated.

Promotional allowances are price reductions granted by a seller in payment for promotional services performed by buyers. To illustrate, a manufacturer of builders' hardware gives a certain quantity of "free goods" to dealers who prominently display its line. Or a clothing manufacturer pays one-half the space charge of a retailer's advertisement that features the manufacturer's product.

The Competition Act and Price Discrimination

The discounts and allowances discussed in this section may result in different prices for different customers. Whenever price differentials exist, there is price discrimination. The terms are synonymous. In certain situations, price discrimination is prohibited by the Competition Act. This is one of the most important federal laws affecting a company's marketing program.

BACKGROUND OF THE ACT

Competition legislation in Canada was first introduced in 1888. Small businessmen who suffered from the monopolistic and collusive practices in restraint of trade by large manufacturers pressured Parliament into setting up a Combines Investigation Commission. Investigators attempting to verify the allegations of the small tradesmen unearthed a widespread range of restrictive practices and measures.

The results of the investigation led Parliament in 1889 to pass an Act for the Prevention and Suppression of Combinations Formed in Restraint of Trade. The intent of the Act was to declare illegal monopolies and combinations in restraint of trade. Although the Act was incorporated into the Criminal Code as section 520 in 1892, it proved ineffectual, because to break the law an individual would have to commit an illegal act within the meaning of the "common law." In 1900 the

Price Competition Takes Many Forms

The average Canadian consumer is exposed to a great deal of price competition every day — in retail stores, through the mail, and in television advertising. Much of the advertising that we see at the retail level is based on price promotions and allowances intended to encourage the consumer to buy or to give one brand or store an advantage over the competition. This is especially the case in product categories in which there is not much differentiation across brands. Rather than resort to price wars, gasoline retailers offer many types of promotions — free glasses, garbage bags, coffee mugs, pantyhose — to encourage customers to stop for gas. Discount carpet retailers use various forms of price competition in order to attract customers — no down payment, low monthly payments, no payments for six months — all factors that ultimately affect the total price paid for the carpet.

Price
differential
+
Injury to
competition
=
Competition Act
violation

unless
Price
differential
=
Quantity
Discount
Structure

Act was amended to remove this loophole and undue restriction of competition became, in itself, a criminal offence.

Additional legislation was passed in 1910 after a rash of mergers involving 58 business firms, to complement the Criminal Code and assist in the application of the Act. In 1919 the Combines and Fair Prices Act was passed, which prohibited undue stockpiling of the "necessities of life" and also prohibited the realization of exaggerated profits through "unreasonable" prices.

In 1923, Canadian combines legislation was finally consolidated and important sections remain in force to this day. Following the presentation of a report by the Economic Council of Canada in 1969,[1] the Government of Canada introduced into Parliament, in 1971 and 1975, a number of important amendments to the Combines Investigation Act to form the basis for a new competition policy for Canada. However, it was not until 1986, when the new Competition Act (the successor to the Combines Investigation Act) became law, that major Economic Council recommendations were implemented.

Below are some of the Competition Act implications for common pricing strategies and policies.[2]

PREDATORY PRICING AS AN OFFENCE

The provisions respecting predatory pricing are contained in paragraph 34(1)(*c*) of the Competition Act, which states:

> 34.(1) Every one engaged in a business who (c)
> engages in a policy of selling products at prices unreasonably low, having the effect or tendency of substantially lessening competition or eliminating a competitor, or designed to have such effect; is guilty of an indictable offence and is liable to imprisonment for two years.

In order for a conviction to result under paragraph 34(1)(*c*), it must be shown that prices are unreasonably low and that such prices have the effect of reducing competition. The amendments to the Combines Investigation Act that were passed in 1975 extended the predatory pricing provisions to the sale of both articles and services. The word "products" is now defined in the Competition Act to include articles *and* services.

PRICE DISCRIMINATION AS AN OFFENCE

At present, price discrimination is regulated under paragraph 34(1)(*a*) of the Competition Act, which states:

> 34.(1) Every one engaged in a business who
> (a) is a party or privy to, or assists in, any sale that discriminates to his knowledge, directly or indirectly, against competitors of a purchaser of articles from him in that any discount, rebate, allowance, price concession or other advantage is granted to the purchaser over and above any discount, rebate, allowance, price concession or other advantage that, at the time the articles are sold to such purchaser, is available to such competitors in respect of a sale of articles of like quality and quantity;
> is guilty of an indictable offence and is liable to imprisonment for two years.

This section goes on to state in paragraph 34(2):

> (2) It is not an offence under paragraph (1)(a) to be a party or privy to, or assist in any sale mentioned therein unless the discount, rebate, allowance, price concession or other advantage was granted as part of a practice of discriminating as described in that paragraph.

The following conditions must, therefore, be met in order for a conviction to be registered for price discrimination: (1) a discount, rebate, allowance, price concession, or other advantage must be granted to one customer and not to another; (2) the two customers concerned must be *competitors*; (3) the price discrimination must occur in respect of *articles* of similar quality and quantity; (4) the act of discrimination must be part of a *practice* of discrimination.

Not all price discrimination is, *per se*, an offence. It is lawful to discriminate in price on the basis of quantities of goods purchased. The cost justification defence which is used in the U.S. — that of a seller differentiating the price to a favoured competitor because of a difference in the costs of supplying that customer — is not viewed as an acceptable basis for discrimination. On the other hand, a seller does not have to demonstrate a cost difference in order to support a quantity discount structure. Rather, the basis for such price discrimination is accepted only on a quantity of goods-purchased basis. Establishing volume discount pricing structures that are available to competing buyers who purchase in comparable quantities is a major basis for discriminating under the provision.

It is also of note that the buyer is seen as being as liable as the seller in cases of discrimination. The legislation applies to those who are party to a sale and this includes both buyer and seller. This wording was intended to restrain large-scale buyers from demanding discriminatory prices. In addition, the buyer (as well as the seller) must know that the price involved is discriminatory.

GRANTING PROMOTIONAL ALLOWANCES AS AN OFFENCE

The Competition Act in section 35 requires that promotional allowances be granted proportionately to all competing customers. This section states:

35.(1) In this section "allowance" means any discount, rebate, price concession or other advantage that is or purports to be offered or granted for advertising or display purposes and is collateral to a sale or sales of products but is not applied directly to the selling price.

(2) Every one engaged in a business who is a party or privy to the granting of an allowance to any purchaser that is not offered on proportionate terms to other purchasers in competition with the first-mentioned purchaser, (which other purchasers are in this section called "competing purchasers"), is guilty of an indictable offence and is liable to imprisonment for two years.

(3) For the purposes of this section, an allowance is offered on proportionate terms only if

(a) the allowance offered to a purchaser is in approximately the same proportion to the value of sales to him as the allowance offered to each competing purchaser is to the total value of sales to such competing purchaser,

(b) in any case where advertising or other expenditures or services are exacted in return therefor, the cost thereof required to be incurred by a purchaser is in approximately the same proportion to the value of sales to him as the cost of such advertising or other expenditures or services required to be incurred by each competing purchaser is to the total value of sales to such competing purchaser, and

(c) in any case where services are exacted in return therefor, the requirements thereof have regard to the kinds of services that competing purchasers at the same time or different levels of distribution are ordinarily able to perform or cause to be performed.

The provisions of section 35 apply to the sale of both articles and services. Discrimination in the granting of promotional allowances is a *per se* offence, not requiring proof of the existence of either a practice of discrimination or a lessening of competition. A company which wishes to discriminate among its customers may do so through the legal practice of granting quantity discounts.

GEOGRAPHIC PRICING STRATEGIES

In its pricing, a seller must consider the freight costs involved in shipping the product to the buyer. This consideration grows in importance as freight becomes a larger part of total variable costs. Pricing policies may be established whereby the buyer pays all the freight, the seller bears the entire costs, or the two parties share the expense. The chosen strategy can have an important bearing on (1) the geographic limits of a firm's market, (2) the location of its production facilities, (3) the source of its raw materials, and (4) its competitive strength in various market areas.

F.O.B. Point-of-Production Pricing

In one widely used geographic pricing strategy, the seller quotes the selling price at the factory or at some other point of production. In this situation the buyer pays the entire cost of transportation. This is usually referred to as **f.o.b. mill** or **f.o.b. factory** pricing. Of the four strategies discussed in this section, this is the only one in which the seller does not pay *any* of the freight costs. The seller pays only the cost of loading the shipment aboard the carrier — hence the term **f.o.b.**, or **free on board**.

Under the f.o.b. factory pricing strategy, the seller nets the same amount on each sale of similar quantities. The delivered price to the buyer varies according to the

Who will pay the freight charges?

freight charge. However, this pricing strategy has serious economic and marketing implications. In effect, f.o.b. mill pricing tends to establish a geographic monopoly for a given seller, because freight rates prevent distant competitors from entering the market. The seller, in turn, is increasingly priced out of more distant markets.

Uniform Delivered Pricing

Under the **uniform delivered pricing** strategy, the same delivered price is quoted to all buyers regardless of their locations. This strategy is sometimes referred to as "postage stamp pricing" because of its similarity to the pricing of first-class mail service. The net revenue to the seller varies, depending upon the shipping cost involved in each sale.

A uniform delivered price is typically used where transportation costs are a small part of the seller's total costs. This strategy is also used by many retailers who feel that "free" delivery is an additional service that strengthens their market position.

Under a uniform delivered price system, buyers located near the seller's factory pay for some of the costs of shipping to more distant locations. Critics of f.o.b. factory pricing are usually in favour of a uniform delivered price. They feel that the freight expense should not be charged to individual customers any more than any other single marketing or production expense.

Zone Delivered Pricing

Under a **zone delivered pricing** strategy, a seller would divide the Canadian market into a limited number of broad geographic zones. Then a uniform delivered price is set within each zone. Zone delivered pricing is similar to the system used in pricing parcel post services and long-distance telephone service. A firm that quotes a price and then says "Slightly higher west of the Lakehead" is using a two-zone pricing system. The freight charge built into the delivered price is an average of the charges at all points within a zone area.

When adopting this pricing strategy, the seller must walk a neat tightrope to avoid charges of illegal price discrimination. This means that the zone lines must be drawn so that all buyers who compete for a particular market are in the same zone. Such a condition is most easily met where markets are widely distributed.

Freight Absorption Pricing

A **freight absorption pricing** strategy may be adopted to offset some of the competitive disadvantages of f.o.b. factory pricing. With an f.o.b. factory price, a firm is at a price disadvantage when it tries to sell to buyers located in markets nearer to competitors' plants. To penetrate more deeply into such markets, a seller may be willing to absorb some of the freight costs. Thus, seller A will quote to the customer a delivered price equal to (1) A's factory price plus (2) the freight costs that would be charged by the competitive seller located nearest to that customer.

A seller can continue to expand the geographic limits of its market as long as its net revenue after freight absorption is larger than its marginal cost for the units sold. Freight absorption is particularly useful to a firm with excess capacity whose fixed costs per unit of product are high and whose variable costs are low. In these cases, management must constantly seek ways to cover fixed costs, and freight absorption is one answer.

The legality of freight absorption is reasonably clear. The strategy is legal if it is used independently and not in collusion with other firms. Also, it must be used only to meet competition. In fact, if practised properly, freight absorption can have the effect of strengthening competition because it can break down geographic monopolies.

SKIMMING AND PENETRATION PRICING

When pricing a product or service, especially a new market entry, management should consider whether to adopt a skim-the-cream pricing strategy or a penetration pricing strategy.

Skim-the-Cream Pricing

The cream-skimming strategy involves setting a price that is high in the range of expected prices. This strategy is particularly suitable for new products because:

- In the early stages of a product's life cycle, price is less important, competition is minimal, and the product's distinctiveness lends itself to effective marketing.
- This strategy can effectively segment the market on an income basis. At first, the product is marketed to that segment that responds to distinctiveness in a product and is relatively insensitive to price. Later, the seller can lower the price and appeal to market segments that are more sensitive to price.
- The strategy acts as a strong hedge against a possible mistake in setting the price. If the original price is too high and the market does not respond, management can easily lower it. But it is very difficult to raise a price that has proven to be too low to cover costs.
- High initial prices can keep demand within the limits of a company's productive capacity.

File 12-2

 Marketing at Work

When Price Takes a Back Seat

Skim-the-cream pricing is most often used in the early stages of the life cycle of a product or service. If the new product or service is perceived by potential customers to be quite attractive, then many of them will want to buy it, almost regardless of price. This was the situation that many Canadian cable television companies encountered when they first introduced their cable TV services. In many cities that were located at some distance from the American border, households could receive only two or three Canadian channels. For them, the availability of several more channels on cable, and improved reception, meant a dramatically improved ''product.'' A cable television company operating in Atlantic Canada conducted a marketing research survey in its licence area prior to the introduction of its first cable service in the late 1970s and found that most consumers were quite price insensitive. As many as 50 percent of households intended to subscribe to the cable TV service, almost regardless of the price to be charged. It was only after 50 percent or more of households had signed on for cable service in the first year or two that many cable companies had to turn to other forms of promotion to encourage others to subscribe.

Penetration Pricing

In penetration pricing, a low initial price is set to reach the mass market immediately. This strategy can also be employed at a later stage in the product's life cycle. Penetration pricing is likely to be more satisfactory than cream-skimming pricing when the following conditions exist:

- The product has a highly elastic demand.
- Substantial reductions in unit costs can be achieved through large-scale operations.
- The product is expected to face very strong competition soon after it is introduced to the market.

The nature of the potential competition will critically influence management's choice between the two pricing strategies. If competitors can enter a market quickly, and if the market potential for the product is very promising, management probably should adopt a policy of penetration pricing. Low initial pricing may do two things. First, it may discourage other firms from entering the field, because of the anticipated low profit margin. Second, low initial pricing may give the innovator such a strong hold on its share of the market that future competitors cannot cut into it. On the other hand, cream skimming may be more feasible when the market is not large enough to attract big competitors.

ONE-PRICE AND FLEXIBLE-PRICE STRATEGIES

Rather early in its pricing deliberations, management should decide whether to adopt a one-price strategy or a flexible-price strategy. Under a **one-price strategy**, a seller charges the *same* price to all similar customers who buy similar quantities of a product. Under a **flexible-price** (also called a **variable-price**) strategy, similar customers may each pay a *different* price when buying similar quantities of a product.

In Canada and the United States, a one-price strategy has been adopted more than variable pricing. Most retailers, for example, typically follow a one-price policy — except in cases where trade-ins are involved, and then flexible pricing abounds. A one-price policy builds customer confidence in a seller, whether at the manufacturing, wholesaling, or retailing level. Weak bargainers need not feel that they are at a competitive disadvantage.

When a flexible pricing policy is followed, often the price is set as a result of

Open-air markets often engage in flexible pricing.

buyer-seller bargaining. In automobile retailing — with or without a trade-in — price negotiating (bargaining) is quite common, even though window-sticker prices may suggest a one-price policy. Variable pricing may be used to meet a competitor's price. Airlines have used an aggressive flexible pricing strategy to enter new markets and to increase their market share on existing routes. Their new business comes from two sources — passengers now flying on other airlines and passengers who would not fly at higher prices. In the second group, especially, the demand for air travel is highly elastic. The trick is to keep the market segment of price-sensitive passengers separate from the business-traveller segment, whose demand is inelastic. Airlines keep these segments apart by placing restrictions on the lower-priced tickets — requiring advance purchases, over-the-weekend stays in destination cities, etc.

A considerable amount of flexible pricing does exist in Canada. On balance, however, a flexible-price strategy is generally less desirable than a one-price strategy. In sales to business firms, but not to consumers, flexible pricing may be in violation of the Competition Act. Flexible pricing also may generate considerable ill will when the word gets around that some buyers acquired the product at lower prices.

UNIT PRICING

Unit pricing is a retail price-information-reporting strategy that, to date, has been employed by some supermarket chains. The method is, however, adaptable to other types of stores and products. The strategy is a business response to consumer protests concerning the proliferation of package sizes (especially in grocery stores). The practice has made it virtually impossible to compare prices of similar products. Regarding canned beans, for example: Is a can labelled "$15^{1}/_{2}$ avoirdupois ounces" for 39 cents a better deal than two "1-pound 1-ounce (482 grams)" cans for 89 cents?

In unit pricing, for each separate product and package size there is a shelf label that states (1) the price of the package and (2) this price expressed in dollars and cents per millilitre, litre, kilogram or some other standard measure.

Studies covering the early years of unit pricing showed that consumers — especially low-income consumers — were not using unit-pricing data. More recent

---

UNSLTD PEANUTS

UNIT PRICE   RETAIL PRICE

$4.52   **$3.89**

PER KILOGRAM

Unit-pricing shelf labels reduce prices to a common basis.

The universal product code label from a beverage six-pack.

studies show an increase in the awareness and usage of unit-pricing information. Unfortunately, however, city residents (typically lower-income markets) still use this information significantly less than do suburban residents (typically higher-income consumers).[3]

Increasingly, supermarkets and other retail stores are using electronic scanners at the checkout stands to read the Universal Product Code on products. Many of these retailers are no longer price-marking each individual item in a store. In such situations, unit-pricing shelf signs clearly are important, if not absolutely essential, to provide consumers with price information.

PRICE LINING

Price lining is used extensively by retailers of all types of apparel. It consists of selecting a limited number of prices at which a store will sell its merchandise. A shoe store, for example, sells several styles of shoes at $29.88 a pair, another group at $39.88, and a third assortment at $49.88.

For the consumer, the main benefit of price lining is that it simplifies buying decisions. From the retailer's point of view, the strategy is advantageous because it helps store owners plan their purchases. A dress buyer, for example, can go into a market looking for dresses that can be retailed for $69.95 or $89.95.

Rising costs can put a real squeeze on price lines, because a company hesitates to change its price line every time costs go up. But if costs increase and prices remain stationary, then profit margins are compressed and the retailer may be forced to seek products with lower costs.

This store followed a price-lining strategy.

"Off-price" strategy is popular today in apparel retailing.

RESALE PRICE MAINTENANCE

Some manufacturers want control over the prices at which retailers resell the manufacturers' products. This is most often done in Canada by following a policy of providing manufacturers' suggested list prices, where the price is just a guide for retailers. It is a list price on which discounts may be computed. For others, the suggested price is "informally" enforced. Normally enforcement of a suggested price, termed resale price maintenance, has been illegal in Canada since 1951. In this country, attempts on the part of the manufacturers to control or to influence upward the prices at which their products are sold by retailers have been considered akin to price fixing.

Section 38 of the Competition Act prohibits a manufacturer or supplier from requiring or inducing a retailer to sell a product at a particular price or not below a particular price. On occasion, a supplier may attempt to control retail prices through the use of a "suggested retail price." Under section 38, the use of "suggested retail prices" is permitted *only* if the supplier makes it clear to the retailer that the product *may* be sold at a price below the suggested price and that the retailer will not in any way be discriminated against if the product is sold at a lower price. Also, where a manufacturer advertises a product, and in the advertisement mentions a certain price, the manufacturer must make it clear in the advertisement that the product *may* be sold at a lower price.

Prior to 1975 it was legal in Canada for a manufacturer to refuse to supply a product to a retailer if that retailer was selling that product as a loss leader or was using the product in "bait advertising" to attract people to his or her store. The 1975 amendments to the Combines Investigation Act eliminated this provision, and it is now illegal for a manufacturer to refuse to supply a product to a retailer because of the pricing policies of the retailer. In other words, a retailer is free to sell a product at whatever price he or she deems appropriate, and the manufacturer of that product is not permitted to exert any pressure on the retailer to sell at a particular price.

LEADER PRICING AND UNFAIR-PRACTICES ACTS

Many firms, primarily retailers, temporarily cut prices on a few items to attract customers. This price and promotional strategy is called **leader pricing**, and the items whose prices may be reduced below the retailer's cost are called **loss leaders**. These leader items should be well-known heavily advertised articles that are purchased frequently. The idea is that customers will come to the store to buy the advertised leader items and then stay to buy other regularly priced merchandise. The net result, the firm hopes, will be increased total sales volume and net profit.

Three provinces, British Columbia, Alberta, and Manitoba, have had legislation dealing with loss leader selling. The approach has been to prohibit a reseller from selling an item below invoice cost, including freight, plus a stated markup, which is usually 5 percent at retail.

The general intent of these laws is commendable. They eliminate much of the predatory type of price-cutting; however, they permit firms to use loss leaders as a price and promotional strategy. That is, a retailer can offer an article below full cost but still sell above cost plus 5 percent markup. Under such acts, low-cost, efficient businesses are not penalized, nor are high-cost operators protected. Dif-

Leader pricing in a grocery store.

ferentials in retailers' purchase prices can be reflected in their selling prices, and savings resulting from the absence of services can be passed on to the customers.

On the other hand, the laws have some glaring weaknesses. In the first place, the provinces do not establish provisions or agencies for enforcement. It is the responsibility and burden of the injured party to seek satisfaction from the offender in a civil suit. Another limitation is that it is difficult or even impossible to determine the cost of doing business for each individual product. The third weakness is that the laws seem to disregard the fundamental idea that the purpose of a business is to make a profit on the total operation, and not necessarily on each sale of each product.

PSYCHOLOGICAL PRICING — ODD PRICING

We have already briefly discussed some pricing strategies that might be called **psychological pricing**. For example, there is price lining, prestige pricing above competitive levels, and *raising* a too-low price in order to *increase* sales. At the retail level, another psychological pricing strategy is commonly used. Prices are set at odd amounts, such as 19 cents, 49 cents, and $19.95. Automobiles are priced at $14,995 rather than $15,000, and houses are listed at $179,950 instead of $180,000.

In general, retailers believe that pricing items at odd amounts will result in larger sales. Thus, a price of 49 cents or 98 cents will bring greater revenue than a price of 50 cents or $1. There is little concrete evidence to support retailers' belief in the value of odd prices. Various studies have reported inconclusive results. Odd pricing is often avoided in prestige stores or on higher-priced items. Thus expensive men's suits are priced at $450, not $449.95.

In the course of developing its marketing program, management has a choice of emphasizing price competition or nonprice competition. This choice can affect various other parts of the firm's marketing system.

Price Competition

In our economy today, there still is a considerable amount of price competition. A firm can effectively engage in price competition by regularly offering prices that are as low as possible. Along with this, the seller usually offers a minimum of services. In their early years, discount houses and chain stores competed in this way. A firm can also use price to compete by (1) changing its prices and (2) reacting to price changes made by a competitor.

Using price appeals.

PRICE CHANGES BY THE FIRM

Any one of several situations may prompt a firm to change its price. As costs increase, for instance, management may decide to raise the price, rather than to cut quality or aggressively promote the product and still maintain the price. If a company's share of the market is declining because of strong competition, its executives may react initially by *reducing* their price. In the long run, however, their best alternative may be to improve their own marketing program, rather than to rely on the price cut. *Temporary* price cuts may be used to correct an imbalance in inventory or to introduce a new product.

From the seller's standpoint, the big disadvantage in price cutting is that competitors will retaliate. This is especially true in oligopolistic market situations. The net result can be a price war, and the price may even settle permanently at a lower level. Note that "oligopoly" does not necessarily imply *large* firms. *Oligopoly* means "a few sellers." Thus a neighbourhood group of small merchants — dry cleaners or hair-styling services, for instance — can constitute an oligopoly. These service retailers will try to avoid price competition, because if one reduces prices, all must follow.

REACTION TO COMPETITOR'S PRICE CHANGES

Any firm can assume that its competitors will change prices. Consequently, every firm should be ready with some policy guidelines on how it will react. If a competitor *boosts* prices, a reasonable delay in reacting probably will not be perilous. Advance planning is particularly necessary in case of a competitive price *reduction*, since time is then of the essence.

Air Canada, Wardair, and Canadian Airlines International will face new pricing strategy challenges under deregulation in Canada. They have closely watched the U.S. airline price wars which have provided a good illustration of a wrong way and a right way to respond to a competitor's price cuts. In the earlier price wars when an airline cut its prices, competitors typically reacted by reducing fares generally across the board — fly anywhere, anytime, for $99. As a result of this unsound strategy, the U.S. airlines suffered heavy financial losses. In recent years, however, the U.S. majors (American, United, Delta) have adopted a better strategy — that of *selective* price cutting — when low-cost carriers reduce their fares. This newer strategy involves cutting airfares only on certain routes, placing restrictions on the discounted fares, and even raising prices on routes that the low-cost carriers do not fly. Canadian carriers will be able to avoid the errors of unwise price strategies thanks to the U.S. demonstration.

Nonprice Competition

In nonprice competition, sellers maintain stable prices. They attempt to improve their market position by emphasizing other aspects of their marketing programs. Of course, competitive prices still must be taken into consideration, and price changes will occur over time. Nevertheless, in a nonprice competitive situation the emphasis is on something *other than* price.

By using terms familiar in economic theory, we can differentiate nonprice competition from price competition. In price competition, sellers attempt to move up or down their individual demand curves by changing prices. In nonprice competition, sellers attempt to *shift* their demand curves to the right by means of product differentiation, promotional activities, or some other device. This point is illustrated in Fig. 12-2. The demand curve faced by the producer of a given model of skis is DD. At a price of $250, the producer can sell 35,000 pairs a year in a ski market. On the basis of price competition alone, sales can be increased to 55,000 if the producer is willing to reduce the price to $230. The demand curve is still DD.

However, the producer is interested in boosting sales without any decrease in selling price. Consequently, the firm embarks upon a promotional program — a form of nonprice competition. Suppose enough new customers are persuaded to buy at the original $250 price so that unit sales increase to 55,000 pairs a year. In effect, the firm's entire demand curve has been shifted to position D'D'.

Two of the major methods of nonprice competition are **promotion** and **product differentiation**. In addition, some firms emphasize the **variety** and **quality** of their services.

Nonprice competition is being used increasingly in marketing. Companies want, at least to some extent, to be the masters of their own destiny. In nonprice com-

FIGURE 12-2

Shift in demand curve for skis in a market.

The use of nonprice competition can shift the demand curve for a product. A company selling skis used a promotional program to sell more skis at the same price, thus shifting DD to D'D'. Volume increased from 35,000 to 55,000 units at $250 (point X to point Y). Besides advertising, what other devices might this firm use to shift its demand curve?

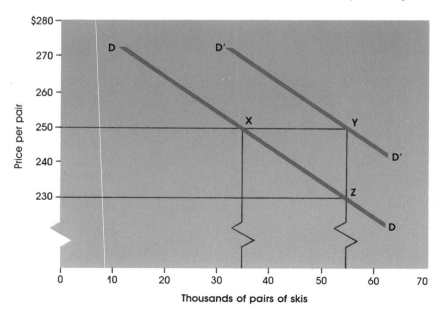

Paying a Price to Send a Message

There is a very important relationship between price and brand name. This is especially obvious in the case of fashion merchandising and personal care items. In some cases, consumers are prepared to pay quite high prices for certain clothing items and then *advertise* the manufacturer's brand name free. The phenomenon of visible brands is an important one in fashion merchandising in recent years and points to the fact that consumers are not particularly interested in the product's functional attributes when they buy some items of clothing. Whereas a student could buy a sweatshirt with a relatively obscure brand name at a local discount clothing store, he or she may be willing to pay two or three times as much for a sweatshirt that has the brand name of Roots, Benetton, or Cotton Ginny. In this case, price seems less important than other motivating factors in influencing the purchase decision. This is a situation where nonprice competition is at work to differentiate one brand from another.

petition, a seller's entire advantage is not removed when a competitor decides to undersell. Furthermore, there is little customer loyalty when price is the only feature that distinguishes the seller. Buyers will stick only as long as that seller offers the lowest price.

Using nonprice appeals.

PRICING OF SERVICES

In the marketing of services, nowhere is there a greater need for managerial creativity and skill than in the area of pricing. Earlier, we noted that services are extremely perishable; they usually cannot be stored, and the demand often fluctuates considerably. All these features carry significant pricing implications. To further complicate the situation, customers may perform some services themselves or get help from friends (auto and household repair, for example).

These considerations suggest that the elasticity of demand for a service should influence the price set by the seller. Interestingly enough, sellers often do recognize inelastic demand. Then they charge higher prices. But they fail to act in opposite fashion when faced with an elastic demand — even though a lower price would increase unit sales, total revenue, utilization of facilities, and probably net profit.

Certainly, perfect competition does not apply to any extent, if at all, in the pricing of services. Because of the heterogeneity and the difficulty of standardizing quality, most services are highly differentiated. Also, it is virtually impossible to have complete market information. Further, in any given market, such as a neighbourhood, often there are geographic limits within which a buyer will seek a service. Consequently, there are not a large number of sellers. The heavy capital investment required to produce some services (transportation, communications, banking) often limits considerably the freedom of entry.

Nevertheless, in recent years price competition in many service areas has increased considerably, partly in response to a deregulatory environment created by government. We can look at three identifiable phases. For example, most professional organizations such as firms of lawyers and accountants still do not stress their prices, even though they may now advertise their services more widely. In the second phase, the seller uses a market segmentation strategy to target a certain market at a specific price. Telephone companies, for example, charge higher rates for long-distance calls during business hours, but offer attractive discounts after 6 P.M. and on weekends to appeal to individuals who make personal long-distance calls. The third phase involves out-and-out price competition as firms stress comparative prices in their advertising. Canadian banks and trust companies have moved into this third phase in recent years and now feature interest rates and rates of return on RRSPs in their advertising.

The *basic* methods of price determination now used for services are generally the same as those for products. Cost-plus pricing is used for regulated service industries. It is also used for repair services where the main ingredient is direct labour and the customer is charged on an hourly basis. For other services (rentals, entertainment, legal counselling, management consulting), prices are determined primarily by market demand and competition.

Many of the pricing strategies discussed in Chapter 11 are applicable to service marketing. Quantity discounts, for example, are used by car-rental agencies. The daily rates are lower if you agree to rent the car for a week or a month at a time. Cash discounts are offered when insurance premiums are paid annually instead of quarterly. Accountants and management consultants can use a variable-price policy. Geographic pricing policies may be involved, although the variable here is time, not freight charges. Mechanics will charge more if they must go out of town, and a hotel will charge higher room rates in a downtown big city location.

Service firms also engage in discount pricing.

PRICING IN NONBUSINESS AND NONPROFIT SETTINGS

Pricing in many nonbusiness organizations is quite different from pricing in a business firm. First, pricing becomes less important when profit making is not an organizational goal. Also, many nonbusiness groups believe there are *no* client-market pricing considerations in their marketing because there is no charge to the client. The organization's basic function is to help those who cannot afford to pay.

Actually, the products or services received by the clients rarely are free — that is, without a price of some kind. True, the price may not be a monetary charge. Often, however, the client pays a charge — in the form of travel and waiting time, and perhaps degrading treatment — that a money-paying client-customer would not incur for the same service. Poor children who have to wear donated, second-hand clothes certainly are paying a price if their classmates ridicule these clothes. Alcoholics Anonymous and some drug rehabilitation organizations which provide ''free'' services do exact a price. They require active participation by their clients, and often a very strongly expressed resolve by clients to help themselves.

Some nonbusiness groups *do* face the same general pricing problems we discussed in Chapter 11. Museums and opera companies must decide on admission prices; fraternal organizations must set a schedule for dues; and colleges must determine how much to charge for tuition. These and other not-for-profit organizations typically face a cash-management problem, the same as in profit-seeking firms. Not-for-profit firms still must generate enough revenue from some source to cover all their costs. For example, an organization may budget a preplanned loss from its own operating revenues. This organization still must price its offerings in such a way that the operating revenues come in at the targeted loss figure. Let's take the case of a private school as an illustration. This school's total operating costs are budgeted at $10 million for next year. The school is expecting to generate $7 million in tuition revenue, leaving a loss of $3 million to be covered by gifts and other grants. Now the school must set its price (tuition) in such a way as to generate enough revenue to meet its $7 million target. Basically this is the same situation that a profit-seeking firm faces when pricing to meet a predetermined profit target. Essentially, not-for-profit organizations must (1) determine the base price for their product offering and (2) establish pricing strategies in several areas of their pricing structure.

SETTING THE BASE PRICE

Here again we are faced with two market situations — pricing in the contributor market and pricing in the client market.

When dealing with the contributor market, nonbusiness organizations really do not set the price of the donation. That price is set by contributors when they decide how much they are willing to pay for the benefits they expect to receive in return for their gifts. However, the organization may suggest a price. A charitable organization, for example, may suggest that you donate one day's pay or that you donate your time for one day a month.

For nonbusiness organizations price is often left to the consumer.

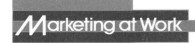

All Benefits Have Costs

The concept of price is one which many not-for-profit and nonbusiness organizations often have difficulty using in their marketing programs. Many tend to think of price only in *monetary* terms and conclude that they do not set prices. The Salvation Army does not set a price on a donation. The Boy Scouts do not tell you how much to pay for an apple (although they may suggest a minimum price). Most churches do not exact a set weekly contribution from their parishioners. Some charitable organizations may not deal in very much money at all. Others do have to make more traditional pricing decisions when they set ticket prices, membership dues, and similar charges.

It may be more useful for a not-for-profit organization to think in terms of *costs* rather than prices. Since much of the activity of such organizations involves attracting volunteers, convincing people to support a particular cause, or to donate their time and interest, it is often appropriate to ask, "What are we costing people to deal with us?" How much are we asking them to commit, not in monetary terms, but in terms of time, effort, and psychic commitment?

Being a Big Brother or Big Sister or a Red Cross blood donor may not cost us anything in dollar terms, but it certainly takes time and a major psychological commitment. Think about how such organizations can use this definition of price in their marketing programs.

Some of our earlier discussion regarding the pricing of services is appropriate to the client market — for example, in pricing admissions to museums, concerts, or college athletic contests. But for the most nonbusiness organizations, the basic pricing methods used by business firms — cost-plus, balance of supply and demand, market alone — simply are not appropriate. Many organizations know they cannot cover their costs with prices charged to client markets. The difference between anticipated revenues and costs must be made up by contributions.

As yet, we simply have not developed any real guidelines — any methodology — for much of our nonbusiness pricing. A major problem here is that most nonbusiness organizations simply do not know the cost of the products and services they offer in their client markets.

PRICING STRATEGIES

Some of the pricing strategies discussed earlier are also applicable in nonbusiness marketing. Discount strategies have widespread use, for example. Some museums offer discount prices to students and to senior citizens. A season ticket for some opera companies or symphony orchestras costs less per performance than tickets purchased on an individual-performance basis. This is a form of quantity discount.

Considerations regarding one price versus variable price also are strategies applicable in nonbusiness marketing. Many nursing homes charge according to the resident's ability to pay — a variable-price strategy. A one-price strategy typically is followed by most universities. That is, all students pay the same tuition for a full load of coursework.

SUMMARY

After deciding on pricing goals and then setting the base (list) price, the next task in pricing is to establish specific strategies in several areas of the pricing structure. One of these areas relates to discounts and allowances — deductions from the list price. Management has the option of offering quantity discounts, trade discounts, cash discounts, and other types of deductions. The factor of freight costs must also be considered in pricing strategy. A producer can pay all the freight (uniform delivered price) or let the buyer pay the freight bill (f.o.b. factory price). Or the two parties can share the cost in some proportion (freight absorption). Any decisions involving discounts or freight allowances must be made in conformity with the Competition Act. This is a major law relating to price discrimination and other aspects of a company's marketing program.

When pricing a product, especially a new product, a company should consider whether to use a cream-skimming or a penetration pricing strategy. Management also should decide whether to charge the same price to all similar buyers (one-price strategy) or to adopt a flexible (variable) pricing strategy. Unit pricing — a relatively new development — can affect a company's marketing program. Some firms, especially retailers, have adopted price lining as a marketing strategy. Many retailers use leader pricing to stimulate sales. Odd pricing is a psychological pricing strategy commonly used by retailers.

Another basic decision facing management is whether to engage primarily in price competition or in nonprice competition. Most firms prefer to use promotion, product differentiation, and other nonprice marketing activities, rather than to rely only on price as a sales stimulant.

NOTES

[1] Economic Council of Canada, *Interim Report on Competition Policy*, Queen's Printer, Ottawa, July 1969.

[2] The materials presented in this section are based on *Competition Law Amendments*, Ministry of Supply and Services 1986 and *A Guide to Competition Law Amendments*, Ministry of Supply and Services 1985. Both are sponsored by the Department of Consumer and Corporate Affairs.

[3] See David A. Aaker and Gary T. Ford, ''Unit Pricing Ten Years Later: A Replication,'' *Journal of Marketing*, Winter 1983, pp. 118–122.

KEY TERMS AND CONCEPTS

Quantity discount: 324	Penetration pricing 332
Noncumulative discount 324	One-price strategy 332
Cumulative discount 324	Flexible-price strategy 332
Trade (functional) discount 325	Unit pricing 333
Cash discount 325	Price lining 334
Competition Act 326	Resale Price Maintenance 335

F.o.b. factory price 329
Uniform delivered price 330
Zone delivered price 330
Freight absorption 330
Skim-the-cream pricing 331

Loss leader 335
Leader pricing 335
Odd pricing 336
Price competition 337
Nonprice competition 338

QUESTIONS AND
PROBLEMS

1. Carefully distinguish between cumulative and noncumulative quantity discounts. Which of these two types of quantity discounts has the greater economic and social justification? Why?

2. A manufacturer of appliances quotes a list price of $800 per unit for a certain model of refrigerator and grants trade discounts of 35, 20, and 5 percent. What is the manufacturer's selling price? Who might get these various discounts?

3. Company A sells to all its customers at the same published price. A sales executive finds that company B is offering to sell to one of A's customers at a lower price. Company A then cuts its price to this customer but maintains the original price for all other customers. Is this a violation of the Competition Act?

4. Name some products that might logically be sold under a uniform delivered price system.

5. "An f.o.b. point-of-purchase price system is the only geographic price system that is fair to buyers." Discuss.

6. An Ontario firm wants to compete in Western Canada, where it is at a significant disadvantage with respect to freight costs. What pricing alternatives can it adopt to overcome the freight differential?

7. For each of the following products, do you recommend that the seller adopt a cream-skimming or a penetration pricing strategy? Support your decision in each instance.
   a. Original models of women's dresses styled and manufactured by Alfred Sung.
   b. A new wonder drug.
   c. An exterior house paint that wears twice as long as any competitive brand.
   d. A cigarette *totally* free of tar and nicotine.
   e. A tablet that converts a litre of water into a litre of automotive fuel.

8. Under what marketing conditions is a company likely to use a variable-price strategy? Can you name some firms that employ this strategy, other than when a trade-in is involved?

9. Distinguish between leader pricing and predatory price cutting.

10. How should a manufacturer of prefinished plywood interior wall panelling react if a competitor cuts prices?

11. What factors account for the increased use of nonprice competition?

12. On the basis of the topics covered in this chapter, establish a set of price

strategies for the manufacturer of a new glass cleaner that is sold through a broker to supermarkets. The manufacturer sells the product at $10 for a case of a dozen 459 mL bottles.

13. Suppose you are president of a company that has just developed a camera and film process somewhat comparable to Polaroid's. The camera is designed to be used only with film produced by your firm. The chief marketing executive recommended that the camera be priced relatively low and the film relatively high. The idea was to make it easy to buy the camera, because from then on the customer would have to buy the company's film. The company's chief accountant said ''no'' to that idea. He wanted to price both camera and film in relation to their full cost plus a reasonable profit. You are mulling over these alternative strategies and also wondering whether there is not a third alternative, better than either of those two. Which pricing strategy would you adopt for the new camera and film?

14. Why is the pricing of services different and generally more difficult than the pricing of tangible products?

15. Identify the various prices and costs that a neighbourhood child-care clinic should consider in developing its marketing program.

CASE 4.1

**UPPER CANADA BREWING
COMPANY (C)
Developing a Pricing
Strategy**

Frank Heaps, president of the Upper Canada Brewing Company, was preparing the pricing section of his marketing plan for the products of his brewery. He realized that the pricing decisions were especially important because they affected both the level of sales the brewery would achieve and how much profit would be earned. He also realized that price often had a psychological impact on consumers and thus could be used symbolically as an indicator of quality to position the products in the consumer's mind. The decision on price was further complicated by its strong interrelationship with the three other elements of the marketing mix: product and packaging, advertising and promotion, and distribution channels. With these important considerations in mind, Mr. Heaps faced the task of setting the retail selling price for his product(s).

THE PRICING OBJECTIVE

Although the Upper Canada Brewing Company was a relatively small and new organization, Mr. Heaps had taken time to carefully prepare a pricing objective. To ensure that the pricing objectives flowed from — and fit in with — the corporate and marketing objectives, Mr. Heaps chose a sales-oriented pricing goal. The specific objective was to capture a 0.1 percent share of the Ontario beer market, growing to 0.3 percent within five years. To achieve this objective, he anticipated that the company would generate a loss for the first one or two years but would obtain an adequate profit and return on investment in the long run.

THE RETAIL SELLING PRICE

Given the unique characteristics of the beer market, Mr. Heaps realized that he did not have complete freedom to set the selling price for his products at any level he desired. This "floor" price was used to establish the retail selling price for Ontario domestic brands (see Table C-1). Mr. Heaps also realized that in the beer industry most buyers and sellers were very familiar with beer prices. Thus, consumers had a good idea of the price that they expected to pay for European-style, top-quality beer products. It was his perception that the target market chosen by the Upper Canada Brewing Company was not price sensitive, but he wondered if they would

TABLE C-1   **ONTARIO DOMESTIC BEER PRICES**

	Keg	**24-Pack**	**12-Pack**	**6-Pack**
1983	$82.00	$15.55	$8.40	$4.50
1984	——	16.50	8.95	4.75

Source: Liquor Control Board of Ontario (L.C.B.O.)

This case was prepared by Donna M. Stapleton and is intended to stimulate discussion of an actual management problem and not to illustrate either effective or ineffective handling of that problem. The author wishes to acknowledge the support provided by the Upper Canada Brewing Company, and particularly by Frank Heaps, President.

TABLE C-2   **ONTARIO IMPORT BEER PRICES**

			1983	**1984**
Bass Pale Ale	(British)	6-pack	$7.15	$7.25
Beck's	(German)	6-pack	5.45	5.90
Carta Blanca	(Mexican)	6-pack	6.15	6.40
Dortmunder Union	(German)	3-pack	3.20	3.20
Genesee Lager	(American)	6-pack	4.55	4.85
Goesser Export	(Austrian)	6-pack	5.55	5.60
Harp Lager	(Irish)	4-pack*	3.95	——
Heineken Lager	(Dutch)	6-pack*	6.20	6.50
Heineken Lager	(Dutch)	6-pack	6.25	6.50
Holston DiaMalt	(German)	6-pack	5.85	——
Kirin	(Japanese)	6-pack	5.65	6.10
Krakaus	(Polish)	6-pack	4.85	5.45
Kronenbourg	(French)	6-pack	6.60	6.65
Lowenbrau Dark Special	(German)	6-pack	6.25	6.30
Lowenbrau Light Special	(German)	6-pack	6.25	6.30
MacEwan's Export Scotch Ale	(British)	6-pack	7.75	——
Michelob	(American)	6-pack	5.75	5.95
Newcastle Brown Ale	(British)	4-pack*	5.75	5.85
Pilsner Urquell	(Czechoslovakian)	4-pack	4.35	4.35
Schlitz	(American)	6-pack	5.45	5.45
Swan Lager	(Australian)	4-pack*	5.40	5.80
Tsing Tao	(Chinese)	6-pack	——	7.25
Tennent's Lager	(British)	4-pack*	4.75	——
Tuborg	(Danish)	6-pack	5.95	6.40
Whitbread Pale Ale	(British)	6-pack	7.00	——

Source: Liquor Control Board of Ontario (L.C.B.O.)
*cans

be willing to pay a price higher than that established for quality imports. The prices for import beers sold in Ontario in 1983 and 1984 are given in Table C-2.

To set the retail selling price for his products, key information on the costs, both fixed and variable, were needed. He had a clear idea of the cost of the project to date. The total budget for the acquisition and installation of the brewery equipment was $1.1 million, and the building acquisition cost was roughly another $1 million.

To forecast an operating statement for the first two years of operation, Mr. Heaps assumed that he could sell the 175,000 gallons of beer needed to achieve his 0.1 percent market share. He also projected that the sales would be 15 percent of annual production in kegs and 85 percent in bottles. To complete the forecast, he chose a selling price of his product in kegs to be $95 per keg based on a 10 percent premium above the 1983 domestic premium brand price of $82 per keg. The selling price for a case of 12 bottles for the year 1985 was projected to be $13. This was based upon the average price of 1983 imported brands. The forecasted operating statement is given in Table C-3 with the notes and assumptions to support the financial projections.

TABLE C-3   FORECAST OPERATING STATEMENT

	1985	1986
Gallons Sold	175,000	250,000
Gross Sales	$2,348,111	$3,522,167
Less P.S.T.	251,583	377,375
Net Sales	$2,096,528	$3,144,792
COST OF SALES		
Opening Inventory	$ 0	$ 70,000
Materials and Manufacturing	630,000	858,000
Federal Excise Taxes	138,801	198,288
Federal Sales Tax	183,153	274,729
Provincial Ad valorem Tax	366,719	550,079
Less: Closing Inventory	70,000	88,000
	$1,248,673	$1,863,096
Gross Margin	847,854	1,281,696
OPERATING COSTS		
Distribution	$ 176,199	$ 264,298
Marketing and Promotion	175,000	175,000
Management and Administration	200,000	225,000
Bank Interest	198,333	171,394
Maintenance	5,000	10,000
Depreciation	145,000	130,000
	899,532	975,692
OPERATING INCOME (LOSS)	$ (51,678)	$ 306,004

*See accompanying notes to support financial projections for details.

THE DECISION

Selecting the final retail selling price was simplified by the fact that Mr. Heaps did not have to consider what type of discount schedule or geographic pricing policy to use. Price deals to middlemen were prohibited in the Ontario beer market, and all products were distributed with a uniform delivered price to all buyers regardless of their location. Even with this added simplification, establishing the retail selling price was not an easy decision. Mr. Heaps debated whether he should set his price equal to the forecasted selling price of $95 per keg and $13 per 12-pack. He realized that if he set a higher price it would mean larger margins and fewer sales required to break even, but it could prevent him from achieving his pricing goal of 0.1 percent market share. If he set a lower price, it would increase his chances of achieving the desired market share but could lead to profitless success. The dilemma he faced was to determine the price which would optimize his profit (minimize his projected loss), yet ensure that the company market share objective was achieved.

NOTES TO SUPPORT FINANCIAL PROJECTIONS

1. Cost of sales for material and manufacturing was estimated at about $3.20 per gallon (which included materials, supplies, labour, utilities, realty and business taxes, and insurance). A 5 percent per annum increase is projected.

2. Provincial retail sales tax was 12 percent.

3. Federal excise duty was $17.31 per hectolitre of beer produced.

4. Federal sales tax was 12 percent of the supplier price.

5. Provincial Ad valorem tax was 21.1/121.2 of the content selling price (i.e., excluding provincial taxes).

6. Brewers' warehousing distribution costs were based on an average service charge of $21 per hectolitre (75 percent Brewers' Retail and 25 percent licensee) with a 5 percent increase per year.

7. Marketing and promotion costs had been estimated at roughly 7.5 percent of gross sales for the first year and 5 percent in the second year.

8. Management and administration costs included projected salaries for the general manager, office manager, brewmaster and office staff, management fees, professional services, overhead, and sundry office expenses.

9. Interest was a rough estimate based at 14 percent on the total of the net long-term loan and the revolving line of credit.

10. Maintenance cost estimates were in addition to plant maintenance personnel wages, which were included in material and manufacturing costs.

11. Depreciation was estimated at 10 percent on a declining balance basis for equipment and 5 percent for building and improvements.

12. 1 hectolitre = 21.9 gallons
    1 hectolitre = 100 litres
    1 litre = 1000 millilitres
    1 keg = 25 gallons

QUESTIONS

1. Evaluate the pricing objective set by Mr. Heaps.

2. What retail selling price would you recommend? What impact will increasing or decreasing the retail selling price have on the company's bottom line and pricing objective?

CASE 4.2

HILLCREST PRODUCTS

The executives of Hillcrest Products were trying to decide what pricing strategy and what retail price they should set for their new product. The new product, a liquid glass cleaner called Shine-Thru, was ready for marketing on a full-scale basis. The product was in liquid form and golden in colour. It was competitive with such brands as Windex, Bon-Ami, and Easy-Off. Market research indicated that Windex held about 70 percent of the market with no other brand reaching over 10 percent of the market.

Management in the Hillcrest company felt that its product was superior to anything else on the market. Market tests had shown that once consumers tried this product, they strongly favoured it over anything they had used previously. The product's main advantage was that it did not leave a film. Also, the Hillcrest product was nontoxic, a distinct advantage in households where there were small children.

The product came in a 500 mL clear plastic bottle with a plunger-type spray dispenser top. The fact that the plastic was unbreakable was another favourable

This case was adapted by Lanita Carter. Used with permission.

differentiating product feature. The product was packed 12 to a case. Hillcrest marketed through supermarket chains in the Atlantic provinces. The company used a separate food broker to reach the chains in each brokerage area.

In setting its own selling price, the company had to have some intended retail price in mind in order to allow for the necessary broker's fee and retailer's margin. The company planned to allow retailers a margin of 25 percent of their selling price and the brokers a fee of 10 percent of Hillcrest's selling price.

The unit variable cost for Shine-Thru packed in case lots was 93 cents. This included the plastic package, the liquid cleaner itself, the shipping carton, freight, and direct labour for filling the packages and preparing the cartons for shipment. It was difficult to estimate overhead very accurately at this stage. Administrative and office salaries would be about $25,000. Other overhead costs, including travel expense but excluding advertising, were figured at $15,000. Of course, the largest single indirect expense was advertising. The company expected to plough all available funds into advertising and display. If necessary, the company would operate at a loss for a few years rather than skimp on advertising. The advertising budget for the first year was set at $30,000.

The usual retail selling prices of competitive products in supermarkets were as follows:

Windex	600 mL bottle	$1.99
Windex	425 g aerosol can	$1.69
Windex	225 mL bottle	$ .99
Easy-Off	425 g aerosol can	$1.59
Bon-Ami	425 g aerosol can	$1.79

QUESTIONS

1. What pricing strategy would you recommend for Shine-Thru? Why?
2. What retail price do you recommend for Shine-Thru? Why?
3. What should Hillcrest's selling price for Shine-Thru be?
4. What is the break-even point in units and in revenue given the selling price you recommended?

CASE 4.3

John Winkleman, president of Winkleman Manufacturing Company, was concerned about the forecast that some of his company's most successful products would experience a declining market share starting next year. He recently had a staff meeting with his managers to discuss the problem.

Winkleman Manufacturing Company was an electronics manufacturer in the Vancouver area. The company produced a wide variety of products. Those that concerned Mr. Winkleman at the moment were three models of the Series A hand-held digital multimeters (DMMs). These multimeters were used to make various types of precision measurements of electronic products and product performance where extreme accuracy of measurement was required.

The three multimeters of concern were model numbers 1010, 1020, and 1030. These three models formed a complementary family line. The 1010 was a low-cost unit containing all standard measurement functions and having a basic measurement accuracy of .5 percent. The 1020 offered identical measurement functions but had an improved basic measurement accuracy of .1 percent. The top of the line was the 1030. In addition to a basic accuracy of .1 percent, the 1030 offered several additional features, one being an audible continuity indicator.

An an innovator in the field of DMMs, Winkleman's business flourished over the past few years. Unit sales for 1988 and projections for 1989 are shown in Table 1. But now, with the company's three most successful products in the maturity stage of their life cycle and the industry facing increasing foreign competition, Mr. Winkleman was worried. That is why he had that staff meeting a few weeks ago.

TABLE 1   UNIT SALES FOR DMMs — SERIES A

Model	1988 actual	1989 forecast	% change
1010	37,455	35,500	− 5.5
1020	67,534	61,800	− 8.4
1030	25,602	35,500	+ 39.0
Totals	130,591	132,800	+ 1.7%

At that meeting he spoke as follows: "Intense competitive pressure is beginning to erode our market share in handhelds. I have documented 11 large orders that have been lost to Backman and Wiston within the past three months. On an annual basis, this amounts to nearly 10,000 units and $1.5 million in lost opportunities. Within the last 18 months at least 16 serious competitors have entered the market. Two-thirds of the competitive models already have continuity indicators.

"Our sales for this year (1989) are forecasted to increase only 1.7 percent. According to industry projections, the handheld DMM market will grow 21 percent over the next five years, and I think even that forecast is conservative. Also our next generation of general-purpose, low-cost handheld DMMs is two years away from introduction. In the meantime, it is essential that we do something to retain

This case was adapted by James G. Barnes from a case originally developed by Jim Dooley. Used with permission.

our profitable position in our traditional channels and markets. At our next meeting I want some ideas from you guys.''

At the next meeting, one of the newer management team members, Dave Haug, made the following proposal for tackling the lost-market problem: ''What we need is a facelift of our existing product line to hold us over for the next two years. Changes in colour, a new deal, some minor case modifications, and most important, an audible continuity indicator in the 1010 and 1020 should give us two more years of product life. We can call this Series B to retain continuity in switching from the old to the new. By including the Series B features, our decline in 1010/1020 sales could be reversed over the next two years. My discussions with our large-order customers indicate that we could have retained 40–60 percent of our lost orders if our entire handheld line had featured audible continuity.

TABLE 2   PROJECTED DMM SALES, 1989, FOR SERIES A AND B

Model	Unit Price ($)	Series A units	Series B units	Increase Units	%	Series B Sales ($000)	Increase ($000)
1010	139	35,500	40,000	4,500	12.6	5,560	626
1020	179	61,800	66,000	4,200	6.8	11,814	752
1030	219	35,500	36,000	500	1.4	7,884	110
Totals	—	132,800	142,000	9,200	6.9%	$25,258	$1,488

''My estimate of sales of Series B (as shown in Table 2) has been generated from discussions with our field sales people, distributors, and customers. Sales of Series B (in units) will be 6.9 percent above the current Series A level. This translates into a marginal revenue increase of $1,488,000, assuming the same list prices as for the Series A models.

''Because of current economic conditions in our industry, our market has become very price sensitive. Now I am aware that our normal pricing policy calls for multiplying our factory cost by three to arrive at our selling price. I also am aware that the added factory cost of an audible continuity indicator is $5. But at this time we should *not* add on this cost to our selling price. My analysis indicates that an increase of $5 in selling price would reduce our incremental sales by 20 percent. An increase of $10 in selling price would cut our sales increase by 80 percent.

''Also, remember that we must pay for some nonrecurring engineering costs, which I estimate will be $96,750. This figure will cover such items as updating our operating instruction manual, new dies, decals, engineering labour, and construction of prototype models. These costs must come out of our contribution margin. As you know, we calculate that margin by taking the total dollar sales less our 28 percent discount to distributors less the factory cost for those units. I believe that increasing our prices will reduce our margins significantly, thus hindering our ability to cover the nonrecurring engineering costs, let alone make a profit. Therefore, I propose we go ahead with Series B and hold the line on prices.''

Dennis Cambelot, a longtime Winkleman employee, spoke up with the following comment on Dave's proposal:

"Dave, I think this Series B idea shows a lot of potential, but price-wise you are way out of line. We have always added the standard markup to our products. We make quality products and people are willing to pay for quality. The only thing your fancy MBA degree taught you was to be impractical. If you had gotten your experience in the trenches like I did, your pricing theories would not be so conservative, and this company could make more money."

At the close of the meeting, Mr. Winkleman asked that each manager consider the Series B proposal. He especially was interested in getting the managers' reactions to the pricing considerations in Haug's proposal.

QUESTION

1. What are your recommendations for pricing the Series B models?

PART 5

DISTRIBUTION

Retailing and wholesaling institutions,
the channels of distribution from
producer to user

We are in the process of developing a marketing program to reach the firm's
target markets and to achieve the goals established in strategic marketing
planning. So far, we have considered the product and the pricing structure
in that marketing program. Now we turn our attention to the distribution
system — the means for getting the product or service to the market.

Our discussion of the distribution ingredient in the marketing mix will
encompass two broad topics: (1) the retailing and wholesaling institutional
structure used in distribution (Chapters 13 and 14) and (2) strategies for
selecting and operating channels of distribution (Chapter 15).

CHAPTER 13

RETAILING: MARKETS AND INSTITUTIONS

The distribution of consumer products begins with the producer and ends with the ultimate consumer. Between the two there usually is at least one middleman — a retailer — who is the subject of this chapter. After studying this chapter, you should understand:

- What a channel of distribution is.
- The functions and importance of middlemen.
- The nature of the retail market.
- The differences between large-scale and small-scale retailing.
- The classification of retailers by:
  a. Product lines carried.
  b. Form of ownership.
- The methods of selling in retailing:
  a. Full-service, in-store.
  b. Supermarket.
  c. Discount.
  d. Nonstore.
- Current trends in retailing.

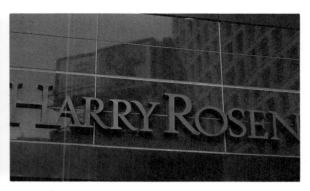

C.N. Woodward   Harry Rosen

Canada has had many successful retail merchants, some of whom became giants in the field over the past century. We have all heard of the founders of major retail companies whose names have become part of our daily lives: Timothy Eaton, Frank Sobey, Henry Birks, Sam Steinberg, A.J. Billes (Canadian Tire), and Garfield Weston, who acquired the Loblaw Companies in the late 1940s. Carrying on that retail tradition are two modern-day retail giants — Harry Rosen and C.N. (Chunky) Woodward.

Harry Rosen is the founder of the chain of high-fashion men's wear stores that carry his name. As a teenager, Rosen was a sales clerk at the Slack Shop in Toronto. After high school, he worked in production at Tip Top Tailors, and in 1954, at the age of 23, he and his brother borrowed $500 to open their own store on Parliament Street in Toronto. In 1961, the brothers moved their store to Richmond Street, at that time an unproven retail district. The store was so successful that, in 1969, Rosen sold out to Wilfred Posluns, one of his customers and co-founder of the Dylex retail empire. Rosen stayed on to manage Tip Top Tailors, one of the Dylex companies. But Rosen missed the day-to-day running of his own stores, and in 1976 he bought back 49 percent of the operation from Dylex and as a partner began to oversee the expansion of the Harry Rosen chain, which now includes more than 20 men's stores and six ladies' wear stores across Canada, with annual sales of more than $100 million.

Chunky Woodward is chairman of the Vancouver-based Woodwards chain and is controlling shareholder of the company that his grandfather founded. Faced with increasing competition and a dramatic downturn in the economies of British Columbia and Alberta, Woodward's experienced difficult times in the early 1980s. Planning to retire in 1985, Chunky Woodward stayed on to oversee the sale of Woodward's real estate assets to Cambridge Shopping Centres and the sale of 23 of its supermarkets to Canada Safeway. Woodward's is now recommitted to a quality department-store business, supplemented by an exclusive agreement to operate the exotic gift and sports wear stores of Abercrombie & Fitch in Canada.

Through a market research study in 1984, Woodward's learned that it had been neglecting the all-important fashion customer and had been devoting too much floor space to furniture, appliances, and hardware. Under Chunky Woodward's leadership, the chain renovated and refurbished all of its department stores and shifted its emphasis clearly toward the fashion market. As Woodward observed, ''Some people will run around for bargains, but sooner or later they are going to say, 'I want a little service,' and I don't want a store that looks like a junk pile all the time.''

Source: Karen Howlett, ''How Success Suits Harry Rosen,'' *Report on Business Magazine*, October 1987, pp. 52—56; and Terry McDonald, ''Woodward's Revival: New Strategy Has Its Risks,'' Financial Post, August 3, 1987, pp. 1, 11.

There are many examples of the fact that the entrepreneurial spirit still prevails in Canadian retailing. This is a fast-moving field, characterized by innovations and new entrants. The exciting world of retailing provides many entrepreneurial opportunities and career openings for university and college graduates. In this chapter, we will discuss the major types of retailing institutions and see where they might fit into the distribution system of a producer's marketing mix.

Even before a product is ready for its market, management should determine what methods and routes will be used to get it there. This task involves the establishment of a strategy covering channels of distribution of the product. Understanding the retailing and wholesaling institutional structure, however, is a prerequisite to doing an effective job of establishing and managing channels of distribution. Consequently, we discuss retailing institutions in this chapter and wholesaling institutions in the next chapter. We begin by defining the terms *middleman* and *channel of distribution*, which we have already used in a more or less intuitive sense.

MIDDLEMEN AND CHANNELS OF DISTRIBUTION

A **middleman** is an independent business concern that operates as a link between producers and ultimate consumers or industrial users. Middlemen render services in connection with the purchase and/or sale of products moving from producers to consumers. Middlemen take title to the merchandise as it flows from producer to consumer, or they actively aid in the transfer of ownership.

What Are Middlemen?

The essence of middlemen's operations is their active and prominent role in negotiations involving the buying and selling of goods. Their income is derived directly from the proceeds of these transactions. Their involvement in the transfer of ownership is what differentiates middlemen from other business institutions, such as banks, insurance companies, and transportation firms. These other institutions help in the marketing process, but they do not take title and are not actively involved in purchase and sale negotiations. A middleman may or may not actually handle the products. Some middlemen store and transport merchandise, while others do not physically handle it at all.

Middlemen are commonly classified on the basis of whether or not they take title to the products involved. **Merchant** middlemen actually take title to the goods they are helping to market. **Agent** middlemen never actually own the goods, but they do actively assist in the transfer of title. Real estate brokers and manufacturers' agents are two examples of agent middlemen. The two major groups of merchant middlemen are wholesalers and retailers. You should note particularly that retailers are merchant middlemen.

What Is a Channel of Distribution?

A **channel of distribution** (sometimes called a **trade channel**) for a product is the route taken by the *title* to the product as it moves from the producer to the ultimate consumer or industrial user. A channel always includes both the producer and the final customer for the product, as well as all middlemen involved in the title transfer. Even though agent middlemen do *not* take actual title to the goods, they are included as part of a distribution channel. Again, this is done because they play such an active role in the transfer of ownership.

A trade channel does *not* include firms such as railroads and banks, which render marketing services but play no major role in negotiating purchases and sales. If a consumer buys apples from the grower at a roadside stand, or if a manufacturer sells a shirt by mail directly to a student, the channel is from producer to consumer. If the shirt manufacturer sold to a department store that, in turn, sold to the student, the channel would be producer → retailer → consumer.

Sometimes we need to distinguish between the channel for the *title* to the goods and the channel for the *physical movement* of the goods. Frequently, these routes are partially different. A contractor might order a large load of sand or gravel from a local building supply house. The product would be shipped directly from the sand and gravel producer to the contractor to minimize freight and handling costs. The channel for the title (and for the invoice), however, would be producer → building supply house → contractor.

The channel for a product extends only to the last person who buys it without making any significant change in its form. When its form is altered and another product emerges, a new channel is started. When lumber is milled and then made into furniture, two separate channels are involved. The channel for the *lumber* may be lumber mill → broker → furniture manufacturer. The channel for the *finished furniture* may be furniture manufacturer → retail furniture store → consumer.

How Important Are Middlemen?

Middlemen are very important in many cases — in fact, in virtually *all* cases where consumers are involved. Usually, it simply is not practical for a producer to deal directly with ultimate consumers. Think for a moment how inconvenient it would be if there were no retail middlemen — no drugstores, newspaper stands, super-markets, or service stations.

There is an old saying in marketing that "you can eliminate the middlemen, but you cannot eliminate their functions (activities)." Someone has to perform those activities — if not the middlemen, then the producers or the final customers. Middlemen serve as purchasing agents for their customers and as sales specialists for their suppliers (see Fig. 13-1). Middlemen frequently provide various financial

FIGURE 13-1
The retailer provides services for consumers on one hand, and for producers and wholesalers in the other.

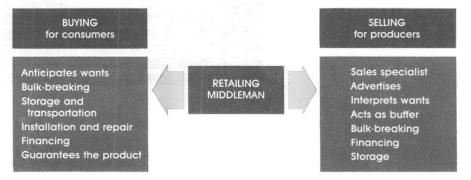

services for both their suppliers and their customers. The storage service of middlemen, their bulk-breaking activities (dividing large shipments into smaller quantities for resale), and the market information they provide benefit suppliers and customers alike.

In the next two chapters, we shall discuss the economic services provided by particular types of middlemen — services that justify their existence and demonstrate their importance. For now, let's look at a couple of broad concepts that illustrate the important role of middlemen in our economy.

CONCENTRATION, EQUALIZATION, DISPERSION

Frequently, the quantity and assortment of goods produced by a firm are out of balance with the variety and amounts wanted by consumers or industrial users. A business needs paper, pencils, word processors, and desks. A homeowner wants grass seed, topsoil, fertilizer, a rake, and eventually a lawn mower. No single firm produces all the items either of these users wants. And no producer could afford to sell any of them in the small quantity the user desires. Obviously there is a need for someone to match what various producers turn out with what the final customers want. This is part of the task of middlemen.

The job to be done involves (1) collecting or **concentrating** the outputs of various producers, (2) subdividing these outputs into the amounts desired by customers and then putting the various items together in the assortment wanted (which together are called **equalizing**), and (3) **dispersing** this assortment to consumers or industrial buyers. In a few cases, these concentrating, equalizing, and dispersing tasks are simple enough to be done by the producer and the final customer working closely together. A copper mine may sell directly to a smelting firm; coal producers may sell directly to steel mills. In most cases, however, the producer and the consumer are not able to work out the proper quantity and assortment. A specialist in concentration, equalization, and dispersion is needed, and this is the middleman.

CREATION OF UTILITY

Middlemen aid in the creation of time, place, and possession utilities. In classical economic theory, production is defined as the creation of utility, and several types of utility are recognized. One is **form utility**, which results from chemical or physical changes that make a product more valuable. When lumber is made into furniture or flour into bread, form utility is created. Other utilities are equally valuable to the final user. Furniture located in Winnipeg in April is of little value to people in Edmonton who want to give the furniture as Christmas presents. Transporting the furniture from Manitoba to Alberta increases its value — **place utility** is added. Storing it from April to December adds another value — **time utility**. Finally, **possession utility** is created when the Alberta families buy the items.

NATURE OF RETAIL MARKET If Safeway or Sobeys sells some floor wax to a gift-shop operator to polish the shop floor, is this a retail sale? When a Shell or Petro-Canada service station advertises that tires are being sold at the wholesale price, is this retailing? Can a wholesaler or manufacturer engage in retailing? Obviously, we need to define the terms *retailing, retail store, retail sales* and *retailers*, to avoid misunderstandings in later discussions.

Retailing includes all activities directly related to the sale of goods or services to the ultimate consumer for personal, nonbusiness use. While most retailing is done through retail stores, retailing may be done by any institution. A manufacturer selling brushes or cosmetics door to door is engaging in retailing, as is a farmer selling vegetables at a roadside stand. Any firm — manufacturer, wholesaler, or retail store — that sells something to ultimate consumers for their nonbusiness use is making a **retail sale**. This is true regardless of *how* the product is sold (in person or by telephone, mail, or vending machine) or *where* it is sold (in a store or at the consumer's home).

A **retailer** or a **retail store** is a business enterprise whose *primary* function is to sell to ultimate consumers for nonbusiness use. The word *dealer* is generally synonymous with *retailer*. In contrast, a *distributor* is a *wholesaler*.

Note the word *primary* in our definition of a retailer. Actually a manufacturer or a farmer can make a retail sale to a consumer. But a manufacturer's primary function is to make a product, and a farmer's job is to grow a product. So in the common usage of terms, we call a textile mill a manufacturer, even though occasionally that mill may sell towels or sheets directly to an ultimate consumer (a retail sale). People who grow potatoes or raise cattle are called farmers or ranchers, not retailers, even though occasionally they do make a retail sale.

Economic Justification for Retailing

The ease of entry into retailing results in fierce competition and better value for the consumer. Except perhaps in a small town, it is rather difficult to establish an unregulated, monopolistic position in retailing. Certainly large-scale enterprises exist in retailing, and in some markets a relatively few large firms account for most of the business. Yet these giants usually compete with one another, so the consumer still benefits.

To get into retailing is easy. To be forced out is just as easy. Consequently, to survive in retailing, a company must do a satisfactory job in its primary role — catering to the consumer — and in its secondary role — serving producers and wholesalers. This dual responsibility is both the justification for retailing and the key to success in retailing.

There are about 208,000 retail stores in Canada, and their total sales volume in 1986 was about $140 *billion* (see Fig. 13-2). In spite of growth in population and rising consumer incomes over the past 25 years, the total number of retail outlets has not increased dramatically. The increase in total sales volume, however, has been tremendous — a nine-fold increase in the 25 years from 1961 to 1986. Even

TABLE 13-1   TOTAL RETAIL TRADE IN CANADA, 1961-1986

	1961	1971	1981	1986
Number of stores (thousands)	152.6	158.2	163.6	207.8
Total sales ($ billions)	$16.07	$32.08	$94.20	$140.00
Average sales per store	$105,504	$202,781	$576,363	$673,706

Source: Statistics Canada. Reproduced with permission of Supply and Services Canada.

FIGURE 13-2
Total retail trade in Canada, selected years.

Sales volume has increased tremendously. In contrast, note the remarkable stability in the number of retail stores. (*Source: Statistics Canada*)

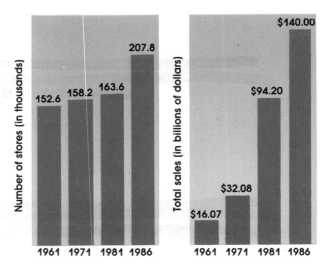

if we adjust for the rate of inflation, we find that total retail sales, and per capita retail sales, have gone up considerably. That is, there has been a huge increase in the volume and value of goods and services sold at the retail level.

File 13-1

The Changing Retail Food Spectrum

Food retailing has become a very competitive business in this country. The major food chains (Loblaws, Sobeys, Steinberg, Safeway, Provigo, etc.) are battling massive superstores at one end and efficient convenience stores at the other. In some cities, superstores that are four times or more larger than conventional supermarkets are grabbing large chunks of the retail food market. Offering customers great variety at low prices, these superstores are different from the no-frills warehouse stores of the late 1970s. They offer brightly decorated surroundings and specialty "boutiques," including in-store bakeries, fish markets, salad bars, flower shops, delicatessens, and cheese shops. Some have their own in-store specialty restaurants.

At the opposite end of the size spectrum, the food chains are being squeezed by convenience stores, which are fast and convenient and are offering an increasing variety to customers. Many are open 24 hours a day and offer specialty services such as small in-store delis and movie rentals. Although prices are higher than at their larger competitors, these stores meet the needs of customers whose time is important.

All of this competition is taking place in what is essentially a no-growth market. When Canada's population was growing during the 1950s and 1960s, there was growth and expansion in the food business. Now, there is no real population growth and the situation is further complicated by the fact that Canadians are consuming close to one-third of all food outside the home.

Costs and Profits of
Retailers

Information regarding the costs of retailing is very meagre. By gleaning data from several sources, however, we can make some rough generalizations.

TOTAL COSTS AND PROFITS

As nearly as can be estimated, the total average operating expense for all retailers combined is about 25 to 27 percent of retail sales. Wholesaling expenses are estimated at about 8 percent of the *retail* dollar or about 10 to 11 percent of *wholesaling* sales. Thus, retailing costs are about $2\frac{1}{2}$ times the costs of wholesaling, when both are stated as a percentage of sales of the middlemen in question. (See Fig. 13-3).

FIGURE 13-3
Average costs of retailing and wholesaling.

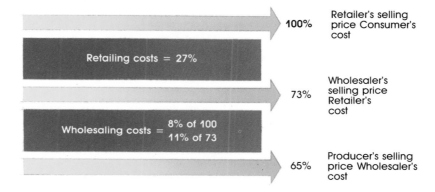

Retailing costs = 27%   100%   Retailer's selling price Consumer's cost

73%   Wholesaler's selling price Retailer's cost

Wholesaling costs = 8% of 100   11% of 73

65%   Producer's selling price Wholesaler's cost

The proportionately higher retailing costs are generally related to the expense of dealing directly with the consumer. In comparison with wholesalers' customers, consumers demand more services. The average retail sale is smaller, the rate of merchandise turnover is lower, merchandise is bought in smaller lots, rent is higher, and expenses for furniture and fixtures are greater. And retail sales people cannot be used efficiently because customers do not come into retail stores at a steady rate.

COSTS AND PROFITS BY KIND OF BUSINESS

The expense ratios of retailers vary from one type of store to another. Table 13-2 shows average gross margins as a percentage of sales for different kinds of stores. These margins range from 15.4 percent for motor vehicle dealers to 51 percent for motor vehicle repair shops. Table 13-2 also shows average net profit (after income taxes) for each type of store.

Retailing Structure in
Metropolitan Areas

As we might expect, retail sales and retailer location tend to follow the population. The bulk of retail sales is concentrated in very small land masses — the Census Metropolitan Areas. These CMA markets account for approximately 60 percent of Canada's population and almost 65 percent of our retail trade.

Within the central city and its adjacent suburbs in a metropolitan area, there are several discernible types of shopping districts. Together, these constitute a retailing structure that should be recognized by marketers. The hub of retailing activity has traditionally been the central downtown shopping district. This is the location of

TABLE 13-2   **GROSS MARGIN AND NET PROFIT AS PERCENTAGE OF NET SALES OF SELECTED TYPES OF RETAILERS**

Gross margin (net sales minus cost of goods sold) is the amount needed to cover a company's operating expenses and still leave a profit. How do you account for the differences in operating expenses among the various types of retailers?

Line of business	Gross margin %	Net profit % after income taxes
Food stores	20.9	1.1
Department stores	29.8	3.2
Variety stores	28.8	1.3
General merchandise	19.3	2.1
Automobile accessories and parts	32.5	2.5
Gasoline service stations	16.9	1.4
Motor vehicle dealers	15.4	1.4
Motor vehicle repair shops	51.0	3.1
Shoe stores	38.5	2.0
Men's clothing stores	42.7	4.5
Women's clothing stores	42.2	3.3
Dry goods stores	40.7	2.6
Hardware stores	32.3	2.6
Book and stationery stores	36.9	2.9
Florist shops	50.1	2.6
Fuel dealers	15.5	2.5
Furniture and appliance stores	30.2	2.5
Jewellery stores	45.8	4.8
Tobacconists	34.9	1.1
TOTAL RETAIL TRADE	26.4	3.3

Source: Statistics Canada, *Corporation Financial Statistics*, 1984, cat. no. 61-207. Reproduced with permission of Supply and Services Canada.

the main units of department stores, major apparel specialty stores, jewellery stores, and other shopping-goods stores.

In the older, larger cities we often find a secondary shopping district with branches of downtown stores. A third type of shopping district is a ''string-street'' development, or a cluster of small, neighbourhood stores. None of these three types of shopping districts is planned or controlled for marketing purposes. Thus they are different from planned suburban shopping centres.

During the past 20 years, many cities have made a concerted effort to revitalize their downtown shopping districts. An especially successful venture in this respect has been the development of planned, controlled downtown shopping centres — the urban shopping mall. Many cities now have such malls — The Rideau Centre in Ottawa, Toronto's Eaton Centre, Scotia Square in Halifax, the Pacific Centre in Vancouver, London Square in London, and new Eaton Centres in Calgary and Edmonton, to name just a few. These malls have brought retail customers back to the downtown areas, provided excellent shopping for the many people who work downtown, and rebuilt an urban tax base.

Toronto's Eaton Centre — drawing shoppers downtown.

SUBURBAN SHOPPING CENTRES

Another significant type of shopping district in metropolitan areas is the suburban shopping centre — a unit that is planned, developed, and controlled by one organization. These planned centres range from (1) a *neighbourhood* centre built around a supermarket, through (2) a *community* centre featuring a discount store or junior department store, to (3) a *regional* centre anchored by a branch of one or more downtown department stores. In the regional centre, ideally there is at least one limited-line store to compete with each department in the department stores.

Many of the regional centres are giant-sized; in effect, they are miniature downtowns. These supercentres may have as many as three department stores, plus many small stores and service operations. They also include hotels, banks, office buildings, churches, and theatres. These centres integrate retail, cultural, and commercial activities, all enclosed under one roof.

In the late 1970s, the building of giant regional centres slowed considerably as the market for shopping centres became saturated in many parts of the country. In the 1980s, energy shortages and concern for more efficient land uses have further discouraged the development of outlying shopping centres. At the same time, increased attention is being devoted to in-city shopping facilities. Many cities from Victoria to St. John's already have built traffic-limited downtown shopping malls or promenades as part of their urban redevelopment programs.

The success of suburban shopping centres lies essentially in their conformity with consumer buying patterns. A wide selection of merchandise is available; stores are open evenings; an informal atmosphere encourages shoppers to dress informally and to bring the children; plenty of free parking space is available. By coordinating their promotional efforts, all stores benefit; one builds traffic for another. Many stores in these centres are too small to do effective, economical advertising on their own. But they can make good use of major advertising media by tying in with the overall shopping-centre advertising.

Suburban shopping malls continue to be popular.

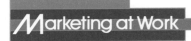

The Mall: For Some, the Centre of It All

One author has depicted the shopping centre as a model for life in North America in the last quarter of the twentieth century. William Kowinski, in his 1986 book, *The Malling of America*, presents the idea that shopping malls have gone well beyond the concept of one-stop shopping and are now closer to the idea of one-stop living. The major shopping malls that have been built in recent years, including Toronto's Eaton Centre and the West Edmonton Mall, reflect society's desire to get everything done at one place. The West Edmonton Mall not only has 828 retail stores, but has added an indoor amusement park (complete with roller-coaster), water park, skating rink, night-club district, aquarium, hotel, movie theatres, Parisian streets, Italian sculpture, and an African safari jungle.

Such major retail developments raise a number of issues of importance to retailers. Clearly, in many cities the downtown or suburban shopping malls now represent a major focal point where parents go to walk their babies, senior citizens stroll during cold winter days, teenagers meet their friends, and people shop. Kozinski's thesis is that shopping has become a major cultural pastime and that malls market experience rather than goods.

Because of the importance of malls as retailing focal points, retailers almost *have* to be there. A retail chain cannot afford to be absent from a mall where the competition has a store. The result is a situation of "sameness" where the same basic mix of stores is offered in most major shopping malls across the country. The challenge then falls to the mall owner or developer to design a centre and provide a mix of stores that will attract shoppers away from other centres.

Source: Adapted from William Thorsell, "The Macabre Malling of a Whole Continent," *Report on Business Magazine*, September 1986, pp. 101-103.

Classification of Retailers

To better explain the role of retailing middlemen in the channel structure, we shall classify and discuss retailers on four bases:

1. Size of store, by sales volume.
2. Extent of product lines handled.
3. Form of ownership.
4. Method of operation.

Any given store can be classed according to all four of these bases. We have done this on page 367, using Sears and a neighbourhood paint store as examples. See also Fig. 13-4.

RETAILERS CLASSIFIED BY SALES VOLUME

Sales volume is a useful basis for classifying retail stores, because stores of different sizes (in terms of sales) present different management problems. Buying, promotion, personnel relations, and expense control are influenced significantly by whether a store's sales volume is large or small. And, as you will see, on the basis of store sales volume, retailing is both a small-scale and a large-scale operation.

Sears	Classification base	Paint store
Large	1. Size of store	Small
General merchandise	2. Product lines carried	Single line of merchandise
Corporate chain	3. Form of ownership	Independent owner
Both in-store and mail order; supermarket method and full service depending on product department	4. Method of operation	In-store selling; full service

FIGURE 13-4
Retailers may be classed in several ways.

By sales volume	By product lines carried	By form of ownership	By method of operation
Large-scale retailers	General merchandise stores:	Corporate chain	Full-service retailing
Small-scale retailers	Department stores	Independents— unaffiliated	Supermarket retailing
	Variety stores	Association of independent retailers	Discount retailing
	Limited-line stores (shoes, furniture, hardware, apparel)		Nonstore retailing (in-home, telephone, mail-order, vending machines)
	Specialty stores (bakery, dairy)		

CLASSIFICATION OF RETAILERS

Quantitative Measurement

Most retail establishments are very small. In 1984, Statistics Canada reported that there were 186,301 retail establishments in Canada. Of these, only 16,233 (8.7%) did more than $1 million in sales. Total retail sales in Canada for that year were $133.8 billion. These larger retailers accounted for 76 percent of total sales, although they operated less than nine percent of the stores. In other words, the 91 percent of Canadian retailers who have annual sales of less than $1 million account for only 24 percent of total retail sales. The concentration in retailing is further illustrated by the fact that in 1984, 434 companies with annual sales of $20 million or more accounted for 39.7 percent of total retail sales with only 2/10 of one percent of stores.

But looking at *individual store sales* does not convey a true picture of concentration in retailing. When we examine *individual company* volume, we get a better understanding of just how much of Canadian retail sales volume is accounted for by just a few companies. A single company may operate a large number of retail outlets, as is the case with national chain stores such as Eaton's, The Bay, Canadian Tire, Birks, and the Dylex Group. When retail stores are analyzed by companies, the high degree of concentration becomes more evident. From Table 13-3, we see that the 20 largest retailers in Canada in 1987 had retail sales in excess of $48 billion, or more than one-third of all retail sales in Canada. The small size of the annual profit of these companies — often less than one percent of sales — may surprise some people who feel that retailers make large profits.

TABLE 13-3   TWENTY LARGEST RETAILERS IN CANADA, 1987
(BY SALES VOLUME)

Company	Sales ($000)	Net Income as % of sales
Loblaws	8,630,750	0.85
Provigo[1]	6,418,100	1.04
Hudson's Bay Company[2]	4,895,128	−1.60
Steinberg	4,491,355	1.02
Sears Canada	4,035,098	2.03
Oshawa Group	3,804,015	1.31
Canada Safeway[3]	3,750,000	n/a
Canadian Tire	2,500,000	3.95
Great Atlantic and Pacific Tea (A&P)	2,286,091	n/a
FW Woolworth	2,025,969	1.64
Groupe Metro-Richelieu	1,915,417	0.46
K-Mart Canada	1,502,523	1.43
Westfair Foods	1,444,453	1.04
Dylex	1,299,856	−9.05
Sobeys Stores	1,056,323	0.99
Woodward's	814,539	−0.22
Grafton	627,700	1.34
Gendis	607,043	3.97
Southland Canada	527,334	n/a
Acklands	414,934	0.76

[1] includes Consumers Distributing
[2] includes the Bay, Simpsons, and Zellers
[3] estimated, includes Woodward's food floors

Source: Adapted from "The Canadian Business 500", *Canadian Business*, June 1988, pp. 68—82

Competitive Positions of Large and Small Retailers

The relative competitive strengths and weaknesses of large and small retailers may be evaluated as follows:

Bases for evaluation	Competitive advantage is generally with:
1. Division of labour and specialization of management	1. Large-scale retailers. This is their major advantage.
2. Flexibility of operations — merchandise selection, services offered, store design, reflection of owner's personality.	2. Small retailers. This is their biggest advantage.
3. Buying power.	3. Large retailers. They can buy in bigger quantities and thus get lower prices.

Bases for evaluation	Competitive advantage is generally with:
4. Effective use of advertising — especially in citywide media.	4. Large retailers. Their markets fit better with media circulation.
5. Development and promotion of retailer's own brand.	5. Large retailers.
6. Feasibility of integrating wholesaling and manufacturing with retailing.	6. Large retailers.
7. Opportunity to experiment with new products and selling methods.	7. Large retailers can better afford the risks and can supply the necessary executive specialists.
8. Cost of operations.	8. Small stores generally have lower expense ratios and lower overhead costs. Large stores pay a price for executive specialization and the large number of employees in non-selling jobs.
9. Financial strength.	9. Large-scale retailers. This advantage also underlies some of the advantages noted above — integration, experimentation, purchase discounts, effective advertising, and executive specialization.
10. Public image and legal considerations.	10. Small merchants enjoy public support and sympathy. But often this same public votes with its pocketbook for (that is, shops at) the big store. Large-scale retailers have been a major target of restrictive legislation.

Improved Position of Small Retailers

With the above evaluation adding up so heavily in favour of large-scale retailing, you might wonder why so many small retailers seem to be succeeding. We find the answer in several developments among both large and small firms. One such development has been the voluntary association of retailers in a chainlike form of organization. This gives the individual members the features of specialized management, buying power, and other advantages of scale listed above. A second development has been the expansion of franchising operations in many fields (by Holiday Inn, Tim Horton's, Japan Camera, and Harvey's hamburgers, for instance). Franchising enables small-scale business people to operate their own businesses under the name and guidance of a large company. This gives some small entrepreneurs the best of both worlds. (Franchising and voluntary associations are discussed later in this chapter.)

Change in the consumer market is another factor working for the smaller retailer. On one hand, huge supermarket-type stores carrying a wide variety of merchandise are catering to consumer's wants. At the same time, small specialty shops are growing in number and apparently doing well, in response to another facet of consumer buying behaviour. Small retailers who take advantage of their flexibility can adapt their merchandise lines to their market. They can also establish an individual image for their store because of their own personality and service as well as by means of unusual store layout and design. The relative position of small stores also is improved when large retailers suffer from the usual problems of large-scale operation — retailing or otherwise. High overhead costs, restrictive union contracts, difficulty in motivating sales people, and organizational inflexibilities all limit the competitive position of the large-scale retailer.

RETAILERS CLASSIFIED BY PRODUCT LINE

In classifying retailers according to the product lines they carry, we group them into two categories — general merchandise stores and limited-line stores.

General Merchandise Stores

As the name suggests, **general merchandise** stores carry a large variety of product lines, usually with some depth of assortment in each line. Department stores are the type of general merchandise stores with the largest sales volume. Variety stores (Woolworth's, The Met, Zellers) are also included in this category.

DEPARTMENT STORES

Department stores are large retailing institutions that carry a *very wide* variety of product lines, including apparel, other soft goods, furniture, and home furnishings. These stores are highly organized business enterprises. Under the merchandising manager are the department buyers. In effect, each department is a business in itself, and the department buyer has considerable autonomy.

In addition to the general advantages and drawbacks of large-scale retailing (specialized management, buying power, and so on) department stores have some other significant merits and limitations. These stores offer a wider variety of products and services than any other type of retail institution where the customer comes to the store. (The mail-order house — a form of nonstore retailing — may carry more lines than a department store.) On the other hand, their operating expenses are considerably higher than those of most other kinds of retail business, running about 35 percent of sales. One of the features of department stores — their many services — contributes significantly to this high operating expense.

A substantial problem confronting the main store of department store chains has been location — typically in the heart of the downtown shopping district. The population growth in the suburbs and the traffic problems downtown have combined to force many department stores to open branches in the suburbs. The big downtown store, with its large investment, high-tax location, and high-cost operations, must be maintained. But it can easily become part of the "downtown problem." In many cities, working with other downtown merchants, the department stores have spearheaded movements to revitalize the downtown areas. Also, as mentioned earlier, urban shopping malls are revitalizing downtown shopping areas, thus benefitting downtown department stores.

Department stores face strong competition on other fronts as well. Some examples of these challenges are (1) the continued expansion of discount selling; (2) the growth of chains of small specialty apparel stores (Dalmys, Harry Rosen, Le Cha-

Large stores have set up specialty departments — such as this designer's salon — to compete with the smaller boutiques.

teau) and (3) the development of specialty stores catering to hobbies, sports, and other leisure-time activities.

But department stores are displaying some innovative, aggressive strategies to meet the competitive challenges. To illustrate, stores are using marketing research extensively to determine current purchasing motives, attitudes, and life-styles. Many stores are trying to appeal to a limited number of market segments — especially the younger, more fashion-conscious groups. These retailers are reducing their merchandise mix — stressing fashion and exclusiveness rather than carrying products in a wide variety of price lines. Some department stores have converted entire floors into groups of specialty shops. Each of these shops features a different line of merchandise, and each has a different decorative display theme or motif. Bargain basements are being revitalized to counter the lower prices in discount stores.

Limited-Line Stores

Only what your computer needs.

Limited-line stores carry a considerable assortment of goods but in only one or a few related lines. We identify these stores by the names of the individual products they feature — food stores, shoe stores, furniture stores, hardware stores, and so on.

This identification is still useful for some types of stores — those selling apparel, furniture, or building materials, for instance. For other types, such as food stores and drugstores, however, to include a single type of product in the store name is inaccurate and misleading. This is the result of a major trend toward **scrambled merchandising** — the practice of adding unrelated lines to the products customarily sold in a particular type of store. Moreover, it is a mistake to interpret food store sales, for example, as being equal to total sales of food products. Supermarkets carry many nonfood lines. Food products, in turn, are sold in drugstores, gas stations, and department stores.

The limited-line category also includes what we call **specialty stores**. These are tobacco shops, bakeries, dairy stores, and furriers, for example — stores that typically carry a very limited variety of products. The name "specialty stores" is an unfortunate, and perhaps even misleading, title. Specialty *stores* should *not* be confused with specialty *products*. Actually, specialty shops do *not* often carry specialty products. Using the word *specialty* in describing the store implies only that it carries a limited line of merchandise.

Limited-line stores usually carry an excellent assortment of goods. In the apparel field, they often feature the newest fashions. Frequently they are the exclusive dealers for certain brands in a given market. Because they limit their merchandise to one or a few lines, these stores can often buy in large quantities and thus secure favourable prices.

RETAILERS CLASSIFIED BY FORM OF OWNERSHIP

The major store-ownership categories are *independent* stores and *corporate chain* stores. A third group consists of *voluntary associations of independents* that band together in chainlike fashion in order to compete more effectively with corporate chain-store organizations.

Corporate Chain Store

A **corporate chain-store system** is an organization of two or more stores, centrally owned and managed, that generally handle the same lines of products. Technically, two or more units constitute a chain. Today, however, many small-scale merchants have opened two or three units in shopping centres and in newly populated areas. These retailers ordinarily do not think of themselves as chains. Having four or more units is a good definitional basis for discussing chain stores.

Central ownership is the key factor that differentiates corporate chains from voluntary associations of independent wholesalers or retailers. The third element in our definition of a chain-store system is central management. Individual units in a chain have very little autonomy. Buying is highly centralized, and there is considerable standardization in the operating policies of the units in a chain.

IMPORTANCE

Organizations with four or more stores did almost 42 percent of all retail business in Canada in 1986. The importance of chains varies considerably from one type of business to another. Chains account for 75 percent or more of total sales in the general merchandise and variety stores categories. Among grocery stores, hardware stores, and pharmacies, however, chains account for less than 30 percent of sales. In the retail food business, there are several giant food chains (Loblaws, Steinberg, A&P, Provigo, Sobeys, Safeway, etc.), yet chains still account for only about 60 percent of all food sales. This is explained in part by the large number of independent food retailers in small towns and neighbourhoods throughout Canada.

Chain store companies have increased their share of the total retail market since

TABLE 13-4   CHAINS' SHARE OF TOTAL RETAIL SALES VOLUME BY KIND OF BUSINESS, 1966, 1974, 1979, 1986

Kind of Business	Percent of Sales			
	1966	1974	1979	1986
Total retail sales	33.4	41.1	41.5	41.5
Grocery and combination stores	44.9	57.5	60.4	
Combination stores (groceries and meat)				64.8
Grocery, confectionery and sundries				29.8
Other food stores	8.7	8.1	8.5	9.4
Department stores[1]	100.0	100.0	100.0	100.0
General merchandise	74.7	80.4	79.8	75.6
Variety stores	86.7	83.2	76.3	87.2
Men's clothing	13.2	18.6	34.3	54.9
Women's clothing	26.5	40.9	53.3	65.6
Family clothing	21.9	28.5	49.9	68.3
Shoe stores	45.0	51.8	66.0	71.7
Hardware stores	15.5	19.0	n/a	21.2
Furniture stores	19.2	19.2	19.5	50.9
Pharmacy stores	13.4	18.5	22.4	29.6
Jewellery stores	33.7	39.4	45.4	49.3

[1] All department stores are considered chains by Statistics Canada.

Source: Statistics Canada, *Market Research Handbook*, cat. no. 63-224, various years. Reproduced with permission of Supply and Services Canada.

the mid-1960s, but the growth has not been uniform in all product categories. In food, for example, chains have increased their share of sales from about 45 percent in 1966 to just over 60 percent in 1986. The growth in the sales of chains in the clothing area and in furniture has been quite dramatic, while there has been relatively little growth in the chains' percentage of sales in hardware. The growth of chains in the drugstore field reflects the way these stores have expanded into a wide variety of merchandise. Further growth in drug chains is likely as they capitalize on potential government- and insurance-sponsored business and the fact that the over-65 segment of the market is increasing in size and buying power.

COMPETITIVE STRENGTHS AND WEAKNESSES

Chain-store organizations are large-scale retailing institutions. As such, they are subject to the general advantages and limitations of all large retailers that we discussed earlier in this chapter. Let's look at a few of these points, especially as they relate to chain stores.

Lower selling prices   Chain stores have traditionally been credited with selling at lower prices than independents. But the claim of lower prices needs careful scrutiny because it can be misleading. It was probably more justified in the past than it is today. Many independents have pooled their buying power so that, in many instances, they can buy products at the same price as the chains.

It is very difficult to compare the prices of chains with those of independents. The merchandise is often not exactly comparable, because many chains sell items under their own brands. It is difficult to compare the prices of Del Monte peaches with Loblaws', Steinberg's or Safeway's brand of peaches. Also, it is not accurate to compare the price of the product sold in a cash-and-carry, no-customer-service store with the price of an identically branded product in a full-service store. The value of services should be included in the comparison.

Multistore feature of chains   Chain stores do not have all their eggs in one basket (or in one store). Even large-scale independent department stores or supermarkets cannot match this advantage of the chains. A multiunit operation has automatically *spread its risks* among many units. Losses in one store can be offset by profits in other units. Multistore organizations can *experiment* quite easily. They can try a new store layout or a new type of merchandise in one store without committing the entire firm.

A chain can make more *effective use of advertising* than even a giant single-unit independent store. To illustrate, a grocery chain may have 15 medium-sized stores blanketing a city. An independent competitor may have one huge supermarket doing three to four times the business of any single unit of the chain. Yet the chain can use the metropolitan daily newspaper as an advertising medium with much less waste in circulation than the independent can. Many chains can also make effective use of national advertising media.

On the negative side   Standardization, the hallmark of a chain-store system and a major factor in its success, is a mixed blessing. *Standardization also means inflexibility*. Often a chain cannot adjust rapidly to a local market situation. Chains are well aware of this weakness, however, and have consequently given local store managers somewhat greater freedom to act in various situations.

*Franchise Systems
Involving Small,
Independent Retailers*

A major competitive factor facing corporate chains is the increased effectiveness of independent retailers and wholesalers that have copied chain-store marketing methods. Independents have improved store appearance and layout; they have sought better locations, including suburban shopping centres; they have improved their merchandising practices by eliminating some slow-moving items and keeping fresh stock; and they have improved their accounting and inventory-control systems.

Probably the most effective measure adopted by small independents is their practice of voluntarily associating with wholesalers, manufacturers, or other retailers in some form of contractual franchise system. These associations sometimes resemble a corporate chain so closely that about the only significant difference is that the member stores are not centrally owned.

NATURE AND EXTENT OF FRANCHISE SYSTEMS

In our discussion here, we use a broad interpretation of franchising. It includes any contractual arrangement between *franchisers* (suppliers, that may be manufacturers or wholesalers) and independent *franchisees* (either wholesalers or retailers). The franchiser grants the right to sell certain goods or services in a stated geographic market. The franchiser usually provides equipment, the products or services for sale, and managerial services. In return, the franchisee agrees to market the product or service in a manner established by the supplier. Within this broad definition we find two main types of franchising systems. One is a voluntary association of retailers, and the other is a retailer network sponsored by a producer.

Voluntary chains help small retailers to compete with big stores.

ASSOCIATIONS OF INDEPENDENT RETAILERS

The two main forms of voluntary associations of independent retailers are **voluntary chains** (sponsored by wholesalers) and **retailer cooperative chains** (sponsored by retailers). Both forms have the same basic purpose — namely, to enable independent wholesalers and retailers to meet more effectively the competition from corporate chain stores. By combining the buying power of their many retailer members, these associations can buy at prices competitive with those of the corporate chains.

Some differences between the two groups are as follows:

Voluntary chain	Retailer cooperative chain
1. Sponsored by wholesalers, with a contract between wholesalers and independent retailer members.	1. Sponsored by retailers. They combine to form and operate a wholesale warehouse corporation.
2. Wholesaler provides a wide variety of management services — buying, advertising, store layout, accounting, and inventory control. Retailers agree to buy all (or almost all) their merchandise from wholesaler. Members agree to use common store name and design and to follow common managerial procedures.	2. Services to retailer members are primarily large-scale buying and warehousing operations. Members maintain their separate identities.
3. Most prevalent in grocery field (IGA). These chains also exist in hardware (Home Hardware), auto supplies (Western Auto), and variety stores.	3. Quite significant in grocery field in local areas, but not in other lines.

PRODUCER-SPONSORED SYSTEMS

In producer-sponsored systems of franchising, a manufacturer (or other producer) sets up a network of retail outlets by contracting with independent retailers. The contract may cover:

- Only one brand within a department (Zenith televisions or Maytag appliances).
- An entire department in a store (Ziggy's Deli).
- The entire retail outlet (auto dealerships or gas stations, Harvey's Hamburgers, Speedy Mufflers, Tilden auto rentals).

We can distinguish between two concepts in producer-sponsored franchise systems. One features franchising as a form of *exclusive distribution* of a product. This type has existed for years and often involves a large-scale retailer. The other concept is the rise of *entrepreneurship franchising*. This practice is relatively new, and it typically has involved small-scale retailers. Enterprise franchising has especially proliferated in the fast-food industry (Pizza Delight, Kentucky Fried Chicken, McDonald's hamburgers)[1] and in service industries (recreation, auto rentals, motels, auto repairs).

The concept of a producer franchising an entire retail outlet (as contrasted with a single department or one brand within a department) is not new — automobile manufacturers have done this for decades. What is new, however, is its substantial growth over the past 20 to 30 years and its spreading into many new fields. In addition to fast-food services, today producer-sponsored franchise selling also embraces such products and services as computers, auto mufflers, putting greens, paint, part-time office help, hearing aids, motels, and dance studios.

Franchising is one way to help a little guy succeed in business.

File 13-3

Marketing at Work

New Franchises for New Segments

Statistics Canada data show that the fast-food segment of the Canadian restaurant industry is now accounting for almost 25 percent of total restaurant sales and is having trouble maintaining the growth experienced in the 1970s. Even if sales volume for this component of the restaurant business continues to grow, its share of the total market has stopped growing. Franchising has always been an important part of the Canadian fast-food industry, but the segments of the market on which the industry has relied for growth are declining in numbers. Also, there are a number of other trends acting against growth in the traditional hamburger-dominated sectors of the fast-food business. As a result, we are likely to see more growth among the newer forms of fast-food franchises in the future. Watch for new Italian, Mexican, Japanese and salad-bar and health-food restaurants.

Competitive advantages   Franchising has many economic and social advantages. A producer-sponsored system offers the producer an opportunity for greater control over the pricing, advertising, and selling of its products or services. Franchising also provides suppliers with the means for rapid market expansion and a wide distribution system at a relatively low cost. Franchisees typically put up some of the money. With their own money at stake, they have more incentive and are likely to be more dedicated entrepreneurs.

When the retailers are identified as a group (through a producer's name), then that producer can make effective use of cooperative advertising programs, display materials, and other promotional features. The group buying power enables the independent retailer-members to obtain lower-cost merchandise and a better selection of the latest products. Furthermore, the retailers are able to do a better job of store management because of the administrative services furnished by the sponsor.

In a producer-sponsored network particularly, franchising enables many people to realize their dream of owning their own business. Also, the franchisees' investment is relatively small, and it is easier for them to borrow the necessary funds when big national firms are behind them. They may be independent, small-scale retailers, but they are backed by the buying power, promotional programs, and management know-how of big companies.

Limitations The biggest competitive weakness of all independent retailers, whether affiliated or not, is their assumption that the sole advantage of the chain is buying power. The real strength of a large-scale institution, however, lies in its superior management personnel and specialized management practices.

Ignorance or disregard of this fact places major limitations on voluntary associations of independents. Too often these retailers reject the management advice given by sponsors. Many retailers think of the association as a buying aid only, and make little use of advertising, accounting, and other association services.

The rapid expansion of producer-sponsored franchising systems during the past 25 years has also brought problems. One is the charge that franchising agreements are grievously one-sided — all in favour of the franchiser. Another threat to continued successful expansion of franchising is the practice whereby the producer-sponsor takes over the ownership of successful units in its franchise system. This, in effect, turns the independent units into a corporate chain system. One unfortunate aspect of this trend is that it reduces the numbers of successful, small, independent entrepreneurs.

RETAILERS CLASSIFIED BY METHOD OF OPERATION

The four types of retailers, classified by method of operation, are listed in Fig. 13-4. The traditional form, *in-store full-service* retailing, is still quite prevalent, although its use has declined considerably over the past 30 years. It probably will continue to be important in retailing high-fashion products and products that require explanation or fitting. The use of the remaining three classes — supermarket, discount, and nonstore retailing (in-home personal selling, telephone selling, mail-order selling, and automatic vending) — has increased considerably during the last two decades.

Supermarket Retailing

It is somewhat difficult to analyze supermarket retailing because there is no universally accepted definition of the term. To some people a supermarket is a *type* of retail store found in the grocery business. To others, the term describes a *method* of retailing and can be used in connection with stores in any product line.

In this discussion, a **supermarket** will be defined as a large-scale departmentalized retailing institution offering a variety of merchandise (including groceries, meats, produce, and dairy products). Such a store operates largely on a self-service basis with a minimum of customer services, and features a price appeal and (usually) ample parking space.

DEVELOPMENT OF SUPERMARKETS

Supermarkets, as we know them today, had their start in the Depression days of the early 1930s. They were owned and operated by *independents* attempting to compete with the chain food stores. The supermarket method of food retailing became an immediate success, and the innovation was soon adopted by chain stores as well as other full-service independents. Today, supermarkets are the dominant institution in food retailing.

The rapidly changing competitive environment in grocery retailing in the 1980s has forced conventional supermarkets to make significant changes in order to survive. The number of supermarkets has reached a saturation point in many communities. Also, today a grocery shopper can choose from among warehouse stores, supermarkets combined with general merchandise stores, convenience stores, gourmet shops, ethnic stores, discount supermarkets, and other institutions.

Supermarkets are expanding their product assortment.

The conventional (or traditional) supermarkets are responding to these competitive pressures in various ways to improve their profits, productivity, and competitive position.[2] Many chains are cutting costs and stressing low prices by offering limited store services, no frills, and generic brands. Many conventional supermarkets are expanding in size and product assortment to become, in effect, superstores — an institution we shall discuss later in this section. These expanded stores often include pharmacies, beauty parlours, restaurants, and automated bank teller machines. Many supermarkets have installed automatic scanners at checkout stands and other technological innovations elsewhere in the store.

At the same time, some of the competitive responses of conventional supermarkets have involved promotional devices such as extra-value coupons, games, and longer store hours. These forms of nonprice competition do, of course, increase operating costs and often the selling prices, but unfortunately not always the profit.

DISCOUNT SUPERMARKETS

The inviting vacancy at the bottom of the supermarket pricing structure has generated discount selling in food and the rise of the *discount supermarket*. This discount food retailer operates with fewer services, lower gross margins, and lower prices than conventional supermarkets. Most food chains have converted some or all of their stores to discount operations.

The **warehouse store** (also called a **box store**) is a form of discount supermarket operation that has appeared in recent years. This type of food store offers a limited assortment of brands and commonly used products on a no-frills basis. There is, especially, a limited offering of fresh produce, fresh meats, frozen foods, and other perishable goods. The products are displayed on pallets or shelves in the original packing boxes whose tops or sides have been cut off. To further reduce costs, these stores typically use computerized price-scanning equipment and other labour-saving equipment.

CONVENIENCE STORES

Other innovative competitors of conventional supermarkets are the **convenience stores** (7-Eleven, Mac's, Beckers, Parsley's, and others). These stores, interestingly enough, have higher prices and a more limited product assortment and are smaller in size. But they do have longer shopping hours and more convenient locations, and they can provide the fill-in type of merchandise when other food stores are closed. In some ways they are a throwback to the corner grocery store of years past.

In recent years, increasing numbers of convenience stores have been adding gasoline, video rentals, and fast foods to their product assortments. In so doing, these stores provide one-stop shopping for customers. Thus they have become effective competition for gas stations and fast-food chains as well as for conventional supermarkets.

SUPERSTORES

The newest and possibly the toughest innovative competitor of the conventional supermarket is the *superstore* — also called a hypermarket or a super-supermarket. Unlike most modern retailing innovations, the superstore concept did not originate in North America; it was imported from France.

Supermarkets and the newer superstores are alike in that they both are low-cost, high-volume, limited-service operations. The key difference between the conventional supermarket and the superstore concepts lies in the breadth of consumer needs to be filled. The supermarket strives mainly to fulfil the consumers' needs for food, laundry, and home-cleaning products. The superstore is designed to provide those same products and to fill other *routine* purchasing needs as well. For example, superstores carry personal-care products, tobacco products, some apparel, low-priced housewares and hardware items, gasoline, consumable lawn and garden products, stationery and sewing supplies, some leisure-time products (books, records, hobby items), and household services (laundry, dry cleaning, shoe repair).

In an effort to boost profits, several supermarket chains are opening new superstores and are expanding existing units into superstore size and product assortment. In general, when compared with conventional supermarkets, we find that the superstore is about double in size, double in customer traffic, and triple in store sales volume. Gross margin and net profit in superstores are higher because they carry more high-margin items in their total product assortment.

Retailing concepts such as the superstore now quickly travel around the world.

Discount Retailing and the Discount House

In this section we really are talking about two things. One is a type of retailing *institution* (the discount house), and the other is a *method* of retail selling that is applicable to almost any type of store. Actually, there is nothing new about discount selling — the practice of selling below the list price. There is also nothing new about discount houses; they have existed in some form for many years. The modern **discount houses** are large stores that are open to the public. They advertise widely, and they carry a reasonably complete selection of wearing apparel and well-known brands of hard goods (appliances, home furnishings, sporting goods, jewellery). They consistently sell below list prices, and they offer a minimum of customer services. Through the years, two major factors led to the success of the modern-day discount houses. Those factors were (1) the traditional high retail markups on appliances and other products that typically are now discounted and (2) consumers' receptivity to a low-price, limited-service appeal.

RECENT DEVELOPMENTS IN DISCOUNT RETAILING

Discount selling has led to a revision of traditional retailing methods. Manufacturers have altered their channels of distribution to include discounting retailers. Small-scale retailers have been forced to drop discounted products or else to meet the discount-house price by offering fewer services and adopting more efficient marketing methods. Large-scale retailers, such as department stores, have realistically lowered their markups on discounted products and have even dropped some of these items.

The discount houses themselves are changing. Some are upgrading their image to that of ''promotional department stores,'' and some have opened stores in suburban shopping centres. In general, all discounters are trading up in products and services. Today, reasonably expensive high-fashion women's apparel is carried in a number of large discount department stores. Separate discount department stores have been established by ''conventional'' retailers such as Woolworth (Woolco), Kresge (K-Mart), and the Hudson's Bay Company (Zellers).

Discount retailers' risks and operating costs do increase, of course, as they add more expensive merchandise, move into fancier buildings and locations, and add more services.

Discount retailing continues to change and continues to be popular.

CATALOGUE SHOWROOMS

The **catalogue showroom** is a form of discount retailing that has expanded considerably in recent years. The showroom features attractive displays of all the merchandise carried in the company's catalogue. Customers can examine the products at their leisure. They place orders by filling out order forms and presenting the forms at a desk. Orders are filled immediately from inventory stock in the store's warehouse area. A limited number of sales people are available to help customers with products such as photographic equipment, television sets, and jewellery. Catalogue showrooms advertise extensively and use their low prices on nationally branded products as their primary selling appeal. In Canada, the undisputed leader in the catalogue showroom business is Consumers Distributing Limited. Although other retailers have tried to break into the market pioneered by Consumers Distributing, none has really succeeded. On the other hand, Consumers has solidified its position in the market and has expanded its product line to include fashion jewellery.

A new form of catalogue selling is represented by the shopping channel on cable television. This approach is in its early stages in Canada and it remains to be seen how it will evolve. In the U.S., the shopping channel has been quite successful so far.

Nonstore Retailing

There are four broad categories of retailing that for the most part occur away from the regular retail store. The four are in-home personal selling, telephone selling, mail-order selling, and automatic vending. Each one may be used by producers and also by retailers. Producers and retailers alike should be well aware of these nonstore retailing methods, because today they constitute a significant proportion of total retail trade.[3]

IN-HOME PERSONAL SELLING

Door-to-door selling is one of the oldest retailing methods in history. Sometimes it simply involves house-to-house canvassing, without any advance selection of prospects. More likely, however, there is an initial contact in a store or by phone, or a mailed-in coupon. "**Party-plan**" selling is also included in this category. A hostess invites some friends to a party. These guests understand that a sales person — say, for a cosmetics or a housewares company — will be making a sales presentation at the party. The sales representative has a larger prospective market under more favourable conditions than if these "guests" were approached individually on a house-to-house basis. And the guests get to do their shopping in a pleasant, friendly atmosphere.

In-home personal selling is used both by producers and by retailers. You probably know of some manufacturing firms that use this method — Mary Kay cosmetics, Tupperware food containers, and Amway household products, for example. Drapery and carpeting departments in department stores often have their sales people call directly on consumers at their homes.

In-home selling offers consumers the convenience of buying at home, but the

As old as time — yet in-home selling thrives as it adapts to the environment.

merchandise assortment is limited and there is no opportunity to shop and compare products. For the seller, in-home selling allows the most aggressive form of retail selling, as well as the chance to demonstrate a product in the customer's home.

On the negative side, in-home selling is the most expensive form of retailing. Sales-force commissions alone usually run as high as 40 to 50 percent of the retail price. Through the years, this method of selling has acquired a bad reputation because some sales people have been nuisances or even fraudulent. Also, managing a door-to-door sales force is a real problem because good sales people are extremely hard to find and the turnover rate is very high.

File 13-4

The Continuous Electronic Catalogue

One of the most important developments in home shopping in recent years has been the introduction of television shopping through cable television. The Canadian Home Shopping Network (CHSN) now reaches more than five million homes. Launched in early 1987, CHSN is licensed by the Canadian Radio-television and Telecommunications Commission to broadcast sales messages using still shots and voice-overs only. The 24-hour continuous commercial sells all manner of merchandise from sporting goods, to jewellery, to cut-glass ashtrays, to floral porcelain centre-pieces. Viewers call a toll-free telephone number to order items and have them charged to their credit card accounts.

By October 1987, CHSN had attracted more than 150,000 members to its Canadian Home Shopping Club. Some industry analysts predict that teleshopping could become a $60 million industry in Canada within a few years. The industry is not without its detractors, however. Some criticize its lack of style; others liken it to direct mail. Andrew Forsyth of CHSN feels the average CHSN shopper is female, aged 35 to 55, with above-average income. Forsyth says, ''They buy from us because they perceive value and because shopping can be a pain. We're not really competing with retailers. We're competing with catalogues, if anything.''

Source: Adapted from John Lownsborough, ''Settle Back, Put Your Feet Up, Turn the Lights Down Low and Get Ready to. . . . SHOP,'' *Canadian Business*, January 1988, p. 61.

TELEPHONE SELLING (TELEMARKETING)

Shopping by telephone is a long-existing method of consumer and industrial buying. And selling by telephone has been around a long time as a method of nonstore, in-home retailing. Yet today it is being used more widely than ever. This is partly because consumers are putting higher values on time saving and convenience in shopping. With so many women now in the outside labour force, traditional consumer shopping patterns are changing. At the same time, sellers are finding that telephone selling — or ''telemarketing,'' as they like to call it — is a productive yet low-cost method of selling.[4]

During the 1990s, however, the real growth in this type of in-home buying and selling is expected to involve sophisticated systems of computer- and television-assisted shopping. This ''teleshopping'' provides the consumer with a two-way communication channel between home and store and removes it from the catalogue selling category.[5]

MAIL-ORDER SELLING

In addition to ordering merchandise from the traditional catalogue, mail-order buying also includes any ordering by mail from an ad or from a direct-mail appeal. Originally designed primarily to reach rural markets, mail-order retailing today is appealing with success to urban buyers. Some of the mail-order houses (such as Sears) are *general merchandise* houses that offer an exceptionally wide variety of product lines. Other mail-order institutions might be termed *specialty* houses in that they limit the number of lines they carry — books, records, garden supplies, or food, for example.

Mail-order retailing enjoys some competitive advantages. Operating costs and prices usually are lower than for in-store retailing. A wide variety of merchandise is offered by general merchandise houses. Also, the consumer can shop at leisure from the catalogue and then place an order without the inconvenience of going to a store.

On the other hand, customers must place their orders without actually seeing the merchandise (unless the items are displayed at catalogue stores). This disadvantage is counteracted to some extent by liberal return privileges, guarantees, and excellent catalogue presentations. Mail-order houses have little flexibility. Catalogues are costly and must be prepared long before they are issued. Price changes and new merchandise offerings can be announced only by issuing supplementary catalogues, which are a weak selling tool.[6]

AUTOMATIC VENDING

Today an amazingly wide variety of products are sold through coin-operated machines that automatically sell merchandise (or services) without the presence of a sales clerk. Statistics Canada reported that, in 1985, 149,000 vending machines across Canada accounted for sales of $367 million. The bulk of this volume comes from cigarettes, soft drinks, candy, and hot beverages. Such products and others sold through vending machines typically have low unit value and low markups, so they are relatively expensive to sell through stores.

Vending machines can expand a firm's market by reaching customers where and when it is not feasible for stores to do so. In addition, many stores use vending machines as a complementary form of retailing. Another major expanding market for automatic vending is in-plant feeding, that is, the provision of meals for employees of factories and offices.

The outlook for this "robot retailing" is promising, but automatic vending still faces major problems. Operating costs are high, and there is a continual need for machine repair. The prices of automatically vended products are frequently higher than store prices for the same products. Products that can be sold successfully by machine must be well-known, presold brands with a high rate of turnover. They must be reasonably low in unit value, small and uniform in size and weight, and generally of a convenience goods nature. Only a limited amount of processing can be accomplished at the vending machine.

Convenient and lots of variety — Sears is Canada's largest general merchandise catalogue marketer.

Sometimes these are the only "stores" that are open.

THE FUTURE IN RETAILING

Looking to the 1990s, retailing management faces unequalled challenges. Population increases and economic growth have slowed down considerably. Competition is particularly fierce and consumers are more demanding. Computer technology is affecting many aspects of consumer and retailer behaviour. Consumerism and government restrictions affecting retailing are not likely to subside. These environmental forces are shaping several broad, significant trends in retailing.[7]

One of these trends is toward more professional management. Traditionally, the presidents of retail organizations came up through the merchandising ranks and were "good merchants." Today's economic and competitive conditions call for executives with a more rounded managerial capability, along with the traditional merchandising skills. Companies are especially stressing profit performance measures (return on investment, for example) and other internal financial controls. Prior to the mid-1980s, strategic planning generally had not been adopted by retailing executives. However, now there seems to be a growing awareness of the value of this management tool.

Out of dangerously low profit margins is also coming an intensified drive for **increased productivity** in retailing. To this end, virtually all kinds of consumer products are being sold, at least to some extent, on a self-service basis. This permits retailers to reduce their salary and wage cost, which typically is their largest single operating expense. Automated materials-handling systems are helping to cut physical distribution expenses. Computers are making retailers' information systems — for accounting, inventory control, and marketing research — more effective. In fact, better information systems are leading to improved information management in all phases of operations in many retailing organizations.

Another trend is the continuing move toward **scrambled merchandising**, which results in more intense competition among traditionally different types of stores. That is, in the constant search for higher-margin items, one type of store will add products that traditionally were handled by other types of outlets. This forces wholesalers and manufacturers to change their channel systems and retailers to adjust their marketing programs to meet the challenge of scrambled merchandising.

An interesting **polarity in store size and merchandise assortment** is developing in retailing. At one pole are the huge mass-merchandising operations of discount stores and department stores, with their tremendously wide variety of products. At the other pole is the small specialty shop — the boutique type of store. As retailers more carefully identify and segment their markets, these specialty stores are increasing in numbers and importance.

File 13-5

Marketing at Work

Consumer Convenience — Every Day

One of the most controversial aspects of retailing in many cities and towns in Canada revolves around the issue of Sunday shopping. Many retailers are already permitted to open on Sundays. These include gasoline retailers, drug stores, small food stores, and retailers who serve a tourist trade. Large department stores and food retailers in some provinces are also permitted to do business on Sundays, while in other jurisdictions there have been battles in and out of court to try to resolve the thorny issue. Those who advocate shopping on Sundays argue that consumers want the convenience of being able to shop seven days a week. Critics oppose this position on religious grounds or on the basis that retail employees need at least one day a week to spend with their families. There is some question of whether total retail sales would be any higher if retailers operated seven days a week, and whether retailers would have to increase prices slightly in order to cover increased costs. We can expect to see both provinces and municipalities wrestling with this issue for several years to come.

We can anticipate a considerable increase in nonstore retailing in the coming years. Mail-order selling and telephone selling are expected to expand much faster than in-store selling. The real potential on the horizon for nonstore retailing is in the area of computer-based ordering systems coupled with television.

Changing life-styles — especially among women, who, incidentally, still do most of the shopping — are a major factor stimulating the growth in nonstore retailing. Close to 60 percent of all women are employed outside the home and have little time to shop. So the timesaving convenience and the product information provided by nonstore retailing are attractive to this growing market segment.

Through the years, many of the evolutionary changes in retailing have followed a cyclical pattern called the **wheel of retailing**. As M.P. McNair has succinctly explained it:[8] ''The cycle frequently begins with the bold new concept, the innovation. The innovator has an idea for a new kind of distributive enterprise. At the outset he is ridiculed, condemned as 'illegitimate.' Bankers and investors are leery of him. But he attracts the public on the basis of a price appeal made possible by the low operating costs inherent in his innovation. As he goes along he trades up, improves the quality of his merchandise, improves the appearance and standing of his store, attains greater responsibility. Then, if he is successful, comes the period of growth, the period when he is taking business away from the established distribution channels that have clung to the old methods. Repeatedly something like this has happened in distribution. . . .

''The maturity phase soon tends to be followed by top-heaviness, too great conservatism, a decline in the rate of return on investment, and eventual vulnerability. Vulnerability to what? Vulnerability to the next revolution of the wheel, to the next fellow who has the bright idea and who starts his business on a low-cost basis, slipping in under the umbrella that the old-line institutions have hoisted.''

Several instances of this familiar cycle can be observed in the past 100 years. First the department stores supplanted small retailers in the cities during the late 1800s and early 1900s. In the 1920s, mail-order houses hit their peak. In that same decade the chain stores grew at the expense of independents, particularly in the grocery store field. In the 1930s, the independents retaliated with supermarkets, which proved so successful that the chain stores copied the method. In the 1950s, the discount houses — young innovators — placed tremendous pressure on department stores, which had become staid, mature institutions. By the early 1960s, the discount houses had passed the youthful stage. In the 1970s, we observed substantial growth in warehouse retailing (catalogue showrooms, furniture warehouse showrooms) and the spread of supermarket-type retailing. In the 1980s we have seen the expansion of superstores and discount retailing, while conventional supermarkets are changing or disappearing. Now we wait to see what will be the innovation of the 1990s — they will almost certainly involve more in-home and automated retailing. Established retailers must be alert to meet the challenge with innovations of their own. Truly, a retailer must be willing to innovate, for the alternative is to die.

SUMMARY

Middlemen balance producers' outputs and consumers' wants through the activities of concentration, equalization, and dispersion. They aid considerably in creating time, place, and possession utilities. Truly, one may eliminate middlemen, but not their functions. Middlemen play a significant role in our social and economic system.

Producers and wholesalers of consumer products must understand the retail market before they can intelligently develop distribution strategies. Retailing is selling to people who are buying for personal, nonbusiness reasons. It is easy to get into retailing, but the mortality rate among retail stores is very high. The national average cost of retailing is 25 to 30 percent of the retail selling price. Costs vary considerably, however, among the different types of retailers, and profits (as a percentage of sales) generally are very low. Retailers tend to locate where the market is, mainly in metropolitan areas. In such areas, there are several types of shopping districts such as planned suburban shopping centres and planned urban shopping malls.

We have classified retailers in four ways. First we looked at the competitive positions of large and small retailers. In the second classification (products carried), we examine the positions of department stores and limited-line stores. The third classification (type of ownership) provided an opportunity to discuss corporate chain stores and independents — especially the associations formed by small independents to compete with the large chains. Franchising in its various forms can also be attractive to independent retailers. In the fourth classification (method of operation), we discussed supermarket retailing, discount selling, and the major types of nonstore retailers.

It is obvious that retailing institutions will continue to change in the future (perhaps at an increasing rate). Retailers' success will depend to a great extent upon their ability to adapt to such change.

NOTES

[1] For an overview of the fast food franchising business in Canada, the reader is referred to Jean-Paul Caron, "Profits to Go," *Canadian Banker*, vol. 95, no. 2, March-April 1988, pp. 11–23.

[2] See Daniel Stoffman, "The Shopping-Cart Sweepstakes," *Canadian Business*, April 1985, p. 40; and Ben Fiber, "Supermarkets Woo Impulse Buyers," *The Globe and Mail Report on Business*, January 10, 1987, p. 1.

[3] In the business world, in-home selling is called *direct selling*, while telephone selling and mail-order selling are called *direct marketing* — an unfortunately confusing use of these terms.

[4] See Kenneth C. Schneider, "Telemarketing as a Promotional Tool — Its Effects and Side Effects," *Journal of Consumer Marketing*, Winter 1985, pp. 29–39; and Joel Dreyfuss, "Reach Out and Sell Something," *Fortune*, Nov. 26, 1984, p. 127.

[5] See George P. Moschis, Jac L. Goldstucker, and Thomas J. Stanley, "At-Home Shopping: Will Consumers Let Their Computers Do the Walking?" *Business Horizons*, March-April 1985, pp. 22–29.

[6] See James R. Lumpkin and Jon M. Hawes, "Retailing without Stores: An Examination of Catalog Shoppers," *Journal of Business Research*, April 1985, pp. 139–151; "Marketing by Mailbox (It's a Revolution, Folks)," a special report on direct-mail selling, *Sales & Marketing Management*, Jan. 14, 1985, pp. 39ff.

[7] For further discussion of the environmental changes that will affect retailing in the future, see Jagdish N. Sheth, "Emerging Trends for the Retailing Industry," *Journal of Retailing*, Fall 1983, pp. 6–18.

For an in-depth look into the future, see Eleanor G. May, C. William Ress, and Walter J. Salmon, *Future Trends in Retailing*, Marketing Science Institute, Cambridge, Mass., report no. 85–102, 1985.

[8] M.P. McNair, "Significant Trends and Developments in the Postwar Period," in A.B. Smith (ed.), *Competitive Distribution in a Free, High-Level Economy and Its Implications for the University*, The University of Pittsburgh Press, Pittsburgh, 1958, pp. 17–18.

KEY TERMS AND CONCEPTS

Middleman 358
Merchant and agent middleman 358
Channel of distribution 358
Concentration, equalization, and dispersion of middlemen 360
Time and place utilities 360
Retailing 361
Retail sale 361
Retailer 361
Cost of retailing 363
Downtown shopping district 363
Planned suburban shopping centre 365
Department store 370
Limited-line store 371
Scrambled merchandising 371
Specialty store 371

Corporate chain store 371
Voluntary chain (wholesaler-sponsored) 374
Retailer cooperative chain 374
Producer-sponsored franchise system 375
Entrepreneurship franchising 375
Supermarket retailing 377
Discount retailing 378
Superstores 379
Nonstore retailing: 381
  In-home personal selling 381
  Telephone selling (telemarketing) 382
  Mail-order selling 383
  Automatic vending 383
Wheel-of-retailing concept 385

QUESTIONS AND PROBLEMS

1. "You can eliminate middlemen, but you cannot eliminate their functions." Discuss.

2. Which of the following institutions are middlemen? Explain.
   a. Avon sales person.
   b. Electrical wholesaler.
   c. Real estate broker.
   d. Railroad.
   e. Auctioneer.
   f. Advertising agency.
   g. Grocery store.
   h. Stockbroker.
   i. Bank.
   j. Radio station.

3. Explain how time and place utility may be created in the marketing of the

following products. What business institutions might be involved in creating these utilities?
   a. Sewing machines.
   b. Fresh peaches.
   c. Hydraulic grease racks used in garages and service stations.

4. Explain the terms *retailing, a retail sale*, and *a retailer* in light of the following situations:
   a. Avon cosmetics sales person selling door to door.
   b. Farmer selling product door to door.
   c. Farmer selling product at a roadside stand.
   d. Sporting goods store selling uniforms to a professional baseball team.

5. How do you account for the wide differences in operating expenses among the various types of retail stores shown in Table 13-1?

6. What is the relationship between the growth and successful development of planned suburban shopping centres and the material you studied in Chapters 4 to 7 regarding the consumer?

7. ''Retailing is typically small-scale business.'' ''There is a high degree of concentration in retailing today; the giants control the field.'' Reconcile these two statements, using facts and figures when appropriate.

8. Of the criteria given in this chapter for evaluating the competitive positions of large-scale and small-scale retailers, which show small stores to be in a stronger position than large-scale retailers? In light of your finding, how do you account for the numerical preponderance of small retailers?

9. What courses of action might small retailers follow to improve their competitive position?

10. What can department stores do to offset their competitive disadvantages?

11. In what ways does a corporate chain (A&P, Loblaws or Eaton's) differ from a voluntary chain such as IGA?

12. With all the advantages attributed to voluntary associations of independents, why do you suppose some retailers are still unaffiliated?

13. ''The only significant competitive advantage that chains have over independents is greater buying power. If buying power can be equalized through antichain legislation or by having the independents join some voluntary association, then independents can compete equally with the chains.'' Discuss.

14. ''The supermarket, with its operating expense ratio of 20 percent, is the most efficient institution in retailing today.'' Do you agree? In what ways might supermarkets reduce their operating expenses?

15. Name some discount houses in your community or in a nearby large city. Is there a distinction between ''discount selling'' and a ''discount house''?

16. ''House-to-house selling is the most efficient form of retail selling because it eliminates wholesalers and retail stores.'' Discuss.

17. ''The factors that accounted for the early growth of mail-order retailing no longer exist, so we may expect a substantial decline in this form of selling.'' Discuss.

18. The ease of entry into retailing undoubtedly contributes to the high mortality rate among retailers, with the resultant economic waste. Should entry into retailing be restricted? If so, how could this be done?

19. What recommendations do you have for reducing the costs of retailing?

CHAPTER 14

WHOLESALING: MARKETS AND INSTITUTIONS

The wholesaling middlemen are the "other" middlemen, the ones that consumers rarely see. After studying this chapter, you should understand:

- The nature and importance of wholesaling:
    a. The meaning of the term *wholesaling*.
    b. The economic justification of wholesaling.
    c. What wholesalers are and how they differ from wholesaling middlemen.
- The major classes of wholesaling middlemen.
- The costs and profits in wholesaling.
- Full-service merchant wholesalers and the services they render.
- The functions of rack jobbers and limited-service wholesalers.
- The several types of agent wholesaling middlemen and the services they provide.

Have you ever wondered how all the merchandise that you see in retail stores actually gets there? In the case of the more than 1,000 Home Hardware stores throughout Canada, thousands of products flow through a modern high-tech warehouse and distribution system.

Home Hardware is owned by its retailers and all of the purchasing for the chain is done through head office in St. Jacob's, Ontario. Almost 400 Home Hardware retailers in western Canada are served by a 450,000-square foot distribution facility in Wetaskiwin, Alberta, with its computerized purchasing, ordering, and shipping system.

A store owner uses an electronic order entry system to identify the items to be ordered each week from the store's inventory system. The order is sent electronically over telephone lines to the central warehouse and computer in St. Jacob's at any time of the day or night. If the order is from a store in the western region, it is transferred to the computer at the regional warehouse in Wetaskiwin. That computer generates a hard copy of the order, which is used by warehouse employees to put the order together.

Each store is served weekly and the shipping department uses colour-coded labels to identify individual orders. More than 300,000 pounds of merchandise a day are shipped from the Wetaskiwin facility. The company uses 25 trucks to make deliveries throughout western Canada.

Source: Adapted from Andy Zielinski, "Hardware Distribution Centre Runs Smoothly," *Materials Management and Distribution*, March 1986, pp. 20-23.

"Let's eliminate the middleman" and "The middleman makes all the profit" are cries that have been echoed by consumers, business people, and legislators through the years. These complaints are most often focussed on the wholesaling segment of the distribution structure. Historically, the wholesaler has been a truly powerful figure in North American marketing. During the past 25 to 50 years, however, many manufacturers and retailers have made successful attempts to eliminate the wholesaler from their trade channels. Yet wholesaling middlemen continue to be important, and in many cases dominant, in the distribution system for many products.

NATURE AND IMPORTANCE OF WHOLESALING

Wholesaling Broadly Defined

Wholesaling or **wholesale trade** includes the sale, and all activities directly related to the sale, of products or services to those who are buying for business use. Thus, *broadly viewed*, sales made by one manufacturer to another are wholesale transactions, and the selling manufacturer is engaged in wholesaling. A retail variety store is engaged in wholesaling when it sells pencils or envelopes to a restaurant. That is, wholesaling includes sales by any firm to any customer except to an ultimate consumer who is buying for personal, nonbusiness use. Thus, in a broad sense, all sales are either wholesale sales or retail sales. The only real criterion for distinguishing between the two is the purchaser's intended use of the product or service.

The Narrower Definition of Wholesaling

While this general definition of wholesaling is accurate, it is too broad to be useful in (1) understanding the role of wholesaling middlemen and (2) establishing channels of distribution. For analytical convenience, the definition must be limited. We are concerned here with companies that are engaged *primarily* in wholesaling. Therefore, we shall ignore retailers who occasionally make a wholesale sale. We shall also exclude the sales of manufacturers and farmers, because they are primarily engaged in production (creating form utility), and not in wholesaling.

Wholesalers and Wholesaling Middlemen

A **wholesaling middleman** is a firm engaged primarily in wholesaling. The more restrictive term **wholesaler** applies only to *merchant* middlemen engaged in wholesaling activities. (Recall that merchant middlemen are those who take title to the goods they handle.) *Wholesaling middlemen* thus is the all-inclusive term, covering both wholesalers and other wholesaling middlemen, such as agents and brokers, that do not take title to the merchandise. Thus a food broker or a manufacturer's agent is not a wholesaler but, rather, a wholesaling middleman.

Sometimes one hears the terms *jobber* and *distributor*. Although usage varies from trade to trade, in this book these terms are considered synonymous with *wholesaler*. Figure 14-1 shows these distinctions.

Economic Justification of Wholesaling

Most manufacturing companies in Canada are small and specialized. They don't have the capital needed to maintain a sales force large enough to contact the many small retailers who are their customers. Even for manufacturers that have sufficient capital, output is too small to justify the necessary sales force. On the other hand, most retailers buy in small quantities and have only a limited knowledge of the market and sources of supply. Thus there is a gap between the retailer (buyer) and the producer (seller). The wholesaler can fill this gap by pooling the orders of many retailers and so furnish a market for the small manufacturer. At the same time, the wholesaler is performing a buying service for small retailers.

From a macromarketing point of view, wholesaling brings to the total distribution system the economies of skill, scale, and transactions. Wholesaling middlemen are marketing specialists. Their wholesaling *skills* are efficiently concentrated in a relatively few hands. This saves the duplication of effort that would occur if the

FIGURE 14-1

Wholesaling institutions.

How the general definition of wholesaling leads to our definition of wholesaling middlemen, wholesalers, and agents and brokers.

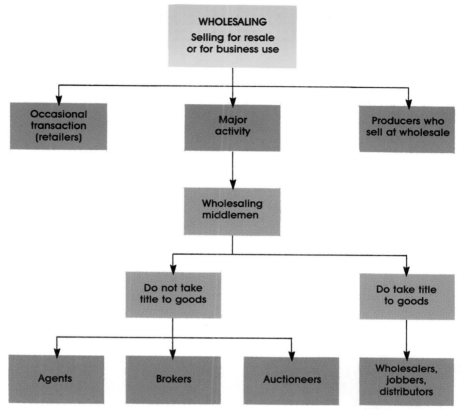

many producers had to perform the wholesaling functions themselves. Economies of *scale* result from the specialization of the wholesaling middlemen who perform functions that might otherwise require several small departments run by producing firms. Wholesalers typically can perform the wholesaling functions at an operating-expense percentage lower than most manufacturers can. *Transition economies* come into play when wholesaling middlemen are introduced between producers and their customers. Assume four manufacturers want to sell to six retailers. Without a wholesaling middleman, there are 24 transactions. With one wholesaler, the number of transactions is cut to 10. That is, four transactions occur when the producers all sell to the wholesaler and another six occur when the wholesaler sells to all the retailers (Fig. 14-2).

Size of the Wholesale Market

In 1984, there were more than 61,000 wholesaling establishments in Canada, with a total annual sales volume of about $213 billion. As was the case in retailing, the sales generated by wholesaling establishments have increased dramatically in recent years. Part of this increase is accounted for by increases in prices that have occurred during the past ten years or so, but even if sales were expressed in constant dollars, we would still see a substantial increase.

Classification of Wholesaling Middlemen

Any attempt to classify wholesaling middlemen in a meaningful way is a precarious project. It is easy to get lost in a maze of categories because, in real life, these

FIGURE 14-2
The economy of transactions in wholesaling.

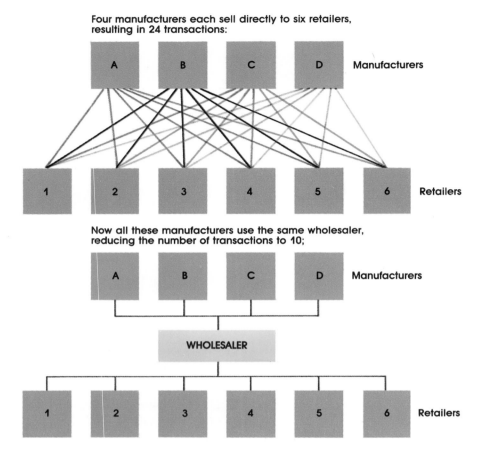

Four manufacturers each sell directly to six retailers, resulting in 24 transactions:

Manufacturers

Retailers

Now all these manufacturers use the same wholesaler, reducing the number of transactions to 10;

Manufacturers

WHOLESALER

Retailers

middlemen vary greatly in (1) the products they carry, (2) the markets they sell to, and (3) the methods of operation they use. To minimize the confusion, we will use the classification scheme shown in Fig. 14-3. There, all wholesaling middlemen are grouped into only four broad categories — wholesale merchants, manufacturers' sales branches and offices, agents and brokers, and primary products dealers. These four groups are the classifications used by Statistics Canada, which is the major source of quantitative data covering wholesaling institutions and markets. Later in this chapter we shall discuss merchant wholesalers, agents and brokers and primary products dealers in more detail.

WHOLESALE MERCHANTS

These are the firms we usually refer to as wholesalers, jobbers, or industrial distributors. They typically are independently owned, and they take title to the merchandise they handle. They form the largest single segment of wholesaling firms when measured either by sales or by number of establishments. Statistics Canada reports that wholesale merchants, along with manufacturers' sales branches and primary-product dealers discussed below, account for almost 85 percent of total wholesale trade.

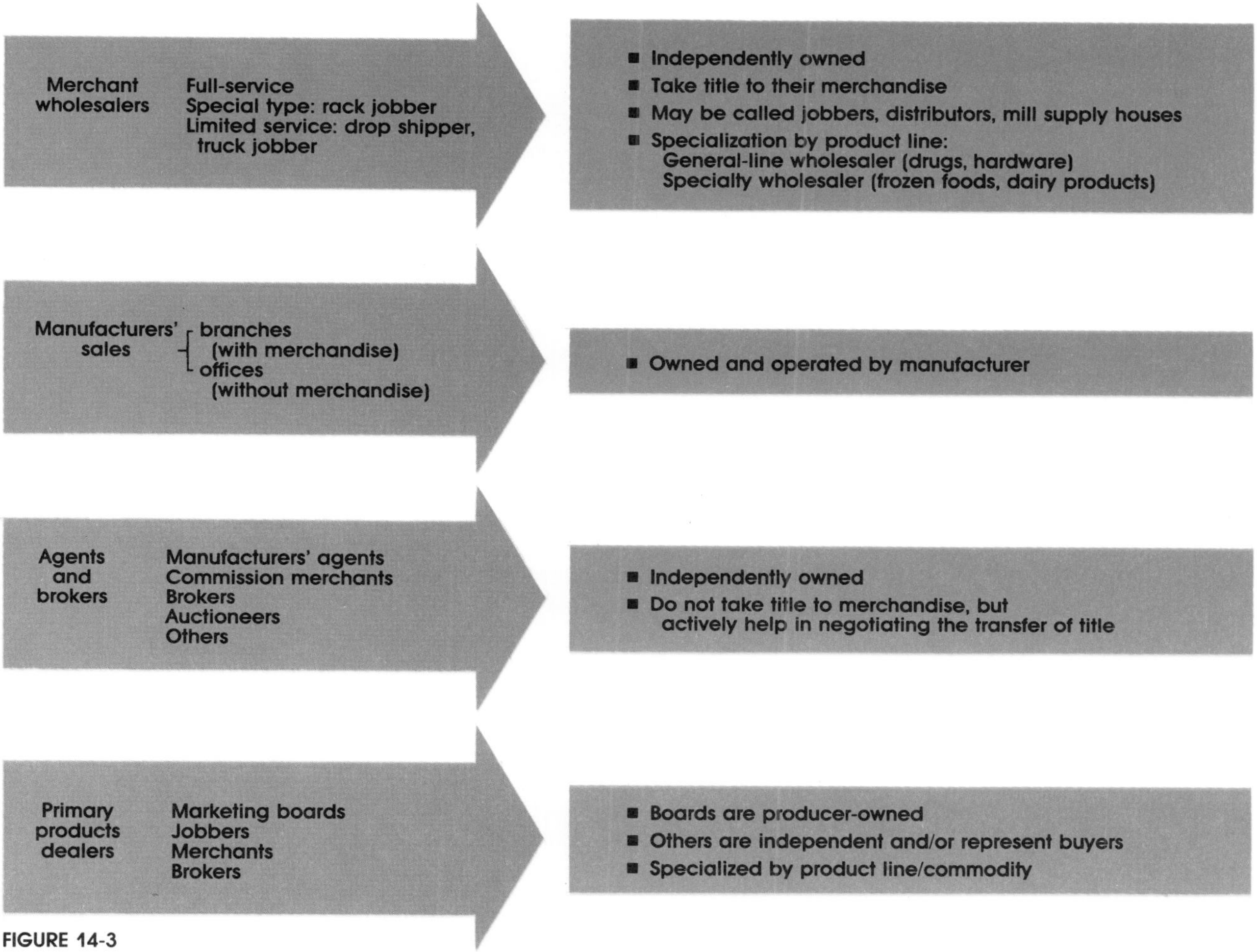

FIGURE 14-3
Types of wholesaling institutions.

TABLE 14-1   **WHOLESALE TRADE IN CANADA, 1984**

	Number of Establishments	Number of Locations	Sales Volume ($ millions)
Wholesale merchants	56,790	68,337	180,161.9
Agents and brokers	4,470	4,737	33,585.6
TOTAL	61,260	73,074	213,747.5

Source: Statistics Canada, *Market Research Handbook*, revised edition 1987-88, cat. no. 63-224, pp. 202-205; and *Wholesale Trade Statistics*, cat. no. 63-226, 1984. Reproduced with permission of the Minister of Supply and Services Canada.

MANUFACTURERS' SALES BRANCHES AND OFFICES

These establishments are owned and operated by manufacturers, but they are phys-ically separated from the manufacturing plants. The distinction between a sales branch and a sales office is that a branch carries merchandise stock and an office does not.

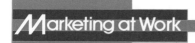

Wholesaling Goes Retailing

A recent development in Canadian distribution is the wholesale or warehouse club. These large bulk merchandisers are located in large urban areas such as Vancouver, Toronto, Edmonton, and Montreal, and sell in volume to retail customers and to small independent businesses, many of whom buy at attractive discounts to resell in their own stores. Costco Wholesale opened the first warehouse club in Burnaby, B.C., in 1985. It now has stores in Edmonton and Calgary. Steinberg opened its first Price wholesale club in Montreal in 1986 and is planning to expand in Quebec and Ontario. Titan Warehouse club is based in Toronto and is expanding from its first stores in Brampton and London.

The wholesale club stocks food and other merchandise and operates on thin margins and no-frills service. Consumers must be members and they buy in bulk at attractive discounts. About 25 percent of warehouse club sales are from food, 20 percent from appliances, and the rest from a wide range of products including sporting goods, automotive products, and toys. The clubs attract small convenience store operators, professionals, restaurant operators, and other small businesses who have no efficient route to buy supplies wholesale. Provided they can show a commercial licence, they buy at special wholesale prices and pay no sales tax. These business customers typically account for between 50 percent and 70 percent of sales. Warehouse clubs also appeal to consumer groups, such as credit unions and government employees.

AGENTS AND BROKERS

Agents and brokers do *not* take title to the merchandise they handle, but they do actively negotiate the purchase or sale of products for their principals. The main types of agent middlemen are manufacturers' agents, commission merchants (in the marketing of agricultural products), and brokers. As a group, agents and brokers represent less than 20 percent of total wholesale trade.

PRIMARY-PRODUCT DEALERS

These firms are principally engaged in buying for resale primary products such as grain, livestock, furs, fish, tobacco, fruit, and vegetables from the primary producers of these products. On occasion, they will act as agents of the producer. Cooperatives that market the primary products of their members are also included in this category.

Some other subcategories used in classifying the wholesaling business are reflected in Fig. 14-3. For example, wholesaling middlemen may be grouped by:

- *Ownership of products* — wholesale merchants versus agent middlemen.
- *Ownership of establishment* — manufacturers' sales branches versus independent merchants and agents.
- *Range of services offered* — full-service wholesalers versus limited-service firms.
- *Depth and breadth of the line carried* — general-line wholesalers (drugs, hardware) versus specialty firms (frozen foods, dairy products).

TABLE 14-2   TOTAL WHOLESALE AND RETAIL TRADE, 1971-1986

Year	Wholesale Trade[1]	Retail Trade
1971	$ 36,892.6	$ 31,390.1
1975	55,284.4	51,408.5
1976	61,176.1	57,166.9
1977	66,541.5	61,651.3
1978	77,231.7	68,859.2
1979	109,633.7*	76,992.5
1980	128,932.6*	84,026.6
1981	176,852.7	95,240.2
1982	170,061.0	97,638.5
1983	189,915.3	106,243.0
1984	213,747.5	116,079.9
1985	n/a	129,446.3
1986	n/a	140,009.3

[1] Wholesale figures for 1971 through 1978 are for the wholesale merchants' category only. This figure represents approximately 80 percent of total wholesale trade.

* Estimates

Source: Statistics Canada, *Market Research Handbook*, cat. no. 63-224; *Canadian Statistical Review*, cat. no. 11-003E; *Corporate Financial Statistics*, cat. no. 61-207; and *Wholesale Trade Statistics*, cat. no. 63-226 (various years). Reproduced with permission of Supply and Services Canada.

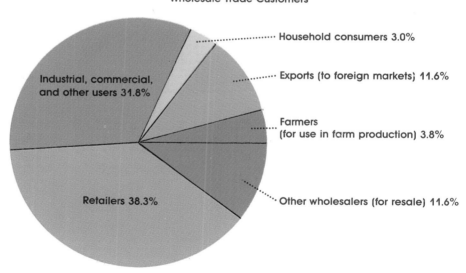

Wholesale Trade Customers

Industrial, commercial, and other users 31.8%

Household consumers 3.0%

Exports (to foreign markets) 11.6%

Farmers (for use in farm production) 3.8%

Other wholesalers (for resale) 11.6%

Retailers 38.3%

Customers of Wholesaling Middlemen

One might expect that total retail sales would be considerably higher than total wholesale trade, because the retail price of a given product is higher than the wholesale price. Also, many products sold at retail never pass through a wholesaler's establishment and so are excluded from total wholesale sales.

Total sales figures belie this particular line of reasoning (see Table 14-2). In each year, the volume of wholesale trade is considerably higher than total retail sales.

The explanation for this seemingly upside-down situation may be found in an analysis of the customers of wholesaling middlemen (Table 14-3).

Most wholesale merchants' sales are made to customers other than retailers. That is, large quantities of industrial products are now sold through wholesale merchants. Moreover, sales by the other types of wholesaling middlemen show this same pattern. Thus, overall, sales to retailers account for less than one-half of total sales by wholesale merchants.

Another trend that has become obvious in recent years is the increase in the percentage of consumer goods sold directly to retailers by manufacturers. Yet, in spite of this increased bypassing of the wholesaler, wholesaling is on the increase, an indication of the usefulness of wholesaling to the business world.

TABLE 14-3   DISTRIBUTION OF SALES OF WHOLESALE MERCHANTS, 1985

Type of Customer	Percentage of Total Wholesale Trade
Retailers (for resale)	38.3
Industrial, commercial and other users	31.7
Exports (to foreign markets)	11.6
Other wholesalers (for resale)	11.6
Farmers (for use in farm production)	3.8
Household consumers	3.0
Total	100.0

Source: Statistics Canada, unpublished data. Reproduced with permission of Supply and Services Canada.

Operating Expenses and Profits of Wholesaling Middlemen

The average total operating expenses for all wholesaling middlemen combined has been estimated at about 17 percent of *wholesale* sales. It has also been estimated that operating expenses of retailers average about 25 percent of *retail* sales (omitting bars and restaurants, which do some processing of products) (see Table 14-4). Therefore, on a broad average, the expenses of wholesaling middlemen take less than 8 percent of the consumer's dollar.

TABLE 14-4   REVENUE AND EXPENSES: WHOLESALE AND RETAIL TRADE, 1984

	Wholesale Trade		Retail Trade	
	$ millions	%	$ millions	%
Income	138,674.7	100.0	124,345.9	100.0
Expenses				
Materials	110,739.2	79.9	89,475.9	71.9
Operating	24,973.9	18.0	30,416.2	24.5
Total	135,713.1	97.9	119,892.1	96.4
Net profit before taxes	3,400.1	2.5	4,828.3	3.9
Net profit after taxes	2,389.3	1.7	4,140.8	3.3

Source: Statistics Canada, *Corporation Financial Statistics, 1984*, cat. no. 61-207. Reproduced with permission of the Minister of Supply and Services Canada.

EXPENSES BY TYPE OF OPERATION

Table 14-5 shows operating expenses as a percentage of net sales for selected categories of wholesaling middlemen. Wholesalers of industrial equipment have the highest average operating expenses at 31.9 percent. Faster-moving, low-margin products such as food and livestock produce much lower levels of operating expenses as a percentage of total income.

TABLE 14-5   **OPERATING EXPENSES AND NET PROFIT AFTER TAXES AS PERCENTAGE OF TOTAL INCOME FOR CATEGORIES OF WHOLESALERS, 1984**

Type of Operation	Operating Expenses as Percentage of Total Income	Net Profit After Taxes as Percentage of Total Income
Industrial equipment	31.9%	2.1%
Scrap and waste dealers	31.3	2.3
Furniture and furnishings	26.5	2.2
Electrical machinery	25.3	2.2
Drug and toilet preparations	23.1	1.9
Motor vehicles and parts	17.7	2.7
Hardware, plumbing and heating	18.7	1.2
Lumber and building products	18.2	1.6
Apparel and drygoods	19.0	2.3
Farm machinery	16.6	1.4
Metal products	13.8	1.7
Livestock	13.7	0.9
Food	12.7	0.9
Petroleum products	10.2	1.1
Paper	15.6	1.3
ALL WHOLESALERS	18.0	1.7

Source: Statistics Canada, *Corporation Financial Statistics, 1984*, cat. no. 61-207. Reproduced with permission of the Minister of Supply and Services Canada.

Care should be exercised when interpreting these figures. For instance, we should not conclude that wholesalers of petroleum products, paper, and food are highly efficient because their operating expenses are low and that wholesalers of industrial equipment and electrical machinery are inefficient. The cost differentials are attributable to the differences in the nature of the products handled and to the nature of the services provided by the various wholesalers. Were more data available, we would likely find that agents and brokers have much lower levels of operating expenses than do wholesale merchants. Similarly, we generally find that manufacturers' sales branches and offices have lower operating expenses as a percentage of sales. Even when merchant wholesalers in given product lines (paper products, machinery) are compared with manufacturers' sales branches in the same line, the branch ordinarily shows a lower operating cost ratio. Careful analysis shows that the comparison is often ''loaded'' in favour of the manufacturers' branch operations. Branches and sales offices are located only in the markets offering the highest potential sales and profits. Thus the manufacturers' operations would get more sales per dollar of effort. Often, too, a branch is not allocated its full share of costs. Many indirect administrative expenses are charged in full to the home office, even though the branches and merchant wholesalers are not always comparable because of differences in services provided.

NET PROFITS

Net operating profit after taxes, expressed as a percentage of total income, is extremely modest for wholesaling middlemen and is considerably lower than that for retailing middlemen. Data collected by Statistics Canada from wholesalers in 1984 showed an average after-tax profit of only 1.7 percent. This compares with an average of 3.3 percent profit after taxes among retailers (see Table 14-4). The highest after-tax profits were reported by wholesalers of motor vehicles and parts. Several categories of wholesalers reported after-tax profits of less than 1.5 percent of total income. These included petroleum wholesalers and those engaged in the wholesaling of paper, food, and livestock products.

WHOLESALE MERCHANTS

As we indicated earlier, wholesale merchants are the wholesaling middlemen that take title to the products they handle, and they account for the largest segment of wholesale trade.

Full-Service Wholesalers

Full-service wholesalers are a vital link in many distribution channels.

Full-service (also called full-function) wholesalers are independent merchant middlemen who generally perform a full range of wholesaling functions. These are the firms that fit the layman's image or stereotype of wholesalers. They may be called simply "wholesalers," or they may be listed as "distributors," "mill supply houses," "industrial distributors," or "jobbers," depending upon the usage in their line of business. They may handle consumer and/or industrial products, and these goods may be manufactured or nonmanufactured, and imported or exported.

Wholesale merchants have accounted for well over one-half of total wholesale trade in Canada for many years. Thus, the full-service wholesalers have held their own in the competitive struggles within the distribution system. In fact, their market share has been relatively constant in the recent past, despite increasing competition from agents and brokers and from direct-selling manufacturers and their sales offices and branches. A presumption is that the wholesalers' existence is maintained by the services they provide both to their customers and to their suppliers (see Table 14-6).

This picture of stability in the full-service wholesaler's share of the market may be a bit misleading. It hides the volatility and shifting competitive positions within various industries. Wholesalers have increased their market share in some industries but have lost ground in other markets where they once dominated. Certainly the aggregate market-share figures are misleading in industries where wholesalers are, and always have been, used very little.

Special Types of Wholesale Merchants

Within the broad category of wholesale merchants, there are a few subclassifications worth observing because of the special nature of their operations. Their titles reflect either the specialized nature of their work or the limited range of wholesaling services that they offer. (Recall Fig. 14-3.)

TABLE 14-6   WHOLESALERS' SERVICES TO CUSTOMERS AND TO PRODUCER-SUPPLIERS

1. Buying: Act as purchasing agents for customers. Anticipate customers' needs and have good knowledge of market and sources of supply. Enable customers to deal with only a few sales people rather than with representatives of many producers.
2. *Selling*: Provide a sales force for producers to reach small retailers and industrial users, at a lower cost than producers would incur to reach these markets. Customers often know and trust their local wholesalers more than distant suppliers.
3. *Dividing, bulk breaking*: Wholesalers buy in carload and truckload lots and then resell in case lots or less, thus providing a saving and a service to customers and producers.
4. *Transportation*. Provide quick, frequent delivery to customers, thus reducing their risks and investment in inventory. Reduce producers' and customers' freight costs by buying in large quantities.
5. *Warehousing*: Provide a service to both customers and suppliers by reducing inventory risks and costs. Wholesalers can warehouse more efficiently than any single customer or producer can do.
6. *Financing*: Grant credit to customers, sometimes for extended periods of time, thus reducing their capital requirements. Producers usually would not offer comparable credit aid to small retailers. Wholesalers also aid producers by ordering well ahead of season and by paying bills on time.
7. *Risk bearing*: We already mentioned some of the ways wholesalers reduce risks for customers and producers. In addition, simply by taking title to products, wholesalers reduce a producer's risk. Losses due to spoilage or fashion obsolescence are then borne by wholesalers.
8. *Marketing information*. For their customers, wholesalers supply information regarding new products, competitors' activities, special sales by producers, etc.
9. *Management services and advice*: By offering managerial services and advice, especially to retailer customers, wholesalers have significantly strengthened their own position in the market. The existence of full-service wholesalers is dependent upon the economic health and well-being of small retailers. Therefore, by helping the retailers, the wholesalers really help themselves.

RACK JOBBERS

These firms are wholesale merchants that began to appear about 40 years ago, primarily to supply grocery supermarkets with nonfood items. Since then, rack jobbers have expanded to serve drugstores, hardware stores, and other stores that have instituted the self-service method of retailing. The many general-line wholesalers carrying these nonfood lines could not easily sell to supermarkets for at least three reasons. First, the wholesalers' regular customers, such as drugstore or hardware stores, would complain loudly and probably withdraw their business. Second, too many different wholesalers would have to call on the supermarket to fill all the nonfood lines, and the retailer would object to seeing so many wholesalers. Third, a single supermarket ordinarily orders too small a quantity in any one nonfood line to make it profitable for a wholesaler to service that line.

One rack jobber (or a very few) can furnish all the nonfood items in a supermarket. Rack jobbers furnish the racks or shelves upon which to display the merchandise, and they stock only the fastest-moving brands on these racks. They are responsible for maintaining full stocked racks, building attractive displays, and price-marking the merchandise. In essence, the retailers merely furnish floor or shelf space and then collect the money as the customers go through the checkout stands.

LIMITED-FUNCTION WHOLESALERS

A small group of wholesale merchants that have received attention in marketing literature through the years — possibly more attention than their numerical importance merits — are the limited-function wholesalers. These are merchant middlemen who do not perform all the usual wholesaling functions. The activities of most of these wholesalers are concentrated in a few product lines. The major types of limited-function wholesalers are truck jobbers, drop shippers, and retailer cooperative warehouses. The retailer cooperative warehouse was discussed in the preceding chapter.

Truck distributors or jobbers (sometimes still called "wagon jobbers" in memory of the days when they used a horse and wagon) are specialty wholesalers, chiefly in the food field. Each jobber carries a nationally advertised brand of fast-moving and perishable or semiperishable goods, such as candies, dairy products, potato chips, and tobacco products. The unique feature of their method of operation is that they sell and deliver merchandising during their calls. Their competitive advantage lies in their ability to furnish fresh products so frequently that retailers can buy perishable goods in small amounts to minimize the risk of loss. The major limitation of truck jobbers is their high operating cost ratio. This is caused primarily by the small order size and the inefficient use of delivery equipment. A truck is an expensive warehouse.

Drop shippers, sometimes called "desk jobbers," get their name from the fact that the merchandise they sell is delivered from the manufacturer to the customer and is called a "drop shipment." Drop shippers take title to the products but do not physically handle them. They operate almost entirely in coal and coke, lumber, and building materials. These products are typically sold in carload quantities, and freight is high in comparison with their unit value. Thus, it is desirable to minimize the physical handling of the product.

Truck jobbers frequently are used in the distribution channels for perishables.

AGENT WHOLESALING MIDDLEMEN

Agents and brokers (agent middlemen) are distinguished from wholesale merchants in two important respects: Agent middlemen do *not* take title to the merchandise, and they typically perform fewer services for their clients and principals. (See Table 14-7.) For these reasons, the operating expenses for agents and brokers average only 3 to 4 percent of net sales, compared with 17 percent for wholesale merchants. On the basis of sales volume, the major types of agent middlemen are manufacturers' agents, brokers, and commission merchants. Other types include auction companies, selling agents, import agents, and export agents.

The relative importance of agents and brokers in wholesale trade has declined over the past 40 years. Although the total number of agents and brokers has not changed appreciably, their market share has dropped to approximately 15 percent. In the wholesaling of agricultural products, agent middlemen are being replaced by wholesale merchants, or by direct sales to retailers and food processors. In the marketing of manufactured goods, agent middlemen are being supplanted by manufacturers' sales branches and offices. As manufacturers' markets grow in sales

TABLE 14-7   SERVICES PROVIDED BY AGENT WHOLESALING MIDDLEMEN

Services	Manufacturers' agents	Selling agents	Brokers	Commission merchants
Provides buying services	Yes	Yes	Some	Yes
Provides selling services	Yes	Yes	Yes	Yes
Carries inventory stocks	Sometimes	No	No	Yes
Delivers the products	Sometimes	No	No	Yes
Provides market information	Yes	Yes	Yes	Yes
Sets prices and terms of sale	No	Yes	No	No
Grants credit to customers	No	Sometimes	No	Sometimes
Reduces producers' credit risks	No	Yes	No	No
Sells producers' full line	Sometimes	Yes	Sometimes	No
Has continuing relationship with producer throughout year	Yes	Yes	No	No
Manufacturer uses own sales force along with agents	Sometimes	No	No	No
Manufacturer uses same agent for entire market	No	Yes	No	No

potential, it becomes more effective for them to establish their own outlets and sales force in these markets.

Manufacturers' Agents   Manufacturers' agents (frequently called *manufacturers' representatives*) are agents commissioned to sell part or all of a producer's products in particular territories. The agents are independent and are in no way employees of the manufacturers. They have little or no control over the prices and terms of sale; these are established by the manufacturer. Because a manufacturers' agent sells in a limited territory, say a province or group of provinces, each producer typically uses several agents. Unlike brokers, manufacturers' agents have continuing, year-round relationships with their principals. Each agent usually represents several noncompeting manufacturers of related products. The agent can pool into one profitable sale the small orders that otherwise would go to several individual manufacturers.

Manufacturers' agents are used extensively in the distribution of many types of consumer and industrial products. the main service offered to manufacturers by these agent middlemen is selling. They seek out and serve markets that manufacturers cannot profitably reach. Furthermore, a manufacturers' agent does not carry nearly so many lines as a full-service wholesaler. Consequently, the agent can offer a higher-calibre, more aggressive selling service. Operating expenses depend upon the product sold and whether the merchandise is stocked. Some representatives operate on a commission as low as 2 percent, while others charge as much as 20 percent. These commissions cover operating expenses and net profit. On an overall basis, the operating expense ratio is about 8 percent for these agents.

There are some limitations to the use of manufacturers' agents. Most agents do not carry merchandise stocks. Also, many agents cannot furnish customers with adequate technical advice or repair service; nor are they equipped to install major products.

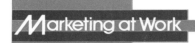

What It Takes to Get on the Shelf

In many cases, manufacturers of food products in Canada have to pay retailers for the use of the space that their products occupy on supermarket shelves. This is a practice that some observers of the industry believe adds 10 percent or more to retail food prices. It is a phenomenon of the highly competitive retail food business, but is an illegal practice in the United States.

In Canada, five retail food chains control about 70 percent of the retail food market. All food manufacturers, from the giants like Pillsbury, General Foods, Robin Hood, and Nabisco to small regional manufacturers, have to pay to get a place for their products on store shelves. In many cases, large retailers charge a listing fee for new products to be carried in the first place, then a second fee for location and space on shelves, and a third fee for a prominent place in newspaper advertisements and flyers. Critics argue that little of this fee income and of the special deals that retailers are also offered by suppliers is passed on to customers. The large food retailers point out that they make a profit after taxes of less than one percent of sales, much lower than most other types of business.

Source: Robert Matas, "Stocking Shelves Has a Hidden Cost," *The Globe and Mail*, February 28, 1987, pp. 1-3.

Manufacturers' agents are most helpful in three characteristic situations:

- A small firm has a limited number of products and no sales force. Then manufacturers' agents may do all the selling.
- A firm wants to add a new and possibly unrelated line to its existing product mix. But the present sales force either is not experienced in the new line or cannot reach the new market. Then the new line may be given to manufacturers' agents. Thus, a company's own sales force and its agents may cover the same geographical market.
- A firm wishes to enter a new market that is not yet sufficiently developed to warrant the use of its own sales force. Then manufacturers' agents familiar with that market may be used.

Brokers   Brokers are agent middlemen whose prime responsibility is to bring buyers and sellers together. They furnish considerable market information regarding prices, products, and general market conditions. Brokers do not physically handle the goods. Nor do they work on a continuing basis with their principals. Most brokers work for sellers although about 10 percent represent buyers.

Brokers have no authority to set prices. A broker simply negotiates a sale and leaves it up to the seller to accept or reject the buyer's offer. Because of the limited services provided, brokers operate on a very low cost ratio — about 3 percent of net sales.

Brokers are most prevalent in the food field. Their operation is typified by a seafood broker handling the pack from a salmon cannery. The cannery is in operation

Brokers are used in selling real estate, securities, and sometimes even fresh celery.

for possibly three months of the year. The canner employs a broker each year (the same one if relationships are mutually satisfactory) to find buyers for the salmon pack. The broker provides information regarding market prices and conditions, and the canner then informs the broker of the desired price. The broker seeks potential buyers among chain stores, wholesalers, and others. When the entire pack has been sold, the agent-principal relationship is discontinued until possibly the following year.

An evolutionary development in the food brokerage field should be noted. Through the years, many brokers have established permanent relationships with some principals. These brokers are now performing activities that would more accurately classify them as manufacturers' agents. They still call themselves ''food brokers,'' however, and they are classed as brokers by Statistics Canada.

Commission Merchants

In the marketing of many agricultural products, a widely used middleman is the commission merchant, also called a *commission man* or *commission house*. (The term *commission merchant* is actually a misnomer. This handler is really an agent middleman who, in many transactions, does not take title to the commodities which are handled.)

The commission method of operation, found mainly in large central markets, may be described briefly as follows: Assemblers in local markets (possibly local produce buyers or grain elevators) consign shipments to commission merchants in central markets. (These firms usually have established working relationships over a period of years.) The commission merchants meet trains or trucks and take charge of the shipments. It is their responsibility to handle and sell the goods. They arrange for any necessary storage, grading, and other services prior to the sale. They find buyers at the best possible prices, make the sales, and arrange for the transfer of shipments. They deduct their commissions, freight charges, and other marketing expenses, and then remit the balance as soon as possible to the local shippers.

Auction Companies

Auctions are important in the marketing of some products.

Auction companies provide (1) the auctioneers who do the selling and (2) the physical facilities for displaying the products of sellers. In this way, auction com-

panies help the assembled buyers and sellers to complete their transactions. Auctioneers account for a very small percentage of total wholesale trade. Yet they are extremely important in the wholesaling of used cars and some agricultural products (tobacco, livestock, fruit, and furs). Their operating expenses usually are quite low — about 3 percent of the sales they handle.

Selling Agents   A selling agent is an independent middleman who essentially takes the place of a manufacturer's entire marketing department. These agents typically perform more marketing services than any other type of agent middleman does. They also have more control and authority over their clients' marketing programs. A manufacturer will employ one selling agent to market the full output of the firm over its entire market. Although selling agents account for a small percentage of total wholesale trade, they are quite important in the marketing of textile products and coal. They are also found to some extent in the distribution of apparel, food, lumber, and metal products. Their operating expenses average about 3 percent of sales.

FUTURE OF THE WHOLESALER

In the 1930s, it was frequently forecast that the full-function wholesale merchant was a dying institution. Statistics in this chapter and elsewhere, however, show that wholesale merchants have enjoyed a resurgent growth rate during the past 35 years. Today they hold a strong and significant position in the economy.

There are two basic reasons for the comeback of wholesale merchant. One is a fuller realization of the true economic worth of their services. The other is the general improvement of their management methods and operations. The bandwagon to eliminate the wholesaler proved to be a blessing in disguise. Innumerable firms tried to bypass the wholesaler and came to realize that the net result was unsatisfactory. In many cases, it became evident that the wholesaler was able to provide manufacturers and retailers with better services, and at a lower cost.

Wholesalers are still the controlling force in the channels used by many firms. We must not conclude, however, that only low-cost wholesalers can survive in the competitive market. Even seemingly high-cost wholesalers are thriving. A high operating cost ratio is not necessarily the result of inefficiency. Instead, it is usually the result of providing more and better service.

Wholesalers are admittedly slow to adopt modern business methods and attitudes. However, they are striving to catch up in this respect. Moreover, the already evident trends shaping the future of wholesale distribution suggest that the wholesaler (1) is responsive to the business environment and (2) can effectively adapt to pressures from suppliers and customers for lower-cost distribution.

SUMMARY

Wholesaling is the selling, and all activities directly related to this selling, of products and services to those who are buying (1) to use the items in their business or (2) to resell them. Thus, in a broad sense, all sales are either wholesale sales or retail sales. The difference depends only on the purchaser's purpose in buying. Is it for a business or a nonbusiness use?

On a narrower scale, the definition of wholesaling encompasses only companies that are *primarily* engaged in wholesaling. Excluded are sales by farmers, retailers, manufacturers (except for their sales branches), and other firms usually called producers (in contrast to resellers).

The institutional structure of wholesaling middlemen (the all-inclusive term) may be divided into four groups: (1) wholesale merchants, (2) manufacturers' sales offices and branches, (3) agents and brokers and, (4) primary products dealers. Total operating expenses of all wholesaling middlemen average about 17 percent of *wholesale* sales and less than 10 percent of *retail* sales (the consumer's dollar). Net profits in wholesaling average only about 2 percent of sales. Less than 40 percent of wholesale sales are made to retailers, and approximately the same percentage go to industrial users and other wholesalers.

Wholesale merchants (also called jobbers or distributors) generally fit the layman's stereotype of a wholesaler. They constitute the largest category of wholesaling middlemen, in both sales volume and number of companies. These middlemen offer the widest range of wholesaling services, and consequently incur the highest operating expenses, of the four major groups of wholesaling middlemen. Wholesale merchants have consistently accounted for more than 50 percent of all wholesale sales over the past 40 years. In spite of persistent attempts to "eliminate the middleman" (namely, the wholesale merchant), these middlemen continue to grow and thrive, thus attesting to their real economic value in our economy.

The use of agents and brokers has decreased over the years. These middlemen have been replaced in distribution channels by wholesale merchants and by manufacturers' sales offices and branches. Agent wholesaling middlemen (manufacturers' agents, brokers, and others) remain strong in certain industries, and in geographic areas where the market potential is still too small for a producer's sales force.

KEY TERMS AND CONCEPTS

Wholesaling 392	Limited-function wholesaler 402
Wholesaling middleman 392	Agent wholesaling middleman 402
Wholesaler 392	Manufacturers' agent 403
Manufacturer's sales office 395	Broker 404
Manufacturer's sales branch 395	Commission merchant 405
Distributor 400	Auction company 405
Jobber 400	Selling agent 406
Rack jobber 401	

QUESTIONS AND PROBLEMS

1. A large furniture warehouse is located in a Saskatchewan city. The following conditions exist with respect to this firm:
   a. All merchandise is purchased directly from manufacturers.
   b. The warehouse is located in the low-rent wholesaling district.
   c. Merchandise remains in original crates; customers use catalogues and

swatch books to see what the articles look like and what fabrics are used.

   d. About 90 percent of the customers are ultimate consumers, and they account for 85 percent of the sales volume.

   e. The firm does quite a bit of advertising, pointing out that consumers are buying at wholesale prices.

   f. Crates are not price-marketed. Sales people bargain with customers.

   g. Some 10 percent of sales volume comes from sales to furniture stores.

   Is the furniture warehouse a wholesaler? Explain.

2. Which of the following are wholesaling transactions?
   a. St. Clair Paint and Paper sells wallpaper to an apartment building contractor and also to the contractor's family for their home.
   b. Canadian General Electric sells small motors to Inglis for its washing machines.
   c. A shrimp fisherman sells shrimp to a local restaurant.
   d. A family has a friend who is a home decorating consultant. The family orders carpet through the consultant at 50 percent off retail. The carpet is delivered directly to the house.

3. Manufacturers' sales offices and branches have maintained a steadily increasing share of total wholesale trade, while the agents' and brokers' share has declined. What conditions account for this fact?

4. How do you account for the substantial variation in operating expenses among the major types of wholesalers shown in Table 14-5?

5. In comparing the operating expense ratio for retailers and for wholesalers in Table 14-4, we see that wholesalers typically have lower operating expenses. How do you account for this?

6. What activities could full-service wholesalers discontinue in an effort to reduce operating costs?

7. What service does a full-service wholesaler provide for a manufacturer?

8. What types of retailers, other than supermarkets, offer reasonable fields for entry by rack jobbers? Explain.

9. Why would a manufacturing firm prefer to use manufacturers' agents instead of its own company sales force?

10. Why is it that manufacturers' agents often can penetrate a market faster and at a lower cost than a manufacturer's sales force?

11. What is the economic justification for the existence of brokers, especially in light of the few functions they perform?

12. Which type of wholesaling middleman, if any, is most likely to be used by each of the following? Explain your choice in each instance.
    a. A small manufacturer of a liquid glass cleaner to be sold through supermarkets.
    b. A small manufacturer of knives used for hunting, fishing, and camping.
    c. A salmon canner in British Columbia packing a high-quality, unbranded product.
    d. A small-tools manufacturing firm that has its own sales force selling to the industrial market and that wishes to add backyard barbecue equipment to its line.

e. A Quebec textile mill producing unbranded towels, sheets, pillowcases, and blankets.

13. Looking into the future, which types of wholesaling middlemen do you think will increase in importance, and which ones will decline? Explain.

CHAPTER 15

CHANNELS OF DISTRIBUTION: CONFLICT, COOPERATION, AND MANAGEMENT

CHAPTER GOALS

A distribution channel is a system — often with very independent parts that may be in conflict. To work effectively, a distribution channel must be well designed and well managed. After studying this chapter, you should understand:

- The distribution channel as a total system.
- The nature of the conflicts in channels of distribution:
    a. Between manufacturers and wholesalers.
    b. Between manufacturers and retailers.
- Vertical marketing systems.
- The major channels of distribution.
- The factors affecting the selection of a channel.
- The concept of intensity of distribution.
- The choice of individual middlemen.
- The legal considerations in channel management.

What do you think of a channel-of-distribution strategy where manufacturers compete with their own best customers? We call this *dual distribution.* A manufacturer sells through its company-owned retail stores at the same time it is selling to independent retailers who are competing against those company stores. For many years, this strategy has been used by Dack's and Florsheim (shoes), Sherwin-Williams (paint), and Singer (sewing machines).

What is new as we move into the 1990s is the upsurge in this risky distribution strategy, especially among relatively small manufacturers of fashion clothing. These are international and American firms such as Ralph Lauren, Yves Saint Laurent, Esprit, and L.A. Gear.

In Canada, Monaco Group provides a good example of a company that has recently become engaged in dual distribution. The company was formed in 1981 and represents a partnership between one of Canada's leading fashion designers, Alfred Sung, and two brothers, Saul and Joe Mimran. The company has been distributing its highly successful lines of Alfred Sung and Sung Sport clothing through major department stores in Canada and the U.S. during the past ten years. The company opened a New York showroom in 1981 and directed its line initially to the professional woman. Sung Sport, a line of less expensive designer sports wear, was introduced in 1982.

By 1985, the company had decided to move into a line of popularly priced clothing and accessories under the Club Monaco label. This line was marketed through the company's own Club Monaco stores, where sweatshirts, belts, sweaters, jeans, and sunglasses are displayed on open shelves. The ambience of the stores has been described as somewhere between "cute and funk." Although the Monaco Group keeps the two elements of its product lines quite separate — Alfred Sung and Sung Sport lines are sold through independent retailers and Club Monaco is sold only in Club Monaco stores — the company is, nevertheless, engaged in dual distribution in that part of its line is sold through one channel and part through another.

The company sees a potential for as many as 70 Club Monaco stores in Canada and 300 or more in the United States. With the opening of its forty-third store in Halifax in late 1988, Club Monaco was operating in ten of the largest metropolitan markets in Canada. Thirty-three of the stores are company-owned and ten are franchised. At the same time, the other components of the Monaco Group's product line, the successful Alfred Sung and Sung Sport labels, continue to be sold in better independent retail stores.

Why would this young company engage in a dual distribution strategy — especially in fashion merchandising, where independent retailers are traditionally so well entrenched? Monaco Group is looking to their retail operations to provide a certain stability to counteract the cyclical nature of wholesaling. All Club Monaco products are designed by the company's own team of designers and marketers who supervise the design, production, marketing and merchandising. This gives them better control over the point of sale and product concept as a whole, including the sourcing of materials, advertising, pricing, inventory control, store presentation, and customer service. It also provides the company better access to the U.S. market where its lines cannot be assured positioning in major department stores.

Source: Adapted in part from John Lownsbrough, "Selling Sung," *Canadian Business*, vol. 59, no. 9, September 1986, pp. 23–31, 147–150; with additional information from Christine Ralphs of Club Monaco.

The task of choosing and managing a distribution channel often begins with a manufacturer or producer. For that reason, we shall approach our discussion of channel design largely from the vantage point of the producer. As you will see, however, the channel problems faced by middlemen are similar to those of a producer. Furthermore, the control of the channels used by manufacturers and the freedom of choice regarding these channels may actually rest with middlemen.

A channel of distribution should be treated as a unit — a total system of action. Producers and middlemen alike should understand that each of them is one component of a system designed to efficiently provide want-satisfaction to the final customer. Thus, there is a real need for coordination throughout the channel. A properly operated distribution system is a significant competitive advantage for each firm that is part of that system.

Unfortunately, a trade channel too often is treated as a fragmented assortment of competing, independently operating organizations. Manufacturers may view their own retailers as competitors. Or middlemen may be in conflict with their suppliers, rather than recognizing that the real threat is other middlemen or the distribution systems of other manufacturers. That is, the real competition is between distribution systems of different producers, rather than among the organizational units within one producer's system.

One possible reason why producers have problems with their channels of distribution is that in most organizations nobody is in charge of the channels. There is no executive with the title of ''distribution channels manager'' in the same sense that there is an advertising manager or a sales manager. In fact, the distribution system is the *only* major element in the marketing mix that typically does not have anyone directly in charge. Perhaps it is time for manufacturers to establish the position of channels manager in their marketing executive structure. The person in this position would be directly responsible for the managerial activities of planning, coordination, and evaluation as they are related to the firm's distribution channels.[1]

CONFLICT AND COOPERATING IN DISTRIBUTION CHANNELS

The systems concept of distribution suggests a need for cooperation among channel members. Yet power structures do exist in trade channels, and there is a continuous tug-of-war among channel members. At the root of this struggle is institutional change, several examples of which were observed in our study of retailing and wholesaling institutions. It is axiomatic that change begets conflict, and conflict very often results in change.[2]

Nature of the Conflicts

Competitive conflicts in channels of distribution may involve middlemen on the same level of distribution (horizontal conflict) or firms on different levels of distribution (vertical conflict).

FIRMS ON THE SAME LEVEL OF DISTRIBUTION

Horizontal conflicts may occur:

- *Between middlemen of the same type*: Hardware store versus hardware store.
- *Between different types of middlemen on the same level*: Hardware store versus paint store.

Perhaps the main source of horizontal conflict has been the competition caused by **scrambled merchandising** — that is, the practice whereby middlemen diversify their product assortment by adding new, nontraditional merchandise lines. Grocery supermarkets, for example, have added toiletries, drugs, clothing, magazines, small appliances, records, and other nonfood lines. The retailers who traditionally sell these lines have become irritated both at the grocery stores for diversifying and at manufacturers for using these ''unorthodox'' channels.

Product proliferation, and the resultant crossing of traditional channel lines, may stem from the market, the middleman, or the manufacturer. Consumers (the *market*) prefer convenient, one-stop shopping, so stores broaden their product offerings to satisfy this want. *Middlemen* constantly seek to add new products with higher gross margins or to add new lines in the hope of increasing customer traffic. *Manufacturers*

Motor oil plus flowers plus fresh vegetables equals scrambled merchandising.

add new types of outlets to expand their markets or to reduce unit production costs. All these efforts toward product or channel expansion only intensify the degree of channel conflict.

FIRMS ON DIFFERENT LEVELS OF DISTRIBUTION

Perhaps the most severe competitive conflicts in distribution systems today are of a vertical nature — that is:

- *Between producer and wholesaler*: Manufacturers may attempt to bypass wholesalers and sell directly to retailers.
- *Between producer and retailer*: Producers compete with retailers by selling directly to the consumer or by selling through their producer-owned retail stores.

The remainder of this section on conflict is devoted to the *vertical* types of conflict.

Who Controls the Channels?

In marketing literature, authors have generally taken a manufacturer-oriented approach to channels of distribution. The implication is that manufacturers are the ones that make the decisions regarding the type of outlet, the number of outlets, and even the selection of individual outlets. This is a one-sided point of view. Actually, middlemen often have considerable freedom to make their own choices in establishing channels. Certainly the names, Eaton's, Loblaws, Safeway, or Sears mean more to consumers than most of the brands sold in these stores. Large retailers today are challenging manufacturers for channel control, just as the manufacturers challenged wholesalers 50 to 60 years ago. Even small retailers may be quite influential in local markets because their prestige may be greater than that of their suppliers.

Actually, the questions of who *is* the channel leader and who *should* be remain largely unsettled. The position that supports leadership by the manufacturer is production-oriented. That is, manufacturers create the new products, and they need increasing sales volumes to derive the benefits of large-scale operations. One can also argue that the retailers should be the leaders under the marketing concept —

standing closest to the consumers, knowing their wants, and being their purchasing agents. Perhaps the best answer to the channel-control question is a compromise — a balance of power — rather than domination by any one level of a distribution channel.

Manufacturer versus Wholesaler

During the past 60 years, a significant channel conflict has occurred between the manufacturer and the wholesaler. The conflict stems from manufacturers' attempts to bypass wholesalers and deal directly with retailers. Ordinarily, this battle is between the producers and wholesalers of manufactured *consumer* products. It usually does not involve wholesaling middlemen for industrial products because there is a tradition of direct sale in industrial marketing. Where middlemen *are* used, the need for their services has long been recognized.

HISTORICAL BACKGROUND OF THE CONFLICT

The clash of interests between wholesalers and manufacturers can be best understood by reviewing (1) the position of the wholesaler before 1920, (2) the changing position of the manufacturer over the years, (3) the changing position of the retailers since 1920, and (4) the net effect these changes have had on the wholesalers and manufacturers.

Historically, *wholesalers* occupied a position of major importance in distribution systems. Before 1920, they were dominant because manufacturers and retailers were small and poorly financed. In addition, retailers were widely dispersed over the country. In effect, the wholesaler serves as a sales force for the manufacturer and as a purchasing agent for the retailer.

As a result of the risks they took and the broad scale of their services, the wholesalers had high operating costs. To cover these costs, they needed a high gross margin. Through the nineteenth century and the early part of the twentieth, wholesaler institutions became complacent. These firms did not adjust to changing economic and social conditions.

During the last half of the nineteenth century and the first part of the twentieth, the position of the *manufacturer* changed substantially. Manufacturing became more efficient. Manufacturers were quick to learn that the best means of achieving increased volume was through a change in marketing methods. Aggressive selling effort, lower prices, product identification through branding, and advertising were recognized as keys to mass markets. Once the manufacturers embarked upon these programs, they balked at giving wholesalers their customary wide margin on sales — sales that the manufacturers' policies were now stimulating.

After World War I, the position of the *retailer* changed considerably. Large-scale retailing institutions developed in great numbers, and retail markets became concentrated in and around metropolitan centres. Large-scale operations entailed increased buying power, well-financed retailers, and better-managed firms. Large-scale retailers thus were economically able to assume many wholesaling functions. All these factors encouraged retailers to purchase their merchandise directly from manufacturers.

Wholesalers were caught between large-scale, direct-buying retailers on the one hand and large-scale, direct-selling manufacturers on the other. The wholesalers saw their importance being reduced. Yet they realized they could not afford to promote aggressively the products of any one manufacturer, and they resented any cut in their discount margin.

THE VIEW FROM EACH SIDE TODAY

When manufacturers prefer to bypass wholesalers and sell directly to retailers or consumers, it is basically because (1) the manufacturers are dissatisfied with the wholesalers' services or (2) the market conditions call for direct sale. The wholesalers, in turn, are often unhappy with the actions of manufacturers. The arguments voiced by each side are summarized in Table 15-1.

TABLE 15-1   MANUFACTURERS VERSUS WHOLESALERS: THE CONTROVERSY TODAY

From manufacturers' point of view:
1. Wholesalers fail to promote products aggressively. Wholesalers generally concur with their charge. Since they usually carry thousands of items, it is not possible for their sales forces even to *mention* each item to a prospective customer, much less try to *sell* each item.
2. Wholesalers no longer perform the storage services that producers were accustomed to. Improvements in transportation and communication enable wholesalers to carry smaller inventories, thus shifting the storage function back to the manufacturers.
3. Some wholesalers promote their own brands in direct competition with manufacturers' brands.
4. Wholesalers' services cost too much. The manufacturers believe they can do the job at a lower cost. However, this may be a mistaken assumption. Many producers have learned the hard way that bypassing wholesalers may actually *increase* the cost of marketing or result in poor market coverage.
5. Manufacturers want closer market contact. They want control over their products for a greater part of the route to the final customer.
6. Some products may need rapid physical distribution because they are perishable or are subject to fashion obsolescence, and the producer → retailer channel is faster.
7. Large-scale retailers usually prefer to buy directly from manufacturers.

From wholesalers' point of view:
1. Manufacturers do not understand that the primary obligation of wholesalers is to serve their customers. Serving the manufacturer is only secondary.
2. Manufacturers expect too much. Wholesalers' discounts are not high enough to justify the level of warehousing and promotion expected by producers.
3. Manufacturers skim the cream off the market. That is, they use wholesalers only in the early stages of territorial development or in the least profitable segments of the market. In the concentrated, profitable areas or after a new market has been developed, manufacturers bypass the wholesalers and sell directly to retailers or industrial users. This observation is accurate. However, wholesalers should understand that their real value lies in their being able to reach markets the manufacturers themselves cannot penetrate profitably.

COURSES OF ACTION OPEN TO MANUFACTURERS

If manufacturers wish to bypass wholesalers, there are four possible courses of action to choose from. Each of these alternatives places a greater financial burden

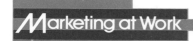

Bringing Retailing Home: Everyone Enjoys a Party

One approach to selling directly to consumers that has proven successful for several well-known companies is the use of the "party plan." This type of distribution is probably most closely associated with Tupperware in housewares and Mary Kay in cosmetics. But now you can buy toys in your home through a party plan.

Two Canadian companies, Creative Kids Inc. and Toy Workshop Inc. now market quality toys through home parties. Frustrated with shopping for toys in retail stores, Ann Corrigan and a partner started Creative Kids in 1985. Less than three years later, her projected sales amounted to $4 million annually.

Creative Kids has more than 350 consultants throughout Canada and they market a hand-picked line of approximately 100 toys. Many of the consultants are former teachers, nurses or child-care professionals who can explain to parents the educational and play value of each item in the line. Consultants get started with an investment of $500 and purchase their toys at a 30% discount. Their success depends on how many parties they schedule and how much effort they expend.

Source: Adapted from Gail Pitney, "Toy Sales Soar," *Canadian*, March 1988, pp. 9, 10. (*Canadian* is the in-flight magazine of Canadian Airlines International.)

---

on manufacturers and adds immeasurably to their management problems. They must operate their own sales force and handle the physical distribution of their products. And direct-selling manufacturers face competition from their former wholesalers, who are now selling competitive products.

■ *Sell directly to retailers*. Under certain market and product conditions, selling directly to retailers is a reasonable alternative. An ideal retail *market* for direct selling is one made up of large-scale retailers who buy in large quantities from central buying offices. In addition, it is often profitable to sell directly to specialty stores (shoes, clothing, photographic equipment) that buy large quantities of a limited line of products.

Direct selling is advantageous when the *product* (1) is subject to physical or fashion perishability, (2) carries a high unit price, (3) is custom-made, or (4) requires mechanical servicing and installation.

■ *Establish sales offices or branches*. This variation of the first alternative is frequently adopted by a producer with a large sales force that can be managed more effectively on a decentralized basis. For such a sales force to operate profitably, essentially the same market and product conditions are required as for the direct-selling course of action.

■ *Sell directly to consumers*. In Chapter 13 we discussed various direct-to-consumer distribution methods. Producers may employ house-to-house or mail-order selling. They may establish their own retail stores or sell directly to consumers at the point of production.

■ *Use a missionary sales force*. As a compromise, when manufacturers prefer to use wholesalers but also want aggressive selling, they may employ missionary sales people. Also known as promotional sales people, detail men, or factory representatives, these missionary sales people perform a number of services. Typically, a missionary sales person calls upon a retailer and aggressively promotes the product of the manufacturer. Any orders the sales person secures are passed on to the jobber, who receives the normal commission. Missionary sales people may be used to install point-of-purchase displays in retail stores or to introduce new items to retailers.

COURSES OF ACTION OPEN TO WHOLESALERS

Wholesalers too can adopt measures to improve their competitive position. These alternatives are attempts (1) to improve the wholesalers' efficiency to such a level that neither suppliers nor customers find it profitable to bypass the wholesaler and (2) to tie the retailers to the wholesaler.

- *Improve internal management.* Many wholesalers have modernized their establishments and upgraded the calibre of their management. New, functional, single-story warehouses have been built outside the congested downtown areas, and mechanized materials-handling equipment has been installed. Electronic data processing equipment has streamlined accounting and reduced inventory losses. Many wholesalers have adopted selective selling. That is, less profitable accounts are visited less frequently, and some customers may be solicited only by mail or telephone. These and other innovations have generally lowered operating costs or have given far better service for the same money.

- *Provide management assistance for retailers.* Wholesalers generally realized that anything they can do to improve retailers' operations is really in the wholesalers' interest. They can help retailers improve store layouts and install better accounting and inventory-control systems. They can also help retailers in selecting and promoting their merchandise.

- *Form voluntary chains.* In a voluntary chain (discussed in Chapter 13), a wholesaler enters into a contract with several retailers, agreeing to furnish management services and large-volume buying advantages. In turn, the retailers agree to do all, or almost all, of their buying from the wholesaler.

- *Develop their own brands.* Many large wholesalers have successfully established their own brand. If a wholesaler is connected with a voluntary chain of retailers, the chain provides the wholesaler's brand with a built-in market.

Manufacturer versus Retailer

Today, perhaps even more significant than the conflict between manufacturers and wholesalers is the struggle for channel control that goes on between manufacturers and retailers. A very basic reason for the conflict is this: "The people who manufacture the goods and the people who move the goods into the hands of the ultimate consumer do not share the same business philosophy and do not talk essentially the same language."[3] In manufacturing corporations, the executives' point of view is typically characterized as a psychology of *growth*. Their goals are essentially dynamic and evolving. In sharp contrast, the psychology of small and medium-sized retailers is essentially *static* in nature. Their goals are well defined and are far more limited than those of manufacturing corporation executives. At some point, the retailer attains (and tends to maintain) a continuously satisfying plateau.

DOMINATION VERSUS COOPERATION

Each group has weapons it can use in its efforts to dominate the other. Manufacturers can use their promotional weapons to build strong consumer preference for their products. Legal weapons are available to them in the form of franchise contracts, consignment selling, or outright ownership of retail stores. As a negative method of domination, the manufacturer may refuse to sell to uncooperative retailers.

Retailers are not necessarily unarmed. By advertising effectively or by establishing their own brands, they can develop consumer preferences for their stores. They can either concentrate their purchases with one supplier or spread their buying among many sources, depending upon which strategy is most effective for them. Over the past several years, larger retailers in particular have strengthened their position in channels of distribution. Retailers have upgraded the quality of their management, improved their computerized information systems, and generally employed more sophisticated marketing programs. As a result, these retailers have generally become stronger and more independent in distribution systems.

On the other side of the coin, fortunately, channel members seem to realize that the returns from cooperating with one another do outweigh any reasons for conflict. Perhaps manufacturers and retailers alike understand that it is in their own best interests to treat a distribution channel as a total system. They must consider the channel as an extension (forward or backward, as the case may be) of their own internal organizations. To implement this concept, manufacturers should do the sort of things for retailers that they do for their own marketing organizations. That is, manufacturers can provide advertising aids, training for dealer sales people, managerial assistance, and so on. Retailers can reciprocate by carrying adequate inventories, promoting the products, and building consumer goodwill.

Vertical Marketing Systems

Some manufacturers own their retail outlets.

Institutional changes in distribution during the past 30 to 40 years have led to the development of vertical marketing systems. These newer vertical marketing systems offer significant economies of scale and increased coordination in distribution. They also eliminate duplication of marketing services. Instead, they enable any given marketing activity to be performed at the most advantageous position in the system.

Vertical marketing systems may be characterized as corporate, administered, or contractual (see Table 15-2). In corporate vertical marketing systems, the production and marketing facilities are owned by the same company. As manufacturers, for example, Benetton (sports wear), Club Monaco (apparel), and Imperial Oil each operate a number of their own retail outlets. Many large food chains run some processing facilities. Sears and Marks & Spencer have ownership interests in manufacturing facilities that supply their stores.

In administered vertical marketing systems, the coordination of production and marketing activities is achieved through the domination of one powerful channel member. This type of distribution is exemplified by Samsonite in luggage, Campbell's in canned soup, and Kraft in cheese. The manufacturer's brand and market position are strong enough to get the voluntary cooperation of retailers in matters of advertising, pricing, and store display.

In contractual vertical marketing systems, independent institutions — producers, wholesalers, and retailers — are banded together by contract to achieve the necessary

A vertical marketing system through franchising.

Voluntary chains — one way wholesalers can compete.

TABLE 15-2   **TYPES OF VERTICAL MARKETING SYSTEMS**

Type of system	Control maintained by:	Examples
Corporate	Ownership	Singer sewing machines, Goodyear tires, Bata shoes
Administered	Economic power	Samsonite luggage, General Electric, Labatt beer
Contractual:		
Wholesaler-sponsored voluntary chain	Contract	IDA and Guardian drug stores, IGA stores
Retailer-owned cooperative	Stock ownership by retailers	Canadian Tire
Franchise systems	Contract:	
	Manufacturer-sponsored retailers	Ford, Chrysler, GM and other auto dealers
	Manufacturer-sponsored wholesalers	Coca-Cola and other soft drink bottlers
	Marketers of services	Harvey's hamburgers, Speedy Muffler, ComputerLand, Tilden car rentals

economic size and coordination of effort. Three types of contractual systems can be identified: wholesaler-sponsored voluntary chains, retailer-owned cooperatives, and franchise systems. All three were discussed in Chapter 13.

Marketing at Work

File 15-2

Service Franchising Assures New Consistency

When we think of franchising, we probably most often think of fast-food outlets, gasoline retailers, or automobile dealerships. But, increasingly, companies are turning to franchising to get *services* to the customers. We can, in fact, define services quite broadly to include all forms of retailing, including the restaurant and hotel businesses, where franchising has been quite common for many years. But more recently, we have seen service franchises established that do not deal in tangible products.

You can now have your shoes repaired at a franchise operation, Moneysworth & Best; have your term paper or report photocopied at Kwik-Kopy, Print Three, or Zippy Print; book a well-earned holiday through franchise travel agents such as Goliger's or Uniglobe.

With the background of the previous sections, we can now look at the major channels used by producers. Then we can discuss the factors that most influence a company's choice of its trade channels.

*Major Channels of
Distribution*

Even to describe the major channels is risky because it may suggest an orthodoxy that does not exist. Nevertheless, what follows is an outline of the most frequently used channels for consumer products and industrial goods. Refer to Fig. 15-1 while reading the following section.

FIGURE 15-1
**Major marketing channels
available to producers.**

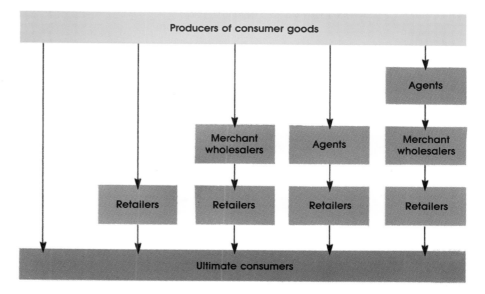

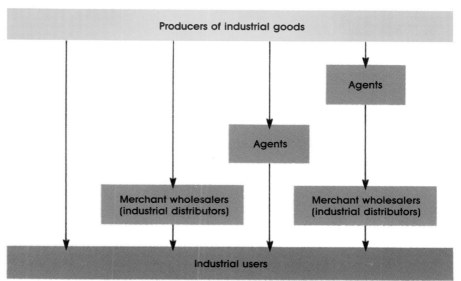

DISTRIBUTION OF CONSUMER GOODS

Five channels are widely used in the marketing of consumer products. In each, the manufacturer also has the alternative of using sales branches or sales offices. Obviously, our suggestion that there are only five major channels is an oversimplification, but one that seems necessary if we are to discuss this unwieldy subject in a few paragraphs.

- **Producer → consumer**. The shortest, simplest channel of distribution for consumer products is from the producer to the consumer, with no middlemen involved. The producer may sell from house to house or by mail.
- **Producer → retailer → consumer**. Many large retailers buy directly from manufacturers and agricultural producers.
- **Producer → wholesaler → retailer → consumer**. If there is a "traditional" channel for consumer goods, this is it. Small retailers and small manufacturers by the hundreds find this channel the only economically feasible choice.
- **Producer → agent → retailer → consumer**. Instead of using wholesalers, many producers prefer to use a manufacturers' agent or some other agent middleman to reach the retail market, especially *large-scale* retailers. For example, a manufacturer of a glass cleaner selected a food broker to reach the grocery store market, including the large chains.
- **Producer → agent → wholesaler → retailer → consumer**. To reach *small* retailers, the producers mentioned in the preceding paragraph often use agent middlemen, who in turn call on wholesalers that sell to small stores.

DISTRIBUTION OF INDUSTRIAL PRODUCTS

Four types of channels are widely used in reaching industrial users. Again, a manufacturer may use a sales branch or a sales office to reach the next institution in the channel. Or two levels of wholesalers may be used in some cases (again see Fig. 15-1).[4]

- **Producer → industrial user**. This direct channel accounts for a greater *dollar* volume of industrial products than any other distribution structure. Manufacturers of large installations, such as airplanes, generators, and heating plants, usually sell directly to users.
- **Producer → industrial distributor → user**. Producers of operating supplies and small accessory equipment frequently use industrial distributors to reach their markets. Manufacturers of building materials and air-conditioning equipment are two examples of firms that make heavy use of the industrial distributor.[5]
- **Producer → agent → user**. Firms without their own marketing departments find this a desirable channel. Also, a company that wants to introduce a new product or enter a new market may prefer to use agents rather than its own sales force.
- **Producer → agent → industrial distributor → user**. This channel is similar to the preceding one. It is used when, for some reason, it is not feasible to sell through agents directly to the industrial user. The unit sale may be too

small for direct selling. Or decentralized inventory may be needed to supply users rapidly, in which case the storage services of an industrial distributor are required.

Factors Affecting Choice of Distribution Channels

Because a channel of distribution should be determined by customer buying patterns, the nature of the market is the key factor influencing management's choice of channels. Other major considerations are the product, the middlemen, and the company itself. Basically, when selecting its channels of distribution, a company should follow the criteria of the three C's — channel *control*, market *coverage*, and a *cost* that is consistent with the desired level of customer service.

SOME GENERALIZATIONS ABOUT DISTRIBUTION CHANNELS

1. Channel design should begin with the final customer and work backward to the producer, because channels of distribution should be determined by buying habits.
2. The channels finally selected must be totally appropriate to the basic objectives of the firm's marketing program. If management sets as its goal the widest possible distribution of its product line, then obviously an exclusive franchise strategy at the retail level is not appropriate.
3. The channels should provide a firm with access to a predetermined share of the market. A manufacturer of golfing equipment seeking the broadest possible market would make a mistake by using a channel that includes only large department stores and sporting goods stores at the retail level.
4. The channels must be flexible enough so that the use of one channel does not permanently close off another. A manufacturer of small appliances (irons, toasters), for example, distributed only through appliance wholesalers, which in turn distributed to appliance retailers. The company had an offer from a drug chain to buy the products directly from the manufacturer. The appliance retailers threatened to discontinue the line if the manufacturer placed it in drug stores. The producer decided to turn down the drug chain's offer. Subsequently, a competitive manufacturer accepted a similar offer and profited considerably.
5. There is a high degree of interdependence among all firms in the channel for any given product. There can be no weak link in the chain if it is to be successful.
6. Channels of distribution and middlemen are always on trial, and changes occur constantly. Middlemen survive only when their existence is economically sound and socially desirable. Furthermore, new middlemen and channels arise to do new jobs or to do the existing jobs better.*

---

*For an interesting discussion of ten conceptual generalizations regarding distribution systems, see Michael M. Pearson, "Ten Distribution Myths," *Business Horizons*, May–June 1981, pp. 17–23. Pearson contends that the ten points he discusses are commonly accepted assumptions that have not been validated by any quantitative measurements.

MARKET CONSIDERATIONS

Perhaps the most obvious point to consider is whether the product is intended for the consumer or industrial market. If it is going to the industrial market, of course retailers will not be included in the channel. In either case, other significant market variables should be considered:

- **Number of potential customers**. With relatively few potential customers, a manufacturer may use its own sales force to sell directly to consumers or industrial users. For a large number of customers, the manufacturer would more likely use middlemen. A related point is the number of different *industries* to which a firm sells. One company, marketing drilling equipment and supplies only to the oil industry, sells directly to users. A paper products manufacturer, on the other hand, makes extensive use of industrial distributors to reach many different industries.

- **Geographic concentration of the market**. Direct sale to the textile or the garment manufacturing industry is feasible because most of the buyers are concentrated in a few geographic areas. Even in the case of a national market, some segments have a higher density rate than others. Sellers may establish sales branches in densely populated markets, but they would use middlemen in the less-concentrated markets.

- **Order size**. A food product manufacturer would sell directly to large grocery chains because the large order size and total volume of business make this channel economically desirable. The same manufacturer, however, would use wholesalers to reach the small grocery stores whose orders are usually too small to justify direct sale.

PRODUCT CONSIDERATIONS

- **Unit value**. The unit value of a product affects the amount of money available for distribution. Thus, the lower the unit value, the longer, usually, are the channels of distribution. However, when products of low unit value are sold in large quantities or are combined with other goods so that the total order is large, shorter channels may be economically feasible.

- **Perishability**. Products subject to physical or fashion perishability must be speeded through their channels. The channels usually are short.

- **Technical nature of a product**. An industrial product that is highly technical is often distributed directly to industrial users. The producer's sales force must provide considerable presale and postsale service; wholesalers normally cannot do this.

Consumer products of a technical nature provide a real distribution challenge for

Perishable products require short distribution channels.

manufacturers. Ordinarily, manufacturers cannot sell the goods directly to the consumer. As much as possible, manufacturers try to sell directly to retailers, but even then the servicing of the product often poses problems.

MIDDLEMEN CONSIDERATIONS

- **Services provided by middlemen**. Each producer should select middlemen that will provide those marketing services that the producer either is unable to provide or cannot economically perform.
- **Availability of desired middlemen**. The middlemen whom a producer desires may not be available. They may be carrying competitive products and may not wish to add another line.
- **Attitude of middlemen toward manufacturers' policies**. Sometimes, manufacturers' choices of channels are limited because their marketing policies are not acceptable to certain types of middlemen. Some retailers or wholesalers, for example, are interested in carrying a line only if they can get an exclusive franchise in a territory.

COMPANY CONSIDERATIONS

- **Financial resources**. A financially strong company needs middlemen less than one that is financially weak. A business with adequate finances can establish its own sales force, grant credit, or warehouse its own products. A financially weak firm would have to use middlemen who could provide these services.
- **Ability of management**. Channel decisions are affected by the marketing experience and ability of the firm's management. Many companies lacking marketing know-how prefer to turn the distribution job over to middlemen.
- **Desire for channel control**. Some producers establish short channels simply because they want to control the distribution of their products, even though the cost of the more direct channel may be higher. By controlling the channel, producers can achieve more aggressive promotion and better control both the freshness of merchandise stocks and the retail prices of their products.
- **Services provided by seller**. Often producers' channel decisions are influenced by the marketing services they can provide in relation to those demanded by middlemen. For example, often a retail chain will not stock a given product unless it is presold through heavy manufacturer advertising.

Use of Multiple Channels of Distribution

A manufacturer is likely to use multiple channels (also called dual distribution) to reach *different* markets when selling:

- The same product (Cooper sports goods; Smith-Corona typewriters) to both the consumer and industrial markets.
- Unrelated products (IBM mainframe and microcomputers; General Electric light bulbs and appliances; CIL paints and chemicals).

Dual distribution is also often used to reach a *single* market, but one in which there are differences in (1) the size of the buyers or (2) the densities within parts of the market. A manufacturer of food products will sell directly to large grocery chains but use wholesalers to reach smaller stores. A producer of industrial machinery may use its own sales force to sell directly to users in concentrated markets. But it may employ manufacturers' agents to reach customers in sparsely populated markets.

A significant development in dual distribution (and a source of channel conflict) is the use of competing channel systems to sell the *same* brand to the *same* market. Dack's (shoes), Ralph Lauren (clothing), Sherwin-Williams (paints), and Goodyear (tires) are examples of manufacturers that distribute through their own retail stores. At the same time, each of these producers reaches its same market by using conventional channels that include independent retailers and possibly wholesalers. Manufacturers may open their own stores (thus creating dual distribution) when they are not satisfied with the market coverage provided by existing retail outlets. Or manufacturers may establish their own stores primarily as testing grounds for new products and marketing techniques.

DETERMINING INTENSITY OF DISTRIBUTION

After selecting their distribution channels, manufacturers should next decide upon the number of middlemen — the intensity of distribution — to be employed at the wholesale and retail levels. There are three strategies to choose from here, but they are not neatly compartmentalized. Instead, they form a continuum, or points on a scale, running from *intensive* distribution through *selective* distribution to *exclusive* distribution. See Fig. 15-2.

FIGURE 15-2
The intensity-of-distribution continuum.

INTENSITY OF DISTRIBUTION		
Intensive	Selective	Exclusive
Many	Limited	One

NUMBER OF WHOLESALERS OR RETAILERS USED

Intensive: Sell your product in every outlet where final customers might reasonably look for it.

Selective: Use a limited number of wholesalers and/or retailers in a given geographic area.

Exclusive: Use only one wholesaler or retailer in a given market.

Intensive Distribution

Ordinarily the strategy of intensive distribution is used by manufacturers of consumer convenience goods. Consumers demand immediate satisfaction with this class of product and will not defer purchases to find a particular brand. Retailers often control the extent to which the strategy of intensive distribution can be implemented. For example, a new manufacturer of toothpaste may want distribution in all supermarkets, but the retailers may limit their assortment to the four fastest-selling brands. Intensive distribution places most of the burden of advertising and promotion on the shoulders of the manufacturer. Retailers will not pay to advertise a product that is sold by all their competitors.

Cosmetic firms often use selective distribution.

Selective Distribution

Selective distribution covers a wide range of distribution intensity. A business that adopts this strategy may have only a few outlets in a particular market. Or it may have a large number but still have something short of intensive distribution. Selective distribution lends itself especially well to consumer shopping and specialty goods and industrial accessory equipment, for which most customers have a brand preference.

A company may decide to adopt a selective distribution strategy after some experience with intensive distribution. The change usually hinges upon the high cost of intensive distribution or the unsatisfactory performance of some middlemen. Certain customers perennially order in small, unprofitable amounts. Others may be poor credit risks. Eliminating such marginal middlemen may reduce the number of outlets, but it can increase a company's sales volume substantially. Many companies have found this to be the case simply because they were able to do a more thorough selling job with a smaller number of accounts.

Exclusive Distribution

Under an exclusive distribution strategy, the supplier agrees to sell only to a particular wholesaling middleman or retailer in a given market. Under an exclusive distributorship (with a wholesaler) or an exclusive dealership (with a retailer), the middleman is sometimes prohibited from handling a directly competing product line.

Exclusive dealerships are frequently used in the marketing of consumer specialty products such as expensive suits. Producers also often adopt an exclusive distribution strategy when it is essential that the retailer carry a large inventory. This form of distribution is also desirable when the dealer or distributor must furnish installation and repair service. Manufacturers of farm machinery and large construction equipment frequently use exclusive distributorships for this reason.

EVALUATION FROM MANUFACTURER'S STANDPOINT

An exclusive distribution policy helps a manufacturer control the retail segment of its channels. The producer is better able to set the retail prices of its products, and it is in a position to approve advertisements featuring its products. The dealers are more likely to be cooperative and to promote these products aggressively, realizing that their future is tied to the success of the manufacturer.

On the other hand, in using this distribution strategy, a company substantially limits the number of its sales outlets. Also, the producer will suffer if its exclusive dealers don't serve its customers well. Essentially, the manufacturer has all its eggs in one basket in each market. The producer is pretty much dependent on its retailers.

Very exclusive distribution.

EVALUATION FROM RETAILER'S STANDPOINT

A significant advantage of being an exclusive dealer is that the dealer reaps all the benefits of the manufacturers' marketing activities in the particular market.

The main drawback to being an exclusive dealer is that the dealer (retailer) may become too dependent upon the manufacturer. If the producer does a good job with the product, the dealer may prosper. But if the manufacturing firm fails, the dealer is powerless to do anything but sink with it, as far as that product is concerned. Dealership agreements often require the retailer to invest a considerable sum of money in equipment and facilities. If the agreement is then cancelled, the retailer stands to lose a major investment. Another hazard is that once the volume has been built up in a market, the manufacturer may add other dealers. The retailer thus is often at the mercy of the manufacturer. It is a one-sided arrangement in this respect, particularly if the brand is strong and the franchise is valuable.

SELECTING AND WORKING WITH INDIVIDUAL MIDDLEMEN

When all is said and done, middlemen can often make or break a manufacturer. Middlemen are the ones who personally contact the final customers — the ultimate consumers or industrial users. Thus the success of manufacturers' distribution efforts depends ultimately upon how well (1) manufacturers select their individual middlemen and then (2) work with their distributors and dealers.

When selecting a middleman, the key factor to consider is whether the middleman sells to the market that the manufacturer wants to reach. Then the manufacturer should determine whether the middleman's product mix, promotional activities, and customer services are all compatible with the manufacturer's needs.

MANUFACTURERS AND MIDDLEMEN: A PERFECT WORKING RELATIONSHIP

The perfect middleman:

1. Has access to the market that the manufacturer wants to reach.
2. Carries adequate stocks of the manufacturer's products and a satisfactory assortment of other products.
3. Has an effective promotional program — advertising, personal selling, and product displays. Promotional demands placed on the manufacturer are in line with what the manufacturer intends to do.
4. Provides services to customers — credit, delivery, installation, and product repair — and honours the product warranty conditions.
5. Pays its bills on time and has capable management.

The perfect manufacturer:

1. Provides a desirable assortment of products — well designed, properly priced, attractively packaged, and delivered on time and in adequate quantities.
2. Builds product demand for these products by advertising them.
3. Furnishes promotional assistance to its middlemen.
4. Provides managerial assistance for its middlemen.
5. Honours product warranties and provides repair and installation service.

The perfect combination:

1. Probably doesn't exist.

There is a community of interests in what each organization — manufacturer and middleman — expects from the other in terms of support for an effective total marketing program. A series of rewards and penalties may be instituted by either party to encourage the other to perform as expected. The major reward for either party is increased profit. Probably the most powerful penalty a manufacturer can impose is to terminate a sales agreement with a dealer. A middleman, in turn, can penalize a manufacturer by not promoting products adequately, by pushing a competitor's products, or ultimately by dropping the manufacturer's line entirely.

LEGAL CONSIDERATIONS IN CHANNEL MANAGEMENT

In various ways, organizations may try to exercise control over the distribution of their product as it moves through the channel. Generally speaking, any attempts to control distribution may be subject to legal constraints. In this section, we shall discuss briefly four control methods that are frequently considered by suppliers (usually manufacturers):

- *Dealer selection.* The manufacturer wants to select its customers, and refuses to sell to some middlemen.
- *Exclusive dealing.* The manufacturer prohibits its dealers from carrying products of the manufacturer's competitors.
- *Tying contracts.* The manufacturer sells a product to a middleman only under the condition that this middleman also buys another (possibly unwanted) product from the manufacturer. Or, at least, the middleman agrees not to buy the other product from any other supplier.
- *Exclusive (closed) territories.* The manufacturer requires each middleman to

sell *only* to customers who are located within the middleman's assigned territory.

None of these arrangements is automatically illegal. The Competition Act deals with such practices under Part VII in which certain dealings between manufacturers and middlemen are deemed illegal if they restrict competition.

Dealer Selection

Under Section 47 of the Competition Act, it is illegal for a manufacturer or supplier to refuse to supply a middleman with the supplier's products. Under certain circumstances, however, a supplier may refuse to deal with retailers or other middlemen if they are unwilling or unable to meet the usual trade terms of the supplier. In other words, for example, if the middleman engaged in a practice of selling the supplier's product as a loss leader, or failed to provide adequate postpurchase service, or in some other way failed to support the product, the supplier could refuse to deal with that company. Generally, it would be illegal to refuse to supply a middleman if the company carried a competitor's product or for resisting a tying contract.

Exclusive Dealing

Exclusive dealing contracts have been declared unlawful if the manufacturer's sales volume is a substantial part of the total volume in a market or if the volume done by the exclusive dealers is a significant percentage of the total business in an area. That is, the law is violated when the competitors of a manufacturer are essentially shut out from a substantial part of the market because of this manufacturer's exclusive dealing contract.

By inference, it is clear that exclusive dealing is not illegal in all situations. In fact, where the seller is just getting started in a market or where its share of the total market is so small as to be negligible, its negotiation of exclusive dealing agreements may not only improve its competitive position but also strengthen competition in general.

Ordinarily there is no question of legality when a manufacturer agrees to sell to only one retailer or wholesaler in a given territory, provided there are no limitations on competitive products. Also, a manufacturer can sell to dealers who do not carry competitor's products, as long as this is a voluntary decision on the part of the franchise holder.

Tying Contracts

A supplier is likely to push for a tying agreement when:

- There are shortages of a desired product, and the supplier also wants to push products that are less in demand.
- The supplier grants a franchise (as in fast-food services) and wants the franchisee to purchase all necessary supplies and equipment from this supplier.
- The supplier has exclusive dealers or distributors (in appliances, for example) and wants them to carry a full line of the supplier's products.

With regard to tying contracts, apparently a dealer can be required to carry a manufacturer's full line as long as this does not impede competition in the market. The arrangement may be questionable, however, if a supplier forces a dealer or a distributor to take slow-moving, less attractive items in order to acquire the really desirable products.

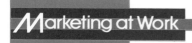

Successfully Tying-Back with Franchising

One example of a tying contract takes place when a franchising company requires that a franchisee buy from the franchiser some or all of the raw materials needed for the operation of the franchise. For example, Tim Horton's Donuts franchisees must buy all ''non-fresh'' ingredients from the franchise company; Pizza Delight franchisees buy all ''dry'' ingredients and meats from a food supply company that is owned by the franchiser; and in the case of Jungle Interiors franchisees, all silk plants and trees must be bought from Jungle Interiors or an authorized supplier.

Such arrangements are not in violation of the exclusive dealing or tied selling provisions in Section 49 of the Competition Act because they do not substantially lessen competition. In addition, the Act specifically exempts from these provisions situations in which the companies involved are affiliated, which they clearly are under a franchise agreement.

Exclusive Territories   Traditionally, the strategy of exclusive (or closed) sales territories has been used by manufacturers in assigning market areas to retailing or wholesaling middlemen. However, closed sales territories can create area monopolies, lessen competition, and restrict trade among middlemen who carry the same brand. Exceptions are generally provided when a company is small or is a new entrant to the market, in order to facilitate market entry.

These limitations on closed sales territories are likely to foster vertical marketing systems, where the manufacturer retains ownership of the product until it reaches the final buyer. That is, the manufacturer could either (1) own the retail or wholesale outlet or (2) consign products on an agency basis to the middlemen but retain ownership. In either of these situations, exclusive territories are quite legal.

SUMMARY   With an understanding of the retailing and wholesaling institutional structure as a foundation, marketing executives are in a position to design and manage distribution-channel systems for their companies. These tasks are likely to be easier if executives realize that a trade channel is a living structure that should be developed as a total system. Channel design and management are often a problem, however, because middlemen in the channel are independent organizations, whose goals may conflict with those of the manufacturer.

Conflicts in channels of distribution can occur on the same level of distribution (horizontal conflict) or between different distribution levels (vertical conflict). Probably the most intensive struggle is between producers and wholesalers of manufactured consumer products. Manufacturers may use alternative channels that bypass the wholesalers. Wholesalers, in turn, can strive to improve their efficiency and to provide services for their retailer customers. Manufacturers and retailers are often in conflict, because there are fundamental differences in the goals and business philosophies of the two groups.

To offset the disadvantages of the traditional, fragmented approach to distribution, many firms (producers, wholesalers, and retailers) are developing vertical marketing systems. These systems are typically controlled by means of corporate ownership, economic power, or formal contract.

In establishing channels of distribution, management faces three tasks. The first is to select the basic channel. This choice is influenced by the market, the product, the middlemen, and the company itself. The second step is to determine the intensity of distribution. How many middlemen will be used on each distribution level in a given market? The third step is to select the individual middlemen and then develop a cooperative working relationship with each of them. Throughout the channel-management activity, executives should be aware of the legal constraints affecting their ability to control their product as it goes through the channel.

NOTES

[1] Donald W. Jackson, Jr., and Bruce J. Walker, "The Channel Manager: Marketing's Newest Aide?" *California Management Review*, Winter 1980, pp. 52–58.

[2] For a report on the status of theory and research regarding power and conflict in channels of distribution, see John F. Gaski, "The Theory of Power and Conflict in Channels of Distribution," *Journal of Marketing*, Summer 1984, pp. 9–29.

[3] Warren J. Wittreich, "Misunderstanding the Retailer," *Harvard Business Review*, May–June 1962, p. 147.

[4] See Donald M. Jackson, Robert F. Krampf, and Leonard J. Konopa, "Factors That Affect the Length of Industrial Channels," *Industrial Marketing Management*, October 1982, pp. 263–268.

[5] See James D. Hlavacek and Tommy J. McCuistion, "Industrial Distributors — When, Who, and How?" *Harvard Business Review*, March–April 1983, pp. 96–101.

KEY TERMS AND CONCEPTS

Conflicts on the *same* level of distribution 413
Conflicts between *different* levels of distribution 413
Scrambled merchandising 413
Channel leader 414
Missionary sales people 417
Vertical marketing systems: 420
    Corporate 420

Administered 420
Contractual 420
Selection of a channel 421
Dual distribution 425
Intensive distribution 426
Selective distribution 426
Exclusive distribution 427
Exclusive dealing 430
Tying contracts 430
Exclusive (closed) territories 430

QUESTIONS AND PROBLEMS

1. "Large manufacturers always control the channels used to reach local markets." Do you agree? In your city or town, are there big manufacturers that are unable to tap the local market except through local independent retailers?

2. Explain the role played by each of the following factors in the conflict between manufacturers and wholesalers, particularly in the marketing of consumer products.
   a. Traditional position of the wholesaler before 1920.
   b. Changing position of the manufacturer since the late 1800s.
   c. Changing position of the retailer since 1920.

3. Why is there considerably less friction between manufacturers and whole-salers in the industrial goods field than in the consumer goods field?

4. Explain the reasons why manufacturers are dissatisfied with the performance of wholesalers. Do you agree with the manufacturers' point of view?

5. Why are full-service wholesalers relatively unimportant in the marketing of women's high fashion wearing apparel, furniture, and large electrical equipment?

6. ''The use of a missionary sales force is a compromise between the use of the wholesaler and the elimination of the wholesaler.'' Discuss this idea, showing how missionary sales people can offset manufacturers' objections to wholesalers.

7. ''The future of wholesalers depends upon their ability to increase their own efficiency and to furnish managerial aids to their retailers.'' Discuss, point-ing out the alternatives if the wholesaler fails to meet this challenge.

8. Explain, using examples, the differences among the three major types of verti-cal systems — corporate, administered, contractual. Which is the best kind?

9. Which of the channels illustrated in Fig. 15-1 is most apt to be used for each of the following products? Defend your choice in each case.
   a. Fire insurance.
   b. Single-family residences.
   c. Farm tractors.
   d. Washing machines.
   e. Hair spray.
   f. Men's shoes.

10. ''The great majority of industrial sales are made directly from the producer to the industrial user.'' Explain the reason for this in terms of the nature of the market, then in terms of the product.

11. A small manufacturer of sports fishing equipment is faced with the problem of selecting its channel of distribution. What reasonable alternatives does it have? Consider particularly the nature of its product and the nature of its market.

12. Is a policy of intensive distribution consistent with consumer buying habits for convenience goods? For shopping goods? Is intensive distribution nor-mally used in the marketing of any type of industrial goods?

13. From a manufacturer's viewpoint, what are the competitive advantages of exclusive distribution?

14. What are the drawbacks to exclusive selling from a retailer's point of view? To what extent are these alleviated if the retailer controls the channel for the particular brand?

15. A manufacturer of a well-known brand of men's clothing has been selling directly to one dealer in an Ontario city for many years. For some time, the market has been large enough to support two retailers very profitably. Yet the present holder of the franchise objects strongly when the manufacturer suggests adding another outlet. What alternative does the manufacturer have in this situation? What course of action would you recommend?

16. ''Manufacturers should always strive to select the lowest-cost channel of distribution.'' Do you agree? Should they always try to use the middlemen with the lowest operating costs? Explain.

CASE 5.1

THE UPPER CANADA BREWING COMPANY (D) Developing a Distribution Strategy

Frank Heaps, president of the Upper Canada Brewing Company, carefully reviewed the decisions for the distribution element of the marketing plan. He sensed that these decisions were of vital importance to the success of the new brewery; if the products were not available where the customers wished to purchase them, it was likely that the sale would be lost. As well, he realized the importance of coordinating the distribution strategies with the other three elements of the marketing mix. The decisions he faced concerned the intensity of distribution, the geographic scope of the initial as well as future distribution, and the type of licensee establishments to serve. The critical decision on the channel structure was solved; in Ontario there existed a very efficient distribution network exclusively for brewery products called Brewers' Warehousing Company Limited ("Brewers' Warehousing").

BREWERS' WAREHOUSING

The sale of beer in Ontario is conducted in almost all cases by Brewers' Warehousing. This company, which is owned by five brewing companies (Labatts, Molson, Carling O'Keefe, Heineken, and Northern Breweries), has the exclusive franchise to distribute domestically-produced beer in Ontario. The producers bring their products to the Brewers' Warehousing depot, from there the products are distributed to the Brewers' Retail outlets, the Liquor Control Board of Ontario (L.C.B.O.) stores, and licensee establishments. The empty bottles and kegs are also returned to the Brewers' Warehousing depot where they are sorted and picked up by the appropriate owner. The charge for this service varied with the distribution agreement. The type of agreement negotiated by the Upper Canada Brewing Company involved the payment of a service charge of $21 per hectolitre (75 percent Brewers' Retail and 25 percent licensee) with a 5 percent increase per year.

THE DECISIONS

The first major distribution decision facing Mr. Heaps was to determine the geographic scope of the market he wished to serve at present and in the future. The alternatives he considered were: (i) Toronto; (ii) Toronto Census Metropolitan Area; and (iii) Southern Ontario. He wondered which of these alternatives was most realistic to help him reach his market share objective of 0.1 percent of the Ontario market (see Table A-2, page 67, for details on the Toronto and Toronto CMA marketplace). He also considered exporting to the United States and Germany as soon as he achieved viability in the Ontario marketplace. Given the fact that there were no taxes on beer in the U.S., the beer could sell at approximately half the domestic selling price, despite the small duty imposed on Canadian beer. He felt that this price differential would help launch the beer on the U.S. market. He also wanted to export the beer to Germany with the hope of being the first Canadian beer to meet the rigid German standards. This achievement would further enhance the quality image of the brewery's product(s).

This case was prepared by Donna M. Stapleton and is intended to stimulate discussion of an actual management problem and not to illustrate either effective or ineffective handling of that problem. The author wishes to acknowledge the support provided by the Upper Canada Brewing Company, and particularly by Frank Heaps, President.

A related decision concerned the intensity of distribution. Should he have the products available in all locations where beer products were sold or should he use more selective distribution? The obvious advantage of using a more selective approach would be to provide a more exclusive image for the product(s) and to concentrate on areas where he felt the target market was located, in areas with the highest socioeconomic profiles, and neighbourhoods with significant ethnic components.

As well, he wondered if he should distribute to all Brewers' Retail outlets. Given the fact that Brewers' Retail stores did not stock imported beer, buyers of imported brands had to go to L.C.B.O. outlets. He wondered if he should concentrate on the Brewers' Retail outlets located adjacent or very close to L.C.B.O. stores. The rationale to support this move was that patrons of Brewers' Retail would be able to buy a quality premium beer (already chilled) in the ''Beer Store'' without having to make a special trip to the L.C.B.O.; conversely, those who were in the habit of going to an L.C.B.O. store for imported products would be able to buy the import-quality Upper Canada Brewery product(s) at the adjacent store. As well, he wondered if he should distribute to the L.C.B.O. stores themselves, given that the Brewers' Retail stores were nearby. If he did decide to distribute at these L.C.B.O. outlets, only one product line from each brewing company could be carried on their shelves.

A final distribution decision centred on the licensee trade — restaurants and taverns. Mr. Heaps projected that the licensee trade would contribute at least 15 percent of gross sales. He wondered which type of establishment he should serve and indeed what intensity of distribution would be ideal for these outlets.

<table>
<tr><td>QUESTIONS</td><td>

1. What geographic market should Mr. Heaps serve initially and in the future? Why?

2. What intensity of distribution would you recommend?

3. What types of licensee establishments should Mr. Heaps use? Why?
</td></tr>
</table>

CASE 5.2

JUNGLE INTERIORS CANADA INC.
Growing a Silk Plant Business

''Jungle Bob'' Thorssen had spent seven years in the jungles of Borneo, making money as a logger, timber trader, and bar owner. He came home to Calgary in 1979, hoping to invest the profits from his Asian businesses in the oil industry. He bought a Calgary machine shop business in 1980 to manufacture drill bits and tools for the oil and gas industry. While his machine shop business was struggling to survive during the recession of the early 1980s, he noticed that the city was almost literally becoming a jungle.

There was greenery everywhere — almost every office building, bar, restaurant, and shopping mall in Calgary had some plants to add colour and warmth. But live plants brought with them their own problems — maintenance and replacement costs, problems with insects, wilted leaves resulting from overwatering (and underwatering), stained carpets, and so on. Bob Thorssen remembered the silk plants he had seen in Asia, maintenance-free, always fresh looking, and cost effective.

Mr. Thorssen commissioned a study to determine whether there was a market

This case was prepared by James G. Barnes and is intended to stimulate discussion of an actual management problem and not to illustrate either effective or ineffective handling of that problem. The author wishes to acknowledge the support provided by Jungle Interiors Canada, and particularly by Robert Thorssen, President; Catherine Robertson, Administrator; and Allan Dagnall, Vice President, Franchise Development.

for silk plants in the Calgary area. Although the answer was clearly "No," Mr. Thorssen went ahead to explore the possibility of establishing a business to supply silk plants, basing his decision on the quality of silk plants he had seen in Asia and on the fact that there was no organized competition in the supply of silk plants for commercial buildings. He made several trips to Hong Kong in 1981 and contracted with a small manufacturer of artificial stems and silk-screened leaves. He opened the first Jungle Interiors in a downtown Calgary mall in December 1982.

The manufacture of "silk" plants, trees, and flowers was perfected by the Chinese more than 3000 years ago. While silk was the raw material most readily available for these early artisans, today's "silk" plants are made from a variety of materials including polyester, to give the most realistic texture and colour possible. Working with suppliers in Hong Kong and China, Bob Thorssen developed the manufacturing process that would provide the highest quality product to his customers and the best rate of return to Jungle Interiors.

To manufacture Jungle Interiors' silk plants, near-perfect leaf specimens of the plant to be duplicated are selected. Colours are chosen to duplicate the original colour of the leaves as closely as possible. The specimen leaves are photographed and photographic plates are made to produce each silk screen needed to obtain the detailed highlights of the leaf. The correct type of polyester is chosen to ensure that the fabric can hold the colour and imitate the texture and sheen of the real leaf. The correct mixture of coloured plastic is determined for the injection moulding of stems and leaf veins. Bolts of the polyester fabric are then rolled out on long tables and each leaf is individually silk-screened onto the material. The fabric is then dried and subsequent silk screenings are applied to give further detail and colour variation. Leaves are hand punched with a cutting die from the completed silk screen. The flat cut leaves are laid in a brass mould where they are heat-formed and bonded with the injection moulded plastic veins to give each leaf its support and stem. Each plant is assembled — leaves, stems, and natural wood trunks — and flat packed into boxes for shipping. The result is a realistic "silk" plant.

Bob Thorssen was aware that some of the sales of his new company would come from household consumers, but he was placing the emphasis on sales to the commercial sector of the market. He wished to reach both residential and commercial customers throughout Canada, as he genuinely believed that "silk" plants represented an untapped market that no other company had begun to address. He knew that some silk plants were sold in florists' shops as a complementary item to real plants. Department stores sold artificial flowers, but their quality could not compete with his silk plants. There was also no advertising of silk plants, and Mr. Thorssen could not help but think that most consumers were probably unaware that quality silk plants even existed.

While he was confident that he could produce the best silk plants available in Canada, Bob Thorssen had to consider how both residential and commercial customers would approach the decision to buy silk plants. Would they buy from stores other than traditional florists? Could he develop among Canadian consumers a brand preference for Jungle Interiors' silk plants? Would his plants be viewed as a substitute for real plants and flowers, or merely as a complementary item? He felt that the commercial sector represented the greatest potential to sell the concept of using silk plants and to generate large volumes of sales.

From his first Jungle Interiors store in Calgary, "Jungle Bob" Thorssen's company has expanded across the country. In 1985, Mr. Thorssen decided to franchise his silk plant retailing concept and a total of 13 stores were opened by 1987 — two company owned and 11 franchised. The company was doing more than $3 million in sales annually, with about 40% of sales going to commercial customers. About 90 percent of the Jungle Interiors' sales come from silk plants, the rest from accessories and gift items, such as wooden masks, ceramics, and wall hangings. Each Jungle Interiors store offers a plant leasing program, a professional commercial representative design service, installation, and fade-resistance guarantees on all plants.

The silk plants are still manufactured in Hong Kong and China and are shipped to the company's Calgary headquarters for assembly and later delivery to franchisees located from Vancouver to Halifax. Statistics available to Mr. Thorssen showed that the Canadian market for silk trees and plants represented approximately 10 percent of the total United States market of $450 million.

Jungle Interiors Canada Inc., with its expansion to 13 outlets and sales in excess of $3 million, now accounted for approximately 7 percent of the total Canadian market. With the addition of newly sourced product lines developed to address the needs of the commercial market and the planned opening of one new store per month, Jungle Interiors planned to attain an overall market share of 10 percent by the end of 1988.

In early 1987, Bob Thorssen and his management team were meeting to discuss the Jungle Interiors' corporate plan for 1987-88. The group had decided that the target for the next couple of years would be to have 39 stores operating coast to coast in Canada by the end of 1989. Obviously, the company would have to open franchised outlets in areas where no stores had yet been established. In order to oversee the expansion of the franchise network, Mr. Thorssen decided to establish a franchise development function within the company. The Vice President, Franchise Development, would be responsible for the marketing and opening of new franchises, including the development and implementation of a franchise marketing plan, and the identification of appropriate franchise locations through location analysis and market research.

The new Vice President, Franchise Development, Allan Dagnall, was appointed in August 1987 and immediately began to develop marketing programs, market analyses, a new business plan, and an information kit to be sent to individuals who might be interested in opening a Jungle Interiors franchised store. One component of that information kit was a "question and answer" sheet that contained answers to most of the questions a potential franchisor might ask (see exhibit).

EXHIBIT   THE JUNGLE INTERIORS FRANCHISE: QUESTIONS AND ANSWERS

Q. **What is Jungle Interiors?**
A. Jungle Interiors is a highly successful marketer of "silk" plants and trees. Our products can be used in place of "live" plants in homes, offices or any other indoor space...and in certain outdoor situations as well.

Q. **Are "silk" plants really made of silk?**
A. No. When artificial plants were created by the Chinese artisans 3000 years ago, silk was just about the only fabric that could be used. Today we use a variety of materials in our fine, hand-made plants and trees. In fact, we spend a great deal of time insuring that the material used in a particular plant allows the most realistic texture and colour possible.

Q. **How are these products sold?**
A. Through professionally designed retail outlets and small teams of outside sales people.

Q. **Are "silks" the only products sold by Jungle Interiors' stores?**
A. No. Each Jungle Interiors' store offers an interesting and unusual assortment of gift items and decorative accessories, such as wooden masks, ceramics, wall hangings, and rattan.

Q. **Do I need a specific kind of experience to succeed in a Jungle Interiors' franchise?**
A. No. But it is critical that you are enthusiastic, hardworking, and dedicated to your own success.

Q. **What type of assistance do I receive to reach my goal?**
A. The Jungle Interiors' training program has been designed to provide you with a thorough understanding of all our marketing, operating, and administrative systems. Afterwards our comprehensive manuals are convenient and practical for reference and staff training purposes. What's more, each member of our corporate staff is interested in your success. You'll see a lot of us in your store and at meetings to which other franchisees are invited. And, should a problem arise, we're never more than a phone call away.

Q. **What has made Jungle Interiors so successful?**
A. That's easy! An innovative product line, aggressive marketing programs, an emphasis on the good old-fashioned traditions of quality and value, strong point-of-sale programs.

Q. **How much is the franchise fee, and what does it cover?**
A. The fee for a Jungle Interiors' franchise is $25,000. This fee gives you the right to operate a full Jungle Interiors' outlet in a mutually agreeable location. It covers training for you and a full-time manager. And it provides you with a variety of

tools and other materials you will need to successfully operate your store. In addition, we help plan your "grand opening," hire and train your staff, and merchandise your store.

Q. **What do I have to pay on an ongoing basis?**
A. Each franchisee is required to pay a monthly royalty equal to six percent of his or her gross sales volume.

Q. **How is advertising handled?**
A. Each franchisee contributes two percent of gross sales to our national advertising fund. This money is used to offset development costs and sponsor promotional events throughout the franchise network. In addition, each franchisee is expected to do some advertising individually, or in conjunction with other franchisees in the same area.

Q. **Where do I purchase my materials and supplies**?
A. All products that are sold or used in your outlet must be purchased from Jungle Interiors or from an authorized supplier. This assures consistency and works to the benefit of the entire network.

Q. **I know nothing about store design and construction. What do I do**?
A. If you wish, Jungle Interiors will look after all the design and construction details. We'll hand you a key to your new store when everything is finished.

Q. **Can I sell my Jungle Interiors' franchise in the future**?
A. Yes. Your Jungle Interiors' franchise can be sold at any time to any company-approved buyer.

Q. **What sort of total investment are we talking about?**
A. Including the franchise fee and inventory, your total investment will be between $100,000 and $130,000. Of this, you will need to put up at least $50,000 in cash. The balance can be financed (if you qualify). For many locations, there are government assistance programs available to help you get started.

QUESTIONS

1. Evaluate the concept that Bob Thorssen has developed to expand the Jungle Interiors company across Canada. Evaluate also the information that is provided to potential franchisors in the "question and answer" sheet.

2. What would you need to know to decide whether a Jungle Interiors store would be successful in the city or town where you live? How would you decide whether or not to apply for a franchise?

CASE 5.3

TAPIS ROYALE
Setting a Brand Apart
Through Retail
Merchandising

Mr. Phillipe Gagnon is president of Tapis Royale Inc., a Canadian manufacturer of carpeting with head offices in a city in eastern Quebec. Mr. Gagnon was giving serious thought to a retail merchandising support program that members of his senior management group had developed. He was not sure how retailers would react to the proposed program; nor was he sure what competing retailers and manufacturers would do if Tapis Royale retailers made effective use of it. He was also giving considerable thought to whether the proposed program would give his firm an edge in the highly competitive retail carpet market.

Tapis Royale is one of the largest manufacturers of carpeting in Quebec and would be considered mid-sized among Canadian-owned manufacturers. The company produces a complete line of household and commercial carpeting, in a range

This case was prepared by James G. Barnes and is intended to present a marketing problem, rather than to illustrate either effective or ineffective handling of that problem.

of fabrics and colours. It also manufactures carpet tiles, primarily for the commercial and industrial markets. The company operates four mills in Quebec, one in Ontario and one in rural New Hampshire, from which carpeting is distributed to retailers in the eastern United States. The Tapis Royale product line is manufactured from a variety of fabrics, including wool and various synthetics such as nylon and Antron and is available at independent carpet retailers and department stores throughout Canada.

The Canadian carpeting industry is characterized by considerable fragmentation, with a large number of companies operating, ranging in size from large multinational companies to somewhat smaller regional firms such as Tapis Royale. Mr. Gagnon was concerned that most consumers who wanted to purchase carpeting for their homes were generally unaware of the brand names available in carpeting stores and department stores. He felt that the lack of awareness might even be greater in the case of Tapis Royale, which would probably not be as well known as some of the large carpet manufacturers, including Burlington, Kraus, and Coronet. He was sure that there was little if any brand loyalty and that consumers generally sought out the retailer first and then decided on the carpet.

Phillipe Gagnon and his management team were concerned that too much reliance in the marketing of carpet was left to the retailer. He knew how important the retailer is in attracting the customer and in directing him or her toward (or away from) a particular fabric or type of carpet. He was also very concerned about the high variability across the country in the manner in which carpet retailers displayed, promoted, and merchandised the carpet that they carried in their stores.

Most carpet retailers point to the high cost of producing effective merchandising programs for particular brands of carpet that they carry in their stores. Other reasons for a less than satisfactory level of support at the retail level included a lack of merchandising expertise on the part of some retailers and time constraints in what is undoubtedly a very competitive business at the retail level. But Mr. Gagnon was confident that the relatively poor quality of promotional activity on the part of independent retailers was hurting the sales of his company. In late 1987, he decided to do something about it. He wanted to bring more customers into Canadian carpet retail stores and he wanted to make sure that they bought Tapis Royale carpeting.

Working with Tapis Royale management group, Mr. Gagnon wanted to develop a new concept in carpet retail merchandising, one that would allow Tapis Royale carpet to stand out in the confusion that exists in most carpet outlets and carpet departments of department stores. Tapis Royale would create a new retail environment that would be much more conducive to the creation of a somewhat unique image for the Tapis Royale brand. It was obvious that the retailers were going to have to be compensated if they were to cooperate in an improved merchandising program for the Tapis Royale line.

The concept developed by Phillipe Gagon and his team was named the ''Tapis Royale Suite.'' The objective of the program was to set up a display environment in larger carpet stores across Canada in which only Tapis Royale carpet was to be displayed. In the vast array of carpet that now is featured in most retail carpet stores, with racks and displays of carpet samples, Tapis Royale wanted to create an island devoted exclusively to the Tapis Royale line.

It was decided that the first phase of the ''Tapis Royale Suite'' program would be the establishment of ''suites'' in more than 100 retail stores across Canada, working first with stores in major markets in Quebec and Ontario where Tapis

Royale sales were better developed, and which were within easy contact by the company's sales staff. The program would then be moved east and west as market acceptance was established over a three-year period. Each "Tapis Royale Suite" was to feature only Tapis Royale carpet and was to look like a small room, with a variety of types of carpeting on floors, stairs, and walls. Each "suite" would be approximately three metres square. The finished look of the room would be enhanced with the use of appropriate furniture, lighting, and pictures on walls. The result would be an "oasis" effect, where Mr. Gagnon was confident Tapis Royale carpet would be more attractively displayed.

The second phase of the retailer merchandising program for Tapis Royale carpet was to involve the distribution of printed flyers that would be made available to retailers by Tapis Royale and that would feature only Tapis Royale carpet, attractively presented and priced. Tapis Royale would prepare four-page, four-colour flyers that qualifying retailers could purchase for $75 per 1,000 flyers. These flyers could be used by the retailers to distribute in their stores or to mail to prospective customers to promote special Tapis Royale sales events. This stage of the merchandising program was to be introduced only after 50 "Tapis Royale Suites" had been established. Mr. Gagnon was convinced that this promotional program, coupled with the "suites," would attract customers to the retail outlets and to the Tapis Royale brand.

The Tapis Royale management group felt it would be a distinct advantage for their company if they could convince Canadian carpet retailers to display and promote their carpet. In order to encourage retailers to participate in the program, Tapis Royale would assume the entire cost of the "Tapis Royale Suite" program — each "suite" was to cost an estimated $1,000. Each retailer who agreed to install a suite would sign an agreement that the store would display only Tapis Royale carpet within the suite and that the area would be properly decorated in a manner consistent with the image of the store and the Tapis Royale line.

Phillipe Gagnon was confident that Tapis Royale was about to make a major breakthrough in the retail merchandising of carpet in Canada. As preparations were being made to install the first Tapis Royale Suites in Montreal and Quebec City, he was looking forward to expanded sales over the next three years.

QUESTIONS

1. Do you agree with Mr. Gagnon's assessment of the process that consumers follow in the purchase of carpet for their homes? How does the proposed Tapis Royale program address the problems inherent in Mr. Gagnon's overview of how consumers buy carpet?

2. Evaluate the "Tapis Royale Suite" concept. How willing would you expect retailers to be to participate in the program? How would you expect consumers to react?

3. To what extent can Tapis Royale exercise control over the "Suite" program once the suites are installed in stores across the country?

4. Can Tapis Royale extend the suite concept into other lines that the company manufactures? Will it or some variation work for industrial and commercial carpeting? Can other manufacturers of carpet do the same thing? Would you now expect manufacturers of furniture, appliances, and other major items for the home to implement similar programs?

PART 6

PROMOTION

The design and management of a
marketing subsystem for the purpose of
informing and persuading present and
potential customers

So far, we have developed three of the four parts of a marketing mix to
reach the organization's target markets and achieve its marketing goals. We
have considered strategies regarding the product, the pricing structure, and
the distribution system. To complete the marketing mix, we now turn to
the task of developing a promotional program.

In Chapter 16 we discuss promotion as a communication process, the
concepts of the promotional mix and a promotional campaign, and finally,
the governmental regulation of promotional activities. Chapter 17 covers
the personal selling process and the management of a sales force. Chapter
18 is devoted to the management of advertising and sales promotion.

CHAPTER 16

THE PROMOTIONAL PROGRAM

This chapter is, essentially, a discussion of what promotion is and how it fits into a firm's complete marketing system. After studying this chapter, you should understand:

- Promotion and its relation to selling and nonprice competition.
- Promotion as a communication process.
- The concept of the promotional mix.
- The factors that shape a company's promotional mix.
- The problems and methods involved in determining the promotional appropriation.
- The concept of a promotional campaign.
- Government regulation of promotional activities.

A company's promotional campaign is a coordinated series of promotional activities built around a central idea or focal point that we call the *campaign theme*. The theme is simply the main promotional appeal dressed up in a distinctive, attention-getting form. Frequently the theme is expressed as a slogan. Now just how effective are these theme-slogans? Well, at this point we are listing 15 promotional slogans and are asking you to identify the brand or company associated with each slogan. The answers are on the next page.

1. Our product is steel. Our strength is people. ~~Dofasco~~ Stelco
2. A diamond is forever.
3. When you care enough to send the very best.
4. A blending of art and machine.
5. Just slightly ahead of our time.
6. We treat you right. DQ
7. The Un-Cola. 7-up
8. Let your fingers do the walking. Yellow Pages
9. Engineered like no other car in the world.
10. A car you can believe in.
11. We are. Canada's department store. Eaton's
12. Giving business our best.
13. Naturally resourceful.
14. The quality goes in before the name goes on.
15. We treat you like a somebody. Midas

ANSWERS TO PROMOTIONAL THEME-SLOGANS:

1. Dofasco
2. DeBeers Diamonds
3. Hallmark Cards
4. Jaguar
5. Panasonic
6. Dairy Queen
7. 7-Up
8. Yellow Pages
9. Mercedes-Benz
10. Volvo
11. Eaton's
12. Air Canada Executive Class
13. Domtar
14. Zenith
15. Speedy Muffler

Product planning, pricing, and distribution are marketing activities that are per-formed mainly within the company, or between the company and its marketing "partners." However, in its promotional activities, the firm gets its chance to communicate with potential customers. Chapters 16 to 18 deal with the management of the **promotional mix** — that is, the combination of personal selling, advertising, sales promotion, publicity, and public relations. These are the promotional tools that help an organization to achieve its marketing objectives. The statement that "nothing happens until somebody sells something" expresses rather well the place of promotional activities in today's business scene.

MEANING AND IMPORTANCE OF PROMOTION

Promotion is the element in an organization's marketing mix that is used to inform and persuade the market regarding the organization's products and services. Many people consider *selling* and *marketing* to be synonymous terms, when, actually, selling is only one of the many components of marketing. We shall treat *selling* and *promotion* as synonymous terms, although promotion is preferred. For many people, selling suggests only the transfer of title or only the activities of sales people and does not include advertising or other methods of stimulating demand. In our definition, promotion includes advertising, personal selling, and all other selling tools. Together, they are basic factors in the marketing mix (see Fig. 16-1).

Promotional Methods

The two most widely used methods of promotion are (1) **personal selling** and (2) **advertising**. Other forms of promotion are:

3. **Sales promotion**, which is designed to supplement and coordinate personal selling and advertising efforts. Sales promotion includes such activities as set-ting up store displays, holding trade shows, and distributing samples, premi-ums, or "cents-off" coupons.

FIGURE 16-1
The role of promotion in the marketing mix.
To reach your target market, coordinate the elements in the promotional mix, and coordinate promotion with the other elements in your marketing mix.

Coupons have become an important part of companies' sales promotion efforts. (Red Rose ® is a registered trademark of Thomas J. Lipton Inc.)

4. **Publicity**, which is a nonpersonal form of demand stimulation and is not paid for by the person or organization benefitting from it. Typically, publicity takes the form of a favourable news presentation — a ''plug'' — for a product, service, or organization. The plug is made in print, on radio or television, or in some form of public address. Typically, publicity is part of a firm's public relations effort.

5. **Public relations**, which is a planned effort by an organization to influence some group's attitude or opinion toward that organization. The target market of the public relations effort may be any given ''public,'' such as customers,

a government agency, or people living near the promoting organization. The firm's public relations department is responsible for a product or for the entire organization.

In addition, there is a group of marketing strategies, discussed in earlier chapters, that are in part promotional. Such strategies as product differentiation, market segmentation, trading up or trading down, and branding belong in this group.

Basic Nature of Promotion

Basically, promotion is an exercise in information, persuasion, and communication. These three are related, because to inform is to persuade, and conversely, a person who is being persuaded is also being informed. Persuasion and information become effective through some form of communication. Many years ago, Prof. Neil Borden pointed out the pervasive nature of persuasion (influence) in our socioeconomic system. He said that "the use of influence in commercial relations is one of the attributes of a free society, just as persuasion and counterpersuasion are exercised freely in many walks of life in our free society — in the home, in the press, in the classroom, in the pulpit, in the courts, in the political forum, in legislative halls and in government agencies for information."[1]

Promotion and Imperfect Competition

The North American marketplace today operates under conditions of imperfect competition. That means there is product differentiation, nonrational buyer behaviour, and less-than-complete market information. Under these conditions, promotional activities are essential. That is, a company needs promotion to aid in differentiating its product, to persuade the buyers, and to bring more information into the buying-decision process.

In economic terms, the basic purpose of promotion is to change the location and shape of the demand (revenue) curve for a company's product. (See Fig. 16-2 and recall the discussion of nonprice competition in Chapter 12.) Through the use of promotion, a company hopes to increase a product's sales volume at any given price. It also hopes that promotion will affect the demand elasticity for the product. The intent is to make the demand *inelastic* when the price increases, and *elastic* when the price goes down. In other words, management wants the quantity demanded

FIGURE 16-2

The goal of promotion: to change the pattern of demand for a product.

Through promotion a company attempts to (a) shift a product's demand curve to the right and (b) change the shape of the curve.

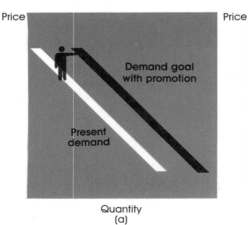
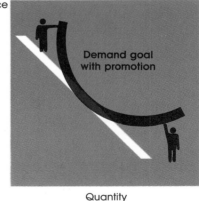

to decline very little when the price goes up (inelastic demand). However, when the price goes down, management would like sales to increase considerably (elastic demand).

Need for Promotion

Several factors illustrate the need for promotion today. In the first place, as the distance between producers and consumers increases, and as the number of potential customers grows, the problem of market communication becomes significant.

Once middlemen are introduced into a marketing pattern, it is not enough for a producer to communicate only with the ultimate consumers or industrial users. It becomes essential that the middlemen, too, be informed about products. Wholesalers, in turn, must promote the products to retailers, and retailers must communicate with consumers. In other words, even the most useful and want-satisfying product will be a marketing failure if no one knows it is available. A basic purpose of promotion is to disseminate information — to let potential customers know!

The intense competition among different industries, as well as among individual firms within an industry, has placed tremendous pressures on the promotional programs of individual sellers. In our economy of abundance, want-satisfaction has generally replaced the necessity of fulfilling only basic physiological needs. Consequently, customers are more selective in their buying choices, and a good promotional program is needed to reach them.

Oddly enough, promotion is also needed during periods of shortages — the opposite of abundance. During periods of shortages, advertising can stress product conservation and efficient uses of the product. The sales force can direct its efforts toward servicing accounts and helping customers solve their shortage-induced problems.

Promotion and Strategic Marketing Planning

In line with the strategic approach to marketing planning, a company should treat all its promotional efforts as a complete subsystem within the total marketing system. This means coordinating sales-force activities, advertising programs, and other promotional efforts. Unfortunately, today in many firms these activities still are fragmented, and advertising managers and sales-force managers often are in conflict.[2]

As we discuss strategic promotional planning, once again we see the interrelationships among the major elements of the marketing mix. Promotional activities must be coordinated with activities in product planning, pricing, and distribution. Promotion is influenced, for example, by the type of product being marketed and by aspects of pricing strategy. Promotion is especially interrelated with distribution strategy. In fact, promotion should be viewed as a distribution-channel activity. It is a mistake for a manufacturer or a middleman to think of developing a promotional program without considering its interdependency with other organizations in that firm's channel. Each firm in a channel should develop strategies that take into consideration the roles played by other firms in the channel. Each firm should view its promotion as part of a total distribution-channel effort. Such a view then would be consistent with our systems approach to marketing.

Promotion also should be strongly influenced by a firm's strategic marketing plan. Suppose, for example, that a company faces production limitations imposed by materials shortages. This firm's marketing goal is simply to hold onto its present customers and its present market share — at least in the short run. Its strategic marketing planning and the strategic planning for its promotional program would be geared toward attaining that objective. The promotional strategies would be quite different from those of a company where a newly developed technology offered bright prospects for market expansion.

THE COMMUNICATION PROCESS

As noted earlier, promotion is basically an exercise in communication. Executives who understand something of the theory of communication should be able to better manage their firm's promotional program.

The word **communication** is derived from the Latin word *communis*, meaning ''common.'' Thus, when you communicate, you are trying to establish a ''commonness'' with someone. Through the use of verbal or nonverbal symbols, you as the source send a message through a channel to a receiver, in an effort to share information. Fundamentally, the communication process requires only four elements — a **message**, a **source** of this message, a communication **channel**, and a **receiver**. However, in practice, additional elements come into play. The information that the sending source wants to share must first be **encoded** into transmittable form, *transmitted*, and then *decoded* by the receiver. Another element to be reckoned with is **noise**, which is anything that tends to distort the message at any stage of the system. The final element in the process — **feedback** — tells the sender whether the message was received and how it was perceived by the target. The feedback is also the basis for planning ahead. The sender learns how the communication may be improved by determining how well the message was received. If the message is not understood, then there is no true ''commonness'' or communication. Thus, **communication** is the verbal and/or nonverbal transmission of information between the sender and the receiver.

These elements constitute a general communications system — a concept that has many practical applications in promotion. In Fig. 16-3 we illustrate a communication system, using as examples some activities in a company's promotional program. The information source may be some marketing executives with ideas to communicate. They will encode these ideas into a transmittable message by putting them in advertisements or sales talks. The encoded message is then carried by a sales force or by advertising media (the message channels) to the destination receivers — perhaps various market segments. These consumer-receivers then decode (interpret) the message in light of their individual frames of reference. The closer the decoded message is to its encoded form (assuming it was encoded fully and accurately), the more effective the communication is. By evaluating the receiver's words or actions (feedback), the sender can judge how well the message got through. At various stages in the communication process, the message is subject to interference (noise) from competitors' advertising, confusion in the receivers' homes, or other disturbances.

DETERMINATION OF PROMOTIONAL MIX

Management has to determine what combinations of advertising, personal selling, and other promotional tools will make the most effective promotional program for a company. This is a tough job. Executives simply do not know exactly how much

FIGURE 16-3

A marketing communication system illustrating activities in promotional program.

To reach customers in a large geographical market requires advertising.

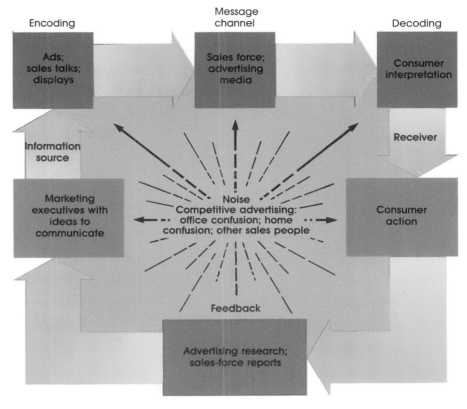

Marketing at Work

Saying It Silently: A Picture Is Worth....

When we think of communicating, we generally think of the use of words or sounds. But some of the best advertising does not use any words to get its message across. In print advertising, for example, some advertisers, particularly those in the fashion business, use no words at all. For example, some advertisements for Chanel rely on the brand name and the illustration to communicate a message. Through the use of the illustration and its various aspects, the advertiser is able to create a certain mood, image, atmosphere, or feeling about the product. No words are needed. The illustration, the setting, and the brand name say it all.

the advertising or any other promotional tool will help achieve the goals of the marketing program.

DO OENOLOGISTS KNOW HOW TO COMMUNICATE — ESPECIALLY WITH THE VAST POTENTIAL MARKET OF PEOPLE WHO KNOW VERY LITTLE ABOUT WINES?

An *oenologist* (also spelled *enologist*) is a specialist in the science and study of wines. Perhaps two oenologists can understand each other. But to the uninitiated outsider, the oenologist's language often seems to be a snobbish jargon that tries to impress us, but really tells us nothing. Consider, for example, the following descriptions of seven French wines displayed at an exhibition:

1. A sturdy, well-balanced white wine.
2. Fresher and with more grace than wine #1. An underlying soundness and sturdiness. Not fresh but more serious in tone.
3. A lively rosé.
4. (Same wine as #3, but a vintage from two years earlier.) This wine has more colour and a more serious rosé (than #3). Exquisite balance and finish, with a nice complexity.
5. A quiet, subdued, elegant wine. But not for greatness.
6. More forward in bouquet. A big wine. A lasting finish.
7. A wine with an earthy quality. A light vintage with deep tones.

Now you tell us what they — the experts — are talking about. The name of the game in promotion is to communicate. If you cannot inform and persuade us, then you can't sell to us. And with wines, we wonder if the oenologists' message is really coming through.

Factors Influencing Promotional Mix

Four factors should be taken into account in deciding on the promotional mix. They are (1) the amount of money available for promotion, (2) the nature of the market, (3) the nature of the product, and (4) the stage of the product's life cycle.

FUNDS AVAILABLE

Regardless of what may be the most desirable promotional mix, the amount of money available for promotion is the real determinant of the mix. A business with ample funds can make more effective use of advertising than an enterprise with limited financial resources. Small or financially weak companies are likely to rely on personal selling, dealer displays, or joint manufacturer-retailer advertising. Lack of money may even force a company to use a less efficient promotional method. For example, advertising can carry a promotional message to far more people and at a lower cost *per person* than a sales force can. Yet the firm may have to rely on personal selling because it lacks the funds to take advantage of advertising's efficiency.

NATURE OF THE MARKET

As is true in most problem areas in marketing, decisions on the promotional mix will be greatly influenced by the nature of the market. This influence is felt in at least three ways.

- *Geographic scope of the market.* Personal selling may be adequate in a small local market, but as the market broadens geographically, greater stress must be placed on advertising.
- *Type of customers.* The promotional strategy is influenced by whether the organization is aiming its promotion at industrial users, household consumers, or middlemen. To illustrate, a promotional program aimed at retailers will probably include more personal selling than a program designed to attract household consumers. In many situations, the middlemen may strongly influence the promotional strategy used by a manufacturer. Often a retail store will not even stock a product unless the manufacturer agrees to do a certain amount of advertising.
- *Concentration of the market.* The total number of prospective buyers is one consideration. The fewer potential buyers there are, the more effective personal selling is, compared with advertising.

To reach customers in a large geographical market requires advertising.

Another consideration is the *number* of different *types* of potential customers. A market with only one type of customer will call for a different promotional mix from that of a market with many different customer groups. A firm selling large power saws used only by lumber manufacturers may be able to use personal selling effectively. In contrast, a company selling hand tools used by thousands of consumers and virtually all types of industrial firms probably will include liberal portions of advertising in its mix. Personal selling would be prohibitively expensive in reaching the many customers.

Finally, even though a firm sells nationally, it may find its market concentrated in relatively few spots. In this type of market concentration, emphasis on personal selling may be feasible. But it would be unrealistic if the potential customers were widely distributed all over the country.

Industrial products require personal selling.

Questions of Basic Promotional Strategy

NATURE OF THE PRODUCT

Consumer products and industrial goods frequently require different strategies. Within the category of consumer goods, a promotional mix is influenced by whether the product is generally considered a convenience, shopping, or specialty item. With regard to industrial goods, installations are not promoted in the same way as operating supplies.

Firms marketing convenience goods will normally rely heavily on manufacturers' advertising in addition to dealer displays. Personal selling plays a relatively minor role. This mix is best because a convenience product is widely distributed and needs no special demonstration or explanation.

In the field of industrial goods, the promotional strategy used to market installations usually features heavy emphasis on personal selling. The unit sales are typically large, products are often made to the customer's specification, and considerable presale and postsale personal service is necessary.

STAGE OF THE PRODUCT'S LIFE CYCLE

Promotional strategies for a product are influenced by the life-cycle stage that a product is in at any given time. Table 16-1 shows how these strategies change as the product moves through its life cycle.

By asking and then answering six questions regarding promotional strategy, we can set some guidelines for determining a company's promotional mix. The answers are related to the four factors that influence the mix.

WHEN SHOULD PERSONAL SELLING BE THE MAIN INGREDIENT?

Personal selling will ordinarily carry the bulk of the promotional load (1) when the company has insufficient funds with which to carry on an adequate advertising program, (2) when the market is concentrated, or (3) when the personality of a sales person is needed to establish rapport. Personal selling will also be emphasized when the product (4) has a high unit value, (5) requires demonstration, (6) must be fitted to the individual customer's needs, as in the case of securities or insurance, or (7) involves a trade-in.

WHEN SHOULD ADVERTISING BE THE MAIN INGREDIENT?

If the market for the product is widespread, as in the case of a national consumer market, advertising should receive heavy emphasis. Advertising also works best when the seller wishes to inform many people quickly, as in the case of an announcement of new store hours or a special sale.

Certainly not every product lends itself to advertising. Many years ago, Prof. Neil Borden identified five criteria that can serve as guides for management in determining the "advertisability" of its product. If all five of these criteria are met, normally there is an excellent opportunity to advertise. However, this ideal situation rarely exists. Ordinarily, a product or service meets some, but not all, of these

TABLE 16-1   **PROMOTIONAL STRATEGY AND PRODUCT LIFE-CYCLE STAGE**

Market situation	Promotional strategy
	Introductory stage
Customers do not realize that they want the product, nor do they understand how it will benefit them.	Inform and educate potential customers. Tell them that the product exists, how it might be used, and what want-satisfying benefits it provides. In this stage, a seller must stimulate **primary demand** — the demand for a type of product — as contrasted with **selective demand** — the demand for a particular brand. For example, manufacturers had to sell consumers on the value of microwave kitchen ovens in general before it was feasible to promote General Electric or some other brand. Normally, heavy emphasis must be placed on personal selling. Trade shows are also used extensively in the promotional mix. Rather than call on customers individually, the company can promote its new product at some type of trade show where prospective customers come to the seller's exhibit. Manufacturers also rely heavily on personal selling to attract middlemen to handle a new product.
	Growth stage
Customers are aware of product benefits. The product is selling well, and middlemen want to handle it.	Stimulate selective (brand) demand. Increase the emphasis on advertising. Middlemen share more of the total promotional burden.
	Maturity stage
Competition intensifies and sales level off.	Advertising is used as a tool of persuasion rather than only to provide information. Intense competition forces sellers to devote larger sums to advertising and thus contributes to the declining profits experienced in the maturity stage.
	Sales-decline stage
Sales and profits are declining. New and better products are coming into the market.	All promotional effort should be cut back substantially, except when attempting to revitalize the product.

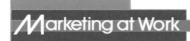

Market Expansion and Extension for Mature Brands

One of the greatest challenges a marketer faces is to increase the sales of a mature brand — one which has reached the mature stage of its life cycle. There are a variety of techniques that can be used to stimulate sales of mature brands that are well established. These include advertising, consumer promotions, and trade promotions.

One objective of a consumer promotion is to encourage the purchaser to buy the brand more often or to buy it instead of a competing brand. Another reason for using promotions is to draw former users back to the brand. Both of these tasks are easier than attracting completely new users. For mature brands, consumer promotions are among the most important marketing tools. There are five major types — coupons, refunds, contests, sampling, and premium offers.

Another strategy to stimulate sales of a mature brand is to create a ''flanker'' or a brand extension. A flanker or line extension is a new variety of the same basic product — tartar-fighting toothpaste, decaffeinated coffee, lemon-scented dish-washing detergent. A brand extension, on the other hand, takes the well-known brand name and applies it to a different, although usually closely related, product. Vicks of Vap-O-Rub fame introduced Vicks cough drops many years ago. Ivory Soap led to Ivory shampoo and conditioner. Tide detergent spawned Tide liquid. Cow Brand baking soda capitalized on another use for the product and led to Cow Brand Carpet and Upholstery Freshener. Sunkist has introduced a line of Vitamin C tablets. In all cases, the launch of the brand extension is made infinitely easier by the fact that the brand name is well known and highly regarded. Advertising and promotions are likely to be effective because the consumer is already sold on the brand.

Source: Adapted from Jo Marney, ''Finding New Words for New-Old Products,'' *Marketing*, January 26, 1987, p. 10.

conditions. Then the decision on whether to advertise becomes more difficult.
 The five criteria are as follows:

■ The primary demand trend for the product should be favourable. In spite of public opinion to the contrary, advertising cannot successfully sell a product

When to stress advertising and when to stress personal selling: a summary.

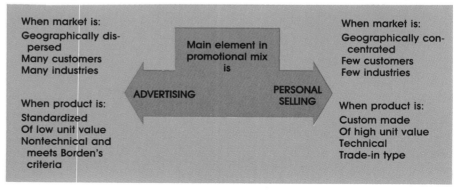

Do these greeting cards, hammer, and clothesline meet the criteria for advertising?

that people do not want. Nor can advertising reverse a declining primary demand.

- There should be considerable opportunity to differentiate the product. Then it is easier to advertise because the company has something to say. For this reason, automobiles or cosmetics are easier to advertise than salt or sugar. Products that are not easy to differentiate by *brand* may still be advertised by a trade association, such as the Dairy Bureau of Canada and the PEI Potato Growers.

- The product should have hidden qualities. This condition affords the seller grounds for educating the market through advertising. On this point, a sofa or a mechanical device is easier to advertise than greeting cards.

- Powerful emotional buying motives should exist for the product. Then buying action can be stimulated by appeal to these motives. It is easier to build an effective advertising campaign for Weight Watchers than for an article such as clotheslines or hammers.

- The company must have sufficient funds to support an advertising program adequately.

WHEN SHOULD PROMOTIONAL EFFORTS BY RETAILERS BE STRESSED?

If the product has important qualities that can be judged at the point of purchase, or if it is a highly standardized item, it lends itself to dealer display. So do products that are purchased on impulse. And retailer promotion is particularly important when the retailer is better known in the market than the manufacturer.

WHEN SHOULD MANUFACTURER-RETAILER COOPERATIVE ADVERTISING BE USED?

There are three questions involved here. These queries and some brief answers follow:

- When should a manufacturer list its dealers' names and addresses in advertisements? The retailers' names should be mentioned particularly when the manufacturer employs selective or exclusive distribution policies. It then becomes important to tell the market where the product may be obtained.

- Under what conditions should a manufacturer pay a retailer to mention the manufacturer's product in the retailer's advertisements? The manufacturer may have to pay the retailer's advertising cost just to get the retailer to carry the commodity. Also, the retailer may be in a position to demand payment when the retailer's name has better selling power than the manufacturer's.

- When should a retailer emphasize the manufacturer's product in the store's advertising and display? A retailer should promote the manufacturer's products when the manufacturer's name is very important.

SHOULD MANUFACTURERS USE A "PUSH" OR A "PULL" PROMOTIONAL STRATEGY?

The questions in the two preceding sections involving retailer promotion and cooperative advertising remind us again that promotion is a distribution-channel activity.

FIGURE 16-4
Push and pull promotional strategies.

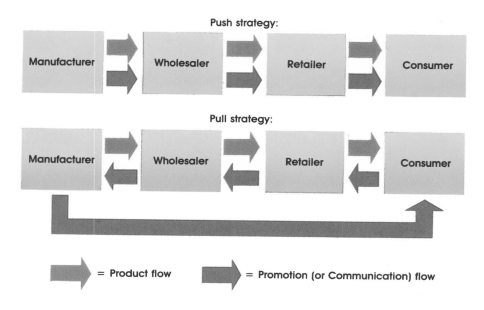

Consequently, manufacturers may aim their promotion either at middlemen or at end users to help move their products through the channels. Promotion aimed at middlemen is called a "push" strategy, and promotion aimed at end users is referred to as a "pull" strategy. Figure 16-4 illustrates these two strategies.

Using a **push strategy** means that the manufacturer will direct its promotion only at the middlemen who are the next link forward in this manufacturer's distribution channel. Let's take the case of a manufacturer who is selling through wholesalers and retailers to reach household consumers. This manufacturer will promote heavily only to the wholesalers. The wholesalers then use a push strategy to the retailers, and the retailers promote to the consumers. A push strategy usually involves the heavy use of personal selling and perhaps sales promotions such as demonstrating the product at trade shows. This promotional strategy is used by a great many manufacturers of industrial products, as well as for various consumer goods.[3]

When a **pull strategy** is used, a manufacturer directs the promotional effort at end users — usually ultimate consumers. The intention is to build up a consumer demand so that these people will ask for the product at retail stores. The retailers, in turn, will demand the product from wholesalers. In effect, the promotion to consumers is designed to *pull* the product through the channels. This strategy typically involves a heavy use of advertising plus possibly various forms of sales promotion such as premiums, free samples, or store demonstrations. Manufacturers of consumer packaged goods often use a pull strategy to get their products stocked on supermarket shelves.

As a practical matter, these push-pull strategies are extremes. Rarely does a company employ one of these strategies exclusively. Most firms — especially those marketing to ultimate consumers — both push and pull their product through the channels. Companies such as CIL, IBM, Johnson & Johnson, Scott Paper, Kodak and Procter & Gamble, for example, advertise heavily to end users. At the same time, these same firms have excellent sales forces who promote their products to wholesalers and large retailers.

SHOULD PROMOTIONAL ACTIVITY BE CONTINUED WHEN DEMAND IS HEAVY OR EXCEEDS CAPACITY?

The answer is a definite "yes." It is important that a manufacturer's name is kept before the public. A market is a dynamic institution, and customer loyalty is a "sometime thing." Old customers leave and new customers must be won. If conditions of high demand persist, they are certain to attract competitors. In any event, the nature of the advertising message may change. When demand is heavy in relation to supply, the advertiser probably will switch to institutional or indirect-action advertising.

DETERMINATION OF TOTAL PROMOTIONAL APPROPRIATION

It is extremely difficult to establish promotional appropriations. Management lacks reliable standards for determining (1) how much to spend on advertising or personal selling in total or (2) how much to spend on specific activities within each area. An even more serious problem is that management normally cannot assess the results of its promotional expenditures. A firm may decide to add ten sales people or increase its trade-show budget by $200,000 a year. But it cannot determine precisely what increase in sales or profits is to be expected from these moves. Nor can anyone measure with a high degree of certainty the relative values of the two expenditures.

Promotional activities usually are budgeted as current operating expenses, implying that their benefits are used up immediately. Through the years, however, several economists and business executives have proposed that advertising (and presumably other promotional efforts) should be treated as a capital investment. Their reasoning is that the benefits and returns on these investments often (1) are not immediately evident and (2) are spread over several years.

Methods of Determining Appropriation

There are four basic methods of determining the appropriation for promotion. These methods are frequently discussed in connection with the advertising appropriation alone, but they may also be applied to the total promotional appropriation.

RELATION TO SALES

The promotional appropriation may be related in some way to company income. The expenditures may be set as a percentage of past or anticipated sales. However, some businesses prefer to budget a fixed amount of money per *unit* of past or expected future sales. Manufacturers of products with a high unit value and a low rate of turnover (automobiles or appliances, for example) frequently use the unit method.

This **percentage-of-sales method** is probably the mostly widely used of all those discussed here. It has achieved broad acceptance because it is simple to calculate.

It also sets the cost in relation to sales income and thus has the effect of being a variable expense rather than a fixed expenditure.

Actually, the method is unsound and logically inconsistent. By setting promotional expenditures on the basis of past sales, management is saying that promotion is a *result* of sales when, in fact, it is a *cause* of sales. Even when promotion is set as a percentage of *future* sales, this method is logically indefensible. By forecasting *future* sales and then setting the promotional appropriation, management is still considering advertising and personal selling to be a *result* of sales. If sales depend upon promotion, as is truly the case, they cannot be forecast until the promotional appropriation has been determined. Another undesirable result of this method is that it reduces promotional expenditures when sales are declining. And this is just when promotion usually is most needed.

TASK OR OBJECTIVE

A much sounder basis for determining the promotional budget is to decide what tasks the promotional program must accomplish, and then to determine what this will cost. Various forms of this method are widely used today. The *task method* forces management to define realistically the goals of its promotional program.

Sometimes this approach is called the *buildup method* because of the way it operates. For example, as one goal, a company may elect to enter a new geographic market. The executives then decide that this venture will require ten additional sales people. Compensation and expenses of these people will cost a total of $520,000 per year. Salary for an additional sales supervisor and expenses for extra office and administrative needs will cost $70,000. Thus, in the personal selling part of the promotional mix, an extra $590,000 must be appropriated. Similar estimates can be made for the anticipated cost of advertising, sales promotion, and other promotional tools to be used. Thus the promotional appropriation is *built up* by adding up the costs of the individual promotional tasks needed to reach the goal of entering a new territory.

USE OF ALL AVAILABLE FUNDS

A new company frequently ploughs all available funds into its promotional program. The objective here is to build sales for the first one to five years. After that period, management expects to earn a profit and be able to budget for promotion in a different manner.

FOLLOW COMPETITION

A weak method of determining the promotional appropriation, but one that is used enough to be noted here, is to match the promotional expenditures of competitors. Sometimes only one competitor is followed. In other cases, management will have access to industry averages through its trade association, and these will become company benchmarks. The system is weak on at least two counts. First, a firm's competitors may be just as much in the dark regarding how to set a promotional budget. Second, one company's promotional goals and strategies may be quite different from those of its competitors, because of differences in the firms' strategic marketing planning.

THE CAMPAIGN CONCEPT:
AN EXERCISE IN
STRATEGIC PLANNING

In planning the total promotional program for an organization, management should make use of the campaign concept. A **campaign** is a coordinated series of promotional efforts built around a single theme and designed to reach a predetermined goal. In effect, a campaign is an exercise in strategic planning.

Although the term *campaign* is probably thought of most often in connection with advertising, we should apply the campaign concept first to the entire promotional program. Then the total promotional campaign can be subdivided into its advertising, personal selling, and sales promotion components. These subcampaigns can then be planned in more detail, to work toward the program goal.

Many types of promotional campaigns may be conducted by a company, and some may be run concurrently. Geographically, a firm may have a local, regional, or national campaign, depending upon the available funds and objectives. One campaign may be aimed at consumers, and another at wholesalers and retailers. The stage of a product's life cycle may determine whether a pioneering or a competitive campaign will be conducted.

In developing a promotional campaign, a firm should first establish the campaign goal. This goal, and the buying motives of the customers, will determine what selling appeals will be stressed. Assume that the goal of a promotional campaign put on by Wardair is to introduce its new air-bus service. Then the appeals might be to the customers' desire for speed, value, a quiet and restful trip, or good and courteous service. The same airline might want to increase its plane loadings of air freight. Then the ads and the personal selling might stress speed of delivery, reduction in losses due to spoilage and handling, or convenient schedules.

A campaign revolves around a central idea or focal point. This ''theme'' permeates all promotional efforts and tends to unify the campaign. A **theme** is simply the promotional appeals dressed up in a distinctive, attention-getting form. It expresses the product's benefits. Some companies use the same theme for several campaigns; others develop a different theme for each new campaign.

For a promotional campaign to be successful, the efforts of the participating groups must be coordinated effectively. This means that:

- The *advertising program* will consist of a series of related, well-timed, carefully placed ads that reinforce the personal selling and sales promotional efforts.
- The *personal selling effort* will be coordinated with the advertising program. The sales force will explain and demonstrate the product benefits stressed in the ads. The sales people will also be fully informed about the advertising part of the campaign — the theme, the media used, and the schedule for the appearance of ads. The sales people, in turn, should carry this information to the middlemen so that they can become effective participants in the campaign.
- The *sales promotional devices*, such as point-of-purchase display materials, will be coordinated with the other aspects of the campaign. For each campaign, new display materials must be prepared. They should reflect the ads and appeals used in the current campaign, to maximize the campaign's impact at the point of sale.
- *Physical distribution management* will ensure that adequate stocks of the product are available in all outlets prior to the start of the campaign.

Red River Cereal, which has been with us for a long time, now uses a natural-healthful theme.

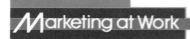

Developing a Successful Advertising Campaign*

Telecom Canada is an association of ten major telecommunications companies across Canada.** The organization was created by its member companies to satisfy the telecommunications and information-handling requirements of Canadians through the cooperative provision of a national fully integrated telecommunications network. In 1981, Telecom Canada launched a national Business Long Distance advertising campaign with the objective of stimulating long distance telephone usage among business subscribers of the member companies — in other words, to expand the market.

The strategy that underlay the campaign was to position long distance as the immediate, effective, efficient communications tool best able to satisfy the productivity demands of Canadian business in the 1980s. This would be done primarily by highlighting applications or uses of long distance in a business context. The key benefit to the consumer was improved productivity and profitability.

The creative strategy was based on an approach used by Southwestern Bell in the United States, in which that company used office situations featuring a "boss" character to demonstrate the applications of business long distance.

McKim Advertising, an agency based in Montreal, in cooperation with the director, Ken Takasaki, recommended having Larry Mann, a Canadian actor, play the role of a boss and use humour to present the message. In the fall of 1981, three commercials were launched — Armbruster (sales applications); Ludlow (collecting accounts receivables); and Dorlinger (stock ordering). The launch was supported by print advertising and direct mail activity. Eventually, Telecom Canada began using Larry Mann, live, for telephone company promotional events and what began as the occasional public appearance evolved into a full-fledged personal appearance program.

In 1985, Telecom Canada conducted an image awareness and assessment study on the "Chief" character. The results were extremely positive, with very high levels of recognition, association with the sponsor, credibility and likability recorded. These results and those of subsequent studies indicated that the "Chief" as played by Larry Mann was becoming a signature for the member companies of Telecom Canada. The mere presentation of his face seemed to communicate a number of messages, including the identification of the member company, the concept of long distance, and, later in the campaign, telemarketing.

The television campaign has gone through a number of phases over the years. In the early 1980s, it was used solely to highlight business uses of long distance. Later, Telecom Canada began to use Larry Mann to promote specific telecommunications products and services. In the mid-1980s, Telecom launched a tele-

*The authors wish to acknowledge the contribution to the preparation of this *Marketing at Work file* by Joanne Stanley, Director — Advertising and Promotion (Business), Telecom Canada.
**The member companies of Telecom Canada are: Alberta Government Telephones, Bell Canada, British Columbia Telephone Company, The Island Telephone Company Limited, Manitoba Telephone System, Maritime Telegraph and Telephone Company Limited, The New Brunswick Telephone Company Limited, Newfoundland Telephone Company Limited, Saskatchewan Telecommunications, and Telesat Canada.

marketing awareness extension to the campaign that took the business applications strategy to the next stage.

Today, the print component of the campaign capitalizes on the recognition of the ''Chief'' by using him as a secondary visual symbol. Larry Mann's image is used in business print media advertising for all Telecom Canada's products and services.

The ''Chief'' character permeates all of Telecom Canada's business promotional activities, as well as a good deal of the material produced for the business market by the member companies of Telecom Canada. He has been used in direct mail, brochures, flyers, airport advertising and, to a limited extent, in radio. The personal appearances program has grown to include not only attendance at member company employee and promotional events, but visits to customer locations organized by Telecom Canada's national sales force.

REGULATION OF PROMOTIONAL ACTIVITIES

Because the primary objective of promotion is to sell something by communicating with a market, promotional activities attract attention. Consequently, abuses by individual firms are easily and quickly noted by the public. This situation in turn soon leads to (1) public demand for correction of the abuses, (2) assurances that they will not be repeated, and (3) general restraints on promotional activities. To answer public demand, laws and regulations have been enacted by the federal government and by most provincial governments. In addition, many private business organizations have established voluntary codes of advertising and promotional standards to guide their own promotional activities. In addition, the advertising industry itself, through the Advertising Advisory Board and its Advertising Standards Councils, does a considerable amount of self-regulation.

The Federal Role   A number of departments of the federal government administer Acts aimed at controlling various aspects of promotion, particularly advertising. The Broadcasting Act established the Canadian Radio-television and Telecommunications Commission (CRTC) in 1968 and provided for sweeping powers of advertising regulation. Under section 16 of the Act, the Commission may make regulations concerning the character of broadcast advertising and the amount of time that may be devoted to it. While the potential for substantial control exists, the Commission did not in reality pass on each commercial message. What it has done is to delegate authority in certain fields to other agencies such as the Health Protection Branch of the Department of National Health and Welfare and the Combines Investigation Branch of the Department of Consumer and Corporate Affairs.

The Health Protection Branch deals with advertising in the fields of drugs, cosmetics, and devices (officialese for birth-control products), and it has sweeping powers to limit, control, rewrite, or ban promotion for the products under its authority. The authority itself is embodied in such Acts, and regulations associated with them, as the Health and Welfare Department Act, the Proprietary or Patent Medicine Act, the Food and Drug Act, the Criminal Code of Canada, and the Broadcasting Act. The various Acts and regulations result in general types of prohibition aimed at preventing the treatment, processing, packaging, labelling, advertising, and selling of foods, drugs, and devices in such a manner as to mislead or deceive, or even to be likely to create an erroneous impression concerning the nature of the products.

The Branch also prohibits the advertising of whole classes of drugs. It has developed a list of diseases or conditions for which a cure may not be advertised under any circumstances. This prohibition stands even if a professionally accepted cure exists. The logic for the prohibition of advertising, in spite of the existence of a cure, is that the Branch does not wish members of the general public to engage in self-diagnosis of the condition that can be treated.

By virtue of the powers delegated to it by the Commission, the Branch has absolute control over radio and television advertisements for the products under its jurisdiction. All such advertisements must be submitted to it at least fifteen days prior to airing, and no radio or television station can air an ad without its having been approved by the Branch and, thereby, the Commission. In practical terms, the Health Protection Branch, even though an appeal route to the CRTC is available, has complete authority and advertisers have no recourse of any consequence.

In contrast to the delegated review powers the Health Protection Branch has over advertisements using the broadcast media, its position with reference to the print media is weak. Its formal control is in terms of alleged Food and Drug violations, which must be prosecuted in court. Given the lack of jurisprudence in this area, the Branch is loath to go to court in case it loses and thus sets a precedent or in case its regulations (many of which have not been tested in court) are found to be illegal. What the Branch does is advise advertisers of its opinion of advertisements that are prepared for the print media. This opinion is not a ruling, and ads submitted, as well as those that are not, are still subject to the regulations for which the Branch has responsibility. This does not mean that the Branch does not monitor the print media. Newspapers and magazines are sampled and advertisements examined.

The Department of Consumer and Corporate Affairs has substantial and major responsibility in the area of regulating promotion. The Combines Investigation Branch of the Department carries the major burden of promotional regulation. The Acts administered include: (1) the Hazardous Products Act (concerning poisonous compounds for household use), (2) the Precious Metals Marketing Act (i.e., definitions of sterling and carat weight), (3) the Trade Marks Act, (4) the Consumer Packaging and Labelling Act, and of greatest significance, (5) the Competition Act. Within the Competition Act, a number of sections pertain directly to the regulation of advertising and promotional activities. Section 35, for example, requires that manufacturers or wholesalers who offer promotional allowances to retailers must offer such allowances on proportionate terms to all competing purchasers. Section 36 of the Act regulates misleading advertising in general, while section 37 pertains specifically to "bait and switch" advertising.[4]

Section 36 of the Competition Act makes it illegal for an advertiser to make any false or misleading statement to the public in advertising or promotional materials or with respect to warranties. This section also regulates the use of false statements regarding the expected performance or length of life of a product and the use of testimonials in advertising. Section 36.2 of the Act regulates the use of "double ticketing" in retail selling and requires that, where a retailer promotes a product at two different prices or where two prices appear on a product or at the point of sale, the retailer must sell the product at the lower of the prices. Businesses or individuals who are convicted of violating section 36 are subject to fines as large as $25,000 or to imprisonment for up to one year.

Paragraph 36(1)(d) of the Competition Act regulates "sale" advertising and would apply particularly to retail advertisers. Section 37 requires that an advertiser who promotes a product at a "sale" price have sufficient quantities of the product on hand to satisfy reasonable market demand. Section 37.1 prohibits an advertiser from selling a "sale" item at a price higher than the advertised "sale" price. Finally, section 37.2 regulates the conduct of contests, lotteries, and games of chance. This section requires that advertisers who promote such contests disclose the number and value of prizes and the areas in which prizes are to be distributed, and further requires that prizes be distributed on a basis of skill or on a basis of random selection.

The provisions of the Competition Act relating to misleading advertising do not apply to publishers and broadcasters who actually distribute the advertising in question to the general public, provided that these publishers have accepted the contents of the advertising in good faith. In essence, this means that a newspaper cannot be prosecuted for misleading advertising if it accepted the advertising on the assumption that its contents were not misleading. Although no newspaper can be prosecuted for misleading advertising if it accepted the advertising in good faith, there is still some question concerning whether media production departments and advertising agencies, which actually participate with the advertiser in the production of misleading advertising, might not in the future be considered jointly responsible with the advertiser for the contents of the offending advertisement. This is a question with which the Canadian courts may deal in the future.

The Provincial Role

In each of the provinces, a considerable variety of legislation exists that is aimed at controlling various promotional practices. For instance, in Ontario, various degrees of control are exercised by the Liquor Control Board of Ontario, the Ontario Board of Film Censors, the Ontario Superintendent of Insurance, the Ontario Human Rights Commission, the Ontario Securities Commission, the Ontario Police Commission, the Ontario Racing Commission, various ministries of the Ontario government responsible for financial, commercial, consumer, and transportation functions and services, and yet more. Most of the provinces have similar sets of legislation, regulatory bodies, and provincial departments. While much of the federal regulation must in the end result in argument and prosecution in a courtroom, the provincial machinery would appear to be much more flexible and potentially regulatory in nature, and if pursued, may have a more substantial effect on undesirable practices.

The powers of provincial governments in relation to the regulation of misleading advertising have been increased considerably in recent years. Since the mid-1970s a number of provinces have passed legislation dealing with unfair and unconscionable trade practices. The "trade practices" Acts passed by British Columbia, Alberta, and Ontario contain "shopping lists" of practices that are made illegal by these Acts. In reality, these pieces of legislation write into law practices that have been considered illegal by federal prosecutors for a number of years. Relating to advertising, these Acts prohibit such practices as advertising a product as new when it is in fact used; advertising that fails to state a material fact, thereby deceiving the consumer; and advertising that gives greater prominence to low down payments or monthly payments rather than to the actual price of the product. The Alberta Unfair Trade Practices Act also contains a provision for corrective advertising. This provision means that a court, upon convicting an advertiser for misleading advertising, can order that advertiser to devote some or all of his advertising for a certain period to informing his customers that he had been advertising falsely in the past and to correcting the misleading information that had been communicated in the offending advertisements.

The Province of Quebec has within its Consumer Protection Act a section that regulates advertising directed at children. This section forbids the use of exaggeration, endorsements, cartoon characters, and statements that urge children to buy. Quebec's Official Language Act also contains a number of sections that govern the use of French and English in advertising in that province.

Regulation by Private Organizations

Several kinds of private organizations also exert considerable control over promotional practices of businesses. Magazines, newspapers, and radio and television stations regularly refuse to accept advertisements that they feel are false, misleading, or generally in bad taste, and in so doing they are being "reasonable" in the ordinary course of doing business. Some trade associations have established a "code of ethics" that includes points pertaining to sales-force and advertising activities. Some trade associations regularly censor advertising appearing in their trade or professional journals. Better Business Bureaus located in major cities all over the country are working to control some very difficult situations. The Advertising Advisory Board administers the Canadian Code of Advertising Standards, a number of other advertising codes, including the Broadcast Code for Advertising to Children (on behalf of the Canadian Association of Broadcasters) and a code regulating the advertising of over-the-counter drugs, which was developed in cooperation with the Proprietary Association and Health and Welfare Canada.

SUMMARY

Promotion is the fourth major component of a company's total marketing mix (along with product planning, pricing, and distribution). Promotion is synonymous with selling. Its intent is to inform, persuade, and influence people. It is a basic ingredient in nonprice competition, and it is an essential element in modern marketing. The three major forms of promotion are personal selling, advertising, and sales promotion.

The promotional activity in marketing is basically an exercise in communication. Fundamentally, the communication process consists of a source sending a message through a channel to a receiver. Some sort of noise is usually present, which tends to interfere with the transmission of the message. For effective promotion, marketers must understand the makeup of their communication channels and the effects of this noise.

When deciding on the appropriate promotional mix (the combination of advertising, personal selling, and other promotional tools), management should be influenced by four factors: (1) money available, (2) nature of the market, (3) nature of the product, and (4) stage of the product's life cycle. A series of six questions relating to basic promotional strategy can be of help in applying the four factors to develop a promotional mix.

It is difficult to set a dollar figure for the total promotional appropriation, but it must be done. The most commonly used method is to set the appropriation as a percentage of sales. Unfortunately, this is an illogical method. A better approach is to decide what promotional goals are to be achieved, and then figure out how much this will cost. These funds and the promotional efforts of the firm should be coordinated into a campaign built around a single theme and designed to reach a predetermined goal.

As a result of criticism and concern regarding the use of advertising and promotional techniques, the federal government has enacted legislation that regulates promotion. The main federal laws are the Competition Act and the Broadcasting Act. The Department of Consumer and Corporate Affairs and the Canadian Radio-Television and Telecommunications Commission are charged with administering the legislation in this area. Promotional practices are also regulated at the provincial level through trade practices legislation, through voluntary codes of businesses and trade associations, and by the advertising industry itself.

NOTES

[1] Neil H. Borden, *The Economic Effects of Advertising*, Richard D. Irwin, Inc., Homewood, Ill., 1942, p. 802.

[2] See Alan J. Dubinsky, Thomas E. Barry, and Roger A. Kerin, "The Sales-Advertising Interface in Promotion Planning," *Journal of Advertising*, vol. 10, no. 3 (1981), pp. 35–41.

[3] For a report on the sales and profit impact of various push marketing strategies, see Michael Levy, John Webster, and Roger A. Kerin, ''Formulating Push Marketing Strategies: A Method and Application,'' *Journal of Marketing*, Winter 1983, pp. 25–34.

[4] For a review of court decisions in misleading advertising cases in Canada, refer to James G. Barnes, ''Advertising and the Courts,'' *The Canadian Business Review*, Autumn 1975, pp. 51–54. The Misleading Advertising Division of the Department of Consumer and Corporate Affairs also publishes a quarterly review of misleading advertising cases entitled the *Misleading Advertising Bulletin*. Individuals interested in receiving this bulletin can have their names placed on the mailing list simply by writing to the Department of Consumer and Corporate Affairs.

KEY TERMS AND CONCEPTS

Promotional mix 446	Primary demand 456
Promotion 446	Push and pull strategies 457
Selling 446	Promotional appropriation 459
Advertising 446	Percentage-of-sales method 459
Personal selling 446	Task or objective method 460
Sales promotion 446	Promotional campaign 461
Publicity 447	Campaign theme 461
Public relations 447	Broadcasting Act 464
Nonprice competition 448	Competition Act 464
Using promotion to shift the demand curve 448	Provincial role in regulating promotion 466
Communication process 450	Regulation by industry itself 466

QUESTIONS AND PROBLEMS

1. What is the difference between selling and marketing?
2. Explain and illustrate a communication system using the following situations:
   a. A teenage girl trying to sell her parents on buying her contact lenses instead of glasses.
   b. A sales person talking to a prospect about buying a car.
3. Explain how the *nature of the market* would affect the promotional mix for the following products:
   a. Contact lenses.
   b. Golf balls.
   c. Plywood.
   d. Colgate toothpaste.
   e. Laser disc record player.
   f. Mainframe computers.
4. Explain how the promotional mix is likely to be affected by the life-cycle stage in which each of the following products is situated.
   a. Television satellite dish.
   b. First Choice Superchannel cable television.
   c. Crest toothpaste.
   d. IBM personal computer.
5. Using Borden's criteria, evaluate the advertisability of each of the following

products. Assume that sufficient funds are available in each case.

a. Automobile tires.   c. Light bulbs.

b. Revlon cosmetics.   d. Sony Walkman.

6. Explain why personal selling is, or is not, likely to be the main ingredient in the promotional mix for each of the following products:

a. Life insurance being considered by   c. Burglar alarm system.
   a young couple.   d. Harvey's hamburger.

b. Tide liquid detergent.

7. Explain why retailer promotional efforts should or should not be stressed in the promotional mix for the following:

a. GWG Jeans.   c. Women's cosmetics.

b. Sunkist oranges.   d. Royal Bank credit card.

8. Why is the percentage-of-sales method so widely used to determine the promotional appropriation when, in fact, most authorities recognize the task or objective method as the most desirable one?

9. Identify the central idea — the theme — in some current promotional campaigns.

10. Assume you are marketing a liquid that removes creosote (and the danger of fire) from chimneys used for wood-burning stoves. Briefly describe the roles you would assign to advertising, personal selling, sales promotion, and publicity in your promotional campaign.

11. Explain the term *proportionally equal basis* in connection with manufacturers' granting advertising allowances. Consider especially the situations where retailers vary in size.

12. Do you think we need additional legislation to regulate advertising? To regulate personal selling? If so, explain what you would recommend.

CHAPTER 17

MANAGEMENT OF PERSONAL SELLING

CHAPTER GOALS

In this chapter we look at personal selling from both the sales manager's and the sales person's viewpoint. After studying this chapter, you should understand:

- The importance of personal selling in our economy and in a company's marketing program.
- How sales jobs are different from other jobs.
- The wide variety of sales jobs.
- The steps involved in the selling process — that is, in making a sale.
- The steps involved in staffing and operating a sales force.
- A little about the evaluation of a sales person's performance.

Is direct marketing the wave of the future? In both the United States and Canada, more and more companies are bypassing the mass media and contacting customers directly. They are using mailing lists, sending catalogues, holding sales parties in living rooms, and selling over the telephone. Customers order directly from the manufacturer or supplier, essentially cutting out middlemen, advertising agencies, and the mass advertising media. Direct marketing companies rely on personal sales contacts, Canada Post and long-distance telephone systems to get their messages across and to deliver their products. Anyone with a major credit card and access to a toll-free 1-800 number can buy almost anything.

One of the fastest growing forms of direct marketing is selling through parties. This has traditionally been the home turf of Tupperware and Mary Kay, but everything from house plants to computers to expensive crystal is being sold at parties these days. Pierre La Traverse, president of the Toronto-based Direct Sellers Association, observed, ''I don't really know of anything that can't be sold this way.''

Cec Girling, president of Toronto's Fashion Party Inc., says, ''Today's customer wants service more than anything else.'' In 11 years, Girling's company has grown to more than $5 million sales annually. It specializes in designer clothes sold at discount prices in the customer's home. Girling noted five tips to keep in mind if you want to operate a successful party-sales operation:

Pick the right product: Any product that needs a demonstration and an explanation is right for party-plan selling, because you don't get that service today in many retail stores. Also, you want a product that will keep customers coming back, like cosmetics or clothing. That way you won't saturate your market too quickly.

Keep your margins up: You have to pay your sales agents a reasonable commission if you are going to keep them. If you don't have high margins, you won't have much left over by the time you pay the agents' commission of 15% to 30%.

Select the right sales representatives: Professional sales experience is not necessary, but being people-oriented is.

Put a business plan together: If things start to take off, you had better know where you are going.

Prepare to delegate. Success brings more sales agents than you can possibly handle. Who is going to make sure that their orders are handled and shipped on time? You won't be able to do it all. Be prepared to have competent people to whom you can delegate.

Source: Adapted from Tim Falconer, "Party Perfect: How to Get Great Sales," *Canadian Business*, March 1987, p. 32.

Selling is essential to the health and well-being of our economic system, and it probably offers more job opportunities than any other single vocation today. Yet, personal selling is frequently criticized, and it is very hard to attract qualified young people into selling jobs. Truly, the task of managing a sales force is a difficult one. But the level of success in this task often has a direct bearing on the level of success of a company's total marketing program.

NATURE AND IMPORTANCE OF PERSONAL SELLING

In personal selling, it is possible to tailor a presentation to an individual customer.

The goal of all marketing efforts is to increase profitable sales by offering want-satisfaction to the market over the long run. *Personal selling* is by far the major promotional method or tool used to reach this goal. More than ever, sales people today are a dynamic power in the business world. They are responsible for directly generating more revenue in our economy than workers in any other single vocation. The efforts of sales people have a direct impact on such diverse activities as:

- The success of new products.
- Keeping existing products in strong market positions.
- Constructing manufacturing facilities.
- Opening new businesses and keeping them open.
- Generating sales orders that result in shipping products to customers all over the world.

The number of people employed in advertising is in the *thousands*. In personal selling, the number is in the *millions*. In many companies, personal selling is the largest single operating expense, often equalling 8 to 15 percent of net sales. In contrast, advertising costs average 1 to 3 percent of sales. Expenditures for sales people's salaries, commissions, and travel expenses, the cost of operating sales branches, and the expenses of managing these sales people all add up to a tidy sum.

Relative Merits

Personal selling is the *personal* communication of information to persuade a prospective customer to buy something — a product, service, idea, or something else. This is in contrast to the mass, *impersonal* communication of advertising, sales promotion, and the other promotional tools.

Compared to these other promotional tools, personal selling has the advantage of being *more flexible* in operation. Sales people can tailor their sales presentations to fit the needs and behaviour of individual customers. Also, sales people can see the customer's reaction to a particular sales approach and then make the necessary adjustments on the spot. A second merit of personal selling is that usually it can be *focussed on prospective customers*, thus minimizing wasted effort. By contrast, in most forms of advertising, much of the cost is devoted to sending the message to people who are not real prospects. In personal selling, a company has an opportunity to pinpoint its target market far more effectively than with any other promotional device.

In most instances, a third feature of personal selling is that it *results in the actual sale*. Advertisements can attract attention and arouse desire, but usually they do not arouse buying action or complete the sale.

The major limitation of personal selling is its high cost. It is true that the use of a sales force enables a business to reach its market with a minimum of wasted effort. However, the cost of developing and operating a sales force is high. Another disadvantage is that personal selling is often limited by a company's inability to get the calibre of people needed to do the job. At the retail level, for example, many firms have abandoned their sales forces and shifted to self-service for this very reason. In spite of the great many job opportunities provided in this field, personal selling is frequently criticized, and it is generally difficult to attract qualified young people into selling jobs.

Nature of the Sales Job

The sales job of today is quite different from that of years gone by. True, high-pressure selling still exists and may always have a role in some fields, but it is no longer typical. Instead, to implement the marketing concept in a manufacturing firm, for example, we see a new type of sales person — a *territorial manager*. Rather than just push whatever the factory has to sell, our new breed of sales person interprets customers' wants. The sales reps either fill these wants with existing products or relay the wants to the producer so that appropriate new products may be developed. They engage in a *total* selling job — missionary selling, servicing customers, being territorial profit managers, and acting as a mirror of the market as they feed back marketing information. Their job includes selling to new customers, obtaining reorders from existing accounts, selling new products, helping customers find new uses for existing products, and helping customers to use the products properly.

By the very nature of this new position, sales people experience problems — role ambiguity and role conflict. Ambiguity enters into a sales job because the sales people fill so many different roles. They persuade prospective customers, service the accounts, set up displays, expedite orders, coordinate deliveries, gather information, collect on past-due accounts, help solve customers' problems, etc.

In performing these many activities, sales people often encounter role conflict. The reps must identify first with their companies and then with their customers. In so doing, they are subject to conflicts regarding whose positions — the company's or the customer's — they are supporting. Also, within the company, several groups with whom sales people interact (credit and production departments, for example) often have differing and even conflicting expectations. The emotional demands stemming from these situations often are great, and they usually must be handled pretty much by the sales people themselves.

Sales Jobs Are Different from Other Jobs

Sales jobs usually are quite different from other jobs in several ways:

- Sales people represent their company to the outside world. Consequently, opinions of a company and its products often are formed from impressions left by the sales force. The public ordinarily will not judge a firm by its office or factory workers.

- Other employees usually work under close supervisory control, whereas a sales force typically operates with little or no direct supervision. Moreover, to be successful, sales people often must be creative and persistent and show great initiative — and all of this requires a high degree of motivation.

- Sales people probably need more tact, diplomacy, and social poise than other employees in an organization. Many sales jobs require the sales person to display considerable social intelligence in dealing with buyers.

- Sales people are among the few employees authorized to spend company funds. They spend this money for entertainment, transportation, and their other business expenses.

- Sales jobs frequently require a considerable amount of travelling and much time spent away from home and family. Being in the field puts sales people in enemy territory, so to speak. There they deal with customers who seem determined not to buy the sellers' products. These mental stresses, coupled with the physical demands of long hours and travelling, combine to require a degree of mental toughness and physical stamina rarely demanded in other types of jobs. Selling is hard work!

Sales People as Strategic Planners

Earlier in this chapter we referred to the modern professional sales person as a territorial manager. Truly, today's sales reps may very well do much of the strategic planning for their individual territories. Sales people typically operate with little or no direct supervision. They usually are given a reasonably well defined geographical territory, a product mix, and a price structure. They also may have been through a company training program. They probably are assigned performance goals in the form of a quota.

Within those general guidelines, however, the reps may have to develop their own specific strategies and tactics to reach their goals. They will make their own strategic decisions regarding (1) what target markets they will solicit, (2) how they will deal with each market segment, and (3) what particular products they will promote.

Wide Variety of Sales Jobs

No two selling jobs are alike. Even when sales jobs are grouped on some basis, we find that the types of jobs and the requirements needed to fill them cover a wide spectrum. Consider, for example, the job of a Pepsi-Cola driver-sales person who calls in routine fashion on a group of retail stores. That job is in a different world from the job of an IBM computer sales person who sells a system for storing and retrieving information to an automobile manufacturer such as Chrysler. An Avon representative selling cosmetics door to door has a job only remotely related to that of an airplane manufacturer's rep selling executive-type aircraft to large firms.

A useful way to classify the many types of sales jobs is to array them on the basis of the creative skills required in the job, from the simple to the complex. One

An inside order-taking sales job.

Successful sales rep for Compaq Canada Inc.

such classification, developed by Robert McMurry, a noted industrial psychologist, is the following:

1. Positions in which the job is primarily to deliver the product — for example, a *driver-sales person* for soft drinks, milk, or fuel oil. The selling responsibilities, if any, are secondary.

2. Positions in which the sales people are primarily *inside order takers* — for example, retail clerks standing behind counters. Most of the customers have already decided to buy; the sales clerks only serve them. The clerks may sell through suggestion, but ordinarily they cannot do much more.

3. Positions in which the sales people are primarily *outside order takers*, going to the customers in the field — for example, wholesale hardware or office supply sales people who call on retail stores.

4. Positions in which the sales people are not expected to solicit orders. Their job is to build goodwill, perform promotional activities, or provide service for customers. These are the *missionary sales people* for a grocery products manufacturer, for example, or the *detail sales people* for a pharmaceutical firm.

5. Positions in which the major emphasis is on the sales person's technical product knowledge — for example, a *sales engineer*.

6. Positions that demand *creative selling of tangible products*, such as vacuum cleaners, airplanes, encyclopedia, or computers. Customers may not be aware of their need for the product. Or they may not realize how the new product can satisfy their wants better than the product they are now using. When the product is of a technical nature, this category may overlap that of the sales engineer.

7. Positions that require *creative selling of intangibles*, such as insurance, advertising services, consulting services, or communication systems. Intangibles are typically difficult to sell because they cannot easily be demonstrated.

Technology and Telemarketing Change Customer Contact

The job of outside selling — the kind where the sales person goes to the customer, in contrast to inside (or across-the-counter) selling — is changing dramatically these days. Instead of the traditional in-person sales call, a growing number of sales reps are using the telephone and/or the computer to talk with customers. In effect, outside selling — especially outside *industrial* selling — is going electronic.

The prime factor accounting for this change is the dramatic increase in the cost of keeping sales people on the road. Some companies estimate that their travel expenses — transportation, hotel, and meals — are higher than their sales reps' compensation (salary, commission, and bonus).

Telephone selling, of course, has been used by many companies for decades. What is new today, however, is the innovative use of communication systems involving the telephone, television, and sometimes the computer to aid a company's selling effort and other marketing activities. The term **telemarketing** has been coined to describe these marketing communication systems.

Some companies have increased sales and reduced costs by taking their field sales people away from their travelling jobs and bringing them into the office. There these reps have been trained to sell by telephone. In effect, personal selling and order taking are being moved from the field to a well-trained inside sales force. The field selling in these firms is shifting to sales promotion work such as instructing customers or providing technical advice and service.

Some companies have turned the telemarketing function around and initiate the customer contact through television or other forms of advertising, relying on the telephone to receive orders. Many direct marketing companies now sell through advertising, rather than through sales people, promoting everything from records to exercise equipment to self-sharpening knives. Interested customers telephone a toll-free 1-800 number, where "operators are standing by" to accept VISA and MasterCard numbers. The purchase price (plus cost of shipping) is charged to the customer's account and the merchandise is mailed.

In some cases, the telemarketing system is tied into a sophisticated computer system that is able to determine inventory status and shipping dates. All of these examples will save millions of dollars in personal selling and other communications expenses.

---

*THE STRATEGIC PERSONAL
SELLING PROCESS*

The personal selling process may be viewed as a logical sequence of actions — called the "5 P's" — that are taken by a sales person in dealing with a buyer.[1] See Fig. 17-1. This process leads, hopefully, to some desired customer action and ends with a follow-up to ensure customer satisfaction. The desired customer action usually is to get that person to buy something. In some cases, however, the desired action may be to get the customer to do some advertising, to display the product, or to reduce the price on the product.

FIGURE 17-1
The personal selling process: the 5 P's.

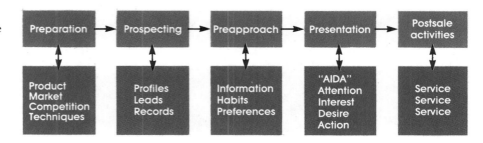

Presale Preparation

In the sequence of events that — it is hoped — will lead to a sale, the first step is to make certain that the sales person is prepared. This means that he or she must be well acquainted with the product, the market, the competition, the techniques of selling — everything that conceivably could pertain to the sale.

Prospecting, or Locating Potential Buyers

The sales person is now ready to locate customers. This second step toward a sale involves drawing up a profile of the ideal prospect. The sales person can examine records of past and present customers in an effort to determine the characteristics of such prospects. From this profile, the seller may develop a list of potential buyers. Sellers also may build a list of prospective customers from people who mailed in a coupon or telephoned a 1-800 number featured in an advertisement.

There are other ways in which sales people can acquire a list of prospects. Their sales manager may prepare a list for them; present customers may suggest new leads; present users may want later or different models of the product. And a little thought will often suggest logical prospects. For instance, sellers of home furnishings or telephone equipment find prospects in the regularly published lists of building permits issued. Sellers of many products find leads among birth or engagement announcements in newspapers.

Preapproach to Individual Prospects

Before calling on prospects, sales people should learn all they can about the persons or companies to whom they hope to sell. They might want to know what products the prospects are now using and the prospects' reactions to these products. Sales people should also try to find out the personal habits and preferences of the prospect.

Presentation — "AIDA"

The actual sales presentation will start with an attempt to attract the prospect's *attention*. The sales person will try to hold the customer's *interest* while building a *desire* for the product. Then the sales person will try to close the sale (*action*). All through the presentation, the sales person must be ready to meet any hidden or expressed objections that the prospect may have.

ATTRACT ATTENTION — THE APPROACH

Several approaches may be used to attract the prospect's attention and start the presentation. The simplest is merely to greet the prospect and state what you are selling. While this is direct, in many situations it is not so effective as other approaches. If the sales person was referred to the prospect by a customer, the right approach might be to start out by mentioning this common acquaintance. Sometimes this is called the "Joe sent me" approach. The sales person might suggest the

Sometimes just getting the prospect to try your product helps to close a sale.

product benefits by making some startling statement. One sales training consultant often greeted a prospect with the benefit question, "If I can cut your selling costs in half, and at the same time double your sales volume, are you interested?" A fourth approach, which can be effective if the sales person has a new product, is simply to walk in and hand the product to the prospect. While the prospect looks it over, the sales person can start the sales presentation.

HOLD INTEREST AND AROUSE DESIRE

After attracting the prospect's attention, the sales person can hold this interest and stimulate a desire for the product by means of the sales talk itself. There is no common pattern here. Usually, however, a product demonstration is invaluable. Whatever pattern is followed in the talk, the sales person must always show how the product will benefit the prospect.

Many companies insist that their sales people use a "canned" sales talk. That is, all representatives of the firm must give essentially the same presentation. Although many people may feel that this is a poor practice, it has been proved time and again that a canned sales talk can be effective. These presentations ensure that all points are covered. They employ tested techniques, and they facilitate the sales training job considerably.

MEET OBJECTIONS AND CLOSE THE SALE

After explaining the product and its benefits, the sales person should try to close the sale and write up an order. As part of the presentation, the sales person may periodically venture a *trial close* to sense the prospect's willingness to buy. By posing some "either-or" questions, a sales person can start to bring the presentation to a head. That is, the sales person may ask, "Would you prefer the grey or the green model?" or "Would you plan to charge this or pay cash?"

The trial close is important because it gives the sales person an indication of how near the prospect is to a decision. A sales person may lose a sale by talking too much. The prospect may be ready to buy at the beginning, and then have a change of mind if the sales person insists on a full presentation. Sometimes sales are lost *simply because the representative fails to ask for the order*.

The trial close also tends to bring out the buyer's objections. A sales person should encourage buyers to state their objections. Then the sales person has an opportunity to answer these objections and to bring out additional product benefits or reemphasize previously stated points.

The toughest objections to answer are those that are unspoken. A sales person must uncover the real objections before hoping to make a sale. Another difficult situation occurs when the prospect wants to "think it over." The sales person must close the sale then and there, or the chances are that it will be lost.

Textbooks on selling discuss different types of sales-closing techniques. The *assumptive close* is probably used as much as any other, and it can be used in a wide variety of selling situations. In this closing technique, the sales person assumes that the customer is going to buy. So it is just a case of settling the details and asking such questions as, "When do you want this delivered?" "Is this a charge sale?" or "What colour have you decided upon?"

Postsale Activities An effective selling job does not end when the order is written up. The final stage of the selling process is a series of postsale services that can build customer goodwill and lay the groundwork for future business. If mechanical installation is necessary, the representative should make certain the job is done properly.

In general, all these activities by the sales person serve to reduce the customer's postdecision anxiety — or cognitive dissonance. The theory of cognitive dissonance holds that after a person has made a buying decision, anxiety (dissonance) will usually occur. This happens because the buyer knows the alternative selected has some disagreeable features, as well as advantages. Consequently, the buyer seeks reassurance that the correct choice was made. Conversely, the buyer wants to avoid anything that suggests that one of the discarded choices really would have been better.

In this final stage of the selling process, it is the sales person's job to minimize the customer's dissonance. The sales person should reassure the customer that the right decision was made by (1) summarizing the product's benefits, (2) repeating why it is better than the discarded alternative choices, and (3) pointing out how satisfied the customer will be with the product's performance.[2]

File 17-2

Marketing at Work

The Big Gains Are in Following Up

Some companies fall down on the job of closing sales by not following up on sales leads. They may spend thousands of dollars generating enquiries from coupons in advertisements, from trade shows, sales calls, telephone calls, direct mail or other sources. In these days when a sales call may cost $200, it is reasonable to expect a company to put a system in place to ensure that sales leads are followed up quickly and efficiently.

A study completed for the Center for Marketing Communications revealed the following startling statistics:

- of all requests for information, 18 percent of those inquiring received no material at all;

- in the case of 43 percent of inquiries, the material was received too late to be of any use;
- a total of 59 percent of those who had received material said they considered some of the material useless and threw it away;
- only 28 percent were ever contacted by a sales person;
- of those who specifically requested a sales person to call, only 25 percent were contacted.

The people who respond to advertising by sending in coupons or calling to request information are interested in buying. In fact, the study showed that 40 percent of those leads resulted in the sale of a product — either the company's or a competitor's. To not respond is to ignore an excellent opportunity to close a sale — often to a customer who is already pre-sold.

Source: Adapted from Michael E. Liepner, "Turning Lead into Gold," *Business to Business Marketing*, September 22, 1986, p. B 22.

STRATEGIC SALES-FORCE MANAGEMENT

Management of the personal selling function is simply a matter of applying the three-stage management process (planning, implementing, evaluating) to a sales force and its activities. The process begins when sales executives set their sales goals and do the strategic planning of sales-force activities. This step involves the forecasting of sales, preparation of sales budgets, establishment of sales territories, and setting up quotas for the sales people.

Then the sales force must be organized, staffed, and operated so as to carry out those plans and reach the predetermined goals. The final stage — performance evaluation — includes evaluating the performance of individual sales people, as well as appraising the total sales performance.[3]

Sales-force management strategies are shaped by a company's strategic marketing planning and its overall promotional planning. For example, a firm that relies heavily on personal selling will use different sales-force strategies from those of a company that depends primarily on advertising.

As another illustration, assume that two companies both have the same marketing goal — to increase their sales volume by 30 percent over the next two years. But they may plan to use different marketing strategies to reach that goal. Company A's strategy may be to open new geographic markets and sell to new classes of customers. Company B's strategy may be to intensify its coverage of its present markets. These different marketing strategies will call for different strategies in such sales-force management activities as quota setting, training, supervision, and compensation.

OPERATING A SALES FORCE

Most sales executives spend the bulk of their time in staffing and operating their sales forces. Consequently, in this section we shall look briefly at the major tasks that are involved in this managerial activity. These tasks are outlined in Fig. 17-2.

FIGURE 17-2
Staffing and operating a sales force.

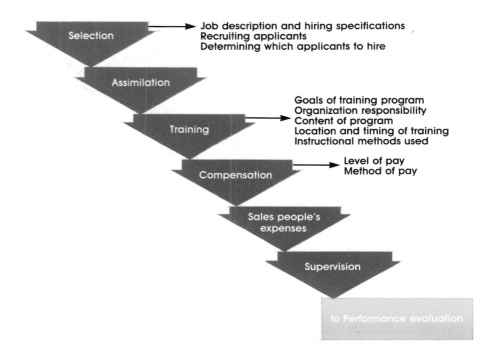

Selection → Job description and hiring specifications
Recruiting applicants
Determining which applicants to hire

Assimilation

Training → Goals of training program
Organization responsibility
Content of program
Location and timing of training
Instructional methods used

Compensation → Level of pay
Method of pay

Sales people's expenses

Supervision

to Performance evaluation

Selecting the Sales Force

The key to success in managing a sales force is to select good sales people. In the authors' opinion, *personnel selection* (staffing) is the most important activity in the management process in any organization. This is true whether the organization is a sales force, an athletic team, a college faculty, a political party, or any other group.

Several benefits accrue from having a good sales-personnel selection program. First, it increases a company's chance of getting the type of sales representatives it needs. This is important because there is a shortage of good sales people, and they are hard to find. Second, when running a sales force, a sales manager's performance can be no better than the material he or she has to work with. No matter how well managed a sales force may be, if it is distinctly inferior in quality to that of a competitor, the competitor will win out. Third, a well-selected sales force will be more productive and will build better customer relations than a poorly chosen group.

SCOPE OF SELECTION TASK

The three major steps in sales-force selection are:

1. Determine the number and type of people wanted. This step includes the preparation of a written job description. Management must also determine what specific qualifications are needed to fill the job as it is described.
2. Recruit an adequate number of applicants.
3. Select the qualified persons from among the applicants.

WHAT MAKES A GOOD SALES PERSON?

The key to success in the first step is to establish the proper hiring specifications, just as if the company were purchasing equipment or supplies instead of manpower. To establish these specifications, management must first know what the particular sales job entails. This calls for a detailed job analysis and a written description. It should include specific statements regarding job duties and applicant qualifications. This written description will later be invaluable in training, compensation, and supervision.

Determining the qualifications needed to fill the job is the most difficult part of the selection function. We still really do not know all the characteristics that make a good sales person. We cannot measure to what degree each quality should be present. Nor do we know to what extent an abundance of one can offset the lack of another.[4]

Over the years, many myths have arisen about what traits lead to success in selling. A good sales representative was supposed to be aggressive, extroverted, articulate, well groomed, and endowed with a great physique. Yet in actual fact many outstanding sales people have been mild-mannered and introverted. Other good ones have been somewhat inarticulate and carelessly dressed. Many good sales people are of average or even small size.

The search for the qualities that make a good sales person continues. As one approach, some companies have analyzed the personal histories of their past sales representatives in an effort to determine the traits common to successful (or unsuccessful) performers.

One psychologist, Robert McMurry, who has worked extensively in sales management, concluded that people who are outstanding sales successes inevitably possess these traits:

- A high level of energy.
- Abounding self-confidence.
- A chronic hunger for money, status, and the good things in life.
- A well-established habit of industry.
- The habit of perseverance — each objection or resistance is a challenge.
- A natural tendency to be competitive.

Moreover, McMurry maintained that the key requirement for sales success is an intuitive sensitivity to people. Supersales people are, in effect, constant and habitual "wooers." They have an inherent flair for winning the acceptance of others.

In another approach to the question of what makes a good sales person, Mayer and Greenberg concluded after some years of research that two personality traits are basic to sales success.[5]

- *Empathy*: The ability to identify with customers and their feelings.
- *Ego drive*: The personal need to make a sale, as a measure of self-fulfillment and not just for the money.

RECRUITING APPLICANTS

A planned system for recruiting a sufficient number of applicants is the next step in selection. A good recruiting system has these characteristics:

- It operates continuously, that is, not only when there are vacancies on the sales force.
- It is systematic, reaching and exploiting all appropriate sources of applicants.
- It provides a continuous flow of qualified applicants in greater numbers than the company can use.

Marketing at Work

File 17-3

Just How Many Sales People Do We Need?

One question that is rarely asked in the management of the sales function is, "How many sales people do we need?"

This question may be interpreted in a number of different ways:

- How many sales people do we want?
- How many sales people can we get?
- How many sales people can we handle?
- How many sales people do we really need?

Unfortunately, in many organizations, the last question is rarely asked, or at least rarely addressed properly. Many Canadian companies have reduced the size of their sales forces in recent years. These reductions were accomplished through the elimination of sales positions or the combining of sales territories — often to conform to corporate mandates to reduce numbers or expenses, and not to adjust to changes in marketing requirements. In many cases, the reductions worked; expenses were reduced, and the companies ended up with smaller sales forces, *but not necessarily the right size of sales force*.

Professor David Burgoyne of the University of Western Ontario has studied the impact on companies of reducing the size of their sales force to the point where there are too few sales people to get the job done properly. For a rational approach to dealing with the question of how many sales people a company should have, you should read his article in *The Business Quarterly*, Summer 1986 issue, page 65.

MATCHING APPLICANTS WITH HIRING SPECIFICATIONS

Sales managers should use all available selection tools in their effort to determine which applicants possess the desired qualifications. These tools include application forms, interviews, references, credit reports, psychological tests, and physical examinations. Probably all companies use application forms. They serve as records of personal histories and can be used to implement interviewing.

The interview is the other most widely used selection device. Virtually no sales person is hired without at least one personal interview, and it is desirable to have several. Ideally, these should be conducted in different physical settings and by different people. The effect of one person's possible bias is reduced by gathering several opinions. And interviewing in different locations allows interviewers to see how the recruit acts under different conditions. An interview should help an employer to determine (1) how badly the applicants want the job, (2) whether the company can assure them of the success they want, and (3) whether they will work to their fullest capacity. Patterned interviews are usually considered most desirable because they overcome many weaknesses found in the typical interviewing process. A patterned interview is one that is planned in advance by preparing a list of questions to ask the applicant.

Assimilating New Sales People into the Organization

When sales people are hired, management should pay close attention to the task of integrating them into the company family. Often this step is overlooked entirely. Potential sales people are carefully selected and are wined and dined in order to recruit them into the firm. Then, as soon as they are hired, the honeymoon is over, and they are left to shift for themselves. In such cases, the new people often become discouraged and may even quit. A wise sales manager will recognize that the new people know very little about the details of the job, their fellow workers, or their status in the firm. A vital need exists to maintain open, two-way channels of communication between new sales personnel and management.

Training the Sales Force

Another major aspect of sales-force operation is training. New sales people obviously need careful indoctrination and guidance. But even experienced reps need some training periodically. Setting up a training program involves answering the following questions: In each instance, decisions will be influenced by the kind of training program involved — indoctrination program, refresher course, or some other type.

1. What are the goals of the program? In very general terms, the aim of the program is to increase productivity and stimulate the sales force. In addition, executives must determine what specific ends they wish to reach. For instance, the goal may be to increase sales of high-profit items, or to improve prospecting methods for generating new accounts.
2. Who should do the training? The training program may be conducted by line sales executives, by a company staff-training department, by outside training specialists, or by some combination of the three.
3. What should be the content of the program? A well-rounded sales training program should cover three general topics: product knowledge, information about company policies, and selling techniques.
4. When and where should training be done? Some companies believe in training new people before they go into the field. Others let new people prove that they have some desire and ability to sell, and then bring them back into the office for intensive training.
   Firms may employ either centralized or decentralized training programs. A centralized program, usually at the home office, may involve a periodic meeting attended by all sales people. A decentralized program may be held in branch offices or during on-the-job training. Decentralized programs generally cost less than centralized programs. The big problem with decentralized programs is that the quality of instruction is often inferior.
5. What instructional methods should be used? The lecture method may be employed to inform trainees about company history and practices. Demonstrations may be used to impart product knowledge or selling techniques. Role playing is an excellent device for training a person in proper selling

techniques. On-the-job training may be used in almost any phase of the program.

Compensating the Sales Force

To compensate their sales forces, companies offer both financial and nonfinancial rewards. The *nonfinancial rewards* involve opportunities for advancement, recognition of efforts, and a feeling of belonging. *Financial rewards* may take the form of *direct* monetary payment or of *indirect* monetary payment (paid vacations, pensions, and insurance plans).

Establishing a compensation system really involves decisions concerning both the *level* of compensation and the *method* of compensation. The *level* refers to the total dollar income that a sales person earns over a period of time. The *method* refers to the system or plan by which the sales person will reach the intended level. The level is influenced by the type of person required and the competitive rate of pay for similar positions.

There are three widely used methods of compensating a sales force: straight salary, straight commission, and a combination plan. Today, well over half the firms in the country use some kind of combination plan.

The **straight-salary** plan offers a maximum of security and stability of earnings for a sales person. Management can expect its sales people to perform any reasonable work assignment because they receive the same pay regardless of the task performed. Under a straight salary, the sales reps can consider the customers' best interests, and the reps are less likely to use high-pressure selling tactics.

A commonly stated drawback of the straight-salary plan is that it does not offer adequate incentive. Thus, management has the added burden of motivating and directing the sales people. The pay plan itself does not provide any appreciable direction or control. Also, under this plan, compensation is a fixed cost unrelated to sales revenue. Straight-salary plans typically are used:

- To compensate new sales people or missionary sales people.
- When opening new territories.
- When sales involve a technical product and a lengthy period of negotiation.

A **straight commission** tends to have just the opposite merits and limitations. It provides tremendous incentive for sales people, and the commission costs can be related directly to sales or gross margin. Sales representatives have more freedom in their work, and their level of income is determined largely by their own efforts. On the other hand, it is difficult to control the sales people and to get them to do a fully balanced sales job. It is particularly difficult to get them to perform tasks for which no commission is paid. There is always the danger that they will oversell customers or otherwise incur customer ill will. Straight-commission plans may work well if:

- Great incentive is needed to get the sales.
- Very little nonselling missionary work is required.
- The company is financially weak and must relate its compensation expenses directly to sales or gross margin.
- The company is unable to supervise the sales force.

The ideal **combination** plan has the best features of both the straight-salary and the straight-commission plans, with as few of their drawbacks as possible. To come close to this ideal, the combination plan must be tailored to the particular firm, product, market, and type of selling.

An important element in the financial affairs of sales people is reimbursement for business expenses they incur in travelling or selling. The importance of sales-force expense control is difficult to overstate. It is essential that sales executives develop a plan both to control these costs and to reimburse the sales people fairly. In principle, sales people should not make or lose money because of their expense accounts. Nor should they forgo any beneficial sales activities because they will not be adequately reimbursed for the attendant expenses.

Supervising the Sales Force

The supervision of a sales force is both difficult and important. It is difficult because sales people often work where they cannot be closely and continually supervised. It is important because supervision serves both as a method of continuation training and as a device to ensure that company policies are being carried out. Still another value of sales-force supervision is that it affords a two-way channel of communication between management and the sales force. Personal supervision by a field supervisor or some other sales executive typically is the most effective supervisory method. Other methods of supervision involve the use of correspondence, reports, and sales meetings.

EVALUATING A SALES PERSON'S PERFORMANCE

Managing a sales force includes the job of evaluating the efforts of the sales people. Until executives know what their sales force is doing, they are in no position to make constructive proposals for improvement. By studying sales people's activities and by establishing standards of performance, management should be able to upgrade the sales force's efforts in general.

Performance analysis can help sales people improve their own efforts. People with poor sales records may know that they are doing something wrong. But they cannot determine what it is if they have no objective standards by which to measure their performance.

Performance evaluation can be of help in determining what should be included in a training program, and it can aid in sales supervision. A supervisor who knows some of the specific strengths and weaknesses of each sales person can do a better job of directing and training. Performance evaluation can also help management decide on salary increases and promotions for individual sales people.

Bases for Evaluation

Both quantitative and qualitative factors should be used as the bases for performance evaluation. The quantitative bases generally have the advantage of being specific and objective. Qualitative factors, unfortunately, require the subjective judgement of the evaluators. For both types of appraisal factors, however, management has the difficult task of setting the standards against which performance can be measured.

QUANTITATIVE BASES

Sales performance should be evaluated on the basis of both input (or efforts) and output (or results). A person's selling effectiveness is a combination of the two — output as measured by sales volume, gross margin, etc., and input as indicated by call rate, nonselling activities, etc.

Some *output* (result) factors that ordinarily are quite useful as quantitative evaluation bases are:

- Sales volume — by products, customer groups, and territory.
- Sales volume as a percentage of quota or territorial potential.
- Gross margin by product line, customer group, and territory.
- Orders:
  a. Number.
  b. Average size (dollar volume).
  c. Batting average (number of orders divided by number of calls).
- Accounts:
  a. Percentage of accounts sold.
  b. Number of new accounts called on and sold.

Some useful *input* (effort) factors to measure are:

- Calls per day (call rate).
- Direct selling expense, in dollars or as a percentage of sales volume.
- Nonselling activities:
  a. Advertising displays set up.
  b. Number of training sessions held with dealers and/or distributors.

The importance of output factors in a performance evaluation is readily recognized. Sometimes, however, the value of input factors is underestimated. Actually, an analysis of the input factors often is effective in locating trouble spots. If a person's output performance is unsatisfactory, very often the cause lies in the handling of the various input factors over which the sales person has control.

One key to a successful evaluation program is to appraise the sales person's performance on as many different bases as possible. Otherwise, management may be misled. A high daily call rate may look good, but it tells us nothing about how many orders per call are being written up. A high batting average (orders divided by calls) may be camouflaging a low average order size or a high sales volume on low-profit items.

QUALITATIVE BASES

It would be nice if the entire performance evaluation could be based only on quantitative factors. This would minimize the subjectivity and personal bias of the evaluators. Unfortunately, this cannot be done. Many qualitative factors must be considered because they influence a sales person's performance and help in the interpretation of quantitative data. These factors include:

- Knowledge of the product, company policies, and the competition.
- Management of the sales person's own time and the preparation for calls.
- Customer relations.
- Personal appearance and health.
- Personality and attitudinal factors, such as:
  a. Cooperation.

This sales rep will be evaluated on the basis of qualitative and quantitative measures of performance.

b. Resourcefulness.
c. Ability to analyze logically and make decisions.

This concludes our coverage of the management of the personal selling effort in a company's promotional mix. In the next chapter we shall consider the other two widely used promotional tools — advertising and sales promotion.

SUMMARY   Personal selling is the major promotional method used in business around the world — whether measured by people employed, by total expenditures, or by expenses as a percentage of sales. The sales job today is not what it used to be. A new breed of professional sales person has been developing over the past few decades. Today the sales jobs are quite different from other jobs in a company. Also, there are a variety of sales jobs. They range from that of a driver-sales person, through jobs like inside order taker, missionary seller, and sales engineer, to the positions that call for highly creative selling of tangible goods and intangible services.

There are five steps in the actual sale of a product or service. The first three involve presale preparation, prospecting for potential buyers, and preapproaching these prospects. Then a sales person is ready to make a sales presentation. This fourth step involves approaching the customer and creating some customer interest. The actual sales talk may be canned or individually tailored for each prospect. The sales person must be prepared to meet customer objections and then try to close the sale. Finally, postsale activities are needed to satisfy the customer and reduce his or her anxieties concerning the purchase.

Strategic sales-force management involves planning and operating a sales force within the guidelines set by the strategic marketing planning. The tasks involved in staffing and operating a sales force present managerial challenges in several areas. The key to successful sales-force management is to do a good job in selecting the sales people. Then plans must be made for assimilating these new people into the company. Sales training and supervision programs have to be developed. Management needs to set up plans for compensating sales people and reimbursing them for their business expenses.

The final stage in strategic sales-force management is to evaluate the performance of the individual sales people.

NOTES

[1] For an in-depth discussion of the personal selling process, see Charles M. Futrell, *ABC's of Selling*, Richard D. Irwin, Inc., Homewood, Ill., 1985.

[2] For suggestions on how a seller can cultivate and better manage its long-term relationships with its customers, see Theodore Levitt, "After the Sale Is Over . . . ," *Harvard Business Review*, September–October 1983, pp. 87–93.

[3] For an in-depth discussion of sales-force management, see William J. Stanton and Richard H. Buskirk, *Management of the Sales Force*, 7th ed., Richard D. Irwin, Inc., Homewood, Ill., 1987.

[4] For a review of research findings regarding factors that are predictive of sales people's performance, see Gilbert A. Churchill, Jr., Neil M. Ford, Steven W. Hartley, and Orville C. Walker, Jr., "The Determinants of Salesperson Performance: A Meta-Analysis," *Journal of Marketing Research*, May 1985, pp. 87–93.

[5] David Mayer and Herbert M. Greenberg, "What Makes a Good Salesman?" *Harvard Business Review*, July–August 1964, pp. 119–125. For an excellent review of recruiting and selecting sales personnel, see James M. Comer and Alan J. Dubinsky, *Managing the Successful Sales Force*, D.C. Heath and Company, Lexington, Mass., 1985, pp. 9–25.

KEY TERMS AND CONCEPTS

Direct marketing 471
Party-plan selling 471
New type of sales person 473
Classification of sales jobs 475
Telemarketing 476
Presale preparation 477
Prospecting for new customers 477
Preapproach 477
The approach 477
AIDA (Fig. 17-1) 477
Canned sales talk 478
Meeting objections in sales talk 478

Cognitive dissonance 479
Postsale activities 479
Sales-force selection tasks 480
Decisions in sales training 482
Financial compensation 483
Nonfinancial compensation 484
Straight-salary compensation 484
Straight-commission compensation 484
Bases for evaluating sales people 486

1. The cost of a full-page, four-colour advertisement in the national edition of *Maclean's* or *Chatelaine* can be as much as $25,000; a two-page spread can cost close to $40,000. A sales-force executive is urging her company to eliminate a few of these advertisements and, instead, to hire a few more sales people. This executive believes that one good sales person working for an entire year can sell more than a couple of ads in these magazines. How would you answer her?

2. "The sales person occupies many roles with many divergent role partners, and this entails heavy emotional demands." Explain.

3. Refer to the seven-way classification of sales jobs in this chapter, and answer the following questions:
   a. In which types of jobs is the sales person most free from close supervision?
   b. Which types are likely to be the highest paid?
   c. Which are likely to involve the most travelling?
   d. For which jobs is a high degree of motivation necessary?

4. What information would you seek as part of your presale preparation to sell each of the following products? In each case, assume you are selling to the users of the product.
   a. Eight-unit apartment complex.
   b. Retail record store.
   c. Minicomputer.
   d. Contributions to the United Way.

5. What are some of the sources you might use to acquire a list of prospects for the following products?
   a. Automobile.
   b. Dental X-ray equipment.
   c. Software for personal computers.
   d. Baby furniture and clothes.

6. How should a sales person respond when customers say that the price of a product is too high?

7. "A good selection program is desirable, but not essential. Improper selection of sales people can be counterbalanced by a good training program, by a good compensation system, or by fine supervision." Discuss.

8. What sources should be used for recruiting sales applicants in each of the following firms? Explain your reasoning in each instance.
   a. A Delta hotel that wants companies to use the hotel's facilities for conventions.
   b. Tupperware, Avon, or Mary Kay Cosmetics, which are selling directly to consumers.
   c. IBM, which needs sales reps for its large computer division.

9. "It is best to hire experienced sales people because they do not require any training." Discuss.

10. What factors should be considered in determining the *level* of sales compensation?

11. Compare the merits of a straight-salary plan and a straight-commission plan of sales compensation. Name some types of sales jobs in which each plan might be desirable.

12. How might a firm determine whether a sales person is using high-pressure selling tactics that may injure customer relations?

13. How can a sales manager evaluate the ability of sales people to get new business?

CHAPTER 18

MANAGEMENT OF ADVERTISING, SALES PROMOTION, AND PUBLICITY

This chapter is a discussion of nonpersonal selling, as distinguished from the personal selling of the last chapter. After studying this chapter, you should understand:

- The nature of advertising and its importance in our economy and in an individual firm.
- The major types of advertising.
- How to develop an advertising campaign and select the advertising media.
- How to evaluate the effectiveness of advertising.
- Sales promotion — its nature, importance, and services rendered.
- Publicity — its nature, benefits, and relation to public relations.

TURN ADVICE INTO ACTION

Royal Trust invites you to take the first step in turning advice into
action by filling in the return card below. We would be pleased to send you information
on specific products or arrange a meeting with one of our advisory staff.

AND EVEN WIN A TRIP
TO SEOUL

All responses are entered in a draw to win a trip for two to the 1988 Summer Olympics
in Seoul, South Korea. Full contest details overleaf. Travel arrangements have been made
courtesy of Canadian Airlines International.

I enjoyed the 88 Advisor. Please enter me in the Seoul Olympics Draw.

Mr. Miss Mrs. Ms. _____

Address _____

City_____ Prov._____ Code_____

Phone: Day_____ Evening_____

I am also interested in the following information.

☐ 1987 Royal Trust Annual Report ☐ RRSPs ☐ Mutual Funds ☐ Personal Line Of Credit ☐ Mortgages
☐ GICs ☐ Credit Cards ☐ RRIFs & Annuities Other_____

**I would also like to arrange an appointment with a Royal Trust
Account Manager to discuss the following:**

☐ Personal Financial Planning ☐ Will & Estate Planning ☐ Investment Management ☐ Tax Planning

The following information will help us better prepare for your appointment.

Are you a Royal Trust client? ☐ Yes ☐ No Your Branch _____

Date of Birth _____ Your approximate income in 1987 _____

Best appointment time for you _____

For an immediate appointment call our toll free number.
1 (800) 668-1990 or 864-6400 in Toronto

ROYAL TRUST

Sales promotion has outgrown its stepchild status and today is treated as an equal partner with advertising and personal selling in the promotional mix of many organizations. Sweepstakes, contests, premiums, coupons, and other promotional devices have long been successful in enhancing sales and building market share when directed at end consumers, the retail trade, distributors, and sales force members.

It is estimated that, in Canada, expenditures on consumer and trade promotions now total more than $8 billion annually. Promotional expenditures are growing at a rate of almost 14 percent per year, as compared with a growth rate in media advertising of less than 7 percent per year. Sales promotions now account for 60 percent of all marketing communications expenses in Canada, and this figure is expected to grow to more than 70 percent within the next few years.[1]

What has led to this increase in interest in the use of sales promotions? There are three major factors: the first relates to the fragmentation of the mass media. With the proliferation of television and radio stations, VCRs, more consumer magazines and billboards, it is simply more difficult to ensure that your advertising message reaches the consumer. Secondly, it is very difficult to measure the effect of media advertising campaigns. In the case of promotions, however, the marketer can much more easily determine how many coupons were redeemed, or how many people entered a sweepstakes contest, or took advantage of the garbage-bag or pantyhose offer when they bought their gas. Finally, some marketers feel that the proliferation of new products in the consumer goods field in recent years has led to a decline in brand loyalty and a perception on the part of consumers that many brands are essentially the same. Sales promotions are more effective at differentiating brands and building short-term brand share.

As a result, we see more and more companies turning to sales promotions.

- *Reader's Digest* is one of the most experienced users of sales promotions in Canada. For more than 25 years, the largest-circulation magazine in the country has been running its annual contest, with prizes now totalling more than $500,000.

- The makers of Gabriel shock absorbers received more than 8,000 entries to a contest open to people who install shock absorbers. The prize was a $58,000 Corvette.

- Spalding Canada printed entry forms on more than one million packages of its Top-Flite II golf balls. The "Discovery Tour" sweepstakes had grand prizes of three two-week trips for two to the Orient.

Hunters ordinarily do not use a rifle to hunt ducks. They need a device that reaches a wider area than a rifle without expending additional effort. Thus, duck hunters ordinarily use a shotgun. By the same token, mass communication is needed to reach mass markets at a reasonable cost. Advertising, sales promotion, and publicity are just the tools for this job. It is too costly and time-consuming to try to do the job with sales people alone.

NATURE OF ADVERTISING

Advertising consists of all the activities involved in presenting to a group a non-personal, oral or visual, openly sponsor-identified message regarding a product, service, or idea. This message, called an **advertisement**, is disseminated through one or more media and is paid for by the identified sponsor.

We should note some important points in connection with this definition. First, there is a significant distinction between advertising and an advertisement. The advertisement is the message itself. Advertising is a process — it is a series of activities necessary to prepare the message and get it to the intended market. Another point is that the public knows who is behind the advertising because the sponsor is openly identified in the advertisement. Also, payment is made by the sponsor to the media that carry the message. These last two considerations differentiate advertising from propaganda and publicity.

Types of Advertising

An organization's objectives in its advertising program determine, to a great extent, what type of advertising that organization will use. Consequently, marketing executives should understand something about the classifications of the various types of advertising.

PRODUCT AND INSTITUTIONAL ADVERTISING

All advertising may be classed as either product or institutional. In **product advertising**, advertisers are informing or stimulating the market about their products

This public service ad illustrates Shell Canada's commitment to supporting the arts.

or services. Product advertising is often further subdivided into direct-action and indirect-action advertising. With **direct-action advertising**, sellers are seeking a quick response to their advertisements. An advertisement with a coupon may urge the reader to send immediately for a free sample. **Indirect-action advertising** is designed to stimulate demand over a longer period of time. Such advertising is intended to inform customers that the product exists and to point out its benefits. The idea is that when customers are ready to buy the product, they will look favourably upon the seller's brand.

Institutional advertising is designed either to present information about the advertiser's business or to create a good attitude — build goodwill — toward the organization. This type of advertising is not intended to sell a specific product or service of an advertiser. Two subdivisions of institutional advertising are:

- **Patronage advertising**: Presents information about the advertiser's business. A retail store may advertise its new store hours or a change in its delivery policy, for example.
- **Public service advertising**: Shows the advertiser as a "good citizen." A company's ads may urge the public to support a Red Cross campaign or to drive carefully. Or a manufacturer's ads may tell what the company is doing to reduce the pollution caused by its factories.

PRIMARY AND SELECTIVE DEMAND ADVERTISING

Primary-demand advertising is that type which is designed to stimulate the demand for a generic category of a product, such as Colombian coffee, or videocassette recorders. This is in contrast to selective-demand advertising, which is intended to stimulate demand for individual brands such as Nabob coffee or Sony or Toshiba videocassette recorders.

Typically, primary-demand advertising is to be used in two situations. The first

We know why they're here.

The richest coffee in the world.™

Colombian coffee uses primary-demand ads to increase the total market.

Nabob uses selective-demand ads to increase their share.

is when a product is in the introductory stages of its life cycle. This is called **pioneering advertising**. An individual firm may run an ad about its new product, explaining the product's benefits, but not emphasizing the brand name. The objective of pioneering primary-demand advertising is to *inform*, and not to *persuade*, the target market. In recent years pioneering-demand ads have been run for such products as backyard satellite dishes for TV reception and compact laser discs for stereo sound systems.

The second use of primary-demand advertising is by trade association or marketing boards to stimulate the demand for their industry's product which is in competition with other product categories. Thus, the Dairy Bureau of Canada's ads urge us to drink milk, instead of some other beverage. The association doesn't care whose brand of milk we drink, just that we drink milk. The Wool Growers' Association urges us to buy clothing made of wool rather than synthetic fibers.

Selective-demand advertising essentially is competitive advertising — it pits one brand against another. This type of advertising typically is used when a product has gone beyond the introductory stage of its life cycle. The product then is sufficiently well known, and several individual brands are competing for a market share. The objective of competitive advertising is to *persuade* the potential customers, and it emphasizes the particular benefits of the brand being advertised.

Comparative advertising is one type of selective-demand advertising that has been used for a wide variety of products in recent years. In comparative advertising, the advertiser mentions rival brands by name and flatly states that the advertised brand is better than the other. Thus, General Mills advertises that one bowl of its cereal, Total, carries the equivalent nutritional benefit found in 12 bowls of Nabisco's Shredded Wheat. Tempo advertises that it gives more effective relief for acid stomach than Tums, Rolaids, or Maalox.

The Bureau of Competition Policy of the federal Department of Consumer and Corporate Affairs has taken the position that truthful comparative advertising can be a pro-competitive force in the marketplace. In fact, the Bureau has periodically published guidelines for the consideration of advertisers.[2] The main point to be learned from the discussion of comparative advertising and its regulation is that a company planning to use the technique had better be very sure that what is being said in its advertising about the competition is completely accurate.

File 18-1

First Create the Ad, Then Review, Review, Review

Government regulatory bodies play a much greater role in regulating the content of advertising in Canada than most consumers realize. It's not just comparative advertising that is subject to scrutiny. The process is particularly strict in the approval of television commercials for food and beverages. For the past 40 years, all radio and television commercials for food and beverage products, including beer, wine and cider, have been approved by the Department of Consumer and Corporate Affairs (CCA) on behalf of the Canadian Radio-Television and Telecommunications Commission (CRTC). Here's how the process works.

After completing a script, the advertising agency sends it to the client to be checked before it is sent to CCA for pre-clearance. Officials at CCA are primarily interested in applying two federal acts: the Food and Drug Act and the Consumer Packaging and Labelling Act. Section 5 of the Food and Drug Act, for example, reads: *No person shall label, package, treat, process, sell or advertise any food in a manner that is false, misleading or deceptive or is likely to create an erroneous impression regarding its character, value, quantity, composition, merit, or safety.*

In addition to the legal regulation of advertising, there are many codes of advertising standards that are administered by the advertising industry itself. For example, in 1982, the Canadian Advertising Foundation developed Guidelines for the Use of Comparative Advertising in Food Commercials. They also developed guidelines for the use of research and survey data in advertising. These guidelines are administered by the Advertising Standards Council and are designed to ensure that comparisons are fair and factual, and based on adequate and proper tests. All comparative claims must be supportable.

When CCA receives a comparative advertisement for approval, it will often ask for substantiation of claims and will examine research results upon which claims are based. It may also refer such commercials to the Advertising Standards Council to determine whether the commercial meets the advertising industry's own standards for comparative advertising.

Source: Adapted in part from "How to Play the Game by the Rules," *Marketing*, vol. 91, no. 43, October 27, 1986, pp. 28, 31.

COOPERATIVE ADVERTISING

In some situations an effective promotional strategy calls for the use of some form of cooperative advertising. **Vertical cooperative advertising** involves firms on different levels of distribution — such as manufacturers and retailers. In fact, the major type of vertical cooperative advertising is a joint venture between a manufacturer and a retailer. The manufacturer and the retailer share the cost of the retailer's advertising that manufacturers' product. The manufacturer of Daks suits, for example, may prepare ads for retail clothing stores, and the stores then pay for the newspaper space that carries these ads.

Another type of vertical cooperative advertising involves an *advertising allowance* — also called a *promotional allowance*. This allowance is an off-invoice or cash discount offered by a manufacturer to a retailer to encourage the retailer to advertise or prominently display the product. This arrangement provides added incentive for the retailer to advertise the manufacturer's product. The producer also benefits from the media rate structure which typically has lower prices for advertising placed by local retail firms than for manufacturer's advertising.

Horizontal cooperative advertising involves a group of firms on the same level of distribution — such as a group of retailers. All stores in a suburban shopping centre, for example, may run a joint ad weekly in a newspaper. The different businesses in a summer resort area — lodges, stores, restaurants, and marinas — often will participate in joint promotional activities.

Cost of Advertising   Advertising in one form or another is used by virtually all manufacturers and retailers in the country. The importance of advertising may be indicated by its cost.

ADVERTISING EXPENDITURES IN TOTAL AND BY MEDIA

One quantitative indication of the importance of advertising is the total amount spent on advertising in Canada. In 1987, the revenues of Canadian advertising media were approximately $7.3 billion. Table 18-1 shows the percentage of the total accounted for by each of the major media. For years, newspapers have been the most widely used medium, based upon total advertising dollars invested, about 80 percent of the expenditures for advertising in Canadian daily newspapers goes for local and classified advertising rather than for national advertising. The revenues generated by television networks and stations and periodicals, while they increased in the past, appear to have peaked.

TABLE 18-1   PERCENT SHARES OF NET ADVERTISING REVENUES BY INDIVIDUAL SECTORS IN BROADCAST AND PRINT, 1974 to 1987

	1974	1978	1982	1986*	1987*
Radio	10%	11%	10%	9%	9%
Television	13	16	17	16	16
Daily newspapers	30	28	26	24	23
Weekly and other newspapers	5	5	5	7	7
General magazines	3	4	5	4	3
Business papers	3	3	4	2	2
Directories	6	6	7	6	6
Direct mail, catalogues	21	20	20	23	23
Outdoor	8	7	6	8	8

*estimates by Maclean-Hunter Research Bureau

Note: Totals may not add up to 100% due to rounding and exclusions.

Source: Maclean-Hunter Research Bureau, *A Report on Advertising Revenues in Canada*, Toronto, November 1988.

ADVERTISING EXPENDITURES AS A PERCENTAGE OF COMPANY SALES

When gauging the importance of advertising, it is often more meaningful to measure expenditures against a benchmark rather than simply to look at the total in an isolated position. Frequently, advertising expenses are expressed as a percentage of a company's sales. Table 18-2 shows the 50 largest advertisers in Canada for 1987. Some of the advertisers who spend a large dollar amount on advertising actually devote a *very* small percentage of sales to advertising. Table 18-3 presents data that permit a comparison of various industries in terms of the percentage of sales devoted to advertising expenses. The data for 1965 (the last year for which Statistics Canada produced figures) are surprisingly still indicative of the patterns, since recent U.S. data are also quite similar. The heaviest expenditures, on a ratio basis, are by the toilet preparations (No. 17) and the soap and cleaning compounds manufacturers (No. 14). At the other extreme are the sugar refiners (No. 16) at 0.19 percent of sales. In general, the consumer goods industries are spending more

TABLE 18-2   **FIFTY LARGEST ADVERTISERS IN CANADA, 1987**

	In $000
1. Government of Canada	66,416.2
2. Procter & Gamble	53,142.9
3. General Motors of Canada	39,739.0
4. The Thomson Group	38,283.0
5. John Labatt — BUDWEISER!!	36,036.0
6. Unilever	31,706.4
7. Chrysler Canada	29,692.0
8. RJR	29,031.2
9. The Molson Companies	28,792.2
10. Ontario Government	27,907.5
11. Bell Canada Enterprises	27,635.5
12. Pepsico	26,869.5
13. Carling O'Keefe Canada	26,827.5
14. McDonald's Restaurants of Canada	25,093.6
15. Kraft	22,290.4
16. Imasco Holdings Canada	21,732.3
17. Ford Motor Co. of Canada	18,871.7
18. Warner Lambert Canada	18,727.8
19. Coca-Cola	18,649.7
20. General Foods	18,398.6
21. American Home Products	18,322.3
22. Kellogg Salada Canada	18,155.2
23. Toyota Canada	15,765.7
24. George Weston	15,307.3
25. Canadian Tire Corporation	14,850.0
26. Rothmans, Benson & Hedges	14,406.2
27. Effem Foods	14,206.3
28. Imperial Oil	13,533.7
29. Canadian Airlines International	12,879.0
30. Quebec Government	12,618.0
31. Johnson & Johnson	11,883.0
32. Dairy Bureau of Canada	11,310.8
33. The T. Eaton Co.	11,052.5
34. Bristol-Myers Canada	10,956.3
35. Nestlé Enterprises	10,847.3
36. Hyundai Auto Canada	10,679.5
37. Nissan Automobile Co. of Canada	10,602.8
38. CKR	10,525.4
39. Mazda Canada	10,202.8
40. Honda Canada	10,051.9
41. Gillette Canada	9,883.4
42. Ralston Purina Canada	9,719.1
43. Provigo	9,655.6
44. Brick Warehouse	9,537.3
45. Quaker Oats Co. of Canada	9,121.7
46. Trilon Financial Corporation	9,100.1
47. General Mills Canada	8,985.9

TABLE 18-2 continued   **FIFTY LARGEST ADVERTISERS IN CANADA, 1987**

48. Sears Canada	8,644.3
49. HJ Heinz Co. of Canada	8,468.8
50. McCain Foods	8,145.4

Source: Marketing, vol. 93, no. 10, March 7, 1988, p. 21. Reprinted by permission, Media Measurement Services, Inc.

TABLE 18-3   **SELECTED ADVERTISING RATIOS, 1965**

	Ratio of Advertising to Sales 1965 (%)
1. Agricultural implement	0.98
2. Breweries	6.56
3. Carpet, mat, and rug	1.11
4. Confectionery manufacturers	4.78
5. Distilleries	2.74
6. Electric lamp and shade	0.31
7. Foundation garments	5.42
8. Hardware, tool, and cutlery manufacturers	3.41
9. Hosiery mills	2.01
10. Pen and pencil manufacturers	7.35
11. Petroleum refining	1.17
12. Pharmaceuticals and medicines manufacturers	8.65
13. Scientific and professional equipment manufacturers	2.06
14. Soap and cleaning compounds manufacturers	10.85
15. Sporting goods	1.37
16. Sugar refineries	0.19
17. Toilet preparations manufacturers	15.22
18. Toys and games	6.50
19. Wineries	3.99
20. Women's clothing factories	0.45

Source: Advertising Expenditures in Canada, 1965, cat. no. 63-216, Table 19.

per sales dollar than are industrial goods manufacturers. One can expect shifts over time for a given industry. Within each industry, of course, a variance exists, with some firms spending quite heavily compared with the industry average and others relying on nonadvertising forms of promotional variables and spending a small amount compared with the industry average.

Sometimes it may seem as if the public is bombarded on all sides by advertising; however, the total amount spent is usually small in relation to sales volume.

One representative study showed that manufacturers of consumer products spend about 3 percent of sales for advertising purposes, while manufacturers of industrial goods spend less than 1 percent. In a summary report, the Conference Board showed advertising as a percentage of sales for various types of manufacturers, retailers, and service industries. In the majority of these industries, advertising was less than 2 percent of sales.

COST OF ADVERTISING VERSUS COST OF PERSONAL SELLING

While we do not have accurate totals for the costs of personal selling, we do know they far surpass advertising expenditures. In manufacturing, only a few industries, such as drugs, toiletries, cleaning products, tobacco, and beverages, have advertising expenditures higher than those for personal selling. In countless companies, advertising runs 1 to 3 percent of net sales. But, in many firms, the expenses of recruiting and operating a sales force run from 8 to 15 percent of sales.

At the wholesale level, advertising costs are very low. Personal selling costs may run 10 to 15 times as high. Even among retailers in total — and this includes those with self-service operations — the cost of personal selling runs substantially higher than advertising.

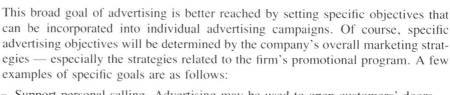

OBJECTIVES OF ADVERTISING

Fundamentally, the only purpose of advertising is to sell something — a product, a service, or an idea. Stated another way, the real goal of advertising is effective communication. That is, the ultimate effect of advertising should be to modify the attitudes and/or behaviour of the receiver of the message.

Specific Objectives

This broad goal of advertising is better reached by setting specific objectives that can be incorporated into individual advertising campaigns. Of course, specific advertising objectives will be determined by the company's overall marketing strategies — especially the strategies related to the firm's promotional program. A few examples of specific goals are as follows:

- Support personal selling. Advertising may be used to open customers' doors for sales people, and to acquaint prospects with the sellers' company.
- Reach people inaccessible to the sales force. Sales people may be unable to reach top executives, or they may not be certain who makes the buying decisions in a company. In either case, there is a good chance that these executives will read a journal that carries the ads.
- Improve dealer relations.
- Enter a new geographic market or attract a new group of customers.
- Introduce a new product.
- Increase sales of a product. An advertising campaign may be destined to lengthen the season for the product (as has been done in the case of soft drinks); increase the frequency of replacement (as is done in campaigns for spark plugs and light bulbs); increase the variety of product uses; or increase the units of purchase.
- Expand the industry's sales.
- Counteract prejudice or substitution.
- Build goodwill for the company and improve its reputation (*a*) by rendering a

An ad in these magazines will help reach industrial buyers inaccessible to the sales force.

public service through advertising or (*b*) by telling of the organization behind the product.

DEVELOPING AN ADVERTISING CAMPAIGN

Once a company decides to advertise (based on the factors discussed in Chapter 16), management can get on with the job of developing an advertising campaign. An advertising campaign is simply one part of a total promotional campaign — identified in Chapter 16 as an exercise in strategic planning. It is a coordinated series of promotional efforts built around a central theme and designed to reach a specific goal.

Initial Planning

The planning in an *advertising* campaign must be done within the framework of the overall strategic marketing plan and the *promotional* campaign planning. Therefore, at the time the advertising campaign is being planned, presumably management already has made decisions in several areas. For example, the specific promotional goals have been established. Also, management has decided what the central campaign theme will be, and what appeals will be stressed in light of consumer buying motives and habits. The total promotional appropriation has been determined and has been allocated among the various promotional tools. And the role of advertising in the promotional campaign has been determined. Management can now make decisions involving (1) the selection of the advertising media and (2) the creation and production of individual advertisements.

Selecting the Media

Three levels of decision making are required in the selection of advertising media. First, management must determine what general types of media to use. Will newspapers, television, or magazines be used? Second, if magazines are to be used, will they be of the special-interest type (for example, exploration magazines such as *Equinox* or business magazines such as *Canadian Business*), or of the general-interest type? Finally, the specific medium must be chosen. The company that decides first on radio and then on local stations now must decide what specific station to use in each city. Some of the factors to consider in making media decisions are as follows:

- *Objective of the advertisement.* Media choices are influenced both by the purpose of a specific advertisement and by the goal of an entire campaign. For example, if the goal of the campaign is to generate appointments for sales people, the advertising company will probably use direct mail. If an advertiser wants to place an ad inducing action within a day or two, newspapers or radio may be used.
- *Media circulation.* Media circulation must match the distribution patterns of the product. Consequently, the *geographic* scope of the market will influence the choice of media considerably. Furthermore, media should be selected that will reach the desired *type* of market with a minimum of waste circulation.

Today many media — even national and other large-market media — can be targeted at smaller, specialized market segments. This reduces waste circulation for an advertiser. For example, many national magazines publish regional editions. Trade and professional journals exist in many fields. Large metropolitan newspapers publish several editions. Some radio stations specialize in rock, country, or classical music.

■ *Requirements of the message.* The medium should fit the message. For example, meat products, floor coverings, and apparel are ordinarily best presented in pictorial form. If the advertiser can use a very brief message, as is possible in advertising salt, beer, or sugar, then billboards may be the best choice.

■ *Time and location of buying decision.* The medium should reach prospective customers near the time they make they buying decisions and the places where they make them. For this reason, outdoor advertising often does well for gasoline products. Many grocery store ads are placed in newspapers on Wednesday or Thursdays in anticipation of heavy weekend buying.

■ *Cost of media.* The costs of the advertising media should be considered in relation to (a) the budget available and (b) the circulation of the media. In the first instance, the budget level could rule out television as a choice. Or possibly the advertiser can afford local television but not a national network. On the second count, the advertiser should try to develop some relationships between the cost of the medium and the size of the audience it will reach.

Chatelaine and *Flare*
© 1988 Maclean Hunter Limited.

CHARACTERISTICS OF MAJOR TYPES OF MEDIA

In the process of selecting the media to use in a campaign, management must consider the advertising characteristics of the main class of media. The term *characteristics* is carefully chosen instead of *advantages* and *disadvantages*. To illustrate, one characteristic of radio as an advertising medium is that it makes its impression through the ear. For many products, this feature is an advantage. For products that benefit from a colour photograph, this characteristic of radio is a drawback.

Newspapers   As an advertising medium, newspapers are flexible and timely. They account for the largest portion of total advertising dollars spent in Canada. They can be used to cover a single city or a number of urban centres. with the development of computer technology and regional printing in the publishing industry, once-local newspapers may now be printed in regional centres for distribution across the country. The daily *Financial Post* and *The Globe and Mail*, for example, are headquartered in Toronto, but are printed regionally and are now true national daily papers.

While newspapers are becoming more attractive to the national advertiser, they remain the principal advertising vehicle for the local advertiser. Ads can be cancelled on a few days' notice or inserted on one day's notice. Newspapers can give an advertiser an intense coverage of a local market because almost everybody reads newspapers. The local feature also helps in that the ads can be adapted to local social and economic conditions. Circulation costs per prospect are low. On the other hand, the life of a newspaper advertisement is very short.

Magazines   Magazines are an excellent medium when high-quality printing and colour are desired in an advertisement. Magazines can be used to reach a national market at a relatively low cost per prospect. Through the use of special-interest magazines or regional editions of national magazines, an advertiser can reach a selected audience with a minimum of waste circulation. Magazines are usually read in a leisurely fashion, in contrast to the haste with which other print media are read. This feature is particularly valuable for the advertiser who must present a message at some length. Some of the less favourable characteristics of magazines are their inflexibility and the infrequency with which they reach the market, as compared with other media.

Direct mail   Direct mail is probably the most personal and selective of all the media. Because it reaches only the market that the advertiser wishes to contact, there is a minimum of waste circulation. Direct mail is not accompanied by articles or other editorial matter, however, unless the advertiser provides it. That is, most direct mail is pure advertising. As a result, a direct-mail ad creates its own circulation and attracts its own readers. The cost of direct mail per prospect reached is quite high compared with other media. But other media reach many people who are not real prospects and thus have higher waste-circulation costs. A severe limitation of direct mail is the difficulty of getting and maintaining good mailing lists. Direct-mail advertising also suffers from the stigma of being classed as ''junk mail.''

Radio   Radio is enjoying a renaissance as an advertising and cultural medium and as a financial investment. When interest in television soared after World War II, radio audiences (especially for national network radio), declined so much that people were predicting radio's demise. But for the past ten years or so, this medium has been making a real comeback. Local radio (as contrasted with national networks) is especially strong. Radio accounts for almost 10 percent of all advertising revenues in Canada, attracting more than $600 million in sales annually.

As an advertising medium, radio's big advantage is its relatively low cost. You can reach almost 100 percent of the people with radio. At the same time, with special-interest programming, some segmented target markets can be pinpointed quite effectively. In the late 1980s for example, many radio stations took a close

Radio advertising can be very creative.

Where else?
On the radio you can show practically any idea you've got swimming around.
From a pipe-puffing pike to a bevy of be-bopping barracudas. And no one's ever going to scream "Holy Mackerel!" when they see the cost.
Get creative and show your stuff with the power of sound. Then everyone will say:
"I saw it on the radio."

"I SAW IT ON THE RADIO."

look at the growth in the 25 to 49 age segment. In 1969, 15 percent of Canadians were teens; by 1986 teens represented only 9 percent of the market. The great bulge of baby boomers represented an attractive target market, and many stations such as CHUM-AM in Toronto departed from their teen-oriented, Top-20-hits format and adopted a much mellower format, such as CHUM's "Favourites of Yesterday and Today."

On the other hand, radio makes only an audio impression. So it is useless where visual impact is needed. As with direct mail, radio advertisers must create their own audiences. And the exposure life of a given radio message is extremely short. Also, audience attention often is at a low level, especially when the radio is being used mainly to provide background for driving, studying, or some other activity.

Television   Television is probably the most versatile of all media. It makes its appeal through both the eye and the ear; products can be demonstrated as well as explained. It offers considerable flexibility in terms of the geographic market covered and the time of message presentation. By making part of its impression through the ear, television can take advantage of the personal, dramatic impact of the spoken word.

On the other hand, television is an extremely expensive medium. The message is not permanently recorded for the message receiver. Thus the prospect who is not reached the first time is lost forever, as far as a particular message is concerned. Television does not lend itself to long advertising copy, nor does it present pictures as clearly as magazines do. As with direct mail and radio, television advertisers must create their own audiences.

Outdoor   Outdoor advertising is a flexible, low-cost medium. Because it reaches virtually the entire population, it lends itself nicely to widely used consumer products that require only a brief selling statement. It is excellent for the reminder type of advertising, and it carries the impact of large size and colour. There is flexibility in geographic coverage and in the intensity of market coverage within the area. However, unless the advertised product is a widely used consumer good, considerable waste circulation will occur. While the cost of reaching an individual prospect

Outdoor billboards are great for short messages.

is low, the total cost of a national campaign is quite high. There also is considerable public criticism of the clutter and landscape-defacing aspects of outdoor advertising.

Marketing at Work

New Ways of Getting the Message Through

Don't be misled into thinking that there are only a few mass media used to reach consumers with advertising messages. While there is still a strong reliance on the traditional print and broadcast media, advertisers in Canada have recently been faced with a dazzling array of new media. There are now more alternatives than ever for getting your message in front of the customer. Many of these media have developed in response to a fragmentation of the mass media. With the proliferation of alternatives competing for the attention of the customer, advertisers have had to look for new ways of getting the message to the target market and getting it there closer to the point of sale. Some of the innovations represent modifications of the existing mass media, others "piggyback" on new technologies, while still others are part of the burgeoning out-of-home advertising business.

- Many advertisers are turning to 15-second television commercials, priced at 60 percent to 70 percent of the cost of a 30-second commercial.
- Bothered by the erosion of their network television audience by videos, some national advertisers have moved their advertising to reach the video watchers by placing ads on rental video movies or by co-sponsoring or co-producing them; Diet Pepsi placed a 60-second commercial on the video version of *Top Gun*; a Calgary company places advertisements on the blank plastic boxes that contain rental video tapes.
- Transit ads now appear on the exterior as well as the interior of buses and subway cars, both on the rear and the front of the bus; in fact, one of the newest forms of transit advertising is to paint the entire bus as a mobile billboard.
- The out-of-home advertising media are the fastest growing. These encompass outdoor billboards, posters in airports, malls, and railway stations, ads on shopping carts, on golf courses, ski lifts, washroom walls, and garbage cans.
- Pixsell is an in-store interactive computer that allows customers to call up recipes or discount coupons, which are then printed right in the store. This system has been tested in Sobeys supermarkets in Atlantic Canada with considerable success, again reaching the customer at the point of sale.
- Coupons and advertising materials are included in egg cartons; home computer owners can access an on-line database called "Free Access Network," complete with news, sports, weather, and classified and display advertising. In Kitchener-Waterloo, Tele-Direct, the publication arm of Bell Canada which publishes the Yellow Pages, has introduced its Talking Yellow Pages service. Users dial a phone number and punch in a four-digit code that is included in a

Yellow Pages ad to hear recorded messages that provide more details on the advertiser's products and services.

These represent a small sample of the "new media" being developed for Canadian advertisers. The choice of where to place one's advertising dollars becomes more difficult all the time.

Creating the Advertisements

Remember once again that the main purpose of advertising is to sell something and that the ad itself is a sales message. The ad may be a high-pressure sales talk, as in a hard-hitting, direct-action ad. Or it may be a very long-range, low-pressure message, as in an institutional ad. In any case, it is trying to sell something. Consequently, it involves the same kind of selling procedure as sales talks delivered by personal sales people. That is, the ad must first attract attention, and then hold interest long enough to stimulate a desire for the product, service, or idea. Finally, the ad must move the prospect to some kind of action.

Creating an advertisement involves the tasks of writing the copy, selecting the illustrations, preparing the layout, and arranging to have the advertisement reproduced for the selected media.

The **copy** in an advertisement is defined as all the written or spoken material in it. Copy includes the headline, coupons, and advertiser's name and address, as well as the main body of the message. The **illustration** is a powerful feature in a printed advertisement. Probably the main points to consider with respect to illustrations are (1) whether they are the best alternative use of the space and (2) whether they are appropriate in all respects to the ad itself. The **layout** is the physical arrangement of all the elements in an advertisement. A good layout can be an interest-holding device as well as an attention getter. It should lead the reader through the entire advertisement in any orderly fashion.

EVALUATING THE ADVERTISING EFFORT

As part of the management of its advertising program, a company should carefully evaluate the effectiveness of (1) what has been done and (2) what is planned for the future.

Importance of Evaluation

Advertising typically is one of the most highly criticized parts of our marketing system. While advertising has been improved greatly through the years, much still remains to be done. We need to increase the effectiveness of advertising, and we must find better ways to evaluate this effectiveness.

Shrinking profit margins and increasing competition, both foreign and domestic, are forcing management to appraise all its expenditures carefully. Top executives want more proof than they now have that advertising really does pay. They want to know whether dollars spent on advertising are resulting in proportionately as many sales as dollars spent on other activities.

Difficulty of Evaluation

It is very difficult to measure the effectiveness of advertising. One problem is our inability to identify the results of any given advertisement or even an entire campaign. Except in the case of mail-order advertising, we cannot attribute a given unit of sales to any specific advertisement or campaign. By the very nature of the marketing mix, all elements — including advertising — are so intertwined that measurement of any one by itself is impossible. Many factors besides advertising influence sales success.

Essentially, there are only two parts to an advertisement — *what* is said and *how* it is said. The first part deals with product attributes to be explained, and the other is made up of the headlines, illustrations, and layouts. A great deal has been done to improve the manner of presentation (the ''how''). This has been possible because research has been able to establish criteria to measure its effectiveness. The most commonly used evaluation methods measure the number of people who saw, read, and remembered the advertisements. But little has been done to aid management in its evaluation of the ''what'' part of an ad.

Many individual advertisements, and even entire campaigns, do not aim primarily at immediate sales results. For example, some advertisements simply announce new store hours or new service policies. Other institutional advertising is intended to build goodwill or to create a company image. It is very difficult to measure the effectiveness of these kinds of advertising.

Methods Used to Measure Effectiveness

Taste this good can only be whipped. It can't be beaten.

Unbeatable offer. 25¢ off
on any size of Nutriwhip

The effectiveness of this Nutriwhip ad can be judged by the number of coupons redeemed compared with redemption norms.

In spite of the difficulties, advertisers do attempt to measure advertising effectiveness simply because they must do so — some knowledge is better than none at all. The effectiveness of an advertisement may be tested before the advertisement is presented to the public, while it is being presented, or after it has completed its run. The sales results test attempts to measure the sales volume stemming *directly* from the advertisement or series of advertisements being tested.

Most other types of tests are *indirect* measurements of effectiveness. One group consists of tests called ''readership,'' ''recognition,'' or ''recall'' tests. They involve showing respondents part or all of a previously run advertisement. That is done to determine (1) whether the ad was read, (2) what parts in it were remembered, and (3) whether the respondent knows who sponsored it. The theory underlying these tests is this: The greater the number of people who see, read, and remember an advertisement, the greater will be the number who do as the advertisement urges them. Another type of test involves measuring the number of coupons or other forms of inquiries that were received from certain advertisements.

Sometimes marketing people use a consumer panel to appraise a group of advertisements. With respect to radio and television advertising, several techniques are used to measure the size and makeup of program audiences. The theory is that the number of people who will buy the sponsor's products varies directly with the number who watch or hear the program.

The basic goal of advertising is to sell something — to modify consumer attitudes or behaviour. Note, however, that most tests measure effectiveness through some variable other than sales. We should be more concerned with measuring advertising's ability to influence attitudes and behaviour than with measuring consumers' recall of given advertisements.

ORGANIZING FOR ADVERTISING

Now let's consider the organization needed to perform and manage the advertising activities in a company. Management has three alternatives. It may (1) develop a company advertising department, (2) use an outside advertising agency, or (3) use both a company department and an advertising agency. Regardless of which alternative is selected, generally the same specialized skills are needed to do the advertising job. Creative people are needed to do the copy writing, generate the photos and other illustrative material, and prepare the layouts. Media experts are needed to select the appropriate media, buy the time and space, and arrange for the scheduled appearance of the ads. Managerial skills are needed to plan and administer the entire advertising program.

Within the Company

All these advertising tasks, only some of them, or none of them can be performed within a company department. When advertising is a substantial part of the marketing mix, a company is likely to have its own advertising department. The head of this department should report to the marketing manager, if the company is to implement the marketing concept. Large retailers, for example, often have their own advertising departments and do not use an advertising agency at all.

Advertising Agency

Many companies, especially producers, use an advertising agency to do some or all of the advertising job. An **advertising agency** is an independent company set up to offer specialized services in advertising in particular and in marketing in general. Today, the term *agency* is a misnomer. These firms are not agents in the legal sense but, instead, are independent companies.

Many agencies offer a broad range of services. In the field of advertising alone, they plan and execute entire advertising campaigns. In radio and television, some agencies produce the entertainment as well as the commercials. Many of these firms are becoming *marketing* agencies, offering services that heretofore were performed by other outside specialists or by the advertisers themselves.

Advertising agencies employ highly skilled professionals to create ads for products and services.

Why Use Both a Department and an Agency?

Many producers have their own advertising department but also use an advertising agency. The advertising department acts as liaison between agency and company. It approves the agency's plans and advertisements, and has the responsibility of preparing and administering the advertising budget. The department also handles direct-mail advertisements, dealer displays, and other activities not handled by an agency.

Using an agency along with a department has other advantages for a company. The agency usually has more advertising specialists than does the company. Also, a company can benefit from the agency's experience with many other products and clients. An agency often can do more for the same amount of money, because the agency can spread the costs of its staff over many accounts.

NATURE OF SALES PROMOTION

Sales promotion is one of the most loosely used terms in the marketing vocabulary. What, then, is sales promotion? Well, in this book we define **sales promotion** as those promotional activities (other than advertising, personal selling, and publicity) that are intended to stimulate customer demand and to improve middlemen's marketing performance.[3] A list of sales promotion activities is a long one. It includes the use of coupons, premiums, in-store displays, trade shows, free samples, contests for consumers or middlemen, and many other activities that we shall discuss later. These activities may be conducted by producers or by middlemen. Sales promotion by producers may be directed at middlemen or at end users — either household consumers or industrial users. Middlemen direct their sales promotion efforts at the end users — consumer or industrial.

While sales promotion is something separate from advertising and personal selling, all three activities often are interrelated. In fact, a major function of sales promotion is to serve as a bridge between advertising and personal selling — to supplement and coordinate efforts in these two areas. For example, an in-store display (sales promotion) furnished by the manufacturer for stores selling Michelin tires may feature a slogan and illustrations from Michelin's current advertising campaign. This effective display then makes the retailers more receptive to talking with the Michelin sales people. Or sales-force prospecting leads may be generated from people who visited the Canon copier exhibit at an office equipment trade show (sales promotion).

IMPORTANCE OF SALES PROMOTION

Traditionally, advertising has been the glamorous promotional tool, attracting much managerial attention in many firms. In contrast, the sales promotion manager of a major oil company once referred to sales promotion as "muddled, misused, and misunderstood." But this situation is changing. As one marketing executive put it, "Sales promotion is moving from being the stepchild to being the Cinderella of marketing."[4] In recent years sales promotion has been the fastest-growing method of promotion, based on percentage increase in annual expenditures. Currently, annual expenditures for sales promotion are estimated to parallel or exceed those for advertising. Sales promotion is also being integrated into the total marketing strategy in many firms. It is being introduced at the inception of a promotion campaign, and not tacked on afterward.

The numbers attached to sales promotion activities are simply mind-boggling. While accurate figures are difficult to calculate because of the vast scope and array of promotions and because many are themselves components of media advertisements, industry estimates of the total amount spent on promotions in Canada range from $7 billion to $8 billion annually. To put this in perspective, the Maclean Hunter Research Bureau estimated total gross advertising revenues in 1988 at $8.3 billion. A dramatic increase in the use of coupons in retail flyers and newspaper ads meant that more than 13 billion coupons were distributed to Canadian consumers in 1987. Millions of people attend trade shows each year and many millions of dollars are spent on point-of-sale displays in retail stores. The number of sweepstakes and contests being run for end consumers and for sales personnel has increased dramatically in the past ten years.

Several factors in the marketing environment account for the surging popularity of sales promotion.[5] One is the proliferation of new products and new brands. This leads to a proliferation of sales promotion activities as sellers work hard to get potential customers to try the new items. A second environmental factor is the state of the economy. Customers' price sensitivity increases as they worry about the economy, especially if the economy is faltering. Then promotions, such as coupons, premiums, cents-off-deals, and sweepstakes, increase in attractiveness to consumers.

The third factor is the low quality of retail selling. Many retailers use self-service (no sales people) or sales clerks who are inadequately trained and informed. In these situations, sales promotion devices (product displays, informational booklets, etc.) often are the only effective promotional tools available at the point of purchase.

The fourth factor is the growing awareness among sellers that many sales promotion devices (cents-off deals, coupons, free samples, product demonstrations) can generate quick buyer action.

File 18-3

Fill Up With Gifts

The use of sales promotions is likely to be at its most competitive in an industry where there is relatively little market growth and where it is difficult to differentiate one brand from another. The retail gasoline business has traditionally been one of the most active users of sales promotions.

Esso tried to build market share recently with scratch-and-win coupons. Texaco offered garbage bags at discount prices. Shell gave children's story books, and Ultramar offered a collection of kitchen knives at $2.99 each.

All of these are examples of fairly typical retail gasoline promotions that are intended to attract customers to the pumps. A much more ambitious sales promotion was that undertaken by Petro-Canada in connection with the Calgary Olympics. The national oil company organized the cross-country Olympic torch relay and outfitted more than 6,000 runners. In the months leading up to the Olympics, Petro-Canada launched a series of Olympic-related promotions at the pumps, including two major glass promotions which sold close to 20 million glasses, with 10 percent of the selling price going to a special fund for amateur athletes.

STRATEGIC MANAGEMENT OF SALES PROMOTION

To avoid the label of being "muddled, misused, misunderstood," sales promotion should be included in the company's strategic marketing planning, along with advertising and personal selling. This means establishing sales promotion goals and selecting appropriate strategies. A separate budget should be set up for sales promotion. A wide variety of promotional tools are available to implement the strategic planning. Finally, management should evaluate the sales promotion performance.

One problem that management faces in this situation is that many sales promotion tools are short-run, tactical actions and devices. Coupons, premiums, and contests, for example, are designed to produce immediate (but short-lived) responses. Thus, to manage sales promotion so that it becomes an effective factor in a company's marketing program over the long run requires some real talent.

Determine Sales Promotion Objectives and Strategies

Early in the strategic planning for sales promotion, management should (1) set the goals for the current sales promotion program, (2) select the appropriate strategies, and (3) identify the target markets at which this promotion will be directed.

The following three broad objectives of sales promotion were identified as we discussed the definition of the term:

- To stimulate end-user demand (industrial user or household consumer).
- To improve the marketing performance of middlemen.
- To supplement and coordinate advertising and personal selling activities.

The more specific objectives of sales promotion are much like those for advertising and personal selling. Some examples are as follows:

- *To get consumers to try a new product or an improved model of an established product.* To get consumers to try a new brand of soap or toothpaste, Procter & Gamble or Lever Brothers may send a free sample through the mail.
- *To attract new customers.* Banks and trust companies have offered small appliances and other premiums to encourage new customers to open an account.
- *To encourage present customers to use the product or service in greater quantities.* Canadian Airlines International, Air Canada, and Wardair have a "frequent flyer" program to encourage travellers to use the given airline more often.
- *To combat a competitor's promotional activity.* One supermarket chain cuts its prices. The competitors retaliate by offering triple-value coupons, a contest, or a premium.
- *To increase the amount of impulse buying by consumers.* Supermarkets have increased their sales of candy bars, magazines, and paperback books by placing these products on display by the checkout stands.
- *To get greater cooperation from retailers.* A sporting goods manufacturer gets additional shelf space and other added support from its retailers by providing excellent point-of-purchase displays, by training of the retailers' sales people, and by giving tote bags to customers.

The specific objectives for a given sales promotion program are derived directly from the objectives and strategies of the total marketing program. The following two case examples illustrate how two different marketing objectives will call for quite different sales promotion objectives, strategies, and tactics.

Case A	**Goal**	**Strategy**
Marketing	Increase sales 10% over last year.	Introduce product into new markets.
Sales promotion	Enter new markets.	Use a pull promotional strategy.

Case B		
Marketing	Maintain market share in face of fierce competition.	Improve retailer performance and build dealer goodwill.
Sales promotion	Improve retailer performance and build dealer goodwill.	Use a push promotional strategy.

The case A pull strategy will call for tactics such as the use of coupons, cash refunds, free samples, and premium gifts. The push strategy in Case B will call for tactics such as training retailers' sales forces, supplying effective point-of-purchase displays, and granting advertising allowances.

Strategic planning also means that a manufacturer must be aware that normally it is dealing with three target markets for its sales promotion efforts. These audiences are the end users (ultimate consumers or industrial users), the middlemen and their sales forces, and the manufacturer's own sales force.

Determining Sales Promotion Budget

Ordinarily the budget for sales promotion should be established in the course of determining the appropriation for the total promotional mix. It is important that the budget for sales promotion be clearly separated from the appropriations for the other major components of the promotional mix. In too many cases, unfortunately, this separation does not occur. Sales promotion often is combined with advertising or public relations for budgetary purposes, or it is included as part of the appropriation labelled ''advertising.''

Carefully setting a clearly separate budget for sales promotion also will help a company do a better job of managing this activity. And a separate budget will help bring to sales promotion a deserved recognition of its growing importance in many organizations.

Select the Sales Promotion Tools

A key step in sales promotion management is to decide which sales promotion tools to use to help the organization reach its promotional goals. The many types of these activities and devices may be divided into three categories, based upon who is the target audience — end users, middlemen, or the manufacturer's own sales force. (See Table 18-3.) Frequently the same tool — contests, premiums, or trade shows, for example — may be used to reach more than one audience category.[6]

Some of the factors that influence the choice of promotional tools are as follows:

- *The organization's promotional objective*: Do we want to use a pull strategy or a push strategy to get middlemen's support?
- *The target market for the promotion*: Are we promoting to ultimate consumers or middlemen?

- *The nature of the product*: Does it lend itself to free samples?
- *The cost of the tool*: Free samples to a wide market are expensive.
- *The current economic conditions*: Coupons, gifts, and cash refund offers are more attractive during periods of recession or inflation.

SALES PROMOTION DIRECTED AT END USERS

The major sales promotion tools directed at ultimate consumers or industrial users by producers and middlemen are listed in Table 18-3. Many of these tools probably are quite familiar to you, but a few words here about some of them still may be useful.

The 1990s equivalent of trading stamps is the frequent-flyer or frequent-shopper program. The use of trading stamps dates back to the early years of the twentieth century, but it was not until the 1950s that they began to have their greatest impact on consumer brand choice. Essentially, stamps were obtained with every purchase and were redeemed for gifts or cash. Today, all major airlines and hotels and several retailers offer similar promotions to their most loyal and frequent customers, allowing them to accumulate points based on their total purchases. These points are later redeemed for free flights, hotel rooms, car rentals, or merchandise. Such programs do seem to offer a competitive advantage to the first firm that uses them in a particular market. Once most of the firms are using them, however, the advantage disappears.

Point-of-purchase displays can serve as a silent sales force, especially in a self-service retailing operation. These displays can attract attention, serve as a buying reminder, stimulate impulse buying, and provide useful information in booklets or signs. **Trade shows and exhibitions** — open to consumers — are put on by many industries. Many of you undoubtedly have heard of, or even attended, an auto show, sporting goods show, boat show, travel and resort show, home and gardens show, flower show, or art exhibition. These shows are a great way to introduce new products, give product demonstrations, and generally create consumer excitement.

"**Advertising specialties**" is a miscellaneous category that includes small, inexpensive items given by manufacturers or by middlemen with the company's name on them. Examples include rulers, pens, calendars, ashtrays, caps, key rings, and paperweights.

Cosmetic firms have found gift certificates to be effective in generating sales. Consumer fills in reverse side of this coupon to take advantage of the special offer.

SALES PROMOTION DIRECTED AT MIDDLEMEN AND THEIR SALES FORCES

Some of the same tools that we just discussed may also be directed at middlemen and their sales forces. (See Table 18-4.) For example, furniture manufacturers and the travel industry periodically will put on a trade show open only to wholesalers and retailers. In addition, some promotional tools are specifically designed for middlemen. For example, many producers spend considerable time and money to **train the sales forces** of their wholesalers and retailers. Producers also provide various forms of advertising allowances for their dealers and distributors.

SALES PROMOTION DIRECTED AT PRODUCERS' OWN SALES FORCES

Again, some of the same promotional tools that a manufacturer aimed at its middlemen's sales forces also can be used for that manufacturer's own sales force. (See Table 18-4.) These tools include **sales contests** and their incentives, and **demonstration models** of the product. In addition, the sales promotion department can prepare visual sales aids for the sales people and **manuals** to be used in company sales training programs.

TABLE 18-4   MAJOR SALES PROMOTION TOOLS, GROUPED BY TARGET AUDIENCE

End users: consumer or industrial	Middlemen and their sales forces	Producers' own sales force
Coupons	Trade shows and exhibitions	Sales contests
Cash refunds	Point-of-purchase displays	Sales training manuals
Premiums (gifts)	Free goods	Sales meetings
Free samples	Advertising allowances	Packets with promotional materials
Contests and sweepstakes	Contests for sales people	Demonstration model of product
Frequent-shopper programs	Training middlemen's sales force	
Point-of-purchase displays	Product demonstrations	
Product demonstrations	Advertising specialties	
Trade shows and exhibitions		
Advertising specialties		

Evaluate Sales Promotion Performance

As was done for the other major components of the promotional mix, management should also attempt to evaluate the productivity — the effectiveness — of sales promotion.[7] Fortunately, for many types of sales promotion, the evaluation task is much easier and likely to be more accurate than is the case with advertising. For example, a company's sales volume or market share in a given market can be measured before, during, and after a particular sales promotion effort. Assume that the sales were $3 million for the 3-month period before the promotion, $4.8 million during the 3-month promotion, and $3.75 million during the 3 months afterward. Then management may assume that the promotion was successful. Sales increased 60 percent during the promotion and settled at a 25 percent increase afterward. If sales had dropped to $2 million after the promotion, management could deduce that the promotion simply had cannibalized sales from a future period. Of course, management also needs to determine whether other factors (competition, economic conditions, etc.) may have accounted for the changes in sales volume.

As other examples, management can examine sales data before and after a training program for retailers' sales forces. When a company exhibits at a trade show, management can measure the sales results coming from leads generated at the show.

PUBLICITY AND PUBLIC RELATIONS

Publicity and public relations are the last two major methods of promotion that we shall briefly discuss in connection with an organization's total promotional program. In most organizations these two promotional tools, much as we said about sales promotion, typically are relegated to stepchild status behind personal selling and advertising.

There are three possible reasons for the lack of marketing management's attention to these two areas. First, in most organizational structures, publicity and public relations activities are not even handled by the marketing department. Instead, they are the responsibility of a separate public relations department. Second, the terms are loosely used by both business and the public. There is no generally accepted definition of the two terms, nor a clear-cut distinction between them. Third, only in recent years have many organizations come to realize the tremendous importance of a good public relations and publicity effort. Companies historically told their executives to maintain a low, or even invisible, profile. Now many firms urge their executives to take part in community affairs and to speak out on issues of concern to the company. Companies realize that they need a good public relations program to offset unfavourable, adverse publicity.

Nature and Scope of Publicity and Public Relations

In Chapter 16 we briefly described the essence of publicity and public relations as promotional methods. **Publicity** is any promotional communication regarding an organization and/or its products where the message is *not* paid for by the organization benefitting from it. Usually the publicity communication is either (1) a nonpersonal news story appearing in a mass medium or (2) a promotional "plug" (for a product or organization) that is delivered by a person in a speech or an interview.

Publicity can be used for a wide variety of purposes in a company. Management may use publicity as one means of promoting the products or services marketed by the organization. A company also may publicize its new policies (credit, price discounting), its people (employee achievements, executive promotions, employee civic activities), research and development successes, financial reports, or its progress on pollution control. A company may use publicity to counteract an unfavourable image, unfavourable reports in the media, or an unfavourable news release from other outside organizations. Publicity is part of the broader communication concept that we call public relations.[8]

Public relations is an organization's broad, overall communications effort intended to influence various groups' attitudes toward that organization. Public relations activities typically are designed to build or maintain a favourable image for an organization and a favourable relationship with the organization's various "publics." These publics may be customers, shareholders, employees, unions, environmentalists, the government, people in the local community, or some other group in society.

There obviously is some overlap among publicity, public relations, and advertising, yet we should differentiate among these three activities. Public relations is the strategic image-building communication force in an organization. Publicity is a major tactical tool used to implement the public relations strategy. In this respect, publicity is part of public relations. As an example, one organizational public relations strategy may be to build a better relationship with local environmentalists. The publicity people then implement this strategy by generating news releases explaining what the company is doing to improve the quality of life in the community. In addition, publicity may be involved in promoting individual products or services, whereas public relations typically does not engage in this activity.

File 18-4

Making Public Relations Work Better

Many successful Canadian companies take their public relations activities very seriously and operate public affairs or public relations departments. It is the responsibility of these departments to involve the company in programs that will reflect positively on the company's image in the community. Many firms donate scholarships to colleges and universities, sponsor the local symphony orchestra, and support hospital foundations. But, in addition to these traditional forms of corporate support, some companies are embarking on new forms of public relations.

- American Express has managed its donations "more strategically . . . to stretch the dollar allocations to charities at the same time as meeting corporate objectives." American Express often cooperates with a charity by donating a small percentage of all purchases made with an American Express card over a certain period of time.*

- Northern Telecom tied its corporate donation to the United Way to the sales of its Priority telephone, donating a percentage of sales (with a minimum of $50,000) to the charitable organization.

- Petro-Canada set up a $4 million academic awards fund for amateur athletes and coaches. The fund was established from the proceeds of special Olympic glasses promotions at Petro-Canada stations.

- Proctor-Silex sponsored a major tennis event featuring Bjorn Borg and John McEnroe and raised $50,000 for the United Way.

- Alcan joined Air Canada as the major sponsors of the Montreal International Jazz Festival.

*"Good Cause Marketing," *Marketing*, November 2, 1987.

Publicity Techniques

Three major communication channels are available for use by an organization in getting its public relations or publicity message to its publics. Different publicity techniques typically are used in each channel. The first channel involves sending a mass communications message through the mass media to reach the intended audience. In using this channel, the public relations or publicity people might prepare a news release or even a longer feature article about the organization. The hope is that the newspapers, the television stations, and other mass media will print or orally report the information. Some companies prepare special tapes or films for publicity purposes.

The second channel involves a personal communication to a group audience. In this situation, an executive or a public relations person might hold a press conference or conduct a tour of the company's physical plant. The people attending might be given a printed or photographic publicity handout. Or someone in the company might make a talk at a civic or professional meeting.

The third channel involves a one-on-one personal communication. In this situation, a company representative, in a lobbying effort, might talk with an elected member or other public official. Or a publicity person might try to get an entertainer to mention the company's new product or put in a plug for a new song or movie.

Benefits and Limitations of Publicity

If the publicity activities in an organization are managed efficiently, they can nicely support and complement the organization's advertising and personal selling efforts. Publicity normally can be done at a much lower cost than advertising or personal selling, because there are no media space or time costs for conveying the publicity messages. Furthermore, the credibility level of publicity typically is much higher than that of advertising. If I tell you my product is great, you may well be sceptical. But if an independent, objective third party says my product is great, you are more likely to believe it.

A publicity message that appears as a newspaper or magazine article is more likely to be read than if the same message appears in a company ad. Readers can skip the ads entirely, but they are likely to read the news and editorial columns, and this is where the publicity messages come through. Another advantage of publicity is that it can provide more information than an ad can. Also, a company can get out a news release very quickly when some event occurs unexpectedly.

Of course, publicity has its limitations. An organization has little or no control over *what* is said in a newspaper article or television report. In fact, a company has no guarantee at all that its publicity message will even appear in print or on radio or television. The media may decide that the message is not of sufficient interest to publicize it. Furthermore, a company cannot control *when* the message will appear, and there is no opportunity for *repetition* as in ads. It is difficult to plan very far ahead in publicity. How do you prepare in advance for a mine explosion, a radiation leak, or a product recall? Finally, even though there are no immediate time and space costs, publicity is by no means free. Significant expenses are incurred in staffing a publicity department and in preparing and disseminating publicity messages.

SUMMARY

Advertising is the impersonal-selling, mass-communications component in a company's promotional mix. The company has the option of running product or institutional types of advertising. The product ads may call for direct or indirect action. Another useful classification of advertising is primary-demand and selective-demand advertising. This classification features pioneering, competitive, and comparative advertising. Manufacturers and their retail dealers often engage in some form of cooperative advertising. Advertising expenditures are large in total, but the cost of advertising in a firm is only 1 to 3 percent of sales, on the average. This is considerably less than the average cost of personal selling. Most advertising dollars are spent in newspaper media, and second place goes to television.

Management should develop an advertising campaign as part of the firm's total promotional program. The first step here is to set the specific goals for the particular campaign. A major task in developing a campaign is to select the advertising media — both the broad media class and the specific individual media. The selection should be based on the characteristics of the media and the way they fit the product and the market. The advertising message — as communicated to the market through the advertising copy, illustrations, and layout — is an integral part of a campaign.

A particularly important, yet difficult, task in advertising management is to measure (evaluate) the effectiveness of the advertising effort — both the entire campaign and individual ads. Several methods are widely used. Except for the sales results test, the commonly used techniques measure only the extent to which the ad was read or recalled. To operate an advertising program, a firm may use its own advertising department, retain an advertising agency, or combine the two organizational structures.

Sales promotion is the third major promotional tool, and the one used to coordinate and supplement the advertising and personal selling programs. Sales promotion has increased considerably in importance in recent years. Sales promotion should receive the same strategic management that a company gives to its advertising and personal selling programs. This means establishing sales promotion objectives and then selecting appropriate strategies. A separate budget should be set up for sales promotion. To implement its strategic planning, management has a wide variety of promotional tools to select from. Finally, the sales promotion performance should be evaluated.

Publicity and public relations were the final promotional methods that we discussed briefly in this chapter. Publicity is any promotional communication regarding an organization and/or its products where the message is not paid for by the companies benefiting from it. Publicity is part of public relations. Public relations is the broad, overall promotional concept that deals with improving or maintaining an organization's image and its favourable relationships with its various publics. Typically these two promotional activities are handled in a department separate from the marketing department in a firm. Nevertheless, the management process of planning, implementing, and evaluating should be applied to a publicity campaign in the same way as for advertising or personal selling.

KEY TERMS AND
CONCEPTS

Advertising 494
An advertisement 494
Product advertising 494
Direct-action advertising 495
Indirect-action advertising 495
Institutional advertising 495
Primary-demand advertising 495

Pioneering advertising 496
Selective-demand advertising 496
Competitive advertising 496
Comparative advertising 496
Cooperative advertising 497
Cost of advertising as a percentage
   of sales 498

NOTES

[1] Miles Nadal and John Puddy, ''No Longer the New Kid on the Block,'' *Marketing*, February 15, 1988, pp. 22, 24.

[2] See for example ''Comparative Price Advertising,'' in *Misleading Advertising Bulletin*, Ottawa: Consumer and Corporate Affairs Canada, no.3, 1987, April/June 1987, pp. 1–5.

[3] Adapted from *Marketing Definitions: A Glossary of Marketing Terms*, American Marketing Association, Chicago, Illinois 1960, p. 20. The American Marketing Association also noted that, in the field of retailing, the term *sales promotion* is used to cover ''all methods of stimulating customer purchasing including personal selling, advertising, and publicity.'' Thus, in retailing, *sales promotion* is used in a broad sense. It is virtually synonymous with *promotion*, as that term is used in this book and also by most manufacturers.

For more on this problem of definition, see Ernest F. Cooke, ''Defining Sales Promotion Difficult, Important,'' *Marketing News*, Nov. 8, 1985, p. 35.

[4] See Curt Schleier, ''Marketing Image Plots Turnaround,'' in a special report on sales promotion, *Advertising Age*, Aug. 15, 1985, pp. 15ff.

[5] See Kenneth G. Hardy, ''Key Success Factors for Manufacturers' Sales Promotions in Package Goods,'' *Journal of Marketing*, vol. 50, July 1986, pp. 13–23; also see a special report on sales promotion in *Marketing*, February 15, 1988, and a special report on premiums and incentives in the same magazine, February 22, 1988.

[6] For a review of several of the sales promotion tools, see Robert J. Kopp, ''Premiums Provide Great Impact, but Little Glamour,'' *Marketing News*, June 7, 1985, p. 12.

[7] See John A. Quelch, ''It's Time to Make Trade Promotion More Productive,'' *Harvard Business Review*, May–June 1983, pp. 130–136; and Thomas V. Bonoma, ''Get More Out of Your Trade Shows,'' *Harvard Business Review*, January–February 1983, pp. 75–83.

[8] David Shamanski, ''The Search for More Effective Publicity,'' *Financial Times of Canada*, May 5, 1986, p. 21.

QUESTIONS AND
PROBLEMS

1. How do you account for the variation in advertising expenditures as a percentage of sales among the different types of companies in Table 18-2?

2. Several specific objectives of advertising were outlined early in the chapter. Bring to class some advertisements that illustrate at least four of these goals. Or be prepared to describe a current radio or television advertisement that is an attempt to achieve these objectives.

3. Which advertising medium is best for advertising the following products?
   a. Grocery carts.
   b. Women's panty hose.
   c. Toys for children 3 to 5 years old.
   d. Jogging shoes.
   e. Microwave ovens.
   f. Plastic clothespins.

4. Many grocery products manufacturers and candy producers earmark a good portion of their advertising appropriations for use in magazines. Is this a wise choice of media for these firms? Explain.

5. Why do department stores use newspapers so much more than local radio as an advertising medium?

6. Why is it worthwhile to pretest advertisements before they appear in the media? Suggest a procedure for pretesting a magazine ad.

7. What procedures can a firm use to determine how many sales dollars resulted from a given ad or from an entire campaign?

8. Many advertisers on television use program ratings to determine whether to continue the sponsorship of a program. These ratings reflect the number of families that watch the program. Are program ratings a good criterion for evaluating the effectiveness of advertising? Does a high rating indicate that sales volume will also be high? Discuss.

9. If a manufacturing firm finds a good advertising agency, should it discontinue its own advertising department?

10. Visit a supermarket, a clothing store, and a hardware store, and then make a list of all the sales-promotion devices that you observed in each store. Which of these devices do you feel are particularly effective?

11. Is sales promotion effective for selling expensive consumer products such as houses, automobiles, or backyard swimming pools? Is your answer the same for expensive industrial products?

12. Explain how sales promotion can be used to offset weaknesses in personal selling in retail stores.

13. How does publicity differ from advertising?

14. Give a recent example of an organization that encountered unfavourable (negative) publicity. Do you think the organization handled this situation satisfactorily?

15. Give some recent examples of what you consider to be effective publicity campaigns. Explain why you rate these campaigns highly.

CASE 6.1

THE UPPER CANADA BREWING COMPANY (E) Developing a Promotion Strategy

The final decision confronting Frank Heaps, president of the Upper Canada Brewing Company, involved the promotion element of the marketing plan. He realized that even the most useful and satisfying product would be a dismal failure if no one knew it was available. It was essential to let the target customers know that the product, with the desired benefits, was available at the price they were willing to pay, in the locations where they would wish to purchase it. Indeed, any promotion decision could be effective only if it was coordinated with strategies for the other three elements of the marketing mix: product, pricing, and distribution.

THE PROMOTION BUDGET

The first decision in planning the promotional strategy was to determine the budget. Mr. Heaps proposed that the promotional appropriation would be 7.5 percent of forecasted gross sales in Year One and 5 percent in Year Two. He felt that these expenditures would support the achievement of the company's market share objectives (see Table E-1). He realized, however, that this proposed promotion investment was dwarfed by the marketing outlays of the three major breweries — Molson, Labatts, and Carling O'Keefe. In fact, research showed that their combined 1984 national advertising expenditures was $87.8 million. Given these massive outlays, he pondered the adequacy of his proposed budget. Knowing that his company could not realistically increase this budget significantly, he knew he had to get real value for each dollar spent. The only problem was, how?

TABLE E-1   **Promotion Budget 1985-86**

	1985	**1986**
Market Share Objective	0.1%	0.15%
Forecasted Gross Sales	$ 2.3M	$ 3.5M
Promotion Budget	$ 175,000	$175,000

THE PROMOTION STRATEGY

To guide the development of an effective strategy, Mr. Heaps knew that he needed a clear set of objectives. The objectives that he identified were: (i) to inform the target audience about the brewery's product(s) and methods; (ii) to persuade the target customer to try the product(s); and (iii) to position the product(s) in the consumer's mind as truly unique, with significantly different benefits. To achieve these objectives, and to prevent head-to-head competition with the major breweries,

This case was prepared by Donna M. Stapleton and is intended to stimulate discussion of an actual management problem and not to illustrate either effective or ineffective handling of that problem. The author wishes to acknowledge the support provided by the Upper Canada Brewing Company, and particularly by Frank Heaps, President.

Mr. Heaps knew that the promotional approach and appeal had to be significantly different from that used by the giant competitors.

A key decision in being different rested with the blend of the promotional mix chosen by the Upper Canada Brewing Company. To decide on the appropriate blend of activities, Mr. Heaps evaluated the different promotional methods at his disposal: advertising, personal selling, sales promotion, and general publicity and public relations. He realized that, given his limited budget, he would not be able to produce expensive print and broadcast advertisements like those of the competition. He felt, however, that some advertising was necessary for a successful entry into this market. As well, given the importance of the licensee trade to the achievement of company sales (projected licensee trade was 15 percent of gross sales), he concluded that some personal selling was also critical.

The location of the brewery site, adjacent to Toronto's booming downtown with visibility from the Gardiner Expressway, the Go Train system, and the C.N.E./Ontario Place complex provided an excellent vehicle to provoke public interest and awareness. Mr. Heaps wondered if he should use this strategic location as a sales promotion tool and actively encourage public tours and sampling of the plant product(s). He knew that Molson offered tours to the public; however, Carling O'Keefe and Labatts did not.

One final activity that he considered using was company-stimulated media coverage such as news releases and articles on the new brewery; he wondered if these methods would be cost effective ways to influence the target market's opinion of the new company and its product(s). Given the nature of the market, the promotional funds available, and the competitive environment, Mr. Heaps wondered what blend of these promotional methods would provide the optimal mix, and indeed how he should allocate his budget among the different mix items.

A related question, to ensure that the approach used at the Upper Canada Brewing Company was different, centred on the marketing theme or appeal to use. Mr. Heaps decided that the primary marketing emphasis was to be on the Upper Canada brand's freshness, natural quality and unique taste, made in a "hands-on" brewery. The slogan he proposed was, " Our beer is as good as the best in the World!" To communicate this message, he wanted to advertise informatively rather than with a life-style appeal. General advertising of a life-style nature was to be avoided because of the cost and Mr. Heaps' conviction of its incompatibility with the Upper Canada Brewing Company corporate and product image. To further support this different market appeal, he decided to promote artistic and cultural activities rather than the sports activities supported by the major breweries. Given the characteristics of his target market and the desired position of the brewery product(s) in the marketplace, he analyzed the appropriateness of this appeal before finalizing decisions on the launch of an advertising campaign.

One final promotion decision to be made concerned media strategy. To ensure that the message reached the target audience, it was necessary to clearly identify the media vehicles to use; the choices available included television, radio, newspaper, magazine, and outdoor. Related to the task of determining media classes and vehicles was the choice of media scheduling and concentration: at what periods throughout the year should the advertising campaign run and should the advertising be concentrated in one medium to gain impact or several media classes to increase reach?

Mr. Heaps realized that any new business must first create awareness and then attract trial if it was to gain customers. The promotional strategy differentiated its products from those of the major competitors, and thus persuaded buyers to give trial support to the products of this new brewery. Ultimately, the success or failure of the venture largely rested with the care taken to devise an appropriate promotion strategy to allow the brewery to obtain 0.1 percent of the market, the estimated market share needed to be viable. Upon gaining initial entry into the market, Mr. Heaps hoped to rely primarily on word-of-mouth advertising for market share development.

QUESTIONS

1. Evaluate the percentage-of-sales method used to establish the promotion budget.
2. Is the promotional budget allocated for the first two years of operation adequate? Why or why not?
3. What blend of promotional methods should Mr. Heaps use? Why?
4. Evaluate the appropriateness of the marketing appeal identified for the product(s) of this new brewery.
5. Which media class(es) should Mr. Heaps choose? Why? What periods of the year should the campaign run? Why?

CASE 6.2

McCAIN FOODS
Drinkin' Boxes

In the spring of 1982, Patrick Sullivan, product manager for McCain's juice line, was developing the promotional plan for McCain's new aseptic juice product, "Drinkin' Boxes." He hoped that the new McCain product would be as successful in Canada as other aseptic juice products had been in the U.K., Europe, and Australia.

McCain Foods had been in business since 1956 and had built its reputation on the production of frozen french fries. They began with 30 employees and sales of $152,678 in the first year. Today, the McCain group of companies employs more than 8,500 people worldwide. Domestic potato processing facilities are located throughout Canada, as well as additional plants producing nonpotato products in Florenceville, Toronto, Grand Falls, and Calgary. The McCain Group has expanded to include companies engaged in transportation, equipment manufacturing, and other areas. McCain products now include not only a complete line of french fries and potato specialties, but also green vegetables, desserts, pizzas, juices and beverages

This case was developed by Lanita Carter and is intended to stimulate discussion of an actual management problem, and not to illustrate either effective or ineffective handling of that problem. The author wishes to acknowledge the support provided by McCain Foods, and particularly by Archie McLean, Vice President of Marketing.

(both frozen and aseptic), oven entrées, boneless chicken, and cheese. McCain Group sales in 1979 were $360 million.

The McCain Foods retail food group in Canada operates in a very competitive environment. Almost all of their products, except for the new aseptic product, are frozen. Since space in the freezer section of the grocery store is limited, McCain must stay very competitive in their product offerings in order to maintain shelf space.

In 1981, McCain Foods decided to explore the opportunity for producing aseptic juice[1] in Canada. At that time, 45 percent of milk and 30 percent of juice was packed aseptically in Europe. In Canada, there were already ten companies producing aseptic juice in Western Canada. Most of these companies were producing the 1-litre size. Though McCain saw the opportunity to produce the 1-litre packages of juice, the management team at McCain felt that the real opportunity was the development of a 250 mL aseptic juice package, already very successful in Europe, the U.K., and Australia.

McCain Foods felt that aseptic packaging had several advantages over canned juices. Aseptic packaging is approximately 40 percent cheaper than cans, as well as being lighter and easier to ship. The cube shape makes packing easier since this shape requires less warehousing and shippers' space. The quality of juices packed aseptically is better than in cans. Also, the package with straw attached is easier to drink out of than the 6 or 10 oz. tins.

Compared to frozen juices, aseptic packed juices are portable (convenient for lunch boxes) and required no special handling in terms of distribution or storage facilities. Compared to refrigerated juices, the aseptic juice has no specialized needs for distributors, it is not required to carry a best-before date (required on all foods with a shelf life of under 90 days), and it has a longer shelf life (4 to 6 months) than refrigerated juices (shelf life of 28 days).

In analyzing this market opportunity, McCain concluded that the 250 mL aseptic

[1]Aseptic processing is similar to pasteurization but processing is done at much higher temperatures (some products such as milk are referred to as UHT milk, for ultra-high temperature processing). This process inactivates the enzymes, producing a self-stable product.

juice did have clear advantages over the competing canned, frozen, and refrigerated juices. The results of sales of aseptic juice in Western Canada indicated that consumers were willing to accept this new packaging idea for the product. The size of the market for juices and drinks is quite large, and thus considered to be one with growth potential.

The problem facing the company now is how to promote the product not only to the consumer market but also to the trade. The packaging format for the product is relatively new and would require some work to ensure acceptance by the trade as well as the consumer market.

In considering the promotional strategy, Patrick Sullivan had to decide how many flavours to introduce. He felt that several flavours would be good choices: orange juice, apple juice, and Revive fruit drink. These three flavours were well known in McCain's juice line and were popular flavours among consumers, based on market sales figures. The name for the product was another issue. Though "aseptic" or "tetra-pak" described the product, Mr. Sullivan felt that these did not reflect a very friendly image of the product. The name "Drinkin' Boxes" was chosen in order to stress the packaging format as well as making the name easy to remember.

In building the market for this product the company also had to first consider possible problems at the trade level. McCain decided to introduce only three flavours of the product in order to reduce the demand for shelf space and by focussing on those flavours that were already best sellers. The efficiency in handling, storage and shelving of the product was stressed in promoting the product. The product was also priced competitively to offer the consumer savings (approximately 15-20 percent per ounce) compared to a canned product.

TABLE 1

	McCain 250 mL Aseptic O.J. (packed 27) — Ontario	Libby's 6 oz. Tin O.J. (packed 48) — Ontario
List Per Case:	$9.00	$13.40
Retail Unit Price:	.44	.37
Per 250 mL Serving:	.44	.54

Now, Mr. Sullivan must develop the promotion campaign for the consumer market.

1. Develop a promotional campaign for this product.
   a. What characteristics of this product should be stressed in order to overcome the resistance of drinking out of a cardboard box?
   b. What other product modifications (changes in packaging, flavours available, etc.) would you suggest?

CASE 6.3

Sun Ice Limited developed from the sewing skills of Sylvia Rempel, who made her first ski outfit for her son, only to find that his friends wanted outfits, too. As news of her expertise spread, she was soon sewing ski suits for neighbours and friends in the basement of her Calgary home. In 1978, she incorporated Sun Ice, a Calgary-based company, to design, manufacture and market superior quality skiwear.

By the time the 1988 Olympic Winter Games were completed in Calgary, millions of people around the world had seen a lot of Sun Ice and its ski clothing, whether they realized it or not. Sun Ice had been selected as the sole licensee and official supplier of outerwear for the Olympics and had outfitted 30,000 Canadian Olympic athletes, officials, sponsors, employees, and volunteers. In addition, Sun Ice had already outfitted the runners who had carried the Olympic torch across Canada in the torch relay sponsored by Petro-Canada. The question in the minds of Sylvia Rempel, president of Sun Ice, and her marketing management group, was how to capitalize effectively on all of this publicity.

Sun Ice produces an extensive line of ski wear, casual outerwear, and active sports and leisure clothing. The company's products are distributed through specialty ski stores, sporting goods stores, fashion boutiques, and department stores throughout Canada and the United States. The Sun Ice collar stripes are an internationally recognized and registered trademark. Since its establishment, Sun Ice has maintained its commitment to the production of outerwear that is both functional and fashionable. The company has been able to carve out a Canadian identity in a market that is extremely competitive and that has been dominated by high-end European imports and by low-end products from Asian countries.

The Sun Ice commitment to quality has paid off. Sun Ice products have been chosen by 12 Canadian national teams in sports such as skiing, skating, bobsled, and canoeing. In addition, Sun Ice garments have been worn by five Mount Everest expeditions since 1982. In late 1986, the company went public, generating funds to construct a $6 million, 68,000 square foot manufacturing facility in downtown Calgary. Company sales in 1988 were $24.3 million with $4 million coming from growing sales in the U.S. market. Sun Ice uses the latest computer technology to design and produce its garments, including computerized pattern making and fabric cutting.

The Sun Ice product line comprises almost 100 styles in more than 20 fashion colours. The "Gold Label" line features Gore-Tex fabrics exclusively. Gore-Tex is produced through a patented process whereby a microthin, microporous Teflon membrane is bonded to special fabrics. The result is a fabric that is waterproof, windproof and breathable. The latest in synthetic, high-performance insulation is used to complement the Gore-Tex fabric, to give this line the unique capacity of adjusting its thermal properties to changing weather conditions and body temperatures.

The "White Label" collection encompasses the widest selection of colours and

This case was prepared by James G. Barnes and is intended to stimulate discussion of an actual management problem, and not to illustrate either effective or ineffective handling of that problem. The author wishes to acknowledge the support provided by Sun Ice Ltd., and particularly by Sylvia Rempel, President, and Victor Rempel, Executive Vice President.

styles, and satisfies the performance and price expectations of a broader range of consumers. The fabrics used in this line are treated with Ultrex, a special coating providing protection against water and wind, while retaining breathability.

The Sun Ice Junior Collection is designed for children and looks and performs like the styles available in the adult Gold Label and White Label lines. All of the styles carrying the Sun Ice label are sold through specialty ski and sporting goods stores, fashion boutiques, and selected high-image retail outlets. The company also manufacturers its "Pod" line, which consists of popular styles in less costly fabrics. This line is named for Steve Podborski, a former member of Canada's National Alpine Ski Team. The Pod Line was introduced in 1983 and is distributed through mid-priced, high-volume department and chain stores.

The Sun Ice product assortment is rounded out by the Olympic Licensee line of insulated and non-insulated jackets, which was developed by the company under its agreement as official licensee for the Calgary 1988 Olympic Winter Games. By 1988, the company had begun to develop an expanded product line to complement its ski wear and outergarments. New products to be introduced in the 1988-89 season included colour- and design-coordinated gloves, headwear, turtlenecks, sweaters, fleece wear, snow boots, and other accessories.

The basis of the Sun Ice marketing program since the establishment of the company has been to become involved as closely as possible in the pursuits of active Canadians, and to support retailers who carry Sun Ice products. Rather than place its marketing emphasis on direct-to-consumer media advertising, the company has promoted to close association with athletes and has been heavily involved in sponsorship. Teams outfitted by Sun Ice include the Canadian National Alpine Ski Team, and national teams in bobsled, luge, ski jumping, nordic combined, speed skating, speed skiing, sailing, canoeing, and kayaking.

During 1987, Sun Ice sponsored major sporting events, including the Molson Men's World Cup Downhill, the Husky Ladies' World Cup Downhill, the American Ski Classic at Vail, Colorado, the Labatt's Interski '87, and the Rothmans/Porsche Challenge car racing series. In 1988, the company's sponsorship program included the Everest Express, the American Ski Classic, the North American Pro Ski Tour, and the Powder 8 World Championships.

In 1983, Sun Ice launched the Adult Lift Ticket Hang Tag promotion and the Junior Learn-to-Ski program. With the purchase of every Sun Ice jacket, the purchaser is given the opportunity to ski free for one day. In cooperation with the retailer, Sun Ice has concentrated on development of the sport of skiing.

The largest promotional program in which Sun Ice has become involved has been its association with the 1988 Winter Olympic Games in Calgary. Research conducted in connection with earlier Olympic Games has shown that 83 percent of adults remember products promoted with Olympic involvement. Almost one-half of respondents to research surveys said that Olympic sponsorship raised their opinion of the sponsors' products and one-third said that they were inclined to buy products that were associated with the Olympics.

The Calgary Olympics were now over and were generally considered to have been a success. Sun Ice jackets had been worn by thousands of officials and athletes and by representatives of corporations such as General Motors, 3M, ABC, Sports Illustrated, Labatt's, IBM, and Petro-Canada, and had been seen by an estimated

1.5 billion television viewers worldwide. Mrs. Rempel and the senior marketing executives of Sun Ice now had to decide how best to capitalize on the exposure their products had enjoyed.

1. Evaluate the promotional programs Sun Ice had been using during recent years to promote its line of ski wear and outerwear. How should this promotional orientation change in light of the new developments in the company's product line and the exposure gained through Olympic sponsorship?
2. Do you think Sun Ice should now re-evaluate its policy of not using media advertising to reach consumers directly?

CASE 6.4

LEGO DIVISION
Promotional Strategy

The Samsonite division of Beatrice International (Canada), Ltd., is the Canadian home for Lego toys. The company's Stratford, Ontario, plant produces, packages, and distributes Lego building bricks and other components to stores all across the country.

Samsonite's association with Lego toys began in the early 1960s when the company entered a licensing agreement with Lego A/G of Billund, Denmark, the parent company which first developed Lego toys in the early 1930s.

Introduction of Lego toys into the Canadian market initially involved a relatively modest promotional campaign, largely restricted to national magazines whose readership included women with children 14 years and younger. These women constituted the main target market and were the focus of an advertising campaign centred on the educational and creative benefits accruing to children who constructed various objects using Lego building bricks. A second element in the promotional mix involved a program encouraging retailers to advertise heavily in local and regional markets.

The early 1970s were marked by an expansion of the promotional campaign to include television advertising, particularly in the period leading up to Christmas. The main target market also expanded modestly to include not only women with children 14 years and younger but also children themselves who were targeted through television advertising on family-oriented shows. The advertising theme was broadened to include both the traditional message (the educational and creative aspects of Lego toys) and the message that construction and disassembly of objects built with Lego bricks was fun for both parents and children (''kids of all ages'').

Throughout the period from the early 1960s to the early 1970s, the overriding objective of the promotional campaign, regardless of changes in media and positioning, was to build the long-term profitability of the operation. ''Selling the Lego system'' implied production and advertising strategies that focussed on the capacity of Lego bricks to build a wide variety of objects rather than a strategy of producing

This case was prepared by William Frisbee and is intended to stimulate discussion of an actual management problem, and not to illustrate either effective or ineffective handling of that problem.

and promoting packages of Lego bricks designed to construct one specific toy, e.g., an airplane. This strategy proved to be highly successful as the Lego division of Samsonite established itself as one of the major toy manufacturers and marketers in Canada.

Circumstances changed significantly for Samsonite's Lego division in the mid-1970s. During that period, the patent on the original Lego brick expired. The remarkable acceptance of Lego toys, in Canada and around the world, quickly brought forth competitors. These competitors ranged from relatively unknown "copy-cat" manufacturers in the Far East to various American toy manufacturing giants.

Given this dramatic change in the competitive environment, marketing management in the Lego division moved quickly to develop a promotional strategy that would accomplish four basic goals: (1) protect the Lego division's share of the Canadian market in the face of an expected promotional challenge from major American toy manufacturers, (2) maintain the hard-earned public perception of Lego bricks as educational, creativity-enhancing, and fun toys for both children and parents, (3) maintain the company's promotional focus on the Lego system and long-term profitability, and (4) not increase the existing, relatively modest promotional budget.

Discussions within the marketing management team ultimately resulted in two options being seriously considered. The first option was to continue the existing promotional strategy. The existing approach had worked extremely well in the past and had succeeded in establishing Lego building bricks as a "childhood necessity" in tens of thousands of Canadian households. Advocates of maintaining the existing strategy felt that the company could rely on its reputation for unparalleled quality and its firmly established place in the Canadian marketplace to withstand any challenge. To deviate from a strategy that had been highly successful seemed unwise in the absence of clear evidence that the strategy was no longer effective.

The second option considered by management involved a radical departure from the existing promotional strategy. This proposal involved the selection of a central educational and creative theme such as space travel. Given the theme, professional engineers would design and construct large-scale Lego objects, which both represented the theme and demonstrated the educational and creative capacity of Lego toys in the hands of experts.

The completed Lego creations would then be organized into a theme show that would travel to major population centres across the country, be set up in major department stores, and opened to the public under the title, "Lego World Show — (Theme Name)".

Properly constructed and organized, the "Lego World Show" concept was projected to exhaust the company's total promotional budget for an entire year. Its adoption, in other words, would preclude all other forms of paid promotion. Proponents of the concept anticipated that the show would require approximately 6000 square feet of floor space to properly accommodate the displays, allow for easy pedestrian travel through the exhibition, and permit a modest but strategically located sales area immediately beyond the exhibition's exit door.

1. Given the objectives outlined in the case, what do you perceive to be the strengths and weaknesses of the two competing options?
2. Can you suggest modifications or additions to either option that would strengthen its capacity to meet the stated objectives?
3. Based on your assessment of the two options (as presented in the case or as modified), which one would you choose if the final decision were yours to make? Why?

PART 7

IMPLEMENTING AND EVALUATING THE MARKETING EFFORT

Implementing a company's marketing
program, evaluating the marketing
performance of a company, and
appraising the role of marketing
in our society

Up to this point in the book, we have dealt primarily with the selection of
target markets and with the development and management of the four segments
of the marketing mix in an individual organization.

Now it is time to tie things together — to take an overview of the firm's
total marketing program, thus integrating the separate elements of the marketing mix. Our approach in Part 7 will be to apply the *implementation* and
evaluation aspects of the management process to the *total* marketing program. Marketing implementation and evaluation in the individual firm are
covered in Chapter 19. Then in Chapter 20 we appraise the current position
of marketing in our socioeconomic system.

MARKETING IMPLEMENTATION AND PERFORMANCE EVALUATION

CHAPTER GOALS

This chapter is concerned with two parts of the management of a company's total marketing program — implementation and evaluation. After studying this chapter, you should understand:

- The importance of the implementation stage in the management process.
- The relationship among strategic planning, implementation, and performance evaluation.
- Organizational structures typically used to implement marketing effort.
- Importance of good selection.
- Significance of delegation, coordination, motivation, and communication in the implementation process.
- The concept of a marketing audit as a complete evaluation program.
- The meaning of misdirected marketing effort.
- Sales-volume analysis.
- Marketing cost analysis.

''I managed good, but boy did they play bad.'' This title from an article many years ago in *Sports Illustrated* may not be excellent grammar, but it surely communicates its message. The coaches (management) of all professional football teams prepare a strategic plan — called a game plan — for every one of their games. When they win a game, often the coaches will say that the team executed well. If the team loses the game, you will hear that the team failed to execute. That is, the team had a strategic plan but failed to carry it out — to execute it or implement it.

Then a day or two later the coaches will study the game films in great detail. In effect, management is evaluating the team's performance as well as the performance of each individual player. This same process of planning, implementing, and performance evaluating can occur in any competitive situation, including marketing by an organization.

In Chapter 3 we defined the management process in marketing as planning, implementing, and evaluating the marketing effort in an organization. See Fig. 19-1, which is a repeat of Fig. 3-1. Most of this book has dealt with the *planning* of a marketing program. We discussed the selection of target markets and the strategic design of a program to deliver want-satisfaction to those markets. This program was built around the components of a strategic marketing mix — the product, price structure, distribution system, and promotional program.

Now we are ready to devote a chapter to the implementation and evaluation stages of the management process in marketing. The implementation stage is the operational stage — the stage during which an organization attempts to carry out (that is, implement or execute) its strategic plan.

At the end of an operating period (or even during the period), management needs to evaluate the organization's performance. In this way management can determine how effectively the organization is achieving the goals set in the strategic planning phase of the management process.

FIGURE 19-1

The management process in marketing systems.

Plans are implemented, and performance results are evaluated to provide information used to plan for the future. The process is continuous and allows for adapting to changes in the environment.

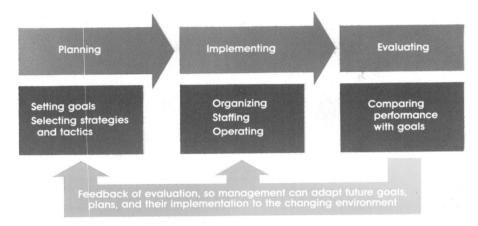

IMPLEMENTATION AND PLANNING INTERRELATIONSHIPS

Obviously there is a close relationship between planning and implementation in the management process. Without planning, a company's operational activities — its implementation — can go off in any direction like an unguided missile. At this point, however, we focus on implementation simply because it ordinarily receives so little attention. Much has been written about strategic planning, but very little has been said about *implementing* these strategies.

No matter how good the strategic planning may be in an organization, it is virtually useless if these plans are not carried out in action — that is, aren't implemented or executed. Stated another way, good planning cannot overcome poor implementation, but effective implementation very often can overcome poor planning or inappropriate strategies.

MARKETING IMPLEMENTATION

In the 1970s and on into the early 1980s, there was a tremendous interest in strategic planning, sparked primarily by some of the leading management consulting firms. Then as we progressed through the 1980s, disenchantment with strategic planning really set in. This cooling off occurred as many companies came to realize that strategic *planning* alone was not enough to ensure a company's success. *These plans had to be effectively implemented*. Management began to realize that the planners are great at telling us *what* to do — that is, designing a strategy. But the planners often came up short with *how* to do it — that is, how to implement the strategy.[1]

''Too often these hot-shot planners could not sell a pair of shoes to a guy who is standing barefooted on a very hot sidewalk with a $50 bill in his hand.''

The implementation stage in the marketing management process includes three broad areas of activity. They are (1) organizing for the marketing effort; (2) staffing this organization; and (3) directing the operational efforts of these people as they carry out the strategic plans.

The first major activity in implementing a company's strategic planning is to organize the people who will be doing the actual implementation work. We must establish an organizational relationship among marketing and the other major functional areas in a firm. And, within the marketing department, we must decide on the form of organization that will most effectively aid our implementation efforts.

COMPANY-WIDE ORGANIZATION

In Chapter 1 we stated that one of the three foundation stones of the marketing concept was to coordinate organizationally all marketing activities. In firms that are production-oriented or sales-oriented, typically we find that marketing activities are fragmented. A sales force is quite separate from advertising; physical distribution is handled in the production department; sales training may be under the personnel department, etc.

In a marketing-oriented enterprise all marketing activities are coordinated under one chief marketing executive who typically is at the vice presidential level. This executive reports directly to the president and is on an equal organizational footing with the chief executives in finance, production, and the other major functional areas of the firm. (See Fig. 19-2.) Under the chief marketing executive, the marketing activities may be grouped into line activities and staff activities. In most firms the chief line activity is personal selling. The supporting staff activities include advertising, marketing research, sales promotion, sales analysis, sales training, and others.

FIGURE 19-2
Company organization embracing the marketing concept.

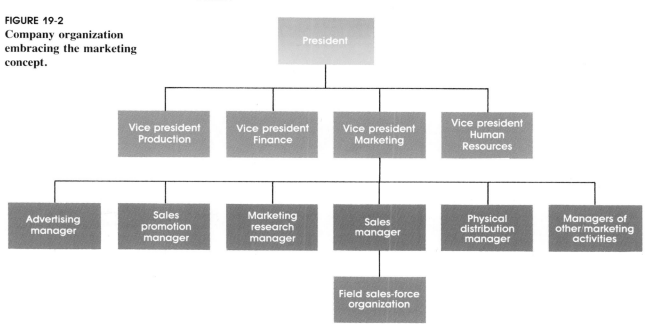

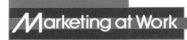

Re-Focussing and Re-Organizing for Productivity

One response to a changing market environment within the Canadian beer industry in recent years has been to make modifications in the way in which the marketing function is organized. The industry, already one of the most regulated in the country, found itself in the late 1980s not only facing additional regulation of its advertising and packaging, but trying to compete in a market that had shown no growth for the past five years.

The major Canadian brewers responded in ways that could have been anticipated. They introduced new brands and packaging to compete for the attention of the consumer. They also paid a great deal more attention to market segmentation and brand positioning, to ensure that each brand was directed toward a viable potential market. But, at the same time, the brewing companies were making changes that were less obvious to the consumer.

Both Molson and Carling O'Keefe centralized their regional marketing operations in Toronto, for all areas except Quebec. They also introduced a brand management system for the first time in the Canadian brewing industry. Each brand group became a profit centre, giving them responsibility for the bottom line. Carling O'Keefe set up a new products group. All companies embarked upon cost-cutting programs, including the dropping of sponsorship agreements for certain major league sports, in favour of increased support for sports at the community level.

ORGANIZATION WITHIN THE MARKETING DEPARTMENT

Within the marketing department — especially in medium-sized or large firms — the sales force frequently is specialized in some organizational fashion. This is done in order to implement more effectively the company's strategic planning. One of the three forms of organizational specialization of line authority typically is adopted. The sales force may be organized by geographical territory, by product line, or by customer type. In very large companies, sometimes other marketing activities such as advertising or sales promotion also are organizationally specialized in one of these same three categories.

Geographical specialization   Probably the most widely used method of specializing selling activities is to organize a sales force on the basis of geographical territories. Under this type of organization, each sales person is assigned a specific geographical area — called a *territory* — in which to sell. Several sales people representing contiguous territories typically are placed under a territorial sales executive who reports directly to the general sales manager. These territorial executives usually are called *district* or *regional* sales managers. (See Fig. 19-3*a*.)

A territorial organization usually ensures better implementation of sales strategies in each local market and better control over the sales force. Customers can be serviced quickly and effectively, and local sales reps can respond better to competitors' actions in a given territory.

Product specialization   Another commonly used basis for organizing a sales

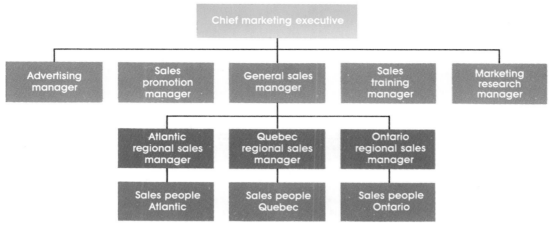

FIGURE 19-3a
Sales organization specialized by geographic territories.

force is some form of product specialization. To illustrate, a company may divide all of its products into three lines. Then one group of sales reps will sell only the products in line A. All sales people in group A will report to a sales manager for product A, who in turn will report to a general sales manager.

This type of organization is especially suited for companies that are marketing:

- A variety of complex technical products — electronics.
- Dissimilar or unrelated products — luggage, folding chairs, and toy building blocks.
- Many thousands of items — hardware wholesale.

The main advantage of this form of organization is the specialized attention each product line can get from the sales force. A potential drawback may occur if more than one sales rep from a company calls on the same customer. This duplication of effort not only is costly but also may irritate the customers.

A variation of product specialization is the use of the product-manager concept that we discussed back in Chapter 8. These people each are given the responsibility of planning and developing a marketing program for a separate group of products. They report to the chief marketing executive. Typically a product manager has no direct authority over a sales force, but acts only in an advisory relationship with the sales force and the line sales executives. (See Fig. 19-3*b*.)

Customer specialization   Many companies today have divided their sales departments on the basis of type of customer. Customers may be grouped either by type of industry or by channel of distribution. Thus, an oil company may divide its markets into such industry customer groups as railroads, auto manufacturers, farm equipment producers, etc. (See Fig. 19-3*c*.) A firm that specializes in sales operations by channel of distribution may have one sales force selling to wholesalers and another that deals directly with large retailers.

As more companies fully implement the marketing concept, customer-specialization organization is likely to increase. Certainly the basis of customer specialization is commensurate with the customer-oriented philosophy that underlies the

FIGURE 19-3b
Sales organization specialized by product.

marketing concept. That is, the organizational emphasis is on the customers and markets rather than on products.

Combination of organizational bases Many medium-sized and large companies typically combine a territorial sales organization structure with one of either product or customer specialization. Thus, a hardware wholesaler operating out of a home base in Winnipeg may establish geographical sales districts for its sales reps. This same sales force also may be divided on a product basis. Consequently, in the one sales district that covers southern Manitoba and southern Saskatchewan, there may be two or three of this company's sales reps. Each of these people will be selling a different group of this wholesaler's products.

Staffing the Organization A key step in implementing strategic planning in an organization is to staff the organization — that is, to select people who will be doing the actual implementation work. *Of all the specific stages in the management process, in your authors' opinion, selection of people is the most important.* We strongly believe this to be true

FIGURE 19-3c
Sales organization specialized by customer.

regardless of what organization is being staffed. A hockey coach's success depends to a great extent upon his ability to recruit the right players. A political party's success depends upon its ability to select the candidate who will attract the most votes. Your career success will depend in great measure upon your ability to pick the right organization (and people) to work with. A sales manager's success depends to a great extent upon the sales people whom the manager selects. Those of you who now are single will learn that your happiness and success in life depends to a great degree upon the person whom you select as a mate.

Yes, selection is critically important in *any* organization! And that's why it is such a tragedy that most people do a poor job in recruiting and selection. Most of us don't know how to pick people — to judge people for the position being filled.

Now let's come back more specifically to the task of implementing a strategic marketing program and the selection of the people who do this job. In most marketing organizations the implementation task is done largely by the sales force. So let's identify the reason why it is important to have a good program for selecting sales people.

- Good sales people are often hard to find — that is, there is a scarcity of qualified recruits.
- Within limits, any manager is no better than the people working under him or her. And managers are judged by the way their subordinates perform.
- A good selection job makes other managerial tasks easier. Well-selected workers are easier to train, supervise, and motivate.
- Good selection typically reduces the turnover rate with all its attendant costs.
- In summary, well-selected sales people will do a better job of carrying out management's strategic plans.

Marketing at Work

Making the Past Work for the Future

One of the most difficult and important responsibilities of a sales manager is to attract and retain good sales people. A large manufacturer of machine tools, with a sales staff of 90 operating in Canada and the Northern U.S., was experiencing a turnover rate among sales people of almost 30 percent annually. Over a ten-year period, almost 400 people had worked in sales positions with the company. The sales manager, Dan Murphy, was concerned that the company could not do a better job of selecting sales people who would meet their quotas and stay with the company.

The company had done a good job of record keeping over the years and had complete files on each of the sales people who had worked for the company during those ten years. They even had the original application form and records of sales activities and performance. A fairly junior staff member in the Human Resources Department decided to construct a computer-based model that would allow the company to determine each applicant's likelihood of sales success at the time that he or she applied for a sales position with the company. Using the historical data, Heather Evans identified ten critical factors that had been highly correlated with sales success in the past. Dan Murphy began to place much greater emphasis on these factors in the selection of sales personnel since they obviously worked. More and more companies are using data that already exist in their files to identify critical factors which could influence marketing performance.

Managing the Marketing Operations

The third broad activity included in the implementation stage of the management process involves actually directing and operating a marketing program. This activity is the guts of the entire implementation process. This is where these strategic plans are actually carried out. This is where the revenue-generating activity occurs in the firm. This is where management directs the efforts of the people who earlier were selected and organized.

The guidelines for operating the marketing-mix components (product, price, distribution, promotion) are probably pretty well set by virtue of the strategic marketing plan. Now it is up to the operating executives in the marketing department to follow these guidelines in practice. The key to success in this stage depends upon how well the executives have put into practice four concepts involving people and the management of these people. These four concepts are delegation, coordination, motivation, and communication.

DELEGATION

Very often much of an executive's success is measured by his or her ability to delegate authority and responsibility in an effective manner. Executives who try to do everything themselves — who for some reason are reluctant to delegate — invariably fail to maximize the potential of their programs or their subordinates in the company.

COORDINATION

Effective coordination will bring about a synergy in the organization whereby the people working together will accomplish more than if they go off on their own in a rudderless fashion. Sales peoples' efforts should be coordinated with the media advertising activities. New-product introduction needs to be coordinated with the physical distribution of this product and the middlemen must be prepared to handle the new product.

MOTIVATION

The success enjoyed by a leader of people in any field — athletics, education, politics, the armed forces, business — is greatly dependent upon that leader's ability to motivate his or her people. Here we can consider economic motivation in the form of monetary payments as well as psychological motivation in the form of nonmonetary rewards.

COMMUNICATION

Finally, all these implementation activities will come together in an effective manner only if the executives involved do an effective job of communicating with their workers. In early chapters we spoke often about effectively communicating with our markets. Now we are concerned with doing a good job of internal communication. It is imperative that an organization maintain open communication channels both upward and downward in the company's hierarchy. Management must communicate with the sales people, and these reps must have an open channel to communicate upward to management. Unfortunately, often it is easier to say these things than to do them. Companies spend untold sums of money to improve the communication abilities of their executives, but the workers often still misunderstand management's messages. Yet this is no reason to stop trying. We all must continue to try to improve our abilities to send and to receive the intended messages through the channels in a communication system.[2]

EVALUATING MARKETING PERFORMANCE

As soon as possible after a firm's plans have been set in operation, the process of evaluation should begin. Without evaluation, management cannot tell whether its plan is working and what the reasons are for success or failure. Planning and evaluation thus are interrelated activities. Evaluation logically follows planning and the execution of the plan. That is, planning sets forth what *should be* done, and evaluation shows what *really was* done. Sometimes a circular relationship exists: Plans are made, they are put into action, the operational results are evaluated, and new plans are prepared on the basis of this appraisal. (See Fig. 19-4.)

Previously we have discussed evaluation as it relates to individual parts of a marketing program — the product-planning process, the performance of the sales force, and the effectiveness of the advertising program, for instance. At this point, let's look at the evaluation of the *total marketing effort*.

The Marketing Audit: A Total Evaluation Program

A marketing audit is the essential element of a total evaluation program.[3] An audit implies a review and an evaluation of some activity. Thus, a **marketing audit** is a systematic, comprehensive, periodic review and evaluation of the marketing function in an organization — its marketing goals, strategies, and performance.

Obviously, a complete audit is an extensive and difficult project. But the rewards from a marketing audit can be great. Management can identify its problem areas in marketing. By reviewing its strategies, the firm is likely to keep abreast of its changing marketing environment. Successes can also be analyzed, so the company can capitalize on its strong points. The audit can spot lack of coordination in the marketing program, outdated strategies, or unrealistic goals. The audit allows management to correctly place responsibility for good or poor performance. Furthermore, an audit should anticipate future situations. It is intended for "prognosis as well as diagnosis. . . . It is the practice of preventive as well as curative marketing medicine."[4]

FIGURE 19-4
The circular relationship among management tasks.

Misdirected Marketing Effort

One of the primary benefits of evaluation activities is that they can help correct misdirected or misplaced marketing effort.

THE "80-20" PRINCIPLE

A company does not enjoy the same rate of net profit on every individual sale. In most firms a large proportion of the orders, customers, territories, or products account for only a small share of the profit. This relationship between selling units and profit has been characterized as the "80-20" principle. That is, 80 percent of the orders, customers, territories, or products contribute only 20 percent of the sales or profit. Conversely, 20 percent of these selling units account for 80 percent of the volume or profit. The 80-20 figure is used simply to epitomize the misplacement of marketing efforts. Actually, of course, the percentage split varies from one situation to another.

The basic reason for the 80-20 situation is that almost every marketing program includes some misdirected effort. Marketing efforts and costs are proportional to the *number* of territories, customers, or products, rather than to their actual sales volume or profit. For example, in a department store, approximately the same order-filling, billing, and delivery expenses are involved whether a mink coat or a necktie is sold. Or a manufacturer may assign one sales person to each territory. Yet there may be substantial differences in the potential volume and profit from the various territories. In each case, the marketing effort (cost) is not in line with the potential return.

REASONS FOR MISDIRECTED MARKETING EFFORT

Many executives are unaware of the misdirected marketing effort in their firms. They do not know what percentage of total sales and profit comes from a given product line or customer group. Frequently executives cannot uncover their misdirection of effort because they lack sufficiently detailed information. The analogy of an iceberg in an open sea has been used to illustrate this situation. Only a small part of an iceberg is visible above the surface of the water, and the submerged 90 percent is the dangerous part. The figures representing total sales or total costs on an operating statement are like the visible part of an iceberg. The detailed figures representing sales, costs, and other performance measures for each territory or product correspond to the important and dangerous submerged segment.

Total sales or costs as presented on an operating statement are too general to be useful in evaluation. In fact, the total figures are often inconclusive and misleading. More than one company has shown satisfactory overall sales and profit figures. But when these totals were subdivided by territory or products, serious weaknesses were discovered. A manufacturer of rubber products showed an overall annual increase of 12 percent in sales and 9 percent in net profit on one product line one year. But management wasn't satisfied with this "tip of the iceberg." When it analyzed the figures more closely, it found that the sales change within territories ranged from an increase of 19 percent to a decrease of 3 percent. In some territories, profits increased as much as 14 percent, and in others, they were down 20 percent.

An even more important cause of misplaced marketing effort is the fact that executives must make decisions based on inadequate knowledge of the exact nature of marketing costs. In other words, management lacks knowledge of (1) the disproportionate spread of marketing effort; (2) reliable standards for determining what should be spent on marketing; and (3) what results should be expected from these expenditures.

As an illustration, a company may spend $250,000 more on advertising this year than last year. But management ordinarily cannot state what the resultant increase in sales volume or profit should be. Nor do the executives know what would have happened if they had spent the same amount on (1) new-product development, (2) management training seminars for middlemen, or (3) some other aspect of the marketing program.[5]

The Evaluation Process

The evaluation process — whether in the form of a complete marketing audit or only an appraisal of individual components of the marketing program — is essentially a three-stage task. In the evaluation process, management's job is as follows:

1. Find out *what* happened — get the facts; compare actual results with budgeted goals to determine where they differ.
2. Find out *why* it happened — determine what specific factors in the marketing program accounted for the results.
3. Decide *what to do* about it — plan the next period's program and activities so as to improve on unsatisfactory performance and capitalize on the things that were done well.

One effective way to evaluate a total marketing program is to analyze the performance results. To do this, two useful tools are available — the sales-volume analysis and the marketing cost analysis. These tools are illustrated in the next two sections.

Our discussion of sales-volume and marketing cost analyses is built around the Great Western Company Ltd. (GW) — a hypothetical firm that markets office furniture. This company's western market is divided into four sales districts, each with seven or eight sales people and a district sales manager. The company sells to office equipment wholesalers and directly to large industrial users. Great Western's products mix is divided into four groups — desks, chairs, filing equipment, and accessories (wastebaskets, desk sets, etc.). Some of these products are manufactured by Great Western, and some are purchased from other firms.

ANALYSIS OF SALES VOLUME

A **sales-volume analysis** is a detailed study of the ''net sales'' section of a company's profit and loss statement (its operating statement). Management should analyze its *total* sales volume, and its volume by *product lines* and by *market segments* (territories, customer groups). These sales should be compared with company goals and with industry sales.

Sales Results versus Sales Goals

We start with an analysis of Great Western's total sales volume, as shown in Table 19-1. The company's annual sales doubled (from $1.8 million to $3.6 million) during the ten-year period ending in 1989. Furthermore, they increased each year over the preceding year, with the exception of 1986. In most of these years the company met or surpassed its planned sales goals. Thus far, the company's situation is very encouraging. When industry sales figures are introduced for comparison, however, the picture changes. But let's hold the industry-comparison analysis until the next section.

A study of total sales volume alone is usually insufficient, and maybe even

TABLE 19-1   ANNUAL SALES VOLUME OF GREAT WESTERN COMPANY, INDUSTRY VOLUME, AND COMPANY'S SHARE IN MARKET

Year	Company volume (in millions of dollars)	Industry volume in company's market (in millions of dollars)	Company's percentage share of market
1989	3.60	30.0	12.0
1988	3.47	27.5	12.6
1987	3.31	25.5	13.0
1986	3.04	22.0	13.8
1985	3.17	23.5	13.5
1984	2.80	20.0	14.0
1983	2.45	17.0	14.4
1982	2.25	15.5	14.5
1981	2.18	15.0	14.8
1980	1.80	12.0	15.0

misleading, because of the workings of the iceberg principle. To learn what is going on in the "submerged" segments of the market, we need to analyze sales volume by market segments — sales territories, for example.

Table 19-2 is a summary of the planned sales goals and the actual sales results in Great Western's four sales districts. A key measurement figure is the *performance percentage* — the actual sales divided by the sales goal. A performance percentage of 100 means that the district did exactly what was expected of it. Thus, from the table we see that B and C did just a little better than was expected. District A passed its goal by a wide margin, but district D was quite a disappointment.

So far in our evaluation process, we know a little about *what* happened in GW's districts. Now management has to figure out *why* it happened, and what should be done about it. These are the difficult steps in evaluation. In the GW situation, the executives need to determine why district D did so poorly. The fault may lie in some aspect of the marketing program, or competition may be especially strong there. They also should find out what accounts for district A's success, and whether this information can be used in the other regions.

TABLE 19-2   DISTRICT SALES VOLUME IN GREAT WESTERN COMPANY, 1989

District	Sales goals (in millions of dollars)	Actual sales (in millions of dollars)	Performance percentage (actual ÷ goal)	Dollar variation (in millions)
A	1.08	1.25	116	+ .17
B	.90	.96	107	+ .06
C	.76	.77	101	+ .01
D	.86	.62	72	− .24
Total	$3.60	$3.60		

This brief examination of two aspects of sales-volume analysis shows how this evaluation tool may be used. In a real business situation, GW's executives should go *much* further. They should analyze their sales volume by individual territories within districts and by product lines. Then they should carry their territorial analysis further by examining volume by product line and customer group *within* each territory. For instance, even though district A did well overall, the iceberg principle may be at work *within* the district. The fine *total* performance in district A may be covering up weaknesses in an individual product line or territory.

Market-Share Analysis   Comparing a company's sales results with its goal certainly is a useful form of performance evaluation. But it does not tell how the company is doing relative to its competitors. We need to compare the company's sales with the industry's sales. In effect, we should analyze, preferably in some detail, the company's share of the market. That is, we should analyze its market share in total, and also by product line and market segment.

Probably the major obstacle encountered in market-share analysis is in obtaining the industry sales information in total, and in the desired detail. Trade associations and government agencies such as Statistics Canada are excellent sources for industry sales-volume statistics in many fields.

The Great Western situation is a good example of the usefulness of market-share analysis. Recall from Table 19-1 that GW's total sales doubled over a ten-year period, with annual increases in nine of those years. *But*, during this decade, the industry's annual sales increased from $12 million to $30 million (a 250 percent increase). Thus, the company's share of this market actually *declined* from 15 to 12 percent. Although the company's annual sales increased 100 percent, its market share declined 20 percent.

The next step is to determine *why* Great Western's market position declined. The number of possible causes is almost limitless, and this is what makes management's task so difficult. A weakness in almost any aspect of Great Western's product line, distribution system, pricing structure, or promotional program may have contributed to the loss of market share. In may be that the real culprit is competition. There may be new competitors in the market who were attracted by the rapid growth rates. Or competitors' marketing programs may be more effective than Great Western's.

File 19-3

Marketing at Work

Tracking Means Knowing Where You're Going

We should not lose sight of the fact that marketing research represents a valuable tool for evaluating the success of marketing programs. Most larger marketing companies will make use of regular "tracking" studies to monitor how their brands are performing in the marketplace. These studies may be conducted every three months, six months, or every year and are intended to provide feedback to brand managers and senior management on the various indicators of marketing success — how many people have heard of our brand? What do they think of it? How many have tried it in the past six months? How many buy it regularly? How many consider it their regular brand? How much of it do they buy?

A manufacturer of baking products found that close to half of the users of flour in an eastern Canadian market named its brand as their first choice. However, the company knew that its sales had been lagging well behind those of its leading competitor in that market. A closer examination of data from a tracking study showed that the regular users of the company's brand used flour very infrequently, for sauces and gravies and for other minor cooking activities. They did very little home baking. On the other hand, the research showed that the competitor's brand was most popular among homemakers who baked regularly and made home-made bread at least once a week. Needless to say, this relevation prompted changes in the marketing strategy for the company's brand.

MARKETING COST ANALYSIS

An analysis of sales volume is quite useful in evaluating and controlling a company's marketing effort. A volume analysis, however, does not tell us anything about the *profitability* of this effort. Management needs to conduct a marketing cost analysis to determine the relative profitability of its territories, product lines, or other marketing units. A marketing cost analysis is a detailed study of the operating expense section of a company's profit and loss statement. As part of this analysis, management may establish budgetary goals, and then study the variations between budgeted costs and actual expenses.

Types of Marketing Cost Analyses

A company's marketing costs may be analyzed:

1. As they appear in the ledger accounts and on the profit and loss statement.
2. After they are grouped into functional (also called activity) classifications.
3. After these activity costs have been allocated to territories, products, or other marketing units.

ANALYSIS OF LEDGER EXPENSES

The simplest and least expensive marketing cost analysis is a study of the "object of expenditure" costs as they appear in the firm's profit and loss statement. These figures, in turn, come from the company's accounting ledger records. The simplified operating statement for the Great Western Company on the left side of Table 19-3 is the model we shall use in this discussion.

The procedure is simply to analyze each cost item (salaries, media space, etc.) in some detail. We can compare this period's total with the totals for similar periods in the past, and observe the trends. We can compare actual results with budgeted expense goals. We should also compute each expense as a percentage of net sales. Then, if possible, we should compare these expense ratios with industry figures, which are often available through trade associations.

ANALYSIS OF FUNCTIONAL EXPENSES

For more effective control of marketing costs, they should be allocated among the various marketing functions, such as advertising or warehousing. Then management can analyze the expenses of these activities.

TABLE 19-3   PROFIT AND LOSS STATEMENT AND DISTRIBUTION OF NATURAL EXPENSES TO ACTIVITY COST GROUPS, GREAT WESTERN COMPANY 1989

Profit and loss statement ($000)			Expense distribution sheet ($000)				
			Activity (functional) cost groups				
Net sales		$3,600					
Cost of goods sold		2,340	Personal selling	Advertising	Warehousing and shipping	Order processing	Marketing administration
Gross margin		1,260					
Operating expenses:							
Salaries and commissions	$271	→	$120	$ 24	$ 42	$ 28	$ 57
Travel and entertainment	144	→	104				40
Media space	148	→		148			
Supplies	44	→	6	3.5	24	7	3.5
Property taxes	13	→	1.6	.5	6	3	1.9
Freight out	350	→			350		
Total expenses	970	→	$231.6	$176	$422	$ 38	$102.4
Net profit		$290					

The procedure here is to select the appropriate groups, and then to allocate each ledger expense among those activities. (See the expense distribution sheet on the right-hand side of Table 19-3.) In our Great Western example, we have decided on five activity cost groups. Some items, such as the cost of media space, can be apportioned directly to one activity (advertising). For other expenses, the cost can be prorated only after management has established some reasonable basis for allocation. Property taxes, for instance, may be allocated according to the proportion of the total floor space that is occupied by each department. Thus, the warehouse accounts for 46 percent of the total area (square metres) of floor space in the firm, so the warehousing-shipping function is charged with $6,000 (46 percent) of the property taxes.

A functional cost analysis gives executives more information than they can get from an analysis of ledger accounts alone. Also, an analysis of activity expenses in total provides an excellent starting point for management to analyze costs by territories, products, or other marketing units.

ANALYSIS OF FUNCTIONAL COSTS BY MARKET SEGMENTS

The third and most beneficial type of marketing cost analysis is a study of the costs and profitability of each segment of the market. Common practice in this type of analysis is to divide the market by territories, products, customer groups, or order sizes. Cost analysis by market segment enables management to pinpoint trouble spots much more effectively than does an analysis of either ledger-account expenses or activity costs.

By combining a sales-volume analysis with a marketing cost study, a researcher can prepare a complete operating statement for each of the product or market segments. These individual statements can then be analyzed to determine the effectiveness of the marketing program as related to each of those segments.

The procedure for making a cost analysis by market segments is similar to that used to analyze functional (activity) expenses. The total of each activity cost (in the right-hand part of Table 19-3) is prorated on some basis to each product or market segment being studied. Let's walk through an example of a cost analysis, by sales districts, for the Great Western Company, as shown in Tables 19-4 and 19-5.

First, for each of the five GW activities, we select an allocation basis for distributing the cost of that activity among the four districts. (See the top part of Table 19-4.) Then we determine the number of allocation "units" that make up each activity cost, and we find the cost per unit. This completes the allocation scheme, which tells us how to allocate costs to the four districts:

- Personal selling activity expenses pose no problem because they are direct expenses, chargeable to the district in which they are incurred.
- We allocate advertising expenses on the basis of the number of pages of advertising that were run in each district. Great Western purchased the equivalent of 88 pages of advertising during the year, at an average cost of $2,000 per page ($176,000 ÷ 88).
- Warehousing and shipping expenses are allocated on the basis of the number of orders shipped. Since 10,550 orders were shipped during the year at a total activity cost of $422,000, the cost per order is $40.
- Order-processing expenses are allocated according to the number of invoice

TABLE 19-4   ALLOCATION OF ACTIVITY COSTS TO SALES DISTRICTS, GREAT WESTERN COMPANY, 1989

Activity	Personal selling	Advertising	Warehousing and shipping	Order processing	Marketing administration
Allocation scheme					
Allocation basis	Direct expense to each district	Number of pages of advertising	Number of orders to be shipped	Number of invoice lines	Equally among districts
Total activity cost	$231,600	$176,000	$422,000	$38,000	$102,400
Number of allocation units		88 pages	10,550 orders	12,667 lines	4 districts
Cost per allocation unit		$2,000	$40	$3	$25,600
Allocation of costs					
District A — units	—	27 pages	3,300 orders	4,600 lines	one
District A — cost	$65,000	$54,000	$132,000	$13,800	$25,600
District B — units	—	19 pages	2,850 orders	3,300 lines	one
District B — cost	$60,600	$38,000	$114,000	$9,900	$25,600
District C — units	—	22 pages	2,300 orders	2,667 lines	one
District C — cost	$54,000	$44,000	$92,000	$8,000	$25,600
District D — units	—	20 pages	2,100 orders	2,100 lines	one
District D — cost	$52,000	$40,000	$84,000	$6,300	$25,600

TABLE 19-5   PROFIT AND LOSS STATEMENTS FOR SALES DISTRICTS ($000), GREAT WESTERN COMPANY, 1989

	Total	District A	District B	District C	District D
Net sales	$3,600	$1,250	$960	$770	$620
Cost of goods sold	2,340	812.5	624	500.5	403
Gross margin	1,260	437.5	336	269.5	217
Operating expenses:					
Personal selling	231.6	65	60.6	54	52
Advertising	176	54	38	44	40
Warehousing and shipping	422	132	114	92	84
Order processing, billing	38	13.8	9.9	8	6.3
Marketing administration	102.4	25.6	25.6	25.6	25.6
Total expenses	970	290.4	248.1	223.6	207.9
Net profit (in dollars)	$ 290	$ 147.1	$ 87.9	$ 45.9	$ 9.1
(as percentage of sales)	8.1%	11.8%	9.2%	6.0%	1.5%

lines typed during the year. Since there were 12,667 lines, then the cost per line is $3.

■ The marketing administration — a totally indirect expense — is divided equally among the four districts, with each district being allocated $25,600.

The final step is to calculate the amount of each activity cost to be allocated to each district. The results are shown in the bottom part of Table 19-4. We see that $65,000 of personal selling expenses were charged directly to district A, $60,600 to district B, and similarly to districts C and D. Regarding advertising, the equivalent of 27 pages of advertising was run in district A, so that district is charged with $54,000 (27 pages × $2,000 per page). Similar calculations provide advertising activity cost allocations of $38,000 to district B, $44,000 to district C, and $40,000 to D.

Regarding warehousing and shipping expenses, 3,300 orders were shipped to customers in district A, at a unit allocation cost of $40 per order, for a total allocated cost of $132,000. Warehousing and shipping charges are allocated to the other three districts as shown in Table 19-4.

To allocate order-processing expenses, management determined that 4,600 invoice lines went to customers in district A. At $3 per line (the cost per allocation unit), district A is charged with $13,800. Allocations to the other districts are shown in Table 19-4. Finally, each district is charged with $25,600 for marketing administration expenses.

After the activity costs have been allocated among the four districts, we can prepare a profit and loss statement for each district. These statements are shown in Table 19-5. The sales volume for each district is determined from the sales-volume analysis (Table 19-2). The cost of goods sold and gross margin for each district is obtained by assuming that the company gross margin of 35 percent (1,260,000 ÷ $3,600,000) was maintained in each district.

Table 19-5 now shows, for each district, what the company profit and loss statement shows for the overall company operations. For example, we note that district A's net profit was 11.8 percent of sales ($147,100 ÷ $1,250,000 = 11.8 percent). In sharp contrast, district D did rather poorly, earning a net profit of only 1.5 percent of net sales ($9,100 ÷ $620,000 = 1.5 percent).

At this point in our performance evaluation, we have completed the ''what happened'' stage. The next stage is to determine *why* the results are as depicted in Table 19-5. As we indicated earlier, it is extremely difficult to pinpoint the answer to this question. In district D, for example, the sales force obtained only about two-thirds as many orders as in district A (210 versus 330). Was this because of poor selling ability, poor sales training, more severe competition in district D, or some other reason among a multitude of possibilities?

After a performance evaluation has determined *why* the district results came out as they did, management can move to the third stage in its evaluation process. That final stage is, *what should management do about the situation?* This stage will be discussed briefly after we have reviewed two major problem areas in marketing cost analysis.

Problems Involved in Cost Analysis

Marketing cost analysis can be expensive in time, money, and manpower. In particular, the task of allocating costs is often quite difficult.

ALLOCATING COSTS

The problem of allocating costs becomes most evident when activity cost totals must be apportioned among individual territories, products, or other marketing units.

Operating costs can be divided into direct and indirect expenses. (These are sometimes called ''separable'' and ''common'' expenses.) Direct, or separable, expenses are those incurred totally in connection with one market segment or one unit of the sales organization. Thus the salary and travel expenses of the sales representative in territory A are direct expenses for that territory. The cost of newspaper space to advertise product C is a *direct* cost of marketing that product. The task of allocating direct expenses is easy. They can be charged in their entirety to the marketing unit for which they were incurred.

The allocation problem arises in connection with indirect, or common, costs. These expenses are incurred jointly for more than one marketing unit. Therefore they cannot be charged totally to one market segment.

Within the category of indirect expenses, some costs are *partially* indirect and some are *totally* indirect. Order filling and shipping, for example, are *partially* indirect costs. They would *decrease* if some of the territories or products were eliminated. They would *increase* if new products or territories were added. On the other hand, marketing administrative expenses are *totally* indirect. The cost of the chief marketing executive's staff and office would remain about the same, whether or not the number of territories or product lines was changed.

Any method selected for allocating indirect expenses has obvious weaknesses that can distort the results and mislead management. Two commonly used allocation methods are to divide these costs (1) equally among the marketing units being studied (territories, for instance) or (2) in proportion to the sales volume in each marketing unit. But each method gives a different result for the total costs for each marketing unit.

Warehousing costs typically are partially indirect.

FULL-COST VERSUS CONTRIBUTION-MARGIN CONTROVERSY

In a marketing cost analysis, two ways of allocating indirect expenses are (1) the contribution-margin (also called contribution-to-overhead) method and (2) the full-cost method. A real controversy exists regarding which of these two approaches is better for managerial control purposes.

In the **contribution-margin approach**, only the direct expenses are allocated to each marketing unit being analyzed. These are the costs that presumably would be eliminated if that marketing unit were eliminated. When these direct expenses are deducted from the gross margin of the marketing unit, the remainder is the amount which that unit is contributing to cover total indirect expenses (or overhead).

In the **full-cost approach**, all expenses — direct and indirect — are allocated among the marketing units under study. By allocating *all* costs, management can determine the net profit of each territory, product, or other marketing unit.

For any given marketing unit, these two methods can be summarized as follows:

Contribution margin	**Full cost**
Sales $	Sales $
less	*less*
Cost of goods sold	Cost of goods sold
equals	*equals*
Gross margin	Gross margin
less	*less*
Direct expenses	Direct expenses
equals	*less*
Contribution-margin (the amount available to cover overhead expenses plus a profit)	Indirect expenses
	equals
	Net profit

Proponents of the *full-cost* approach contend that the purpose of a marketing cost study is to determine the net profitability of the units being studied. They feel that the contribution-margin approach does not fulfil this purpose. The advocates of the full-cost approach point out that management may be deluding itself with the contribution-margin approach. A given territory or product may be showing a contribution to overhead. Yet, after the indirect costs are allocated, this product or territory may actually have a net loss. In effect, say the full-cost people, the contribution-margin approach is the iceberg principle in action. That is, the visible tip of the iceberg (the contribution margin) looks good, while the submerged part may be hiding a net loss.

Contribution-margin supporters contend that it is not possible to accurately apportion indirect costs among product or market segments. Furthermore, items such as administrative costs are not all related to any one territory or product. Therefore the marketing units should not bear any of these costs. These advocates also point out that a full-cost analysis may show that a product or territory has a net loss, whereas this unit may be contributing something to overhead. Some executives might recommend that the losing product or territory be eliminated. But they are overlooking the fact that the unit's contribution to overhead would then have to be borne by other units. Under the contribution-margin approach, there would be no question about keeping this unit as long as no better alternative could be discovered.

Use of Findings from Combined Volume and Cost Analysis

So far in our discussion of marketing cost analysis, we have been dealing generally with the first stage in the evaluation process. That is, we have been finding out *what happened*. To conclude this section, let's look at some examples of how management might use the results from a combined sales-volume analysis and a marketing cost analysis.

TERRITORIAL DECISIONS

Once management knows the net profit (or contribution to overhead) of the territories in relation to their potential, there are several possibilities for managerial action. The executives may decide to adjust (expand or contract) territories to bring them into line with current sales potential. Or territorial problems may stem from weaknesses in the distribution system, and changes in channels of distribution may be needed. Some firms that have been using manufacturers' agents may find it advisable to establish their own sales forces in growing markets. Intensive competition may be the cause of unprofitable volume in some districts, and changes in the promotional program may be advisable.

Of course, a losing territory might be abandoned completely. An abandoned region may have been contributing something to overhead, however, even though a net loss was shown. Management must recognize that this contribution must now be carried by the remaining territories.

PRODUCT DECISIONS

When the relative profitability of each product or group of products is known, a product line may be simplified by eliminating unprofitable models, sizes, or colours. The sales people's compensation plan may be altered to encourage the sale of high-margin items. Channels of distribution may be altered. Instead of selling all its products directly to industrial users, for example, a machine tools manufacturer shifted to industrial distributors for standard products of low unit value. The company thereby improved the profitability of these products.

In the final analysis, management may decide to discontinue a product. Before this is done, however, consideration must be given to the effect this will have on other items in the line. Often a low-volume or unprofitable product must be carried simply to round out the line. Customers expect a seller to carry the article. If it is not available, the seller may lose sales of other products.

DECISIONS ON CUSTOMER CLASSES AND ORDER SIZES

By combining a volume analysis with a cost study, executives can determine the relative profitability of each group of customers. If one group shows a substandard net profit, changes in the pricing structure for these accounts may be required. Or perhaps accounts that have been sold directly should be turned over to middlemen.

A common problem plaguing many firms today is that of the **small order**. Many orders are below the break-even point. The revenue from each of these orders is actually less than the allocated expenses. This is true because several costs, such as billing or direct selling, are the same whether the order amounts to $10 or $10,000. Management's immediate reaction may be that no order below the break-even point should be accepted. Or small-volume accounts should be dropped from the customer list. Actually, such decisions may be harmful. Management should determine first *why* certain accounts are small-order problems and then adopt procedures to correct the situation. Proper handling can very often turn a losing account into a satisfactory one. A small-order handling charge, which customers would willingly pay, might change the profit situation entirely.

SUMMARY   The management process in marketing may be defined as the planning, implementation, and evaluation of the marketing effort in an organization. The implementation stage is the operational stage in which an organization attempts to carry out its strategic planning. Strategic planning is virtually useless in an organization if these plans are not implemented effectively.

The implementation stage includes three broad areas of activity — organizing, staffing, and operating. In organizing, the company first should coordinate all marketing activities into one department whose chief executive reports directly to the president. Then, within the marketing department, the company may utilize some form of organizational specialization based on geographical territories, products, or customer types. Regarding staffing, our philosophy is that selecting people is the most important step in the entire management process. To operate an organization effectively, management needs to do a good job in delegation, coordination, motivation, and communication.

The evaluation stage in the management process involves measuring performance results against predetermined goals. Evaluation enables management to determine the effectiveness of its implementation efforts and to plan future corrective action where necessary.

A marketing audit is extremely important in a total marketing evaluation program. Most companies are victims of at least some misdirected marketing effort. That is, the 80-20 situation and the iceberg principle are at work in most firms. This is so because marketing efforts (costs) are expended in relation to the *number* of marketing units rather than to their profit potential. Fundamentally, companies do not know how much they should be spending for marketing activities, or what results they should get from these expenditures.

Two useful tools for controlling these misdirected marketing efforts are a sales-volume analysis and a marketing cost analysis. Given appropriately detailed analyses, management can study its sales volume and marketing costs by product lines and by market segments (sales territories, customer groups). One major problem in marketing cost analysis is that of allocating costs — especially indirect costs — to the various marketing units. But the findings from these analyses are extremely helpful in shaping decisions regarding several aspects of a company's marketing program.

NOTES

[1] See Walter Kiechel III, "Corporate Strategists Under Fire," *Fortune*, Dec. 27, 1982, pp. 34–39; and "The Future Catches Up with a Strategic Planner," *Business Week*, June 27, 1983.

[2] For some guidelines to aid in identifying implementation difficulties and some suggestions for remedying them, see Thomas V. Bonoma, "Making Your Marketing Strategy Work," *Harvard Business Review*, March-April 1984, pp. 69–76.

[3] See *Analyzing and Improving Marketing Performance: "Marketing Audits" in Theory and Practice*, American Management Association, Management Report no. 32, New York, 1959; see especially Abe Schuchman, "The Marketing Audit: Its Nature, Purpose, and Problems," pp. 11–19; and Alfred R. Oxenfeldt, "The Marketing Audit as a Total Evaluation Program," pp. 25–36.

[4] Schuchman, ibid., p. 14.

[5] For some ideas on how to correct an 80-20 situation of misdirected marketing effort, see Alan J. Dubinsky and Richard W. Hansen, "Improving Marketing Productivity: The 80/20 Principle Revisited," *California Management Review*, Fall 1982, pp. 96–105.

KEY TERMS AND CONCEPTS

Implementation (in the management process) 536
Organizational structures for implementing strategic planning 537
Importance of good selection 540
Delegating authority and responsibility 542
Coordinating marketing activities 542
Motivating people 542
Communicating inside a company 542
Marketing audit 543
Misdirected marketing effort 543
80-20 principle 544

Iceberg principle 544
Sales-volume analysis 545
Market-share analysis 547
Marketing cost analysis 548
Direct costs 552
Indirect costs 552
Full-cost versus contribution-margin allocation 553

QUESTIONS AND PROBLEMS

1. Explain the relationship among planning, implementation, and evaluation in the management process.

2. "Good implementation in an organization can overcome poor planning, but good planning cannot overcome poor implementation." Explain, using examples.

3. How is the organizational placement of marketing activities likely to be different in a marketing-oriented firm as contrasted with a production-oriented firm?

4. What benefits can a company expect to gain by organizing its sales force by geographical territories?

5. Give some examples of companies that are likely to organize their sales force by product groups.

6. What are some of the reasons why this book's authors believe that selecting people is such an important aspect of the management process?

7. Why is effective delegation of authority and responsibility so important in operating a marketing program?

8. Give some examples of how advertising and personal selling activities might be coordinated in a company's marketing department.

9. A sales-volume analysis by territories indicates that the sales of a roofing materials company have increased 12 percent a year for the past three years in the territory comprising Atlantic Canada and Quebec. Does this indicate conclusively that the company's sales-volume performance is satisfactory in that region?

10. A manufacturer found that one product accounted for 35 to 45 percent of the company's total sales in all but two of the 18 territories. In each of those two territories, this product accounted for only 15 percent of the company's volume. What factors might account for the relatively low sales of this article in the two districts?

11. Explain how the results of a territorial sales-volume analysis may influence a firm's promotional program.

12. What effects may a sales-volume analysis by products have on training, supervising, and compensating the sales force?

13. "Firms should discontinue selling losing products." Discuss.

14. Should a company discontinue selling to an unprofitable customer? Why or why not? If not, then what steps might the company take to make the account a profitable one?

CHAPTER 20

MARKETING: SOCIETAL APPRAISAL AND PROSPECT

CHAPTER GOALS

We have looked at marketing within the individual *firm* and within our *economic system*. Now, in this final chapter, we shall look more closely at the place of marketing within our *social system*. After studying this chapter, you should understand:

- The major criticisms of marketing and the phenomenon of consumerism.
- Some basic yardsticks for evaluating these criticisms and our marketing system in general.
- Government and business responses to consumer discontent.
- The emerging societal orientation in marketing and the social responsibilities of marketing management.
- Some forces that will shape marketing in the next ten years.
- The broadened, socially responsive marketing concept.

In recent years, marketing activities in two industries, beer and tobacco, have been creating quite a bit of controversy. The brewing industry has been criticized primarily for its use of "life-style" advertising that usually shows attractive young people having fun in the outdoors or at parties. A criticism that the advertising of beer leads to increased consumption seems to have run out of steam in recent years as per capita consumption of beer in Canada has declined, although advertising expenditures have been increasing.

It is a concern over alcohol abuse that has prompted much of the criticism levelled at beer advertising. Some critics have proposed an outright ban on the advertising of beer and other alcohol beverage products. Others have advocated warning labels on bottles. The Brewers' Association of Canada and the individual brewers themselves have responded with public interest campaigns warning against overconsumption and the dangers of drinking and driving.

In the marketing of cigarettes, tobacco companies have been bound by a self-imposed ban on advertising on radio and television. More recently, the companies have been accused of trying to counteract a decline in consumption by directing their products toward young consumers who may be beginning to smoke. The industry imposed a voluntary code which includes not placing billboards in the vicinity of schools and limiting the total amount that they will spend on advertising.

During the past couple of years, the Canadian Parliament has passed legislation that essentially prohibits smoking in certain public buildings and that will eventually lead to the elimination of all advertising and promotion for cigarettes in this country; many cities have enacted no-smoking by-laws, business and government offices have adopted a no-smoking policy, and airlines have banned smoking during most flights. The problem again is abuse of the product. Both tobacco and beer are legal products. But there are problems associated with their use. If the product is the problem, do you ban the advertising?

In the first two chapters of this book, we touched on the broader, societal dimension of marketing and examined briefly the role of marketing in the total economy. For the most part, however, we have approached marketing from the viewpoint of the firm, as we discussed the problems facing an individual producer or middleman in managing its marketing activities. Now in this final chapter, we will once again look at marketing from a broader, societal perspective.

First we shall appraise our marketing system by examining (1) the criticisms of the system, (2) the phenomenon of consumerism, and (3) the responses to these criticisms. Then we shall consider some of the societal aspects of marketing management, including a broadened view of the marketing concept.

BASIS FOR EVALUATING OUR MARKETING SYSTEM

MARKETING:

Does it satisfy consumers' wants — as consumers themselves define or express those wants?

Now here is a satisfied customer!

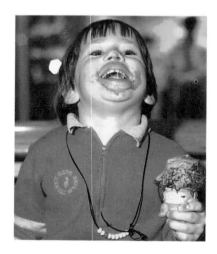

The present-day economic system of Canada is a reasonably free market system, but an *imperfect* one. Price is a major determinant of resource allocation. We call our system ''imperfect'' because it is not composed of the elements basic to the theoretical model of perfect competition. Those elements are great numbers of well-informed buyers and sellers, always acting rationally. Each is so small that one individual's activities have no appreciable influence on total supply, demand, or price. Another imperfection is the structural rigidity of our system. Also, in the interest of the general welfare, the various levels of government and their boards and agencies often act so as to decrease the free play of market forces.

We shall appraise our marketing system, using this imperfect economic system as our frame of reference. Before we engage in this evaluation, however, we need to agree on what is the *objective* of the system. Throughout this book we have stressed the philosophy of the marketing concept. The goal of the marketing concept is to develop a customer orientation on the part of management. In line with this philosophy, *it seems reasonable to establish as our objective the satisfaction of consumers' wants as they are expressed by the consumers themselves*. Then marketing should be appraised on the basis of how well it achieves this goal, that is, how effectively it satisfies consumers' wants. We grant that this is not everyone's idea of the ultimate goal. Some feel that consumers do not know what is good for them — that some group (usually the government) should take over the responsibility for setting standards. Others believe that the social and economic goals should be to build the social ''safety net,'' to promote the growth of its less developed regions, or to clean up the environment.

Regardless of how worthy these or other goals may be, our basis for evaluating our marketing system will be: *Does it satisfy consumers' wants — as consumers themselves define or express those wants?*

CRITICISMS OF MARKETING

For many years, critics of our marketing system have raised a variety of thought-provoking questions and have generated numerous lively discussions. Let us examine their criticisms, try to determine the true nature of these charges, and consider one key question: Does marketing cost too much?

What Are the Criticisms?

We can summarize the major charges against marketing by grouping them in relation to the components of the marketing mix — product, price structure, distribution system, and promotional activities.

Some people object to the proliferation of products.

THE PRODUCT

Critics allege that many products are of poor quality or are unsafe. Parts fall off cars, zippers jam, food products are adulterated, trains run late, wash-and-wear clothing really needs ironing, appliances do not perform as advertised, etc., etc. Also, these products are backed up by confusing and worthless warranties, and repair service is inadequate. Packaging is deceptive, and labels do not carry sufficient information concerning product contents, operating instructions, or care of the product.

Furthermore, heavily promoted product improvements are often trivial. Planned style obsolescence encourages consumers to get rid of products before they are physically worn out. Moreover, too many different types of goods, and too many different brands of each type, are produced. As a result, the buyer is confused and unable to make accurate buying decisions, and much production capacity is wasted in unnecessary duplication.

PRICE STRUCTURE

We hear that prices are too high, or too inflexible, or that they are controlled by the large firms in an industry. Some people feel that price competition has been largely replaced by nonprice competition.

DISTRIBUTION SYSTEM

Probably the main objection to the distribution system is that it is unnecessarily complex and includes too many middlemen. This is a two-part charge — there are too many different types of middlemen, and too many of each type.

PROMOTIONAL ACTIVITIES

The strongest and most bitter indictments against marketing are in the area of promotional activities — especially in personal selling and advertising. Most of the complaints about personal selling are aimed at the retail level. We find that both consumers and business people often are disenchanted with the poor quality of retail selling. Objections are also voiced against the poor services offered by many retailers.

File 20-1

Coordinated Service Equals Success

Many retailers are realizing that the key to their success in the future lies in better customer service. Not only is the marketplace becoming increasingly competitive, but Canadian consumers are placing renewed emphasis on the way they are treated in the store — discount prices and distinctive products are no longer enough to get them coming back; nor is the automatic, plastic type of customer service — "Thank you for shopping at _____."

This interest in ensuring good, sincere service at the point of sale has spawned a new industry — the customer service consultant. Following a period of rapid expansion in the early 1980s, Mark's Work Wearhouse found itself caught in the midst of the recession and headed for losses. By 1986, the economy had turned around and the company had climbed back to profitability. CEO Mark Blumes attributes much of his success to the fact that they rediscovered how to serve customers.

In 1983, Blumes took his executives on a retreat with Art McNeil, president of Achieve Enterprises of Toronto. McNeil delivered the message that senior managers, not just front-line staff, must be involved with customer service. Blumes' team realized that they had to put in place a well-trained, motivated sales team with a supportive organization behind them. To train employees across the country, Mark's Work Wearhouse introduced correspondence courses in basic selling. The more employees learn, the faster they are given added responsibilities; for example, as product managers, with responsibility for selecting items for their stores.

Blumes admits that while deciding to improve customer service was easy, "living it has been quite a different thing. We still have a long way to go. . . . For every store that works, there is one that isn't there yet."

Source: Adapted from Patricia Davies, "Standards Bearer," *Canadian Business*, March 1988, pp. 123–129.

The general criticisms of advertising may be divided into two groups — social and economic. From a *social* point of view, advertising is charged with overemphasizing our material standard of living and underemphasizing our cultural and moral values. Advertising also is charged with manipulating people — making them want to buy things they should not have, cannot afford, and do not need.

A major social criticism of advertising today, and one that has some justification, is that advertising is often false, deceptive, or in bad taste. Exaggerations, overuse

This print advertisement for Calvin Klein's Obsession for Men fragrance has been very successful.

of sex and fear appeals, inane claims, excessive numbers of commercials on radio and television, and poor choice of the placement of commercials are examples of this criticism. As with most criticisms in marketing, this one applies to a small segment of advertising. The main offenders are advertisers of a limited number of consumer goods, and the advertising medium causing most of the furor is television. The charge of misleading and offensive advertising is rarely made against advertisers of industrial products or companies that advertise consumer products in trade journals. Most retail display advertising is not subject to this charge, nor is most classified advertising in newspapers and magazines.

The *economic* criticisms of advertising have taken an interesting turn in recent years.[1] We still hear that advertising costs too much — that it increases the cost of marketing and therefore raises the prices of products. Recently, however, the economic charge drawing the most interest is that advertising leads to restraint of competition, economic concentration, and monopoly.[2]

The line of reasoning behind the economic-concentration complaint goes something like this. (1) The big companies can afford to spend much on advertising to differentiate their products, and thus they are able to acquire a large share of the market; (2) in this way, advertising creates a barrier to market entry by new or smaller firms; (3) a high level of market concentration then results; (4) the firms enjoying this protected position can charge high prices, which in turn lead to high profits.

A challenge to the economic-concentration charges was carefully spelled out in a study by Prof. Jules Backman.[3] He concluded that there is no relationship between advertising intensity and high economic concentration. Nor does there seem to be any link between advertising intensity and (1) price increases or (2) high profit rates. Advertising is highly competitive, Backman states, not anticompetitive.

Understanding the True Nature of Criticisms

In evaluating the charges against marketing, we should be careful to recognize the differences in the nature of the various points. We should understand what fundamentally is being criticized. In a company, is it the marketing department or some other department that is the cause of the complaints? In the economy, is it the marketing system or the general economic system that is being criticized? It is also helpful to know when the critics (1) are misinformed, (2) are unaware of the services performed by the marketing system, or (3) are trying to impose their own value judgements on consumers. That is, the critics may not agree that the goal of the marketing system should be consumer want-satisfaction, as the consumers *themselves* define and express their wants.

In some cases, the criticisms of marketing are fully warranted. They point out weaknesses and inefficiencies in the system and call for improvement. By most people's standards, there are instances of deceptive packaging and of misleading and objectionable advertising. There are weaknesses in marketing, just as there are in any system developed and operated by human beings.

The real key to the evaluation of our marketing system lies in the answers to two fundamental questions. First, is the present system of marketing achieving its goal (that is, satisfying consumers' wants as the consumers themselves express those wants) better than any other known alternative could? The answer is an unqualified ''yes.'' Second, is constant effort being devoted to improving the system and increasing its efficiency? Generally speaking, the answer to this question is also a strong ''yes.''

Progress sometimes may seem slow. Companies that operate in a socially undesirable manner even over a short period of time are harmful. Price fixing and objectionable advertising are intolerable and inexcusable. Instances of this nature, though widely publicized, are few relative to the totality of marketing effort. In essence, we are saying that weaknesses exist in marketing and that a continuing effort must be devoted to their elimination. However, at the same time, we should not overlook the improvements in marketing and consumer want-satisfaction over the years. The way to correct existing weaknesses is not to destroy or heavily regulate the existing system.

Does Marketing Cost Too Much?

Many of the censures of marketing can be summarized in the general criticism that marketing costs too much. However, the question of whether marketing costs too much should be analyzed and answered from two points of view. The first is within the *macro* context of our total socioeconomic system, and the second is within the *micro* context of an individual organization.

IN OUR SOCIOECONOMIC SYSTEM

It is estimated that the total cost of marketing for all products is about 50 percent of the final price paid by ultimate consumers. Admittedly, marketing costs are a substantial portion of the total sales value of all products. However, the question of whether marketing costs too much is somewhat academic, because we do not have sufficient information to make comparisons. Even if we had accurate data on marketing costs, we would still have no objective criteria for determining whether these expenses are too high or not high enough. As we noted in Chapter 19, we have not yet developed adequate tools for measuring the return (output) that is derived from a given marketing expenditure (input). To say that marketing costs are too high implies that one or more of the following situations prevail: (1) Marketing institutions are enjoying abnormally high profits; (2) more services are being provided than consumers and business people demand; (3) marketing activities are performed in a grossly inefficient manner; (4) consumption is declining; and (5) total costs (production plus marketing) are increasing. Actually, there is no reasonable evidence that any of these conditions exist.

Total marketing costs have indeed risen substantially over the past 100 years. At the same time, careful studies indicate that these costs have been leveling off for the past three or four decades. Still, it is important that we understand the reasons for this increase in marketing expenses. Certainly it would be a mistake simply to jump to the conclusion that the cost increase indicates growing inefficiencies in marketing.

Actually, the rise in marketing expense is traceable to several factors, some of which are external environmental influences. As an example, one reason for the increase in the number of people employed in marketing relative to production is simply that the workweek in marketing has been shortened relative to that in production. In the latter part of the nineteenth century, people employed in wholesaling and retailing worked about 66 hours a week. Those employed in production worked about 52. Today, both groups work 40 hours or less. This shift toward equality has meant that relatively more employees were added in marketing.

Another factor is that consumers are demanding more services and more marketing refinements today than in the past. Consumers today demand credit, delivery, free parking, attractive stores, merchandise return privileges, and other services. A related point is the rise in consumer demand for products emphasizing style. And consumers want merchandise assortments covering considerable breadth and depth. Certainly we could cut marketing costs substantially if consumers would buy on a cash-and-carry basis in stores displaying small quantities of standardized merchandise in boxes.

It is a mistake to study the trend in marketing costs alone. A total-cost approach should be adopted. In many instances, a firm can reduce its *total* costs by increasing its *marketing* costs. To illustrate, an increase in advertising expenditures may so expand a firm's market that the unit *production* cost can be reduced more than the *marketing* costs have increased. Thus, the net effect is to reduce total expenses. In another situation, production economies can result when a company locates near sources of raw materials or low-cost power. Yet *marketing* costs (transportation) may be increased in the new location.

It is understandable that productivity in marketing may never match the level attained in manufacturing or agriculture. Marketing offers far fewer opportunities for mechanization. It is one thing to control the input and output of machines. But it is quite another problem when the activity largely involves dealing with people. Until a better system for satisfying consumer wants is proposed, however, we shall continue with the existing system. Its benefits in both the private and public sectors of our economy are bounteous by almost any measure used. Canadian business must continue to improve the efficiency of marketing and to seek accurate measures of its cost. Most important of all, business must explain to Canadians the essential role marketing plays in our economy.

Today we demand services and conveniences—like "free" parking—but that adds to the cost of marketing.

IN AN INDIVIDUAL ORGANIZATION

Unquestionably, in some individual firms, marketing *does* cost too much. In firms that market inefficiently or that are production-oriented in their management and operations, marketing probably costs too much. The high rate of mortality among retail businesses attests, in part, to their inefficiencies in marketing. A high rate of new-product failure raises the cost of marketing in a firm.

Marketing costs undoubtedly are too high — that is, marketing efficiency is too low — in firms that:

- Do not carry a product mix that customers want.
- Use obsolete distribution channels.
- Are totally cost-oriented (ignore demand) in their pricing.
- Cannot manage a sales force effectively.
- Waste money with ineffective advertising.

Fortunately, in many firms, marketing does *not* cost too much. These firms have strategically planned and implemented the customer-oriented type of marketing program that has been discussed and advocated throughout this book.

CONSUMERISM: A CRITICISM OF OUR MARKETING SYSTEM

"Consumerism" became a significant social movement in the 1960s, although its growth has slowed down considerably during the past five years or so. There is every reason to expect, however, that actions and programs to protect the interests of consumers will continue to be popular well into the future. In this section, we discuss what consumerism is and why it came to be. Then, in the following section, we consider the responses of government and business to this phenomenon.

Meaning and Scope of Consumerism

We may define consumerism as both (1) a consumer protest against the perceived injustices in exchange relationships and (2) efforts to remedy those injustices. Consumers clearly feel, in exchange relationships between buyers and sellers, that the balance of power lies with the sellers. Consumerism is an expression of this opinion, and an attempt to achieve a more equal balance of power between buyers and sellers.

SCOPE OF CONSUMERISM

Consumerism today includes three broad areas of consumer dissatisfaction and remedial efforts. The original, and still the major, focus of consumerism involves discontent with direct buyer-seller exchange relationships between consumers and business firms.

The second area of discontent extends beyond business. Consumerism extends to *all* organizations with which there is an exchange relationship. Therefore, consumerism involves such diverse organizations as hospitals, schools, and government agencies (police departments, tax assessors, street maintenance departments, etc.).

The third area of consumerism involves the *indirect* impact that an exchange relationship between two social units (a person, a business, etc.) has on a third social unit. Consumer Jones may buy steel from mill A. But in producing the steel for that exchange, the mill pollutes the river used by consumer Smith for fishing and swimming. Smith becomes upset and protests. In other words, an exchange between two people or groups has created a problem for a third person or group.

CONSUMERISM YESTERDAY AND TODAY

Consumerism really is not a new phenomenon. In the early 1900s and again during the Great Depression in the 1930s, there was a "consumer movement." Efforts were made to protect the consumer from harmful products and from false and misleading advertising.

The movement that began in the 1960s, however, is different in three ways from earlier consumer movements. First, the consumerism of the past 20 years has occurred in a setting of higher incomes and largely fills subsistence needs, in contrast to the harsher economic conditions which surrounded earlier movements. Second, the consumer-movement legislation since the 1960s has been intended first and foremost to protect the consumer's interests. Emphasis in earlier legislation was placed on the protection of competition and competitors.

Third, today's consumerism is much more likely to endure, because it has generated an institutional structure to support it. Government agencies have been established to administer the consumer-oriented laws and to protect consumer interests. The social sensitivity of many businesses has increased, and various consumer- and environment-oriented organizations have developed.

Why did consumerism take hold in the 1960s, when the factors of social and economic discontent (pollution, unsafe products, and others) had been with us for some time? It just so happened that a series of issues converged in the mid-1960s to touch off the "social conflagration" that we call consumerism.

BROAD CULTURAL CHANGES

Two broad cultural changes occurred to provide the setting for consumerism. The first was a dramatic shift in the social and economic goals of Canadian consumers as we entered a more advanced stage of cultural and economic development. In the decades preceding the 1960s, our emphasis was on improving our material standard of living. Today, with our materialistic needs more or less satisfied, we are more sensitive to social and environmental needs. The second cultural change underlying consumerism was the active role of young people. Compared with previous generations, today's young people are better educated, more articulate, and more inclined (less afraid) to speak out and take action.

CONSUMER DISCONTENTS AND FRUSTRATIONS

This changing cultural setting converged with a series of highly flammable issues that generated much consumer discontent and frustration. There were economic discontent (inflation), social discontent (unemployment, language issues), and ecological discontent (pollution, diminishing quality of life).

In the business area, discontent was focussed on the marketing system as people perceived that their consumer rights were being violated. Consumers were frustrated and indignant because of unfulfilled promises and expectations. Nobody seemed willing to listen to the consumers' complaints or to do anything about them. "We can't get past the computer to deal with real people."

Parents want products that are safe.

Conditions Leading to Consumerism

Consumers want to know what they are eating.

Consumerism Today

Many people thought that consumerism would decline, and even disappear, once the initial interest and support burned out. On the contrary, however, the fires of consumerism have continued to burn through the 1980s, although in a different form than in the 1960s and 1970s. Instead of marching in the streets, today more people are working within the existing political, legal, and social systems in order to bring about change.

One reason why consumerism will not disappear is that many consumer demands of earlier years are now set in legislation. Also, in spite of the remedial progress of the past 20 years, the major areas of consumer discontent are substantially the same as they were then.

In their research on consumerism, Paul Bloom and Stephen Greyser concluded that consumerism is in the maturity stage of its product life cycle — but, again showing few signs of decline. Originally, the consumerism ''industry'' consisted of a few organizations interested primarily in generating regulatory legislation. This industry has evolved into ''an enormous web of organizations and institutions, each trying to serve the interests of consumers with its own distinctive set of offerings or brands.''[4]

RESPONSES TO THESE CRITICISMS

Significant action-oriented efforts to remedy the conditions leading to consumerism have come from the consumers themselves, from government activities, and from business organizations.

Responses of Consumers and Consumer Organizations

Consumers have reacted in a wide variety of ways to vent their frustrations and to correct what they consider to be injustices. In Canada, they have not tended to demonstrate particularly violent responses to marketing programs with which they do not agree. For the most part, they are now more willing than ever before to complain at the retail level and to take their complaints to manufacturers and senior officials of companies. In extreme circumstances, there have been occasional boycotts against the products of certain companies and against particular retailers. Consumers as a group have become more politically active since the late 1960s, and organized consumer groups now maintain full-time lobbyists in Ottawa and bring considerable influence to bear on politicians when legislation of interest to consumers is introduced.

Consumers are becoming increasingly, and better, organized in their social and economic protests. In Canada, the major consumer organization is the Consumers' Association of Canada. This association had its origins in 1947, and its membership today numbers more than 100,000. The major objectives of the CAC involve representing the consumer viewpoint to governments. In recent years many other organizations such as church groups, labour unions, and student groups have become involved in consumer issues, whereas in previous years their efforts were in quite different directions.

While some consumers have shown themselves to be much more interested today in becoming involved in consumer issues, it is not clear that all consumers have become so interested. Research has shown that consumers who join consumer organizations and who become involved in consumer issues tend to be nonrepresentative of consumers in general. For the most part, the consumer activists come from a higher social stratum, tend to be better educated, have higher incomes, and

Marketing at Work

Consumer Satisfaction: Are They Happier Now?

With the enactment of many pieces of consumer legislation at the federal and provincial levels in recent years, is it possible that the Canadian consumer is now adequately protected? Have Canadians lost interest in the consumer movement? Has business reacted so well that consumers no longer feel that they need the type of protection that was demanded in the 1960s?

In early 1988, the Consumer' Association of Canada (CAC) was suffering from cash flow problems. With an annual budget of $4 million and a staff of 45, the association had to suspend publication of its magazine *The Canadian Consumer* for two months, and it had defaulted on payments to its pension plan. While membership in the organization stood at 130,000, the CAC had lost about 30,000 members in the preceding 18 months. The association is financed primarily through membership fees and it found itself short of cash to meet its obligations. It was looking to the federal government for a grant to allow it to overcome its financial difficulties.

Do Canadian consumers need this type of consumer organization as we move into the 1990s? Why do you suppose membership in the CAC is on the decline? Should the federal government ensure that funds are made available to keep the organization afloat?

---

tend to be more cosmopolitan in their outlook on life.[5] Such results suggest that a large mass of consumers have been considerably slower in adopting a consumerist viewpoint. There can be no denying, however, that consumers in general are far more active than they have ever been before, and the results of this activism are quite obvious in the amount of legislation that has been passed in recent years and in the growing influence of consumer opinion in this country.

Government Responses   Consumerism is not likely to fade away. The main reason for this forecast is that today it is politically popular to support consumers. Politicians may generally have been unresponsive to consumer needs in the years prior to the mid-1960s. Since then, however, consumer-oriented activity at both the federal and provincial levels has been carried on at an unprecedented rate. All the provinces and many cities have created some kind of office for consumer affairs.

LEGISLATION

Since the mid-1960s, federal and provincial legislatures have been passing for the first time laws whose primary purpose is to aid the consumer. In contrast, very often in the past marketing legislation was generally business-oriented, not consumer-oriented. As we have pointed out earlier, often the intent of such legislation was to protect competition or to benefit some segment of business, and any benefit or protection to the consumer occurred in an indirect manner, if it occurred at all. In contrast, recent years have seen the introduction of a large number of pieces of consumer-oriented legislation at both the federal and provincial levels in Canada.

A significant number of these laws are designed to protect the consumer's "right to safety'' — especially in situations where the consumer cannot judge for himself the risk involved in the purchase and use of particular products. In Canada, we have such legislation as the Food and Drugs Act, which regulates and controls the manufacture, distribution, and sale of food, drug, and cosmetic products. A very important piece of legislation, which also protects the consumer's right to safety, is the Hazardous Products Act. This law establishes standards for the manufacture of consumer products designed for household, garden, personal, recreational, or child use. Regulations under the Hazardous Products Act require that dangerous products be packaged as safely as possible and labelled with clear and adequate warnings. This law also makes provision for the removal of dangerous products from the marketplace.

One controversial area of product safety legislation is the paternalistic type of law that is intended to protect the consumer, whether he or she wants that protection. Thus, it is now mandatory to equip automobiles with seat belts, and in most provinces it is illegal to operate an automobile unless the seat belts are fastened. In effect, somebody else is forcing a consumer to accept what the other person feels is in the consumer's best interests — truly a new and broadening approach to consumer legislation.

Another series of laws and government programs supports the consumer's ''right to be informed.'' These measures help in such areas as reducing confusion and deception in packaging and labelling, identifying the ingredients and nutritional content in food products, advising consumers of the length of life of certain packaged food products, providing instructions and assistance in the care of various textile products, and determining the true rate of interest.

At the federal level, government has passed a number of pieces of legislation designed to provide consumers with more information. Possibly the most important of these is the Consumer Packaging and Labelling Act, which regulates the packaging, labelling, sale, and advertising of prepackaged products. The Textile Labelling Act requires manufacturers of textile products to place labels on most articles made from fabrics. These labels must name the fibres, show the amount of each fibre in the product by percentage, and identify the company for whom or by whom the article was made. In addition, federal government programs assist the consumer in providing information on the care of textile products. For example, most textile products sold in Canada today carry care labels, which provide instructions on the washing and ironing of textile products. Similarly, the Canada Standard Sizes program for children's clothing ensures that all children's clothing manufactured in Canada by participating manufacturers is sized in a standard manner so that consumers can feel confident that sizes are standard across manufacturers.

At the provincial level, a number of programs exist that provide information to consumers. For example, all provinces have passed consumer protection legislation, which requires that all consumer lending agencies and retail stores provide consumers with information concerning the true rate of interest that they are paying on borrowed money and on purchases made on credit.

Also at the provincial level there has been considerable interest in recent years in the passage of new consumer-oriented legislation. At the present time all provinces, for example, have on their books a number of laws that offer protection to the consumer. Each province has passed a general Consumer Protection Act, which deals primarily with the granting of credit. All provinces also have legislation that provides for a ''cooling off'' period during which the purchaser of goods or services in a door-to-door sale may cancel the contract, return any merchandise, and obtain a full refund. In addition, most provinces have legislation that provides for the disposal of unsolicited goods and credit cards received through the mail. All provinces also administer legislation that regulates particular industries such as collection agencies, automobile dealerships, and insurance agents.

The consumer is also protected at both the federal and provincial levels in Canada in the area of misleading and dishonest advertising. The federal Competition Act contains a number of provisions dealing with misleading advertising; these have been discussed in Chapter 18. Protection is also offered for certain special interest consumer groups in a number of areas. For example, the Province of Quebec, through its Consumer Protection Act, prohibits advertising that is directed to persons under 13 years of age, except under certain limited circumstances.

A development of the late 1970s in many provinces was the passage of a new form of legislation designed to protect the consumer against certain unfair business practices that had not been covered under legislation existing at that time. This relatively new form of consumer legislation is generally described as ''trade practices legislation'' since it prohibits certain unfair, deceptive, or unconscionable trade practices.[6] Trade-practices or business-practices acts are now on the books in most provinces. The passage of such legislation provides additional protection for Canadian consumers, in that these laws are designed to protect consumers against such illegal practices as advertising that claims that goods are new if in fact they have been reconditioned; representations on the part of service companies that service, parts, replacement, or repairs are needed if in fact this is not so; the sale of products at grossly excessive prices; practices that tend to take advantage of consumers who are unable to protect their own interests because of physical infirmity, ignorance, illiteracy, inability to understand the language of an agreement, or similar factors; and trade practices that tend to subject consumers to undue pressures to enter into the transaction.

These new trade-practices laws have broken new ground in a number of areas. For example, the Alberta legislation provided, for the first time in Canada, for class action suits that may be brought against a supplier on behalf of all wronged consumers. The Alberta law also provides that a court may order corrective advertising by a supplier who has been convicted of an unfair trade practice, and further provides that the court may issue an interim injunction that restrains the company from carrying on certain acts or practices while court action is pending.

GOVERNMENT REGULATORY AGENCIES[7]

One of the most significant responses to the consumer movement on the part of government has been a strengthened and expanded role of regulatory agencies involved in consumer affairs. At the provincial level, Public Utilities Boards hold public hearings and receive briefs from concerned citizens and consumer groups whenever a telephone or hydro company is seeking a rate increase or a change in its services. It has become quite common for organized consumer associations and ratepayer groups to intervene at such hearings as representatives of the consumer interest.

Federally, two major regulatory agencies have emerged as powerful arms of government in recent years. The Canadian Transport Commission (CTC) regulates all aspects of interprovincial travel and companies that operate nationally, such as Canadian National and the major airlines. Applications for route changes and fare increases must be filed with the CTC, and opportunities are presented at public hearings for consumer groups to make representations. Similarly, the Canadian Radio-television and Telecommunications Commission (CRTC) regulates the broadcasting industry in this country. This regulatory body has become very much involved in marketing-related areas in recent years. It is responsible for awarding broadcasting licenses to AM and FM radio stations, television stations, and cable television operators. The CRTC also regulates these broadcasters in terms of the content of the programming they use and also administers numerous codes of advertising standards in its role as the agency responsible for regulating broadcast advertising.

Also, at the federal level, many government departments play important regulatory roles that have a major impact on the way in which marketers do business. From the point of view of a marketer of consumer products, the two most important would likely be the Department of Consumer and Corporate Affairs and Health and Welfare Canada. Various branches of these departments administer federal regulations and legislation such as the Competition Act, the Hazardous Products Act, the Consumer Packaging and Labelling Act, and the Food and Drugs Act.

Finally, in all provinces and at the federal level in Canada there exist marketing boards that, to varying degrees, control the production, distribution, and pricing of products. These marketing boards, such as the Ontario Milk Marketing Board, the British Columbia Fruit Board, and the Canadian Egg Marketing Agency, wield considerable power over the marketing of the products that fall under their responsibility. Most of these boards are involved in the distribution of agricultural products and were established to represent the interests of producers. However, through their efforts to promote marketing efficiency, marketing boards generally attempt to represent the best long-term interests of consumers.[8]

EFFECTIVENESS OF GOVERNMENT ACTION

How effective have government efforts been in improving the consumer's position? In many cases, government has stepped in during the past 20 years to enact consumer protection legislation when the pace at which business was moving was deemed to be too slow. The nature of the demands being placed upon government are different today than they were in the 1960s when Canada was the first western country to establish a ministry for consumer affairs at the federal level. Now, consumers may be clamouring for government to *deregulate* in certain instances, where some feel that marketing boards or other government programs interfere with the free market economy, possibly contributing to higher prices and less choice at the retail level.

Since the late 1970s, the cry for more government regulation and consumer protection has been subsiding. Consumers, economists, and even some politicians are questioning the value of certain health, safety, and other regulations. Soaring costs are being imposed on business, and the regulations of the many federal and provincial regulatory agencies are alleged to add to the rate of inflation. Knowledgeable people outside business are joining business leaders in asking whether the benefits are worth the costs. Often the answer appears to be ''no.'' Consequently, for the first time in many years, pressure is being applied to governments at all levels to ''de-regulate.''

Certainly government regulations protecting consumers' interests are not going to be eliminated. But the regulators are likely to be forced to take a more responsible, realistic, cost-benefit approach than often has been the case in the past.

Business Responses

Business apathy, resistance, or token efforts in response to consumerism simply increase the probability of more government regulation. It is as simple as this today: Consumerism is sufficiently entrenched and well organized so that consumer complaints will be answered. The only question is: Answered by whom — business or government? If business cannot or will not do the job, the only alternative is additional government intervention.

''The reaction of many businessmen who have been caught by consumerism, is like good old Charlie Brown's bafflement when his team lost its 43rd consecutive game: 'How can we lose when we're so sincere?' Good intentions don't impress anyone. The public wants good intentions translated into effective action, and they're going to get it, one way or another.''

Source: Elisha Gray II, chairman of Whirlpool Corporation, as quoted in *Newsweek*, July 26, 1971, p. 44.

The response to consumerism on the part of business often tended to be superficial, negative, unplanned, and uncoordinated, even among some larger companies. This was especially the case during the early days of the consumer movement, when many businesses seemed to regard consumer activism as a passing fad, a problem that would eventually pass from the scene. Such, of course, has not been the case. On the contrary, many of the demands of the consumer movement have been acted upon and enshrined in law. For the most part, business people no longer ignore its importance. Most now realize that the road to success in business lies in producing satisfied customers and that satisfaction is more likely to occur when a company is responsive to the concerns of its customers.

File 20-3

Marketing at Work

Social Responsibility Provides Extra Satisfaction for Some Segments

Do consumers prefer to do business with companies that are socially responsible? Will you cross a street to buy from a retailer who makes a donation to the local symphony? Will you choose the brand of a manufacturer who you know employs minority groups, or cleans up pollution, or refuses to do business with South Africa? To what extent do consumers take matters such as these into consideration when making purchasing decisions? There is growing evidence that at least some do.

In the United States, the Council on Economic Priorities has produced a guidebook that rates 130 consumer goods companies on their social policies. The Canadian Network for Ethical Investing has developed criteria for evaluating corporate social responsibility as a guide for investors who wish to buy stock in companies that behave in a socially responsible manner. According to Richard Finlay, chairman of Unimarc Limited, a Toronto management consulting firm that advises clients on social responsibility, the ethical shopping movement has considerable potential. He says, ''If consumers form an alliance with investors, they could become a powerful force for reshaping the corporate responsibility landscape.''

Source: Adapted from Ellen Roseman, ''Shoppers Favor Firms with a Heart,'' *Globe & Mail Report on Business,* February 24, 1987, p. B1.

POSITIVE RESPONSES OF INDIVIDUAL FIRMS

There is a growing executive awareness of the dangers accompanying a negative response to consumer issues. Consequently, we are seeing an increasing number of positive and substantive responses to consumer problems.

Here are just a few examples of how individual firms are responding to consumerism.

- *Better communication with consumers.* Many firms have responded positively to the consumers' ''right to be heard.'' Appliance and insurance companies have established 24-hour ''cool lines.'' This enables customers to call free of charge from anywhere in the country to register a complaint, ask about service, or get product-usage information. Other firms have speeded up and otherwise improved their responses to consumers' written inquiries or complaints.
- *More and better information for consumers.* Point-of-sale information has been improved by a number of firms. Manufacturers are publishing instructional booklets on the use and care of their products. In many instances, labelling is more informative now than it was in the past. Many supermarkets have instituted unit pricing.
- *Product improvements.* Companies have introduced many product-safety changes and pollution-reduction measures. Warranties have been simplified and strengthened. Nutritional elements have been added to some foods. In response to increased diet consciousness, food manufacturers have introduced low-salt and sugar-free products.
- *More carefully prepared advertising.* Many advertisers are extremely cautious in approving agency-prepared ads, in sharp contrast to past practices. Advertisers are involving their legal departments in the approval process. They are sensitive to the fact that the CRTC may reject a commercial or the Advertising Standards Council may find that the advertisement violates some particular code of advertising standards. The advertising industry and the media are doing a much more effective self-regulation job than ever before, especially through the Advertising Advisory Board and its Advertising Standards Councils.[9]

ORGANIZING FOR EFFECTIVE RESPONSE

Many firms have made organizational changes to implement their response programs. Most of these moves have been directed toward establishing an ''ombudsman'' position — sometimes a high-level executive and sometimes a separate department of consumer affairs. The responsibilities of this position or department typically are (1) to serve as a listening post for consumer inquiries and complaints, and to see that they are answered; (2) to represent the consumers' interests when policies and programs are being formulated; and (3) to ensure that the firm maintains the necessary degree of societal orientation in its planning.

The ombudsman position or department must be an independent unit, preferably reporting directly to the chief executive. Placing the consumer affairs group in the marketing department is ordinarily a mistake. When profit or competitive crises arise, marketing executives may not place the consumer's interest foremost in their decision making.

Experience so far shows that consumers' reactions to consumer affairs representatives are mixed. Some programs get high ratings, and others are looked upon simply as "paper consumerism" and "corporate hypocrisy."

TRADE ASSOCIATION RESPONSES

Many trade associations have responded to consumerism by setting industry standards, stimulating consumer education, and promoting research among the association members. Of course, trade associations have not been neglecting their time-honoured activity as parliamentary lobbyists. In that role they are viewed (1) by business people as seekers of moderation in government antibusiness legislation, but (2) by consumer advocates as negative defence mechanisms striving to defang consumer-oriented legislation.

LIMITATIONS TO BUSINESS SELF-REGULATION

Generally speaking, the efforts at self-regulation by business have met with some success, although possibly less so in the eyes of consumer activists. Many of the self-regulatory steps taken by business have been in response to threats of government legislation being imposed.

If an industry depends upon the *voluntary* compliance of its members toward meeting industry standards, the results are likely to be ineffective. For self-regulation to have any real chance of success, an industry must be able to *force* its members to comply with the industry standards. The problem is, however, that any enforcement measure strong enough to be effective (a boycott against an offender, for example), may be considered a violation of the restrictive trade practices provisions of the Competition Act. One reasonable solution to this problem might involve some form of joint business-government cooperation in the formulation of regulations. For example, the Canadian Code of Advertising Standards was formulated following consumer-government-industry consultation and is administered by the Advertising Standards Council. Similarly, this council administers the Broadcast Code for Advertising to Children on behalf of the Canadian Association of Broadcasters. These and other codes of advertising standards apparently have the support of the federal government, since the government has not yet moved to impose legal regulations in those areas covered by the codes.

Two additional situations limit the effectiveness of self-regulation. The first is that often it is difficult to get a consensus among industry members regarding an acceptable set of product or promotion standards. The net result is that the industry settles for the least common denominator as the level for its standards. A second limitation is that executives often fail to see anything wrong with various business practices in their industry — practices that are highly criticized by outside observers.

Effective self-regulation by business can serve to balance consumer advocates and governmental action in setting and enforcing industry standards. For business to be effective in this respect, however, it must generate much more confidence among consumers than it does now.

BUSINESS DISCONTENT WITH CONSUMER FRAUD

Discontent is not a one-way street. In growing measure, what might be called a ''reverse consumerism'' is developing. That is, business people are increasingly concerned and vocal about consumer-initiated fraud against business. Shoplifting, fraudulent redemption of coupons, fraudulent cashing of cheques, and other consumer abuses, especially against retailers, are costing businesses billions of dollars each year.[10]

A SOCIETAL ORIENTATION IN MARKETING

Out of consumerism and our changing consumer goals has emerged a new approach to marketing — a societal orientation. (This point was discussed briefly in Chapter 1.) This new approach — societal marketing — is both a broadening and a logical extension of the managerial systems approach to marketing.

Societal Marketing and Managerial Marketing

Societal marketing is a broadening of, but not a replacement for, managerial marketing. In societal marketing, we still must develop a marketing program to plan, price, promote, and distribute products and services to satisfy consumers' wants. But we must also consider the societal consequences of this marketing program. In managerial marketing, for example, we are concerned with marketing automobiles to people. In societal marketing, in addition, we worry about the societal aspects of auto production and use — air pollution and traffic congestion.[11]

Conflicts in Consumer Goals

We want the convenience of disposable packaging, but we also want no litter.

The consumers' shift to socially oriented goals is not proving to be easy to implement. As consumers, we have not abandoned our desire for things — but we have complicated our wants with a social concern. Here is the difference, possibly oversimplified, between pre-1970s goals and today's goals. Then, we wanted big cars that would go fast. We paid little attention to air pollution, traffic congestion, or depleting oil resources. Now, we still want autos, but we also want clean air, no traffic jams, clean water, and limited dependence on foreign oil resources. Certainly the former goal — a desire for autos only — was much easier to achieve, because the element of *conflict in goals* was largely absent.

The greater the number of target markets (publics) a company must deal with, the more difficult it becomes to satisfy them all. Often, the goals of the different markets are in conflict. One group may want a plant closed because it pollutes the air and water. But another of the target markets wants it kept open because it provides jobs.

Perhaps a key point to keep in mind is that we are dealing with consumers — human beings — with all their attendant contradictions and self-interests. Thus we cry out for safer autos; but, given the chance, a large percentage of people still do not use their seat belts regardless of provincial legislation. We want more energy-generating facilities, but we won't allow anyone to build a power plant in our town.

Social Responsibilities of Marketing Mangement

A recurring theme in this chapter has been the broadened perspectives in marketing. Continuing in this vein, we now shall focus on the social responsibilities of marketing executives, both in concept and in practice.

WHAT IS SOCIAL RESPONSIBILITY?

Marketing executives have a threefold responsibility — to their firms, to their employees, and to their customers. For their firms, their job is to provide a satisfactory net profit over the long run. For their employees, their responsibility is to provide a good working environment. For their customers, the executive's job is to market want-satisfying goods and services at the lowest reasonable cost.

The substance of social responsibility is much broader, however. It emphasizes the effect of executive actions on the entire social system. Without this broader viewpoint, personal and institutional acts tend to be separated. Marketing executives can lead model personal lives, but they continue to justify their company's pollution of a river because there is no direct personal involvement. To them, river pollution is a public problem to be solved by governmental action.

The concept of social responsibility, however, requires executives to consider their acts within the framework of the whole social system. And the concept implies that executives are responsible for the effects of their acts anywhere in that system. Executives must realize (1) that business does not exist in isolation in our society and (2) that a healthy business system cannot exist within a sick society.[12]

REASONS FOR CONCERN ABOUT SOCIAL RESPONSIBILITY

Marketing executives should have a high degree of social responsibility simply because it is the morally correct thing to do. While this is simple and attractive in concept, it is far more difficult to put into operation. Let's look at four points that have a more pragmatic flavour — four practical reasons for social responsibility in business.

To reverse declining public confidence in business   The image of business is tarnished — at least in the eyes of many people. To compound the consumerism problem facing business in the 1970s, Canadians were exposed to revelations that business executives (often in large multinational corporations) had participated in political kickback schemes, payoffs to agents in foreign markets, illegal and unethical gifts, and a few other unsavoury practices. Opinion polls showed that the public's confidence in business leadership had declined. Some of these same polls also reported a very low opinion of several other institutions — government, labour unions, education, and the news media, for example.

Now the question is, how do we reverse this decline in public confidence? Business leaders must demonstrate in convincing fashion that they are aware of, and will *really* fulfil, their social responsibility. A cosmetic, lip-service treatment will only worsen an already bad situation. Companies must set high ethical standards and then enforce them. Failure to act in this fashion will lead inevitably to further government intervention. Indeed, most of the government limitations placed on marketing throughout the years have been the result of management's failure to live up to its social responsibilities. Moreover, once some form of government control has been established, it is rarely removed.

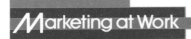

Community Relations and Charity: Part of Marketing

Many companies operate regularly in a socially responsible manner. Some fast-food restaurants have voluntarily stopped using plastic food containers once it was determined that their use was contributing to an erosion of the Earth's ozone layer. Many small Canadian companies are voluntarily cleaning up the environment around their plants and disposing of chemicals and industrial waste in a responsible manner. The Royal Bank of Canada adopted a policy of publishing a detailed list of all the service charges that the bank charges on its accounts and making a commitment that the charges will remain in effect without change for at least a year. Businesses regularly make financial contributions to charities, the arts, universities and colleges, hospital foundations, and organizations such as Junior Achievement.

Can you distinguish between ethical behaviour and acting in a socially responsible manner? Are they part of the same thing? Can a company act ethically without being socially responsible? Why do you suppose some of Canada's largest companies donate millions to charitable and public organizations annually? Do consumers notice? How can you evaluate the success of a ''corporate giving'' program?

Price of economic freedom and flexibility   Marketing executives must act in a socially desirable manner in order to justify the privilege of operating in our relatively free economic system. No worthwhile privilege or freedom comes without a price. Our economic freedoms sometimes have a high price, just as our political freedoms do. Moreover, it is very much in management's self-interest to be concerned with social problems, for these problems affect both the firm and its customers. Also, a concern for the quality of life may very well lead to change, and this change may present opportunities for new business.

The power-responsibility equation   The concept that social power begets social responsibility helps to explain why business executives have a major responsibility to society. Marketing executives do wield a great deal of social power as they influence markets and speak out on matters of economic policy. In business, we see many practical applications of the idea of a reasonable balance between power and responsibility. A management axiom holds that authority and responsibility should be matched. Since responsibility is tied to power, we may reason that the avoidance of social responsibility will lead to an erosion of social power. That is, ''In the long run, those who do not use power in a way that society considers responsible will tend to lose it.''[13]

Marketing department represents company   Procter & Gamble put this point nicely in an annual report that is paraphrased here: ''When a Procter & Gamble sales person walks into a customer's place of business — whether calling on an individual store or keeping an appointment at the headquarters of a large group of stores — that sales person not only represents Procter & Gamble, but in a very real sense, that person is Procter & Gamble.''[14]

Action Programs Regarding Social Problems

For marketers who are genuinely interested in working to solve major social problems, there are opportunities for action both within their firms and in their communities. This entire book has been devoted to developing a consumer-oriented, socially responsible marketing program in the firm. In the community, marketing can play an active role in such areas as:

- Hiring and training disadvantaged people.
- Contributing to education and the arts.
- Reducing food shortages in the Third World.
- Removing discrimination against women, seniors, and minority groups.
- Reducing the marketing problems of low-income consumers.
- Reducing environmental pollution.

In the next section we shall discuss briefly some practical examples of marketing's involvement in the last of these problem areas. But first, note that marketing executives should let the public know about their social-action programs and accomplishments. With all the criticism being heaped on business today, it is not enough just to *do* some good in the social arena. Business executives must start to *tell* people about it instead of hiding their light under a bushel. In the past, many executives went out of their way to maintain a low profile. Now they are urged to be more visible in their community and in the public media. They should explain what they are doing to improve the quality of life, as well as the standard of living.

REDUCING ENVIRONMENTAL POLLUTION

One of the major social problems facing us today is the pollution of our physical environment. Our ecology — the relationship of people to their environment — is being disturbed, and in some cases seriously, by air, water, or noise pollution.

Who are the polluters?   Marketing has contributed to the pollution problem. By stimulating a demand for products and by satisfying consumers' wants, marketing has helped to build mountains of solid wastes. Making and using these products pollutes air and water. Promotional efforts in marketing have generated a ''throwaway'' society and have contributed to a ''no-deposit, no-return'' behavioural pattern.

However, our ecological problems are far more complex than many people realize. Marketing alone did not cause pollution. Production technology is responsible for air and water pollution from steel mills, chemical plants, pulp and paper mills, oil refineries, and utility power plants. Cattle-feed lots and various mining operations contribute their share of wastes. Various government agencies have inadequate control over their own pollution-producing operations — and yet, the critics of business want the government to control pollution. Selfish consumer behaviour adds to the problem. We want clean air, but we won't pay to tune up our auto engines. As a group, we demand highway beautification, but as individuals, we toss trash out the car window and often leave picnic grounds a shambles.

We are dealing with a complex assortment of technological, economic, and even cultural and psychological factors. Furthermore, contrary to the belief held by many critics, pollution is *not* restricted to capitalistic economies and big business. Pollution is a by-product of any industrialized urban society.

Marketing's contribution to pollution reduction   Because of the complexity of ecological problems, effective solutions require cooperation from producers, marketers, and consumers, with the government serving as a coordinating and enforcement agency. The costs of pollution reduction and control are enormously high. Prices will have to be increased to pay for these efforts.

Just as marketing alone did not cause pollution, so too marketing alone cannot cure it. But marketing can and does contribute to the "solution of pollution." To do so is simply a part of our social responsibility. Moreover, there are many profitable business opportunities in pollution abatement. Pollution reduction is *not* limited to shut-down-the mill, don't-drive-your-car, and return-that-bottle type of negative alternatives. Some illustrations of positive efforts by marketers revolve around product planning, channels of distribution, and promotion.

The major polluting industries and many of the lesser culprits provide golden market opportunities for new pollution-control products. A little innovative thinking also helps. As we run out of land for garbage dumps, some cities are generating electricity by using solid wastes for fuel. Marketing is also challenged to develop products that will *not* contribute to solid-waste matter. The disposal of solid wastes is a monumental problem, and one way to cope with it is not to accumulate so much waste in the first place. Thus, biodegradable or recyclable products, and returnable or reusable containers, are desirable.

The key in recycling is to develop a distribution system that will move waste products from consumers back to a producer who can use them in manufacturing new products. Marketing's challenge is to find the incentive needed to stimulate the consumer to start this reverse-channel movement. Marketers can use their skills in persuasion to urge consumers to conserve our natural resources by using them in a less wasteful manner. Promotion also can be used to impress upon consumers the seriousness of our pollution and waste-disposal problems.

BROADENING THE MARKETING CONCEPT

In Chapter 1 we introduced the idea of broadening the marketing concept to make it more relevant and useful in today's social and economic environment. Now we are at the end of this book and you are about to finish your course in marketing. As the final section of this book, we return to what has been our guiding philosophy throughout the entire book — namely, the marketing concept. We especially need to review the marketing concept to determine whether it is compatible with a societally oriented marketing perspective.

The philosophy of the marketing concept holds that a company should (1) develop an integrated marketing program (2) to generate profitable sales volume (3) by satisfying consumers' wants. The fact that consumerism exists today means that the marketing concept has to some extent failed. The customer-orientation theme in the marketing concept implies that business should find out what consumers want, and then try to satisfy those wants profitably. Consequently, carried to their original logical extremes, consumerism and the marketing concept are mutually exclusive; if one exists, the other does not. Yet most business people probably would claim that they are consumer-oriented. They look on in wounded surprise at the wave of consumer discontent engulfing them.

Okay, then, what went wrong? Is it simply that the marketing concept has outlived its usefulness and is not compatible with today's societal orientation in marketing? In our opinion, there is nothing wrong with the marketing concept that a broader interpretation won't cure. It is as viable as it ever was. It is quite compatible with a societal orientation to marketing and with a marketing executive's social responsibility.

However, three things did occur that have hurt the credibility of the marketing concept. The first was that too many marketing executives, while professing whole-hearted agreement and support of the philosophy, were in actual practice giving it only token implementation. In some cases, these executives were simply too production- or engineering-oriented to fully comprehend the idea of customer orientation. In other cases, short-run crises have forced operating executives to put their self-interest ahead of consumer satisfaction.

The two other factors affecting the implementation of the marketing concept revolve around the narrow interpretation of consumer want-satisfaction. Who is a consumer, and what is meant by want-satisfaction? The answers to both these questions have been too narrow and too short-run-oriented. Most human beings — whether in the role of producer or consumer — tend to be short-run-oriented in most situations. We fail to see the long-run implications of our actions. Thus, I may want certain foods, and be satisfied when marketers cater to these wants. But these foods may be fattening, and thus bad for me, so there is a negative personal effect on me in the long run.

If the goal is defined as consumer want-satisfaction *in the long run*, then the marketing concept is more in line with the societal perspective of marketing. Of course, the problem of goal conflict crops up here again. To sell me fattening foods is contrary to society's view of socially desirable want-satisfaction. But non-fattening food (while socially desirable and healthy for me) is just not what I want. So the marketer of this food loses my business. My short-run wants and long-run interests conflict.

Besides extending the *time* dimension in the marketing concept, we need to extend its *breadth*. To view only the direct buyers of a company's product as being the consumers — a view generally held in the past — is too narrow a dimension. We must broaden our definition of target markets to include other groups affected by the direct buyer-seller exchange. Thus, someone may buy an auto and be satisfied with it. But the negative social effects of pollution and traffic congestion from the auto displease other groups. In the broader context, we have not generated customer satisfaction and thus have not successfully implemented the marketing concept.

In summary, the marketing concept can be compatible with a societal perspective of marketing if we define the marketing concept as follows:

THE BROADENED MARKETING CONCEPT IS:

A philosophy whereby a company strives:
- to develop an integrated marketing program
- that generates long-run profitable sales volume
- by satisfying the long-run wants of:
  - the customers of its products and services
  - the other parts of society affected by the firm's activities.

SUMMARY

In this final chapter, we appraised marketing from a broad, societal perspective, in contrast to the individual-company approach followed in the preceding chapters of this book. When evaluating our marketing system, the key point to recognize is the socioeconomic yardstick we used as the basis for the appraisal. We evaluated marketing on the basis of its ability to satisfy consumers' wants *as consumers themselves define or express those wants*. We reviewed some of the common criticisms of marketing, structuring this review around the four components of the marketing mix. Several aspects of the complex question "Does marketing cost too much?" were discussed.

Then we moved to the topic of consumerism. Consumerism is a protest against perceived business injustices, combined with the efforts to remedy these situations. Actually, consumerism is not limited to business alone. It also includes consumers' relations with government and other public organizations in our society. We have experienced consumer movements in the past, but the current one is significantly different in several respects. Consumerism, as we know it today, stemmed from some broad cultural changes and from consumer discontents and frustrations.

Consumers, individually and in consumer organizations, have responded to perceived injustices. The government, through legislation and the actions of regulatory agencies, also has responded to consumers' cries. Some companies have resisted consumerism, and others have come up with token or apathetic responses. However, there also have been strong positive responses from a significant number of companies and from trade associations. The current consumer movement shows every indication of continuing into the future.

There is an emerging societal orientation in marketing, and a growing social responsibility on the part of marketing management, for some very practical reasons. A societal orientation is needed to build the public's confidence in business and to justify the privilege of operating in our economic system. A socially responsible attitude is needed if business is to retain its social power. Perhaps the overriding reason for operating in a socially responsible manner is that the alternative is further government intervention. This would be unfortunate, because business people are best qualified to solve our social problems.

Finally, in line with this emerging societal orientation in marketing, we broadened our definition of the marketing concept. Our broadened restatement now makes the marketing concept a responsive philosophy that will be compatible with the social and economic environment of the coming decade.

NOTES

[1] The topic of the economic effects of advertising in Canada is dealt with in O.J. Firestone, *The Economic Implications of Advertising*, Methuen Publications, Toronto, 1967.

[2] For a review of the criticisms of advertising, see Jacques C. Bourgeois and James G. Barnes, "Does Advertising Increase Alcohol Consumption?" *Journal of Advertising Research*, August 1979, pp. 19–29; and James G. Barnes and Chris R. Vaughan, "Taxation of Advertising: The Newfoundland Experience," in *Market Place Canada: Some Controversial Dimensions*, Stanley J. Shapiro and Louise Heslop (eds.), McGraw-Hill Ryerson Limited, Toronto, 1981.

3 Jules Backman, *Advertising and Competition*, New York University Press, 1967.

4 Paul N. Bloom and Stephen A. Greyser, *Exploring the Future of Consumerism*, Marketing Science Institute, Cambridge, Mass., report no. 81–102, p. 7. For the essence of this report, see the authors' article, "The Maturing of Consumerism," *Harvard Business Review*, November-December 1981, pp. 130–139.

For an excellent group of papers dealing with current issues in consumerism and future prospects for the consumer movement, its organizations, and the social environment of marketing, see Paul N. Bloom (ed.), *Consumerism and Beyond: Research Perspectives on the Future Social Environment*, Marketing Science Institute, Cambridge, Mass., report no. 82–102, 1982.

For a discussion of the extent to which consumers are knowledgeable concerning their rights, see John Liefeld, Louise Heslop, and Ann Hammond, "Consumer Knowledge of Their Marketplace Rights," *Proceedings* of the Marketing Division, Administrative Sciences Association of Canada, vol. 3, part 3, 1982, pp. 117–126.

5 Jacques C. Bourgeois and James G. Barnes, "Viability and Profile of the Consumerist Segment," *Journal of Consumer Research*, March 1979. For a comprehensive study of the consumer movement in the United States, see *Consumerism at the Crossroads*, Sentry Insurance Company, in collaboration with the Marketing Science Institute, Cambridge, Mass., 1977.

6 Jacob S. Ziegel, "The New Trade Practices Legislation," *Canadian Consumer*, February 1975, pp. 18–20.

7 For an insight into the regulatory process in Canada, see Sylvia Ostry, "Government Intervention in Democratic Economies: A Comparison of Canada and the United States," in *Conference on Canadian–U.S. Economic Relations*, Institute for Research in Public Policy, Montreal, 1978, pp. 1–12; W.T. Stanbury (ed.), *Government Regulation: Scope, Growth, Process*, Institute for Research in Public Policy, Montreal, 1980; and T. Gregory Kane, *Consumers and the Regulators*, Institute for Research in Public Policy, Montreal, 1980.

8 Bank of Nova Scotia, "Marketing Boards in Canada," in James G. Barnes and Montrose S. Sommers (eds.), *Current Topics in Canadian Marketing*, McGraw-Hill Ryerson Limited, Toronto, 1978, pp. 216–224; and R.M. A. Loyns, "Marketing Boards: The Irrelevance and Irreverence of Economic Analysis," in Donald N. Thompson et al. (eds.), *Macromarketing: A Canadian Perspective*, American Marketing Association, Chicago, 1980, pp. 196–224.

9 Robert E. Oliver, "Ethics in Advertising — A Shared Responsibility," in *Advertising Self-Regulation: Who Benefits Most, the Advertiser or the Consumer?* Thirtieth World Congress of the International Advertising Association, Chicago, May 29, 1986.

10 See Robert E. Wilkes, "Fraudulent Behavior by Consumers," *Journal of Marketing*, October 1978, pp. 67—75; this article reports on consumer attitudes and rationale involving 15 fraud situations and the extent of consumer participation in these situations.

11 For a very thoughtful, but also very provocative, notion that societal marketing is an erroneous and counterproductive idea — that "for marketers to attempt to serve the best interests of society is not only undemocratic but dangerous as well" — see John F. Gaski, "Dangerous Territory: The Societal Marketing Concept Revisited," *Business Horizons*, July-August 1985, pp. 42–47.

12 This and the preceding paragraph adapted from Keith Davis, "Understanding the Social Responsibility Puzzle," *Business Horizons*, Winter 1967, p. 46; see also Donald P. Robin and R. Eric Reidenbach, "Social Responsibility, Ethics, and Marketing Strategy: Closing the Gap Between Concept and Application," *Journal of Marketing*, vol. 51, no. 1, January 1987, pp. 44–58.

[13] Keith Davis and William C. Frederick, *Business and Society*, 5th ed., McGraw-Hill Book Company, New York, 1984, p. 34.

[14] For an empirical survey that (1) identifies the nature and extent of ethical problems confronting marketing managers and (2) examines the effectiveness of top management in reducing these ethical problems, see Lawrence B. Chonko and Shelby D. Hunt, "Ethics and Marketing Management: An Empirical Examination," *Journal of Business Research*, August 1985, pp. 339–359.

KEY TERMS AND CONCEPTS

Basis for evaluating our marketing system 560
Criticisms of marketing 561
Consumerism 566
Scope of consumerism 566
Causes of consumerism 567
Consumer affairs department in a firm 574

Self-regulation by business 575
Societal marketing 576
Social responsibility of marketing management 577
The broadened marketing concept 580

QUESTIONS AND PROBLEMS

1. Some people feel that too much power is concentrated in big business in Canada and that large firms should be broken up. Yet these same people will drive a General Motors car, buy groceries at a large chain supermarket, buy appliances made by an industry giant, wash with a brand of Procter & Gamble soap, and brush their teeth with the leading brand of toothpaste. How do you reconcile the behaviour of these people with their opinion concerning big business?

2. "Middlemen make unfairly high profits." Do you agree?

3. Some people believe that there are too many fast-food outlets in their communities. Suggest a method for reducing the number of these retailers. How many should be eliminated in your city or town?

4. Evaluate the following criticisms of advertising:
   a. It creates a false sense of values.
   b. It costs too much.
   c. It is in bad taste.
   d. It is false, misleading, and deceptive.
   e. It tends to create monopolies.

5. What proposals do you have for regulating advertising?

6. What specific recommendations do you have for reducing the costs of marketing?

7. What information do you think should be included in advertisements for each of the following products or services?
   a. Snack foods.   c. Nursing homes.
   b. Jogging shoes.   d. Credit cards.

8. What suggestions do you have for an appliance manufacturing company that wants to improve the service of its products? An automobile manufacturing company?

9. What is the social and economic justification for "paternalistic" laws — like auto seat-belt regulations — that require us to do something because the government says it is in our best interest?

10. What proposals do you have for resolving some of the consumer goal-conflict situations discussed in this chapter?

11. You are vice president of marketing in a company heavily involved in outdoor advertising. Your company owns billboards and handles the outdoor advertising for many manufacturers. Currently, in your provincial legislature there is a bill pending that would eliminate all outdoor advertising on all major highways in your province. Several key members of the committee considering the bill have received major campaign contributions from your company over the years. Should you tell them that your firm will cut off further financial support if they approve the bill? Assume they do approve the bill. Then what position should your company take at the next election when these legislators seek your campaign contributions?

CASE 7.1

BEAM OF CANADA INC. Development of a Strategy for Creating a New Market

Beam of Canada is a manufacturer of built-in home vacuum systems, with head-quarters in Oakville, Ontario. The company was established by Gill and Paul Muser in Regina, Saskatchewan, in 1976, when the Musers began to retail built-in central vacuum systems that they imported from a manufacturer in the United States.

In 1979, the Musers decided to move east to the much larger market of southern Ontario. At that time, the company consisted of the Musers and one installer. The company operated out of a rented 1500 square foot warehouse in a small industrial mall in Mississauga. By the end of that first year, the company had achieved sales levels of more than $400,000.

In the late 1970s, the Canadian vacuum cleaner market was dominated by a number of well-established multinational manufacturers of conventional vacuum cleaners, including Electrolux, Hoover, Filter Queen, and Eureka. The few manufacturers of central, built-in vacuum systems were also well established and had positioned their products as luxury items at the high end of the price scale. As the market for central vacuum systems expanded through the mid to late 1980s, the large manufacturers of conventional vacuum cleaners also turned to the manufacture of central systems. In addition, by 1987 a total of 28 small regional manufacturers of central vacuum systems were operating in Canada.

Conventional, electric vacuum cleaners had changed very little since they were first developed in the early 1900s. They were primarily of two types: canisters and uprights, both of which consisted of an electric motor, connecting hoses or pipes, and various floor and carpet tools used to clean different surfaces.

Paul Muser referred to these conventional vacuums as ''lug-arounds.'' The products that Beam of Canada was marketing were built-in vacuum systems that consisted of a centralized electric motor and collection pail that were connected to a series of suction pipes running within or behind the walls of a house. At convenient locations throughout the house, inlet valves were placed that allowed the homeowner to connect a flexible hose to permit the cleaning of the particular level or area. The average home normally required no more than three inlet valves — one for every 1000 to 1500 square feet of living area. In other words, the centralized system eliminated the heavy vacuum cleaner which had to be pulled or pushed from room to room, and replaced it with conveniently located wall outlets into which a vacuum hose was plugged.

MARKET ANALYSIS

The Musers determined that an opportunity existed for a small creative, aggressive company to take advantage of the current state of the market. After researching the competitive and market environment, the Musers developed a marketing strategy

This case was prepared by James G. Barnes and is intended to stimulate discussion of an actual management problem, and not to illustrate either effective or ineffective handling of that problem. The author wishes to acknowledge the support provided by Beam of Canada, Inc., and particularly by Gill Muser, President, Paul Muser, Executive Vice President, and Darcy Spencer, Vice President of Sales Promotion and Advertising.

for Beam, based on five distinct opportunities that they identified in the Canadian vacuum cleaner market.

First, the Musers felt they could take advantage of the fact that consumers had to contend with heavy, noisy equipment that had to be dragged throughout the house, up and down stairs. They were sure that consumers were ready for a more modern and more affordable home cleaning method.

Second, basic research that Paul Muser conducted on the Canadian market confirmed that a startling number of these old-technology vacuum cleaners were being sold at retail outlets and door-to-door for prices as high as $750 or more.

Third, the Musers observed that the large multinational companies that manufactured conventional vacuum cleaners had grown complacent and inflexible. They had introduced very few innovations in recent years and the Musers felt that, with their heavy investment in relatively old technology, they would be slow to react to a small Canadian company aggressively marketing a new technology at a reasonable price.

Fourth, in 1979 central vacuum systems were positioned in the Canadian market as luxury items, selling for an average price of $1200.

Finally, practically all of the built-in vacuum systems then being sold in Canada were being installed in homes under construction, prior to the erection of walls. Neither the equipment, nor the expertise, nor the techniques existed in 1979 to install central vacuum systems in homes already built. Do-it-yourself installation was unheard of. The Musers considered the eight million homes in Canada to be a vast potential market for the company that could develop the products and techniques that would be required for a do-it-yourself central vacuum market.

THE MARKETING PROGRAM

Armed with their analysis of the competitive market for vacuum cleaners, the Musers set out to develop a central vacuum system that would allow Beam to take advantage of the market opportunities they had identified. They hired a retired marketing executive, Stu Smith, from Westinghouse Canada to serve as a consultant to assist them in addressing these opportunities and in achieving their corporate objectives for market development and growth. Together, they developed a strategy to distance Beam from the existing image of the vacuum cleaner industry. The Musers decided to position the Beam central vacuum as a major appliance, not as a vacuum cleaner.

By 1982, sales had increased to more than $2 million annually, and constant product improvements were being made. The company implemented a program of competitive product analysis. Paul Muser observed, ''You have to know the competitors' products better than they know them themselves.'' Beam kept more than 100 competitive machines in stock for comparative purposes and invested heavily in research and development. The result was the modification of existing central vacuum technology and the development of some unique features for the Beam system, features such as a clog-free ducting system for which patent protection was obtained.

Further market analysis in 1982 led to the formulation of the company's first five-year marketing plan, the objective of which was to have Beam selling one central vacuum system for every 200 homes in Canada by the end of 1987 — a target of 42,000 units in 1987. To implement this plan, the company planned to establish a system of national distribution through regional distributors, franchised dealers, company-owned stores, and private branding programs. The company

would rely heavily on intensive advertising directed at builders and architects, as well as homeowners, local promotions, trade shows, and a large co-op advertising program. The main thrust of the competitive effort would be directed at conventional vacuum cleaners in the early years of the plan, with added emphasis in 1986 and 1987 on competitive claims against other central vacuum systems.

The Beam marketing group anticipated as early as 1982 that the market would become increasingly competitive as the initial five-year plan was being implemented. New manufacturers of central vacuum systems could be expected to enter the market and the large manufacturers of conventional vacuum cleaners could still rely on their large network of established dealers, thereby impeding Beam's goal of obtaining national distribution. The bright side to the increasing competition, in the minds of Gill and Paul Muser, was that Canadian consumers would hear more about central vacuum systems, thereby expanding the market.

The key to Beam's success throughout the 1980s was the development of an efficient built-in vacuum system that could be installed by a homeowner in his or her existing home. This new technology greatly expanded the central vacuum market and enabled Beam to target its promotional program at owners of existing homes, as well as at builders and architects who would be interested in installing central vacuum systems in homes under construction. A further element in the attractiveness of the Beam system was its price — a popular $399.

The built-in kit came complete with fittings and clear instructions which allowed for easy do-it-yourself installation. Beam also offered a one-year money-back guarantee on all built-in systems, even those which were self-installed. The entire Beam ducting system carried a lifetime guarantee, even against clogging, and each customer was called three months after installation to determine whether any problems were being experienced.

Beam central vacuum systems were distributed through a network of private and company-owned regional distributors and retail stores across Canada. Beam also established a private label manufacturing program, producing private label central vacuum systems for major retailers including Eaton's, Simpsons, and The Bay.

The company's products are promoted through direct and dealer-sponsored advertising in newspapers and on television. Promotion is also achieved through major consumer home shows and demonstrations in shopping malls. A national co-op advertising program was added in 1985, and television was added to the media mix in 1986. By 1987, the company was spending $3 million on advertising annually. All advertising materials are tested on a single market before being released for regional or national use. All print advertisements are coded for telephone response, so that store managers and the marketing group can tell immediately which advertisements and which appeals are most successful in generating enquiries. Many of the company's advertisements present the results of its exhaustive testing program and compare the suction and air power of Beam vacuum systems against competitors' products.

THE RESULTS

By 1987, all of Beam's corporate objectives that had been set in 1982 had been met or exceeded. Approximately 300,000 Beam vacuum systems had been installed in Canadian homes. The company held a larger share of the total built-in vacuum market in Canada than its four largest competitors combined, and was exporting its products to approximately 20 countries. They were spending more than $500,000 annually on research and development. Beam employed more than 150 employees and distributed its products through more than 1000 outlets across Canada. The Musers had recently overseen the expansion of their company's facilities to include a 64,000 square foot manufacturing and sales complex in Oakville, strategically located on a major highway between Toronto and Hamilton.

Gill and Paul Muser were pleased with the progress that their company had made in less than ten years since they had moved to Oakville. Throughout that period, the Musers had insisted on a "cash only" policy on sales as part of their normal trading terms. As a result, even in 1987, all Beam customers bought their vacuum systems on a "cash with order" basis. The company was free of debt and the Musers had never had to approach a bank or other financial organization for external financing or capital. The expansion to Beam's facilities in Oakville had been financed entirely through profits. In 1987, the company was awarded the Gold Medal in the Marketing Division of the Canada Awards for Business Excellence.

QUESTIONS

1. Evaluate the approach that Gill and Paul Muser took to the development of the built-in vacuum cleaner market in Canada.
2. As the market for built-in vacuum cleaner systems begins to mature, what changes would you expect to take place in that market over the coming years?
3. As the first five-year marketing plan of Beam of Canada, Inc., comes to an end, how would you advise the Musers on the development of the company's second five-year plan?
4. What information would you need to have in order to be able to prepare the plan?

CASE 7.2

It had been three weeks since the Vancouver Symphony Orchestra suspended its season on Tuesday, January 27, 1988 (see Case 1-2, p. 68). At the time, the symphony organization was nearly $1.7 million in debt. Officials had made their announcement just as 84 musicians tuned up in the rehearsal hall prior to a concert. The audience had been dumbfounded. Michael Adam, who had attended that evening's performance, had known that the VSO was in trouble but the announcement had shocked him as well. He knew that as vice president of marketing for Pan Pacific Forest Products, he would have to deal with some of the fallout of the suspension in the days that followed.

His first task had been to provide some long overdue professional marketing advice to Jesse Saunders, Pan Pacific's legal counsel and member of the VSO board of directors. Michael had provided Jesse with a detailed analysis format of what he believed the culture, leisure, and entertainment market could look like, if the format was used to guide the collection and organization of information. He also had extensive discussions with Jesse concerning what the marketing concept could mean for a symphony. Initially he believed Jesse was not too receptive so he was quite surprised to see him moving quickly and decisively. As a result of one of Jesse's decisions, he had just taken part in the recruiting of the company's first Director for Public and Community Affairs, Annie Lee. He expected that she would soon approach him with formal proposals about what the company role and his department's role could be in the VSO situation. Since he had already expressed his ideas to Jesse, he was interested in hearing what Annie would come up with and whether her thinking would be consistent with his. Regardless of what he thought, they would both have to deal with Jesse Saunders as company patron of the VSO when it came to their respective responsibilities.

While Michael was wondering when the VSO affair would be behind him, Annie began pulling together materials on Canadian corporate support for the arts. She had to continue with the VSO situation as well as the development of the Department of Public Affairs and Community Relations. Since her arrival in Vancouver eight months ago, she had been looking for the right opportunity and now the VSO's misfortune had become her good luck. She had left a fairly senior contract job with the Council for Business and the Arts in Canada to come to Vancouver to visit her mother's family and look for new career opportunities. She had always wanted to work in Vancouver but the economy was slow and she had almost given up when the Pan Pacific opening came up.

Now that she was in the job, she was wondering whether a forest products company was the right place to be. She felt secure about her background in community and public affairs as well as in dealing with the arts as a result of her work in Montreal and Toronto. But this was different. Before her arrival, community relations were handled at the local operations and plant level, and public affairs was looked after by the president and a few interested members of Pan Pacific's

This case was prepared by Montrose S. Sommers and was drawn from: Liam Lacey, "Courting Culture," Matthew Fraser, "Francophone Companies Lag Behind in Donations," and Stephen Godfrey, "West's Resource Firms Among the Stingier Givers," *Globe and Mail*, April 2, 1988.

board. Public affairs and community relations in this industry had to deal with every issue imaginable, ranging from the environmental hazards and effects of logging, transporting and milling lumber through to the chemical and other treatment of various forest products. Then there were the problems of community disruption and the support for community projects. The problems in the various locations in B.C. and Alberta where the company operated were quite different from those in the rest of the country where it marketed its products. To add to her growing unease, she had quickly discovered that the people she had to deal with — Michael Adam excepted — were a pretty rough and ready lot when it came to business matters and, most particularly, her area of responsibility.

Annie had a fair amount of information on Canadian corporate support for the arts, so she began reviewing her materials in order to be able to propose a policy framework as well as an approach to dealing with the VSO situation. In general, there seemed to be two strategies that companies used. One was the well established donations approach. It had been used for a long time and was simply the provision of funds for good works and good deeds with the view to being perceived as a good corporate citizen in general. From time to time Pan Pacific had used this approach. Annie knew that it was rather a common one with large Canadian firms. What it amounted to was sitting back and waiting for an arts or performing or social action group to approach the company and make a presentation for a donation or some other form of support. Typically, no measures of success or effectiveness beyond the word of the person or group making the request were involved. Jesse Saunders seemed to be an ardent practitioner of this approach. He had been instrumental in seeing to it that Pan Pacific consistently supported the VSO almost to the exclusion of anything else. However, Annie felt that he was reasonably open minded. After all, he had been instrumental in her being hired so quickly.

The donations approach, while still popular, had seemed to be a problem lately. When firms did not do well financially, donations dropped drastically. The hard times many companies faced in the early 1980s had caused sponsorship or "event" marketing to grow in popularity in place of donations. Whereas the donations approach could be seen as altruistic and the epitome of good corporate citizenship (some said paternalism), the sponsorship approach was viewed as the fourth arm of marketing after advertising, public relations and public affairs (some said too commercial). It was clearly seen as serving specific corporate and marketing objectives. Sponsoring an event could mean getting the company name on the program and providing tickets for employees, clients, or special public groups. It could mean being recognized by those who attend, work with the event, or believe it to be useful and important. Sometimes it can mean the only way of attracting the attention of a select group whose opinions may be important. As far as Annie could find out, Pan Pacific had never taken this approach.

Annie knew of an oil company that sponsored a playwriters' workshop in Calgary, a steel company that underwrote certain local orchestra performances, a pipeline that sponsored a national tour of a string quartet. She had quickly glanced at the entertainment section of the Toronto and Montreal Saturday newspapers and saw Olivetti sponsoring the Canadian Opera Company's production of Don Giovanni and Honeywell sponsoring the production of Ariadne. There was also an Opera Hamilton advertisement for Faust listing Texaco, Stelco, Alexanian Carpets, Taylor

Steel and Westinghouse as sponsors of different parts of the total production. She knew that the Royal Bank had developed a corporate sponsorship model to help decide which groups to work with; that Mobil Oil had contracted for a study of all major artistic events in Canada during the next five years complete with details on both their public and company sources of funds and their likelihood of success — all to allow the company to decide what to sponsor.

Now she came to some material that was quite current; she had never seen it before. It reported on the differences in approaches used in various parts of the country as well as across industries. A study conducted by a Montreal group concluded that in Anglophone Canada a mixed model based on the American (patrons) and English (local financing) approaches was used whereas in Quebec, the French and Italian models of majority state funding was the main approach. It did not please Annie to see that the resource sector, which includes forest product firms located primarily in B.C. and Alberta, was the least generous of industries. In fact, apart from Chevron Canada's sponsorship of a children's cultural program, Alberta fared much better than did B.C. with substantial sponsorship provided in Alberta by Nova, Shell, and Petro-Canada.

While Annie was somewhat familiar with the story, the starkness of it caused her to shiver and she continued with some apprehension. Commentators attributed the lack of activity in B.C. to the boom and bust nature of the resource industry and the fact that 70 to 90 percent of wood is exported. This seemed to mean that there was not much incentive for forest product firms to sponsor large urban groups. MacMillan Bloedel, B.C.'s biggest company — a forest products giant with a net income in 1987 of $281 million — had no clear formula and no set goals. Its donations were aimed at the locations of its operations but not necessarily its markets. B.C. Forest Products, another Pan Pacific competitor, was said to have donated not more than $25,000 annually at the best of times.

Annie stopped reading. Was her job possible? Had Jesse Saunders made an error? Should anything be done about the VSO? Were she and Michael ahead of their time at Pan Pacific? What did Jesse really expect from her? Should there be a blend of donations and event sponsorship in Vancouver? At operations sites? In large urban markets removed from production centres? What kinds of events? What kinds of donations? But really, to satisfy what purposes?

QUESTIONS

1. Should Annie recommend to Jesse Saunders that a systematic donations and sponsorship program be embarked upon?
2. If so, what objectives should she state and what policy should she recommend?
3. How should she proceed in dealing with Jesse and Michael?
4. What presentation format and type of content should she use in making her case? Should this be different from what she might do in the future?

MARKETING ARITHMETIC

Marketing involves people — customers, middlemen, and producers. Much of the business activity of these people, however, is quantified in some manner. Consequently, some knowledge of the rudiments of business arithmetic is essential for decision making in many areas of marketing. This appendix is intended as a basic review. It contains discussions of three accounting concepts that are useful in marketing: (1) the operating statement, (2) markups, and (3) analytical ratios. Another useful concept — discounts and terms of sale — was reviewed in Chapter 12 in connection with price policies.

THE OPERATING
STATEMENT

An operating statement — often called a *profit and loss statement* or an *income and expense statement* — is one of the two main financial statements prepared by a company. The other is the balance sheet. An **operating statement** is a summary picture of the firm's income and expenses — its operations — over a period of time. In contrast, a **balance sheet** shows the assets, liabilities, and net worth of a company at a given time, for example, at the close of business on December 31, 1989.

The operating statement shows whether the business earned a net profit or suffered a net loss during the period covered. It is an orderly summary of the income and expense items that resulted in this net profit or loss.

An operating statement can cover any selected period of time. To fulfill income tax requirements, virtually all firms prepare a statement covering operations during the calendar or fiscal year. In addition, it is common for business to prepare monthly, quarterly, or semiannual operating statements.

Table A-1 is an example of an operating statement for a wholesaler or retailer. The main difference between the operating statement of a middleman and that of a manufacturer is in the cost-of-goods-sold section. A manufacturer shows the cost of goods *manufactured*, whereas the middleman's statement shows net *purchases*.

Major Sections

From one point of view, the essence of business is very simple. A company buys or makes a product and then sells it for a higher price. Out of the sales revenue, the seller hopes to cover the cost of the merchandise and the seller's own expenses

TABLE A-1   ALPHA-BETA COMPANY LTD., OPERATING STATEMENT, FOR YEAR
             ENDING DECEMBER 31, 1989

Gross sales			$87,000
Less: Sales returns and allowances		$ 5,500	
Cash discounts allowed		1,500	7,000
Net sales			$80,000
Cost of goods sold:			
Beginning inventory, January 1 (at cost)			18,000
Gross purchases		49,300	
Less: Cash discounts taken on purchases		900	
Net purchases		48,400	
Plus: Freight in		1,600	
Net purchases (at delivered cost)		50,000	
Cost of goods available for sale		68,000	
Less: Ending inventory, December 31 (at cost)		20,000	
Cost of goods sold			48,000
Gross margin			32,000
Expenses:			
Sales-force salaries and commissions		$11,000	
Advertising		2,400	
Office supplies		250	
Taxes (except income tax)		125	
Telephone and telegraph		250	
Delivery expenses		175	
Rent		800	
Heat, light, and power		300	
Depreciation		100	
Insurance		150	
Interest		150	
Bad debts		300	
Administrative salaries		7,500	
Office salaries		3,500	
Miscellaneous expenses		200	
Total expenses			27,200
Net profit			$ 4,800

and have something left over, which is called *net profit*. These relationships form
the skeleton of an operating statement. That is, *sales minus cost of goods sold
equals gross margin*; then *gross margin minus expenses equals net profit*. An
example based on Table A-1 is as follows:

	Sales	$80,000
less	Cost of goods sold	− 48,000
equals	Gross margin	32,000
less	Expenses	− 27,200
equals	Net profit	$ 4,800

SALES

The first line in an operating statement records the gross sales — the total amount sold by the company. From this figure, the company deducts its sales returns and sales allowances. From gross sales, the company also deducts the discounts that are granted to company employees when they purchase merchandise or services.

In virtually every firm at some time during an operating period, customers will want to return or exchange merchandise. In a *sales return*, the customer is refunded the full purchase price in cash or credit. In a *sales allowance*, the customer keeps the merchandise, but is given a reduction from the selling price because of some dissatisfaction. The income from the sale of returned merchandise is included in a company's gross sales, so returns and allowances must be deducted to get net sales.

NET SALES

This is the most important figure in the sales section of the statement. It represents the net amount of sales revenue, out of which the company will pay for the products and all its expenses. The net sales figure is also the one upon which many operating ratios are based. It is called 100 percent (of itself), and the other items are then expressed as a percentage of net sales.

COST OF GOODS SOLD

From net sales, we must deduct the cost of the merchandise that was sold, as we work toward discovering the firm's net profit. In determining the cost of goods sold in a retail or wholesale operation, we start with the value of any merchandise on hand at the beginning of the period. To this we add the net cost of what was purchased during the period. From this total we deduct the value of whatever remains unsold at the end of the period. In Table A-1 the firm started with an inventory worth $18,000, and it purchased goods that cost $50,000. Thus the firm had a total of $68,000 worth of goods available for sale. If all were sold, the cost of goods sold would have been $68,000. At the end of the year, however, there was still $20,000 worth of merchandise on hand. Thus, during the year, the company sold goods that cost $48,000.

In the preceding paragraph, we spoke of merchandise "valued at" a certain figure or "worth" a stated amount. Actually, the problem of inventory valuation is complicated and sometimes controversial. The usual rule of thumb is to value inventories at cost or market, whichever is lower. The actual application of this rule may be difficult. Assume that a store buys six footballs at $2 each and the next week buys six more at $2.50 each. The company places all 12, jumbled, in a basket display for sale. Then one is sold, but there is no marking to indicate whether its cost was $2 or $2.50. Thus the inventory value of the remaining 11 balls may be $25 or $24.50. If we multiply this situation by thousands of purchases and sales, we may begin to see the depth of the problem.

A figure that deserves some comment is the *net cost of delivered purchases*. A company starts with its gross purchases at billed cost. Then it must deduct any purchases that were returned or any purchase allowances received. The company should also deduct any discounts taken for payment of the bill within a specified period of time. Deducting purchase returns and allowances and purchase discounts

TABLE A-2   COST-OF-GOODS-SOLD SECTION OF AN OPERATING STATEMENT FOR A MANUFACTURER

Beginning inventory of finished goods (at cost)		$18,000
Cost of goods manufactured:		
Beginning inventory, goods in process	$24,000	
Plus: Raw materials $20,000		
Direct labour 15,000		
Overhead 13,000	48,000	
Total goods in process	72,000	
Less: Ending inventory, goods in process	22,000	
Cost of goods manufactured		50,000
Cost of goods available for sale		68,000
Less: Ending inventory, finished goods (at cost)		20,000
Cost of goods sold		$48,000

gives the net cost of the purchases. Then freight charges paid by the buyer (called "freight in") are added to net purchases to determine the net cost of *delivered* purchases.

In a manufacturing concern, the cost-of-goods-sold section has a slightly different form. Instead of determining the cost of goods *purchased*, the company determines the cost of goods *manufactured*. (See Table A-2.) Cost of goods manufactured ($50,000) is added to the beginning inventory ($18,000) to ascertain the total goods available for sale ($68,000). Then, after the ending inventory of finished goods has been deducted ($20,000), the result is the cost of goods sold ($48,000).

To find the cost of goods *manufactured*, a company starts with the value of goods partially completed (beginning inventory of goods in process — $24,000). To this beginning inventory figure is added the cost of raw materials, direct labour, and factory overhead expenses incurred during the period ($48,000). The resulting figure is the total goods in process during the period ($72,000). By deducting the value of goods still in process at the end of the period ($22,000), management finds the cost of goods manufactured during that span of time ($50,000).

GROSS MARGIN

Gross margin is determined simply by subtracting cost of goods sold from net sale. Gross margin, sometimes called *gross profit*, is one of the key figures in the entire marketing program. When we say that a certain store has a "margin" of 30 percent, we are referring to the gross margin.

EXPENSES

Operating expenses are deducted from gross margin to determine the net profit. The operating expense section includes marketing, administrative, and possibly some miscellaneous expense items. It does not, of course, include the cost of goods purchased or manufactured, since these costs have already been deducted.

NET PROFIT

Net profit is the difference between gross margin and total expenses. A negative net profit is, of course, a loss.

MARKUPS   Many retailers and wholesalers use markup percentages to determine the selling price of an article. Normally the selling price must exceed the cost of the merchandise by an amount sufficient to cover the operating expenses and still leave the desired profit. The difference between the selling price of an item and its cost is the **markup**, sometimes referred to as the "mark-on."

Typically, markups are expressed in percentages rather than dollars. A markup may be expressed as a percentage of either the cost or the selling price. Therefore, we must first determine which will be the *base* for the markup. That is, when we speak of a 40 percent markup, do we mean 40 percent of the *cost* or of the *selling price*?

To determine the markup percentage when it is based on *cost*, we use the following formula:

$$\text{Markup } \% = \frac{\text{dollar markup}}{\text{cost}}$$

When the markup is based on *selling price*, the formula to use is:

$$\text{Markup } \% = \frac{\text{dollar markup}}{\text{selling price}}$$

It is important that all interested parties understand which base is being used in a given situation. Otherwise, there can be a considerable misunderstanding. To illustrate, suppose Mr. A runs a clothing store and claims he needs a 66⅔ percent markup to make a small net profit. Ms. B, who runs a competitive store, says she needs only a 40 percent markup and that A must be inefficient or a big profiteer. Actually, both merchants are using identical markups, but they are using different bases. Each seller buys hats at $6 apiece and sets the selling price at $10. This is a markup of $4 per hat. Mr. A is expressing his markup as a percentage of cost — hence, the 66⅔ percent figure ($4 ÷ $6 = .67, or 66⅔ percent). Ms. B is basing her markup on the selling price ($4 ÷ $10 = .4, or 40 percent). It would be a mistake for Mr. A to try to get by on B's 40 percent markup, as long as A uses cost as his base. To illustrate, if Mr. A used the 40 percent markup, *but based it on cost*, the markup would be only $2.40. And the selling price would be only $8.40. This $2.40 markup, averaged over the entire hat department, would not enable A to cover his usual expenses and make a profit.

Unless otherwise indicated, markup percentages are always stated as percentage of selling price.

Markup Based on Selling Price   The following diagram should help you understand the various relationships between selling price, cost, and markup. It can be used to compute these figures regardless of whether the markup is stated in percentages or dollars, and whether the percentages are based on selling price or cost:

		Dollars	Percentage
	Selling price		
less	Cost		
equals	Markup		

As an example, suppose a merchant buys an article for $90 and knows the markup based on selling price must be 40 percent. What is the selling price? By filling in the known information in the diagram, we obtain:

		Dollars	Percentage
	Selling price		**100**
less	Cost	90	
equals	Markup		**40**

The percentage representing cost must then be 60 percent. Thus the $90 cost is 60 percent of the selling price. The selling price is then $150. [That is, $90 equals 60 percent of the selling price. Then $90 is divided by .6 (or 60 percent) to get the selling price of $150.]

A common situation facing merchants is to have competition set a ceiling on selling prices. Or possibly the sellers must buy an item to fit into one of their price lines. Then they want to know the maximum amount they can pay for an item and still get their normal markup. For instance, assume that the selling price of an article is set at $60 (by competition or by the $59.95 price line). The retailer's normal markup is 35 percent. What is the most that the retailer should pay for this article? Again, let's fill in what we know in the diagram:

		Dollars	Percentage
	Selling price	**60**	**100**
less	Cost		
equals	Markup		**35**

The dollar markup is $21 (35 percent of $60). So, by a simple subtraction we find that the maximum cost the merchant will want to pay is $39.

Series of Markups

It should be clearly understood that markups are figured on the selling price at *each level of business* in a channel of distribution. A manufacturer applies a markup to determine its selling price. The manufacturer's selling price then becomes the wholesaler's cost. Then the wholesaler must determine its own selling price by applying its usual markup percentage based on its — the wholesaler's — selling price. The same procedure is carried on by the retailer, whose cost is the wholesaler's selling price. The following computations should illustrate this point:

Producer's cost	$ 7	**Producer's markup = $3, or 30%**
Producer's selling price	$10	
Wholesaler's cost	$10	**Wholesaler's markup = $2, or $16⅔%**
Wholesaler's selling price	$12	
Retailer's cost	$12	**Retailer's markup = $8, or 40%**
Retailer's selling price	$20	

Markup Based on Cost

If a firm is used to dealing in markups based on cost — and sometimes this is done among wholesalers — the same diagrammatic approach may be employed that was used above. The only change is that cost will equal 100 percent. Then the selling price will be 100 percent plus the markup based on cost. As an example, assume that a firm bought an article for $70 and wants a 20 percent markup based on cost. The markup in dollars is $14 (20 percent of $70). The selling price is $84 ($70 plus $14):

		Dollars	Percentage
	Selling price	**84**	**120**
less	Cost	**70**	**100**
equals	Markup	**14**	**20**

A marketing executive should understand the relationship between markups on cost and markups on selling price. For instance, if a product costs $6 and sells for $10, there is a $4 markup. This is a 40 percent markup based on selling price, but a 66⅔ percent markup based on cost. The following diagram may be helpful in understanding these relationships and in converting from one base to another.

If selling price = 100%   **If cost = 100%**

$10 = 100% {60% → **Cost = $6.00** ← 100% {
         {40% → **Markup = $4.00** ← 66⅔% { $10 = 166⅔%

The relationships between the two bases are expressed in the following formulas:

$$(1)\ \%\ \text{markup on selling price} = \frac{\%\ \text{markup on cost}}{100\% + \%\ \text{markup on cost}}$$

$$(2)\ \%\ \text{markup on cost} = \frac{\%\ \text{markup on selling price}}{100\% - \%\ \text{markup on selling price}}$$

To illustrate the use of these formulas, let us assume that a retailer has a markup of 25 percent on *cost*. This retailer then wants to know what the corresponding figure is, based on selling price. In formula 1 we get:

$$\frac{25\%}{100\% + 25\%} = \frac{25\%}{125\%} = .2, \text{ or } 20\%$$

A markup of 33⅓ percent based on *selling price* converts to 50 percent based on cost, according to formula 2:

$$\frac{33\frac{1}{3}\%}{100\% - 33\frac{1}{3}\%} = \frac{33\frac{1}{3}\%}{66\frac{2}{3}\%} = .5, \text{ or } 50\%$$

The markup is closely related to the gross margin. Recall that gross margin is equal to net sales minus cost of goods sold. Looking below the gross margin on an operating statement, we find that gross margin equals operating expenses plus net profit. Normally, the initial markup in a company, department, or product line must be set a little higher than the overall gross margin desired for the selling unit. The reason for this is that, ordinarily, some reductions will be incurred before all the articles are sold. For one reason or another, some items will not sell at the original price. They will have to be marked down, that is, reduced in price from the original level. Some pilferage and other shortages also may occur.

ANALYTICAL RATIOS

From a study of the operating statement, management can develop several ratios that are useful in evaluating the results of its marketing program. In most cases, net sales is used as the base (100 percent). In fact, unless it is specifically mentioned to the contrary, all ratios reflecting gross margin, net profit, or any operating expense are stated as a percentage of net sales.

Gross Margin Percentage

This is the ratio of gross margin to net sales. In Table A-1, the gross margin percentage is $32,000 ÷ $80,000, or 40 percent.

Net Profit Percentage

This ratio is computed by dividing net profit by net sales. In Table A-1, the ratio is $4,800 ÷ $80,000, or 6 percent. This percentage may be computed either before or after federal income taxes are deducted, but the result should be labelled to show which it is.

Operating Expense Percentage

When total operating expenses are divided by net sales, the result is the operating expense ratio. In Table A-1, the ratio is $27,200 ÷ $80,000, or 34 percent. In similar fashion, we may determine the expense ratio for any given cost. Thus we note in Table A-1 that the rent expense was 1 percent, advertising was 3 percent, and salesforce salaries and commissions were 13.75 percent.

Rate of Stockturn

Management often measures the efficiency of its marketing operations by means of the **stockturn rate**. This figure represents the number of times the average inventory is "turned over," or sold, during the period under study. The rate is computed on either a cost or a selling-price basis. That is, both the numerator and the denominator of the ratio fraction must be expressed in the same terms, either cost or selling price.

On a *cost* basis, the formula for stockturn rate is as follows:

$$\text{Rate of stockturn} = \frac{\text{cost of goods sold}}{\text{average inventory at cost}}$$

The average inventory is determined by adding the beginning and ending inventories and dividing the result by 2. In Table A-1, the average inventory is ($18,000 + $20,000) ÷ 2 = $19,000. The stockturn rate then is $48,000 ÷ $19,000, or 2.5. Because inventories usually are abnormally low at the first of the year in anticipation of taking physical inventory, this average may not be representative. Consequently, some companies find their average inventory by adding the book inventories at the beginning of each month, and then dividing this sum by 12.

Now let's assume the inventory is recorded on a *selling-price* basis, as is done in most large retail organizations. Then the stockturn rate equals net sales divided by average inventory at selling price. Sometimes the stockturn rate is computed by dividing the number of *units* sold by the average inventory expressed in *units*.

Wholesale and retail trade associations in many types of businesses publish figures showing the average rate of stockturn for their members. A firm with a low rate of stockturn is likely to be spending too much on storage and inventory. Also, the company runs a higher risk of obsolescence or spoilage. If the stockturn rate gets too high, this may indicate that the company maintains too low an average inventory. Often, a firm in this situation is operating on a hand-to-mouth buying system. In addition to incurring high handling and billing costs, the company is liable to be out of stock on some items.

Markdown Percentage

Sometimes retailers are unable to sell articles at the originally stated prices, and they reduce these prices to move the goods. A **markdown** is a reduction from the original selling price. Management frequently finds it very helpful to determine the markdown percentage. Then management analyzes the size and number of markdowns and the reasons for them. Retailers, particularly, make extensive use of markdown analysis.

Markdowns are expressed as a percentage of net sales and *not* as a percentage of the original selling price. To illustrate, assume that a retailer purchased a hat for $6 and marked it up 40 percent to sell for $10. The hat did not sell at that price, so it was marked down to $8. Now the seller may advertise a price cut of 20 percent. Yet, according to our rule, this $2 markdown is 25 percent *of the $8 selling price*.

Markdown percentage is computed by dividing total dollar markdowns by total net sales during a given period of time. Two important points should be noted here. First, the markdown percentage is computed in this fashion, whether the markdown items were sold or are still in the store. Second, the percentage is computed with respect to total net sales, and not only in connection with sales of marked-down articles. As an example, assume that a retailer buys 10 hats at $6 each and prices them to sell at $10. Five hats are sold at $10. The other five are marked down to $8, and three are sold at the lower price. Total sales are $74, and the total markdowns are $10. The retailer has a markdown ratio of $10 ÷ $74, or 13.5 percent.

Markdowns do not appear on the profit and loss statement because they occur *before* an article is sold. The first item on an operating statement is gross sales. That figure reflects the actual selling price, which may be the selling price after a markdown has been taken.

Return on Investment

A commonly used measure of managerial performance and the operating success of a company is its rate of return on investment. We use both the balance sheet and the operating statement as sources of information. The formula for calculating return on investment (ROI) is as follows:

$$\text{ROI} = \frac{\text{net profit}}{\text{sales}} \times \frac{\text{sales}}{\text{investment}}$$

Two questions may quickly come to mind. First, what do we mean by "investment"? Second, why do we need two fractions? It would seem that the "sales" component in each fraction would cancel out, leaving net profit divided by investment as the meaningful ratio.

To answer the first query, consider a firm whose operating statement shows annual sales of $1,000,000 and a net profit of $50,000. At the end of the year, the balance sheet reports:

Assets	$600,000	Liabilities		$200,000
		Capital stock	$300,000	
		Retained earnings	100,000	400,000
	$600,000			$600,000

Now, is the investment $400,000 or $600,000? Certainly the ROI will depend upon which figure we use. The answer depends upon whether we are talking to the stockholders or to the company executives. The stockholders are more interested in the return on what they have invested — in this case, $400,000. The ROI calculation then is:

$$\text{ROI} = \frac{\text{net profit } \$50,000}{\text{sales } \$1,000,000} \times \frac{\text{sales } \$1,000,000}{\text{investment } \$400,000} = 12\tfrac{1}{2}\%$$

Management, on the other hand, is more concerned with the total investment, as represented by the total assets ($600,000). This is the amount that the executives must manage, regardless of whether the assets were acquired by the stockholders' investment, retained earnings, or loans from outside sources. Within this context the ROI computation becomes:

$$\text{ROI} = \frac{\text{net profit } \$50,000}{\text{sales } \$1,000,000} \times \frac{\text{sales } \$1,000,000}{\text{investment } \$600,000} = 8\tfrac{1}{3}\%$$

Regarding the second question, we use two fractions because we are dealing with two separate elements — the rate of profit on sales and the rate of capital turnover. Management really should determine each rate separately and then multiply the two. The rate of profit on sales is influenced by marketing considerations — sales volume, price, product mix, advertising effort. The capital turnover is a financial consideration not directly involved with costs or profits — only sales volume and assets managed.

To illustrate, assume that our company's profits doubled with the same sales volume and investment because management operated an excellent marketing program this year. In effect, we doubled our profit rate with the same capital turnover:

$$\text{ROI} = \underbrace{\frac{\text{net profit } \$100,000}{\text{sales } \$1,000,000}}_{10\%} \times \underbrace{\frac{\text{sales } \$1,000,000}{\text{investment } \$600,000}}_{1.67} = 16\tfrac{2}{3}\%$$
$$= 16\tfrac{2}{3}\%$$

As expected, this 16⅔ percent is twice the ROI calculated above.

Now assume that we earned our original profit of $50,000 but that we did it with an investment reduced to $500,000. We cut the size of our average inventory, and we closed some branch offices. By increasing our capital turnover from 1.67 to 2, we raise the ROI from 8⅓ percent to 10 percent, even though sales volume and profits remain unchanged:

$$\text{ROI} = \underbrace{\frac{\$50,000}{\$1,000,000}}_{5\%} \times \underbrace{\frac{\$1,000,000}{\$500,000}}_{2} = 10\%$$
$$= 10\%$$

Assume now that we increase our sales volume — let us say we double it — but do not increase our profit or investment. That is, the cost-profit squeeze is bringing us "profitless prosperity." The following interesting results occur:

$$ROI = \frac{\$50,000}{\$2,000,000} \times \frac{\$2,000,000}{\$600,000} = 8\frac{1}{3}\%$$

$$2\frac{1}{2}\% \times 3.33 = 8\frac{1}{3}\%$$

The profit rate was cut in half, but this was offset by a doubling of the capital turnover rate, leaving the ROI unchanged.

QUESTIONS AND PROBLEMS

1. Construct an operating statement from the following data, and compute the gross-margin percentage:

Purchases at billed cost	$15,000
Net sales	30,000
Sales returns and allowances	200
Cash discounts given	300
Cash discounts earned	100
Rent	1,500
Salaries	6,000
Opening inventory at cost	10,000
Advertising	600
Other expenses	2,000
Closing inventory at cost	7,500

2. Prepare a retail operating statement from the following data and compute the markdown percentage:

Rent	$ 9,000
Closing inventory at cost	28,000
Sales returns	6,500
Gross margin as percentage of sales	35
Cash discounts allowed	2,000
Salaries	34,000
Markdowns	4,000
Other operating expenses	15,000
Opening inventory at cost	35,000
Gross sales	232,500
Advertising	5,500
Freight in	3,500

3. What percentage markups on cost correspond to the following percentages of markup on selling price?
   a. 20 percent.   c. 50 percent.
   b. 37½ percent.   d. 66⅔ percent.

4. What percentage markups on selling price correspond to the following percentages of markup on cost?

a. 20 percent.

c. 50 percent.

b. 33⅓ percent.

d. 300 percent.

5. A hardware store bought a gross (12 dozen) of hammers, paying $302.40 for the lot. The retailer estimated operating expenses for this product to be 35 percent of sales, and wanted a net profit of 5 percent of sales. The retailer expected no markdowns. What retail selling price should be set for each hammer?

6. Competition in a certain line of sporting goods pretty well limits the selling price on a certain item to $25. If the store owner feels a markup of 35 percent is needed to cover expenses and return a reasonable profit, what is the most the owner can pay for this item?

7. A retailer with annual net sales of $2 million maintains a markup of 66⅔ percent based on cost. Expenses average 35 percent. What are the retailer's gross margin and net profit in dollars?

8. A company has a stockturn rate of five times a year, a sales volume of $600,000, and a gross margin of 25 percent. What is the average inventory at cost?

9. A store has an average inventory of $30,000 at retail and a stockturn rate of five times a year. If the company maintains a markup of 50 percent based on cost, what are the annual sales volume and the cost of goods sold?

10. From the following data, compute the gross margin percentage and the operating expense ratio:
Stockturn rate = 9
Average inventory at selling price = $45,000
Net profit = $20,000
Cost of goods sold = $350,000

11. A ski shop sold 50 pairs of skis at $90 a pair, after taking a 10 percent markdown. All the skis were originally purchased at the same price and had been marked up 60 percent on cost. What was the gross margin on the 50 pairs of skis?

12. A men's clothing store bought 200 suits at $90 each. The suits were marked up 40 percent. Eighty were sold at that price. The remaining suits were each marked down 20 percent from the original selling price, and then they were sold. Compute the sales volume and the markdown percentage.

13. An appliance retailer sold 60 radios at $30 each after taking markdowns equal to 20 percent of the actual selling price. Originally all the radios had been purchased at the same price and were marked up 50 percent on cost. What was the gross margin percentage earned in this situation?

14. An appliance manufacturer produced a line of small appliances advertised to sell at $30. The manufacturer planned for wholesalers to receive a 20 percent markup, and retailers a 33⅓ percent markup. Total manufacturing costs were $12 per unit. What did retailers pay for the product? What were the manufacturer's selling price and percentage markup?

15. A housewares manufacturer produces an article at a full cost of $1.80. It is sold through a manufacturers' agent directly to large retailers. The agent

receives a 20 percent commission on sales, the retailers earn a margin of 30 percent, and the manufacturer plans a net profit of 10 percent on the selling price. What is the retail price of this article?

16. A manufacturer suggests a retail selling price of $400 on an item and grants a chain discount of 40-10-10. What is the manufacturer's selling price? (Chain discounts are discussed in Chapter 12.)

17. A building materials manufacturer sold a quantity of a product to a wholesaler for $350, and the wholesaler in turn sold to a lumberyard. The wholesaler's normal markup was 15 percent, and the retailer usually priced the item to include a 30 percent markup. What is the selling price to consumers?

18. From the following data, calculate the return on investment, based on a definition of *investment* that is useful for evaluating managerial performance:

Net sales	$800,000	Marksup	35%
Gross margin	$280,000	Average inventory	$ 75,000
Total assets	$200,000	Retained earnings	$ 60,000
Cost of goods sold	$520,000	Operating expenses	$240,000
Liabilities	$ 40,000		

accessory equipment In the industrial market, capital goods used in the operation of an industrial firm. Accessory equipment is shorter-lived than installations and does not materially affect the scale of operations in a company.

administered vertical marketing system A distribution system in which channel control is maintained through the economic power of one firm in the channel.

adoption curve The distribution curve showing when various groups adopt an innovation.

adoption process The stages that an individual goes through in deciding whether or not to accept an innovation.

advertisement The nonpersonal message in advertising that is disseminated through media and is paid for by the identified sponsor.

advertising The activities involved in presenting a paid, sponsor-identified, nonpersonal message about an organization and/or its products, services, or ideas.

advertising agency An independent company set up to provide specialized advertising services to advertisers and to the advertising media.

advertising appropriation The amount of money allocated for an organization's advertising program for a specific period of time.

advertising media The vehicles (newspapers, radio, television, etc.) that carry the advertising message (the advertisement) to the intended market.

agent middleman An independent business that does not take title to goods but actively assists in the transfer of title.

agents and brokers A broad category of wholesaling middlemen that do not take title to products. The category includes manufacturers' agents, selling agents, commission merchants, auctioneers, brokers, and others.

agribusiness The business side of farming. Usually involves large, highly mechanized farming operations.

AIDA The sales presentation stage of the personal selling process. Consists of steps to attract *A*ttention, *I*nterest, arouse *D*esire, and generate buyer *A*ction by meeting the buyer's objections and closing the sale.

annual marketing plan A master plan covering a year's marketing operations. It is one part — one time segment — of the ongoing strategic marketing planning process.

area sample A statistical sample that is selected at random from a list of geographic areas.

attitude A person's enduring cognitive evaluation, feeling, or action tendency toward some object, idea, or person.

auction company An independent agent wholesaling middleman that (1) provides the physical facilities for displaying products to be sold, and (2) does the selling in an auction.

automatic vending The nonstore, nonpersonal selling and delivery of products through coin-operated vending machines.

base price The price of one unit of a product at its point of production or resale. Also called *list price*.

battle of the brands Market competition between manufacturers' brands and middlemen's (store) brands. In recent years, "no-brand" (generic) brands have entered this competitive struggle.

benefit segmentation A basis for segmenting a market. A total market is divided into segments based on the customers' perceptions of the various benefits provided by a product.

blanket branding A strategy used for branding a group of products. Also called *family branding*.

box store A low-cost, low-price, low-service, no-frills supermarket. Offers a limited assortment of staple food products displayed in their original packing boxes. Also called a *warehouse store*.

brand A name, term, symbol, special design, or some combination of these elements that identifies the product or service of one seller.

brand manager A product manager responsible for one or more brands.

brand mark The part of a brand that appears in the form of a symbol, picture, design, or distinctive colour.

brand name The part of a brand that can be vocalized — words, letters, and/or numbers.

breadth of product mix The number of product lines offered for sale by a firm.

break bulk To divide a large quantity of a product into smaller units for resale to the next customer in the distribution channel. This is usually done by middlemen.

break-even point The level of output at which revenues equal costs.

broker An independent agent wholesaling middleman whose main function is to bring buyer and seller together and to furnish market information.

business portfolio analysis An evaluation to determine the present status and future roles of a company's strategic business units (SBUs).

buy classes Three typical buying situations in the industrial market – namely, new task, modified rebuy, and straight rebuy.

buyer's market A situation in which the supply of a product or service greatly exceeds the demand for it.

buying centre All the people who participate in the buying-decision process.

buying decision-making process The steps that a buyer goes through in the course of deciding whether to purchase a given item.

campaign In promotion or advertising, a coordinated series of promotional efforts built around a theme and designed to reach some goal.

canned sales talk A form of sales presentation consisting of a company-provided speech that a sales representative is supposed to deliver verbatim during a sales call.

cartel A group of companies that have banded together to regulate competition in the production and marketing of a given product.

cash discount A deduction from list price for paying a bill within a specified period of time.

catalogue showroom A retail store that displays the merchandise in a showroom, takes orders out of a catalogue, and fills these orders from inventories stored on the premises.

chain store One in a group of retail stores that carry the same type of merchandise. Corporate chain stores are centrally owned and managed. Voluntary chains are an association of independently owned stores.

channel captain The firm (producer or middleman) that controls a given distribution channel.

channel conflicts Friction in a channel

of distribution occurring because the channel members are independent, profit-seeking organizations often operating with conflicting goals. Conflict may occur among middlemen on the same level of distribution (horizontal conflict) or among firms on different levels (vertical conflict).

channel of distribution The route that a product, and/or the title to the product, takes as it moves to its market. A channel includes the producer, the consumer or industrial user, and any middlemen involved in this route.

closing In personal selling, the stage in the selling process when the sales person gets the buyer to agree to make the purchase.

cognitive dissonance Postpurchase anxiety often experienced by buyers.

cognitive theory of learning A refinement of the stimulus-response theory of learning: Learning is not a mechanistic process but is influenced by mental (thought) processes.

commission merchant An independent agent wholesaling middleman used primarily in the marketing of agricultural products. This middleman physically handles the seller's products in central markets and has authority regarding prices and terms of sale.

commission plan A method of compensating a sales force whereby a sales person is paid for a unit of accomplishment (measured as sales volume, gross margin, or a nonselling activity). It provides much incentive for a sales rep, but little security or stability of income.

communication process A system by which an information source (sender) transmits a message to a receiver.

community shopping centre A shopping *centre* that is larger than a neighbourhood centre but smaller than a regional centre. Usually includes one or two department stores or discount stores, along with a number of shopping-goods stores and specialty stores.

company planning Setting broad company goals and then deciding on company strategies to reach these goals. See *strategic planning*.

comparative advertising Ads compare the advertiser's brand with those of specifically named competitors.

concentration In distribution, an activity of middlemen in which the outputs of

various producers are brought together. These outputs then are equalized with the market demand and later dispersed to markets.

concept testing The first three stages in the new-product development process — pretesting of the product idea, in contrast to later pretesting of the product itself and the market.

consumer goods Products intended for use by ultimate, household consumers for personal, nonbusiness purposes.

consumerism A protest by consumers against perceived injustices in marketing, and the efforts to remedy these injustices.

contractual vertical marketing system A distribution system in which control is exercised through contracts signed by the producer and/or middlemen members of the channel.

contribution-margin approach In marketing cost analysis, an accounting approach in which only direct expenses are allocated to the marketing units being studied. A unit's gross margin minus its direct costs equal that unit's contribution to covering the company's indirect expenses (overhead).

convenience goods A class of consumer products that people buy frequently and with the least possible time and effort.

convenience store A type of retail outlet that stresses its accessible location, long shopping hours, and the quickness and ease of shopping there.

''cooling-off'' laws Provincial or municipal laws that permit a consumer to cancel an order for a product — usually within a period of three days after signing the order.

cooperative advertising Two or more firms share the cost of an ad. When firms are on the same level of distribution (a group of retailers), we call this *horizontal* cooperative advertising. When producers and middlemen share the costs, we call this *vertical* cooperative advertising.

corporate vertical marketing system A distribution system wherein control is maintained by one company (usually a manufacturer) owning the other (retailing and/or wholesaling) firms in the channel.

correlation analysis A form of the market-factor of sales forecasting, more mathematically exact than the direct-derivation method.

cost of goods sold A major section in an operating statement, showing calculations to determine the cost of products sold during the period covered by the statement.

cost-plus pricing A major method of price determination. The price of a unit of a product is set at a level equal to the unit's total cost plus a desired profit on the unit.

cues Stimuli, weaker than drives, that determine the pattern of responses to satisfy a motive.

culture The symbols and artifacts created by people and handed down from generation to generation as determinants and regulators of human behaviour in a given society.

cumulative quantity discount A discount based on the total volume purchased over a period of time.

dealer Same as a *retailer*.

decline stage of the product life cycle The stage when sales and profits decline sharply. Management must decide whether to abandon the product or to rejuvenate it in this stage.

demography The statistical study of human population and its distribution characteristics.

department store A large retailing institution that carries a very wide variety of product lines, including apparel, furniture, and home furnishings.

depth of product line The assortment within a product line.

derived demand A situation in which the demand for one product is dependent upon the demand for another product. Found in the industrial market, where the industrial demand is derived from the demand for consumer products.

descriptive label A label that gives information regarding the use, care, performance, or other features of a product.

desk jobber Same as a *drop shipper*.

diffusion of innovation A process by which an innovation is communicated within social systems over time.

direct-action advertising Advertising that is designed to get a quick response from the potential customer.

direct derivation A relatively simple form of the market-factor method of sales forecasting.

direct expenses Expenses incurred totally in connection with one market segment or one unit (product, territory) of the company's marketing organization. Also called *separable costs*.

direct mail An advertising medium whereby the advertiser contacts prospective customers by sending some form of advertisement through the mail.

direct selling A vague term that may mean selling directly from producer to consumer without any middlemen; or it may mean selling from producer direct to a retailer, thus bypassing wholesaling middlemen. Also called *direct marketing* or *direct distribution*.

discount house A general-merchandise retailer featuring self-service and prices that are below list prices or regularly advertised prices.

discount in pricing A reduction from the list price. Usually offered to buyers for buying in quantity, paying in cash, or performing marketing services for the seller.

discount retailing The practice of selling below the list price or regularly advertised price.

discretionary buying power The amount of disposable income remaining after fixed expenses and household needs are paid for.

dispersion In distribution, the middlemen's activities that distribute the correct amount of a product to its market.

disposable personal income Income remaining after personal taxes are paid.

distribution The channel structure (institutions and activities) used to transfer products and services from an organization to its markets.

distribution centre A large warehousing centre that implements a company's inventory-location strategy.

distributor Same as a *wholesaler*.

drive A strong stimulus that requires satisfaction. Same as a *motive*.

drop shipper A limited-function wholesaler that does not physically handle the product. Also called a *desk jobber*.

early adopters The second group (following the innovators) to adopt something new. This group includes the opinion leaders, is respected, and has much influence on its peers.

early majority A more deliberate group of innovation adopters that adopts just before the "average" adopter.

economic order quantity (EOQ) A concept in the inventory-control phase of the physical distribution system that identifies the optimum quantity to reorder when replenishing inventory stocks.

economy of abundance An economy that produces and consumes far beyond its subsistence needs.

ego In Freudian psychology, the rational control centre in our minds that maintains a balance between (1) the uninhibited instincts of the id and (2) the socially oriented, constraining superego.

80-20 principle A term describing the situation in which a large proportion of a company's marketing units (products, territories, customers) accounts for a small share of the company's volume or profit, and vice versa.

elastic demand A price-volume relationship, such that a change of one unit on the price scale results in a change of more than one unit on the volume scale. That is, when the price is decreased, the volume increases to the point where there is an increase in total revenue. When the price is increased, demand declines and so does total revenue.

EOQ See *economic order quantity*.

equalization In distribution, the activity of middlemen that balances the output of producers with the demands of consumers and industrial users.

exchange (in marketing) The voluntary act of offering a person something of value in order to acquire something of value in return.

exclusive dealing The practice by which a manufacturer prohibits its retailers from carrying products that are competitive with that manufacturer's products.

exclusive distribution The practice in which a manufacturer uses only one wholesaler or retailer in a given market.

exclusive territories The practice by which a manufacturer requires each middleman to sell only within that middleman's assigned geographic area.

executive judgement A sales forecasting method based on estimates made by the firm's executives. Also called *jury of executive opinion*.

"expected" price The price at which customers consciously or unconsciously value a product; what customers think a product is worth.

experimental method A method of gathering primary data in a survey by establishing a controlled experiment that simulates the real market situation.

fabricating materials Industrial goods that have received some processing and will undergo further processing as they become a part of another product.

fabricating parts Industrial goods that have already been processed to some extent and will be assembled in their present form (with no further change) as part of another product.

facilitating agencies Organizations that aid in a product's distribution, but they do not take title to the products or directly aid in the transfer of title. They include such organizations as transportation agencies, insurance companies, and financial institutions, as distinguished from retailing and wholesaling middlemen.

fad A short-lived fashion that is usually based on some novelty feature.

family branding A branding strategy in which a group of products is given a single brand. Also called *blanket branding*.

family life cycle The series of life stages that a family goes through, starting with young single people and progressing through married stages with young and then older children, and ending with older married and single people.

family packaging The use of packages with similar appearance for a group of products.

fashion A style that is popularly accepted by groups of people over a reasonably long period of time.

fashion-adoption process The process by which a style becomes popular in a market; similar to diffusion of innovation. Three theories of fashion adoption are trickle-down, trickle-across, and trickle-up.

fashion cycle Wavelike movements representing the introduction, rise, popular acceptance, and decline in popularity of a given style.

feedback In the communication process, the element that tells the sender whether and how the message was received.

field (custodian) warehousing A form of public warehousing that provides a financial service for a seller.

fixed cost A constant cost regardless of how many items are produced or sold.

F.O.B. (free on board) pricing A geographic pricing strategy whereby the buyer pays all freight charges from the F.O.B. location to the destination.

focus-group interview Interviewing 5 to 10 people who are gathered together as a group in an informal setting.

forward dating A combination of a seasonal discount and a cash discount. The buyer places an order and receives shipment during the off-season, but does not have to pay the bill until after the season has started and some sales income has been generated.

franchise system A system wherein one organization (the franchisor) grants a number of independent operators (franchisees) the right to sell the franchisor's products or services, in exchange for meeting certain conditions laid down by the franchisor.

freight absorption A geographic pricing strategy whereby the seller pays for (absorbs) some of the freight charges in order to penetrate more distant markets.

full-cost approach In a marketing cost analysis, an accounting approach wherein all expenses — direct and indirect — are allocated to the marketing units being analyzed.

full-function wholesaler A merchant wholesaling middleman that performs all the usual wholesaling activities.

functional (activity) costs The grouping of operating expenses into categories that represent the major marketing activities. In a marketing cost analysis, the ledger expenses are allocated to these various activity categories.

functional discount Same as a *trade discount*.

generic product A product that is packaged in a plain label and is sold with no advertising and without a brand name. The product goes by its generic name, such as ''tomatoes'' or ''paper towels.''

generic use of brand names General reference to a product by its brand name — aspirin, cellophane, kerosene, zipper, for example — rather than its *generic name*. The owners of these brands no

longer have exclusive use of the brand name.

gestalt theory of learning The theory stating that, in learning, people sense the ''whole'' of a thing rather than its component parts.

grade label Identification of the quality (grade) of a product by means of a letter, number, or word.

gross margin Net sales minus cost of goods sold. Also called *gross profit*.

growth stage of the product life cycle The stage when sales continue to increase, and profits increase, peak, and start to decline.

horizontal industrial market A situation where a given product is usable in a very wide variety of industries.

horizontal information flow A theory that holds that people take their cues from opinion leaders in their own social class.

human-orientation stage An emerging stage of marketing management that stresses quality of life rather than material standard of living.

hypermarket A very large retail store that sells a wide variety of products intended to satisfy all of a consumer's routine needs. Also known as a *superstore* or a super-*supermarket*.

iceberg principle The concept that uses the analogy of an iceberg to represent a company's situation. Analyzing only total sales and costs is like looking at the tip of an iceberg and can be misleading.

id In Freudian psychology, the part of the mind that houses the basic instinctive drives, many of which are antisocial.

image utility The emotional or psychological value in a product or service, usually derived from its reputation or social standing.

imperfect competition Same as *monopolistic competition*.

impulse buying Purchasing without planning the purchase in advance.

indirect-action advertising Advertising that is designed to stimulate demand slowly over a long period of time.

indirect expenses Costs that are incurred jointly for more than one marketing unit (product, territory, market). Also called *common costs*.

industrial buying process The series of steps which an industrial user goes through when deciding whether or not to buy a given industrial product.

industrial distributor A full-service merchant wholesaler that handles industrial goods and sells to industrial users.

industrial marketing The marketing of industrial goods to industrial users.

industrial products Products intended for use in producing other goods or in rendering services in a business.

industrial users People or organizations who buy products to use in their own businesses or as aids in making other products.

inelastic demand A price-volume relationship such that a change of one unit on the price scale results in a change of less than one unit on the volume scale. That is, when the price is increased, the volume demanded goes down but total revenue increases. When the price is decreased, the volume goes up, but not enough to offset the price increase; so the net result is a decrease in total revenue.

informal investigation The stage in a marketing research study that involves informal talks with people outside the company being studied.

in-home retailing Retail selling in the customer's home. A personal sales representative may or may not be involved. In-home retailing includes door-to-door selling, party-plan selling, and selling by television and computer.

innovation Anything that is perceived by a person as being new.

innovators The first group — a venturesome group — of people to adopt something new (product, service, idea, etc.).

installations Long-lived, expensive, major industrial capital goods that directly affect the scale of operation of an industrial user.

institutional advertising Advertising designed to generate an attitude toward a company, rather than toward a specific product marketed by that company.

intensity of distribution The number of middlemen used by a producer at the retailing and wholesaling levels of distribution.

intensive distribution A manufacturer sells its product in every outlet where a customer might reasonably look for it. Also known as *mass distribution*.

introduction stage of the product life cycle The stage in which a product is

launched into its market with a full-scale production and marketing program. In this stage, sales are low and losses usually are incurred.

inventory stockturn rate The number of times that a company's average inventory is sold during a year.

inverse demand A price-volume relationship such that the higher the price, the greater are the unit sales. Thus, an increase in price results in an increase in unit sales volume.

jobber Same as a *wholesaler*.

jury of executive opinion A sales forecasting method based on estimates made by a firm's executives.

"just-in-time" (inventory-control system) The process of buying parts and supplies in small quantities "just in time" for use in production.

kinked demand curve The type or shape of demand curve existing (1) when prices are determined entirely by market demand or (2) when a "customary" price prevails for a given product. The kink occurs at the level of the market price.

label The part of the product that carries information about the product or the seller.

laggards Tradition-bound people who are the last to adopt an innovation.

late majority The sceptical group of innovation adopters who adopt a new idea late in the game.

leader pricing Temporary price cuts on well-known items. The price cut is made with the idea that these "specials" (loss leaders) will attract customers to the store.

learning Changes in behaviour resulting from previous experiences.

leasing A growing behavioural pattern in the industrial market (as well as in the consumer market) of renting a product rather than buying it outright.

ledger expenses A company's operating expenses as they appear in the usual accounting system. Also called "natural" expenses and "object-of-expenditure" costs.

licensing An arrangement whereby one firm sells to another firm (for a fee or royalty) the right to use the first company's patents or manufacturing processes. This is a common method of entering a foreign market: A company

grants (licenses) manufacturing rights to a firm in the foreign country.

limited-function wholesaler A merchant wholesaling middleman that performs a limited number of the usual wholesaling functions.

limited-line store A retailing institution that carries an assortment of products, but in only one or a few related product lines.

list price The official price as stated in a catalogue or on a price list. The price of one unit of a product at the point of production or resale. The price before any discounts or other reductions. Also known as *base price*.

local (retail) advertising Advertising that is placed by retailers.

long-range planning Planning that covers a period of 3, 5, or 10 years, or even longer.

loss leaders See *leader pricing*.

lower-lower class The social class that includes unskilled labourers and workers in nonrespectable jobs.

lower-middle class The social class that includes white-collar workers, such as teachers, sales people, small-business owners, and office workers.

lower-upper class The social class that includes the socially prominent, newly rich people in a community.

mail interview The method of gathering data in a survey by means of a questionnaire mailed to respondents and, when completed, returned by mail.

mail-order selling A type of nonstore, nonpersonal retail or wholesale selling in which the customer mails in an order that is then delivered by mail or other parcel-delivery system.

mall-intercept interview Personal interview conducted in a shopping centre mall.

management The process of planning, implementing, and evaluating the efforts of a group of people toward a common goal. In this book, the terms *management* and *administration* are used synonymously.

management process Activities involved in planning, implementing, and evaluating a program.

manufacturers' agent An independent agent wholesaling middleman that sells part or all of a manufacturer's product mix in an assigned geographic territory.

The agent sells related but noncompeting products from several manufacturers.

manufacturer's brand A brand owned by a manufacturer or other producer. Also called a *national brand*.

marginal analysis A major method of setting a base price. Involves balancing market demand with product costs to determine the best price for profit maximization.

marginal cost The cost of producing and selling one more unit; that is, the cost of the last unit produced or sold.

marginal revenue The income derived from the sale of the last unit — the marginal unit.

markdown A reduction from the original retail selling price, usually made because the store was unable to sell the product at the original price.

market People or organizations with wants to satisfy, money to spend, and the willingness to spend it.

market aggregation A marketing strategy in which an organization treats its entire market as if that market were homogeneous.

market-based pricing A pricing strategy in which a company sets the price of its product only in relation to the competitive market price. The firms' costs have no influence at all on this price.

market factor An item that is related to the demand for a product.

market-factor analysis A sales forecasting method based on the assumption that future demand for a product is related to the behaviour of certain market factors.

market index A market factor expressed in quantitative form relative to some base figure.

market potential Total expected industry sales for a product in a given market over a certain time period.

market segmentation The process of dividing the total market into one or more parts (submarkets or segments), each of which tends to be homogeneous in all significant aspects.

market segmentation (with multiple segments) A segmentation strategy that involves identifying two or more different groups of customers as target-market segments. The seller then develops a different marketing mix to reach each segment.

market segmentation (with a single seg-

ment) A segmentation strategy involving the selection of one homogeneous group of customers within the total market. The seller develops one marketing mix to reach this single segment.

market share One company's percentage share of the total industry sales in a given market.

marketing (macro societal dimension) Any exchange intended to satisfy human wants or needs.

marketing (micro organizational definition) Total system of activities designed to plan, price, promote, and distribute want-satisfying goods and services to markets.

marketing audit A total evaluation program consisting of a systematic, objective, comprehensive review of all aspects of an organization's marketing function. An evaluation of the company's goals, policies, results, organization, personnel, and practices.

marketing concept A philosophy of business based on customer orientation, profitable sales volume, and organizational coordination.

marketing cost analysis A detailed study of the operating expense section of a company's profit and loss statement.

marketing information system (MkIS) An ongoing, organized system for gathering and processing information to aid in marketing decision making.

marketing mix A combination of the four elements — product, pricing structure, distribution system, promotional activities — that constitute the core of an organization's marketing system.

marketing plan See *annual marketing plan*.

marketing planning Setting goals and strategies for the marketing effort in an organization. See *strategic marketing planning*.

marketing research The systematic gathering and analysis of information relevant to a problem in marketing.

marketing system A regularly interacting group of ideas forming a unified whole. These items include the organization that is doing the marketing, the thing that is being marketed, the target market, marketing intermediaries helping in the exchange, and environmental constraints.

markup The dollar amount that is added

to the acquisition cost of a product to determine the selling price.

markup percentage The dollar markup expressed as a percentage of either the selling price or the cost of the product.

maturity stage of the product life cycle The stage wherein sales increase, peak, and start to decline. Profits decline throughout this stage.

merchandising manager An executive position commonly found in retailing. See *product manager*.

merchant middleman An independent business that takes title to the product it is helping to market.

message In communication, the information sent from the source to the receiver.

middleman The business organization that is the link between producers and consumers or industrial users. Renders services in connection with the purchase and/or sale of products as they move from producer to their ultimate market. Either takes title to the products or actively aids in the transfer of title.

middleman's brand A brand owned by a retailer or a wholesaler. Also called a *private brand*.

misdirected marketing effort A marketing effort (cost) that is expended in relation to the number of marketing units (products, territories, or customers) rather than in relation to the potential volume or profit from these units.

missionary sales person A type of manufacturer's sales job that involves non-selling activities such as performing promotional work and providing services for customers. The sales rep ordinarily is not expected or permitted to solicit orders.

MkIS See *marketing information system*.

modified rebuy An industrial purchasing situation between a new task and a straight rebuy in terms of time required, information needed, and alternatives considered.

money income The amount of income a person receives in cash or cheques from salaries, wages, interest, rents, dividends, or other sources.

monopolistic competition A market situation in which there are many sellers. Each seller tries to differentiate its product or its marketing program in some way to suggest that its market offering is distinctive. Also known as *imperfect competition.*

monopoly A market situation in which one seller controls the supply of a product.

motivation The force that activates goal-oriented behaviour.

motive A stimulated need that an individual seeks to satisfy with goal-oriented behaviour.

multiple influence on purchases The situation where the purchasing decision is influenced by more than one person in the buyer's organization.

multiple packaging The strategy of packaging several units of a product in one container in the hope of increasing the product's sales volume.

national advertising Advertising sponsored by a manufacturer or some other producer. Also called *general advertising.*

national brand A brand that is owned by a manufacturer or other producer.

neighbourhood shopping centre A small group of stores situated around a supermarket and including other convenience-goods stores and specialty stores. Draws from a market located perhaps within 10 minutes by car.

net profit Gross profit minus all operating expenses. Or, sales revenue less both the cost of the goods sold and all operating expenses.

net sales Gross sales less sales returns and sales allowances.

new product A vague term that may refer to (1) really innovative, truly unique products; (2) replacements for existing products that are significantly different from existing ones; or (3) imitative products that are new to the given firm.

new-product development process Developmental stages that a new product goes through. Starts with idea generation and continues through idea screening, business analysis, limited production, test-marketing, and eventually commercialization (full-scale production and marketing).

new task In the industrial buying process, the situation in which a company for the first time considers the purchase of a given item.

nonbusiness organizations A category that covers a wide spectrum of organizations that do not perceive themselves to be in business (even though they really are). Includes such groupings as educational, religious, charitable, social cause, cultural, health-care, and political organizations.

noncumulative quantity discount A discount based on the size of an individual order of products.

nonprice competition Competition based on some factor other than price — for example, promotion, product differentiation, or variety of services.

nonprofit, or not-for-profit, organization An organization in which profit making is not a goal. The organization neither intends nor tries to make a profit.

nonstore retailing A type of retail selling in which the customer does not go to the store.

observational method The method of gathering primary information in a survey by personal or mechanical observation of respondents. No interviewing is involved.

odd pricing Pricing at odd amounts ($4.99 rather than $5, for example) in the belief that these seemingly lower prices will result in larger sales volume. A form of psychological pricing that is also called "penny pricing."

off-price retailer Retailer whose standard pricing policy is to sell branded products below the manufacturer's suggested retail price.

oligopoly A market situation in which only a few sellers control all (or most) of the supply of a product.

one-price policy The pricing strategy by which the seller charges the same price to all customers of the same type who buy the same quantity of goods.

operating ratio A ratio between any two items on an operating statement. Most commonly used are the ratios between some item and net sales.

operating statement The financial statement that shows an organization's revenues and expenses over a period of time. Also called an *income statement* or *profit and loss statement.*

operating supplies The "convenience goods" of the industrial market — short-lived, low-priced items purchased with a minimum of time and effort.

opinion leader The member of a reference group who is the information source and who influences the decision making of others in the group.

organizational portfolio analysis Same as *business portfolio analysis.*

packaging The activities in product planning that involve designing and producing the container or wrapper for a product.

party-plan selling A form of in-home retailing in which a personal sales rep makes a presentation to a group of potential customers gathered in a party setting in a person's home. The rep writes orders at this party, and the host or hostess receives a commission based on these sales.

patronage buying motives The reasons why a person or an organization patronizes (shops at) a certain store or some other supplier.

patterned interview A standardized list of questions used by all interviewers when interviewing a group of applicants for a given job.

penetration pricing Setting a low initial price on a product in an attempt to reach a mass market immediately.

percentage-of-sales promotional appropriation A method of determining the promotional appropriation. The amount is set as a certain percentage of past or forecasted future sales.

perception The meaning we attribute to stimuli received through our five senses, or the way we interpret a stimulus. Our perceptions shape our behaviour.

personal interview A face-to-face method of gathering data in a survey.

personal selling The activity of informing and persuading a market on a person-to-person basis (face to face or on the telephone).

personal selling process Activities involved in making a personal sale, starting with presale preparation and including prospecting, the preapproach, the sales presentation, and postsale activities.

personality An individual's pattern of traits that are determinants of behavioural responses.

physical distribution Activities involved in the flow of products as they move physically from producer to consumer or industrial user.

physical distribution system The concept of treating all physical distribution activities as a total, interacting system, rather than as a series of fragmented, unrelated elements.

pioneer advertising Same as primary-demand advertising — stimulates demand for a product category.

planned obsolescence As used in this book, the same as *fashion* or *style* obsolescence, in contrast to technological or functional obsolescence. The altering of the superficial characteristics of a product so that the new model is easily differentiated from the old one. The marketer's intention is to make people dissatisfied with the old model.

planned shopping centre A group of retail stores whose activities are coordinated and promoted as a unit to consumers in the surrounding trade area. The centre is planned, developed, and controlled by one organization, typically called a shopping-centre developer.

planning The process of deciding in the present what to do in the future.

preapproach The stage in the personal selling process when a sales rep learns as much as possible about prospective customers and plans the best way to approach a given prospect.

presentation In personal selling, the activities that involve approaching the customer, giving a sales talk, meeting objections, and closing the sale. This is the AIDA stage in personal selling. See AIDA.

pretesting Field-testing a questionnaire, a product, an advertisement (or whatever item is being studied) by trying out the item on a limited number of people, prior to a full-scale market introduction of the item.

price What you pay for what you get. Value expressed in dollars and cents.

pricing lining A retail pricing strategy whereby a store selects a limited number of prices and sells each item only at one of these prices.

pricing objectives The goals that management tries to reach with its pricing structure and strategies.

primary data Original data (information) gathered specifically for the project at hand.

primary demand The market demand for a general category of products (in contrast to the selective demand for a particular brand of the product).

primary-demand advertising Intended to stimulate the demand for a generic product category, rather than a specific brand.

private brand A brand that is owned by a middleman.

product A set of tangible and intangible attributes which provide want-satisfying benefits to a buyer in an exchange. Such attributes include colour, price, packaging, and the reputation and services of the manufacturer and the middleman. A "product" may be a physical good, a service, an idea, a place, an organization, or even a person.

product assortment Full list of products sold by a firm. Same as *product mix*.

product buying motives The reasons for buying a certain product.

product deletion The discontinuance of the marketing of a product; withdrawal of the product from the company's product mix.

product development The technical activities of product research, engineering, and design.

product differentiation A product strategy wherein a company promotes the differences between its products and those of its competitors.

product life cycle The stages a product goes through from its introduction, through its growth and maturity, to its eventual decline and death (withdrawal from the market or deletion from the company's offerings).

product line A group of similar products intended for essentially similar uses.

product manager An executive responsible for planning the entire marketing program for a given product or group of products.

product mix The full list of products offered for sale by a company.

product planning All the activities that enable an organization to determine what products it will market.

product positioning The decisions and activities involved in developing the intended image (in the customer's mind) for a product in relation to competitive products.

product warranty — express A statement in written or spoken words regarding compensation by the seller if its product does not perform up to reasonable expectations.

product warranty — implied The concept of what a warranty was intended to cover, even though it was not actually stated or written in words.

production orientation The first stage in the evolution of marketing management. The basic assumption is that making a good product will ensure business success.

promotion The element in an organization's marketing mix that is used to inform and persuade the market regarding the organization's products and services.

promotional allowance A price reduction granted by the seller as payment for promotional services rendered by the buyer.

promotional mix The combination of elements that constitute the promotion ingredients in an organization's marketing mix.

prospecting The stage in the personal selling process that involves developing a list of potential customers.

psychic income The intangible income factor related to climate, neighbourhood, job satisfaction, etc.

psychoanalytic theory of personality Sigmund Freud's theory that behaviour is influenced by the action and interaction of three parts of the human mind — the id, the ego, and the superego.

psychogenic needs Needs which arise from psychological states of tension.

psychographics A concept in consumer behaviour that explains a market in terms of demographics, as well as consumers' attitudes and life-styles.

public relations A planned effort by an organization to influence some group's attitude toward that organization.

public service advertising Advertising (possibly by a manufacturer or a retailer) that urges people to support some public cause, such as a Red Cross drive or a campaign to drive carefully.

public warehouse An independent firm that provides storage and handling facilities.

publicity Nonpersonal promotion that is not paid for by the organization benefitting from it.

"pull" promotional strategy Aiming

product promotion at end users so they will ask middlemen for the product.

"push" promotional strategy The producer directs its promotion at middlemen that are the next link forward in distribution channels.

quantity discount A reduction from list price when large quantities are purchased; offered to encourage buyers to purchase in large quantities.

questionnaire A data-gathering form used to collect the information in a personal, telephone, or mail survey.

quota sample A nonrandom sample that is "forced" in some way to be proportional to something.

rack jobber A merchant wholesaler that primarily supplies food stores with non-food items. This middleman provides the display case or rack, stocks it, and prices the merchandise.

random sample A sample chosen in such a way that every unit in the whole has an equal chance of being selected for the sample.

raw materials Industrial products that have not been processed in any way and that will become part of another product.

readership test An indirect measure of the effectiveness of an ad that measures how many people saw or read the ad.

real income Purchasing power; that is, what money income will buy in goods or services.

recall test An indirect measure of the effectiveness of an ad. Determines how many people remember seeing a given ad.

reciprocity The situation of "I'll buy from you if you'll buy from me." A very controversial buying pattern in the industrial market.

recognition test An indirect measure of the effectiveness of an ad. Determines how many people can identify a given ad.

reference group A group of people who influence a person's attitudes, values, and behaviour.

regional shopping centre The largest type of planned suburban shopping centre (sometimes large enough to be a mini-downtown). Usually includes two or more department stores and many limited-line

stores, along with service institutions such as banks, theatres, restaurants, hotels, and office buildings.

reinforcement In learning theory, the positive result of a rewarding (satisfying) behavioural reaction to a drive.

resale price maintenance A pricing policy whereby the manufacturer sets the retail price for a product.

response In learning theory, the behavioural reaction to cues.

retail sale The sale by any organization (producer, wholesaler, retailer, or non-business organization) to an ultimate consumer for nonbusiness use.

retailer A business organization that sells primarily to ultimate consumers.

retailer cooperative chain A retailer-sponsored association of independent stores carrying essentially the same product lines.

retailing Activities related to the sale of products to ultimate consumers for their nonbusiness use.

return on investment (ROI) A measure of managerial performance and operating success in a company. The ratio of net profit to total assets or net worth. It is determined by multiplying the percentage of profit on sales by the rate of asset (or capital) turnover.

salary plan (or straight salary) A sales-force compensation plan that pays a representative a fixed amount per period of time. Provides security and stability of income but generally does not provide much incentive.

sales branch A manufacturer's regional office that carries inventory stocks and performs the services of a wholesaling middleman.

sales-force composite A sales forecasting method based on estimates compiled by the field sales force.

sales forecast The estimate of what a company expects to sell in a given market during a specified future time period.

sales management The managerial efforts involved in planning, implementing, and evaluating the activities of a sales force.

sales office A manufacturer's regional location that does not carry merchandise stocks, but otherwise performs the services of a wholesaling middleman.

sales orientation The second stage in the evolution of marketing management, wherein the emphasis is on selling whatever the organization produces.

sales potential A company's expected sales of a given product in a given market over some time period.

sales promotion Activities that supplement and coordinate personal selling and advertising. Includes such elements as store displays, trade shows, and product samples.

sales-results test A method of measuring the effectiveness of advertising. Measure the sales volume stemming directly from an ad or a series of ads.

sales-volume analysis A detailed study of a company's sales volume over a given period of time.

sample A limited portion of the whole of a thing.

sampling principle The concept that, if a small number of parts (a sample) is chosen at random from the whole (the universe or population), the sample will tend to have the same characteristics, and in the same proportion, as the universe.

SBU See *strategic business unit.*

scrambled merchandising The practice of adding new product lines, quite unrelated to the products usually sold in a given type of store.

seasonal discount Discount for placing an order during the seller's slow season.

secondary data Information already gathered by somebody else for some other purpose.

selective demand The market demand for an individual *brand* of a product, in contrast to the primary demand for the broad product category.

selective-demand advertising Intended to stimulate the demand for a specific brand, in contrast to a generic product category.

selective distribution The strategy wherein a manufacturer uses a limited number of wholesalers and/or retailers in a given geographic market.

selectivity in perceptions The process that limits our perceptions. We perceive only part of what we are exposed to, and we retain only part of what we selectively perceive.

self-concept (self-image) The way you

see yourself, and also the way you think others see you. The concept includes your actual self-image and your ideal self-image.

seller's market The situation in which the demand for a given item greatly exceeds the supply of that item.

selling Informing and persuading a market about a product or service; synonymous with *promotion*.

selling agent An independent agent wholesaling middleman that serves as an entire marketing department for a manufacturer. The agent markets the entire output of the manufacturer, and often influences the pricing and design of the products.

services Separately identifiable, intangible activities that provide want-satisfaction and are not tied to the sale of a product or another service.

shopping centre A cluster of retail stores in a limited geographic area. Planned suburban shopping centres typically are planned, developed, and controlled by one organization. Their geographic market may be neighbourhood, community, or regional.

shopping goods Consumer products that are purchased after the buyer has spent some time and effort comparing the price, quality, colour, etc., of alternative products.

short-term planning Planning that typically covers a period of one year or less.

situation analysis The stage in a marketing research study that involves getting acquainted with the organization and its problems by means of library research and interviewing the organization's officials.

skimming pricing Setting a high initial price on a product, hoping to quickly recover new-product development costs.

small-order problem Individual sales orders that are so small as to be unprofitable relative to the cost of filling the orders.

social class A major division of society based on people's status in their communities.

social (societal) marketing A broadening and extension of managerial marketing. An organization must consider the social and environmental consequences of the production, marketing,

and use of its products.

social responsibilities of marketing management Management's broad responsibilities for the effects that executive actions produce on our society.

specialty goods Consumer products with perceived unique characteristics, such that consumers are willing to expend special effort to buy them.

specialty store A retailer that carries only part of a given line of products. Or, in an alternative interpretation, a store that stresses its reputation, quality of merchandise, and abundant and excellent services.

stabilizing prices A pricing goal designed to stabilize prices in an industry. Often found in industries where one firm is a price leader. Other firms price so as to follow the leader and thus not "rock the boat."

stimulus-response theory of learning Learning occurs as correct responses to a given stimulus are reinforced with want-satisfaction and as incorrect responses are penalized.

stockturn rate The number of times the average inventory is sold (turned over) during a given period of time. It is calculated by dividing net sales by average inventory at retail, or by dividing cost of goods sold by average inventory at cost.

storage The marketing activity that creates time utility. Involves holding and preserving products from the time they are produced until they are sold.

straight rebuy In the industrial market, a routine purchase with minimal informational needs.

strategic business unit (SBU) A separate major product and/or market division in a company. A separate strategic plan is prepared for each SBU.

strategic marketing planning The process of setting marketing goals, selecting target markets, and designing a marketing mix to satisfy these markets and achieve these goals.

strategic planning The managerial process of matching an organization's resources and abilities with its marketing opportunities over the long run.

strategy A broad, basic plan of action by which an organization intends to reach one or more goals.

style A distinctive presentation or construction in any art, product, or activity.

style obsolescence Same as *planned obsolescence*.

subculture A part of a total culture that is reasonably homogeneous with regard to race, religion, nationality, geographic location, or some other factor.

superego In Freudian psychology, the part of the mind that houses the conscience and directs instinctive drives into socially acceptable channels.

supermarket A large, departmentalized, self-service retailing institution offering a wide variety of food products, as well as an assortment of nonfood items. Emphasizes low prices and ample parking space.

superstore A large store carrying all that a supermarket typically carries plus a much wider assortment of the nonfood products that are usually purchased on a routine basis and at a low price. Also called *hypermarket* or *super-supermarket*.

survey of buyer intentions A method of sales forecasting in which a sample of potential customers is asked about their future plans for buying a given product.

survey method A method of gathering data by interviewing a limited number of people (a sample) in person or by telephone or mail.

tactic A detailed course of action by which a strategy (or a strategic plan) is to be implemented and activated.

target market A group of customers at whom an organization specifically aims its marketing effort.

target return A pricing goal that involves setting prices so as to achieve a certain percentage return on investment or on net sales.

task or objective method A method of determining the promotional appropriation. First, the organization decides what is to be accomplished, and then it calculates how much it will cost to reach this goal.

telemarketing A marketing communication system involving use of telephone, television, and computer to aid in a company's selling effort.

telephone selling/shopping Selling via telephone. The seller contacts a customer and makes a sales presentation over the phone. Or the customer contacts the seller and places an order over the phone. It is used in both retailing and wholesaling.

telephone survey or interview A method of gathering data in a survey by interviewing people over the telephone.

teleshopping In-home retailing where the consumer shops with the aid of a television set and possibly a home computer.

test marketing Commercial experiments in limited geographic areas, to determine the feasibility of a full-scale marketing program. The seller may test a new product, a new feature of an existing product, or some other element in the marketing mix.

theme In promotion, the central idea or focal point in a promotional campaign. The promotional appeals are dressed up in some distinctive attention-getting form.

total cost The sum of total fixed costs and total variable costs, or the full cost of a specific quantity produced or sold.

total-cost approach In physical distribution, the optimization of the overall cost-customer service relationship of the entire physical distribution system.

trade channel Same as a *channel of distribution*.

trade (functional) discount A reduction from the list price, offered by a seller to buyers in payment for marketing activities that they will perform.

trademark A brand that is legally protected — essentially a legal term.

trading down A product-line strategy wherein a company adds a lower-priced item to its line of prestige goods, to reach the market that cannot afford the higher-priced items. The seller expects that the prestige of the higher-priced items will help sell the new, lower-priced products.

trading stamps Stamps that are given to the purchaser of a product or service and that can later be exchanged for merchandise. This is a form of nonprice competition.

trading up A product-line strategy wherein a company adds a higher-priced, prestige product to its line in the hope of increasing the sales of the existing products in that line.

trend analysis A sales forecasting method that projects future sales on the basis of past trends.

trickle-across concept In fashion adoption, a fashion cycle moves horizontally within several social classes at the same time.

trickle-down concept In fashion adoption, a given fashion cycle flows downward through several socioeconomic classes.

trickle-up concept In fashion adoption, a style becomes popular (fashionable) first with lower socioeconomic classes and then, later, with higher socioeconomic groups.

truck jobber or truck distributor A limited-function wholesaler, usually carrying a limited line of perishable products that are delivered in the jobber's own truck to retail stores. Also called *wagon jobber* or truck wholesaler.

tying contract A contract under which a manufacturer agrees to sell a product to a middleman only if this middleman also buys another (possibly unwanted) product from the manufacturer.

ultimate consumers People who buy products or services for their personal, nonbusiness use.

uniform delivered price A geographic price strategy whereby the same delivered price is quoted to all buyers regardless of their location. Sometimes referred to as *postage-stamp pricing*.

unit pricing A form of price reporting where the price is stated per gram, per litre, or per some other standard measure — a consumer aid in comparison shopping.

upper-lower class A social class that includes blue-collar workers and the politicians and union leaders whose power base is with these workers.

upper-middle class A social class that includes successful executives in large firms and professionals.

upper-upper class A social class that includes the "old wealth" in a community.

utility The characteristic in an item that makes it capable of satisfying wants.

variable cost A cost that varies or changes directly in relation to the number of units produced or sold.

variable-price policy A pricing strategy in which a company sells similar quan-

tities of merchandise to similar buyers at different prices. The price is usually set as a result of bargaining.

vending See *automatic vending*.

venture team An organizational structure for new-product planning and development. A small group that manages the new product from the idea stage to full-scale marketing.

vertical industrial market A situation where a given product is usable by virtually all the firms in only one or two industries.

vertical marketing system A distribution arrangement whereby a given channel of distribution is treated as a coordinated, integrated unit. Three common types of vertical systems are corporate, administered, and contractual.

voluntary chain A wholesaler-sponsored association of independently owned retail stores carrying essentially the same product lines.

wagon jobber Same as a *truck jobber*.

warehouse store Same as a *box store*.

warehouse/wholesale club A low-price, no-frills wholesaler/retailer that charges a membership fee and sells to small retailers (wholesaling transactions) and to ultimate consumers (retailing transactions).

warehousing A broad range of physical distribution activities including storage, assembling, bulk breaking, and preparing products for shipping.

wheel-of-retailing theory A theory which holds that (1) a new type of retailing institution gains a foothold in the retailing structure by competing on a low-status, low-price, low-service basis; (2) then, to expand its market, this retail institution increases its services and product offerings, thus increasing its costs and prices; (3) this leaves room at the bottom for the next low-price, low-service type of retailer to enter the retailing structure; and (4) the "wheel of retailing" continues to turn as new institutions enter the retail market.

wholesaler A merchant middleman (takes title to the products) whose primary purpose is to engage in wholesaling activities. Also may be called a *jobber*, *industrial distributor*, or *mill-supply house*.

wholesaling All activities involving sales to organizations that buy to resell or to use the products in their businesses.

wholesaling middleman The broad category that includes all middlemen engaged primarily in wholesaling activities.

world enterprise The most advanced form of international marketing structure. Both foreign and domestic operations are fully integrated and are no longer separately identified.

zone delivered pricing A geographic price strategy whereby the same delivered price is charged at any location within each geographic zone. Sometimes called *parcel-post pricing*.

PHOTO CREDITS

SUBJECT INDEX

COMPANY AND BRAND INDEX

STUDENT REPLY CARD

In order to improve future editions, we are seeking your comments on
FUNDAMENTALS OF MARKETING, Fifth Canadian Edition, by Sommers, Barnes, Stanton, and Futrell.
After you have read this text, please answer the following questions and return this form via Business Reply Mail. *Thanks in advance for your feedback!*

1. Name of your college or university: _____

2. Major program of study: _____

3. Your instructor for this course: _____

4. Are there any sections of this text which were not assigned as course reading? If so, please specify those chapters or portions:

5. How would you rate the overall accessibility of the content? Please feel free to comment on reading level, writing style, terminology, layout and design features, and such learning aids as chapter objectives, summaries, and appendices.

6. What did you like *best* about this book?

7. What did you like *least*?

If you would like to say more, we'd love to hear from you. Please write to us at the address shown on the reverse of this card.

- *CUT HERE* -

CUT HERE

- *FOLD HERE* -

**BUSINESS
REPLY MAIL**

No Postage Stamp
Necessary If Mailed
in Canada

Postage will be paid by

Canada Post   Postes Canada

7115

Attn: Sponsoring Editor, Business and Economics

The College Division
McGraw-Hill Ryerson Limited
330 Progress Avenue
Scarborough, Ontario
M1P 2Z5

TAPE SHUT